Structured Programming in FORTRAN

LOUIS A. HILL JR.

Arizona State University

Prentice-Hall, Inc.

Englewood Cliffs, New Jersey 07632

Library of Congress Cataloging in Publication Data

Hill, Louis A., Jr. (date)
    Structured programming in FORTRAN.

    (Prentice-Hall software series)
    Includes index.
    1. FORTRAN (Computer program language)
2. Structured programming.   I. Title.   II. Series.
QA76.73.F25H54   001.64'24   80-39567
ISBN 0-13-854612-6

© 1981 by Prentice-Hall, Inc., Englewood Cliffs, New Jersey 07632

Printed in the United States of America

10 9 8 7 6 5 4 3 2 1

Editorial/production supervision and interior design:
    Nancy Milnamow and Marianne Thomma Baltzell
Cover design: Jorge Hernandez
Manufacturing buyer· Joyce Levatino and Gordon Osbourne

Prentice-Hall International, Inc., *London*
Prentice-Hall of Australia Pty. Limited, *Sydney*
Prentice-Hall of Canada, Ltd., *Toronto*
Prentice-Hall of India Private Limited, *New Delhi*
Prentice-Hall of Japan, Inc., *Tokyo*
Prentice-Hall of Southeast Asia Pte. Ltd., *Singapore*
Whitehall Books Limited, *Wellington, New Zealand*

Dedicated to:

My wife, Jeanne,

and

Lee P. Thompson, Emeritus
Founding Dean, Arizona State University

Contents

Chapter 10   THE DATA STATEMENT, ARRAYS, AND NESTED DO-LOOPS   241

Chapter 11   EXAMPLES INVOLVING TWO-DIMENSIONAL ARRAYS   272

Chapter 12　UTILIZING CHARACTERS 293

Chapter 13　RECAPITULATION AND SYNTHESIS 321

Chapter 14   SUBROUTINES   332

Chapter 15   FUNCTIONS   381

Chapter 16   ADDITIONAL FEATURES   403

Chapter 17   ADDITIONAL INPUT/OUTPUT   425

Preface

To the Student

This book has been class-tested by over 5,000 students from nearly every department on the Arizona State University campus. It is written to satisfy your present and future needs by helping you through various levels of programming skill and serving you as a ready reference.

Chapter exercises are chosen to clarify your thinking and to reinforce your knowledge; most exercises have answers provided in the appendix. Words for the glossary have been carefully chosen to help you communicate in the computer center and computer community, as well as in book-related activities. The index is comprehensive. Boldface entries in the index point to elements of the book which summarize the rules of FORTRAN 77.

The ultimate objective of this book is to help you develop sufficient knowledge and skill to use computers to provide humankind with pertinent information and to free time for creative endeavors.

To the Instructor

This book is designed to support a broad spectrum of teaching techniques. Several chapters and sections may easily be omitted or reordered to suit your style.

It is my intention that all FORTRAN, unless specifically noted (rare), conform to ANSI X3.9-1978, FORTRAN 77. In general, when Full Language is not specified, Subset Language is implied. Because the ANSI Standard is written by and for experienced programmers, the ANSI format is not incorporated directly into this text. Rather, the format for explaining FORTRAN 77 is based upon the results of extensive experimentation, by using different techniques with students from essentially every academic discipline. Although I have gone to great lengths to insure accuracy, I am aware that some errors have probably not been detected. Your comments, corrections, and suggestions are most welcome.

An Instructor's Manual is available to facilitate your use of this text. A Typical Course Schedule in the Instructor's Manual lists subjects for each lecture and shows text sections that the student should read and/or study before coming to class. A quiz and laboratory schedule is included, with suggested point values.

Lesson plans in the Instructor's Manual state objectives, give a summary lecture outline, and present a detailed lecture outline keyed to transparencies or slides.

Laboratory projects in the text, designed for very early use, are ample for several semesters. Individual laboratory projects allow each student to write a different computer program, yet these programs are accurately and quickly graded with aids presented in the second half of the Instructor's Manual.

ACKNOWLEDGEMENTS

This text is the outgrowth of three previous versions which were class-tested and critiqued by over 5,000 students and fifty laboratory instructors. From the large group who provided extraordinary help, the following deserve special mention: George C. Beakley, III, Carolyn Brown, Hugh Bynum, David Eyestone, Clayton Knight, John Krobock, Kathy Levandowsky, Peter K. Piascik, and Rajiv Sachdeva.

The critique and criticism of the reviewers, Dr. Lionel E. Deinel, Jr. and Dr. Brian Kernighan, was extremely helpful and especially appreciated. Linda Thompson did an excellent and timely job of copyediting. The late Marianne Baltzell and Nancy Milnamow were most pleasant and helpful in expediting the book through the production stage. Karl Karlstrom and Steve Cline, my computer science editors, have been consistently supportive. To all of them, my thanks.

Special thanks are due to Dr. Robert Lovell and Dr. James Wilson, professors who gave excellent critiques from their experience gained while classroom-testing the material. Thanks are also due to Dr. George C. Beakley, Jr., for his consistent encouragement and support.

For more than a decade, I have been able to count on my son, David A. Hill (presently a systems programmer), for critique, enlightening suggestions, and lively discussion on relevant but sometimes obscure points. He has added appreciably to the quality of this book.

Louis A. Hill Jr.

Chapter 1

Overview – A Look Ahead

Welcome to an exciting and profitable study—one that can greatly increase your contribution to society and add new dimension to your personality. Not only will the computer save you hours and energy, it will eventually free you from mundane tasks so that you will have time to be creative. The study of computer programming also can increase your ability to define and organize problems in other spheres of your life.

It does take work, as well as courage and stick-to-itiveness—courage to overcome fear of the unknown, and stick-to-itiveness to overcome frustration when a "perfect" computer does what you say and not what you mean. You will face the ever present temptation to forget your ultimate "human" goals and to concentrate upon pleasing an uncompromising impersonal machine. However, if you work and persevere, you will soon be using the computer to truly optimize attainment of your goals.

As in any new subject, you will encounter new vocabulary (or words used in an unfamiliar context), new rules, and new techniques. A glossary is provided to give you ready definitions (words in italics are in the glossary); by the end of your study, the full meaning of these terms will become clear.

1-1 SITUATIONS YOU CAN EXPECT TO ENCOUNTER

In a first computer course, you will encounter a new set of problems. You will have to define each project for yourself and work carefully in defining a program. You will be dependent not only upon the machine, but upon other human beings every time you work toward a solution. You will be constantly beckoned by the siren's call to other, "better," "faster," and "easier" ways of doing things which all too often lead to hours of extra effort.

The computer is a machine—a very, very fast one. It is error-free almost beyond comprehension. But it does only what it is told to do and only when you ask in a "perfect" way. The computer will not read your mind; it will not do what you mean. In addition, the rules for its use must be followed exactly. A comma or a period in the wrong place will probably lead to a program that does not function properly, if at all.

Probably your biggest frustration will be that your work is not solely dependent upon you. In almost every case you will have to depend upon other people who run the machine and handle your program and subsequent results. You will always be dependent upon the availability of a computer and constrained by the *turn-around time* associated with each run that you make. To enjoy programming, you need to allow time in case things—often not of your own doing—go wrong. In general, you should start work early enough so that you will have sufficient slack time to overcome these almost certain untoward occurrences. Many novice programmers feel that everything is under control and do not allow contingency time; in the long run they cost themselves excessive time and effort.

In every computer center there are people willing to suggest other ways to write your program. Unfortunately, these excursions into "other ways" can be very time-consuming distractions. If you are tempted to try another "better, faster, or easier" way of doing things, at least be sure you understand the process involved. Blind use of any computer technique is certain to cause more trouble than it overcomes.

1-2 EFFECT OF YOUR PERSONAL BACKGROUND

Student concern about lack of experience and background when first learning to program a computer generally falls into three categories: experience level, area of interest or expertise, and age.

1-2.1 Experience Level

Experience has convinced the author that it is inconsequential whether you are a high school junior, college junior, graduate student, or professional. Students with no mathematics beyond high school algebra, as well as those who have completed courses in partial differential equations, have consistently mastered programming techniques. Prior industrial or educational experience does not seem to have any major effect on your ability to learn computer programming. The primary advantage to be gained from prior experience is an ability to satisfactorily define a project. Yet students with little background, either academic or professional, often formulate exciting problems that are extremely interesting and practical.

1-2.2 Area of Interest or Expertise

No one comes to a study of computer programming with built-in handicaps. A variety of experience lends unexpected benefits, since stereotyped concepts often found among civil engineers, botanists, nurses, wildlife biologists, psychologists, electronic technicians or business people tend to melt away as they work together with computer programming as a common bond. The computer not only provides a powerful tool for your specialty, it is also an important vehicle for enhancing communication among students and practitioners of the various disciplines.

1-2.3 Age

A younger student usually learns to program effectively with relatively more ease. Middle-aged students, with a wealth of education and experience, often suffer real trauma in the learning process, although in the end they usually are highly successful. This apparent anomaly can be explained by noting that the less experienced student has little concept of what to expect and therefore accepts everything at face value. By contrast, the more educated and experienced learner constantly tries to relate the elements of computer programming to past situations, and these prior relationships often do not help until a higher stage of programming ability has been reached.

Using concepts and techniques that are not completely understood can be a very frustrating experience, but not nearly so frustrating as wasting time and effort in trying to understand them in depth before the proper foundation in rudimentary programming experience has been built. Thus if you do not try to understand everything at once, in time you will develop understanding—and in the meanwhile, you will succeed.

1-3 HOW THIS TEXT RELATES TO YOUR FUTURE

Your approach to this text depends somewhat on how you expect to use the electronic computer. Your own future could contain one of five paths: extensive programming in school, work, or research; middle management with some programming; middle management with problem formation; upper management with problem formation only; or further formal courses in programming.

Of the four nonstudy paths, only one involves extensive programming, whether at school, at work, or in your research. The second path involves middle management with some computer programming. In the third path, the only contact with computer programming is in problem formulation. In an upper management position, contact with the computer is probably limited to the problem definition. Many management personnel do not have a comprehensive knowledge of computer usage. Although many short courses designed to teach appreciation of computer facilities exist, experience seems to indicate that most managers need the discipline and training of actual programming to insure effective use of computer facilities.

This text is designed to provide you with adequate background to function effectively along any of these possible paths. It also provides you with sufficient programming skill to do fundamental computer programming jobs with reasonable facility.

1-4 CONFRONTING THE COMPUTER

Programming does not have to be a traumatic conflict, although *hardware bugs,* *software* bugs, computer-center personnel, or the ever-present need to have things "perfect" can sometimes make it feel that way. Remember that this text is designed to put you in the role of David and the computer in Goliath's shoes; you are going to be the winner.

*When first used, words contained in the Glossary are italicized.

1-4.1 What the Computer Reads From

An electronic computer can obtain information from many sources, but the two most common *input* media are punched cards and remote terminals. Characters typed on cards are simply for human convenience; the computer actually uses the corresponding holes punched in the cards. A computer's card reader, therefore, reads only holes punched in computer cards and completely overlooks the following factors.

1. The color of the card.
2. Any printing (or lack of printing) on the card.
3. Rounding or clipping of any corners of the cards.

With a remote terminal, the characters are displayed for your convenience and corresponding computer characters are transmitted to or from the computer. The printed characters may be activated by the keyboard as you type while the computer symbols are being transmitted (one way only) more or less simultaneously (*half-duplex*). In other cases, the computer character is sent to the machine when you strike the keyboard; the character is read and an "*echo*" is sent back. This echo activates the printing of the character for your observation (*full-duplex with echo on*). When using the half-duplex system, you can never type ahead of the machine's capacity to accept data. With the latter system, it is possible to type a great deal of information before any typed output is echoed to your remote terminal.

In this text, the word *card* is usually synonymous with a *line* at a remote terminal. In the following discussion, however, the only fact that applies to lines is the spacing of columns.

(a) *A typical card* is shown in Figure 1-1. The alphabet, numerals, and several auxiliary symbols are punched in this card. The printing across the top of the card is simply for convenience and corresponds to the holes read by the computer. Each card has a total of 80 columns and 12 rows. The top row of punched holes is called the *12 row* and the second is called the *11 row*. The third row from the top is called the *zero row* and is followed sequentially by the first through ninth rows.

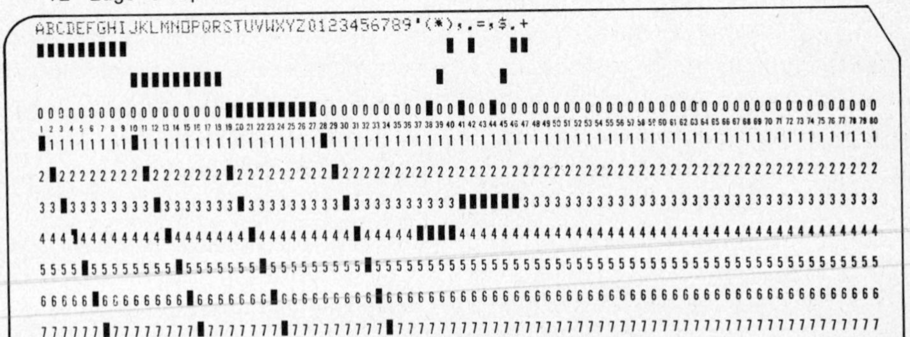

"12" Edge is Top of Card

FIGURE 1-1 A typical card

The first nine letters of the alphabet, letters *A* through *I,* require two punches, one in the 12 row and one in the row corresponding to the letter of the alphabet. Thus *C,* the third letter of the alphabet, is punched in the third column with a hole in the 12 row and another hole in the 3 row. Letters *J* through *R* use the 11 row in conjunction with sequential numerical punches 1 through 9. The last letters of the alphabet are represented by a zero punch used in conjunction with the numbers 2 through 9 sequentially.

The numerals zero through 9 are represented by a single punch in the appropriate row. Other symbols are represented by various combinations of holes and may vary from one installation to the next. Although cards usually contain printing, a person can also learn to read the holes without much difficulty.

(b) *Control cards* are used to determine valid users, establish the computer language being used, distinguish between programs and input data, and so on. These control cards vary between machines and installations and usually have very specific rules about the way they are formatted. Many require a multipunch (two or more symbols punched in the same location) in Column 1. Figure 1-2 shows some typical control cards for various machines.

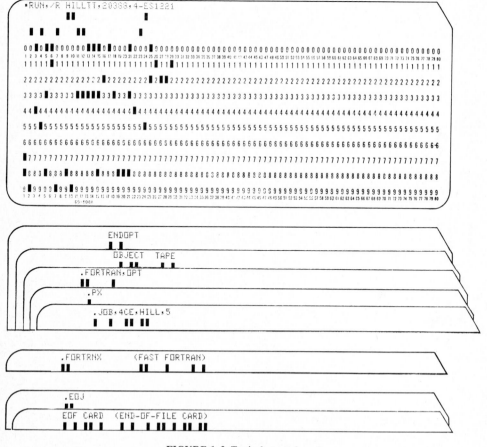

FIGURE 1-2 Typical control cards

(c) *FORTRAN cards* are used to write the statements that comprise your program. The 80 columns of a FORTRAN computer card are divided into four primary fields (see Figure 1–3). Any time the letter *C* (or *) occurs in the first column of a FORTRAN card, everything will be read and output with no other action by the computer. This technique is employed to write comments for human observers on FORTRAN output listings without detracting from the computer's operation.

Columns 1 through 5 are reserved for *statement label* numbers of the FORTRAN statements if the statements are, in fact, labeled. Up to five digits may be used; blanks placed anywhere and leading zeros are not significant. Column 6 is used to signal the continuation of any FORTRAN statement that cannot fit on one card.

Columns 7 through 72 are reserved for a single FORTRAN statement. In general, spaces within FORTRAN statements are ignored by the computer and can be used to make the printing more readable and corrections easier to make. Columns 73 through 80 are ignored by the computer and may be used to code cards with the name of the FORTRAN program and a set of sequence numbers. Typically, Columns 73 through 76 are used for the name of the FORTRAN program in abbreviated form, leaving the last four columns to number the cards, usually by tens. Numbering by tens makes it possible to insert additional cards with intermediate numbers that are still in sequence.

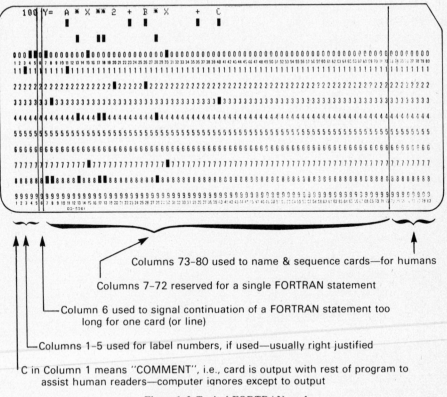

Columns 73–80 used to name & sequence cards—for humans

Columns 7–72 reserved for a single FORTRAN statement

Column 6 used to signal continuation of a FORTRAN statement too long for one card (or line)

Columns 1–5 used for label numbers, if used—usually right justified

C in Column 1 means "COMMENT", i.e., card is output with rest of program to assist human readers—computer ignores except to output

Figure 1–3 Typical FORTRAN card

The same column allocation is reserved for FORTRAN statements typed on a remote terminal, except that Columns 73–80 are sometimes unavailable. Also, to facilitate editing, most remote terminals provide some sort of numbering system for each line typed.

(d) *Data cards* may use any or all of the 80 columns on a card; the number used depends upon the number of values to be read and the FORMAT statement employed.

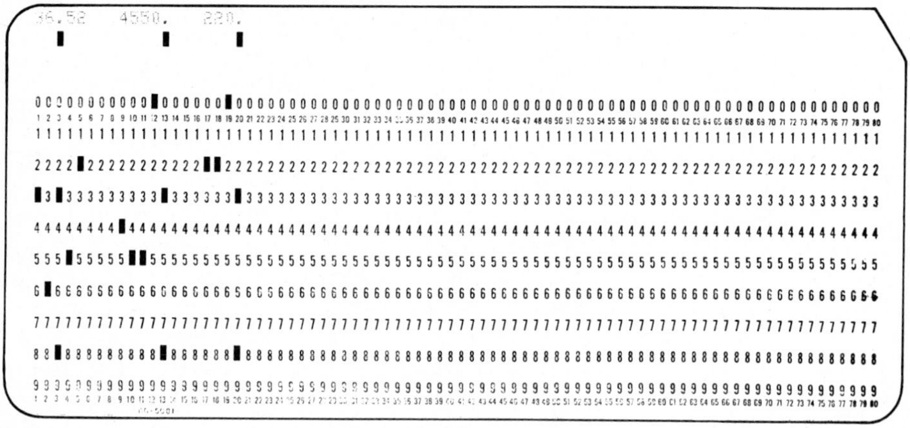

FIGURE 1–4 Typical data card

Figure 1–4 depicts a typical data card. READ and FORMAT statements are discussed briefly in Chapter 2 and thoroughly examined in Chapter 6. At this point, you should recognize that certain cards are read as data, that such data cards can use any or all of the 80 columns, and that the columns actually used on any data card are dependent upon the READ statement of the FORTRAN program (which causes the data card to be read) and its corresponding FORMAT statement (which establishes the form to be used).

Thus, for our purposes, there are three types of cards.

1. Control cards, which are machine- and installation-dependent.
2. FORTRAN cards, which have a specified form.
3. Data cards.

In general, each of these three types of cards is represented by a line on a remote terminal.

1–4.2 What the Computer Writes On

If the computer is used in the *batch* mode with computer cards, the most common output is obtained from the high-speed printer. Such a printer outputs an entire line at a time, with some models exceeding 1200 lines per minute. A high-speed printer going at this speed can print a complete novel in 2 to 4 minutes.* Output is normally returned to the remote terminal if one is used to input the program and data to the computer.

*(1200 lines per minute)×(25 words per line)×(4 minutes) = 120,000 words

1-4.3 Basic Machine Configuration

A schematic drawing of a typical computer configuration is shown in Figure 1-5.

The control unit passes commands between the other four basic units: input, output, arithmetic unit (which actually does the calculations), and memory unit (which stores necessary information).

The arithmetic unit consists of a series of accumulators for storing intermediate results of computations. The arithmetic unit may be hard-wired to provide especially fast service, or it may consist of *software* components. (Note that the arithmetic unit may provide logic and character capabilities.)

The memory unit contains loading instructions for utilizing the computer, the FORTRAN 77 compiler that translates FORTRAN coding into machine language (after successful compilation), the translated program, and storage locations assigned for numbers and names used within a given program.

Thus, basic configuration for an electronic computer consists of five parts: (1) the control unit; (2) the input unit; (3) the output unit; (4) the arithmetic unit; and (5) the memory unit. Although you can use an electronic computer without understanding how it works, it is sometimes helpful to know more of the hardware and software details associated with your local computer center so that you can make more efficient use of your computer facilities.

1-5 INSIGHTS TO EXPEDITE YOUR LEARNING

This section should give you insight into what to expect while running your initial programs.

1-5.1 Running a FORTRAN Program

Before a FORTRAN program can be run on any computer, the machine must be readied. This preparation includes providing a *loader* that enables the computer to read your material and store it in appropriate locations. In addition, the computer must have ready access to a "processor" which, speaking loosely, translates your FORTRAN 77 coding into the machine's language.

After the machine is made ready, it can accept your deck. The normal sequence for composition of such a program deck is: (1) leading control cards; (2) the FORTRAN deck; (3) intermediate control cards; (4) data to be used by the program when compiled; and (5) a terminal control card. Often, the same sequence can be used on a remote terminal.

When you submit your deck, the computer first reads what is often called a RUN card to see if you have been authorized to use the system. If not, your program is aborted immediately; otherwise, some sort of accounting system is activated so that appropriate charges can be made.

Assuming that you are a valid user, the second card (or line if you are using a remote terminal) is read and signifies that the program (punched in the cards or lines) that follow is written in FORTRAN 77 and must be translated into the machine's language.

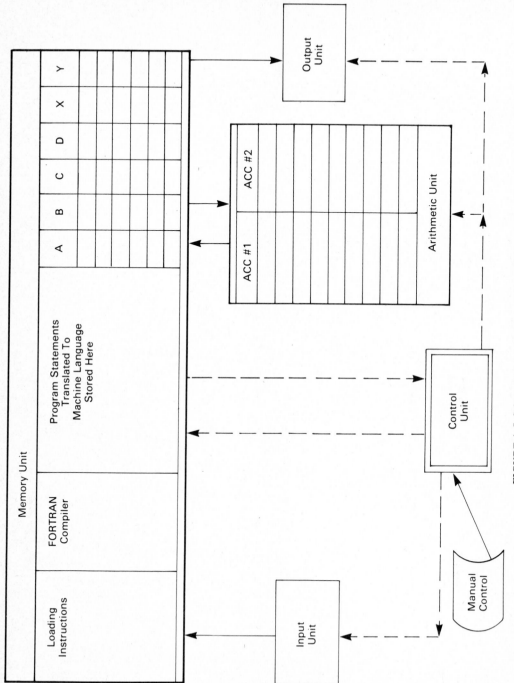

FIGURE 1-5 Schematic of computer configuration

9

Usually your FORTRAN deck follows these two leading control cards, with each card or line of the FORTRAN program read sequentially. As a card is read, the computer (*processor*) checks to see if it is a valid FORTRAN statement. If not, an appropriate error message is output on the high-speed printer or at your remote terminal. In some cases, such an error causes the computer to reject everything else in the deck. In other cases, the computer attempts to remedy the error—or overlooks it—and continues with the remainder of the deck.

When a statement is valid, the computer (processor) performs two tasks: it translates the statement into its own language, and it allocates storage spaces for all *variable names* and *constants,* which it reads from the FORTRAN statement.

Normally, each individual FORTRAN statement must be represented by a series of statements written in the machine's language. This process of reading, translating, and storing continues until END—physically, the last card of the FORTRAN deck—is read. The word END signals the computer to stop translating and allocating storage; if no errors have been found the program is compiled and ready to execute.*

When no errors are found, you may use an "execute" control card to request the computer to execute the program. When the execute control card is reached, the computer program that you wrote in FORTRAN 77 is actually executed on a one-to-one basis by the program that was translated into the machine's language. Whenever a READ statement is encountered in the program, data is read from the succeeding data cards, in order. The execution process continues until a run-time error occurs or until the program arrives at a STOP statement. The final control card terminates the execution of your program. Figure 1-6 summarizes this process in *flow diagram* form. As you progress in your study of FORTRAN, this figure will often prove helpful.

In practice, at different installations and with different computers, this procedure actually varies somewhat. The primary external difference is in the form of control cards that are used. In reality, few modern high-speed computers do all of the translating and storage allocation in one pass. Instead, they go through the FORTRAN deck several times, optimizing the code used in their own language so that your program will be more efficient.

1-5.2 What Kind of Trouble Can You Expect?

Three types of errors occur in any programming efforts. These are logic, compilation, and run-time errors.

Logic errors are those in which you ask the computer to do something—which it does correctly—that you did not really mean for it to do. Often beginning programmers have the mistaken impression that if a program runs without any errors being detected by the computer, then the program is correct. Nothing could be further from the truth! A computer solves a problem just as you tell it to, even when you give it incorrect directions.

Compilation errors occur when the processor is translating your FORTRAN program into the machine's language and allocating storage spaces. These errors represent violations of the formal rules of FORTRAN and are called *syntactic* errors. The majority of such errors are detected by the processor and are listed with high-speed printer output of your program, along with some succinct comments about what you may have

---

*At many installations, a collection or linkage step will also be required.

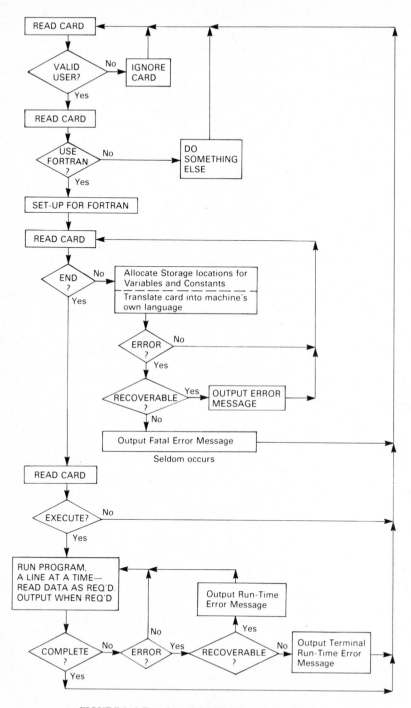

FIGURE 1-6 Running a FORTRAN computer program

done wrong. The bulk of syntactic errors committed by both beginning students and experienced programmers seem to be the fault of poor proofreading (see Section 1-5.4). Although FORTRAN 77 syntactic rules are very precise, there are relatively few of them and they are fairly easily mastered.

Even if the logic of a program is correct and it has been compiled correctly, there is still the possibility of run-time errors. Run-time errors can be caused by many circumstances, but the most prevalent is that input or output commands, used in conjunction with their formats, simply do not match the data cards or the desired output.

In general, compilation errors and run-time errors can be greatly reduced by carefully proofreading your program. Logic errors should be caught during the formulation of the problem. When we let logic errors creep into a program, the results are quite wrong—but the computer has no way to detect or correct them.

When things go wrong, the first thing to determine is what type of trouble you are having—logic, compilation, or run-time. Often, when you arrive at the answer to that question, the means for correcting the trouble will be readily evident.

Another type of annoying trouble is in the confusion of certain characters: the number 1 and the letter *I*, the number 2 and the letter *Z*, the number 5 and the letter *S*, and the number 0 and the letter *O*. To compound this difficulty, it is not always easy to discern the difference between the letter *O* and the number 0 on high-speed printer or remote terminal output. Furthermore, to distinguish between the two, some installations use a slash through the letter *O*, while others use a slash through the number 0. It is good practice to put bars on the top and bottom of capital *I*'s to distinguish them from the numeral 1.

1-5.3 Saving Yourself Time and Trouble

Any study in computer programming can require an inordinate amount of time unless you discipline yourself. Five areas need particular attention.

(a) *Start Early*   If you wait until deadlines approach, you may find that you have to wait in long lines to receive help and gain access to equipment and that computer *turn-around time* has increased. A minor error, caught early, is easy to correct. A minor error discovered near the deadline for turning in a project usually costs a great deal of time and wasted effort.

(b) *Keep Up in Everything*   An absence from class is often unavoidable. But, if you are absent, seek help quickly and get caught up in the areas that you missed. The lectures, text, and laboratory projects often are coordinated; being out of step with any of the three can make it much more difficult to receive optimum advantage from the other two. If you have not completed the required laboratory projects by the required date, lectures will be less valuable because you will not have the background necessary to understand them well. If you miss a lecture, it may cause you difficulties when you start on the next laboratory project.

(c) *Do Not Shortcut Basic Procedures*   If you slight any of the basic formulation steps, you can be sure that you will pay the price of extra time on the project. In the early examples, it may appear that following a basic formulation procedure is costing you time;

however, it is important to recognize that you are perfecting techniques in a simple setting so that the techniques will be useable tools when they are essential to the solution of more complex problems.

(d) *Use Consultants Properly* Use consultants when they are available. But do not expect consultants to study for you, write your program, or do your work. They are usually instructed to help you learn to become a good computer programmer, not to solve your computer problems. On the other hand, be frank with the consultants. They often can find some means to give you special assistance if you are in difficulty.

If you must wait to see a consultant, play consultant with the others in line. Often you can see the mistakes others are making much more clearly than you can see your own and learn from the process.

(e) *Do Not Rush to the Computer* Every time you run a program on the computer, it takes *your* time. Be sure of your formulation before you even think of *coding*. Proofread before you make your run. If you punch cards rather than use a remote terminal, then try to run your deck through a *lister* so you can proofread from a printed sheet rather than directly from the cards. A few extra minutes spent making that final check or *tracing* that part you are not quite sure of will, in the long run, save a great deal of time.

1-5.4 Proofreading and Turn-Around Time

An efficient, effective, and inexpensive way to check punched cards is by use of a *verifier*, which looks very much like a keypunch but which accepts punched cards and compares their punched holes with retyped material. Cards that agree, column to column, for full card width are clipped on one end to show that they have been verified. If an error is detected, the machine stops until the necessary corrective action occurs.

If a verifier is not available, then you must use optical proofreading. Usually you can save time and reduce costly errors if you proofread with another person. For maximum efficiency, proofread from a listing of the program and not the computer deck of cards. For the very best results, proofread from the machine-oriented flow diagram or *Nassi-Shneiderman chart* to a listing of the program.

To shorten verbal communication and make the meaning more precise, use *par* and *close* for leading parenthesis and closing parenthesis, respectively. Thus ((X–3.)**2) would be read, "Par, par, X minus 3 point, close, star, star, 2 close." (Commas indicate slight pauses and are not vocalized.) Proofread where there are no distractions. Although proofreading may be boring and may seem to be an unnecessary burden, it is essential to proofread, thus avoiding potential waste of computer time, dollars, and personal time.

Just one more precaution: Schedule your work to make sojourns to the computer center fruitful, remembering that turn-around time is sure to increase near maintenance periods, down-times, and toward the end of any term. Try to schedule your time so that you can use the computer constructively.

1-6 OBJECTIVES

The overall objective of this book is to give you a *structured, modular, systems approach* to problem definition, formulation, and solution by computer with FORTRAN 77. Specifically, this text is designed to develop your skill in defining and formulating problems, to use FORTRAN 77 to master *syntactic* skills, and to obtain an overall view of generalized computer usage.

1-6.1 Structured Programming

Structured programming is a technique devised to optimize human efforts with only a slight reduction of computer efficiency. A structured program is basically composed of a series of *modules,* each with only one entrance and exit point. Thus a structured program has a "straight-line flow" which proceeds sequentially, step-by-step, until the problem is solved. In contrast, "rat's nest" programs allow the control of flow to change rapidly from one portion of the program to another, often in a manner that is very difficult to follow.

Structured programming techniques became the subject of active debate among many programmers in the mid 1970's. The time and cost advantages of structured programming seem to far outweigh its disadvantages, and lack of acceptance usually appears to be psychological. A structured program is easy to follow, easy to update or change, and easy to correct. Its inherent disadvantage is that there is not quite as much machine efficiency and not as much room for "sophisticated" tricks.

Although FORTRAN is a widely used computer language, it is one of the poorest for the application of structured programming. Nonetheless, structured programming can be used efficiently and effectively with FORTRAN 77 while enhancing the learner's progress and ultimate programming skill.

1-6.2 Module; Modular

A module is a set of statements which, when acting together, complete a specific task, and must have only one entrance and one exit point. As used in this text, the term *modular* is very closely allied to the term *structured program.* That is, a structured program is a linked set of modular elements, called modules, which act one after the other in a straight-line path. Programs presented early in this text often are composed of only a single module because they are designed to illustrate a specific point.

1-6.3 Systems Approach

With increased systems size and improved storage access, all problems may eventually be formulated within a systems context. A systems approach puts heavy emphasis on efficient and effective use of independent programs, called *subprograms,* as components of other subprograms and specialized programs. The systems approach emphasizes the need for structured programming, using modules in a straight-line configuration.

Examples, practice, and additional comments will clarify the terms *structured, modular,* and *systems approach.* They have been introduced at this point so that you can see their applications in subsequent discussions.

1-7 EXERCISES

1. Figure 1-7 shows two computer cards with holes, but without typing. Read the holes in these cards to show that you understand how the computer reads. (Refer to Figure 1-1, or punch a similar card for your use.)

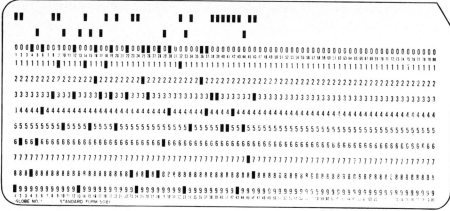

(a)

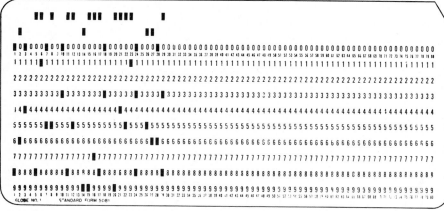

(b)

FIGURE 1-7 Nondecoded computer cards

FIGURE 1-8 Nondecoded numbers on computer card

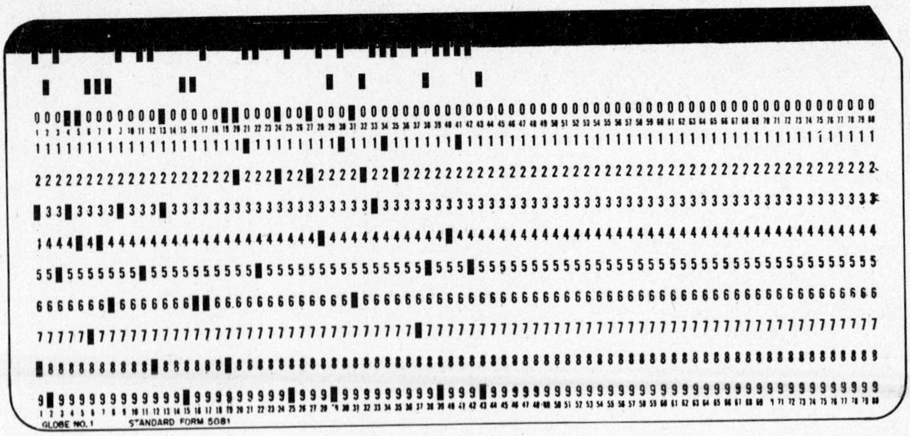

FIGURE 1-9 Nondecoded message

2. Figure 1-8 shows a computer card with several numbers punched in it. How might this card be read by the computer if it were turned upside down?

3. Figure 1-9 shows a computer card with a message punched on it. What would the computer read if the card were turned backwards?

(Your instructor will provide necessary instructions for exercises 4 and 5.)

4. Make yourself a *drum card* for the keypunch that allows you to tab to Columns 7, 12, 19, and 73. This is an excellent card to have available as you type your FORTRAN deck. Alternately, set these tabs on a remote terminal.

5. Make a drum card for the keypunch that tabs to locations 9, 17, 25, 33, 41, 49, 57, 65, and 73. This is an excellent drum card to keep for use in preparing numerical input data for 10F8.0 format. Alternately, set these tabs on a remote terminal. Is there room? (On some remote terminals the number of characters per line is limited so that input of numerical data is by 10F7.0, requiring tabs at 8, 15, 22, 29, 36, 43, 50, 57, and 64.)

6. Finite limits are placed on the magnitude and number of significant figures that a computer can represent. Yet, comparisons of widely diverse values are often made with zero. Can you think of a situation in which the number 1000 might be "close to zero"? Can you visualize a case where 0.0000000001 might not be "close to zero"?

Programming by Concept and Example

Chapter 1 presents an overview of what to expect while learning computer programming, as well as insight into the process that occurs each time a composite deck (containing control cards, the FORTRAN deck and corresponding data cards) is entered in (read by) the computer. Chapter 3 discusses various formulation procedures and compares strengths and weaknesses of two systems used in this book. Chapters 4 through 6 each deal with a specific aspect of the FORTRAN language: Chapter 4 defines the basic rules used to form syntactic items, expressions, and arithmetic assignment statements; Chapter 5 concentrates on control of flow within a FORTRAN computer program; and Chapter 6 formalizes rules for input/output. The concepts of Chapters 3 through 6 are synthesized by a series of examples in Chapter 7. Chapter 2 shows the fundamentals developed in Chapters 3 through 6 and summarized in Chapter 7, thus giving you a framework into which you can fit the appropriate details.

In Section 2–1, a program for doing computations for simple interest using two different formulations is presented. The first formulation illustrates the modified DO-WHILE, used in conjunction with logical IF statements. This program is then rewritten to improve the readability of output using the block IF (IF-THEN-ELSE) and the classical DO-WHILE. These are simple programs which are not too difficult to read.

Section 2–2 introduces a program called CUB, which uses two *nested* DO-WHILEs. Except for a discussion on how to formulate the problem, descriptive matter is somewhat limited and you will need to study the diagrams quite carefully if you are to understand the process. Program CUB may be too much of a challenge on the first time through. If so, you may want to study Section 2–3, a similar program with each step carefully described. If you find Section 2–2 easy to understand, you can probably omit Section 2–3.

Section 2–4 is optional, illustrating a small program which *calls* a *subroutine*. Traditionally, subroutines are introduced very late in a first course. With increasing emphasis on *top-down programming*, however, it seems prudent to show an example as early as possible. This example describes the computation of a factor needed in building design to mitigate against earthquake hazards. Interestingly, no mathematical or engineering background is needed to understand the problem. The program accomplishes the description taken from one of the most commonly used building codes.

In the remainder of this chapter, many new terms and concepts are introduced very rapidly. Remember that you will study the details more precisely in subsequent chapters, so concentrate on getting a feel for the overall process.

2-1 READING PROGRAM IEQPRT

The FORTRAN statement needed to evaluate i from the simple interest formula $i = prt$ is

$$I = P * R * T$$

Capital letters are used because FORTRAN does not include lower-case letters. Multiplication is represented by * rather than the more traditional · or ×.

Mathematical or algebraic symbols can be represented by descriptive names. Thus the simple interest equation can be represented by

$$EARN = PRIN * RATE * TIME$$

Because it is common to give rate as a percentage, conversion to a decimal is required (rate as percentage / 100 equals rate as a decimal). Thus in FORTRAN, a better form of the simple interest formula is

$$EARN = PRIN * RATE/100. * TIME$$

where the slash represents division.

In a computer program, the symbolic names refer to storage locations within the computer. The mathematical computations are performed using the numbers stored at these locations. In order to find EARN (the amount of interest earned), appropriate numerical values must already be stored at the locations named PRIN, RATE, and TIME.

One way to store numerical data in computer locations represented by symbolic names is by use of a READ statement. Thus, to enter data, our computer program becomes

```
READ(LR,1000) PRIN, RATE,TIME
EARN = PRIN * RATE/100. * TIME
```

(The parenthesized expression after the word READ signifies read from a device specified by the symbol LR, and present the data in a form specified by some statement numbered 1000.) The program now reads three numerical values, stores them sequentially in locations symbolized by PRIN, RATE, and TIME, and uses the stored values to compute an answer which is stored in the location named EARN.

A WRITE statement is used by the computer program to display the results stored in EARN.

```
READ (LR,1000) PRIN, RATE, TIME
EARN = PRIN* RATE/100. * TIME
WRITE(LW,1001) EARN
```

(The parenthesized expression after the word WRITE signifies write on a device specified by the symbol LW, and show the value stored in location EARN in the form specified by the statement labeled 1001.)

The symbols LR and LW used in the READ and WRITE statements must be given values so that the correct input/output devices will be used.† Although installation dependent, LR is often 5 to signify input from cards and LW is 6 to specify the high-speed printer. So the program becomes

```
LR = 5
LW = 6
READ (LR,1000) PRIN, RATE, TIME
EARN = PRIN * RATE/100. * TIME
WRITE (LW,1001) EARN
```

We need to include the two labeled (numbered) statements used in the READ and WRITE statements (their precise meaning will be discussed later).

```
        LR = 5
        LW = 6
        READ (LR, 1000) PRIN, RATE, TIME
        EARN = PRIN * RATE/100. * TIME
        WRITE (LW, 1001) EARN
1000 FORMAT (3F8.0)
1001 FORMAT(' EARN = ', F8.3)
```

It is desirable to name the program (first line) and to tell it when to stop executing. So the final program takes the following form:

```
        PROGRAM FIRST
        LR = 5
        LW = 6
        READ (LR, 1000) PRIN, RATE, TIME
        EARN = PRIN * RATE/100. * TIME
        WRITE (LW, 1001) EARN
1000 FORMAT (3F8.0)
1001 FORMAT (' EARN = ', F8.3)
        STOP
        END
```

The word END signifies the physical end of a FORTRAN program and must always be the very last statement in any program. By contrast, the word STOP indicates the logical end, the point at which the program is to stop executing.

Although the program is complete, it seems hardly worth the effort required to write it. Therefore, a more useful form of a program used for simple interest calculations is desirable. In developing the process, auxiliary elements of computer programming are presented and discussed.

†LR stands for Logical unit number for Read and LW is Logical unit number for Write.

In writing a computer program, a file is started that eventually becomes *documentation* for the completed program. The tables, figures, and listings of this section represent typical elements of such documentation and represent a very important part of computer programming.

2-1.1 Definition Sheet

The program IEQPRT is defined by the definition sheet of Table 2-1. This definition sheet has three main parts: (1) the program name; (2) a definition of the problem; and (3) a list of descriptive items used, shown both by symbols in general use (if such exist) and by names used to represent these symbols in the FORTRAN computer program.

(a) *Program Name*   Although it may appear trivial, it is important to display the program name prominently on each sheet. In this case, the program name, shown on the first line of the definition sheet, comes from $i = prt$, that is, I̲ Equals P̲ $\times$ R̲ $\times$ T̲.

(b) *Problem Definition*   Read the definition of Table 2-1. It has sufficient detail so that you can understand the problem in its entirety. The definition can be separated into four parts:

1. For each problem to be computed, four values, P, r, t and i, are always read in sequence.
2. Here P, r, t, and i represent symbols commonly used for the simple interest equation, $i = Prt$.
3. To work any problem involving this equation, three values of P, r, t, and i must be input with magnitudes greater than zero; the one remaining must be input as zero. The value input as zero will then be computed using the other three values.
4. When both P and r are input as zero, this acts as a signal that tells the program to stop computations.

(c) *Descriptive Items List*   In Table 2-1, the commonly used symbols P, r, t, and i are listed with the names used to represent their locations in the FORTRAN computer

---

Table 2-1 Definition Sheet for Program IEQPRT

Program: IEQPRT (I̲ EQUALS P̲ $\times$ R̲ $\times$ T̲)

Definition: This program reads values of P, r, t, and i for use in the general simple interest equation $i = Prt$. If three values are input, the fourth (input as a zero) will be computed. When both P and r are input as zero, the program will stop execution.

Descriptive Items:

Variable Name	Symbol	Meaning
PRIN	P	Principal or present worth.
RATE	r	Rate of interest (%)*.
TIME	t	Time or period over which interest is earned.
EARN	i	Interest or interest earned over time period of calculation.

*RATE is input and output as a percentage, but must be a decimal fraction in the equation $i = Prt$. This requires that RATE always be used as RATE/100.

---

program: PRIN, RATE, TIME, and EARN, respectively. Each symbol and *variable name* (or simply *variable†*) is given a meaning. Thus PRIN, representing the symbol *P*, stands for the principal or present worth and RATE, corresponding to *r*, signifies rate of interest as a percent. The letters used for the variable names are underlined in the column defining their meanings.

It may seem odd that interest, indicated by the common symbol *i*, was not stored in the variable name INT. Chapter 4 discusses this matter thoroughly; we shall simply state that numbers that may have decimal fractional parts must use variable names beginning with a letter of the alphabet other than *I, J, K, L, M,* or *N*. Therefore INT cannot be used because the location represented by this variable name must be able to store decimal fractions.

2-1.2 Solutions to $i = Prt$

The basic equation $i = Prt$ can be written four ways, solving for a different unknown each time. These combinations are shown in Table 2-2, using symbols rather than the variable names of the program.

Table 2-2 Algebraic Combinations of Simple Interest Formula $i = Prt$

Given	Find (Meaning)	Solution*
r, t, and *i*	*P* (Principal)	$P = 100i/(rt)$
t, i, and *P*	*r* (rate)	$r = 100i/(Pt)$
i, P, and *r*	*t* (time)	$t = 100\,i/(Pr)$
P, r, and *t*	*i* (interest, %)	$i = P(r/100)t$

*The constant 100 is necessary to convert rate *(r)* from a percent to a decimal fraction, and vice versa.

2-1.3 First Solution to Program IEQPRT

Listing 2-1 shows a FORTRAN computer program for the simple interest computations using the equation $i = Prt$. Each line of the listing represents a single FORTRAN card or a single line typed on a remote terminal. The first line names the program. The second line defines what the program does. The next four lines define the four variables used in the program. The letter *C* in the first column of these five lines indicates that everything on these lines are Comments to be ignored by the computer (except that each line is to be output along with the remainder of the program as an aid to human users). These leading six lines are followed by a blank line to make the program easier to read.

The two cards LR = 5 and LW = 6 define the *logical unit numbers* to be used for reading data and writing output by the FORTRAN program. These two values are isolated near the beginning of the program so that they can be changed readily if the program is to be run on another machine or at another installation. In this text, logical

†See Section 4-2.3.

unit number 5 stands for either read from cards to obtain input data or read from the remote terminal, and logical unit number 6 signifies either write any output values on the high-speed printer or write on the remote terminal.

It is important to remember that two stages occur when the program deck represented by Listing 2–1 is read into the computer: (1) storage locations are allocated and the FORTRAN program is translated into the machine's language; and—only then— (2) the program that has been completely translated executes so that the FORTRAN program appears to be performing the operations. This, of course, means that the FORTRAN program neither reads input data nor writes output information until the first stage is complete.

When the next line of Listing 2–1, the READ statement, is encountered, this FORTRAN will be translated into the machine's language and storage will be allocated for the four variables PRIN, RATE, TIME, and EARN. No data is actually read until the program has been compiled through the last statement in the program, the word END.

When the program has completely compiled in Stage 1, it is executed. In Stage 2, the READ statement will cause the computer to read from the unit specified by LR; (since LR was set to 5, the computer will expect the input data to come from cards). Data on the input cards must have the form shown by statement 100, the FORMAT statement. The four values on the data card (or on the line submitted from the remote terminal) will be stored sequentially into the locations PRIN, RATE, TIME, and EARN.

Although the READ statement starts in Column 7, it is preceded in Columns 4 and 5 by the constant 10. Such a number, located within the first 5 columns of a FORTRAN card, represents a label for the statement on this line. Such labels are used when more than one path exists to any given single FORTRAN statement. During Stage 2 execution, this statement will be executed immediately following any FORTRAN statement, anywhere in the program, stating GO TO 10.

```
1     5 6 7
      |PROGRAM IEQPRT
C     |DOES SIMPLE INTEREST COMPUTATIONS I=PRT
C     |WHERE   PRIN -MEANS- PRINCIPAL($)                        =P
C     |        RATE -MEANS- INTEREST RATE AS PERCENT            =R
C     |        TIME -MEANS- TIME CORRESPONDING TO RATE          =T
C     |        EARN -MEANS- EARNINGS OR INTEREST EARNED ($)     =I
      |
      |LR=5
      |LW=6
      |
   10 |READ(LR,100) PRIN,RATE,TIME,EARN
      |IF(PRIN .NE. 0. .OR.  RATE .NE. 0.) THEN
      |     IF(PRIN .EQ. 0.) PRIN=100.*EARN/(RATE * TIME)
      |     IF(RATE .EQ. 0.) RATE=100.*EARN/(PRIN * TIME)
      |     IF(TIME .EQ. 0.) TIME=100.*EARN/(PRIN * RATE)
      |     IF(EARN .EQ. 0.) EARN=PRIN*RATE/100.* TIME
      |     WRITE(LW,101) PRIN,RATE,TIME,EARN
      |     GO TO 10
      |END IF
      |
  100 |FORMAT(10F8.0)
  101 |FORMAT(' PRIN=' , F8.2 , '  RATE=' , F6.2 ,
     1|'  TIME=' , F5.1 , '  EARN=' , F8.2)
      |
      |STOP
      |END
```

LISTING 2–1 Program IEQPRT listing

Chapter 2 Programming by Concept and Example

In Listing 2–1, the READ statement labeled 10 is the first line of a *modified DO-WHILE*. The last line of this modified DO-WHILE is the statement several lines below, END IF. This group of statements is preceded and followed by a blank card to facilitate reading the program.

Once the four values for PRIN, RATE, TIME, and EARN have been read and stored during the execution stage, control will go to the following line, a block IF (IF-THEN) statement. The meaning of this IF-THEN statement is almost intuitively clear: if the value of PRIN (just read) is not equal to zero or if the value of RATE (also just read) is not equal to zero, then do the following sequence of statements until the sequence is altered or the statement END IF is reached.

When solving a problem of the type $i = Prt$, either the value read into PRIN or the value read into RATE during execution would not be zero. (Often neither PRIN nor RATE would be zero.) Flow would then be to the next statement, a logical IF.

During execution, the statement following each of the indented parenthetical expressions is performed if, and only if, the expression within the parentheses is true. If the expression is false, then control simply *flows* to the next statement with no other action. The logical IF, therefore, provides a way to perform or skip during execution, an operation that is dependent on values that change from time to time while the program is running.

Thus, on the first indented line of Listing 2–1, which starts IF(PRIN.EQ. . ., if the value currently stored in PRIN is zero the positive values currently stored in EARN, RATE, and TIME (assuming correct input) are used to calculate the value of PRIN. This is done by multiplying (indicated by *) 100 times the value currently stored in EARN and dividing (indicated by /) by the product of the values currently stored in the locations RATE and TIME. Once this calculation is performed, the result is stored in location PRIN. Because RATE, TIME, and EARN are not zero, none of the next three indented statements of Listing 2–1 would involve calculations, since in each case the expression within parentheses would be false.

As another example, if we wish to compute the time needed to earn a specified interest for a specified rate and principal, we would input the values of PRIN, RATE, and EARN; the value to be read and stored in TIME would be zero. Then, following the sequence of

Five typical lines (or cards) of input:

```
1        8 9      16 17     24 25  ◄──Column numbers on data cards
8000.    6.       3.        0.
0.       5.       4.        180.
6000.    0.       7.        3360.
4000.    7.       0.        980.
0.       0.
```
↙Data card that terminates run

Four lines of output from data above:

```
PRIN= 8000.00    RATE=  6.00    TIME=  3.0    EARN= 1440.00
PRIN=  900.00    RATE=  5.00    TIME=  4.0    EARN=  180.00
PRIN= 6000.00    RATE=  8.00    TIME=  7.0    EARN= 3360.00
PRIN= 4000.00    RATE=  7.00    TIME=  3.5    EARN=  980.00
```

LISTING 2–2 Typical I/O for program IEQPRT

indented statements of Listing 2–1, PRIN and RATE are not computed because they are not zero; TIME is computed using values currently stored in PRIN, RATE, and EARN because it has been read and stored as zero, and EARN is not computed because it is not zero. Thus every time this sequence is executed, only one computation is performed—the one that determines the missing fourth value, which was input as zero.

The four logical IF statements are followed by a WRITE statement which outputs the four values currently stored in PRIN, RATE, TIME, and EARN. The device used for output is controlled by the number stored in location LW, which was set to 6. (This is usually considered to represent the high-speed printer or remote terminal in this text.)

Flow through the program of Listing 2–1 is sequential except for *branches* caused by statements such as GO TO 10. At this branch, control is transferred to the READ statement labeled 10 and the usual sequential execution is resumed. This branching results in a loop, a portion of a program that is usually used more than once during execution.

In summary, when the program of Listing 2–1 is executing, it will start by reading and storing four values for PRIN, RATE, TIME, and EARN. The program will then check to see if either the value stored in PRIN or the value stored in RATE is zero. If at least one of PRIN or RATE is not zero, then the program will proceed through the four logical IF statements. One of the logical IF's will compute the unknown value; the other logical IF's will be essentially inoperative assuming data are entered correctly. Once the four logical IF's have been executed, the four values are output—the three nonzero values and the one which was read as zero and then computed. Since this problem is complete, control is transferred to Statement 10 by the GO TO and a new set of four values, at least one of which must be zero, is read and stored.

At any time that the values read and stored in PRIN and RATE are both zero, the (first) block IF statement will be false and none of the succeeding statements will be performed. Control will then conceptually transfer to the END IF. The END IF is followed by a STOP statement, which terminates execution of the program. The last statement of the program is END, used during first stage compilation to indicate the physical end of the FORTRAN computer program.

Listing 2–2 shows typical input read by program IEQPRT, together with the resulting output. Because of the simple input data, the answers are easy to verify.

2–1.4 Aids Used to Formulate Program IEQPRT

Figure 2–1 shows a Nassi-Shneiderman diagram and a machine-oriented flow diagram for program IEQPRT, two typical aids used by programmers in formulating computer programs. Program IEQPRT is so simple that these tools may appear to complicate the program rather than clarify it. In complex programs, however, these aids can be of great value.

As you read the following subsections, relate the commentary to the diagrams. This will help you understand the process of writing computer programs.

(a) *The modified Nassi-Shneiderman Chart for IEQPRT* is contained within a rectangle on the left side of Figure 2–1. Statements such as LR = 5 and LW = 6 that do not involve branching are placed in "*process boxes,*" which are formed by drawing horizontal lines completely across the major rectangle.

The modified DO-WHILE is represented by a rectangle divided into two primary parts; its extent is signified by an open space in the shape of an inverted L. Double horizontal lines at the beginning and end of the DO-WHILE highlight its limits. The number 10 at the top of the DO-WHILE rectangle is a statement label number, used in conjunction with the READ statement. This is followed by WHILE with an expression in parentheses. As long as the expression within the parentheses is true, everything in the remainder of the box—the four logical IF statements, the WRITE statement, and the GO TO statement—is executed.

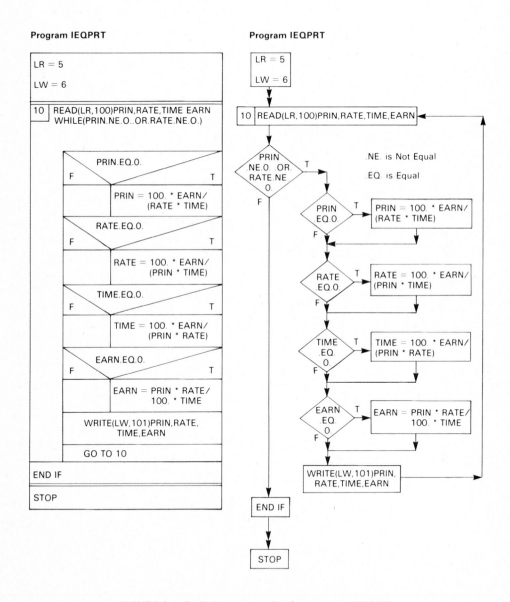

FIGURE 2-1 Typical documentation for program IEQPRT

The last statement in the rectangle bounded by the inverted L is always GO TO, which, in this case, transfers control back to READ statement 10 at the beginning of the modified DO-WHILE.

Within the DO-WHILE rectangle, the logical IF statements are represented by a rectangle cut into three triangles with a common vertex. The upper triangle contains the expression to be tested. The left triangle contains the letter F, indicating what action is to be performed if the statement in the upper triangle is false. The lower right triangle has the letter T, indicating the path to be taken if the statement in the upper triangle is true. Below each triangle is a box containing the corresponding statements to be performed.

The logical IF statement used in this fashion always has an empty box under the "false" path and a single statement in the box under the "true" path.

Flow proceeds through the boxes, checking each of the four IF statements in turn; then the WRITE statement is performed. Finally, the GO TO statement passes control back to the top of the DO-WHILE.

When the READ statement obtains zeros from input data for PRIN and RATE, the DO-WHILE statement (in parentheses) is no longer true. Control then passes to the next box, which terminates the DO-WHILE with END IF.

The final statement, STOP, is shown in the last process box.

(b) *The Machine-Oriented Flow Diagram for IEQPRT,* depicted on the right side of Figure 2–1, is a sequence of operations connected by a series of flow arrows. The flow diagram is read by following the arrows, branching at diamond-shaped boxes. At the first diamond, if the values of PRIN and RATE are both zero, the expression within the diamond is false; therefore flow would be to END IF, followed by STOP. When at least one of the current values of PRIN or RATE is not zero, control flows to the right. The next logical IF statement is represented by a diamond containing the expression PRIN.EQ.O. If the value of PRIN equals zero, flow is to the right and the calculation is performed; control then flows to the next diamond. If PRIN is not equal to zero, flow is straight down to the next diamond.

After each of the four logical IF's are checked, control passes to the WRITE statement. An arrow directs us back to the original READ statement, which contains a statement label (10 in this case). This arrow is represented in FORTRAN by GO TO 10.

The DO-WHILE is initiated and terminated by double arrowheads, corresponding to the double horizontal lines on the modified Nassi-Shneiderman charts and the blank cards within the FORTRAN coding.

2–1.5 Modifying IEQPRT into EEQPRT

In EEQPRT, the program is modified so that the output shows clearly which values are known and which is unknown for each data card read. The basic difficulty in IEQPRT is that the logical IF allowed for only one action when the logical expression was true and none when the logical expression was false. This is easily overcome by using the block IF, in this case, IF-THEN-ELSE.

Listing 2–3 combines the FORTRAN coding, input data, and output for program EEQPRT. The program is somewhat longer but the results are much more informative. (Compare with Listing 2–2.)

We convert program IEQPRT to program EEQPRT for two other reasons. Many acceptable programs can be written to do identical tasks. It is highly unlikely that two people will write the same program in the same way. Also, instructors, installations, and employees may specify acceptable programming forms. IEQPRT uses a "modified" DO-WHILE which works well in FORTRAN but, as we shall see, may not be an allowed technique. EEQPRT overcomes such a difficulty by using the "classical" DO-WHILE, which is a required technique in certain circumstances.

Program EEQPRT

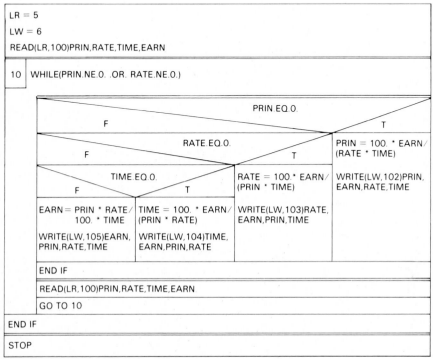

FIGURE 2-2 Modified Nassi-Shneiderman chart for program EEQPRT

(a) *The Modified Nassi-Shneiderman Chart for EEQPRT.* In Figure 2–2, the initial process box assigns 5 to LR and 6 to LW. Next, four values are read and stored, sequentially, into locations PRIN, RATE, TIME, and EARN.

The double horizontal line signifies the start of a classical DO-WHILE, which is terminated by the last set of double horizontal lines following END IF.

While either PRIN or RATE is not equal to zero, the rectangle defined by the inverted L is executed through GO TO 10. The chart in this rectangle is read in the following manner.

> IF PRIN is equal to 0, THEN
>> Compute PRIN, and
>> Output results along with corresponding input values.

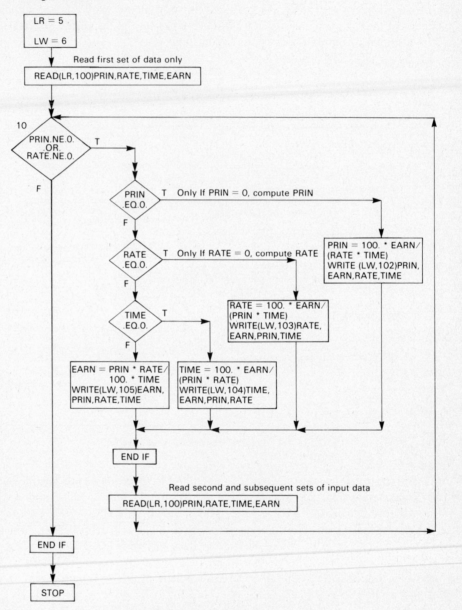

Program EEQPRT

LR = 5

LW = 6

Read first set of data only

READ(LR,100)PRIN,RATE,TIME,EARN

10

PRIN.NE.0.
.OR.
RATE.NE.0.   T

F

PRIN
.EQ.0.   T   Only If PRIN = 0, compute PRIN

F

RATE
.EQ.0.   T   Only If RATE = 0, compute RATE

F

PRIN = 100. * EARN/
(RATE * TIME)
WRITE (LW,102)PRIN,
EARN,RATE,TIME

TIME
.EQ.0.   T

F

RATE = 100. * EARN/
(PRIN * TIME)
WRITE(LW,103)RATE,
EARN,PRIN,TIME

EARN = PRIN * RATE/
100. * TIME
WRITE(LW,105)EARN,
PRIN,RATE,TIME

TIME = 100. * EARN/
(PRIN * RATE)
WRITE(LW,104)TIME,
EARN,PRIN,RATE

END IF

Read second and subsequent sets of input data

READ(LR,100)PRIN,RATE,TIME,EARN

END IF

STOP

FIGURE 2-3 Machine-oriented flow diagram for program EEQPRT

Chapter 2 Programming by Concept and Example

```
      PROGRAM EEQPRT
C     DOES SIMPLE INTEREST COMPUTATIONS I=PRT
C     WHERE   PRIN -MEANS- PRINCIPAL($)                    =P
C             RATE -MEANS- INTEREST RATE AS PERCENT        =R
C             TIME -MEANS- TIME CORRESPONDING TO RATE      =T
C             EARN -MEANS- EARNINGS OR INTEREST EARNED ($) =I

      LR=5
      LW=6
      READ(LR,100) PRIN,RATE,TIME,EARN

   10 IF(PRIN .NE. 0. .OR.  RATE .NE. 0.) THEN

         IF(PRIN .EQ. 0.) THEN
            PRIN= 100.*EARN/(RATE * TIME)
            WRITE(LW,102) PRIN,EARN,RATE,TIME
         ELSE IF(RATE .EQ. 0.) THEN
            RATE= 100.*EARN/(PRIN * TIME)
            WRITE(LW,103) RATE,EARN,PRIN,TIME
         ELSE IF(TIME .EQ. 0.) THEN
            TIME=100.*EARN/(PRIN * RATE)
            WRITE(LW,104) TIME,EARN,PRIN,RATE
         ELSE
            EARN= PRIN*RATE/100.*TIME
            WRITE(LW,105) EARN,PRIN,RATE,TIME
         END IF

         READ(LR,100)PRIN,RATE,TIME,EARN
         GO TO 10
      END IF

  100 FORMAT(10F8.0)
  102 FORMAT(/9X,'PRIN',3X,'=',5X,'100 X   EARN',4X,'/ (RATE    X TIME)'/
     1F15.2,' =',5X,'100 X',F8.2,'   / (',F7.2,' X',F5.2,')'/)
  103 FORMAT(/9X,'RATE',3X,'=',5X,'100 X',F8.2,'   / (',F7.2,' X',F5.2,')'/)
     1F15.2,' =',5X,'100 X',F8.2,'   / (',F7.2,' X',F5.2,')'/)
  104 FORMAT(/9X,'TIME',3X,'=',5X,'100 X   EARN',4X,'/ (PRIN    X RATE)'/
     1F15.2,' =',5X,'100 X',F8.2,'   / (',F7.2,' X',F5.2,')'/)
  105 FORMAT(/9X,'EARN',3X,'=',2X,'PRIN',3X,'X  TIME',4X,'X RATE / 100'
     1/F15.2,' =',F8.2,' X',F8.2,'   X',F7.2,' / 100'/)

      STOP
      END
```

Input data:

```
|1       8|9      16|17     24|25    ← Columns on input data card
|8000.   |6.      |3.      |0.
|0.      |5.      |4.      |180.
|6000.   |0.      |7.      |3360.
|4000.   |7.      |0.      |980.
|0.      |0.
          └ Terminal data card
```

Output:

```
EARN    =  PRIN    X  TIME    X  RATE / 100
1440.00 = 8000.00 X   6.00   X   3.00 / 100

PRIN    =    100 X   EARN    / (RATE    X TIME)
900.00  =    100 X  180.00   / (  5.00 X 4.00)

RATE    =    100 X   EARN    / (PRIN    X TIME)
8.00    =    100 X 3360.00   / (6000.00 X 7.00)

TIME    =    100 X   EARN    / (PRIN    X RATE)
3.50    =    100 X  980.00   / (4000.00 X 7.00)
```

LISTING 2-3 Program EEQPRT with typical I/O

ELSE, IF RATE is equal to 0, THEN
>   Compute RATE, and
>   Output results along with corresponding input values.

ELSE, IF TIME is equal to 0, THEN
>   Compute TIME, and
>   Output results along with corresponding input values.

ELSE

>   Compute EARN, and
>   Output results along with corresponding input values.

Every time a statement is true, a positive action is taken and flow proceeds directly to the first END IF process box.

The first two IF's lead to secondary IF's when the expression is false. The last IF branches to one of two action statements, each of which flows directly to the first END IF process box. (Compare the modified Nassi-Shneiderman diagram of Figure 2–2 to Listing 2–3.)

(b) *The Machine-Oriented Flow Diagram for EEQPRT* Figure 2–3 shows a modification of the $i = Prt$ program that permits output to show clearly which values were known and which were computed for each set of data.

The primary difference is in the sequence of IF statements. A change to the block IF overcomes the limitation of the logical IF, where only one statement is performed when the expression is true, none when the expression is false.

Starting with the second diamond, this flow diagram is read as follows.

If PRIN is equal to 0, THEN
>   Compute PRIN, and
>   Output results along with corresponding input values.

ELSE, IF RATE is equal to 0, THEN
>   Compute RATE, and
>   Output results along with corresponding input values.

ELSE, IF TIME is equal to 0, THEN
>   Compute TIME, and
>   Output results along with corresponding input values.

ELSE

>   Compute EARN, and
>   Output results along with corresponding input values.

Every time a statement is true, a positive action is taken and flow proceeds directly to the first END IF process box.

The first two IF's lead to secondary IF's only when the expression is false. The last IF branches to one of two action statements, each of which flows directly to the first END IF process box. Compare the machine-oriented flow diagram of Figure 2–3 to Listing 2–3.

2-1.6 DO-WHILE Variations

In many high-level languages similar to FORTRAN, the classical DO-WHILE exists as a single command, which eliminates the need for the GO TO statement. Because of this, many programmers insist on using only the classical form of DO-WHILE. Thus the modified DO-WHILE of IEQPRT has been changed to a classical form in EEQPRT by adding an auxiliary READ statement. Using the classical method, the initial READ statement is used only for the first set of data—all subsequent data is read by an identical READ statement located within the confines of the classical DO-WHILE itself. In later chapters, the significance of such variations will become clearer.

2-1.7 Enhancing Readability

The DO-WHILE and block IF are described as *mini-modules* in Chapter 5. The limits of such mini-modules are highlighted. At the beginning, we use:

a double horizontal line	in modified Nassi-Shneiderman charts;
a double arrowhead	in machine-oriented flow diagrams;
a blank line (card)	in FORTRAN coding.

The mini-modules are all terminated by:

a double horizontal line immediately following an END IF	in modified Nassi-Shneiderman charts;
a double arrowhead immediately following an END IF	in machine-oriented flow diagrams;
a blank line (card) immediately following an END IF	in FORTRAN coding.

Mini-modules are also indented in FORTRAN coding.

In the program EEQPRT, the block IF mini-module is *nested* within the confines of the classical DO-WHILE mini-module. The limits of each, however, are quite clear.

In the modified Nassi-Shneiderman charts (see Figure 2–2) the double horizontal lines initiating and terminating the classical DO-WHILE extend across the complete rectangle. The double lines initiating and terminating the block IF extend across only the rectangle defined by the inverted L, and are inside the initial and terminal marks of the DO-WHILE.

In the machine-oriented flow diagram (see Figure 2–3), the double arrows indicating the beginning and end of the classical DO-WHILE are on the vertical line at the far left. The double arrowheads beginning and ending the block IF are both on the vertical line

```
      PROGRAM FEQPRT

C         POORLY STYLED PROGRAM
C
C         -- NOT --THIS WAY
C         *******
C
      LR=5
      LW=6
      READ(LR,100) PRIN,RATE,TIME,EARN
   10 IF(PRIN .NE. 0. .OR. RATE .NE. 0.) THEN
      IF(PRIN .EQ. 0.) THEN
      PRIN= 100.*EARN/(RATE * TIME)
      WRITE(LW,102) PRIN,EARN,RATE,TIME
      ELSE IF(RATE .EQ. 0.) THEN
      RATE= 100.*EARN/(PRIN * TIME)
      WRITE(LW,103) RATE,EARN,PRIN,TIME
      ELSE IF(TIME .EQ. 0.) THEN
      TIME=100.*EARN/(PRIN * RATE)
      WRITE(LW,104) TIME,EARN,PRIN,RATE
      ELSE
      EARN= PRIN*RATE/100.*TIME
      WRITE(LW,105) EARN,PRIN,RATE,TIME
      END IF
      READ(LR,100)PRIN,RATE,TIME,EARN
      GO TO 10
      END IF
  100 FORMAT(10F8.0)
  102 FORMAT(/9X,´PRIN´,3X,´=´,5X,´100 X  EARN´,4X,´/ (RATE     X TIME)´/
     1F15.2,´ =´,5X,´100 X´,F8.2,´   / (´,F7.2,´ X´,F5.2,´)´/)
  103 FORMAT(/9X,´RATE´,3X,´=´,5X,´100 X  EARN´,4X,´/ (PRIN     X TIME)´/
     1F15.2,´ =´,5X,´100 X´,F8.2,´   / (´,F7.2,´ X´,F5.2,´)´/)
  104 FORMAT(/9X,´TIME´,3X,´=´,5X,´100 X  EARN´,4X,´/ (PRIN     X RATE)´/
     1F15.2,´ =´,5X,´100 X´,F8.2,´   / (´,F7.2,´ X´,F5.2,´)´/)
  105 FORMAT(/9X,´EARN´,3X,´=´,2X,´PRIN´,3X,´X  TIME´,4X,´X  RATE / 100´
     1F15.2,´ =´,F8.2,´ X´,F8.2,´  X´,F7.2,´ / 100´/)
      STOP
      END
```

LISTING 2-4 Poorly styled EEQPRT

second from the left. The diagram shows that the block IF is contained within the DO-WHILE.

Can you identify the nested block IF within the classical DO-WHILE on Listing 2-3? Does the use of indentation and blank lines (cards) help? If you are not sure, compare the readability of Listing 2-3 with Listing 2-4.

2-2 PROGRAM CUB

This section shows four steps often used in writing computer programs. The example program computes y using the formula $ax^2 + bx + c$ for different sets of a, b, and c and for different values of x for each set of a, b, and c.

2-2.1 Understanding the Problem

It is important to be sure you completely understand any problem whose solution you wish to program, since anything that is unclear is certain to cause you difficulty and cost you time later.

Table 2-3 Program CUB Example Problems

Given: Evaluate $ax^2 + bx + c = y$ for y in each case.

a	b	c	$ax^2 + bx + c$	x	$ax^2 + bx + c = y$
3	-4	7	$3x^2 - 4x + 7$	2	$3(2)^2 - 4(2) + 7 = 11$
				-2	$3(-2)^2 - 4(-2) + 7 = 27$
				1	$3(1)^2 - 4(1) + 7 = 6$
5	2	-9	$5x^2 + 2x - 9$	2.16	$5(2.16)^2 + 2(2.16) - 9 = 18.648$
				-4.7	$5(-4.7)^2 + 2(-4.7) - 9 = 92.050$

Often it helps to lay out a sample of what you have in mind. Table 2–3 illustrates this technique for program CUB. The final table is orderly, but it is a culmination of several false starts. The equation in general form is followed by a table with typical input values. The first three columns represent different values of a, b, and c that reduce the general form to an equation with x as the only remaining variable. According to the initial description, each set of values is to be used with one or more values of x. Column 5 shows typical values of x to be used with the particular values of a, b, and c. Column 6 shows the generalized equation with a, b, c, and x replaced by their appropriate numerical values.

Although situations vary, this process of defining the problem by a sample table has wide generality. The biggest deterrent to using this process is the time required to do the layout. Time spent at this point is very often repaid by the time saved during subsequent steps in developing a correctly functioning computer program.

As you study the table, it becomes clear that the program must have several parts. Values for one set of a, b, and c must be read. (It might appear reasonable to use these values as a "flag" to tell the computer to stop executing.) For each set of a, b, and c, the program must (1) read a value of x, and (2) do the computations for y.

2–2.2 Evolution of Human-Oriented Flow Diagram

Sometimes it helps to think through the steps to a single solution before adding a system to loop through multiple problems. Figure 2–4 represents a possible way that this can be done for program CUB. The boxes and arrows provide a means of identifying individual steps. Boxes 2, 4 and 5 come directly from conclusions about the program discussed earlier. Box 1 insures that headings are put in place, while Box 3 is added because it is always wise to *echo* input to be sure the computer is using the data we had in mind. Box 6 gives an echo of individual values of x and outputs corresponding answers computed for y.

If only one set of a, b, and c were to be used with any number of x values, Figure 2–4(a) could be altered by drawing an arrow from the last box back to Box 4 to read another x (see Figure 2–4(b)). With this diagram, however, the program would never know when to stop. Thus the value of each x should be checked after it is read to see if more solutions are desired. We could then decide that if x is input as zero, the program should stop. A diamond (signifying a question during program execution) is therefore inserted between Boxes 4 and 5 to check on x, as shown in Figure 2–4(c).

To allow for different sets of a, b, and c, the STOP of Figure 2–4(c) could be replaced by an arrow to Box 2, where new values of a, b, and c could be read (see Figure 2–4d).

Finally, the addition of the IF statement in the diamond in Figure 2–4(e) gives the program a way to stop executing. Note that each loop of the nested DO-WHILE is now clearly discernible.

Sketching such diagrams becomes second nature with practice, and many of the intermediate steps can be eliminated. Figure 2–5(c), on page 37, represents the desired results in an improved, structured format. It may be helpful at this point to think through the steps in writing Figure 2–5(c) directly. Start in the upper left corner. Anticipate questions and represent them with diamonds. Flow from diamonds is down when the answer is false, to the right when the answer is true. Loops flow counterclockwise.

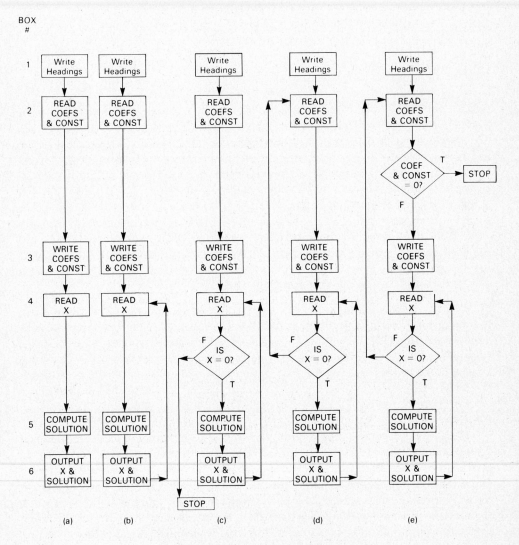

FIGURE 2-4 Evolution of human-oriented flow diagram

Chapter 2 Programming by Concept and Example

2-2.3 Summary

Figure 2–5 is a composite diagram of four elements of programming applied to the solution of program CUB. Figure 2–5(a) contains the definition sheet, while (c) displays the human-oriented (gross) flow diagram. Figure 2–5(d) pictures the machine-oriented (detailed) flow diagram, and (b) has the FORTRAN coding. In practice, the definition sheet and human-oriented flow diagram are usually developed simultaneously. Both should be completed, except for the descriptive item list, before starting the machine-oriented flow diagram. Typical input/output is shown in Listing 2–6, page 41.

It is usually simple to make the transition from the human-oriented flow diagram to the machine-oriented diagram and subsequently to FORTRAN coding. To provide further assistance, Listing 2–5, page 40, explains many important details. In addition, Listing 2–6 contains only comments taken from the human-oriented flow diagram.

Programmers disagree on the optimum number of comments a program should contain. Compare the codings of Figure 2–5, Listing 2–5, and Listing 2–6. Which do you prefer? See if your preference changes as you become more proficient at programming.

2-2.4 Alternate Approach

Figure 2–6, on page 42, illustrates modified Nassi-Shneiderman charts, both human and machine-oriented. A detailed discussion of their use in formulating a computer program is not presented because they require a more precise concept of the DO-WHILE and block IF to be used efficiently. (See Chapter 5.)

2-2.5 A Simple WRITE Statement to Output a Title

Within the FORTRAN program of Listing 2–6, the statement

$$\text{WRITE (LW, 1003)}$$

when associated with an appropriate FORMAT statement, causes the computer to output a title on the high-speed printer.

The letter *W* of the word *WRITE* must start in, or beyond, Column 7 on the computer card or line of remote terminal. (See also Section 1–4.1(c).) WRITE is normally written without imbedded blanks. Although such blanks are legal and are ignored, it is good practice not to write words with imbedded blanks. Thus, if $\triangle$ is a blank, we avoid writing expressions such as

$$\text{W}\triangle\text{R}\triangle\triangle\text{IT}\triangle\text{E} \hspace{3cm} \text{[poor]}$$

Any number of spaces can occur to the right or left of the parentheses symbols.

LW gives the logical unit number, signifying the unit to write to—the high-speed printer, a remote terminal, a tape, a *drum,* and so on. As usual, 6 identifies the high-speed printer, so the statement LW = 6 occurs in Listing 2–6 prior to the WRITE statement.

As an alternate form, LW may be replaced by the device number itself. In such a case, the WRITE statement would appear as WRITE (6, 1003). Use of LW (an integer variable) rather than the unit number itself (an integer constant) simplifies running programs on different machines or in different computer centers where logical unit numbers differ. Any integer variable name could be used for the purpose of defining the logical number for an output unit, but LW is used in this text.

The comma between the LW and the 1003 is mandatory. The comma itself may be preceded and followed by any number of blanks.

The integer constant 1003 represents a statement label number that identifies the FORMAT statement to be used with the WRITE statement. Clearly, the number of the FORMAT statement label need not always be 1003. Many programmers do, however, prefer to label all formats as 1001, 1002, or by some other such scheme. An integer constant rather than a variable name is used for the statement number.

The last parenthesis is mandatory and must occur before Column 73 on the card, unless a continuation card is used. Again, however, arbitrary blanks may precede or follow the last parenthesis.

Thus WRITE (LW, 1003) commands the computer to write the information formatted by the statement labeled 1003 on the output unit defined by LW. Unless the contents of the FORMAT statement are known, it is impossible to tell what will be written on the high-speed printer. That is, the WRITE statement is *executable,* it says to do something, but it does not say what form the "something" is to take.

2-2.6 Basic Concepts of FORMAT Statements

With reference to the high-speed printer, the FORMAT statement corresponding to WRITE (LW, 1003) can control four things: vertical position on the output page, blank lines, blank spaces within lines, and textual material to be output.

(a) *Vertical Position* is controlled by the first space (column) of every line to be output on the high-speed printer. It often *does not print*. That is, the value in column 1 controls the high-speed printer carriage. Attempting to write a 1 in Column 1 of an output line causes the high-speed printer to advance to the top of the next page. This is called *slueing*. To slue to the top of the next page, simply try to write a 1 in Column 1.

Program: CUB (a novice or learner program)

Purpose :   Compute y by formula $ax^2 + bx + c = y$ for (1) Different sets of
            a,b and c and (2) Different values of x within each set.

Descriptive Items:

Variable Name	Symbol	Description
COXS	a	coefficient of x squared*
COX	b	coefficient of x
CON	c	constant within equation*
X	x	variable x
SOL	y	solution to $ax^2 + bx + c$
LR		logical unit number for Reading Cards
LW		logical unit number for Writing on HSP (High Speed Printer)

*Some programmers would oppose these variable names because they could be confused with one another if the mnemonic meanings were forgotten.

FIGURE 2–5(a) Program CUB—Definition sheet

(b) *Blank lines* are produced by slash marks encountered outside of the text material within a FORMAT statement. Actually, a slash simply causes a carriage return, and a blank line is obtained only if nothing is to be output on the line immediately after the carriage return.

(c) *Blank spaces* within lines are obtained by two methods. The simplest is by imbedding spaces in text material. Another way, often very convenient, is to use nX, where n is a positive integer constant equal to the number of blank spaces desired and X is the character for "leave blank spaces." Thus $3X$ means leave three blank spaces, $7X$ means leave seven blank spaces, and so on.

Human-Oriented Flow Diagram: CUB

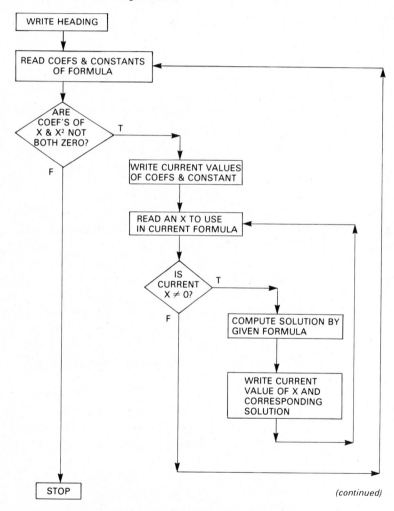

(continued)

FIGURE 2-5(c) Program CUB—Human-oriented flow diagram

```
1     5 6 7
      |   PROGRAM CUB
      |   LR=5
      |   LW=6
      |
      |   WRITE(LW,1003)
   10 |   READ(LR,1000)COXS,COX,CON
      |   IF(COXS.NE.0. .OR. COX .NE. 0.) THEN
      |       WRITE(LW,1001) COXS, COX, CON
   50 |       READ(LR,1000) X
      |       IF(X.NE.0.) THEN
      |           SOL=COXS*X**2 + COX*X + CON
      |           WRITE(LW,1002) X, SOL
      |           GO TO 50
      |       END IF
      |
      |       GO TO 10
      |   END IF
      |
      |   STOP
 1000 |   FORMAT(10F8.0)
 1001 |   FORMAT(1X  , F9.3 ,  2F10.3)
 1002 |   FORMAT(30X,  F14.3  ,  F16.3  )
 1003 |   FORMAT('1' , 2X , 'COXS' , 7X , 'COX' , 7X , 'CON' ,
      | 1 13X , 'X' , 13X , 'SOL' //)
      |
      |   END
```

FIGURE 2-5(b) Program CUB—Coding

(d) *Text material* is output by using apostrophes to precede and follow the copy exactly as it is to appear.

2-2.7 Typical FORMAT Statement for WRITE (LW, 1003)

Listing 2–6 combines all of the considerations of Subsection 2–2.6 in the statement labeled 1003, a typical FORMAT statement for WRITE (LW, 1003). The following refer to Statement 1003 of Listing 2–6.

1. '1' means output the character (the number 1) located between the apostrophes exactly as shown. Because the 1 would appear in Column one, it will not print; also, because the symbol that is "trying" to be printed in Column 1 is a 1, slue to the top of the next page before doing anything else (first *edit descriptor*).
2. $\triangle\triangle,\triangle$ separates edit descriptors. ($\triangle$ means a blank.) The number of blanks to the left and right of the comma may be any number (including none) and are used to simplify key punching and to aid in correcting erroneously punched cards (first edit descriptor separator).
3. $2X$ means to leave two blank spaces on the line to be output (second edit descriptor).
4. $\triangle,\triangle$ is a comma with an arbitrary number of blanks to separate edit descriptors (second edit descriptor separator).
5. 'COXS' means output the characters COXS on the line immediately following the two blanks specified by the previous $2X$ (third edit descriptor).
6. $\triangle,\triangle$ (third edit descriptor separator).
7. $7X$ means to leave seven spaces following COXS (fourth edit descriptor).

Chapter 2 Programming by Concept and Example

Machine-Oriented Flow Diagram: CUB

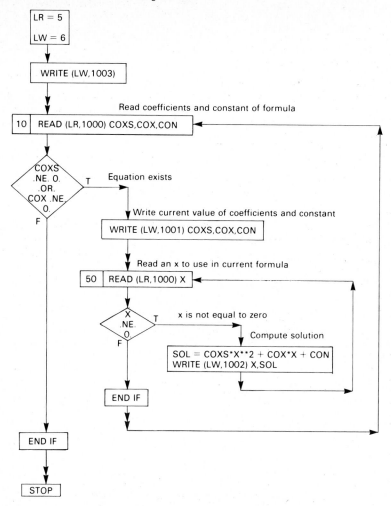

FIGURE 2–5(d) Program CUB—Machine-oriented flow diagram

8. △,△ (fourth edit descriptor separator).
9. 'COX' means output COX following the seven spaces after COXS following the initial two spaces on the line (fifth format edit descriptor), and so on.
10. 'SOL' means output SOL.
11. // means return carriage twice, which has the effect of leaving two blank lines.

The output from WRITE (LW, 1003) is the line containing COXS, COX, CON, X, and SOL with proper spacing near the bottom of Listing 2–6. Note that this line would be the first line on a new page of output because of the first edit descriptor '1'.

The position of FORMAT statements within a FORTRAN program is not critical to program flow. Some machines, however, work more efficiently with the FORMAT

```
1|2   5|6|7
          PROGRAM CUB
C            --- LR IS TO DEFINE DEVICE TO BE USED FOR READING INPUT DATA
          LR=5
C            --- LW IS TO DEFINE DEVICE TO BE USED FOR WRITING OUTPUT INFO
          LW=6
C            --- YOU MAY NEED TO CHANGE 5(FOR CARDS)AND 6(FOR HSP) TO AGREE
C            --- WITH LOGICAL UNIT NUMBERS OF YOUR INSTALLATION

          WRITE(LW,1003)

C            --- STORE VALUES READ FROM A SINGLE CARD OR LINE AT REMOTE TERMINAL
C            --- SEQUENTIALLY INTO LOCATIONS COXS,COX AND CON
C            --- WHEN EITHER COXS OR COX IS ZERO--THEN STOP
       10 READ(LR,1000)COXS,COX,CON

C            --- WHEN COXS AND COX ARE NOT BOTH ZERO--THEN--
          IF(COXS.NE.0. .OR. COX .NE. 0.) THEN
C            --- WRITE CURRENT VALUE OF COEFS AND CONSTANT
             WRITE(LW,1001) COXS, COX, CON

       50    READ(LR,1000) X

C            --- IF CURRENT X IS NOT ZERO--THEN--
             IF(X.NE.0.) THEN

C            --- COMPUTE SOLUTION BY FORMULA AS GIVEN
                SOL=COXS*X**2 + COX*X + CON
                WRITE(LW,1002) X, SOL

C            --- GO BACK AND READ ANOTHER X TO GO WITH THE CURRENT SET OF
C            --- COEFS AND CONSTANT, COXS, COX AND CON
                GO TO 50

             END IF

             GO TO 10
          END IF
C            --- THIS IS LOGICAL END OF PROGRAM AND SIGNALS TERMINATION DURING
C            --- PHASE 2, CALLED EXECUTION ON RUNNING
C            --- STOP MAY OCCUR AT ANY PHYSICAL LOCATION IN PROGRAM
          STOP
     1000 FORMAT(10F8.0)
     1001 FORMAT(1X  , F9.3 , 2F10.3)
     1002 FORMAT(30X,  F14.3  , F16.3  )
     1003 FORMAT('1' , 2X , 'COXS' , 7X , 'COX' , 7X , 'CON' ,
        1 13X , 'X' , 13X , 'SOL' //)
C            --- END IS THE PHYSICAL END OF THE PROGRAM (ALWAYS LAST STATEMENT)
C            --- AND SIGNALS TERMINATION OF COMPILATION DURING STATE 1
          END
```

LISTING 2-5 Program CUB—Excessive comments?

statements collected together, either at the beginning or at the end of the program. Some programmers prefer that FORMAT statements always be adjacent to READ/WRITE statements. (Some compilers do not permit the first program statement to be a FORMAT statement).

The total output that can be displayed on any line is limited by the output device. High-speed printers range from about 108 to 142 spaces per line. Remote terminals usually have at least 72 spaces available per line, and often more. If edit descriptors accumulate output to a width greater than permitted, some anomaly will occur and the output portion of the program will have to be rewritten.

```
 1    5 6 7
              PROGRAM CUBC
              LR=5
              LW=6
       C                                          ... WRITE HEADINGS
              WRITE(LW,1003)

       C                                          ... READ COEFS AND CONSTANT
       C                                              OF FORMULA
          10  READ(LR,1000)COXS,COX,CON
       C                                          ... ARE COEF'S OF X AND X ** 2
       C                                              NOT BOTH ZERO (QUESTION)
              IF(COXS.NE.C. .OR. COX .NE. 0.) THEN
       C                                          ... WRITE CURRENT VALUE OF
       C                                              COEFS AND CONSTANT
                 WRITE(LW,1001) COXS, COX, CON

       C                                          ... READ AN X TO JSE IN CURRENT
       C                                              FORMULA
          50     READ(LR,1000) X
       C                                          ... IS CURRENT X NOT = C(QUEST)
                 IF(X.NE.0.) THEN
       C                                          ... COMPUTE SOLUTION BY FORMULA
                    SOL=COXS*X**2 + COX*X + CON
       C                                          ... WRITE CURRENT VALUE OF X
       C                                              AND CORRESPONDING SOLUTION
                    WRITE(LW,1002) X, SOL
                    GO TO 50
                 END IF

                 GO TO 10
              END IF

              STOP
        1000  FORMAT(10F8.0)
        1001  FORMAT(1X  , F9.3 ,  2F10.3)
        1002  FORMAT(30X,  F14.3 ,  F16.3  )
        1003  FORMAT('1' , 2X , 'COXS' , 7X , 'COX' ,  7X , 'CON' ,
             1 13X ,  'X' ,  13X  , 'SOL' //)
              END
```

Input data:

```
1        8 9      16 17  ◄────Column locations on cards
3.       -4.       7.
2.
-2.
1.
C.
5.       2.       -9.
2.16
-4.7
C.
0.
```

Corresponding output:

COXS	COX	CON	X	SOL
3.000	-4.000	7.000		
			2.000	11.000
			-2.000	27.000
			1.000	6.000
5.000	2.000	-9.000		
			2.160	18.648
			-4.700	92.050

LISTING 2–6 Program CUB with "human-oriented
flow" comments plus I/O

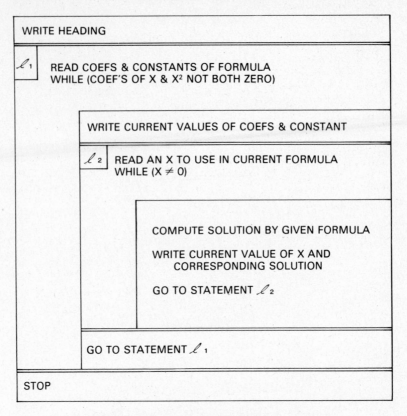

FIGURE 2-6(a) Program CUB—Human-oriented
Nassi-Shneiderman chart

2-2.8 Typical Statements to Input Data

To enable a FORTRAN program to input data, both a READ (executable) and a corresponding FORMAT (*nonexecutable*) statement are required. Consider the READ of the statement of Listing 2-6 labeled 10 and the corresponding FORMAT statement labeled 1000.

The READ statement differs from the WRITE statement of the previous subsections in three ways: the word READ is used rather than the word WRITE, the logical unit number is specified by LR rather than LW, and a list of variable names, separated by commas, follows the entities in parentheses.

The FORMAT statement (10F8.0) permits reading of up to 10 real variables; F8.0 stands for floating point using 8 columns for each number, with no decimal point unless one is punched in the data. When a decimal point is punched in the data, the decimal point of the format (.0) is overridden. That is, when a decimal point is punched in the data, it will be used without regard to the format.

The format 10F8.0 is used frequently in this text because it makes keypunching easier and helps minimize errors. Tabs are set at 9, 17, 25, 33, 41, 49, 57, 65, and 73 on a remote

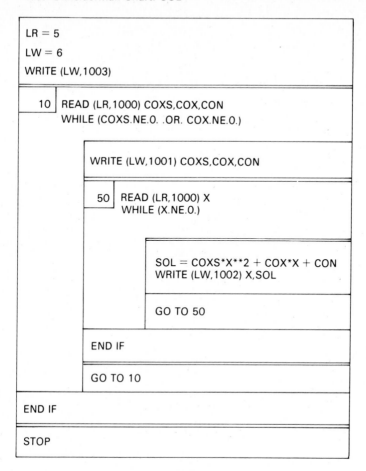

**FIGURE 2-6(b) Program CUB—Modified
Nassi-Shneiderman chart**

terminal or on a key-punch by a *drum card*. Data can then be punched *left-justified* when a decimal point is used with real numbers. Although some programmers prefer 8F10.0, we shall use 10F8.0 because it usually provides sufficient field width while making it easy to locate values in tables or matrices with more than 10 columns. (This is discussed further in later chapters.)

After compilation of program CUB of Listing 2-6, execution proceeds and the READ statement is executed. Listing 2-6 shows typical input. When the READ is encountered the first time, 3. is stored in location COXS, −4. in COX, and 7. in CON. That is, input values are stored on a one-to-one basis with the order of the variable list of the READ statement being used to identify storage locations.

When Statement 10 is encountered the second time, values 5., 2., and −9. are read from the sixth line (or card) of input and stored sequentially in COXS, COX, and CON. Intermediate lines of data are, of course, read into the variable name *X* from Statement 50.

2-2.9 Typical Output

Coefficients are echoed by program CUB of Listing 2-6 by

WRITE (LW, 1001) COXS, COX, CON

FORMAT statement 1001 has three edit descriptors that state the following. On a line of output write:

1. a space in Column 1 (from $1X$);
2. the contents of COXS within 9 columns and containing 3 digits after the decimal point (If all 9 columns are not needed, use leading blanks to fill the space.);
3. the contents of COX and CON using 10 columns each, and with 3 digits after a decimal point.

Results of activating the WRITE statement twice are shown in the three left columns of Listing 2-6, corresponding to the two sets of input from lines 1 and 6. Note that the READ statement is activated three times, but the last set of input data fills COXS and COX with zeros and causes a branch to terminate execution of the program.

Listing 2-6 shows READ and WRITE statements for program CUB in conjunction with typical input and resulting output data. Note in particular that a slash causes a carriage return only when it is acting as an edit descriptor. (A slash located between apostrophes would simply be a character to be output on the line.)

To avoid confusion, it is important to understand the distinction between continuation lines on output and continuation lines in the FORTRAN program itself. A slash used as a format specification causes a carriage return on output during the execution of the program. To continue a line in FORTRAN for compilation, any nonzero character is entered in Column 6 of the second card required for the statement. Thus statement 1003 of Listing 2-6 uses two lines for the single FORTRAN FORMAT statement.

2-3 PROGRAM COMP

This is an optional section that is included to provide detailed commentary for those who need additional clarification. Again, it is important that you relate the comments of this section to Figure 2-7.

Although some comments of this section may be redundant, they are included in order to give a complete picture of a typical process that takes place in formulating a problem for solution by electronic computer. Figure 2-7, on page 46, illustrates four elements of a formulation procedure. Part (a) is the definition sheet for program COMP, Part (b) contains the FORTRAN coding, Part (c) is the human-oriented flow diagram, and Part (d) is a machine-oriented flow diagram.

The FORTRAN statements shown in Part (b) comprise a program, that is, a series of related statements that accomplish some preconceived purpose. The ordered set of cards resulting when a card is created for each line is called a FORTRAN deck. When appropriate control cards and data are added to this FORTRAN deck, it becomes a composite deck, or simply "the deck."

2–3.1 Definition Sheet

The name COMP is prominently displayed on the definition sheet, which states the problem that the program solves.

Table 2–4 shows some typical solutions for program COMP. The process is quite similar to that discussed in detail for program CUB. In this case, however, an input value for a determines a y. This y is used (in conjunction with a) with an indefinite number of input values for b to compute corresponding values of x.

The descriptive items are defined so that the following are true.

Storage location A contains the current value of the first independent variable, named a.

Storage location B contains the current value of the second independent variable that is read, called b.

Storage location Y contains the current value of the solution of the first equation, involving only a.

Storage location SOL contains the current value of the final solution, represented symbolically as x. SOL is obtained from the second equation, which uses the computed value of y (location Y) and the input values of a and b (Locations A and B).

The first column of the list of descriptive items on the definition sheet of Figure 2–7 represents variable names used by the computer. The variables store numerical values associated with the symbols in the second column. The third column defines the meaning of these symbols for this particular program. The letters used to form the mnemonically named variables can be underlined in the third column to help reinforce the significance of their meaning.

Table 2–4 Example Solution of Program COMP

Problem:

From $y = 27a^3 - 47a^2 + 13a + 7$, find y for a given value of a.

Then—

From $\quad x = \left[\dfrac{y^2}{(a - y)} \right] \dfrac{a}{b}$, find x for (1) the given value of a (2) the previously computed value of y, and (3) successive values of b.

a	$27a^3 - 47a^2 + 13a + 7 = y$	b	$\left[\dfrac{y^2}{(a-y)} \right] \dfrac{a}{b} =$	x
2	$27(2)^3 - 47(2)^2 + 13(2) + 7 = 61.00$	1	$\left[\dfrac{(61.00)^2}{(2-61)} \right] \dfrac{2}{1} =$	−126.14
		2	$\left[\dfrac{(61.00)^2}{(2-61)} \right] \dfrac{2}{2} =$	−63.07
		3	$\left[\dfrac{(61.00)^2}{(2-61)} \right] \dfrac{2}{3} =$	−42.05
3	$27(3)^3 - 47(3)^2 + 13(3) + 7 = 352.00$	1	$\left[\dfrac{(352.00)^2}{(3-352)} \right] \dfrac{3}{1} =$	−1065.08
		2	$\left[\dfrac{(352.00)^2}{(3-352)} \right] \dfrac{3}{2} =$	−532.54

2-3.2 Human-Oriented Flow Diagram

Flow diagrams are read by following paths indicated by arrows. Starting with the top box, a heading is written by the computer on the high-speed printer (or at the remote terminal). Next, a numerical value is read and stored in Location A. Values are usually read sequentially from data cards that follow the FORTRAN deck. (See Section 17–2.2 for exceptions.) Data can also be input from a remote terminal. This value of A will remain unchanged until a new value is read.

Program: COMP

Purpose : Evaluate the equations $y = 27a^3 - 47a^2 + 13a + 7$
and $x = [y^2/(a - y)]\, a/b$ to get y and x, respectively,
for (1) different values of a and (2) for different
values of b for each value of a.

Descriptive Items:

Variable Name	Symbol	Definition
A	a	Input value, first independent variable
B	b	Input value, second independent variable
Y	y	Solution to $27a^3 - 47a^2 + 13a + 7$
SOL	x	Solution to $[y^2/(a - y)]a/b$

Input:

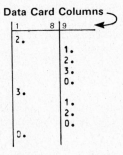

Data Card Columns

Output:

```
SOLUTION OF Y=27A**3 - 47A**2 + 13A + 7 AND
           SOL=(Y**2/(A-Y))* A/B  --- WHERE ---
    A         Y                 B           SOL


  2.00      61.00
                              1.00        -126.14
                              2.00         -63.07
                              3.00         -42.05
  3.00     352.00
                              1.00       -1065.08
                              2.00        -532.54
```

FIGURE 2-7(a) Program COMP—Definition sheet with I/O

The diamond signifies a question within the computer program during run-time (Stage 2, execution). If A is zero, program execution will terminate. Otherwise, flow proceeds to the next box (to the right) where the value of y is computed by the given formula, using the current value stored in A. Once this is accomplished, both the value of A (as read in) and the value of Y (as computed) are output on the high-speed printer.

Following the arrows, another numerical value is read and stored in Location B. Once B is read, another question is asked: Is B not equal to 0? When B is not zero, a value is computed for x (SOL in the program). This computation involves the two numerical values that were read in for A and B, plus the numerical value previously computed and stored in Y.

When the computation is complete, the numerical values of B (as read in) and SOL (as computed) are output on the high-speed printer.

Flow then returns to the box that reads a new value for B. When a new value is read for B, the previous value is automatically erased. Note, however, that the values of A and Y are still unchanged.

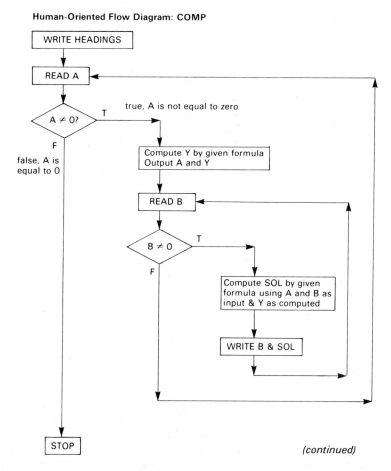

Human-Oriented Flow Diagram: COMP

FIGURE 2-7(c) Program COMP—Human-oriented
flow diagram

(continued)

```
PROGRAM COMP
C     --- SOLVE FOR:
C             (1) Y = 27*A**3 - 47*A**2 + 13*A + 7  -- AND --
C             (2) SOL = (Y**2/(A-Y)) * A/B
C     --- FOR :
C             (1) FOR DIFF VALUES OF A --AND--
C             (2) FOR DIFF B'S FOR EACH DIFF A

      LR=5
      LW=6

      WRITE(LW,1000)

  100 READ(LR,1001) A
      IF ( A .NE. 0.0) THEN
          Y = 27. * A ** 3 - 47.*A**2 + 13.*A + 7.
          WRITE(LW,1003) A ,Y

  300     READ(LR,1002) B
          IF (B . NE. 0.) THEN
              SOL = ( Y ** 2 /(A-Y)) * A/B
              WRITE(LW,1004) B , SOL
              GO TO 300
          END IF

          GO TO 100
      END IF

      STOP

 1000 FORMAT('1SOLUTION OF Y=27A**3 - 47A**2 + 13A + 7 AND' /
     1   11X,'SOL=(Y**2/(A-Y))* A/B  --- WHERE ---'/
        24X, 'A' , 9X , 'Y' , 16X, 'B' , 10X , 'SOL' //)
 1001 FORMAT(F8.0)
 1002 FORMAT(8X, F8.0)
 1003 FORMAT(1X,F6.2,F10.2)
 1004 FORMAT(28X,  F6.2 ,  F11.2  )

      END
```

FIGURE 2-7(b) Program COMP—Coding

Following the path indicated by the arrow, the diamond is entered again and the question is repeated: Is the current value of B not equal to 0? If the answer is true, a new computation is performed for SOL giving a new result, the latest B read and the corresponding solution stored in SOL (as just computed) are output, and the flow proceeds back to read in a new value of B.

At some time, the numerical value of B (as read) will be zero to indicate that no more solutions (using different B's with the current A and Y) are desired. Flow from the diamond will then go back to the initial READ statement: Read a numerical value and store it in the location named A. At this time, the value of A is changed.

There are two built-in controls to program COMP. An unlimited number of values can be read for A, and the program does not stop until A is read as zero. Likewise, an unlimited number of values of B can be used (read) with any specific numerical value stored in A. The computations involving x (Location SOL) continue with the same numerical value for A and Y until B is input as zero.

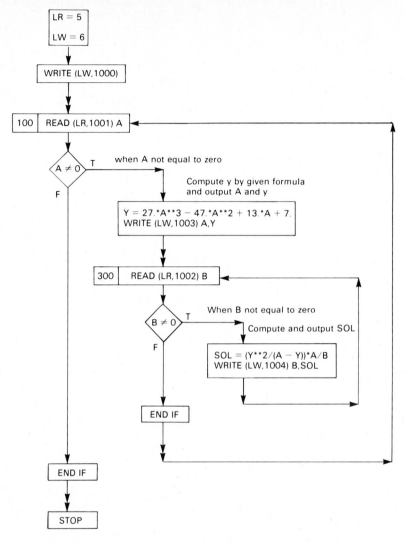

FIGURE 2-7(d) Program COMP—Machine-oriented flow diagram

Data must be prepared for COMP using the following rules.

1. Enter the first A on a data card.
2. Enter all B's associated with the first A, each on a separate data card.
3. Follow the last valid B with a zero on a separate data card. (This signals the computer to read a new A.)
4. Enter the next A on a data card (if a new A exists; if not go to step 8).
5. Enter all B's associated with this next A, each on a separate data card.

6. Follow the last valid B with a zero on a separate data card. (This signals the computer to read a new A.)
7. If another set of A and corresponding B values is to be read, return to Step 4.
8. If no other A and B values exist, enter a zero on the final data card. (This signals the computer that all data has been read and corresponding problems solved so that the program can terminate.)

Suppose we desire to use the following combinations of A and B: A = 2 and B = 1; A = 2 and B = −1; A = 1 and B = 2; A = 1 and B = −2; A = 1 and B = −3. Values would be input, a card at a time, in the following manner.

Card Number	Numerical Value	Stored in Location	Case
1	2.	A	Read first A.
2	1.	B	First computation.
3	−1.	B	Second computation.
4	0.	B	(Change A.)
5	1.	A	Read new A.
6	2.	B	Third computation.
7	−2.	B	Fourth computation.
8	−3.	B	Fifth computation.
9	0.	B	(Change A.)
10	0.	A	(Stop.)

From the first card, 2. is read and stored in A; 1. is read from Card 2 for the first B. Because A does not change for the second problem, Card 3 contains −1., which is stored in B. Card 4 contains a zero to indicate that there are no more B's with this particular A.

Because A changes, a new value of A (1.) is read from Card 5. This is followed by Card 6 with a new value of B (2.), then by Card 7 with another value of B (−2.), and finally by Card 8, with B equal to −3. To indicate that all B's have been read that are to be used in computations with A defined as 1., a zero is entered on Card 9. Because all of the equations have been evaluated, a zero is read from the last data card so that the program will terminate.

If Figure 2–7 has a good human-oriented flow diagram, you should be able to "see" how everything works. In general, if you put yourself in place of the computer, you should get correct results by following the steps of the human-oriented flow diagram. (See Exercises of Section 3–8.1 for examples.)

2–3.3 Machine-Oriented Flow Diagram

The machine-oriented (detailed) flow diagram (See Figure 2–7(c)) repeats the human-oriented flow diagram, but the statements are written so that they can be punched directly into computer cards.

The first box establishes the values for LR and LW specifying which devices the computer is to read from and write upon. The second box, which corresponds to the first box on the human-oriented flow diagram, calls for the output of headings. The FORTRAN command is the word WRITE followed by two symbols, separated by commas, located within parentheses. LW tells the computer to write on the high-speed printer because it was filled with a 6 in the previous box. The second symbol is a label number pointing to the appropriate FORMAT statement. 1000 FORMAT is shown in the listing of Part (b); the "how" is located within the parentheses following the word FORMAT. The FORMAT statement, labeled 1000, tells the computer what the output should look like. Therefore, we say that WRITE statements are *executable* because they cause something to happen—that is, they cause output to be written on the high-speed printer. FORMAT statements, on the other hand, are *nonexecutable* statements and they simply tell how something is going to look.

The material in the parentheses after 1000 FORMAT in Figure 2–7(b), is composed of a series of "edit descriptors," separated by commas. In each case, the number in front of an X signifies how many spaces to leave at that particular location in the output line. Characters contained between two apostrophes are to be output exactly as shown. Slashes tell the printer to go to the next line before printing any more material. (For complete details, refer to Chapter 6.)

The third box of the flow diagram has a statement label, the number 100. This box contains a typical READ statement. LR (which was set equal to 5 in the first box of this program) tells the computer to read from cards because 5 is the logical unit number used for the card reader at the computer center (and for the computer) where this program is to be run. The number 1001 is the statement label of the FORMAT statement that contains information about how the numerical values are to be punched on the data cards to be read.

In Figure 2–7(b), 1001 FORMAT (F8.0) is a typical FORMAT specification used to read data. The capital F signifies that the numbers to be read are "floating point" (real) numbers, to distinguish them from "fixed point" (integer) numbers. Because they are real, floating point numbers, they must contain a decimal point. A number preceding the capital F tells the maximum number of values that can be read in F8.0 format—in this case, a one is assumed because no number is used. The number after F but before the decimal point defines the *field width* for each number on the data card. The number following the decimal point states the number of digits that are to follow the decimal point if no decimal point is punched in the card. That is, if no explicit decimal point is present in the data, one will be implicitly inserted.

Thus 10F8.0 means to read a maximum of 10 floating point numbers, the first from the first eight locations on a data card (field of eight), the second from the next eight locations, the third from columns 17 through 24, and so on. When a decimal point is punched in a field on a data card, such a decimal point will override the edit descriptor. Blanks read by *F*-format are treated as zeros. (For more details, refer to Chapter 6.)

Once A has been read, flow proceeds to the diamond representing an IF statement. If the current numerical value stored in location A is zero, the program flows to END IF and then STOP, and execution terminates. If the current value stored in location A is not zero—it may be either positive or negative—then flow of the program proceeds to the right and a computation is performed using the current value stored in location A for the sought value of y.

The computation is $27 \times a^3 - 47 \times a^2 + 13 \times a + 7$. In the machine-oriented flow diagram, multiplication signs are replaced by asterisks and powers are indicated by double asterisks and the given power. In addition, because the numbers are real, that is floating point numbers, all (except exponents) must have a decimal point. The computational statement therefore shows the following.

1. The current value stored in location A is cubed, multiplied by 27, and this intermediate result is stored in an accumulator.
2. The current value stored in A is squared, multiplied by 47, and stored in another accumulator.
3. The current value in A is multiplied by 13 and the result is stored in still another accumulator.
4. The values stored in the accumulators are combined with the constant 7. This final result is then stored in location Y.

After output of A and Y by the WRITE statement, control proceeds to the statement labeled 300, where a new value is read and stored in location B. The second diamond is then reached; it asks if B is not equal to zero. If B has either a positive or negative value, x is computed by the given formula and the result is stored in location SOL. The computation is performed using the current values stored in locations A and B, as read in, and the current value stored in Y, as previously computed.

The WRITE statement is then executed and tells the computer to output the current values stored in locations B and SOL on the high-speed printer. Control then returns to statement number 300, where a new value of B is read.

The part of the flow diagram below and including statement 300 represents a DO-WHILE mini-module. Within this mini-module, every time a value is read it is stored in location B, erasing the previous value. Then, if that value as read and stored is not zero, a computation is performed, output is displayed on the high-speed printer, and a new value of B is read. Therefore this DO-WHILE is operative as long as the value of B is not zero.

Once B becomes zero, the program flows back to statement 100 and a new value of A is read. Thus the program is essentially composed of two *nested* DO-WHILE mini-modules. The innermost mini-module is the one that depends upon the value of B. The outer mini-module depends upon the value of A. The program continues to operate as long as A is not zero; once A is zero, the program terminates. For each valid value of A, the inner mini-module will operate only so long as the value of B is not zero. If B is read as zero, a new value must be read for A and a new test must be performed upon A to determine if the program is to continue execution.

2–3.4 Coding

Each rectangular box is coded into FORTRAN by writing the contents of the box within Columns 7 through 72 on a computer card or on a line at a remote terminal. Statement labels are often *right justified* to Column 5.

A diamond is replaced by a FORTRAN statement consisting of IF followed by the contents of the diamond, enclosed in parentheses, followed by THEN. If the contents of the diamond (the expression within the parentheses of the FORTRAN statement) are true, flow is to the right and computations occur; if false, flow is down to an END IF, which terminates the DO-WHILE.

When a box has more than one entrance point, it must be labeled like Statement 300. In this case, Statement 300 physically follows WRITE (LW, 1003) A, Y, and is always executed directly after the computation for Y is complete. To get from the WRITE statement that outputs B and SOL to Statement 300, however, requires the statement GO TO 300. This requirement is clearly evident from the machine-oriented flow diagram by the arrows leading back to Statement 300.

FORMAT statements are not executable and may be placed at any location within the FORTRAN program (see comments in Section 2-2.7). STOP must be used to logically terminate the program during run-time (execution) and END is physically the last FORTRAN statement of the program (to signify the end of compilation).

2-3.5 Comment

It may appear that the amount of work involved in using this four-element process for such a simple program is excessive—but that is precisely why it is used with simple programs at first. In this way, the mechanical methodology of using such a procedure becomes second nature before the technique itself is required as an essential tool for the solution of more complex problems. If you wait to develop skills in writing definition sheets and flow diagrams until you actually need them in order to succeed, you will then be trying to learn too many new things at once. Note that modified Nassi-Shneiderman charts (see Figure 2-8) can be used rather than flow diagrams.

Nassi-Shneiderman Chart: COMP

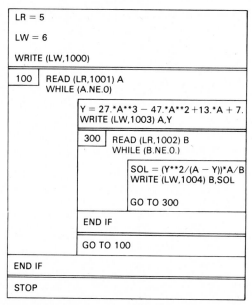

FIGURE 2-8 Modified Nassi-Shneiderman chart for program COMP

2-4 A PROGRAM THAT CALLS A SUBROUTINE

This section is optional. It is included because of the stress often placed on top-down programming. There are a few more concepts and the program logic is more complex than that of previous examples, but it can be understood with no mathematical or engineering background.

2-4.1 Genesis of the Program

Table 2–5 is taken verbatim from the 1976 edition of the *Uniform Building Code*. The meaning of *S* is unimportant to our present study; the important concept is that its value must be computed for essentially every physical structure that is designed to resist earthquake forces. The logic needed to compute *S* is somewhat complex. For this reason, we want to write a *subroutine* (an independent program that can be executed only when it is "called" by another program) that can be used by many different programs.

We must write a subroutine that solves for *S* in accordance with the rules in Table 2–5. Because the subroutine is written to "find *S*," it is given the name FINDS. Because the subroutine needs to be tested and cannot be run by itself, a test program must also be written to "Test FINDS"; it is given the name TFINDS.

Table 2-5 Extract from *The Uniform Building Code**

The value of *S* shall be determined by the following formulas, but shall be not less than 1.0:

$$\text{For } T/T_s = 1.0 \text{ or less } \quad S = 1.0 + \frac{T}{T_s} - 0.5 \left[\frac{T}{T_s}\right]^2$$

$$\dots\dots\dots\dots\dots\dots\dots\dots\dots\dots\dots (12\text{--}4)$$

$$\text{For } T/T_s \text{ greater than } 1.0 \quad S = 1.2 + 0.6\frac{T}{T_s} - 0.3 \left[\frac{T}{T_s}\right]^2$$

$$\dots\dots\dots\dots\dots\dots\dots\dots\dots\dots\dots (12\text{--}4A)$$

Where:

T in Formulas (12–4) and (12–4A) shall be established by a properly substantiated analysis but *T* shall be not less than 0.3 second.

The range of values of T_s may be established from properly substantiated geotechnical data, in accordance with U.B.C. Standard No. 23–1, except that T_s shall not be taken as less than 0.5 second nor more than 2.5 seconds. T_s shall be that value within the range of site periods, as determined above, that is nearest to *T*.

When T_s is not properly established, the value of *S* shall be 1.5.

Exception: Where *T* has been established by a properly substantiated analysis and exceeds 2.5 seconds, the value of *S* may be determined by assuming a value of 2.5 seconds for T_s.

---

*This material is reproduced from Section 2312, page 135, of the 1976 Edition of *The Uniform Building Code,* copyright 1976, with permission of the publisher, the International Conference of Building Officials, Whittier, CA 90601.

```
1 2    5 6 7
│ │     │ │ │ PROGRAM TFINDS
│ │
│ C              ** THIS PROGRAM TESTS SUBROUTINE FINDS
│ │     LR=5
│ │     LW=6
│ │
│ │ 10  READ(LR,100)T,TS1,TS2
│ │
│ │     IF(T.GT.0.) THEN
│ │         WRITE(LW,101) T, TS1, TS2
│ │         CALL FINDS( S, TS, T , TS1, TS2)
│ │         WRITE(LW,102) S,TS,T,TS1,TS2
│ │         GO TO 10
│ │     END IF
│ │
│ │     STOP
│ │
│ │ 100 FORMAT(10F8.0)
│ │ 101 FORMAT(//15X,'VALUES OF ' ,3X, 'S' , 6X, 'TS' , 5X , 'T' ,
│ │    1 5X, 'TS1' , 4X , 'TS2' / 18X,'AS READ' , 14X,3F7.3)
│ │ 102 FORMAT(' AS COMPUTED AND ADJUSTED', 5F7.3/)
│ │
│ │     END
```

**LISTING 2-7 Program to test subroutine FINDS,
named TFINDS**

2-4.2 Program TFINDS

The program written to test subroutine FINDS is shown in Listing 2–7. This is a very simple program that reads three input values, T, TS1, and TS2 defined in Table 2–6. Once these are read, it "calls" the subroutine by the statement.

CALL FINDS(S, TS, T, TS1, TS2)

At this point, during execution, control is transferred from program TFINDS to the

---

Table 2-6 Definition Sheet for Program TFINDS

Program: TFINDS

Definition: This program tests a subroutine named FINDS which:
1. Establishes a legitimate site period T_s from a range of site periods input by giving the lowest and highest possible values, if known.
2. Computes a value named S using the legitimate site period T_s and the period of the structure T as input.

Descriptive Items:

Variable Name	Symbol	Meaning
S	S	A value to be computed for use in a formula to help mitigate against earthquake hazards in the design of buildings.
TS	T_s	Site period.
T	T	Period of building.
TS1	none	Lowest value within range of site periods.
TS2	none	Highest value within range of site periods.

---

first statement of subroutine FINDS, with values of T, TS1, and TS2 (called actual arguments) available for reference by the subroutine. When the subroutine has finished its job, control will be transferred back to the statement immediately following the "call" in the test program TFINDS, with values of S and TS computed and returned to the test program.

To insure that the subroutine has performed correctly, WRITE statements are used immediately before and after the call. Typical input data and results are output by the test program as shown in Listing 2–8. Interestingly, this output can be used to see if the subroutine works correctly without ever seeing the subroutine itself.

Before proceeding, study the requirements specified in Table 2–5 to check the results presented in Listing 2–8. In this way, you can become more familiar with the logic which must be used in the subroutine.

2–4.3 Subroutine FINDS

If you have checked the output of program TFINDS with the requirements of the Uniform Building Code, you should be able to follow the logic of the modified Nassi-Shneiderman charts of Figure 2–9 or the machine-oriented flow diagram of Figure 2–10 on page 62.

The first process box contains what is also the first statement of the subroutine:

SUBROUTINE FINDS (S, TS, T, TS1, TS2)

As an independent program, the word SUBROUTINE tells the computer that it is a subprogram rather than a main program, with the name FINDS. The names in parentheses (called *dummy arguments*) separated by commas act as the "door" between this subroutine and the calling program. That is, information can be transferred between the subroutine and main program, and vice versa, only by these arguments. (For more details and the inevitable exception, refer to Chapter 14 and following chapters.) Since the calling program reads values of T, TS1, and TS2, they can be used within the subroutine to calculate TS and S, which are "returned" to the main program.

The first IF corresponds to the fourth line from the bottom of Table 2–5: "When T_s is not properly established, the value of S shall be 1.5." When the value of T_s is not properly established, no range of values is known, so TS1 and TS2 are input as zero and S becomes 1.5. If TS1 and TS2 could be negative, the first IF statement would require the more complex form IF (TS1.EQ.O..AND.TS2.EQ.O.).

The next two IF's become active if something is known about T_s. Sometimes only one value is input so that the range is simply TS1 = TS2.

By the fourth IF, T, TS1 and TS2 all have numerical values other than zero. Then if T is greater than 2.5, TS becomes 2.5 by the exception at the end of Table 2–5.

When T is not greater than 2.5, the third paragraph from the bottom of Table 2–5 is developed. First, limits are applied to TS1, TS2, and T (fourth paragraph from the bottom of Table 2–5). Then TS is chosen as the value of TS1 or TS2 which is closest to T.

At this point, T and TS are established to be used in formulas (12–4) or (12–4A) of Table 2–5 depending upon the ratio of T to TS which is computed and stored in TTS.

The value of TTS is *local* to the subroutine and cannot be transferred back to the

```
          VALUES OF      S      TS       T      TS1     TS2
          AS READ                      1.510    .000    .000
AS COMPUTED AND ADJUSTED  1.500   .000  1.510    .000    .000


          VALUES OF      S      TS       T      TS1     TS2
          AS READ                      1.520   1.100    .000
AS COMPUTED AND ADJUSTED  1.456  1.100  1.520   1.100   1.100


          VALUES OF      S      TS       T      TS1     TS2
          AS READ                      1.530    .000   1.200
AS COMPUTED AND ADJUSTED  1.477  1.200  1.530   1.200   1.200


          VALUES OF      S      TS       T      TS1     TS2
          AS READ                      2.700   2.100   2.200
AS COMPUTED AND ADJUSTED  1.498  2.500  2.700   2.100   2.200


          VALUES OF      S      TS       T      TS1     TS2
          AS READ                       .310    .300   2.900
AS COMPUTED AND ADJUSTED  1.428   .500   .310    .500   2.500


          VALUES OF      S      TS       T      TS1     TS2
          AS READ                      2.150    .400   2.110
AS COMPUTED AND ADJUSTED  1.500  2.110  2.150    .500   2.110


          VALUES OF      S      TS       T      TS1     TS2
          AS READ                       .990    .030   1.610
AS COMPUTED AND ADJUSTED  1.500   .990   .990    .500   1.610


          VALUES OF      S      TS       T      TS1     TS2
          AS READ                      2.100    .420   1.980
AS COMPUTED AND ADJUSTED  1.499  1.980  2.100    .500   1.980


          VALUES OF      S      TS       T      TS1     TS2
          AS READ                      1.920    .400   1.980
AS COMPUTED AND ADJUSTED  1.500  1.920  1.920    .500   1.980


          VALUES OF      S      TS       T      TS1     TS2
          AS READ                      1.930   1.040   2.490
AS COMPUTED AND ADJUSTED  1.500  1.930  1.930   1.040   2.490
```

LISTING 2–8 Typical output for program TFINDS

main program because it is not listed with the arguments (variables in the parentheses) in the statement

SUBROUTINE FINDS (S, TS, T, TS1, TS2)

It is used, however, because it reduces the number of calculations that must be made by either Formula 12–4 or 12–4A (see Table 2–5).

Human Oriented Nassi-Shneiderman Chart: FINDS

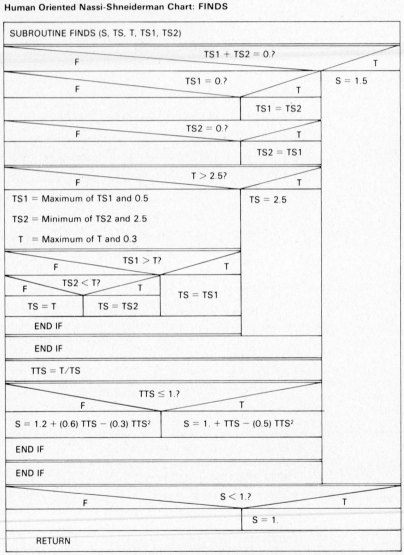

FIGURE 2–9(a) Subroutine FINDS—Human-oriented Nassi-Shneiderman chart

The last IF statement performs the first sentence of Table 2–5. The logical ending statement of a subroutine is usually RETURN rather than STOP, meaning "return control to the calling program." The last statement of a subroutine must, of course, be END.

The subroutine is coded with and without comments in Listing 2–9. Note that this

Nassi-Shneiderman Chart: FINDS

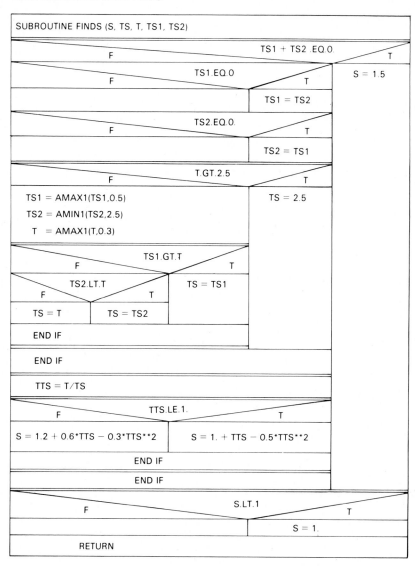

**FIGURE 2–9(b) Subroutine FINDS—Modified
Nassi-Shneiderman chart**

Machine-Oriented Flow Diagram: FINDS

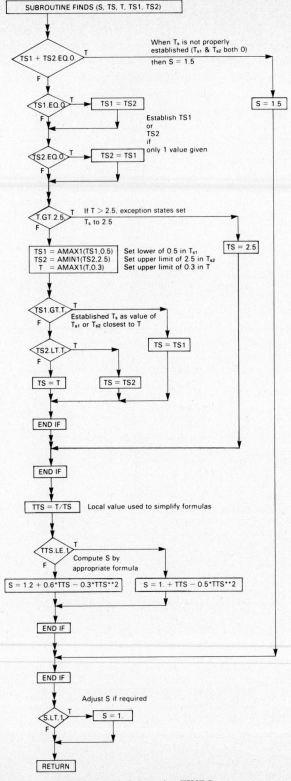

FIGURE 2-10 Subroutine FINDS

```
      SUBROUTINE FINDS(S,TS,T,TS1,TS2)
C   SUBROUTINE COMPUTES S AND TS FROM T, TS1 AND TS2 WHERE
C   SYMBOLS CORRESPOND TO EXCERPT FROM PG. 135 OR UBC-76 -- AND --
C      TS1 = LOWER RANGE OF TS
C      TS2 = UPPER RANGE OF TS

C                    ** IF TS NOT PROPERLY ESTABLISHED, TS1 AND TS2
C                    ** ARE INPUT AS ZEROS--AND-- S =1.5

      IF(TS1+TS2.EQ.0.) THEN
          S=1.5
      ELSE

C                    ** IF RANGE OF TS IS A SINGLE VALUE,TS1 OR
C                    ** TS2 WILL BE 0. IF SO, SET TO SINGLE VALUE

          IF(TS1.EQ.0.) TS1=TS2
          IF(TS2.EQ.0.) TS2=TS1

C                    ** EXCEPTION-WHERE T ESTABLISHED BY A PROPERLY
C                    ** SUBSTANTIATED ANALYSIS AND EXCEEDS 2.5 SEC,
C                    ** DETERMINE S USING TS=2.5

          IF(T.GT.2.5) THEN
              TS=2.5
          ELSE

C                    ** TS SHALL NOT BE TAKEN AS LESS THAN 0.5

              TS1=AMAX1(TS1,0.5)

C                    ** TS SHALL NOT BE TAKEN AS MORE THAN 2.5

              TS2=AMIN1(TS2,2.5)

C                    ** T SHALL NOT BE LESS THAN 0.3 SEC

              T=AMAX1(T,0.3)

C                    ** TS SHALL BE THAT VALUE WITHIN THE RANGE
C                    ** OF SITE PERIODS(BTW TS1 AND TS2) THAT
C                    ** IS NEAREST TO T

              IF(TS1.GT.T) THEN
                  TS=TS1
              ELSE IF(TS2.LT.T) THEN
                  TS=TS2
              ELSE
                  TS=T
              END IF

          END IF

C                    ** DECIDE WHICH FORMULA TO USE

          TTS= T/TS
          IF(TTS.LE.1.) THEN
              S=1. + TTS - 0.5*TTS**2
          ELSE
              S=1.2 + 0.6 * TTS - 0.3 * TTS ** 2
          END IF

      END IF

C                    ** S SHALL NOT BE LESS THAN 1

      IF(S.LT.1.) S=1.
      RETURN
      END
```

LISTING 2-9(a) Subroutine FINDS with comments

```
SUBROUTINE FINDS(S,TS,T,TS1,TS2)

IF(TS1+TS2.EQ.0.) THEN
     S=1.5
ELSE
     IF(TS1.EQ.0.) TS1=TS2
     IF(TS2.EQ.0.) TS2=TS1

     IF(T.GT.2.5) THEN
          TS=2.5
     ELSE
          TS1=AMAX1(TS1,0.5)
          TS2=AMIN1(TS2,2.5)
          T=AMAX1(T,0.3)

          IF(TS1.GT.T) THEN
               TS=TS1
          ELSE IF(TS2.LT.T) THEN
               TS=TS2
          ELSE
               TS=T
          END IF

     END IF

     TTS= T/TS

     IF(TTS.LE.1.) THEN
          S=1. + TTS - 0.5*TTS**2
     ELSE
          S=1.2 + 0.6 * TTS - 0.3 * TTS ** 2
     END IF

END IF

IF(S.LT.1.) S=1.
RETURN
END
```

LISTING 2-9(b) Subroutine FINDS without comments

listing contains no READ or WRITE statements. Because it does not have these, access to the "outside world" is only through the "door" provided by the dummy arguments that compare in a one-to-one order with the actual arguments.

This example is a simple one. Subroutines can do very powerful things. They can, for instance, read and write as well as call or be called by other subroutines. Because of the way they are formed, the names (arguments) used in the list of the subroutines are *dummy* names and do not have to be the same as the actual arguments used in the main program. This provides tremendous flexibility, which will be discussed in detail starting with Chapter 14.

2-5 EXERCISES

1. Do you prefer the output from IEQPRT or EEQPRT? Why? Which do you feel is more oriented toward humans? Why? Does the output from EEQPRT give you more confidence in the program than that of IEQPRT? Do you think the additional time spent is worthwhile?

2. In program CUB, many programmers would rewrite the computation for SOL as

$$SOL = X * (A * X + B) + C.$$

This is called the *nested form*. The nested form for computing *y* in program COMP is

$$Y = 7. + A * (13. + A * (-47. + 27 * A))$$

Can you give a good reason for using the nested form? (*Hint:* Count the number of arithmetic operations required by the nested form as compared to the expanded form used in the programs. Can you think of any good reasons not to use the nested form?)

3. Program COMP could be changed in the following way.

```
      Y = 7. + A * (13. + A * (-47. + 27. * A))
      COEF = (Y ** 2/(A - Y)) * A
      WRITE(LW, 1006) A, Y, COEF
  300 READ(LR, 1002) B
      IF(B.NE.O.) THEN
              SOL = COEF/ B
                        .
                        .
                        .
```

How much of an improvement is this? Do you believe that the time saved by computing $AY^2/(A-Y)$ only once for each A offsets the extra storage location required by COEF? Are these matters too trivial to consider? If so, can you think of some cases where a slight increase in speed by using more storage spaces would be good? Would be bad?

4. Look at subroutine FINDS. The first IF statement sets S = 1.5 when TS1 = TS2 = 0. Yet, in the last IF statement, S is checked to see if it is less than 1., even when it has been previously set to 1.5. Alter subroutine FINDS so that the check to see if S is less than 1. will not occur when S has already been set to 1.5 because TS1 = TS2 = 0.

5. When you studied the programs, did you notice that changes suggested by the previous questions might be desirable? Two attitudes are often expressed: (1) Almost any working program can be improved, and (2) Never touch a working program. What might be behind such opposite statements? Why would people hold such opposite views? Do you think that either side would relax its rule? If so, for what reasons?

Chapter **3**

Formulation
Procedures

Programmers have developed many different formulation procedures in an attempt to minimize the time and effort required to obtain efficient and effective programs. Typically, seasoned programmers choose a procedure which "feels right" to them. Many swear by flow diagrams, while others derisively call flow diagrams "training wheels." A number espouse Nassi-Shneiderman charts, while still others prefer pseudocode or to formulate problems directly with FORTRAN 77 statements. Several alternative procedures are presented in this chapter.

3-1 PROBLEM DEFINITION

One of the most difficult tasks is to develop a clear, precise, complete definition of the problem to be solved, based on all of the contingencies that might arise. Computer programs usually stop executing when impossible mathematics—such as taking the logarithm of a negative number or dividing by zero—is encountered.

Sometimes a problem cannot be defined completely until elements of the solution have been partially programmed; even so, do not give in to the temptation to use the computer too soon. As a minimum, write down the specific type of input you wish the computer to use and exactly how the output should look—being sure that it is meaningful to the intended users. Then define how output depends upon input to develop the concept that will be used by the program.

It is a good idea to formulate input data in a manner that is familiar to potential users. It is also important to prepare data cards with a minimum amount of wasted time and effort. For this reason, format 10F8.0 (See chapter 6) will often be recommended for numerical input data.

Output is adequate if the results can be read by someone unfamiliar with the program without referring to the program, *documentation,* or input. That is, output must include input data in readable form, explain the process taking place in the program, and clearly indicate the solutions.

64

3-2 A FORMAL DEFINITION SHEET

Many programmers feel that a formal definition sheet clarifies their thinking, affords logical, straightforward, orderly progression, and provides a permanent record when the job is done. Often the definition sheet is entered directly into the program in the form of comment lines.

3-2.1 Composition

In this text, a formal definition sheet is composed of three parts: a title, a definition, and the descriptive items. The title should stand out on the definition sheet and, if possible, suggest the subject of the program.

A good definition should clearly and completely state the purpose of the program. It should also indicate any special aspects or limitations of the program. The following are definitions for the same program, each more complete and precise.

1. This program solves the quadratic equation $y = ax^2 + bx + c$.
2. This program solves the quadratic equation for all real roots.
3. This program solves the quadratic equation—including the degenerate forms— for all real roots.
4. This program solves the quadratic equation for all real, imaginary, or complex roots for any quadratic or degenerate quadratic equation with real coefficients.

Each additional item in this list removes an unknown condition. The fourth definition shows thought about the type of acceptable input and the three types of expected roots, and that the problem will be solved even when the coefficient of x^2 is zero so that the equation degenerates to the linear form $y = bx + c$. Many published programs to solve the quadratic equation do not consider all possibilities and produce run-time errors with data that appears to be valid. It is much easier to write a program based on the fourth definition than on the first because the fourth definition is complete enough to point out problems that will be encountered.

3-2.2 How Definition Sheets Are Developed

The title and problem definition should be written on the formal definition sheet before anything else is started. The descriptive items list, however, will grow throughout the development of the program. On a descriptive list, it is helpful to use three columns: one for the *mnemonic* variable name used in the computer program; a second for the symbol generally used; and a third for the descriptions of the variable used in the program. To avoid errors or difficulties in completing the program, descriptive items lists are usually started concurrently with human-oriented flow diagrams or modified Nassi-Shneiderman charts, kept up-to-date, and generally not finished until the flow diagrams or charts are completed.

Long descriptive items lists can be segmented into input, output, and internal groupings. It is also helpful to arrange descriptive items in alphabetical order, although this is not essential.

Typical definition sheets are shown for program IEQPRT in Table 2–1, for CUB in Figure 2–5, and for COMP in Figure 2–7. If the definition sheets of these programs are well done, you should understand the purpose of each program and know what variables are used within the program, as well as what each variable represents.

3-3 DIAGRAMS AND CHARTS

Flow diagrams and Nassi-Shneiderman charts provide a means for visualizing the logical flow of computer programs. Many forms of flow diagrams are in use; in this text, we use a readable style that is particularly well-adapted to use in the formative stages of program development.

Nassi-Shneiderman charts were presented in 1973* and soon became the focal point for controversy about the "best" technique to use. We shall use "modified" Nassi-Shneiderman charts that can be directly applied to FORTRAN 77. Nassi-Shneiderman charts, as presented, did not have facility for branch instructions so that the GO TO statement was eliminated. The form developed and used in this text is "modified" because it does use the GO TO, but only under strict conditions. (The nature of FORTRAN necessitates the modification.)

Although these techniques are in parallel use throughout much of the text, specific discussions of the techniques themselves are normally isolated from one another. This makes it possible to ignore either flow diagrams or modified Nassi-Shneiderman charts without losing continuity.

3-3.1 Flow Diagrams

Flow diagrams provide a graphical representation of the step-by-step procedure required to solve a particular problem; such a representation makes a complex, logical sequence of events easy to see and comprehend. Flow diagrams seem to have less benefit for theoretical mathematicians than for engineers. For specialists in social science, natural science, business, architecture, and so on, flow diagrams can be a very efficient and effective learning tool.

Flow diagrams can involve varied amounts of detail. In this text, two basic types are used: the human-oriented (gross) flow diagram and the machine-oriented (detailed) flow diagram. A human-oriented flow diagram is good if it can be understood by a person knowledgeable in the field but without computer programming experience. In this text, a good machine-oriented flow diagram is one from which the program can be punched directly without intermediate coding, except for input/output statements.

The American Standards Association has accepted a standard set of symbols for flow diagrams. We shall use a system of three symbols to simplify understanding and mastery of programming. If you continue with programming, standard symbols are easily adopted. Within the first seven chapters of this text, only two of the symbols are used: a rectangular box, signifying that an action is to occur, and a diamond-shaped box, representing a question. These boxes are connected by flow-arrows, straight lines with arrowheads at all junctions, corners, and points of arrival into boxes. It is important that

*I. Nassi and B. Shneiderman, "Flowchart Techniques for Structured Programming," SIGPLAN Notices (August, 1973), pp. 12–26.

arrowheads be used only at junctions and arrival points and that no gaps exist in any lines on the diagram. Strict adherence to these simple rules is important to improve your chance of finding random mistakes. In fact, errors seem to stand out in carefully constructed flow diagrams.

Emphasis on flow diagrams is not intended to minimize the importance of other powerful techniques such as good style, structured programming, or use of *decision tables*. Rather, the emphasis on flow diagrams is to help you, as a novice, to become an experienced programmer as rapidly, effectively, and efficiently as possible.

3-3.2 Modified Nassi-Shneiderman Charts

Modified Nassi-Shneiderman charts are a reasonable alternative to flow diagrams. They are quite easy to read, although more forethought may be required to use them during program formulation.

Modified Nassi-Shneiderman charts represent a complex, logical sequence of events in a form that is easy to comprehend. In this text, two types are used: the human-oriented (gross) modified Nassi-Shneiderman chart and the machine-oriented (detailed) modified Nassi-Shneiderman chart. Human-oriented charts should be easy for nonprogrammers to read, while machine-oriented charts should have sufficient detail for direct keypunching without intermediate coding.

Nassi-Shneiderman charts are also advantageous because they illustrate the three basic constructs (process box, DO-WHILE, and block IF) used almost universally in languages of both higher and lower level than FORTRAN 77.

In the first seven chapters of this text, all three basic constructs are displayed in modified Nassi-Shneiderman charts: a rectangular box, signifying "do-something", a rectangular box divided into three triangles representing a question, and a rectangle divided into two spaces, an inverted L and a smaller rectangle signifying "do something WHILE something else is true". All of the rectangles in a modified Nassi-Shneiderman chart fit within an overall rectangle, usually on a single sheet of paper, representing the entire program.

3-4 HUMAN-ORIENTED (GROSS) DIAGRAMS AND CHARTS

Human-oriented diagrams or charts are used during the preliminary thinking stages and the developmental process and are finally maintained as a permanent record. They are used to clarify the thought processes necessary to develop an appropriate *algorithm* and to help the programmer arrive at a complete and concise definition of the problem. At the very least, human-oriented diagrams and charts can insure that every facet of the problem has been considered before developing the more detailed machine-oriented diagram or chart and subsequent coding.

Human-oriented diagrams and charts can be used by the programmer when communicating with a client who has requested that the program be written and by the client in describing the problem to the programmer.

The amount of information needed in the human-oriented chart or diagram depends upon who will use it. It is not uncommon to use a gross-gross diagram and then show independent human-oriented diagrams that fill in details of the boxes. Any reasonable combination of verbal descriptions or mathematical formulations is appropriate on a human-oriented diagram or chart so long as it presents a clear, precise picture of the process taking place.

3-4.1 Human-Oriented Flow Diagrams

The elements of a good human-oriented (gross) flow diagram are shown in Table 3-1. Although the rules seem almost trivial, when used rigorously they lead to successful programs developed with a minimum of time and effort. Figures 2-5(c) and 2-7(c) show human-oriented flow diagrams for programs CUB and COMP, respectively.

Table 3-1 Elements of a Human-Oriented Flow Diagram

To give a direction, enclose the statement(s) in a
                rectangular box.

Enclose a question in a diamond-shaped box.

Enclose "automatic repetitive" statements in a
                hexagonal box.

Connect boxes by flow-arrows
        Use arrowheads at:
             each corner;
             entry into box;
        Do not use arrowheads along the line.

Comments:

1. The name should stand out prominently on each sheet.

2. The main line should stand out clearly.

3. No gaps should occur:
    in circumference of boxes;
    in flow-arrows;
    between flow-arrows and boxes.

4. A person unfamiliar with the program should be able to solve the type of problem involved by carefully following the diagram.

3-4.2 Human-Oriented Modified Nassi-Shneiderman Charts

The primary difference between human- and machine-oriented Nassi-Shneiderman charts is in the type of statements used in them. In general, the former uses any combination of words, mathematical formulation and symbols that can be easily and quickly understood. The latter uses *syntax* directly related to FORTRAN 77.

    Table 3-2 summarizes the elements of Nassi-Shneiderman charts. Figures 2-6(a) and 2-9(a) show human-oriented modified Nassi-Shneiderman charts for program CUB and subroutine FINDS, respectively.

Table 3-2 Elements of a Nassi-Shneiderman Chart

To give a direction, enclose the statement(s) in a
        rectangular box.

Enclose questions in the upper triangle of rectangles divided
        into 3 triangles; the lower left triangle
        leads to action to be taken if question is
        false; the lower right triangle leads to
        action to be taken if question is true.

Enclose "repetitive" statements in a box divided into an
        inverted L and the remaining rectangle.

Nest rectangles into an all-encompassing rectangle. Flow
        proceeds from top to bottom.

Comments:

1. The name should stand out prominently on each sheet.
2. A person unfamiliar with the program should be able to solve the type of problem involved by carefully following the chart.

3-4.3 Constructing Diagrams and Charts During the Development of Program

To construct a human-oriented flow diagram or chart, formulate the step-by-step procedure needed to solve the problem. It is usually easier to construct a straight-line program for the solution of a single example before considering the techniques necessary to solve many problems of a similar type. (See Figure 2–4.) Conceptually, put yourself in place of the flow diagram: for example, if you wished to add *a* and *b*, you would need to know what numbers to use for *a* and *b*. Thus, if the flow diagram is to add *a* and *b*, it will first have to read the numerical values currently associated with *a* and *b*. Then the results must be stored some place. Thus the human-oriented steps for this process could be: (1) read the values of *A* and *B*; (2) add *A* and *B*; (3) store the results of such addition into location *C*, and (4) output the results stored in *C*.

As your programs become more involved, the human-oriented flow diagram or chart is the best insurance that the program does exactly what you want it to do for any input. If you cannot exactly determine the next step at any stage in the program, then the flow diagram or chart is not complete.

3-5 MACHINE-ORIENTED (DETAILED) FLOW DIAGRAMS AND CHARTS

Machine-oriented flow diagrams or charts are used in overall program development and as a permanent record. Machine-oriented flow diagrams are also used by the coder, the key-punch operator, or the remote terminal operator (often the same person who does the programming).

A program can be punched from a good machine-oriented diagram without any intermediate coding. Thus all required statement numbers (labels) must be shown and formats must be listed separately, preferably on *coding forms.* The practice of coding directly from machine-oriented diagrams without intermediate longhand coding is not endorsed by many programmers and instructors. However, it can be a very economical procedure. Coding errors can be reduced when card punching or remote terminal operation is performed from machine-oriented diagrams by the programmer. Even more efficiency has been achieved when the program is punched directly by a keypunch operator. Using only the minimum symbols developed in this text, a keypunch operator can be trained to do an effective job in less than two hours.

It is also easy and cost effective to punch a program in ALGOL, *PL/I,* or *BASIC* from the machine-oriented flow diagrams or charts used in this text. Comment lines are taken from the human-oriented flow diagram used in parallel with the machine-oriented flow diagram, or from annotated machine-oriented flow diagrams.

Table 3-3 shows the elements of a machine-oriented flow diagram and comments on items—including the terms GO TO, END, and IF—that are usually omitted. In addition, FORMAT statements are usually put on an auxiliary coding form rather than being listed directly on the flow diagram.

A detailed discussion of Nassi-Shneiderman charts is deferred until the formal presentation of mini-modules in Chapter 5. Examples of machine-oriented modified

Table 3-3 Elements of Machine-Oriented Flow Diagram

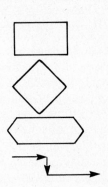

FORTRAN statement(s) go in a rectangular box.

IF (block IF, logical IF, arithmetic IF and computed GO TO) statements go into a diamond-shaped box.

DO-loops are indicated by a hexagonal box.

Boxes are connected by flow-arrows which sometimes represent GO TO statements. (When a flow-arrow leads to another portion of the program, it represents a GO TO, and the statement to which it points must be labeled.) Use arrowheads at each corner, at entry to a box. Do not use arrowheads along lines.

Comments:

1. The name should stand out prominently on each sheet.
2. The main line should be clearly evident.
3. No gaps should occur in boxes, flow-arrows, or their connections.
4. Show necessary statement labels.
5. List formats on separate coding form.
6. The FORTRAN words GO TO, IF, and END do not belong on the flow diagram.
7. A machine-oriented flow diagram is adequate when a program can be punched directly from it, without intermediate coding, by an experienced person familiar with this system of notation. (Not recommended for slow typists! — or persons with little key punch or remote terminal experience)

Nassi-Shneiderman charts are given in Figure 2–1 for program IEQPRT and Figures 2–6(b) and 2–9(b) for program CUB and subroutine FINDS, respectively.

Examples of machine-oriented flow diagrams are found in Figures 2–5(d) and 2–7(d) for programs CUB and COMP, respectively. Figure 2–10 contains a machine-oriented flow diagram for subroutine FINDS.

3–6 PROGRAM TRACING

To verify that a machine-oriented flow diagram or chart works correctly, it is often advisable to "trace" the flow using a "typical" set of data. Program tracing actually does three things: It helps you learn to construct your own machine-oriented diagrams and charts, it helps you increase your speed in program development, and it helps you find errors that have gone undetected or to verify that an algorithm is correct.

The simple rules for program tracing summarized in Table 3–4 have been perfected by extensive class-testing. To keep tracing reasonably compact, values are entered on the same horizontal line until a previously entered value needs changing. This rule may be relaxed only if additional spacing actually helps clarify the process. Once you have gone to a new line, never make an entry on the preceding line. This rule should never be violated. The additional lines needed are more than offset by the reduction in errors. Furthermore, adhering to this rule means the trace can be easily followed and retraced, often a necessary procedure.

Program CSFN is used to illustrate program tracing. A definition sheet (Table 3–5), a machine-oriented flow diagram (Figure 3–1(a)), a modified Nassi-Shneiderman chart

---

Table 3-4 TECHNIQUE for PROGRAM TRACING

1. Use tabular form.
2. List variable names horizontally as column headings.
3. It is often helpful to show some expressions as well, usually in parentheses.
4. On each row, in turn, continue making entries until the value of a variable changes. Then go to the next row.
5. Never make an entry on a preceding row once you have moved to a new one.

Table 3-5 Definition Sheet for Program CSFN

Program:	CSFN (Counting and Summing Fibonacci Numbers)
Definition:	1. Determine Fibonacci numbers, with first, third, . . . , terms in I and second, fourth, . . . , terms in J.
	2. Sum odd valued Fibonacci numbers.
	3. Count even valued Fibonacci numbers.
	4. Stop with the first ten Fibonacci numbers.

Descriptive Items:

Variable Name	Meaning
I, J	Fibonacci numbers (odd and even terms, respectively).
KTR	Counter that controls the number of loops.
LSUM	Location where sum of odd valued Fibonacci numbers is stored.
KOUNT	Location where count of even valued Fibonacci numbers is stored.

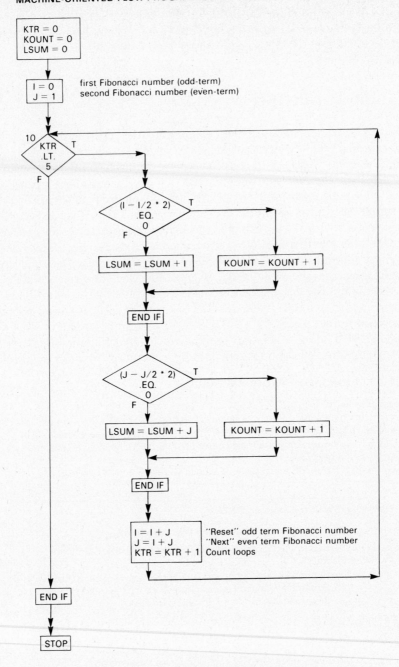

FIGURE 3–1(a) Program CSFN, machine-oriented flow diagram: Counting even, summing odd-valued Fibonacci numbers

(Figure 3–1(b)), and FORTRAN listing (Listing 3–1) are provided. The program is traced in Table 3–6 with Rule 4 relaxed; it is then traced again in the tightest possible form.

From the program it is clear that a Fibonacci number is formed from the sum of the two previous Fibonacci numbers, as illustrated below.

$$0 + \underbrace{1 = 1}$$
$$1 + \underbrace{1 = 2}$$
$$1 + \underbrace{2 = 3}$$
$$2 + 3 = 5$$

This process can be continued indefinitely, although the program indicates that we shall stop after the first ten numbers.

Line 1 of Table 3–6 comes from the first five program statements which initialize: (1) the loop counter; (2) the counter for Fibonacci numbers with even values; (3) the location for summing Fibonacci numbers with odd values; (4) the first Fibonacci number; and (5) the second Fibonacci number.

Line 2 shows computations performed in the second IF-THEN.

$$I/2 * 2 = 0/2 * 2 = 0$$

and

$$I - I/2 * 2 = 0.$$

Table 3-6 Trace of Program CSFN

KTR	KOUNT	LSUM	I	J	(I/2 * 2)	(I – I/2 * 2)	(J/2 * 2)	(J – J/2 * 2)
0	0	0	0	1				
	1				0	0		
		1					0	1
1			1	2				
		2			0	1		
	2						2	0
2			3	5				
		5			2	1		
		10					4	1
3			8	13				
	3				8	0		
		23					12	1
4			21	34				
		44			20	1		
	4						34	0
5			55	89				
0	0	0	0	1	0	0		
1	1	1	1	2	0	1	0	1
2	2	2	3	5	2	1	2	0
		5					4	1
3	3	10	8	13	8	0	12	1
4		23	21	34	20	1		
5	4	44	55	89			34	0

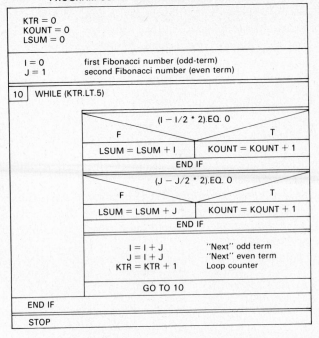

PROGRAM CSFN: NASSI-SHNEIDERMAN CHART

FIGURE 3-1(b) Program CSFN: Nassi-Shneiderman chart

Because the last calculation is zero, the IF is true and 1 is added to location KOUNT. Line 3 shows computations executed during the third IF-THEN.

$$J/2 * 2 = 1/2 * 2 = 0$$

and

$$J - J/2 * 2 = 1.$$

The factor $1/2$ is 0 because fractional parts are discarded in integer division. (Other examples of this are $4/2 = 2$, $5/2 = 2$, $6/2 = 3$, and $7/2 = 3$.) Within FORTRAN programs, multiplication and division is performed before addition and subtraction. Because the IF is false (that is, not equal to zero), this Fibonacci number is added to location LSUM for accumulation.

On the fourth line, I and J are recomputed and the loop counter is incremented by 1. The fifth line repeats the major DO-WHILE loop with $I = 1$ and $J = 2$.

The trace is repeated below the double line in a more compact form using the rules of Table 3-4. In both traces, the Fibonacci numbers 55 and 89 are not included in the KOUNT and LSUM computations because the loop counter, KTR, is set to 5 immediately after they are computed. Using computers to trace programs is discussed further in later sections.

```
      PROGRAM CSFN
C     COUNTING AND SUMMING FIBONNACI NUMBERS
C     *          *          *          *
C
C              --- KTR IS COUNTER WHICH CONTROLS
C                    NUMBER OF LOOPS
C              --- KOUNT STORES COUNT OF EVEN VALUED
C                    FIBONACCI NUMBERS
C              --- LSUM STORES SUM OF ODD VALUED
C                    FIBONACCI NUMBERS
C              --- FIBONACCI NUMBERS GENERATED:
C                    --- I FOR ODD TERMS
C                    --- J FOR EVEN TERMS

      KTR=0
      KOUNT=0
      LSUM=0
      I=0
      J=1

   10 IF(KTR.LT.5 )THEN

         IF((I-I/2*2).EQ.0)THEN
            KOUNT=KOUNT+1
         ELSE
            LSUM=LSUM+I
         END IF

         IF((J-J/2*2).EQ.0)THEN
            KOUNT=KOUNT+1
         ELSE
            LSUM=LSUM+J
         END IF

         WRITE(6,'('' I='',I3,''   J='',I3,''   KOUNT='',I2,
     1   ''   LSUM='',I3)') I,J,KOUNT,LSUM
         I=I+J
         J=I+J
         KTR=KTR+1
         GO TO 10
      END IF

      STOP
      END
```

Output:
```
 ENTERING USER PROGRAM
 I=  0  J=  1  KOUNT= 1  LSUM=  1
 I=  1  J=  2  KOUNT= 2  LSUM=  2
 I=  3  J=  5  KOUNT= 2  LSUM= 10
 I=  8  J= 13  KOUNT= 3  LSUM= 23
 I= 21  J= 34  KOUNT= 4  LSUM= 44
 END PROGRAM EXECUTION
```

LISTING 3-1 Program CSFN with output

3-7 CODING IN FORTRAN 77

Elements of the FORTRAN language are formally developed in the next three chapters. The following seven basic types of statements are discussed.

1. Arithmetic assignment statements
2. STOP statements

3. CONTINUE statements
4. END statements
5. Control-of-flow statements
6. READ/WRITE statements
7. FORMAT statements

Types 1 through 4 are considered in Chapter 4. Control-of-flow is treated in Chapter 5. The last two types are the subject of Chapter 6.

3-8 EXERCISES

Make a human-oriented flow diagram or Nassi-Shneiderman chart for the following nonmathematical situations.

1. Getting up in the morning.

2. Getting in and starting an automobile.

3. Getting a date.

4. Getting the best courses for the next term.

Prepare a human-oriented flow diagram in each case.

5. Solution of the quadratic equation.

6. Averaging test scores.

7. Optimizing scales for plotting. (This is a very difficult but extremely useful human-oriented flow diagram. The idea is to establish a scale that has exactly 101 points so that it can fit any particular range of numbers and use the maximum possible range of points on this 101-point scale. In addition, the scale values used with each ten divisions must be either 1, 2, 4, or 5 times some power of 10. Figure 3-2 illustrates some possibilities.)

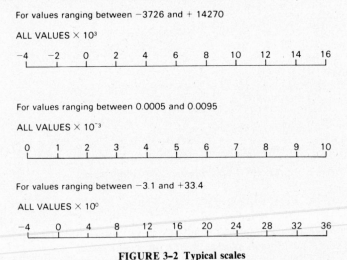

For values ranging between −3726 and + 14270

ALL VALUES × 10^3

| −4 | −2 | 0 | 2 | 4 | 6 | 8 | 10 | 12 | 14 | 16 |

For values ranging between 0.0005 and 0.0095

ALL VALUES × 10^{-3}

| 0 | 1 | 2 | 3 | 4 | 5 | 6 | 7 | 8 | 9 | 10 |

For values ranging between −3.1 and +33.4

ALL VALUES × 10^0

| −4 | 0 | 4 | 8 | 12 | 16 | 20 | 24 | 28 | 32 | 36 |

FIGURE 3-2 Typical scales

Figures 3-3 through 3-6 each contain a flow diagram, a chart, and a corresponding tracing table.

8. Trace the flow of Figure 3-3.

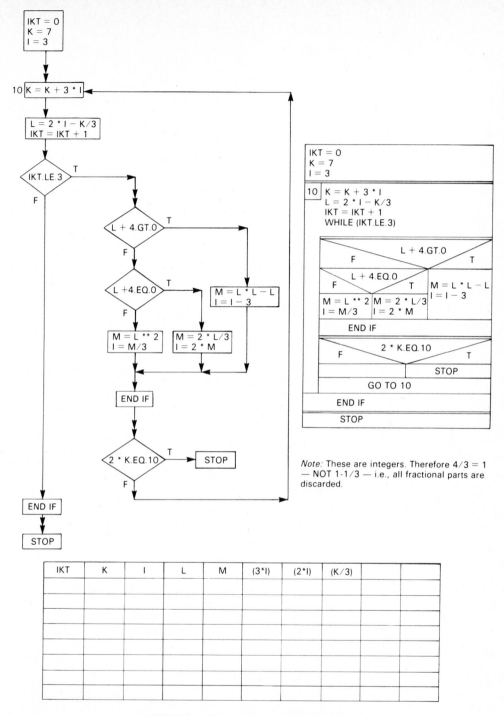

Note: These are integers. Therefore $4/3 = 1$ — NOT $1\text{-}1/3$ — i.e., all fractional parts are discarded.

IKT	K	I	L	M	(3*I)	(2*I)	(K/3)		

FIGURE 3-3 Trace involving integer numbers

9. Trace the flow of Figure 3–4.

10. Trace the flow of Figure 3–5.

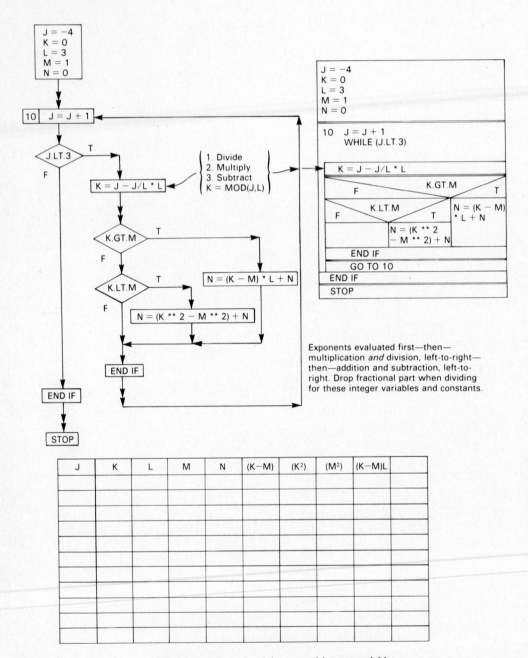

Exponents evaluated first—then—multiplication *and* division, left-to-right—then—addition and subtraction, left-to-right. Drop fractional part when dividing for these integer variables and constants.

J	K	L	M	N	(K−M)	(K²)	(M²)	(K−M)L

FIGURE 3-4 Trace involving several integer variables

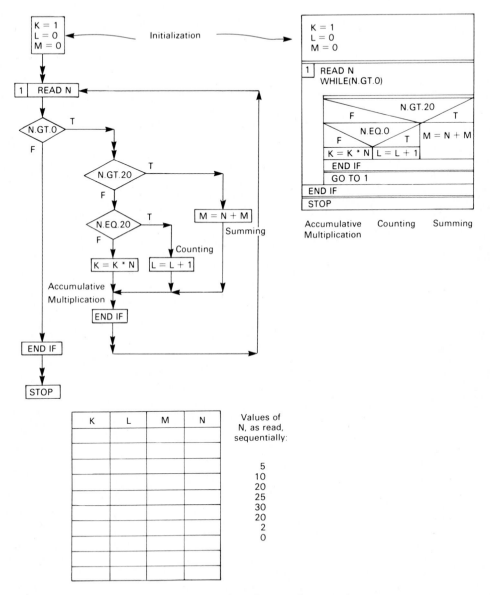

FIGURE 3-5 Trace involving counting, summing,
and accumulative multiplication

11. Trace the flow of Figure 3–6.

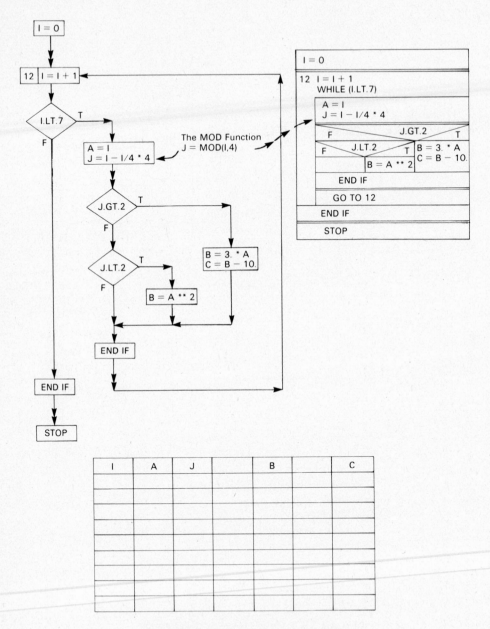

FIGURE 3-6 Trace involving real numbers

Figures 3–7 through 3–10 each represent a series summation equation,* the corresponding machine-oriented flow diagram and modified Nassi-Shneiderman chart, and a table to trace the steps as they occur in the program. In each case, trace using the variable in an algebraic expression, even though the computer would actually perform the calculations using the numerical value currently stored in the location defined by the variable name.

12. Trace $\displaystyle\sum_{i=1}^{5} (i+1)^2 x^{(i-1)}$

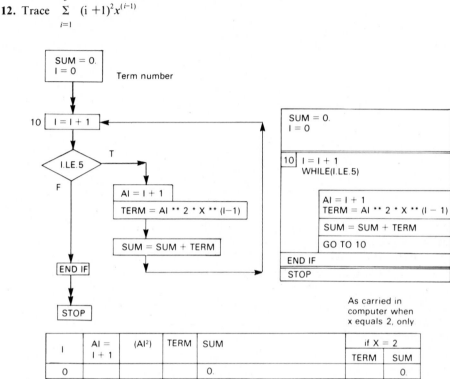

FIGURE 3-7 Simple series expansion and summation

*The symbol Σ is defined in the glossary.

13. Trace $\displaystyle\sum_{i=1}^{5} \frac{x^{(2i-1)}}{(2i-1)}$.

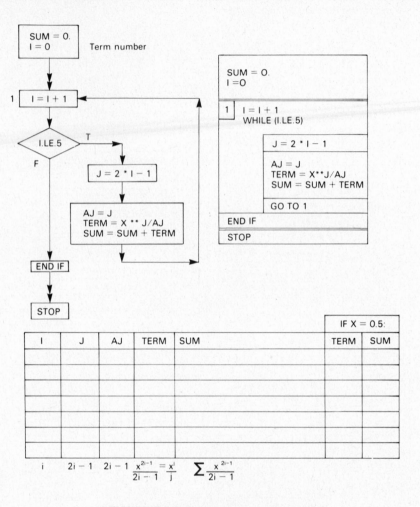

FIGURE 3–8 Series expansion and summation

14. Trace $\sum\limits_{i=1}^{5} K!$. (Note: The symbol $K!$ is read "*K-factorial*" and represents

the product $1\cdot2\cdot3\cdots K$. Thus $3! = 1\cdot2\cdot3 = 6$, and $5! = 1\cdot2\cdot3\cdot4\cdot5 = 120$.)

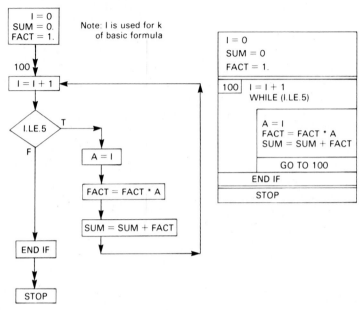

I	A	FACT		SUM	
		EXPANDED	AS STORED	EXPANDED	AS STORED
0		1.	1.	0.	0.
1	1.	1. * 1.	1.	1.	1.
2	2.	1. * 2.	2.	1. + 2.	3.
k	k	k^{th} term		$k! = \Sigma k$	

FIGURE 3-9 Simple factorial series expansion and summation

15. Trace $\sum\limits_{i=1}^{5} L!(2L-1)(2L+1)$.

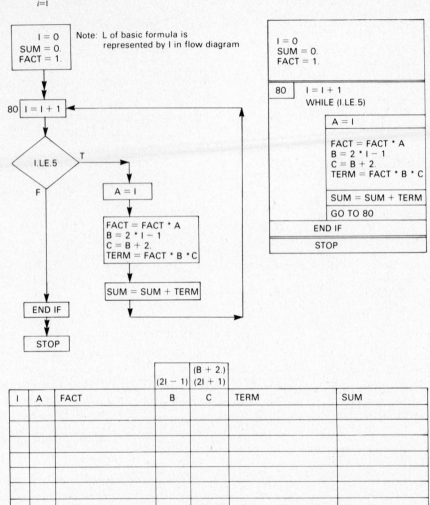

FIGURE 3–10 Factorial series expansion and summation

Essential Rules of FORTRAN Programming

This chapter gives a formal introduction to FORTRAN.

4-1 FORMULA TRANSLATION

FORTRAN is an acronym composed of the first three letters of the word *formula* plus the first four letters of the word *translation*. It is a near-mathematical language that attaches specific (sometimes nontraditional) meanings to words and symbols. It is important to understand the distinction between the two stages of FORTRAN programming, compilation and execution. These concepts are described in Table 4–1 (and Figure 1–6).

Table 4–2 illustrates an analogy between English and the FORTRAN language. The

---

Table 4-1 FORTRAN, Formula Translation

FORTRAN (FORmula TRANslation) is a two-stage procedure.

(Stage 1)   COMPILATION

1. Locations established for variables and constants.
2. FORTRAN translated into machine's own language. (Line-by-line)
3. Appropriate error messages produced when FORTRAN is used incorrectly.

(Stage 2)   EXECUTION

1. Program "runs."
2. Data (cards) read.
3. Results output (high-speed printer — HSP)
4. Appropriate messages for "run-time" errors produced.

Note: An intermediate stage, linkage or collection, often occurs between compilation and execution.

Table 4-2 An Analogy Between English and FORTRAN

An Analogy

English	*FORTRAN*
Character set	Character set
Letters (capital and lowercase)	"Alpha" characters
Punctuation	A → Z (capitals only)
Numbers	"Numeric" characters*
	0 → 9
	"Special" characters
	blank (usually denoted as Δ or b)
	= (equals) + (plus)
	– (minus) * (asterisk)
	/ (slash) ((left parenthesis)
	) (right parenthesis) , (comma)
	. (decimal point or period)
	' (apostrophe)
	Full Language also includes $
	(currency symbol or dollar sign)
	and : (colon).
Words	Syntactic Items (partial list)
	Arithmetic Operators
	Constants
	Variable Names
Phrases	Expressions
	(Ordered combination of
	of syntactic items)
Sentences	Arithmetic (Replacement) Statements
	variable name = expression
	↑
	replacement symbol

Analogy suggested by Dr. Robert E. Lovell.

character sets for English and FORTRAN are similar, but FORTRAN uses only capital letters. Letters and digits are collectively called alphanumeric characters.† In addition, FORTRAN contains several special symbols which, from time to time, take on special meanings. A detailed discussion of selected syntactic items, expressions, and arithmetic statements follows in the first three parts of the next section. (See also Section 13–1.1.)

4-2 THREE KINDS OF FORTRAN SYNTACTIC ITEMS

The arithmetic operators have previously been used: + for addition, − for *negation* or subtraction, * for multiplication, / for division, and ** for raising a number to a power. We have also used two other kinds of syntactic items, constants and variable names.

Constants are the numbers that occur in a FORTRAN program. There are several kinds of constants, two of which are integer (fixed point) and real (floating point). An

†An alphanumeric character is defined as either a letter (alpha) or digit (numeric).

integer constant never contains a decimal point and can, therefore, be readily distinguished from a real constant which always—even as a whole number—has a decimal point.* Other types of constants are introduced in later chapters.

The third type of syntactic item used in previous programs is the variable name. A variable name is the symbolic name assigned to a specific storage location for a particular FORTRAN program; the variable name represents the place where numerical data are stored so that data can be retrieved whenever the variable name is used. As the name variable implies, such locations are used for numerical values that are expected to change while the program is running. By contrast, constants maintain the same value throughout the running of any given program.

4-2.1 A Valid Integer (Fixed Point) Constant

The value of an integer constant never has an associated decimal point. The maximum possible range of values of integer constants varies from machine to machine. The smallest range is from -9999 to $+9999$. Other machines have extremely larger limits, such as the range between plus and minus 34,359,738,367 (which is $2^{35} - 1$). Caution must be exercised when using integers in programs to be sure that the limits of the machine are not exceeded. If an integer "attempts" to exceed maximum upper or lower limits, an anomaly will occur—one which is usually not easy to detect.

Typical valid integers include the following.

$$3 \qquad -76 \qquad 1843 \qquad -1926 \qquad +17$$

4-2.2 A Valid Real (Floating Point) Constant

A basic real constant must always contain a decimal point, even if it is a whole† number. Real constants are usually limited to eight significant figures, scaled by a power of 10. The range of the power of 10 varies among machines. The smallest known range is from 10^{-28} to 10^{28} and one of the largest ranges varies from 10^{-243} to 10^{243}.

Typical basic real constants include the following.

$$-183.2 \qquad 0.0000243 \qquad 163. \qquad 9.$$

Real constants can be written in scientific notation by writing the letter E and an integer constant—which may or may not be signed—after a basic real or integer constant. The value of such a real constant is the product of the constant preceding the E times the power of ten indicated by the integer following the E. Typical examples include the following.

$$6.2E5 \quad (6.2 \times 10^{5}) \qquad +7E-3 \quad (7.0 \times 10^{-3})$$
$$-7.6E4 \;(-7.6 \times 10^{4})$$

---

*Real numbers may be written in scientific notation without using a decimal point, but they are still distinguishable as real constants because integer constants cannot be written in scientific notation.

†Contrary to the usual mathematical convention, whole number is used for both positive and negative values. The word integer is more appropriate mathematically, but cannot be used because of FORTRAN conventions.

4-2.3 Variables and Variable Names

An algebraic variable is represented by a symbol and can assume different values. In FORTRAN 77, a variable is defined as an *entity* that has both a name and a type, while a variable name is a symbolic name of a datum. A variable name is, therefore:

1. the name of a storage location;
2. used in the same manner as the value of a variable in an algebraic expression. For example, if the variable name IT is used in a FORTRAN program, then every time IT occurs, the current value stored in IT will be used in the computation.

(a) *Rules*   Variable names must be constructed following several simple rules.*
1. Variable names must start with a letter of the alphabet.
2. Variable names must contain only letters of the alphabet or numbers. These can be arranged in any order as long as the first character is a letter.
3. Variable names are limited to a maximum of six characters.

Mnemonics are useful in forming valid FORTRAN variable names. Thus to represent the symbol π, it is appropriate to use PI. To represent the symbol θ, it is appropriate to use THETA. Likewise Yearly CASH Flow might be represented by YCASHF. Use of appropriate mnemonics and clear variable name definitions on the definition sheet can eliminate many troubles.

(b) *Type*   Although variables are of several types, for the present we shall consider only two types: integer (fixed point) and real (floating point). To make a variable name represent and store only integers, make the first letter an I, J, K, L, M, or N. (Notice that this sequence of letters is easy to remember because the first letter, I, and the last letter, N, are the first two letters of the word *integer*.) Any variable name that does not start with the letters I through N is, by definition, a floating point variable. All numbers stored in such a location, therefore, always include a decimal point.

These facts about syntactic items are summarized in Table 4–3.

(c) *Valid Examples*   Typical integer variable names include:

I   N2B3   MMC3D

These show allowable variations in formation and that a single letter can be a variable name. Mnemonics such as the following are preferable.

INDEX   JOBNUM   (for JOB NUMber)   LOC (for LOCation)

Typical real variable names include the following.

A   AJAK   A3B2   A134

Again, use of mnemonics is desirable.

AREA (for AREA) DIA (for DIAmeter) CSTPUN (for CoST Per UNit)

*These same three rules apply to all *symbolic names*.

Table 4-3 Constants and Variables and Their Definitions

Syntactic Items (Partial list)

Constants ("numbers")*

    Integer

        No decimal point.

    Real, basic†

        8 Significant figures (typically).
        Power of 10.
        Always a decimal point, except when using scientific notation.

Variable names

    Concept: Name of location where data is stored when this program is executing (running).

    Rules‡:

        1. Must start with a letter.
        2. Can contain only letters and numbers.
        3. Number of characters is limited to a *maximum* of 6.

    Type

        Integer (Fixed point)
            Must start with
            I, J, K, L, M, or *N.*

        Real (Floating point)
            Must start with a letter other than *I, J, K, L, M,* or *N.*

* Precision and rounding are not ANSI specified.

† Real constants are of three kinds: a basic real constant, a basic real constant followed by E and an integer representing a power of 10, and an integer followed by E and an integer representing a power of 10.

‡ These rules are applicable to all *Symbolic Names.*

4-2.4 Type

In FORTRAN, integer and real (fixed and floating point) values are stored differently. The word *type* is used to distinguish between them. Table 4-4 summarizes concepts of type.

4-2.5 Scientific Notation

Table 4-5 shows the representation of real numbers using scientific notation in FORTRAN. Column 1 of the table shows the appearance of the computer output, Column 2 shows the typical scientific notation format, and Column 3 shows usual decimal notation. Notice that both the decimal portion of the number and the power of ten can have either positive or negative signs. A conceptual model of the storage of such real numbers is discussed in Section 4-3.

Table 4-4 Concept of Type

Concept of Type
(Representation of Numerical Data)

Integer (Fixed point)

No decimal fractions.

No decimal point.

Positive or negative.

Size is machine dependent.

Typical small machine : maximum 9999

Typical large machine : maximum $2^{35}-1 = 34,359,738,367$

Real (Floating point)

Whole numbers and decimal numbers.

Always a decimal point (24. not 24).

Positive or negative.

Size is machine dependent.

Typically: 8 (some have only 6 or 7) significant figures multiplied by power of ten with variations from 10^{-38} to 10^{+38} up to 10^{-243} to 10^{+243}.

Table 4-5 Scientific Notation

Scientific Notation
(E-FORMAT)

Computer Output	Scientific Notation*	Standard Form
.10+02 or 0.10E 02	0.10×10^2	10.
–.10+02 or –0.10E 02	-0.10×10^2	–10.
.216+05 or 0.216E 05	0.216×10^5	21600.
.52–01 or 0.52E –01	0.52×10^{-1}	
	or $0.52 \times \dfrac{1}{10}$	0.052
.43–05 or 0.43E –05	0.43×10^{-5}	
	or $0.43 \times \dfrac{1}{10^5}$	0.0000043
.99999999–14 or 0.99999999E–14	$0.99999999 \times 10^{-14}$ or $0.99999999 \times \dfrac{1}{10^{14}}$	0.0000000000000099999999
6+03 or 6E 03	0.6×10^4	6000.
6.+03 or 6.E 03	0.6×10^4	6000.

*Scientific notation by common mathematical notation requires $1 \le x < 10$ in $x \cdot 10^a$. In FORTRAN, by contrast, scientific notation requires $0.1 \le x < 1.0$ in $x \cdot 10^a$. See Section 4–3 for an indication of the reasons for this change.

Chapter 4 Essential Rules of FORTRAN Programming

4-2.6 Exceptions

FORTRAN has many exceptions and possible modifications. The following are examples of valid integer (fixed point) variable names (chosen to illustrate "legally" permissible characteristics).

$$K \qquad K3J9 \qquad L333 \qquad KABC$$

Examples of valid real (floating point) variable names are these.

$$R \qquad RJLK \qquad R3IT \qquad R134$$

However, the type of all of these variable names can be changed by use of special declaration statements. (See Section 4–4.) In general, however, type is set by the first letter of the variable name—additional letters or numbers in the word do not affect the type in any way. Some instructors encourage use of the type statements of Section 4–4 to foster use of names that are appropriate to the problem rather than names modified for implicit FORTRAN type.

4-3 STORAGE OF DATA—A CONCEPTUAL MODEL

For most students, it is much too early in the study of computer programming to discuss how variables and constants are actually stored. On the other hand, it is quite important to have a "conceptual model." This model will help you to input and output with reasonable acumen, have some concept of the problems associated with roundoff, and have a better feel for the size of numbers that you can use in the programs you write. So, although the computer is really a *binary* machine, often using *octal* or *hexadecimal* representation for numbers, the conceptual model is based on a decimal (base 10) number system.

You may visualize that integers are stored exactly as they appear, always right-justified. That is, think of integers in storage as having no trailing zeros unless the zeros are actually part of the number.

Table 4–6 shows several numbers each written in standard form as a real number, repeated in scientific notation, and then represented as a conceptual model for storage in the computer.

Consider the number 1, expressed in scientific notation in FORTRAN as 0.1×10^1. Conceptually, storage for the number is divided into four distinct areas. The first area is simply the first space, and stores the sign of the number. The second area embodies the next eight spaces and stores the eight significant figures of the number. The third area is the tenth space, which stores the sign of the exponent. The last two spaces comprise the fourth area and store the exponent to be used with a power of 10 for scaling. An implied decimal point is always assumed to exist just in front of the eight significant figures. Thus, for the number 1: (Area 1) the sign is $+$; (Area 2) to eight significant figures 1 is expressed as a decimal as .10000000 with the decimal point implied; (Area 3) the exponent is positive; and (Area 4) the power of 10 is 1. Therefore 1 is stored as $+.10000000 \times 10^{+01}$.

Several more examples are shown in table 4–6, using a combination of positive and negative numbers and a mixture of positive and negative exponents. The last value, -37.034, is shown in scientific notation and in the conceptual stored form in the

Table 4-6 A "Conceptual Model" of the Storage of Real Numbers

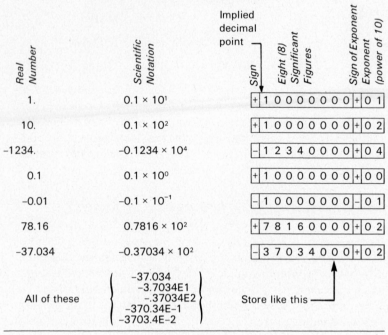

Conceptual Model:
Storage of Real (Floating point) Numbers

Real Number	Scientific Notation	Sign	Eight (8) Significant Figures	Sign of Exponent	Exponent (power of 10)
1.	0.1×10^1	+	1 0 0 0 0 0 0 0	+	0 1
10.	0.1×10^2	+	1 0 0 0 0 0 0 0	+	0 2
-1234.	-0.1234×10^4	-	1 2 3 4 0 0 0 0	+	0 4
0.1	0.1×10^0	+	1 0 0 0 0 0 0 0	+	0 0
-0.01	-0.1×10^{-1}	-	1 0 0 0 0 0 0 0	-	0 1
78.16	0.7816×10^2	+	7 8 1 6 0 0 0 0	+	0 2
-37.034	-0.37034×10^2	-	3 7 0 3 4 0 0 0	+	0 2

All of these $\left\{ \begin{array}{l} -37.034 \\ -3.7034E1 \\ -.37034E2 \\ -370.34E-1 \\ -3703.4E-2 \end{array} \right\}$ Store like this ⟶

computer. This number can be read as input data or can be output as results in real or scientific form in any of the following manners (assuming the FORMAT specification is consistent).

$$-37.034 \qquad -3.7034E1 \qquad -.37034E2 \qquad -307.34E-1 \qquad -3703.4E-2$$

Can you see other ways?

4-4 DECLARATION OF VARIABLES

Many higher-level languages require variables to be declared before they are used. At this point, declaration means to specify the type of each variable. In FORTRAN, all variables are automatically assigned a type based on their first letter unless the type is changed by a declaration statement.

Variables may be declared by use of an IMPLICIT statement or by use of explicit statements.

4-4.1 Explicit Type Statements

Any variable name can be assigned as type real, integer, or logical by using an explicit type statement. Form of the explicit statement is REAL, INTEGER, or LOGICAL followed by the variable names to be typed, separated by commas (also COMPLEX and DOUBLE PRECISION, followed by array names, array declarators, function names, and dummy procedure names as well as variable names). Thus the statements

INTEGER RR1, RR2
REAL INT

override the standard convention that variable names starting with I through N are type integer and all others are type real. RR1 and RR2 can store only integers. Conversely, INT is now type real and stored numbers, even if whole numbers, would always contain a decimal point.

4-4.2 IMPLICIT Type Statements

An IMPLICIT type statement is used to establish type by the first letter of the variable name. Form of the IMPLICIT statement is IMPLICIT *typ*( ), *typ*( ) where *typ* is REAL, INTEGER, or LOGICAL and the parentheses contain either a single letter or end point letters of a sequence, separated by a hyphen (full language also allows COMPLEX and DOUBLE PRECISION). The standard FORTRAN convention would be expressed as

IMPLICIT REAL (A–H), INTEGER (I–N), REAL (0–Z)

This signifies that all variables starting with the letters A through H are type real, all variables starting with the letters I through N are type integer, and all variables starting with the letters O through Z are type real. The statement could be written in the alternate form

IMPLICIT REAL (A–H, O–Z), INTEGER (I–N)

If the two explicit statements of Section 4–4.1 were included in the program, RR1, RR2 and INT would be exceptions.

4-4.3 Combination of Type Statements

Consider the following FORTRAN statements located in a single program.

IMPLICIT REAL (M), INTEGER (X–Z), INTEGER (A)
REAL ALL, INT, X3
INTEGER MAX, BEST

The order of establishing variable types is as follows.

1. The Standard Convention types variables starting with A through H and O through Z as real and those starting with I through N as integer.
2. The Standard Convention is modified by the IMPLICIT statement so that variables starting with B through H, M, and O through W are real. Variables starting with A, I through L, N, and X through Z are integer.
3. The Standard Convention as modified by the IMPLICIT statement is further modified by the explicit statements so that the preceding is true except for the specific variables ALL, INT, and X3, which are type real. MAX and BEST are type integer.

The IMPLICIT statement could be written in an alternate form as

IMPLICIT REAL (M), INTEGER (X–Z, A)

4-4.4 When to Declare Variables

Many instructors believe that students should quickly form the habit of declaring all variables because they feel it makes students more aware of all variable names being used, fixes the idea of "type" in their minds, and is more compatible with other high level languages.

For simplicity, and to ensure that the *default* status (the Standard Convention) of type is well mastered, no declarations are used in the early programs of this text without some specific comments.

IMPLICIT statements must be located at the very beginning of the program, just after the PROGRAM statement. All other declarations, including explicit type statements, follow immediately after any IMPLICIT statements. For more details on the order of statements, see Section 13–1.4.

4-5 EXPRESSIONS

A FORTRAN expression is defined as a combination of syntactic items (or perhaps just a single syntactic item or letter) used together in a meaningful way, often linked together by mathematical characters. The following are typical examples of valid expressions.

PI * R ** 2
AMPS * RESIS
ROGER (Degenerate form; a single syntactic item used as an expression)
J (Degenerate form; a single character used as a syntactic item that is, in turn, used as an expression).
RATE * TIME * PRINC

Expressions are found within FORTRAN programs to the right of an equal sign in a replacement or arithmetic assignment statement, and as logical expressions within IF statements, represented by diamond-shaped boxes on flow diagrams. Rules for expressions are summarized in Table 4–7.

In general, every constant and variable within any given expression should be of the same type; that is, all constants and variables in any given expression should be all real values or all integer values. For further discussion, see Section 4–6.1.

In addition, arithmetic expressions may not use implied multiplication or have two arithmetic symbols adjacent to each other. Thus if you want to multiply the contents currently stored in location FIRST by the contents currently stored in location THIRD, you may *not* write an expression such as (FIRST)(THIRD). Rather, the legal expression is FIRST * THIRD. In addition, if you want to multiply the contents stored in FIRST by the negative of the contents stored in THIRD, it would be invalid to write FIRST * −THIRD. Arithmetic symbols cannot be adjacent and must be separated by the use of parentheses. Thus a valid form would be

FIRST * (−THIRD)   or   (FIRST) * (−THIRD)

Table 4-7 Rules for Valid Arithmetic Expressions

Arithmetic Expressions

Typical Uses

1. Right of equal sign in arithmetic (replacement) statements.

2. In IF statements (within diamond shaped boxes on flow diagrams).

Restrictions

1. No mixed modes (legally permissible but undesirable because they foster difficulties).

2. No arithmetic operators adjacent to each other (even if separated by blanks).

Typical Precedence of Evaluation (For exceptions, see Section 13-1.4.)

1. Innermost parentheses first.

2. If no parentheses exist, or within parentheses at a particular level:

     (a) Evaluate functions first.

     (b) Evaluate all exponents right to left.

     (c) Do multiplication and division, in order, left to right.

     (d) Then, do addition and subtraction, in order, left to right.

Most Simple

     Sometimes an expression is only a single constant or variable name.

4-5.1 Exponentiation

Many processors use the type of exponent to determine the process to be used in raising a number to a power.

1. An integer exponent specifies sequential multiplication. That is, $6. ** 4$ means $6. \times 6. \times 6. \times 6.$

2. A real exponent signifies the use of logarithms. That is, $6. ** 4.$ means take the antilog of the quantity 4. times the log of 6., or antilog $[4. \times \log(6.)]$. Because of this significance of exponential mode, severe restrictions are necessary when using exponentiation to insure correct results.

In general:

1. Integer exponents should be positive (sometimes zero is allowed) and may, therefore, be used with either positive or negative integers or real numbers.

     $J**(-3)$ means $1/(J**3) = 0$ (1 if $J = 1$; -1 if $J = -1$)

2. Real exponents may be either positive or negative, but they can be used only with positive real numbers because logarithms are involved. (On some machines, a real exponent of 0. is valid, while 0. is not allowed on others.) The number to be raised to a power must be positive because logarithms are not defined for zero or negative numbers. Integers raised to a real power are first converted to real numbers. Table 4-8 illustrates several examples of valid and invalid exponentiation.

Table 4-8 Valid and Invalid Exponentiation

VALID

± integer ** (+ integer)

   I ** K   All right if $K>0$; however, can lead to values that exceed limits of Integer (fixed point) words.

   3 ** 4   Means $3 \times 3 \times 3 \times 3$

± real ** (+ integer)

   3. ** 2   Means $3. \times 3.$ (not mixed mode; see Section 4-6.1).

   A ** K   Generally all right if $K>0$ (not mixed mode).

+ real ** (± real)

   A ** A   Means take antilog (A log A) where value of A is not changed during operation. A must be greater than zero.

   A ** B   All right if $A>0$.

   3.1 ** (−1.3)   All right; means antilog (−1.3 × log (3.1)).

± integer ** (± real)   Integer will be changed to real before exponentiation and mode is no longer integer. (This is mixed mode.)

INVALID

(−real) ** (± real)

   −3.1 ** 1.3   Cannot take log of negative numbers.

   0. ** 1.   Cannot take log of zero.

All right, but caution:

± real ** (− integer)

   +A ** (−I)   Means 1./(+A**I).

± integer ** (− integer)

   3 ** (−4)   Means 1/(3**4) = 0

   I ** (−4)   Means 1/(I**4) = 0 (1, I = ±1)

4-5.2   Scientific Notation versus Exponentiation

Confusion often exists between the use of scientific notation (a constant) and an expression that raises a number to a power. This distinction is shown in Table 4–9.

Thus 16.E−03 means 16. times 10^{-3} and is a constant, not an expression. When using scientific notation, a decimal point is usually included with the number in front of the capital E but the number representing the exponent of 10 following the E must be type integer. Both numbers may be with or without a sign.

To write an expression of equal value using exponentiation, it is necessary to write 16.*10.**(−3.), which also means 16. times 10^{-3}. In the first case, a constant is expressed in scientific notation and no computation is involved. In the second case, 10 must be raised during execution to the power −3 power and this result multiplied by 16.

$$10.**(-3) \quad \text{means} \quad 1./(10.**3.) = 1./1000. = 0.001$$

4-5.3   Hierarchy of Computations

General rules for the sequence used to evaluate expressions in the FORTRAN language were summarized in Table 4–7. Considering the sequence of calculations when writing computer programs is important in at least three particular contexts.

Table 4-9 Scientific Notation versus Exponentiation

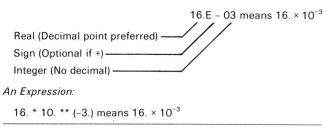

A Constant (in Scientific Notation):

16.E – 03 means 16. × 10^{-3}

Real (Decimal point preferred)

Sign (Optional if +)

Integer (No decimal)

An Expression:

16. * 10. ** (–3.) means 16. × 10^{-3}

1. In doing integer (fixed point) computations.
2. In certain esoteric computations.
3. In eliminating an excessive number of parentheses.

Typically, in evaluating an expression, the expression in the innermost parentheses is worked on first, with the intermediate results stored in an accumulator. Within the level of any particular expression in parentheses, or if no parentheses exist, functions are evaluated before exponents. Multiplications and divisions are performed from left to right. Finally additions and subtractions are done from left to right. (For exceptions, see Section 13–1.4.)

Thus $4.0 - 6.0/4.0 * 4.0$ is evaluated by first dividing 6.0 by 4.0, which gives 1.5. This is then multiplied by 4.0 to obtain 6.0. Finally the subtraction is done, giving an answer of -2.0.

The expression $(2. *3. + 4.) ** 2 - (6. + 3. * (2. + 1.))$ is evaluated as follows: The innermost parentheses contain the sum of 2.0 and 1.0, or 3.0, which is stored in an accumulator. This leaves two parenthesized expressions at the same level. The left expression is evaluated by multiplying 2.0 times 3.0 (6.0) and adding 4.0, which gives 10.0 to be stored in another accumulator. The right expression is evaluated by multiplying 3.0 times the 3.0 from (2.0 + 1.0) for 9.0, adding 6.0, and storing the resulting 15.0 in an accumulator. With quantities within all the parentheses evaluated, exponentiation of the quantity in the left parentheses, 10.0, leads to 10.0^2, or 100.0. Finally, subtract $100.0 - 15.0$ to yield the final result, 85.0.

Table 4–10 shows several examples. Numbers that must be temporarily stored in an accumulator during the process are indicated at the point of the bracket enclosing the expression represented by that single number. Several special problem areas are treated in the next few paragraphs.

(a) *Negative exponentiation* can cause untoward difficulties because negation occurs after exponentiation. The expression

$$-PI ** 4$$

means

$$-(PI**4)$$

Table 4-10 Examples of Hierarchy of Computations

Example 1

Equation: $F = \left(\dfrac{AB}{C}\right)D + \dfrac{EG}{H}$

FORTRAN Statement: F = A * B/C * D + E * G/H

Evaluated with: A = 4., B = 8., C = 2., D = 3., E = 5., G = 6., H= 3.

$$F = 4. * 8./2. * 3. + 5. * 6./3.$$

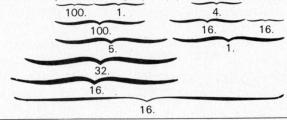

Example 2

Equation: $F = \dfrac{A/B}{C/D/E}$

FORTRAN Statement: F = A/B/(C/(D/E))

Evaluated with: A = 120., B = 2., C = 3., D = 5., E = 4.

$$F = 120./2./(3./5./4.))$$

Example 3

Equation: $R = \dfrac{ab^{x^2 \log(x)/y}}{c\sqrt{d}/Rg}$

FORTRAN Statement:

R = A*B**(X**2*ALOG(X)/Y)/(C*SQRT(D)/(R*G))

Evaluated with: A = 0.5, B = 2., X = 10., Y = 20., C = 4., D = 16., R = 8.0, G = 2.

$$R = 0.5*2.**(10.**2*ALOG(10.)/20.)/(4.*SQRT(16.)/(8.0*2.))$$

so that the result is always negative. If the sign is to be associated with PI, then the expression must be written as

$$(-PI) ** 4$$

(b) *Sequential exponentiation* uses the reverse of normal evaluation order, going right to left. Thus

$$4 ** 2 ** 3$$

means

$$4 ** (2 ** 3) = 4 ** 8 = 65536$$

This is different than the left-to-right order of evaluation mandated by parentheses. Thus

$$(4**2)**3 = 16**3 = 4096$$

The difference in these two answers illustrates why it is so important to understand this concept and why many programmers consistently use parentheses to avoid ambiguity.

(c) *Delineation of denominators* is important. Always enclose denominators within parentheses so that operations are performed correctly. Thus

$$\frac{ANUM}{DEN1 * DEN2}$$

must be written as

$$ANUM/(DEN1 * DEN2)$$

because

$$ANUM/DEN1 * DEN2$$

would represent

$$\frac{ANUM}{DEN1} * DEN2$$

(d) *Compound division* can cause trouble to the careless programmer. In Example 2 of Table 4–10, the same result can be obtained in a number of ways. For example,

$$\frac{\dfrac{A}{B}}{\dfrac{C}{\dfrac{D}{E}}} = \frac{\dfrac{A}{B}}{\dfrac{CE}{D}} = \frac{AD}{BCE}$$

or

$$A*D/(B*C*E)$$

When

$$B * C * E = 2. * 3. * 4. = 24 \quad \text{and} \quad A * D = 120. * 5. = 600$$

the result is again $600./24. = 25$.

4-6 ARITHMETIC ASSIGNMENT (REPLACEMENT) STATEMENTS

Table 4–11 summarizes the following comments on arithmetic assignment statements.
Assignment statements are composed of three separate parts, consisting of a *variable*

Table 4-11 Arithmetic Assignment (Replacement) Statement

Arithmetic Assignment (Replacement) Statement

Form:

VARIABLE NAME = EXPRESSION

Meaning:

1. Evaluate expression (in its mode), that is, do the computations shown in the expression using the constants (numbers) shown and the values currently stored in the locations represented by the variable names.
2. Observe type of variable name located left of the equal sign.
3. Change type of the single number that represents the result of evaluating the expression located right of the equal sign if it does not agree with type of the variable name located left of the equal sign.
4. Store results obtained from evaluating the expression (right of equal sign) in proper type into variable name (left of equal sign).

Values Changed:

1. Variable name (left of equal sign) has any old value erased and replaced by the new one representing the results of evaluating the expression (right of equal sign).
2. All values right of equal sign are unchanged except in cases where variable name (left of the equal sign) is also used in the expression (right of the equal sign).

---

name, which is always at the left of an *equal sign* with an *expression* to the right of the equal sign. Thus $A = I$ has the following meaning.

1. Take the current integer value stored in location I.
2. Convert the result to a real number.
3. Store this result (in type real) in location A.

Likewise,

$$AREA = PI * R ** 2$$

has this meaning.

1. Take the current value stored in R and square it.
2. Multiply this result by the current value stored in location PI.
3. Note that the *mode* of operation is identical to the type of the variable name found left of the equal sign.* Therefore store the result into location AREA.

The equal sign is not used to mean equality. Rather, the equal sign signifies the following.

1. Evaluate the expression to the right of the equal sign until it is expressed as a single number.
2. Check the type of the result obtained for the evaluated expression right of the equal sign against the type of the single variable left of the equal sign. If the types

*When operations are performed in an expression, the term *mode* is frequently used to indicate the *type* of arithmetic being processed.

do not agree, change the type of the result obtained for the evaluated expression so that it agrees with the type of the variable located left of the equal sign.

3. Store the final result in the location named by the single variable left of the equal sign.

Because of this meaning of the equal sign, a valid arithmetic assignment statement might appear as

$$A = (A + A ** 2) ** A$$

This instructs the computer to do these steps.

1. Square (but do not change) the current value of A.
2. Add the unchanged current value of A to A^2 (do not change the value stored in A).
3. Raise this sum to the Ath power (the value of A is still unchanged).
4. Store the final result in A, which now changes the value stored in location A.

This technique is particularly valuable in counting and related operations. For instance, the expression $I = I + 1$ adds 1 to the current value of I and stores the result back in I each time the statement is executed. This, of course, results in a counting sequence for successive values of I.

4-6.1 Mixed Mode

When two or more data types are used within the same expression, the resulting computations are said to be in *mixed mode*. Mixed mode is poor practice because it can, and does, lead to undetected errors within programs even when very careful work is done. Often these errors are very subtle and extremely difficult to locate.

Mixed modes occur when an expression contains combinations of both fixed and floating point words, such as these.

$$I * B \qquad 3 * B \qquad I * 3.16 \qquad 3. + A * 4 \qquad \text{[MIXED MODE]}$$

Mixed mode occurs in arithmetic assignment statements (replacement statements) only when mixed mode occurs in the expression found right of the equal sign. That is, mixed mode is a characteristic of an expression, not of an arithmetic assignment statement. Thus $A = B + K$ is mixed mode since the expression $B + K$ contains a real variable plus an integer variable. Likewise, $I = R - J$ is mixed mode because the expression right of the equal sign contains a real variable and a fixed variable. By contrast, the expression $A = K * L$ is not mixed mode, even though A is real and both K and L are integers. Likewise, $K = A/B$ is not mixed mode.

In the common operations such as $I+R$ and $I*R$, integer values are converted to type real and operations are performed in real mode. However, because of the seriousness of the subtle errors that can occur, the author requires students to refrain from mixing modes in their first courses. Typically,

$$A = 1/J * B$$

always yields $A = 0$ if J is not a positive or negative one and

$$A = 1./J * B$$

yields a decimal fraction B/J (with J converted to real). For more details, see Section 13–1.4.

In summary, although mixing modes is legal, mixed mode is poor practice and leads to errors that are difficult to find. Mixed mode occurs only in expressions and, therefore, occurs in arithmetic statements only within the expression located right of an equal sign. Mixed mode does not apply across equal signs.

An apparent exception is found in exponentiation, when raising a real number to an integer power. As previously explained, however, this is not true mixed mode because the mode of the exponent often determines the algorithm to be used.

4–6.2 Integer Computations

Troubles related to integer computations are limited to two specific cases.

1. When an integer goes out of range during a computation, no error is indicated; however, the answer will be wrong.
2. When an integer is divided by another integer, the result is always integer—any fractional part is discarded (a process called *truncation*). Thus 16/3 is 5 and 21/5 is 4. Interestingly, 3/4 is zero.

Program C5, partially coded in Listing 4–1, shows the differences obtained by using real versus integer computations as well as the differences inherent in orders of computation altered by parentheses.

Table 4–12 is a schematic of the input and resulting computations for Program C5. The first column of Table 4–12 shows symbols for variables and a symbolic representation for temporary computations stored in accumulators. Column 2 shows current numerical values stored in these locations. Thus the numerical value of $A/B + C$ (that is, $2./4. + 6.$) is stored in accumulator AC as 6.5. This accumulated value of 6.5 is then multiplied by the value stored in location D (currently equal to 8.) to obtain 52.0 in the temporary accumulator AD, representing

$$(A/B + C) * D$$

For Case 1, small values, G2 and G1 are computed in identical sequence, even though they have different sets of parentheses. G3, however, is computed in an alternate sequence

```
PROGRAM C5
LR=5
READ(LR,1)A,B,C,D
1 FORMAT(10F8.0)
G1=  (((A/B+C)*D )/A)*B
G2=   ((A/B+C)*D )/A *B
G3=    (A/B+C)*D  *B/A
I=A
J=B
K=C
L=D
M1=  ((((I/J+K)*L )/I)*J
M2=   (((I/J+K)*L )/I *J
M3=    (I/J+K)*L  *J/I
COMMENT *** ASSUME MAX INTEGER SIZE
C       ***       IS 32000  *******
```

LISTING 4–1 Program C5: Comparing real and integer computations

Table 4-12 Input and Results of Program C5 in Schematic Form

Case 1 Small values

	Type Real Computations			Type Integer Computation		
Input	A		2.	I		2
	B		4.	J		4
	C		6.	K		6
	D		8.	L		8
	A/B	= 2./4.	0.5	I/J	= 2/4	0
	A/B+C ≡ AC	= (.5+6.)	6.5	I/J+K ≡ IK	= (0+6)	6
	AC*D ≡ AD	= (6.5*8.)	52.0	IK*L ≡ IL	= (6*8)	48
	AD/A ≡ AE	= (52.0/2.)	26.0	IL/I ≡ IE	= (48/2)	24
G1:	AE*B	= (26.0*4.)	104.0	M1: IE*J	(24*4)	96
G2:	= G1		104.0	M2: = M1		96
	AD*B ≡ AB	= (52.0*4.)	208.0	IL*J ≡ IB	= (48*4)	192
G3:	AB/A	= (208.0/2.)	104.0	M3: IB/I	= (192/2)	96

Case 2 Large values

	Type Real Computations			Type Integer Computations		
Input	A		40.	I		40
	B		60.	J		60
	C		80.	K		80
	D		100.	L		100
	A/B	= 40./60.	0.66666666	I/J	= 40/60	0
	A/B+C ≡ AC	= (.66666666+80.)	80.666666	I/J+K ≡ IK	= (0+80)	80
	AC*D ≡ AD	= (80.666666*100.)	8066.6666	IK*L ≡ IL	= (80*100)	8000
	AD/A ≡ AE	= (8066.6666/40.)	201.66665	IL/I ≡ IE	= (8000/40)	200
G1:	AE*B	= (201.66665*60.)	12099.999	M1: IE*J	= (200*60)	12000
G2:	= G1		12099.999	M2: = M1		12000
	AD*B = AB	= (8066.6666*60.)	483999.99	IL*J = IB	= (8000*60)	too large
G3:	AB/A	= (483999.99/40.)	12099.999	M3: IB/I	= (?/40)	???

Note: Maximum integer size is assumed to be 32,000.

because of parentheses. All results are correct and identical: G1 = G2 = G3 = 104.0.

The second two sets of columns show the same computations with real A, B, C, and D changed to integer I, J, K, and L, respectively. Division of A by B gave 0.5, but I divided by J yields zero. This "error" is propagated throughout the program, leading to a final result which is not the same as the one obtained by ordinary mathematics. That is, 104. is not the same as 96. Although the mathematical computation involved using the integer form is numerically incorrect, it is not syntactically wrong. (In fact, availability of both real and integer computations is a very powerful tool for developing adequate logic in complicated programs, but consideration of such application is premature in this chapter.)

For Case 2, large values of A, B, C, and D result in an answer that should be 12,100. Because of roundoff errors, however, the computer output 12,099.999 (eight significant figures).

Integer computation of Case 2 using large numbers assumes that the maximum size for an integer is 32,000. Thus when using these larger values of A, B, C, and D converted to integer form in the second part of the program, results not only yield incorrect arithmetic, but real trouble is encountered in the computation of M3.

The sequence is as follows: $I/J + K = IK (= 80)$. Then $IK*L = IL = (80 * 100 = 8000)$. When IL is multiplied by J (8000×60), the result is greater than 32,000 and is "out of range." Another number is, however, actually obtained and no error message is given. (It is possible to use these results if the representation of integers in a particular machine is fully understood and reasonable care is taken, although the results bear no resemblance to the expected arithmetic answer.) When this result is divided by I, the answer stored into M3 is essentially a random number bearing no discernable relation to the desired answer.

4-6.3 Built-In Library Functions

The FORTRAN language contains a set of built-in *library function* subprograms (*intrinsic functions*) which can be used to evaluate many common algebraic functions. Typical examples are shown here.*

SIN(R) supplies the real (floating point) answer for the sine of R, where R is a real expression in radians.

COS(R) supplies a real answer for the cosine of an expression defined by R, where R is in radians.

ALOG(E) supplies the natural logarithm for the expression defined by E.

EXP(E) computes e^E, where the real answer is obtained by evaluation of the real expression represented by E and $e \doteq 2.7182818$ is the base of the natural logarithms.

SQRT(E) computes the square root of the real expression represented by E and supplies a type real, positive answer.

ATAN(E) computes the arctangent of the expression represented by the symbol E; the answer is in radians.

ABS(E) returns the absolute value of the number obtained by evaluating the expression represented by E; the answer is positive and type real. It may, of course, also be zero.

A short program to illustrate use of these function subprograms contained in the library associated with a FORTRAN 77 processor and some of their important characteristics are shown in Listing 4-2. These functions work only if the arithmetic of the expression is mathematically legal. For instance, if you ask the computer to take the square root of a negative number, it will not comply—it will give you an error at run time. Thus, although the expression A = SQRT(B) is valid syntactically and will compile correctly during the compilation stage, it will give an error message at run time if the value stored in B at that time is negative. In such a case, A = SQRT(−B) would execute because the product of two negative numbers is positive and would store a positive real number (that represents an imaginary root) in A.

In Listing 4-2, the operations are performed as follows. First, a value is read in for A. This number is squared and its sine is taken and stored in location B. Notice that A^2 (written as A * A) is assumed to have radian units when the sine is taken. The cosine of A raised to the 0.416 power is taken and the results are stored in C. (This statement causes a

*A full list of FORTRAN 77 intrinsic functions is given in Table 15-1.

```
    5|6|7
C  |  |PROGRAM FUNCT
   |  |LR = 5
   |  |LW = 6
   |  |READ (LR,10) A
10 |  |FORMAT (F10.0)
   |  |B = SIN (A*A)
   |  |C = COS (A**.416)      } here, A must not be 0 or negative
   |  |D = ALOG (SQRT(A))
   |  |E = ABS (B)
   |  |F = ABS (B*C*D)  ⟵—C may be +, −, or 0
   |  |G = SQRT (B*B+C**2+D**2.)      ⟵D must ≥ 0
   |  |WRITE (LW,20) A, B, C, D, E, F, G
20 |  |FORMAT (7(E16.8,1X))
   |  |STOP
   |  |END
```

LISTING 4–2 Illustration of built-in library function rules

run-time error if A is not positive because an attempt would be made to take the logarithm of a negative number or zero.) The value stored in D comes from the use of two intrinsic functions, one acting on the result of the other. First, the square root of A is taken, then the antilog of the value obtained from SQRT(A) is computed and stored in D. If the value of A is not positive, a run-time error will occur.

The value previously stored in B could be plus or minus; as stored in E it will always be plus. The absolute value function is also used for the product of $B \times C \times D$, which assures that the value stored in F is positive. G takes the square root of $B^2 + C^2 + D^2$, using three different methods for squaring the numbers. B * B works whether B is positive or negative. C ** 2 also works for C positive or negative, because this form of exponentiation signifies multiplication of C by itself. In the third case, D ** 2., the value of D must be positive. Otherwise an attempt would be made to take the logarithm of a negative number in the exponentiation process, which is impossible.

What is mathematically correct and what is syntactically correct are not always the same thing. For instance, in Listing 4–2, suppose the following statements were written after the computation for E.

$$E = ABS(B)$$
$$R = -E$$
$$T = SQRT(-R)$$

Then E would always be positive, R would always be negative, and T would be a positive real number representing the positive imaginary root of −R.

During the compilation stage, indiscriminant use of signs or radian measure is not detected and does not cause compilation errors. During run-time, however, any such faults are detected and usually cause the program to abort.

4-7 THREE CONTROL STATEMENTS

Chapter 5 discusses several statements that control flow for various branching mechanisms. Chapter 16 introduces the remaining control statements except for

CONTINUE, STOP, and END, which are the subject of this section. The PROGRAM statement is optional. When used, the PROGRAM statement must be the first statement and the symbolic name following the word PROGRAM must not be used for any other purpose.

4-7.1 The CONTINUE Statement, Continuation Lines, and Comment Lines

The CONTINUE statement means *do nothing and proceed.* In this text, the CONTINUE statement is used to terminate various mini-modules, including DO-loops (introduced in Chapter 8). In a sense, the CONTINUE statement is a "dummy" statement used to add clarity and flexibility to FORTRAN programs, as will be demonstrated in subsequent chapters.

Occasionally, neophyte programmers confuse CONTINUE statements with comment lines. There is a distinction, however. The CONTINUE statement is an executable statement of the FORTRAN language. A comment line, on the other hand, is used solely to provide documentation and does not affect the computer programs in any way. A comment line has three forms: (a) blanks in columns 1–72 inclusive, (b) a C in column 1 followed by any sequence of characters, or (c) an asterisk in column 1 followed by any sequence of characters.

A FORTRAN statement is composed of exactly one initial line and up to nine continuation lines (19 for Full Language). (Continuation lines are not related to CONTINUE statements.) Any line that contains a blank or zero in Column 6 (and is not a comment line) is an initial line. Continuation lines must have blank characters in Columns 1 through 5 and a character other than blank or zero in Column 6. Thus a single FORTRAN statement is limited to a maximum of 660 characters (1320 characters for Full Language) because FORTRAN statements must be located within 66 columns on a line (7 through 72).

4-7.2 STOP and END

In a sense, a FORTRAN program has two terminal points. The first is a physical termination, indicated by the word END (which must be the last card of the FORTRAN deck). This card signifies termination of the compilation stage. The second type of termination is a logical ending of the program during the execution. This logical terminator is the word STOP. STOP can be followed by a five-character or five-digit constant that can be made accessible by the processor. The meaning of *accessible* is purposefully vague to facilitate accommodation to different systems.

Thus the word END must physically always be the last statement in any FORTRAN program or subprogram without regard to statement labels (except on some computers that generously supply it for you). The word END indicates to the processor that the FORTRAN program is complete and that the computer should stop translating and assigning storage locations. After reading the word END in the compilation stage, the computer either will be ready to execute your program (including reading data and writing answers), or will have found errors in your FORTRAN program and will be too confused to proceed.

When your FORTRAN program has been successfully translated into the machine's own language, the translated program will proceed to Stage 2 and execute (run) in precisely the order specified by your FORTRAN program. Logic must be written into the program to cause execution to stop at a timely point. The logical terminator STOP is standard and can appear at any physical location within a FORTRAN program, even at multiple locations. Because the effect of STOP is to cause the program to stop executing, such statements must be placed at logical locations where program termination is desired. (The END statement also can act as a STOP statement, although such usage is discouraged.)

Some programmers choose a specific label number for a single STOP statement within every program, although to keep programs structured, many programmers would discourage this practice. Many use 9999; others use 30 (adopted from journalism). This technique facilitates termination from any place in the program by the statement GO to 9999 or GO TO 30. Of course, STOP could also be used at any of these locations. Sometimes a useful modification is to place the 9999 label on an output statement ahead of the logical terminator. Using this technique, it is possible to output values of selected variables, along with the location of the logical termination point, using a single WRITE statement.

4-8   COMMENTS ON THE FORTRAN LANGUAGE

Many varieties of FORTRAN exist, most of which contain unique and locally powerful techniques. Experience indicates that a great deal of time and money is lost attempting to convert programs when machines are altered or replaced. Therefore emphasis is placed on writing programs that are machine-compatible throughout industry and throughout various installations. For this reason, in this text many elements of FORTRAN are expressed in terms of "good practice" rather than as "legally possible." Except when specifically noted, Subset FORTRAN 77 is used consistently.

4-9   EXERCISES

1. Complete Table 4-13.
2. Complete Table 4-14.
3. Complete Table 4-15.
4. Complete Table 4-16.
5. Evaluate the following.
    (a) $I = 3/4 * 6. = ?$
    (b) $J = 3/4 + 6. = ?$
    (c) $R = 4. + 8/6 + 2. = ?$
    (d) $A = 3/4 * 6. = ?$
    (e) $B = 3 * 6./4 = ?$
    (f) $M = 3 * 6./4 = ?$
6. Evaluate the following.
    (a) If $I = 2$, $J = 3$ and $A = 5.$, find $D = I/J * A$.
    (b) If $A = 5.$, $B = 6.$, $C = 7.$, $K = 4$ and $J = 3$, find $E = A * B + K/J * C$.

Table 4-13 Constants and Variables

If the following constants or variable names are correct, check the appropriate column. If they are invalid, state why.

| | Valid Constant | | Valid Variable | | Why Invalid |
	Integer	Real	Integer	Real	
$12.61					
121.34E-17					
JO+1					
FORM2					
26E-4					
(JOHN)					
126,314.					
JOHNSON					
12					
1.+KL					
6.E431					
.31E.26					
JACK					
SUM$					
BK					
KB					
2.61E4					
IAAI					
.24E+8					
DIAMETER					
2DKS					
1286954					
AI23					
F3B6					
RUN					

(c) Given the values for the variables in (a) and (b), find $F = (A + 2) * (B + J) * ((I + J)/(K - 2))$.

7. Show how the following numbers would be stored, conceptually.
   (a) 123.67
   (b) −12.3
   (c) −0.00201
   (d) 0.0313
   (e) 101.101
   (f) −101.101
   (g) −0.00000000000074021

8. The sine of 30 degrees is 0.5. Why doesn't SIN(30.) yield 0.5?

9. Location TEST has −3.0 stored in it. To take the square root, therefore, should you use

SQRT(TEST) or SQRT(ABS(TEST)) or SQR(−TEST)? If you get an answer, what does it mean?

10. Which of the following are incorrect? Why?
   (a) 36 ** 4
   (b) 36. ** 4
   (c) −36 ** 4
   (d) −36. ** 4
   (e) 36 ** 4.
   (f) 36. ** 4.
   (g) −36 ** 4.
   (h) −36. ** 4.
   (i) 36 ** (−4)
   (j) 36. ** (−4)
   (k) −36 ** (−4)
   (l) −36. ** (−4)
   (m) 36 ** (−4.)
   (n) 36. ** (−4.)
   (o) −36 ** (−4.)
   (p) −36. ** (−4.)

Table 4-14 Expressions

If the following expressions are correct, check the appropriate columns. Otherwise, write a corrected version. (Do not allow mixed modes.)

| | Valid | | |
	Real	Integer	Corrected Version
CURR*RES			
15.**4			
JK3+321			
PRIN+INT			
Y−Y**2			
L/3.2			
6A−5B			
K+1,237			
4−K+L/7			
15**4			
15**4.			
I**J			
B**(A/3.16)			
π*D			
(A)(B)/C			
15.**4.			
I*J/B			
J*−K			
4+SUMT			
R+3.2E4/16.31			

Table 4-15   Arithmetic Assignment Statements

If the following arithmetic statements are valid, put a check in column captioned "valid." Otherwise rewrite the statement correctly.

	Valid	Statement Rewritten Correctly
COST = $18.62		
JNV = A*–B		
MAN = I+J+K+4		
AREA = π*R**2		
AREA = π*R*R		
V = (R+U/T)**(T+V/G)		
MAN = A+B+C+4		
ROOT = JVK**.5		
PI = A+G+K+V+7.21		
A(RECT) = B*H		
AREA = BH		
HYPOTENUSE = (A**2+B*B)**.5		
AREA = L*W		
K = 2.16E14/(A*B)		
R*B = C		
R*B = L		
A = A+A**2		
R = N*(–4)		
N = N–3		
C = A/B/(A/B/C)		

Table 4-16   Anomalies of Integer Arithmetic

Given:	Then:
R = 21/4 + 6/4	R =
J = 2/3	J =
I = 2000*2000	I =
A = 2000*2000	A =
N = 10.E2+699.	N =
L = 3.*(2.E4/7.)	L =
R = 3.*(2.E4/7.)	R =
S = 21./4.+6./4.	S =
N = 21./4.+6./4.	N =
T = (1/8)*40	T =

Note: Assume the range of integers is from –32000 to +32000.

11. In a certain FORTRAN 77 program, the following declarations are made:

IMPLICIT   REAL(R,T),   INTEGER(K)

How does this change the default declaration?

12. In a certain FORTRAN 77 program, the following declarations are made:

IMPLICIT   REAL(I–N),   INTEGER(O–Z)
REAL OUT1, OUT2, OUT3
INTEGER E1, E2

State the type (integer or real) of each of the following variables located within the program.

ART	E3	J	OUT2	Q12RT
BOY	G76	KOUNT	OUT4	ZONE
D1	HEAD	LIMIT	P27	
E1	HEAD2	NUMB	POUT1	

Control of Flow

Chapter 5 is divided into three main parts. First, two fundamental control statements are presented in a formal manner, along with relational and logical *operators*. Then structured programming is discussed with additional details. Finally, the formal rules for the block IF and DO-WHILE mini-modules are developed, using the fundamental control statements within the context of structured programming.

5-1 FUNDAMENTAL CONTROL

Normal flow through a FORTRAN program is top to bottom, card by card (or line by line) sequentially. This normal sequence can be changed by several instructions that perform logical operations. In this section, only two such statements—the GO TO and the logical IF—are defined.

5-1.1 Unconditional GO TO Statement

The GO TO statement is the most direct branching construct in FORTRAN and is also the most controversial. The general form of the GO TO is shown in Figure 5-1. The symbol ℓ represents a statement label that must always be an integer constant. The statement label indicates the next statement the program is to GO TO and execute. (FORTRAN has three types of GO TO statements: the assigned GO TO, the computed GO TO, and the unconditional GO TO. When the words GO TO are used without a modifier, the unconditional GO TO is always signified.)

The GO TO statement is controversial because, when used in an unthinking and sporadic manner, it can lead to "rat's nest programming." In fact, a number of influential computer experts have seriously suggested adding sufficient control structures to eliminate it from every computer language. In this text, the GO TO is used judiciously in the context of structured programming, primarily in the development of the DO-WHILE. (Given the current structure of FORTRAN, the GO TO cannot be eliminated.)

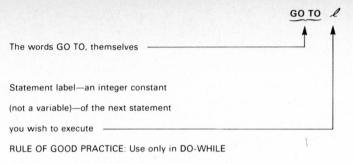

The words GO TO, themselves

Statement label—an integer constant

(not a variable)—of the next statement

you wish to execute

RULE OF GOOD PRACTICE: Use only in DO-WHILE

FIGURE 5-1 Summary of the controversial
Unconditional GO TO statement

GO TO statements are used in FORTRAN coding to replace flow-arrows going from one statement box to another labeled statement box of a flow diagram. The words GO TO do not appear on a machine-oriented flow diagram; the arrow suffices. In modified Nassi-Shneiderman charts, GO TO is always the last statement of the "true" part of a DO-WHILE (see Section 5-4).

5-1.2 Logical and Relational Operators and Expressions

In addition to arithmetic operators, FORTRAN 77 supplies both relational and logical operators, as illustrated in Table 5-1.

(a) *Logical constants and variable names* can be true or false. The form of a logical constant having the value *true* is .TRUE.; the form for *false* is .FALSE.. Type of a logical variable name must be established by an explicit LOGICAL statement or by an IMPLICIT statement. (See Section 4-4.) Thus

$$\text{IMPLICIT LOGICAL (L-M)}$$
$$\text{LOGICAL TR,FLS}$$

would establish all variable names starting with either the letter L or M, as well as the variable names TR and FLS, as type logical.

(b) *Logical assignment statements* take the form

$$var_L = exp_L$$

where var_L is the name of a logical variable (or logical array element) and exp_L is a logical expression (summarized in Table 5-2).

(c) *Relational operators* are used between two arithmetic expressions to form a relational expression that compares the two arithmetic expressions and yields only the logical results .TRUE. or .FALSE.. It is recommended that the two arithmetic expressions be of the same type, that is, mixed modes are undesirable in relational expressions. Relational expressions can also be used within logical expressions where they yield either the answer .TRUE. or .FALSE.. Thus 3.GT.1 yields .TRUE. and I.LE.5 yields .FALSE. when I is greater than 6 and .TRUE. when I is 5 or less.

Table 5-1 Summary of Relational and Logical Operators

Relational Operators

.EQ.	equal to
.LT.	less than
.GT.	greater than
.LE.	less than or equal to
.GE.	greater than or equal to
.NE.	not equal to

Logical Operators

.AND.   True only if all logical terms are true.

IF e_1:	e_2:	Then e_1 .AND. e_2
T	T	T
T	F	F
F	T	F
F	F	F

.OR.   True if any logical term is true.

IF e_1:	e_2:	Then e_1 .OR. e_2
T	T	T
T	F	T
F	T	T
F	F	F

.NOT.   True becomes false; false becomes true.

IF e_1:	Then .NOT. e_1
T	F
F	T

Full Language Only:

.EQV.   True when both expressions are either true or false.

IF e_1:	e_2:	Then e_1 .EQV. e_2
T	T	T
T	F	F
F	T	F
F	F	T

.NEQV.   True when one expression is true and the other is false.

IF e_1:	e_2:	Then e_1 .NEQV. e_2
T	T	F
T	F	T
F	T	T
F	F	F

(d) *Logical operators* of Subset FORTRAN 77 are of three types: .AND., .OR., and .NOT.. (Full Language also provides .EQV. and .NEQV..) The truth values of these logical operators are summarized in Table 5–1. Logical operators serve only as *operands* with logical constants and variables (in much the same way as the arithmetic operands such as +, −, and * serve with real and integer constants and variables). The result of a logical computation can only be .TRUE. or .FALSE..

The simplest *logical expression* is a single constant or variable of type logical (that is, value only .TRUE. or .FALSE.). Logical operators are used within logical expressions to perform logical computations between entities with values of either .TRUE. or .FALSE.. Because a relational expression always yields a result of either .TRUE. or .FALSE., a relational expression can stand alone or be used as part of a logical expression.

To summarize, both relational expressions and logical expressions yield only the results .TRUE. or .FALSE.. They differ in that relational expressions compare arithmetic expressions, whereas logical expressions relate only expressions which reduce to type logical (i.e., .TRUE. or .FALSE.).

5–1.3   Logical IF Statement

Figure 5–2 shows a typical Nassi-Shneiderman chart and flow diagram for a simple logical IF statement with corresponding FORTRAN coding. The symbols e_1 and e_2 stand for any arithmetic expressions of any complexity. The symbol .L. stands for any of the relational operators defined in Table 5–1. The statement following the parentheses can be almost any FORTRAN statement that is executable; it is executed if and only if the comparison of expressions within the parentheses is true. (The statement following a logical IF cannot be a DO (see Chapter 8), a block IF, ELSE IF, ELSE, END IF (see Section 5–3), nor another logical IF.)

As an example, Figure 5–3 illustrates the human-oriented flow, Nassi-Shneiderman chart, machine-oriented flow, and FORTRAN coding used to compare L and K, setting L equal to the current value of M only if L and K are not equal. Branches from the diamond-

A SIMPLE LOGICAL IF

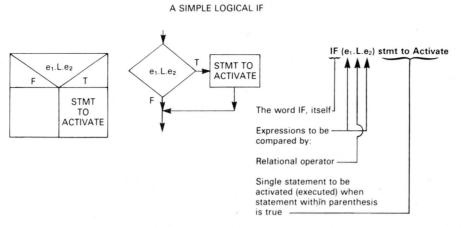

FIGURE 5–2 Simple logical IF using a relational expression

shaped logical IF box (or from the upper triangle in the three-triangle IF rectangle of the Nassi-Shneiderman chart) have only two possibilities: .TRUE. or .FALSE.. If the expression within the diamond-shaped box (upper triangle) is false, no action takes place and flow is automatically to the next statement. If the expression within the diamond-shaped box (upper triangle) is true, then the statement to the right is executed, after which flow automatically continues to the next statement.

Thus, if L is not equal to K, L is filled by the current value stored in M and then the subsequent statement is executed. If L is equal to K, the statement L = M is not executed—the logical IF "acts" as if it were a CONTINUE statement—and the subsequent statement is executed directly.

Although it is neither illegal nor bad practice to use real variables within logical IF statements, special precautions must be taken to insure that the proper result is obtained. For instance, the expression AN.GT.O. in Figure 5–4 can yield wrong results if AN has been computed and contains *roundoff error* (AN might then be, for example, 0.00000001, which is not zero).

A more general form of the logical IF is shown in Figure 5–5, with a Nassi-Shneiderman chart to the left, a machine-oriented flow in the center, and FORTRAN 77 coding on the right.

Relational expressions can be combined within the parentheses of a logical IF statement. Several examples are shown by the program segments in Listing 5–1. Part (a) shows utilization of a logical IF statement to terminate execution of a program when three values are simultaneously equal to zero. Spacing is used to make the IF statement easy to read.

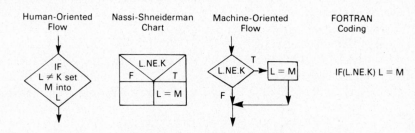

FIGURE 5–3 Example of logical IF

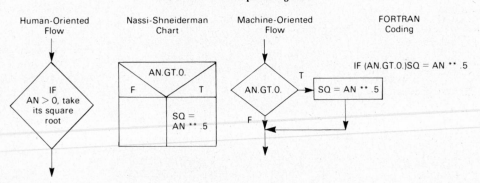

FIGURE 5–4 Example of logical IF using real variables in relational expressions

LOGICAL IF, GENERAL FORM:

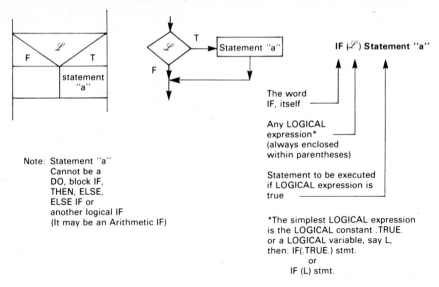

FIGURE 5-5 General form of the logical IF
statement

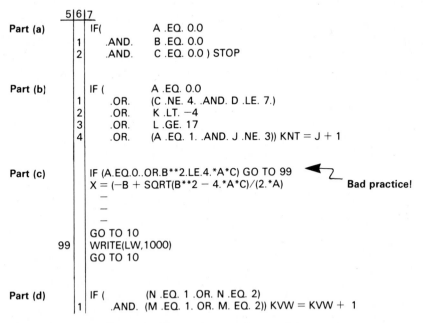

LISTING 5-1 Logical IF examples containing related relational expressions

Part (b) combines the .OR. and .AND. logical operators. Parentheses are used to make the order of operation clear. In this case, KNT is computed from the current value stored in the location J + 1 if and only if at least one of the following five statements is true:

1. If the current value stored in location A is equal to zero.
2. If the current value stored in C is not equal to 4 and the current value stored in D is less than or equal to 7.
3. If the current value stored in location K is less than −4.
4. If the current value stored in L is greater than or equal to 17.
5. If the current value stored in location A is equal to 1 and the current value stored in J is not equal to 3.

If any of these five cases is satisfied, the operation KNT = J + 1 is executed. Whether KNT = J + 1 is executed or not, flow continues directly to the next statement.

Part (c) represents poor practice, although it has been used for the quadratic equation. The first statement indicates that when $A = 0$ (that is, $y = Bx + C$, a linear equation) or B^2 is less than $4AC$ (that is $\sqrt{B^2 - 4AC}$ yields an imaginary number), the program is to proceed to a statement 99. Otherwise, the next statement is executed and the quadratic equation is solved for one value of x. The GO TO 99 transfers flow to 99 WRITE. Using the GO TO for such erratic "jumps" destroys structure and is therefore strongly discouraged by many knowledgeable programmers.

The last example, part (d) of Listing 5–1, executes the statement KVW = KVW + 1 if N is equal to either 1 or 2 and M is equal to either 1 or 2. Thus the four possible occurrences precipitating execution of this statement are N = 1 and M = 1; N = 1 and M = 2; N = 2 and M = 1; or N = 2 and M = 2.

5–1.4 More About Logical Expressions

Logical expressions that use the logical operators .NOT., .AND. and .OR. do logical computations only on type logical variables, constants and expressions that reduce to only .TRUE. or .FALSE..

To illustrate, we evaluate the following logical expression (assuming I is greater than J, that B is not less than C and G = 3.0).

$$((I.GT.J) .OR. (B.LT.C)) .AND. (3.0 .EQ.G)$$
$$(.TRUE. .OR. .FALSE.) .AND. \quad (.TRUE.)$$
$$(.TRUE.) \qquad .AND. \quad (.TRUE.)$$
$$(.TRUE.)$$

Inside the parenthesized expression on the left, each relational expression is evaluated within its own parentheses. Because I is greater than J, the result of I.GT.J is .TRUE.. Because B is not less than C, B.LT.C is .FALSE.. Inside the parenthesized expression on the right, the relational expression yields .TRUE. because G = 3.0. Inside the expression left of the .AND., a logical computation results in .TRUE. .OR. .FALSE., which is .TRUE. (because if any element computed with .OR. is .TRUE., the result is .TRUE.). The final logical computation of .TRUE. .AND. .TRUE. yields .TRUE., because neither is .FALSE..

Now reconsider the left part of the logical expression:

$$((I.GT.J) .OR. (B.LT.C)) .AND. (3.0 .GT.G)$$

I and J are type integer; B and C are type real. This is not mixed mode, however, because the relational expression I.GT.J is not mixed mode and yields a type logical answer. Likewise, B.LT.C and 3.0 .GT.G are both type real and yield type logical answers. Therefore the expression reduces to logical computations involving type logical variables operated upon by logical operators.

Consider, however,

$$((I.GT.P) .OR. (J.LT.T)) .AND. (G.GT.O) \qquad \text{(Mixed Mode)}$$

Each relational expression is mixed mode and the program may function erroneously. Observe that G.GT.O is mixed mode; it must be G.GT.O., G.GT.O.O, G.GT..O, or some similar form containing a decimal point with the zero.

Although it may seem reasonable to simplify

$$IF(A.GT.O. .AND. B.GT.O.) \qquad \text{(Valid)}$$

to

$$IF((A .AND. B) .GT.O.) \qquad \text{(Invalid)}$$

the "simplification" does not work because the expressions left and right of the logical operator .AND. are not type logical. (The invalid expression could be made valid if A and B were declared as type logical, but then it would not have the same meaning as the original valid expression.)

A summary of logical expressions is presented in Table 5–2.

5–2 STRUCTURED PROGRAMS AND MODULES

Structured programs were introduced in Chapter 1 and illustrated in subsequent chapters. They are composed of linearly connected modules forming a straight-line flow path. By definition, modules are composed of several related FORTRAN statements acting in a group with only one entrance point and one exit point. In a gross flow diagram,

---

Table 5-2 Summary of Logical Expressions

1. Logical expressions return only the type logical operands .TRUE. or .FALSE..
2. Computations involving logical operators (.NOT., .AND., .OR.) must use only type logical *operands*.
3. Type logical operands can be obtained from Relational Expressions.
   a. Relational expressions return only .TRUE. or .FALSE..
   b. Relational expressions compare arithmetic statements* with the relational operators.
   c. Arithmetic statements compared by relational operators should be of the same type. If mixed, I.G.T.B. is evaluated as (I-B). GT.O. (Only .EQ. and .NE. compare complex expressions.)
4. Because a relational expression yields a single type logical result, it can be used in place of a more complex logical expression.

*For type character statement, see Chap. 12.

---

modules may be represented by a single process box entered and exited by only one path.

To distinguish between modules for various constructs and of different sizes, in this text the following distinctions are sometimes made. A module consisting of a few interrelated FORTRAN statements is called a mini-module. Module often refers to subprograms, usually consisting of 50 or fewer FORTRAN statements. The portion of a program construct consisting of combinations of subprogram modules and mini-modules is sometimes called a maxi-module. This section introduces only mini-modules.

Some combinations of FORTRAN statements may appear to form a mini-module when they could more aptly be called *pseudo-modules*. These pseudo-modules have more than one entrance or more than one exit. Use of pseudo-modules is undesirable because they destroy the inherent advantages of structured programming.

Figure 5–6 illustrates the gross flow diagram of a typical rat's nest program; here M represents a true module and PM signifies a pseudo-module that differs from a true module because it has more than one entrance or more than one exit point. Such programming is extremely difficult to follow and therefore hard to change in any way or to have complete confidence in.

On Figure 5–6, the words *change, error message* and *boom* illustrate the type of trouble inherent in rat's nest programs. A small change was made in pseudo-module PM_3 to correct its performance. On the subsequent run, PM_3 apparently worked well, but an error message showed up in pseudo-module PM_5—that part of the program in which the programmer had the most confidence. Suddenly, in PM_2, the program aborted and no solution was obtained. How can the program be fixed? Even more importantly, where should the program be fixed? In a rat's nest program, the repair might be just as likely in PM_6 as in PM_2, PM_3 or PM_5. Since the program does not have linear flow, it "circles back on itself" and each attempt to fix the *bug* produces far-reaching changes.

By contrast, a structured program is readily followed because of its straight-line flow and is relatively easy to debug, update, correct, and maintain. A structured program also lends itself to thorough checking. A summary of the concepts of structured programs is shown in Table 5–3.

5–3 BLOCK IF MINI-MODULE

Although the logical IF provides a powerful mechanism for control of flow, it has one severe shortcoming: only one statement can be executed when the IF statement is true. Because of this, the logical IF statement can lead very quickly to rat's nest programming unless extreme care is employed. To offset this disadvantage, FORTRAN 77 uses the block IF.

The block IF works essentially as the logical IF except that a group of statements can be acted upon as a single block. Formally, the block IF takes the form

IF (logical expression) THEN

The IF-block may also contain the ELSE IF statement

ELSE IF (logical expression) THEN

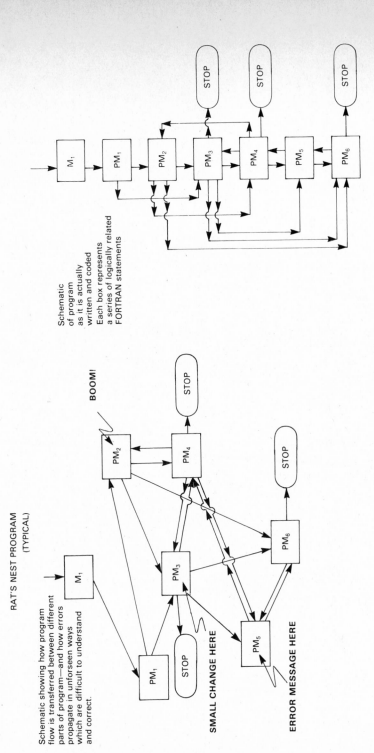

RAT'S NEST PROGRAM
(TYPICAL)

Schematic showing how program
flow is transferred between different
parts of program—and how errors
propagate in unforseen ways
which are difficult to understand
and correct.

BOOM!

STOP

STOP

STOP

M_1

PM_1

PM_2

PM_3

PM_4

PM_5

PM_6

SMALL CHANGE HERE

ERROR MESSAGE HERE

Schematic
of program
as it is actually
written and coded
Each box represents
a series of logically related
FORTRAN statements

FIGURE 5–6 Typical rat's nest program

121

and the ELSE statement

ELSE

Each block IF statement is terminated by the END IF statement

END IF .

which has no effect upon execution. The manner in which these statements are combined is the subject of this and the following section.

In general

Entity	Consists of all executable statements following the	up to, but not including the next
IF-block	block IF	ELSE IF, ELSE, or END IF statement
ELSE IF-block	block ELSE IF	ELSE IF, ELSE, or END IF statement
ELSE block	block ELSE	END IF statement

5-3.1 IF-THEN

Figure 5–7 illustrates the IF-THEN with a modified Nassi-Shneiderman chart shown to the left, a machine-oriented flow diagram depicted in the center, and the corresponding FORTRAN coding listed on the right. This figure is almost identical to Figures 5–2 and 5–5. The difference is that when the logical expression is true, a series of statements is performed. In order for the processor to know how many statements are to be included,

---

Table 5-3 Summary of Structured Programming

STRUCTURED PROGRAMS

are composed of

MODULES

connected linearly in a

STRAIGHT-LINE PATH.

MODULES (BY DEFINITION)

HAVE ONLY ONE ENTRANCE POINT
AND ONLY ONE EXIT POINT.

In this text, the following are sometimes used:

MINI-MODULE ~ PROCESS BOX

MODULE ~ SUBPROGRAM (≤50 STATEMENTS)

MAXI-MODULE ~ (PORTION) PROGRAM CONSTRUCT

PSEUDO-MODULES

"LOOK LIKE" MODULES

BUT HAVE MORE THAN ONE

ENTRANCE OR EXIT.

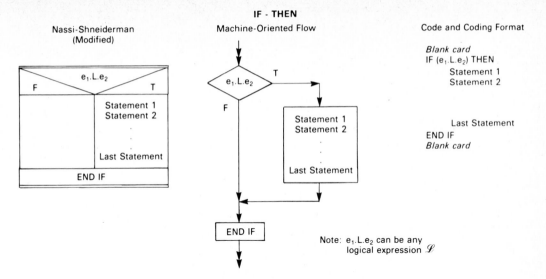

FIGURE 5-7 General form of IF-THEN

the "block" of statements is set off by the special words THEN and END IF. Thus if the logical expression is true, the numbered statements are done until the END IF is reached. On the other hand, if the logical expression is false, control passes immediately to the END IF statement and then on to the next statement in sequence.

To emphasize that this is a mini-module, the modified Nassi-Shneiderman chart utilizes two horizontal lines at the beginning of the rectangle and two horizontal lines following the END IF. This notation corresponds to the double arrowheads starting the mini-module on the machine-oriented flow diagram and the END IF followed by the double arrowheads. To make these distinctions in the coding, the IF-THEN mini-module is preceded and followed by a blank card. Also, the statements in the block to be executed when the IF is true are all indented (usually 4 or 5 spaces).

Although the relational expression $e_1 .L. e_2$ is used in Figure 5-7, the general form can use any logical expression, denoted by $\mathscr{L}$. (Compare Figures 5-2 and 5-5.) In this text, the false path is always to the left or down and the true path is always to the right.

5-3.2 IF-THEN-ELSE

The block IF also provides another important advantage. The IF-THEN-ELSE allows for executing one set of statements if the expression is true and another set of statements if the expression is false. Figure 5-8 illustrates the modified Nassi-Shneiderman chart, machine-oriented flow diagram and the FORTRAN Coding for the IF-THEN-ELSE.

When the logical expression is true, then the block of numbered statements is performed; flow is then directly to the END IF. When the logical expression is false, the *true* path is skipped and Statements a, b, . . ., are each performed sequentially. Again, it is necessary to have special words to set off the block of statements so that the compiler can determine your meaning.

The block of statements in the true path is preceded by the word THEN and followed

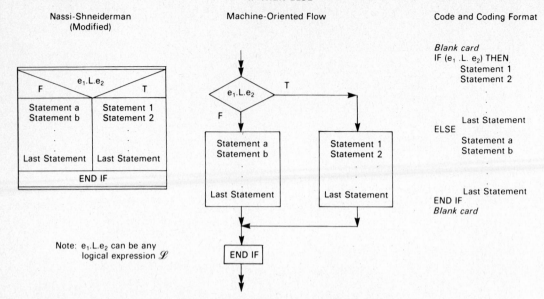

FIGURE 5–8 General form of IF-THEN-ELSE

by the word ELSE. The block of statements in the false path is preceded by the word ELSE and followed by END IF.

The same delimiters are used to signify the beginning and end of the mini-modules in IF-THEN-ELSE as in IF-THEN. The block of statements for both the true and the false paths are again indented and the words IF, ELSE, and END IF are aligned.

On machine-oriented flow diagrams in this text, the tops of the true block of statements and the false block of statements are always aligned horizontally.

5–3.3   IF-ELSE IF-ELSE IF-ELSE

Though purist advocates of structured programming might stop with the IF-THEN and the IF-THEN-ELSE, FORTRAN 77 allows additional constructs so that more than two blocks of statements can be considered at a single time. Figure 5–9 is an illustration of a typical formulation. (It is typical because the number of ELSE IF's in the construct is variable.)

IF-THEN-ELSE allows for only two branches because use of a sequence of ELSE statements would have no meaning; it would be impossible to specify a particular path. In order to distinguish additional paths, there must be additional questions asked. This leads to the creation of the statement ELSE IF ($\mathscr{L}$) THEN. Refer to Figure 5–9 and look at the modified Nassi-Shneiderman chart, machine-oriented flow diagram, and the FORTRAN coding as you consider the operation that takes place.

If the expression $e_1 .L. e_2$ is true, then Statements 1, 2, . . . , are executed, and control passes to the final END IF and on to the next statement in the program.

On the other hand, when the logical expression $e_1 .L. e_2$ is false, another question is asked. This time the question is asked in a slightly different form because the series of questions is not complete. Figure 5–9 shows that if the first block of statements (numbered numerically) is not performed, then something else is to be done. This may be more than one thing; therefore ELSE IF (e_3 .L. e_4). When the first logical statement (IF-THEN) is false, the second logical statement (ELSE-IF) is tested. If the ELSE-IF (e_3 .L. e_4) is true, then Statements a, b, . . . , are performed, after which control passes to the final END IF and on to the next statement of the program. If ELSE IF (e_3 .L. e_4) is false, then the final question is asked.

If the final logical expression (e_5 .L. e_6) is true, then Statements I, II, . . . , are executed and control is transferred to END IF and on to the next statement.

If the final ELSE IF (e_5 .L. e_6) is false, then do Statements A, B, . . . , with control going to the final END IF after the last block has been executed and from there to the next statement.

Again, observe the double lines in the modified Nassi-Shneiderman chart which indicate the beginning and the end of the mini-module. In the machine-oriented flow

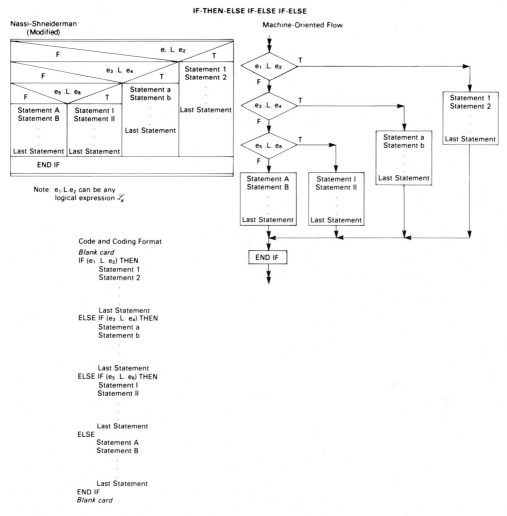

FIGURE 5-9 General form of IF-ELSE IF---

diagrams of this text, the block of statements to be executed when a logical expression is true is aligned horizontally with either the succeeding ELSE IF diamond shaped box or the block of statements to be executed when the final ELSE IF is false. As usual, in the FORTRAN coding the mini-module is preceded and followed by a blank card and each block of statements to be executed is indented.

Notice how easy it is to do the FORTRAN 77 coding directly from either the modified Nassi-Shneiderman chart or the machine-oriented flow diagram. The control statements used in FORTRAN 77 are very descriptive of the process that is taking place. When a sequence of blocks of statements are to be executed, depending upon different criteria, then a series of ELSE IF's is required. The FORTRAN control statement before the last block to be executed, however, is usually a simple ELSE.

5-4 DO-WHILE MINI-MODULES

Many high-level languages have the DO-WHILE implemented as a statement, but FORTRAN 77 does not. In FORTRAN 77, however, the DO-WHILE can be implemented by combining the IF-THEN and the GO TO.

5-4.1 The Classical DO-WHILE

Figure 5-10 illustrates the modified Nassi-Shneiderman chart, a machine-oriented flow diagram, and FORTRAN 77 coding for the classical DO-WHILE.

(a) *The Nassi-Shneiderman chart* was developed, in part, to eliminate the GO TO. In order to use Nassi-Shneiderman charts with FORTRAN 77, however, it is necessary to

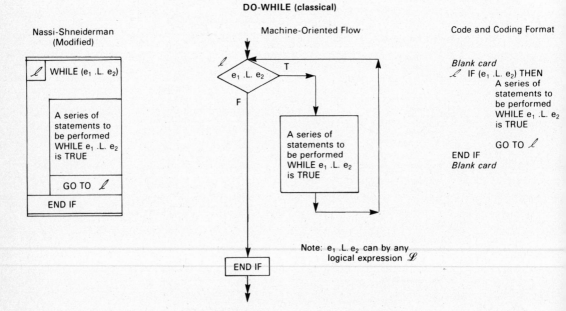

FIGURE 5-10 General form of classical DO-WHILE

incorporate the GO TO, which accounts for the name *modified*. Furthermore, the DO-WHILE is the only mini-module where a nonlegal FORTRAN 77 expression (WHILE) is used in this text in Nassi-Shneiderman charts. The ℓ in the upper lefthand corner of the modified Nassi-Shneiderman chart represents the statement number corresponding to the classical DO-WHILE. The logical expression in parentheses following the WHILE is checked; while it is true, the series of statements in the rectangle is executed through—and including—the final statement, GO TO ℓ. Therefore the loop is executed each time the first statement yields a true answer for the logical expression. When the logical expression yields a false answer, control passes to the end of the DO-WHILE mini-module, which is the END IF statement.

(b) *The machine-oriented flow diagram* shows that the DO-WHILE mini-module is composed of an IF-THEN, a series of statements to be performed while the logical IF is true, a GO TO statement, and finally an END IF statement that terminates the mini-module.

(c) *The coding* uses typical delimiters: (1) a blank card to initiate the DO-WHILE; (2) indentation for the series of statements executed in the loop, and (3) an END IF followed by a blank card to terminate the mini-module.

The program CUB (illustrated in Figures 2–5 and 2–6) is altered to use the classical DO-WHILE in the modified Nassi-Shneiderman chart and machine-oriented flow diagrams of Program CUBALT in Figure 5–11 and Listing 5–2. Each DO-WHILE mini-

Nassi-Shneiderman Chart: **CUBALT**

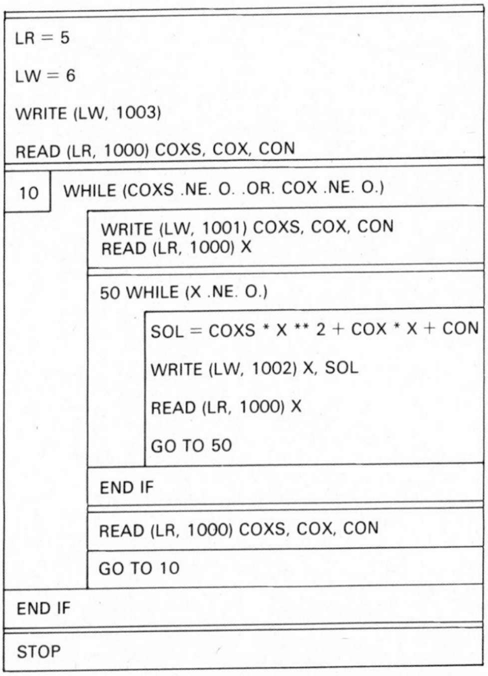

FIGURE 5-11(a) Modified Nassi-Shneiderman
chart: CUBALT

module of Figure 5–11 is preceded by a single READ statement. The first READ statement obtains the first set of coefficients and the constant. The first READ statement in the inner mini-module reads the first *x* for any particular set of coefficients and constant. Within the outer mini-module, a second (and subsequent) set of two coefficients and a constant is read within the loop. Likewise, a second (and subsequent) value of *x* is read within the inner DO-WHILE mini-module loop for each independent set of two coefficients and single constant.

Such additional (and duplicate) READ statements are required by the strict form of the classical DO-WHILE. Although the classical form may appear artificial at first, it is

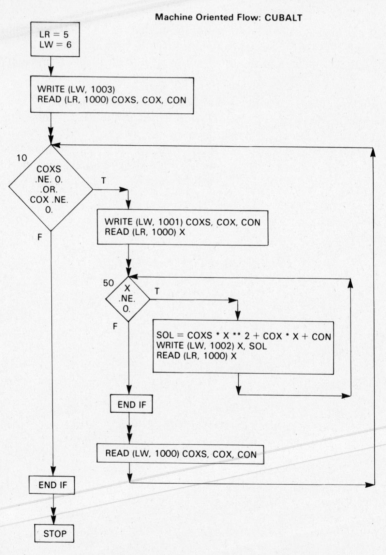

Machine Oriented Flow: CUBALT

FIGURE 5–11(b) Machine-oriented flow: CUBALT

```
      PROGRAM CUBALT
C           --- SOL= COXS*X**2 + COX*X + CON
C           --- FOR: (1) DIFFERENT SETS OF COXS, COX, AND CON -- AND --
C           ---      (2) FOR DIFF VALUES OF X WITHIN EACH SET
      LR=5
      LW=6

      WRITE(LW,1003)
      READ(LR,1000) COXS,COX,CON

   10 IF(COXS .NE. 0. .OR.  COX .NE. 0.) THEN
          WRITE(LW,1001) COXS, COX, CON
          READ(LR,1000) X

   50     IF(X.NE.0.) THEN
              SOL=COXS*X**2 + COX*X + CON
              WRITE(LW,1002) X, SOL
              READ(LR,1000) X
              GO TO 50
          END IF

          READ(LR,1000) COXS, COX , CON
          GO TO 10
      END IF

      STOP

 1000 FORMAT(10F8.0)
 1001 FORMAT(1X  , F9.3 ,  2F10.3)
 1002 FORMAT(30X,  F14.3 ,  F16.3  )
 1003 FORMAT('1' , 2X , 'COXS' , 7X , 'COX' , 7X , 'CON' ,
     1 13X , 'X' , 13X , 'SOL' //)

      END
```
Output with echoed input:

COXS	COX	CON	X	SOL
3.000	-4.000	7.000		
			2.000	11.000
			-2.000	27.000
			1.000	6.000
5.000	2.000	-9.000		
			2.160	18.648
			-4.700	92.050

LISTING 5-2 Program CUBALT

essentially the only method used by many programmers or allowed by some establishments or languages. Also, the literal translation of the modified DO-WHILE of the following subsection into other languages may introduce GO TO's into that language that are not otherwise needed.

5-4.2 Modified DO-WHILE Mini-module

Figure 5-12 illustrates the modified DO-WHILE mini-module by a modified Nassi-Shneiderman chart, a machine-oriented flow diagram, and FORTRAN 77 coding. Although "purists" would probably object to this form of the DO-WHILE, it provides reliable results within the context of structured programming when used judiciously.

Note that the double horizontal lines of the modified Nassi-Shneiderman chart and the double arrowheads of the machine-oriented flow diagram precede the beginning of

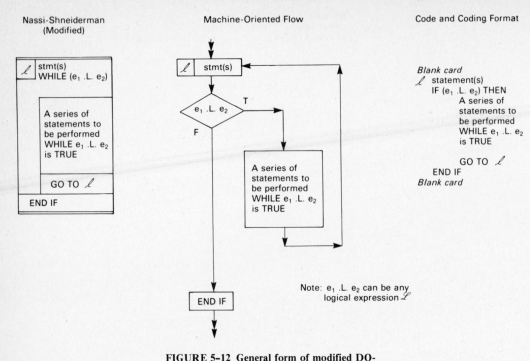

FIGURE 5-12 General form of modified DO-WHILE

the mini-module, that is, precede the beginning of the loop proper. In the FORTRAN coding, these symbols are replaced by a blank card. No blank card is inserted just prior to the IF-THEN statement because it is not the beginning of the mini-module.

Program CUB of Figures 2–5 and 2–6 illustrates use of the modified DO-WHILE in nested form.

5-5 COMPOUND MINI-MODULES

Mini-modules may be compounded in a number of ways, but it is extremely important that their beginnings and endings are clearly delineated and easily discernible. Figure 2–1 is an example of a modified DO-WHILE.

Figures 2–2 and 2–3 illustrate IF-THEN and IF-THEN-ELSE mini-modules nested within a classical DO-WHILE. On the modified Nassi-Shneiderman chart, components of the innermost mini-module are shown by the initial double line across its portion of the rectangular box corresponding to similar lines across the same horizontal distance following the END IF. On the machine-oriented flow diagram, the same delimiters are shown by double arrowheads on a vertical, contiguous line. The listing of program EEQPRT uses blank cards wherever these double horizontal lines of the modified Nassi-Shneiderman charts or the double arrowheads of machine-oriented flow diagrams appear.

Figures 2–9 and 2–10 illustrate more complex nesting of block IF statements within a subroutine.

5-6 EXERCISES

1. Listing 5–3 shows a simple program containing twelve alternate forms of logical IF statements, with a set of typical data. For form a, b, c, d, e, f, g, h, i, j, k, or l of the logical IF, determine the

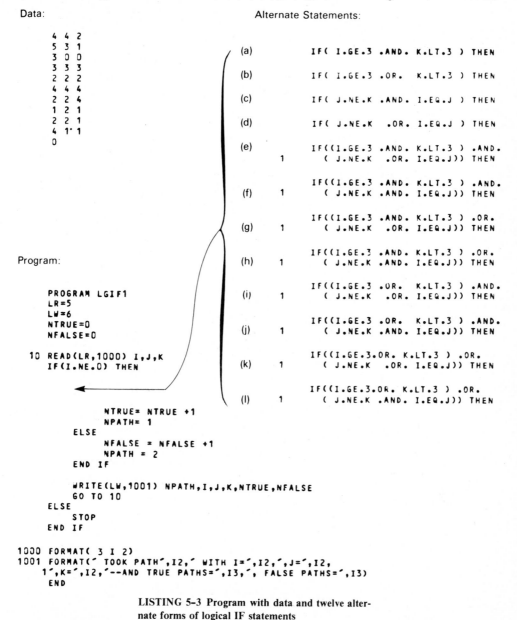

Data:

```
4 4 2
5 3 1
3 0 0
3 3 3
2 2 2
4 4 4
2 2 4
1 2 1
2 2 1
4 1 1
0
```

Alternate Statements:

```
(a)     IF( I.GE.3 .AND. K.LT.3 ) THEN

(b)     IF( I.GE.3 .OR.  K.LT.3 ) THEN

(c)     IF( J.NE.K .AND. I.EQ.J ) THEN

(d)     IF( J.NE.K  .OR. I.EQ.J ) THEN

(e)     IF((I.GE.3 .AND. K.LT.3 ) .AND.
     1     ( J.NE.K  .OR. I.EQ.J)) THEN

        IF((I.GE.3 .AND. K.LT.3 ) .AND.
(f)  1     ( J.NE.K .AND. I.EQ.J)) THEN

(g)     IF((I.GE.3 .AND. K.LT.3 ) .OR.
     1     ( J.NE.K  .OR. I.EQ.J)) THEN

(h)     IF((I.GE.3 .AND. K.LT.3 ) .OR.
     1     ( J.NE.K .AND. I.EQ.J)) THEN

(i)     IF((I.GE.3 .OR.  K.LT.3 ) .AND.
     1     ( J.NE.K  .OR. I.EQ.J)) THEN

(j)     IF((I.GE.3 .OR.  K.LT.3 ) .AND.
     1     ( J.NE.K .AND. I.EQ.J)) THEN

(k)     IF((I.GE.3.OR. K.LT.3 ) .OR.
     1     ( J.NE.K  .OR. I.EQ.J)) THEN

(l)     IF((I.GE.3.OR. K.LT.3 ) .OR.
     1     ( J.NE.K .AND. I.EQ.J)) THEN
```

Program:

```
        PROGRAM LGIF1
        LR=5
        LW=6
        NTRUE=0
        NFALSE=0

    10  READ(LR,1000) I,J,K
        IF(I.NE.0) THEN

                NTRUE= NTRUE +1
                NPATH= 1
        ELSE
                NFALSE = NFALSE +1
                NPATH = 2
        END IF

        WRITE(LW,1001) NPATH,I,J,K,NTRUE,NFALSE
        GO TO 10
        ELSE
            STOP
        END IF

    1000 FORMAT( 3 I 2)
    1001 FORMAT(' TOOK PATH',I2,' WITH I=',I2,',J=',I2,
       1',K=',I2,'--AND TRUE PATHS=',I3,', FALSE PATHS=',I3)
        END
```

LISTING 5–3 Program with data and twelve alternate forms of logical IF statements

output. This exercise illustrates use of .AND. and .OR. in logical expressions composed of a series of relational expressions.

2. Change the modified DO-WHILE to a classical DO-WHILE by changing the necessary GO TO's and adding appropriate READ statements for each of the following:
   (a) Figure 2–7, flow diagram of program COMP.
   (b) Figure 2–8, modified Nassi-Shneiderman chart of program COMP.
   (c) Figure 3–3, 3–4, 3–5, 3–6, 3–7, 3–8, 3–9, or 3–10.
   (d) List 2–7, program TFINDS.

Chapter **6**

Input/Output

Discussion of input/output in many textbooks is often delayed until near the end, which is logical only from the standpoint of programming ease. To write good programs, however, input/output must be considered early—and consistently—so that input/output techniques become deftly used tools even in the hands of the novice programmer.

(In Chapter 17, Section 1 and the first two parts of Section 2 are designed so that they can be used immediately after completion of this chapter for those who need early facility with file management.)

6-1 FORMAL RULES FOR I/O

It is helpful to perform a simple laboratory project using the "example and imitative mode" before reading this section.

6-1.1 Executable Statements

Input and output statements are executable because they tell the computer to read or write something. The statement that specifies how material must be organized to be read properly, or how material is to appear on output, is a nonexecutable FORMAT statement and is discussed in Section 6-1.2.

FORTRAN 77 input/output (I/O) statements are summarized in Tables 6-1 and 6-2. Table 6-1 presents a symbolic representation for the READ statement. A READ statement always starts with the word READ itself, usually followed by two syntactic items in parentheses, separated by a comma. The first syntactic item within the parentheses specifies the logical unit number of the input device and can be either an integer variable or constant. The second syntactic item specifies the statement label of the FORMAT statement and is always an integer constant. No comma follows the parentheses.

The output statement (Table 6-2) is almost identical to the input statement except

Table 6-1 General Form of Input Statement

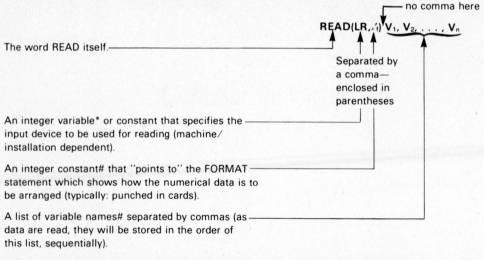

The word READ itself.

An integer variable* or constant that specifies the input device to be used for reading (machine/installation dependent).

An integer constant# that "points to" the FORMAT statement which shows how the numerical data is to be arranged (typically: punched in cards).

A list of variable names# separated by commas (as data are read, they will be stored in the order of this list, sequentially).

*LR is used in this text for Logical unit for Read. Any other integer would be satisfactory.
#For general rules refer to Section 12–2.1.

Table 6-2 General Form of Output Statement

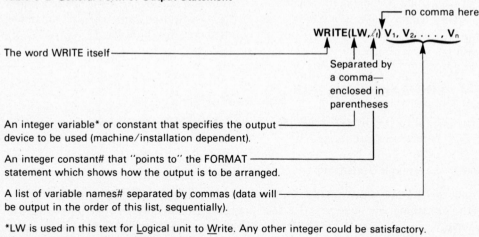

The word WRITE itself

An integer variable* or constant that specifies the output device to be used (machine/installation dependent).

An integer constant# that "points to" the FORMAT statement which shows how the output is to be arranged.

A list of variable names# separated by commas (data will be output in the order of this list, sequentially).

*LW is used in this text for Logical unit to Write. Any other integer could be satisfactory.
#For general rules refer to Section 12–2.1.

---

that the word READ is replaced by WRITE. Also, because a WRITE is often used with a FORMAT statement only, it may have no list of items. That is, items, separated by commas, follow a WRITE statement only if the current contents of such specified storage locations are to be output.

6–1.2 FORMAT Statements

The general form of a FORMAT statement is illustrated in Table 6–3. The leading symbol, ℓ_f stands for a statement label that must always be an integer constant. The word

FORMAT is used, in capital letters, starting in Column 7 or beyond, preferably without imbedded blanks. Following the word FORMAT are a series of edit descriptors, separated by commas and enclosed in parentheses.

Before discussing format specifications in detail, study Table 6–4. The term *field width* refers to the exact number of spaces allowed on any device for the representation of any piece of I/O information. Field width is an important consideration because it must always be related to the size of the value being input/output and it is fundamental in developing appropriate FORMAT specifications.

Total field width is limited to 80 spaces on any given card and to the width of the local

Table 6-3 General Form of FORMAT Statement

Note: It may be desirable to leave several spaces on each side of commas to ease key punching and alteration.

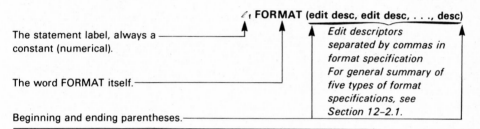

The statement label, always a constant (numerical).

The word FORMAT itself.

Beginning and ending parentheses.

Edit descriptors separated by commas in format specification
For general summary of five types of format specifications, see Section 12–2.1.

Table 6-4 Summary of Field Width Concepts

Field Width

Field width indicates the exact number of spaces to be used on a card, line, or other device for a given piece of I/O information.

Counting Field Width

1. Field width is always counted from the leftmost possible position.
2. Field width for the first edit descriptor *starts* in column 1.
3. Field width for the second edit descriptor *starts* in the column *immediately* following the end of the first specified field width.
4. Subsequent field widths *start* in the column *immediately* following the end of the preceding one.

Limits on fields

Cards, teletypes, CRT's, high speed printers, and most other devices are limited in combined total field width.

1. Cards are limited to a combined total of field widths of 80 columns.
2. HSP output is limited to a combined total of field widths varying from a low of about 108 to a high of about 142 (120 and 132 and more common).
3. Remote terminals are often limited to 72 columns; a large variation is not unlikely (72 and 80 are most common).

printer for any high-speed printer output. At remote terminals, field width is sometimes restricted to a width less than found on cards. If format specifications are combined so that total required field width exceeds that available, error messages will occur and portions of the program will have to be rewritten.

6–1.3 Format Specifications

The format specification of a FORMAT statement encloses a series of edit descriptors, separated by commas. These edit descriptors are summarized in this section.

Mixed modes are not allowed between input/output statements and their corresponding FORMAT statements. Thus to input or output an integer, the FORMAT statement must contain a corresponding integer edit descriptor. Likewise, I/O of a real value requires a corresponding floating point, or scientific floating point, edit descriptor. (Some machines make necessary conversions when mixed modes are used, but several large-scale machines neither convert nor flag such mixed mode operations. Anomalies produced by such occurrences are treated in Section 6–1.5.)

(a) *I/O of Numerical Data* Tables 6–5, 6–6 and 6–7 show common edit descriptors for the input/output of numbers. The capital letters (I, F, or E) represent themselves; lowercase letters, however, are symbols used to represent integer constants. A lowercase *n* preceding I, F, or E represents an integer constant that specifies the number of times which that particular format specification is to be used repeatedly and sequentially. The capital letters I, F, or E tell the type of I/O data, respectively: fixed point (integer), floating point (real), or floating point, scientific notation (real).

The *w* following each capital letter represents an integer constant that states the field width allocated for the numerical representation of data taken from or placed into a storage location.

A decimal point follows the integer constant represented by *w*, followed by *d*. For real numbers (not using scientific notation), *d* is an integer constant that specifies the number of decimal places to be used. For scientific notation, *d* represents a fixed point constant specifying the number of significant figures to be displayed. On input only, the integer

---

Table 6-5 General Form of Integer Edit Descriptor

Integer Edit Descriptor

(Used for I/O of numbers into or out of locations specified by variable names in READ/WRITE type statements.)

$$n \quad I \quad w$$

An integer constant representing the number of times I*w* is to be used, sequentially (assumed to be 1 if not shown).

This is the letter I itself–the symbol representing an integer (fixed point) number (one that does not contain a decimal point).

An integer constant representing the specified field width.

(Caution: Input data *must* be right justified!)

Table 6-6 General Form of Real Edit Descriptor

Real Edit Descriptor

(Used for I/O of numbers into or out of locations specified by variable names in READ/WRITE type statements.)

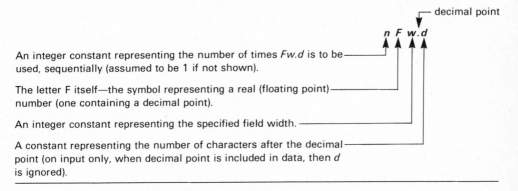

An integer constant representing the number of times *Fw.d* is to be used, sequentially (assumed to be 1 if not shown).

The letter F itself—the symbol representing a real (floating point) number (one containing a decimal point).

An integer constant representing the specified field width.

A constant representing the number of characters after the decimal point (on input only, when decimal point is included in data, then *d* is ignored).

Table 6-7 General Form of Scientific I/O Specification

Real Edit Descriptor Using Scientific Notation

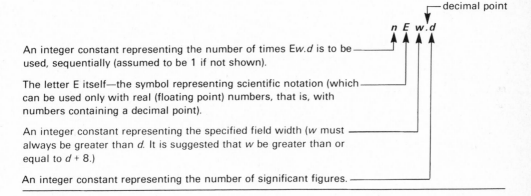

An integer constant representing the number of times E*w.d* is to be used, sequentially (assumed to be 1 if not shown).

The letter E itself—the symbol representing scientific notation (which can be used only with real (floating point) numbers, that is, with numbers containing a decimal point).

An integer constant representing the specified field width (*w* must always be greater than *d*. It is suggested that *w* be greater than or equal to *d* + 8.)

An integer constant representing the number of significant figures.

---

constant represented by *d* in the edit descriptor is ignored if a decimal point is included within the input data.

To determine the field width to specify, always count decimal points used within input data or printed on output. On input only, if *d* is used to establish the decimal point (because a decimal point is not used within input data) the resulting decimal point is not counted as part of the field width. On output, of course, the decimal point will be printed and always takes one place of field width.

(b) *I/O of Text Material* Two character specifications are shown in Tables 6–8 and 6–9. Use of H editing is discouraged because it requires counting and will probably be completely deleted in the next version of FORTRAN.

In both cases, blanks embedded within the character *string* count as part of the field

**Table 6-8 Edit Descriptor to Output Captions
and Headings**

Apostrophe Editing
(Used to output titles, captions, and so on. Not valid for input.)

$$'\downarrow\downarrow\downarrow...\downarrow\downarrow\downarrow'$$

Initiation character—shows beginning of string of characters.———————

Any combination of characters (including blanks) that are to be output ————
exactly as shown. (To output an apostrophe, use two apostrophes adjacent to
one another. Only one will print; therefore the field width for '' is 1, not 2)

Termination character—shows end of string of characters.———————————

Table 6-9 Format Being Phased Out

(Alternate) Hollerith, H-edit Descriptor

(Used to output titles, captions, and so on. Not valid for input.)

$$n\,H\downarrow\downarrow\downarrow...\downarrow$$

An integer constant representing the exact number of characters (including————
blanks) to be output exactly as shown in the spaces immediately following
H (must be specified).

This is the letter H itself—the character indicating Hollerith output. ————

Any combination of characters (including blanks and single apostrophes)————
that are to be output exactly as shown (starting immediately after H and
not ignoring blanks).

---

width. Also, to reduce possibility of error, character edit descriptors should not be continued from one card to the next, even though this is "legally" permissible. For ease in correcting typographical errors, several spaces may be left on each side of the commas that separate edit descriptors.

(c) *Spacing and Other Typical I/O Editing* The spacing edit descriptor provides spacing within a line of output and is valuable because it allows adjustments with a minimum of effort. This descriptor is summarized in Table 6–10.

Some typical edit descriptors are shown in Table 6–11. Edit descriptors can be used in any order so long as they agree sequentially with the corresponding list of items in the READ/WRITE statement.

(d) *Carriage Control* To *slue* to the top of a new page on output, attempt to write the number 1 in the first location of that line. The expression "attempt to write" is used because on a computer using the FORTRAN language, the first space on any line of high-speed printer output usually does not print.

This form for controlling the carriage embodies a hidden pitfall for the unwary. For instance, if the number 1234 is stored in location J and is output in format I4, and if it is the first edit descriptor on that line with no spaces preceding, the page will automatically slue and the output will often show 234, not 1234. The same anomaly occurs if the number 123.45 is stored in variable location A and is output in format F6.2. With no blank space at the beginning of the line, output on that line will start with 23.45 after the page has slued; the hundreds digit will often be lost.

FORTRAN 77 offers additional carriage control. A plus (+) in Column 1 causes the machine to print without advancing the paper. A zero (0) in Column 1 is used to double space lines. (At some installations, nonstandard characters are used for a variety of spacings. Thus attempting to print a 9 in Column 1 may cause 9 lines to be skipped. Since use of such nonstandard carriage controls can quickly destroy the machine-independent characteristics of programs, their use is not recommended.)

On the high speed printer, slash editing is used to cause a carriage return. Several slashes can be used collectively to produce any desired number of blank lines. More formally, the slash edit descriptor indicates the end of data transfer for the current record.

6-1.4 Format Rules

Twelve basic format rules for input and output of data are summarized in Table 6-12. Several of these rules are highlighted within this section by pertinent examples. Although these rules are expressed with respect to input cards and high-speed printer output, they also usually apply to remote terminals.

(a) *Input read from cards* Rule 1 states that the READ and its corresponding FORMAT statement are irrevocably tied together each time the READ statement is

---

Table 6-10 Specification for Spaces Within Lines

Spacing Edit Descriptors [*X-Editing*]

(Used to insert blanks within lines of output)

$$n \quad x$$

An integer* constant representing the number of blank spaces to be used. ——————

The letter X itself–the symbol indicating "leave blank space(s)." ——————

*This integer must be positive.

Table 6-11 Typical Edit Descriptors

Edit Descriptors (Typical)

1. For contents of variable name locations, that is, for variables:

Integer Variables	6I3, I5, 7I1
Real Variables	10F8.0, F6.1, F19.3
	E20.8, 3E18.4

2. For type character and blanks:

Character	'IS', 'THIS', 'Δ='
Blanks	3X, 6X, 9X

3. To go to next card or line:

Carriage Return*	/// or /,/,

*It is suggested that commas not be used to set off slash marks.

Table 6-12 Fundamental Rules of Formats

FORMAT RULES

<table>
<tr><td>

*Input Read
From Cards*

</td><td>

*Output Written
on High Speed Printer*

</td></tr>
<tr><td>

1. For any given READ, the same FORMAT will be used until all values have been read from cards.

</td><td>

1. For any given WRITE, the same FORMAT will be used until all values have been printed on HSP.

</td></tr>
<tr><td>

2. If the end of the FORMAT is reached (exhausted) before all values have been read from cards, a *new* card will be read and the FORMAT will start at the beginning again.

</td><td>

2. If the end of the FORMAT is reached (exhausted) before all values have been printed on HSP, a *new* line will be printed and the FORMAT will start at the beginning again.

</td></tr>
<tr><td>

3. If values are punched in an input data card in an area not covered by the FORMAT, the values will be ignored and essentially "lost."

</td><td>

3. Character labels and captions will be correct only if variables in WRITE statements correspond correctly to FORMAT.

</td></tr>
<tr><td>

4. No error occurs if all values have been read by a READ even if the FORMAT statement has not all been used.

</td><td>

4. No error occurs if all values have been printed by a WRITE even if the FORMAT statement has not all been used.

</td></tr>
<tr><td>

5. A decimal point punched in a data card overrides the FORMAT specification, using one space of field width.

</td><td>

5. A decimal point (or a minus sign) always requires one space of the specified field width on HSP.

</td></tr>
<tr><td>

6. A FORMAT-specified decimal point does *not* use a space of field width on a data card.

</td><td>

6. If field width is not large enough, entire field will be filled with asterisks.

</td></tr>
</table>

executed. Stated another way, the FORMAT statement is locked into the READ statement.

Rule 2 is illustrated in Table 6–13. A program segment reads values into four storage locations named A, B, C, and D, respectively. The format specification, however, allows for reading only three variables from a single card.

Thus, with the typical data cards shown, values for A, B, and C are read from the first card. A has 19.2 stored because the decimal point in the card overrides the *d* specification in F10.2. The value of B is 80,000, with the decimal point taken from the *d* specification (which is zero); blanks are read as zeros in such circumstances. The number 17623 has a decimal point inserted according to the *d* specification 3, and is stored in location C as 17.623. Once these three values are read, the format is exhausted, but the READ statement is not complete.

Therefore the FORMAT statement is reactivated and applied to a new card. The value of D is read from the first location of the second card and stored as 16.00. The decimal point is implied by the FORMAT specification 10.2 (where *d* is 2), and the blanks are read as zeros.

Confusion often persists about Rule 3. The FORMAT actually controls what column (or columns) of any given card are read. Thus, if a value is read into location BOY by FORMAT statement 123 of Table 6–14 from a data card with the numbers 123456789, the value of 1234.56 is stored in BOY. Field width specified by the edit descriptor is 6, and 2 places are to follow the decimal point. The numbers 7, 8, and 9 punched in the card are ignored because they are outside the format specification and are essentially lost forever.

Cards can be numbered in any set of columns that are consistently not read by format specifications. For instance, card numbers can be included within X formats. For example, a large set of data can be numbered in columns 1 through 5 if the FORMAT statement starts with edit descriptor 5X. (Of course, these numbers could be input by using a suitable I or F edit descriptor.)

Rule 4 is illustrated in Table 6–15. The fact that the format can read ten values is of no consequence. If only three values are specified by the READ statement, only three will be read.

Rules 5 and 6 have been covered by the above discussion.

(b) *Output On the High Speed Printer* Output rules are similar to those for input. Rule 2 is illustrated by Table 6–16. In this case, the current values stored in locations A, B, C, and D are shown, followed by a program segment that provides for output of these four

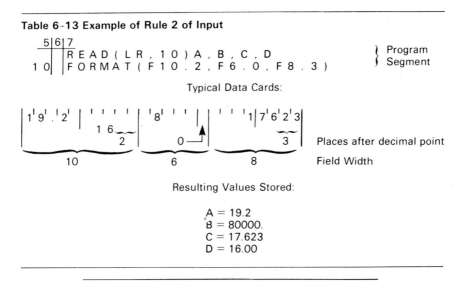

Table 6-13 Example of Rule 2 of Input

```
   5 6 7
        R E A D ( L R , 1 0 ) A , B , C , D          } Program
 1 0    F O R M A T ( F 1 0 . 2 , F 6 . 0 , F 8 . 3 )   } Segment
```

Typical Data Cards:

| | | Places after decimal point |

| 10 | 6 | 8 | Field Width |

Resulting Values Stored:

$$A = 19.2$$
$$B = 80000.$$
$$C = 17.623$$
$$D = 16.00$$

Table 6-14 Example of Rule 3 of Input

```
     5 6 7
          R E A D ( L R , 1 2 3 ) B O Y      } Program
 1 2 3    F O R M A T ( F 6 . 2 )             } Segment
```

Data Card:

1 2 3 4 5 6 7 8 9   ignored & lost

Stored Value:

$$BOY = 1234.56$$

Table 6-15 Example of Rule 4 of Input

```
5|6|7
   |R E A D ( L R , 1 0 ) B , C , D      } Program
1 0||F O R M A T ( 1 0 F 8 . 0 )        } Segment
```

Typical Data Card:

|1 3 . 1 6| 1 7 . 3 2 | − 1 7 . 2 1 |

    8   8   8   Field Width

Resulting Value Stored:

B =	13.16	*Note:* Decimal point
C =	17.32	punched in card over-
D =	−17.21	rode format specification.

Table 6-16 Example of Rule 2 for Output

Typical Values Stored:

A = 19.2
B = 80000.
C = 17.623
D = 16.00

```
5|6|7
   |W R I T E ( L W , 1 0 ) A , B , C , D              } Program
1 0||F O R M A T ( F 1 0 . 2 , F 6 . 0 , F 8 . 3 )     } Segment
```

Resulting HSP Output:

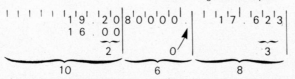

       2   0   3   Places after decimal point

    10   6   8   Field Width

---

values. The FORMAT statement allows for only three values per line. After the values stored in locations A, B, and C have been output, the format specification is exhausted. It is then initiated again for the succeeding line of output.

Rule 3 is a curious one and causes many people a great deal of concern. Character strings, as written in the FORMAT statement, have no built-in relation to the values that they identify unless the programmer makes it so. Thus the example of Table 6–17 shows a syntactically correct program that gives misleading results, at best. Variable location I has a current value of 6 while location J, concurrently, has a value of 12. But, upon output, it "appears" that I has a value of 12. The character J has been lost because an attempt was made to write it in the first column.

Rule 4 is illustrated by Table 6–18, and Rule 5 was discussed earlier.

(c) *Examples* Listing 6–1 is a "do nothing" program that utilizes most of the format rules presented in the preceding section. Listing 6–2 shows input cards used by the program, with corresponding output. These two listings are designed to help you understand the format rules.

6-1.5 Mixed Mode in Input/Output

Although some machines allow I/O statements to differ in type from their corresponding format specifications, such mixing of modes is not good practice. Built-in type conversion is not standard, even on large-scale machines.

For example, two real and two integer variables are read in Listing 6-3. The

---

Table 6-17 Example of Rule 3 for Output

Stored Variables:

I = 6
J = 12

Program Segment:

(CORRECT SYNTAX —
INCORRECT LOGIC)

```
5 6 7
   |WRITE(LW,69)I,J
69 |FORMAT('J=',I4,2X,'I=',I4)
```

HSP Output:

```
   =      6      =     1 2
   2     I4    2X 2    I4
```

Table 6-18 Example of Rule 4 of Output

Typical Values Stored:

RT = 18.17
AV = 19.03
SQ = −1.114

```
   5 6 7
      |WRITE(LW,1000)RT,AV,SQ   } Program
1000  |FORMAT(10F8.4)           } Segment
```

Resulting HSP Output:

```
   1 8 . 1 7 0 0   1 9 . 0 3 0 0   − 1 . 1 1 4 0
        4              4              4            Places after decimal
   8              8              8                 Field Width
```

Note: Both decimal point and minus sign take 1 place of Field Width.

DANGEROUS! What if value stored in RT exceeds 99.9999?

```
PROGRAM IOTEST
   LR=5
   LW=6

   READ(LR,14) ABLE,C1,C2,ROGER
   WRITE(LW,14) ABLE,C1,C2,ROGER
   WRITE(LW,14) C1,C2,C2,C2,ROGER
   WRITE(LW,14) C2
14 FORMAT(F8.2,F10.4,F9.3,F12.6)

   WRITE(LW,15) ABLE,C2,ROGER
15 FORMAT(F12.6,´  C1=´, F8.0)

   WRITE(LW,16) ABLE,C1,C2,ROGER
16 FORMAT(11H ABLE=,F8.2,F8.0,F6.2,´ROGER=´,F10.3)

   READ(LR,17) A,B,C
   READ(LR,18) D,E,F
17 FORMAT(F8.0)
18 FORMAT(10F8.0)
   WRITE(LW,18) A,B,C
   WRITE(LW,17) D,E,F

   WRITE(LW,19) A,B,C,D,E
19 FORMAT(´ A AND B=´,2F8.4,´C=´,F14.2/
  1F8.4,F18.4)

   STOP
   END
```

LISTING 6-1 I/O program IOTEST

Input:

```
11.11      22.22      -33.33           0444
10.10    20.20    30.30
40.40    50.50    60.60
70.70    80.80    90.90
12.34    56.78    13.57
```

Output:

```
11.11      22.2200    -33.330       .000444
22.22    -33.3300    -33.330   -33.330000
 .00
-33.33
11.110000    C1=      -33.
   .000444    C1=
ABLE=,F8.2      11. 22.22ROGER=    -33.330
ABLE=,F8.2      0.
   10.      40.      71.
   12.
   57.
   14.
A AND B= 10.1000 40.4000C=        70.70
12.3400              56.7800
```

LISTING 6-2 Output from program I/O of Listing 6-1

corresponding FORMAT statement mixes types for the second and third variables that are read. Contents of each variable name location are written out using both floating and fixed point edit descriptors.

When A is read and output with floating point format, the correct value of 1 is shown. When A is output using integer format, however, it appears to the computer to be a very large integer (too large for the field width) so that warning asterisks are printed.

When B is read in integer format, it appears to be a zero when output in floating point format. When B is output using integer format, the true value of 2 is displayed. This demonstrates that mixing modes between READ/WRITE statements and their corresponding formats results in error, but no error message is given.

The second line of output using integer values results in similar difficulties. An integer both read and written in floating point format appears to be correct, even though its value as stored cannot be used for computations.

Refer to Listing 6–4, where the value for floating point A is read in integer format. When A is written using the same mixed mode format, its value is output as 4. This appears to be the correct value as read in. Thus numbers read and echoed by the same wrong mode (wrong type) of edit descriptor appear correct. Both errors are undetectable and are not flagged by the computer.

In the seventh line of Listing 6–4, the value stored in location A is multiplied (by 10.). This should mean that the product (40.) is stored in location B. From output of the WRITE statement, however, it can be seen that this computation did not result in a correct answer.

```
      PROGRAM IOTYPE
      LR=5
      LW=6

      READ(LR,10) A,B,I,J
      WRITE(LW,10) A,A, B,B, I,I, J,J
   10 FORMAT(F4.0,I4,F4.0,I4)

      STOP
      END
```

Output:

```
   1.****  0.    2
   3.****  0.    4
```

LISTING 6–3 Mixed type on I/O, Program IOTYPE

```
      PROGRAM IOERR
      LR=5
      LW=6

      READ(LR,10) A
      WRITE(LW,10) A
   10 FORMAT(I4)

      B= 10. * A

      WRITE(LW,11) A,A,  B,B
   11 FORMAT(2(I6,F8.0))

      STOP
      END
```

Output:

```
         4
         4      0.******     0.
```

LISTING 6–4 Calculations performed with mixed type I/O, Program IOERR

In summary, if the type of a format specification does not agree with the type of a corresponding variable in the READ/WRITE statement, both stored and output results are likely to be incorrect. If a value is read and echoed using the same mixed mode, output makes it appear that the correct value has been stored, but any ensuing computations using such values result in incorrect answers; the value actually stored in that location is different than shown in the erroneous output. In these cases, the computer does not flag the error and serious consequences may result.

6-2   PRINT-CONTROL

Print-control is a technique and is not a part of the FORTRAN language. This technique is based upon a widely observed phenomenon: the desirable quantity of output from any given program is quite likely to vary between runs. Several typical uses for print-control are discussed in the following subsections.

The concepts of print-control are summarized in Table 6–19. The most important criterion is that the print-control value is always read as part of the data and is then used in IF statements that control the activation of output statements.

6-2.1   Use in Business

An accounting department may be required to produce summary output on a daily basis, more detailed output on a weekly basis, comprehensive output on a monthly basis, and complete and total accounting output on a yearly basis. In such a case, a print-control value read in with data can satisfy output requirements for the day, week, month, or year, without the necessity of changing the program itself at any time.

6-2.2   Use in Design

On preliminary runs, an engineer using a computer program for trial-and-error sizing of members may be interested only in overstressed and highly understressed members. Subsequently, as the design improves, the engineer may be interested in stresses for all members, thus requiring additional output. Near final stages of the design process, the engineer may become interested in deflection characteristics related to vibration and proper camber, requiring still more output. When the design is complete, the engineer may want a complete set of output showing detailed computations that can be sealed for review by an appropriate governmental authority. The engineer's needs are readily met by adjusting the print-control variable, along with other data. Output volume, which can

---

Table 6-19   Concept of Print-Control

1. A value that controls quantity or type of output is read in as data.

2. Output statements are executed only if activated by the print-control value which is always input as data.

3. Variable quantity or type of output provided by print control is desirable because of the following.

   (a). Required output is dependent upon the users' needs and often varies from time to time.

   (b). Debugging, maintaining, updating, and machine conversion are facilitated.

---

become quite large, is kept to a minimum by showing only required information at each stage of the design.

6–2.3 Use in Monitoring Programs

Print-control is also useful for monitoring computer programs. Compilation errors that cause a program to abort can often be detected by changing the print-control variable to increase the output.

6–2.4 A Specific Example of Print-Control

The computer program discussed in this section is run numerous times each year at a certain installation. For illustrative purposes, the mathematical formulation has been reduced and simplified. Also, descriptive items that are actually read as input data have been shown as constants. Table 6–20 presents one of the formulas used by the program in three different ways: (1) in its basic form, (2) in a reduced form with most of the parenthetical expressions replaced by a single letter and (3) in a much reduced form using only two letters to represent the equation.

Figure 6–1 shows a flow diagram for this segment of the program. First, coefficients A through D are computed. When the print-control value read into location NP (as data) is equal to or greater than 5, the current values stored in X and the four intermediate locations A, B, C, and D are output. Next, E and F are computed; if the value of NP (as read in) is equal to or greater than 4, the value of X is repeated along with secondary values E and F. Finally the answer, G, is computed using values stored in E and F. In this case, if NP is equal to or greater than 3, X is output in conjunction with G. (X was written

---

Table 6–20 Example for Print-Control

Basic equation:

$$G = \sqrt{\left\{\sqrt{\frac{(3x^2-4)(4\sin 2x)^2}{\sqrt{3e^{4x}}+(8x^2-4)^2}}\right\}^2 + \sin^2\left[(\sqrt{3e^{4x}})(8x^2-4)^3\right]}$$

Reduce form of equation using substitutions:

A for $3x^2-4$
B for $4\sin 2x$
C for $\sqrt{3e^{4x}}$
D for $8x^2-4$

Basic equation becomes:

$$G = \sqrt{\left(\frac{(A)(B)^2}{\sqrt{C+D^2}}\right)^2 + \sin^2(CD^3)}$$

Reduce equation further by using additional substitutions:

E for $\dfrac{(A)(B)^2}{\sqrt{C+D^2}}$

F for $\sin(CD^3)$

So that equation reduces to simple form:

$$G = \sqrt{E^2 + F^2}$$

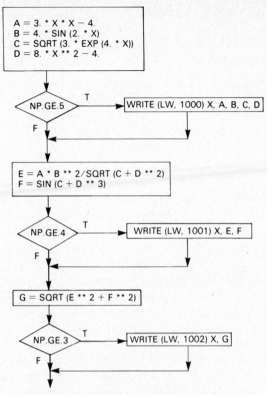

FIGURE 6-1 Program segment illustrating print control for example of Table 6-20

with each output although it could be eliminated from the first two WRITE statements.)

When using the total program, which includes the segment shown in Figure 6–1, the input data can include a print-control less than 3 because even *G* is an unnecessary intermediate answer. On other occasions, values of E and F are important and data includes a value of 4 for NP. On rare, but highly important occasions, values of A through D are critical so that NP is read as 5.

Although this example represents only a small segment of the program, it does highlight the value of print-control. The total program, of which the program segment of Figure 6–1 is only a small part, outputs only one page when NP is input as 1. When NP is read from data as 6, over 1300 pages of output are obtained. When intermediate values of NP are input as data, an intermediate number of pages, corresponding to the precise needs of the user for that particular run, is output. This does more than save paper; it helps emphasize the important characteristics needed by the user from that particular run.

6-3 END and ERR Used in Control Information Lists

Input and output rules are summarized in Tables 6–1 and 6–2. The entities within the parentheses, (LR, ℓ_f) or (LW, ℓ_f), are elements of a *control information list*. Further flexibility can be gained by adding additional items to such control information lists. (For complete details, refer to Chapter 17.)

Two of the more important additional controls are illustrated in Listing 6–5: end-of-file specifier END (found in both Full and Subset FORTRAN 77) and error specifier ERR (found only in Full Language FORTRAN 77).

The input statement of Listing 6–5 can be written in several ways, including the following.

$$\text{READ (LR, 1000, ERR = 10, END = 20) I}$$
$$\text{READ (LR, 1000, END = 20, ERR = 10) I}$$

In Full Language FORTRAN 77 only, we can use

$$\text{READ (UNIT = LR, FMT = 1000, ERR = 10, END = 20) I}$$
$$\text{READ (ERR = 10, FMT = 1000, UNIT = LR, END = 20) I}$$

The first and second forms of the preceeding input statements are most common, requiring the first symbol (always the first) to represent the logical unit number* and the second symbol (always the second) to represent the FORMAT statement label number†. Order for ERR and END is immaterial so long as the first and second entities are ordered properly. In the third and fourth forms, entities are defined for the logical unit number by UNIT = LR and for the FORMAT statement label number by FMT = 1000. When all

```
      PROGRAM ERREND
      LR=5
      LW=6

    5 READ(LR,1000,ERR=10,END=20) I
      WRITE(LW,1000) I
      GO TO 5

   10 WRITE(LW,1001)
      GO TO 5

   20 WRITE(LW,1002)

 1000 FORMAT(I4)
 1001 FORMAT(' ERROR ENCOUNTERED, DATA SKIPPED')
 1002 FORMAT(' DATA ALL READ, HAD TO MOVE ON')

      STOP
      END
```

Input: Output:

```
1                   1
2                   2
3                   3
4                   4
5.                  ERROR ENCOUNTERED, DATA SKIPPED
6                   6
7.                  ERROR ENCOUNTERED, DATA SKIPPED
8                   8
9                   9

                    DATA ALL READ, HAD TO MOVE ON
```

LISTING 6–5 Program ERREND with I/O

*Formally a unit specifier; specifically an external unit identifier or an internal file identifier.
†Formally a format identifier; see Section 12–2.1 for all permissible forms.

entities are defined in the manner of the third and fourth examples, order of the control information list is immaterial. Most programmers seem to prefer the restrictions and simplicity of the first two examples.

The program of Listing 6–5 reads and writes a single integer value on each loop. Note, however, that the fifth and seventh data entries are real rather than integer—mixed type. In both cases, the value read in is in error and control passes to Statement 10 because of ERR = 10 in the control information list. General form would be ERR = ℓ_f, where ℓ_f is the label of any executable statement to which control should transfer. Thus, even though the program does not use the incorrect data, it does proceed to operate after output of the error message of Statement 10. Without ERR, data may be read incorrectly (mixed mode) or the trouble may be so serious (two periods, or alphabetical characters in I field) that execution will terminate.

When the last data card (line) is read, a control card (line) is encountered by the program. But, rather than giving an error message, control simply passes to Statement 20, or whatever numbered statement is specified. The end-of-file specifier, though popular, does not provide the flexibility of *trailer cards* when using different groupings of data.

6–4 LIST-DIRECTED I/O

Although list-directed I/O is not a part of Subset FORTRAN 77, it is likely to be an early *local extension*. List-directed I/O is quite helpful when using the computer simply as a giant calculator and during the debugging process. Though list-directed input is sometimes useful for service programs, list-directed output is usually inferior to formatted output.

Listing 6–6 is an example of list-directed I/O. Two forms of READ and WRITE (PRINT) are shown. For the standard READ/WRITE, the FORMAT statement label number is replaced by an asterisk. When an asterisk is used instead of a FORMAT statement label, the processor automatically chooses an appropriate format.

The second form of I/O statement does not require a control information list. (Also see Chapter 17.) To input, the word READ is followed by an asterisk, a comma, and the list of variables separated by commas. To output, the word PRINT is followed by an asterisk, a comma, and the list of items separated by commas. READ and PRINT without control information lists is often called a FORTRAN II I/O form. Output is always returned to a specified device (cards to HSP, remote terminal to remote terminal, and so on).

The first READ statement of Listing 6–6 inputs values for A, B, and C, with data delineated by use of blanks between the numbers. Also, integer values are considered to be real whole numbers, even though they do not include a decimal point. (*Note:* Integer variables cannot be used to read real numbers.) The second READ statement uses data delineated by commas.

The first two output statements display values using the two possible methods. The next two output statements show that characters can be output directly.

Finally, the last group of statements shows that the result of expressions can be output by both the WRITE and PRINT statements using Full FORTRAN 77. (This

```
PROGRAM LDIO
LR=5
LW=6

READ(LR,*) A,B,C
READ *,E,D,L,M

WRITE(LW,*) A,B,C,E,D,L,M
PRINT *, M,L,D,E,C,B,A
PRINT *, ´A=´,A,´B=´,B,´C=´,C
WRITE(LW,*) ´L AND M=´,L,M

WRITE(LW,*) ´A+B=´,(A+B)
PRINT *, ´M+L´, (L+M)
PRINT *, ´RESULT OF (A+B)*(L+M)=´,((A+B)*(L+M))

STOP
END

2  3. 12
4.,5., 4, 10
```

Output:

```
2.0000000      3.0000000      12.000000      4.0000000      5.0000000                    4           10
        10            4 5.0000000      4.0000000      12.000000      3.0000000      2.0000000
A= 2.0000000      B= 3.0000000      C= 12.000000
L AND M=          4                10
A+B= 5.0000000
M+L            14
RESULT OF (A+B)*(L+M)=  70.000000
```

LISTING 6-6 List-directed I/O

is not possible in Subset FORTRAN 77, probably not even if list-directed I/O is implemented.) For additional discussion see Section 12–2.2.

In summary,

1. Data for list-oriented I/O may be separated by:
   (a) commas or slashes (when encountered, a slash terminates execution of that input statement);
   (b) any number of blanks;
   (c) any number of blanks (including none) on either or both sides of commas or slashes.
2. Data for real variables may be in integer form; data for integer variables must be in integer form.
3. Each READ starts reading from a new card (line) and reads until all variables have been defined even if it must go to additional lines (cards).
4. Each WRITE and PRINT starts output on a new line. If all values cannot fit on a line, additional lines will be used automatically.
5. Each I/O value is either a constant, a null value, r*c, or r* (r is a positive integer constant which specifies the number of times the constant c, or null values if the r* form is used, is to be I/O sequentially).

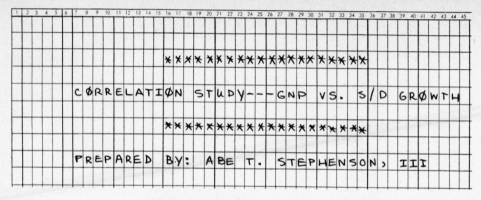

LISTING 6-7 Typical heading laid out on coding form

```
     5 6 7
       READ(LR,1000) G,H,I        } Program
1000   FORMAT(10F8.0)             } Segment
```

Typical Data Card(s):

```
|9. 1 6 |   -3 . 2 1  | 7 6   |
```

(a)

```
     5 6 7
       READ(LR,1000) T,U,V        } Program
1000   FORMAT(10F8.0)             } Segment
```

Typical Data Card(s):

```
|  1 2 . 3  1 7 . 6  1 2 3 4 5 |   4 1 3 2   |
   1 2 7 3   1 8 9 6   1 2 3 . 4    4 1 . 3 2
```

(b)

```
      5 6 7
        READ(LR,1000)T,U,V,W,X      } Program
1000    FORMAT(F6.2,5X,F5.1)        } Segment
```

Typical Data Card(s):

```
|1 2 3 4 5|6 7 8 9 0|1 2 3 4 5|6 7 8 9 0|
 1 2 3 4 5 6 7 8 9 0 1 2 3 4 5 6 7 8 9 0
 1 2 3 4 5 6 7 8 9 0 1 2 3 4 5 6 7 8 9 0
```

(c)

```
     5 6 7
       READ(LR,1000)T,U,V,W,X      } Program
1000   FORMAT(F6.2,5X,F5.1)        } Segment
```

Typical Data Card(s):

```
| 1 8 . 3 |     1 2 3 4   |
  1 2 3 4     1 2 . 7
    1 2 3 4 5 6
```

(d)

LISTING 6-8 Program segments with data to be read

6-5 EXERCISES

1. Listing 6-7 shows a heading laid out on a coding form. Prepare the minimum number of necessary WRITE and FORMAT statements to produce this heading in each case.
   (a) Only one WRITE statement is to be used.
   (b) One WRITE statement is to be used for each independent line, including blank lines.
   (c) One WRITE statement is to be used for each independent line followed by a blank line.

2. Listing 6-8 illustrates four sets of input data corresponding to four program segments. Indicate the values stored in appropriate computer locations for (a), (b), (c), or (d).

3. Listing 6-9 illustrates four sets of stored data to be used with four program segments. Indicate the appearance of the output for (a), (b), (c), or (d).

4. Listing 6-10 is a "do nothing" I/O program. Four possible sets of data are listed in (a)-(d). Show how output would appear from the statements of set (a), (b), (c), or (d).

Typical Values Stored in Variable Name Locations

```
R Z       1 3 . 6      T 3       0 . 0 0 2    Z 1 B      1 7 8
  A   =   6 3 1 9 2 .   R I       1 2 0 4      R K 3        8 3    1 6 9
```

```
5 6 7
      WRITE ( LW , 1 0 0 1 ) R Z , T 3 , Z 1 B , A , R I , R K 3   } Program
1 0 0 1  FORMAT ( 3 F 6 . 0 , 3 F 8 . 2 )                          } Segment
```

(a)

Typical Values Stored in Variable Name Locations:

```
  I D 4  =  4          I D 7   7          I D 9  =  9
```

```
5 6 7
      WRITE ( LW , 1 0 0 1 ) I D 9 , I D 4 , I D 7
1 0 0 1  FORMAT ( 1 X , ' I D 4 = ' , 2 X , I 4 , ' I D 4 = ' , I 4 ,  } Program
      1 2 X , 4 H I D 7 = , I 4 ,                                      } Segment
```

(b)

Typical Values Stored in Variable Name Locations:

```
  M A  =  2 3 6 0     W O  =  3 1 7 2        B O  =  1 6 9 5
  G I  =  1 8 3 2
```

```
5 6 7
      WRITE ( LW , 1 0 0 1 ) M A , W O , B O , G I   } Program
1 0 0 1  FORMAT ( I 4 , 3 F 6 . 1 )                  } Segment
```

(c)

Typical Values Stored in Variable Name Locations:

```
  A  =  - 1 2 . 3    B  =  1 . 2 6 4    C  = - 1 8 3 .
  D  =  + 1 8 3 .    E  =  1 7 . 6      F  =  - 9 . 0 1 3
```

```
5 6 7
      WRITE ( LW , 1 0 0 1 ) A , B , C , D , E , F   } Program
1 0 0 1  FORMAT ( 2 F 5 . 0 )                        } Segment
```

(d)

LISTING 6-9 Program segments with stored data to be output

```
      5 6 7
C         PROGRAM INOUT
          LR=5
          LW=6
1000      FORMAT(F8 2)
1001      FORMAT(3F8 4)
1002      FORMAT(10F8 0)
1003      FORMAT(F6 1,F10 3,F7 2,F11 4)
          READ(LR,1003)  VAR1,VAR2,VAR3,VAR4
          WRITE(LW,1003) VAR1,VAR2,VAR3,VAR4
          WRITE(LW,1003) VAR4          VAR1
          WRITE(LW,1003) VAR4,VAR3,VAR3,VAR2,VAR3,VAR1
          WRITE(LW,1000) VAR1,VAR2,VAR3
          WRITE(LW,1001) VAR1,VAR2,VAR3
          WRITE(LW,1002) VAR1,VAR2,VAR3,VAR4
          READ(LR,1002)  VAR1,VAR2,VAR3,VAR4
          WRITE(LW,1002) VAR1,VAR2,VAR3,VAR4
          STOP
          END
```

Data Set (a)
```
  ' 1 6 3 2 ' ' ' '1 8  4 7' ' '  9 1 7 6 ' '  8 3 2 '  ' ' '
1 6 3  2       1 8  4 7    9 1  7 6     8 3 2
```

Data Set (b)
```
    1 0 0     −   8 3 2       1 2 3 4 5                  1 2
1 0 0         −   8 3 2   1 2 3 4 5      0 0 1 2
```

Data Set (c)
```
  − 5 0       − 6            7          8 0
− 5 0         − 6 0      7 0            8 0
```

Data Set (d)
```
    − 5       − 6            7                          8
−   5         −   0 0 6      0 7        0 0 0 8
```

LISTING 6-10 "Do nothing" I/O program with data sets

Synthesis and Examples

The examples of this chapter provide a synthesis of the material in Chapters 1 through 6. Particular attention is given to program development, loop control, program limitations, selection of appropriate test data, and motivation for the use of subroutines. Variables and constants of type *complex* are introduced in (optional) Section 7–5.

7–1 PROGRAM SIMLR—SIMPLE LINEAR REGRESSION

Linear relationships exist in many sets of data pairs relating such items as height and weight of students, or rainfall and yield of corn per acre. We want to create a program, SIMLR, to obtain the equation of the straight line that best represents any such set of data pairs. Later in this book, the program will be improved and expanded for additional capabilities.

7–1.1 Understanding the Problem of Relating Data Pairs

As with every computer program, it is first necessary to obtain a complete understanding of the problem. In this case, it is assumed that the following equations and relationships are provided (linear regression formulas):

$$y = a + bx \quad \text{(equation of a straight line)}$$

where

$$a = \frac{\Sigma y - b\Sigma x}{N} \quad \text{and} \quad b = \frac{(\Sigma x)(\Sigma y) - N(\Sigma xy)}{(\Sigma x)^2 - N(\Sigma x^2)}$$

and where

$$N \quad = \text{number of } (x,y)\text{-coordinate pairs used}$$
$$x \quad = x\text{-coordinate of a point}$$

$$y \quad = y\text{-coordinate of the same point}$$
$$\Sigma x \quad = \text{sum of all } (N) \ x\text{-coordinates}$$
$$\Sigma y \quad = \text{sum of all } (N) \ y\text{-coordinates}$$
$$\Sigma x^2 \quad = \text{sum of the squares of all } (N) \ x\text{-coordinates}$$
$$\Sigma xy \quad = \text{sum of the product of all } (N) \ (x,y)\text{-coordinate pairs}$$

The idea is to find coefficients a and b so that for any given x, the corresponding y-coordinate can be approximated. The coefficient a involves the summation of all of the y-coordinates, the summation of all the x-coordinates, and a count of the total number of (x, y)-coordinate pairs used. The coefficient b involves these same terms, plus the summation of the products of all xy and then of the squares of the x-coordinates.

Before writing the program, we shall work through a simple example longhand to insure that the problem is well understood and to provide test data for validating the program after it is written.

Simple values for a and b are chosen, $a = 2$ and $b = 3$; these values are used in the equation $y = a + bx = 2 + 3x$ to compute several coordinate pairs. For example, when $x = 0$, $y = 2$, and when $x = 2$, $y = 2 + 3(2) = 8$. Several values of x and the corresponding values of y are plotted in Figure 7–1.

Since the formulas for linear regression require summations, the values of x and y are put in columns in Table 7–1. (Note that the order in which the coordinates are written does not follow the order along the straight line.) Two additional columns are added, one to show the values of x^2, the other to show each product xy. Thus on the second line of the table, $x^2 = 2^2 = 4$ and $xy = 2 \times 8 = 16$.

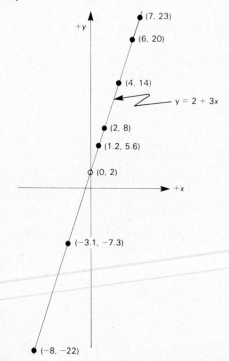

FIGURE 7–1 Graph of some x, y pairs for $y = 2 + 3x$

Table 7-1 Calculations for Linear Equation from Set of
x, y pairs

x	y	x^2	xy
0.0	2.0	0.00	0.00
2.0	8.0	4.00	16.00
6.0	20.0	36.00	120.00
1.2	5.6	1.44	6.72
-3.1	-7.3	9.61	22.63
4.0	14.0	16.00	56.00
7.0	23.0	49.00	161.00
-8.0	-22.0	64.00	176.00
$\Sigma x = 9.1$	$\Sigma y = 43.3$	$\Sigma x^2 = 180.05$	$\Sigma xy = 558.35$

Basic equation: $y = a + bx$

$$b = \frac{(\Sigma x)(\Sigma y) - N(\Sigma xy)}{(\Sigma x)^2 - N(\Sigma x^2)} = \frac{(9.1)(43.3) - 8(558.35)}{(9.1)^2 - 8(180.05)} = 3.000$$

$$a = \frac{\Sigma y - b\Sigma x}{N} = \frac{43.3 - (3.000)(9.1)}{8} = 2.000$$

The final equation is $y = 2.000 + 3.000(x)$.

Each of the columns is added to give the four summations required by the given formulas for eight sets of coordinate pairs ($N = 8$). These values are then substituted into the formulas for b and a to yield 3 and 2, respectively. From these results the final equation $y = 2 + 3x$ is obtained.

Realistic sets of data will seldom lie exactly on the straight line that they approximate, but that is precisely the reason for choosing test data in a manner which provides a positive check.

7-1.2 Developing Program SIMLR

Working an example by hand helps to delineate the steps necessary to develop a program. Obviously, the x- and y-coordinates must be read by the computer program. Because there are several sets, we would probably consider the possibility of a loop. Two (from among many) possibilities are: (1) read all of the x- and corresponding y-coordinates first and then do the calculations; or (2) read a set of x- and corresponding y-coordinates and perform the calculations before reading the next set of (x,y)-coordinates. The second method is chosen for the following development.

Look at Table 7-1 again. In order to obtain the summations and to count the number of (x,y)-pairs, locations for accumulating the results must be initialized. Next, a loop must be entered to: (1) read a set of (x, y)-pairs; (2) accumulate a count of the sets read; (3) sum the x's; (4) sum the y's; (5) sum the x^2 values; and (6) sum the xy values. Once the loop is completed, a final computation must be performed to obtain a and b and the answers must be output.

Such a process can often be clarified by sketching a human-oriented flow diagram such as the one of Figure 7-2. At the same time, it is desirable to create a definition sheet for the program SIMLR. Mnemonics should be chosen for the variables. One possibility is to use COUNT to represent N, a count of the (x,y)-pairs; SUMX for the sum of the x's; SUMY for the sum of the y's; SUMX2 for the sum of the x^2 values; and SUMXY for the accumulated sum of the xy values. It seems reasonable to call the x-and-y coordinates simply X and Y. Figure 7–2 suggests that five values must be initialized: COUNT, SUMX, SUMY, SUMX2 and SUMXY. The read box inputs a coordinate pair and stores the values of x and y in locations X and Y, respectively.

How will the program know when to stop? A trailer card with zeros for X and Y is probably not desirable because the straight line often passes through the origin. So, in this case, the unlikely simultaneous values of +9999.99 for X and −9999.99 for Y are utilized to terminate the program.

It could be helpful to sketch a machine-oriented flow diagram for this problem from the information obtained so far. Then, check your flow diagram against the program coding of Listing 7–1.

Note that the data used to test the program yields the required answer. Are you satisfied that this single test is adequate? How many and what kinds of additional tests would you require to have complete faith in this program?

In summary, program SIMLR has four basic elements: (1) an initialization block; (2) a primary loop that counts the number of (x,y)-pairs and accumulates the sums of x, y, x^2 and $xy;$ (3) a loop termination technique; and (4) final calculations with output.

7–1.3 Applicability of SIMLR as a Subroutine

Program SIMLR of Listing 7–1 is unsuitable for conversion into a subroutine because of the large and variable amount of input required. This points up the need for a method to represent tables by a single name so that their elements can be referred to by subscripts. Such a technique, use of arrays and array elements, is introduced in Chapter 9 and developed in the subsequent chapters. Once arrays and array elements have been

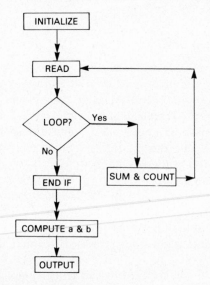

FIGURE 7–2 Human-oriented flow diagram for program SIMLR

```
      PROGRAM SIMLR
      LR=5
      LW=6


*******************************************************************
*                                                                 *
*  PROGRAM SIMLR COMPUTES A AND B FOR EQUATION Y= A + BX          *
*               FROM SETS OF X, Y COORDINATES INPUT AS DATA.      *
*               Y = A + BX IS EQUATION OF STRAIGHT LINE           *
*               WHICH GIVES THE BEST LINEAR REPRESENTATION        *
*               OF THE DATA.                                      *
*     X,Y       COORDINATE PAIRS INPUT                            *
*               (RUN TERMINATES WHEN TRAILER CARD CONTAINS)       *
*               (X= 9999. AND SIMULTANEOUSLY Y = -9999.  )        *
*     COUNT     COUNTS NUMBER OF COORDINATE PAIRS INPUT           *
*     SUMX      ACCUMULATES SUM OF X COORDINATE VALUES            *
*     SUMY      ACCUMULATES SUM OF Y COORDINATE VALUES            *
*     SUMX2     ACCUMULATES SUM OF X-SQUARED                      *
*     SUMXY     ACCUMULATES SUM OF PRODUCT OF X TIMES Y           *
*                                                                 *
*******************************************************************


      SUMX2= 0.
      SUMXY= 0.
      SUMY = 0.
      SUMX = 0.
      COUNT= 0.

   10 READ(LR,100) X,Y
      IF(X.NE.9999. .AND. Y.NE.-9999.) THEN
          COUNT = COUNT + 1.
          SUMX2 = SUMX2 + X**2
          SUMXY = SUMXY + X*Y
          SUMY  = SUMY  + Y
          SUMX  = SUMX  + X
          GO TO 10
      END IF

      B=(SUMX*SUMY-COUNT*SUMXY)/(SUMX**2-COUNT*SUMX2)
      A=(SUMY-B*SUMX)/COUNT
      WRITE(LW,101) A,B

  100 FORMAT(2F8.0)
  101 FORMAT('1 BEST STRAIGHT LINE THRU DATA GIVEN BY'/
     1 1X,F10.3,' + ',F10.3,' * X = Y' )

      STOP
      END
```

Input:

	2.	SHOULD GIVE
2.	8.	Y = 2 + 3 X
6.	20.	
1.2	5.6	
-3.1	-7.3	HW--
4.	14.	ALTER SO ON EACH CYCLE
7.	23.	COUNT,X,Y,X**2,X*Y AND
-8.	-22.	SUMY,SUMX2 AND SUMXY
9999.	-9999.	

Output:

```
BEST STRAIGHT LINE THRU DATA GIVEN BY
    2.000 +        3.000 * X = Y
```

LISTING 7-1 Program SIMLR, input data and output

Section 7-1 Program SIMLR—Simple Linear Regression   **159**

considered, the solution to fitting a straight line to a set of data pairs can be substantially improved.

As written, program SIMLR also has a severe limitation because it does not indicate how well the straight line actually fits the data points supplied. Obviously, many sets of data cannot be represented adequately by any straight line. With additional FORTRAN techniques presented in subsequent chapters, an improved subroutine can be developed that makes it possible to choose the best curve or straight line to fit any given set of data pairs.

Program SIMLR has been developed in an incomplete form and will be perfected in subsequent sections; however, program QUAD (Section 7–2) is essentially complete.

7-2 PROGRAM QUAD— ROOTS OF THE QUADRATIC EQUATION

Although the quadratic equation, usually introduced in elementary algebra, is easy to use, programming the solution for a general quadratic equation is not as simple as it appears to be. At first glance, a program to solve the quadratic formula emphasizes the need for a complete understanding of this familiar process and the need to plan for all of the special cases.

7-2.1 Understanding and Developing a Solution to the Quadratic Equation

Program QUAD is to be written to solve equations of the type

$$y = ax^2 + bx + c$$

which has the general solution

$$x = \frac{-b \pm \sqrt{b^2 - 4ac}}{2a}$$

where a, b, and c are real numbers that may be positive, negative, or zero.

If a is zero, the quadratic equation degenerates to the linear form $bx + c = 0$ so that $x = -c/b$. In such a case, the general quadratic formula does not provide a solution for x because the coefficient a appears in the denominator, which would require division by zero.

If b is zero, then the quadratic equation reduces to

$$x = \frac{\pm \sqrt{-4ac}}{2a} = \pm \sqrt{-\frac{c}{a}}$$

If the quantity under the radical sign is positive, then two real answers are obtained; they have equal magnitudes but opposite signs. If the value of c is zero, then the value of x is, of course, zero. If the value under the radical sign is negative, then two imaginary answers (of the form zi) of equal magnitude and opposite signs are obtained.

When neither a nor b is zero, then the form of the two answers (roots) is determined by the sign of the expression under the radical, $b^2 - 4ac$, called the discriminant. When the discriminant is positive, two real and unequal roots are obtained. When the discriminant is zero, two real and equal roots are obtained. When the discriminant is negative, complex conjugates are obtained.

7-2.2 Spacing of Output

Because solutions to quadratic equations have answers in several different forms, special attention should be given to spacing the output. Four forms of roots are possible: one real root, two real roots, two imaginary roots, or two complex conjugates. Of several possible schemes, the one illustrated by the output shown in Listing 7–2 is used, with answers in the last four columns (4 through 7). Columns 4 and 5 represent the first x (called X1 in the program) with the real part in the fourth column and the imaginary part in the fifth. The second x (X2) is displayed in the next two columns, the real part in the sixth column and the imaginary part in the last (seventh) column. (Listing 7–2 is on page 165.)

Four different format schemes are required so that blank columns are skipped over. Blank columns rather than zeros are desirable because such zeros would not truly be a part of the answers. Properly spaced solutions are provided, however, by only three FORMAT statements: 1002, 1003, and 1004 of Listing 7–2. (Why do only three FORMAT statements provide the four required format schemes?) Typical output is shown at the bottom of Listing 7–2, with input values in the first three columns and the solutions in columns four through seven, as appropriate.

7-2.3 Formulating the Program

Sometimes it is useful to formulate a program using words that are somewhat similar to FORTRAN coding, called *pseudocode*. Before going any further, refer to the discussion of Section 7–2.1 and write a series of *pseudocode* statements to indicate exactly what program QUAD is suppose to do. No rules are given for pseudocode because words meaningful to you should be used. The following "solution" is typical and may not agree precisely with your pseudocode. It is, however, important that all operations are treated.

When A and B are both zero, terminate run.
ELSE IF A = 0, solve linear equation.
ELSE IF B = 0, compute discriminant $4ac$ and if:
$4ac < 0$, get 2 imaginary roots (equal magnitude but opposite signs);
$4ac = 0$, get 2 zero roots;
$4ac > 0$, get 2 real roots (equal magnitude but opposite in sign).
ELSE A $\neq$ 0, B $\neq$ 0, compute discriminant $b^2 - 4ac$ and if:
$b^2 - 4ac < 0$, get complex conjugates;
$b^2 - 4ac = 0$, get 2 identical real roots;
$b^2 - 4ac > 0$, get 2 real, unequal roots.

To visualize the process, you may find it advantageous to sketch this information into a human-oriented flow diagram. The final steps are shown in the machine-oriented flow diagram of Figure 7–3 and the modified Nassi-Shneiderman chart of Figure 7–4. The program is coded in Listing 7–2. Would you prefer to have more comments in the main body of the program?

Program QUAD

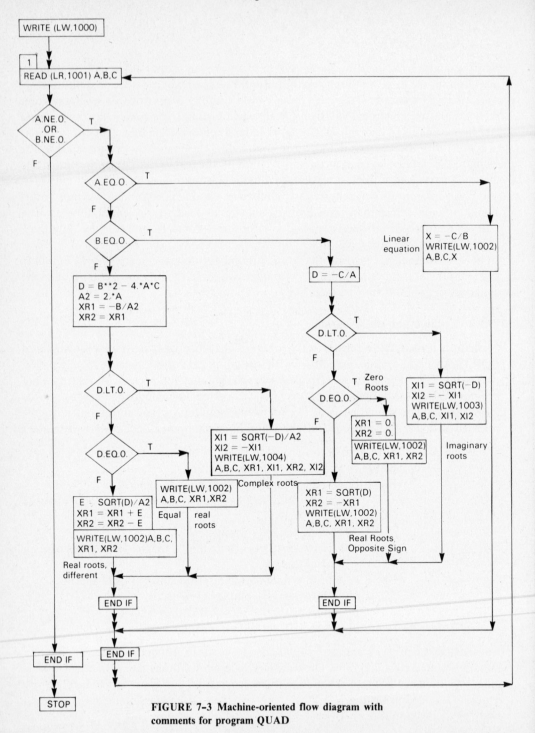

FIGURE 7-3 Machine-oriented flow diagram with comments for program QUAD

7-2.4 Choosing Test Data by "Reverse" Formulas

It is almost impossible to thoroughly test program QUAD by employing a random set of equations using arbitrary values of a, b, and c. However, a thorough test can be performed with only seven sets of data by using the following easily found "reverse" relationships.

$$x_1 + x_2 = \frac{-b}{a}$$

$$x_1 x_2 = \frac{c}{a}$$

From these relationships, the coefficients a, b, and c can be obtained for any given x_1 and x_2. Thus if $x_1 = 4$ and $x_2 = -3$

$$4 + (-3) = 1 = \frac{-b}{a}$$

$$4(-3) = -12 = \frac{c}{a}$$

Program QUAD

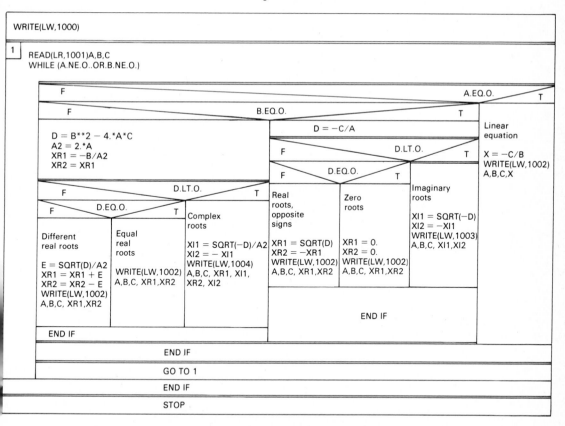

FIGURE 7-4 Modified Nassi-Shneiderman chart for program QUAD

```
      PROGRAM QUAD
C                 --- THIS PROGRAM SOLVES THE QUADRATIC
C                 --- FORMULA FOR X IN EQUATIONS OF THE
C                 --- FORM: A*X**2 + B*X + C = 0
C                 --- CONSTRAINTS:
C                       A,B AND C MUST BE REAL NUMBERS
C                       IF A=0, SOLUTION FOR B*X + C = 0
C                       IF BOTH A=0 AND B=0, RUN TERMINATES
C                 --- ANSWERS
C                       FIRST X: XR1= REAL PART
C                                XI1= IMAGINARY PART
C                       SECOND X: XR2= REAL PART
C                                 XI2= IMAGINARY PART
C                 --- OTHER VARIABLES
C                                D= DISCRIMINANT
C                                A2= 2 TIMES A

      LR=5
      LW=6

      WRITE(LW,1000)

    1 READ(LR,1001)A,B,C
      IF(A.NE.0. .OR. B.NE. 0.)THEN

          IF(A.EQ.0.) THEN
              X= -C/B
              WRITE(LW,1002)A,B,C,X
          ELSE IF(B.EQ.0.) THEN
              D = -C/A

              IF(D.LT.0.) THEN
                  XI1= SQRT(-D)
                  XI2= -XI1
                  WRITE(LW,1003)A,B,C,XI1,XI2
              ELSE IF(D.EQ.0.) THEN
                  XR1= 0.
                  XR2= 0.
                  WRITE(LW,1002)A,B,C,XR1,XR2
              ELSE
                  XR1= SQRT(D)
                  XR2= -XR1
                  WRITE(LW,1002)A,B,C,XR1,XR2
              END IF

          ELSE
              D= B**2 -4.*A*C
              A2= 2.*A
              XR1= -B/A2
              XR2= XR1

              IF(D.LT.0.) THEN
                  XI1= SQRT(-D)/A2
                  XI2= -XI1
                  WRITE(LW,1004)A,B,C,XR1,XI1,XR2,XI2
              ELSE IF(D.EQ.0) THEN
                  WRITE(LW,1002)A,B,C,XR1,XR2
              ELSE
                  E= SQRT(D)/A2
                  XR1= XR1+E
                  XR2= XR2-E
                  WRITE(LW,1002)A,B,C,XR1,XR2
              END IF

          END IF
          GO TO 1
      END IF
```

LISTING 7-2 Program QUAD with I/O

```
1000 FORMAT('1SOLUTION OF QUADRATIC EQUATION'/
     15X,'A',10X,'B',10X,'C',15X,'X1',20X,'X2'/
     236X,'REAL',8X,'IMG',7X,'REAL',8X,'IMG'/)
1001 FORMAT (10F8.0)
1002 FORMAT(1X,4E11.4,11X,E11.4)
1003 FORMAT(1X,3E11.4,2(11X,E11.4))
1004 FORMAT(1X,7E11.4)

     STOP
     END
```

Input:

0.	4.	12.	LINEAR EQUATION(CHG DATA***)	CARD 1
2.	0.	-8.	A*X**2 + C=0 --REAL ROOTS	CARD 2
12.	0.	0.	A*X**2 + C=0 --ZERO ANSWER	CARD 3
1.	0.	4.	A*X**2 + C=0 --IMAGINARY(+,-)	CARD 4
2.	-2.	-24.	COMPLETE QUAD--TWO,REAL	CARD 5
-3.	-18.	-27.	COMPLETE QUAD--TWO,IDENTICAL	CARD 6
1.	-2.	5.	COMPLETE QUAD--TWO,COMPLEX	CARD 7
0.	0.		TERMINATE RUN	CARD 8

Output:

```
SOLUTION OF QUADRATIC EQUATION
      A          B          C              X1                  X2
                                       REAL     IMG       REAL      IMG

   .0000      .4000+001  .1200+002 -.3000+001
   .2000+001  .0000     -.8000+001  .2000+001            -.2000+001
   .1200+002  .0000      .0000      .0000                 .0000
   .1000+001  .0000      .4000+001            .2000+001             -.2000+001
   .2000+001 -.2000+001 -.2400+002  .4000+001            -.3000+001
  -.3000+001 -.1800+002 -.2700+002 -.3000+001            -.3000+001
   .1000+001 -.2000+001  .5000+001  .1000+001  .2000+001  .1000+001 -.2000+001
```

LISTING 7-2 (*continued*)

Assume $a = 2$. Then

$$b = -2$$
$$c = -24$$

Thus, for each case discussed in Section 7–2.1, answers (x_1 and x_2) were selected. From these selected values of x, the coefficients of a, b, and c were then computed. These seven carefully chosen sets of a, b, and c were then read into the computer program to provide a thorough test. Because the coefficients a, b, and c were computed from known values of x_1 and x_2, the answers provided by the computer program are readily checked by inspection.

Would you be confident that this program would solve any quadratic equation for which you supplied data? What further testing is required?

Program testing is extremely important but can be quite time consuming and very complex. Often the complexity can be sharply decreased by using the "reverse" approach, minimizing the number of runs required to insure program validity.

Programs SIMLR and QUAD were straightforward solutions to mathematical formulations. Program RATE requires a search for the right answer by solving the same formula a number of times, with continuously changing parameters.

7–3   PROGRAM RATE—DETERMINING UNKNOWN COMPOUND INTEREST RATE

The program of this section is to solve problems of this type: "If I invest $15,000 now and am repaid at the rate of $2800 per year for 10 years, what is the rate of compound interest that I am earning?" Obviously, answers to this type of question are very important when considering different types of investments or when purchasing different types of production equipment having various rates of yield.

7–3.1   Understanding the Problem of Unknown Interest Rate

The value of an investment now is called Present Worth (PW). For this particular problem the necessary formula is:

$$\text{present worth} = -(\text{investment now}) + \text{yearly return} \left(\frac{1}{\dfrac{\text{int. rate}}{(1 - \text{int. rate})^{\text{years}} - 1} + \text{int. rate}} \right)$$

or, for the particular example used in this section,

$$PW = -15{,}000 + 2{,}800 \left(\frac{1}{\dfrac{i}{(1 - i)^{10} - 1} + i} \right)$$

Thus, present worth can be determined by substituting any interest rate (i) into the formula for PW. (Note that interest must be used in decimal form.)

This formula presents little difficulty when i is known and PW is to be calculated. Our requirement, however, is to determine i when PW is known. Before a method of solution can be formulated, it is necessary to gain some insight into the relationship between i and PW. The easiest way to do this is use values of i to compute a series of values of PW.

If the interest rate is 1%, then PW is $11,519.63. (Results shown Listing 7–4, p. 172.) Using an interest rate of 2%, PW is $10,151.23. As the interest increases, the value of PW decreases. When PW is zero, the interest that gave the result of zero is the compound interest rate being earned by the investment of $15,000 for 10 years with $2800 annual payments.

When the interest rate is 14%, PW is negative (−$394.88), showing that the actual interest rate is less than 14%.

This suggests a technique to be used by this program: start with an interest rate of 1%, and change the interest rate by increments of 1% until the value of PW changes sign and becomes negative. The change in sign will indicate that the correct interest rate lies between the last two percentages used to compute present worth.

To increase the accuracy, once PW changes sign, the increments in the interest rate could be decreased by a power of 10 and the search restarted from the last interest rate that gave a positive PW. For example, an interest of 13.2% gives PW = $72.81, an interest of 13.3% gives PW = $13.04, and an interest rate of 13.4% gives PW = −$46.34. This change of sign now indicates that the correct interest rate must lie between 13.3% and 13.4%. (In actual practice, such an answer is more than adequate. For purposes of illustration for the computer program, however, more accuracy is desired.)

Since the interest rate that makes PW zero lies between 13.3% and 13.4%, the search can continue with an increment of 0.01%. Values of present worth are then checked at 13.31%, 13.32%, and so on, until the sign changes again. If this technique is unclear, a graph of PW versus the interest rates may be helpful. For simplicity, you can use the output of program RATE as shown in Listing 7-4 (See page 172).

7-3.2   A Solution with Program RATE

The number of statements required to solve this problem is not large. On the other hand, if you do not completely understand the problem it will take an excessive amount of time to write a valid program. Sometimes it helps to start a formulation "in the middle."

The value of PW must be computed from a changing interest rate, which we call R_2. (Prior to the first calculation, some initialization will be required; before considering initialization, however, it may be desirable to obtain a better concept of how to construct the loop.) From the previous discussion, it is evident that interest rate is incremented by a small value before each calculation. Do not overlook the fact that there are times when two sequential interest rates must be known simultaneously! Therefore, it may be reasonable to precede the calculation of PW using R_2 by a statement that increments the previous rate: $R_2 = R_1 + CHGR$, where CHGR signifies the change in rate and R_1 the "old" rate.

The statement $R_2 = R_1 + CHGR$ would appear at the top of the loop. Thus, initialization would be required for R_1 (to 0) and CHGR (to 1., signifying 1%).

Inside the loop, immediately following the calculations of PW, it is necessary to check the answer for accuracy. An IF statement, which is discussed in more detail below, seems desirable for either implementing a subsequent loop or terminating the loop process.

To continue the loop process, there are two possibilities. If the computed value of PW is greater than zero, then we should again try the same change in the interest rate and place the current interest rate R_2 in the "old" interest rate R_1, loop back to the statement $R_2 = R_1 + CHGR$ and recalculate PW. On the other hand, if PW is less than zero (it has changed sign), then the answer is bounded between the previous interest rate R_1 and the present interest rate R_2. In order to continue with the search, it is necessary to "go back" to the previous interest rate, which requires setting $R_1 = R_2 - CHGR$. Also, the rate of change of interest must be altered, so that $CHGR = CHGR/10$. The loop should then recycle for another calculation of a new interest rate R_2 and subsequent present worth PW. (It may be helpful to put this information in the form of a human-oriented flow diagram.)

A complete solution of the unknown interest rate problem is given in final form. Table 7-2 defines the terms used in the program RATE, the machine-oriented flow diagram is shown in Figure 7-5, the modified Nassi-Shneiderman chart is given in Figure 7-6, a listing of program RATE is given in Listing 7-3, and output is presented in Listing 7-4.

In summary, excluding the termination process, the basic procedure is as follows:

1. Define the initial rate (R_1).
2. Define the initial change of rate (CHGR) as 1 (percent).
3. Enter the loop.

4. At Statement 10, compute the new rate (called R_2) from the old rate (R_1) plus the change in rate (CHGR).
5. Compute the present worth, (PW), using the new rate (R_2).
6. Go forward if PW is positive by:
   (a) Placing R_2 (the newly computed rate) into R_1 (the "old" interest rate).
   (b) Cycling back to Statement 10.
   Go backward if PW is negative by:
   (a) Placing R_2 − CHGR (the newly computed rate minus the change in rate supplies the rate used to calculate the last positive PW) into R_1 (the "old" interest rate).
   (b) Changing CHGR (the change in interest rate) by a factor of ten.
   (c) Cycling back to Statement 10.

Should the sixth step above have an additional criteria for the case when PW is equal to zero? Why, or why not?

7-3.3 Control of the Looping Process

The looping process is controlled by values that are read in, that is, by input data. Control values are not built into the program directly.

The numerical value read into location ERR establishes the limit on PW. ERR states how close to zero the computed value of present worth (PW) must be for the answer to be "good enough." The value of ERR depends upon user requirements for any given problem.

The value read into location SIZER establishes the limit on how precisely the interest

---

Table 7-2 Definition Sheet for Program RATE

Program: RATE

Definition: Program RATE seeks the compound interest rate yielded by an investment that pays equal annual payments for a set number of years. Accuracy is prescribed both by present worth (PW) and interest rate.

Descriptive Items:

Variable Name	Symbol	Meaning
BEGINV		Initial investment (in dollars)
YCASHF		Yearly payment, uniform amount (in dollars)
YRS	*N*	Years for repayment
ERR		Establishes permissible error on PW in relation to zero
SIZER		Establishes permissible error on compound interest earned (%)
PR		Print Control PR>0 output during each cycle
R1		"Old" rate (set to 0 and incremented to 1 for first calculation)
R2		"New" rate used in calculations
CHGR		Change in rate used to adjust between R1 and R2
PW		Present Worth, solution obtained as PW approaches zero

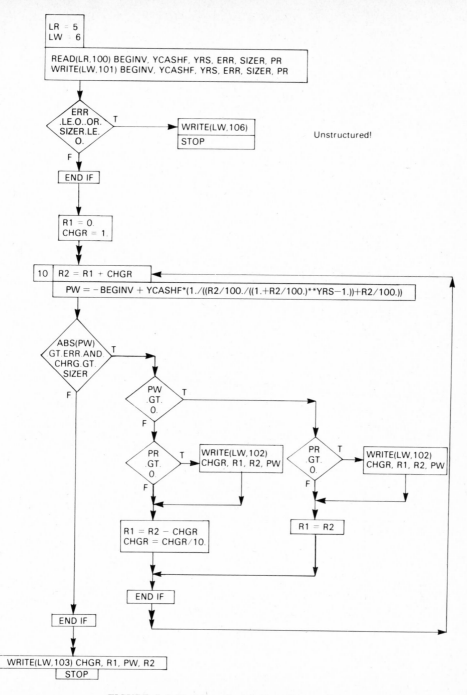

FIGURE 7-5 Machine-oriented flow diagram for program RATE

Program RATE

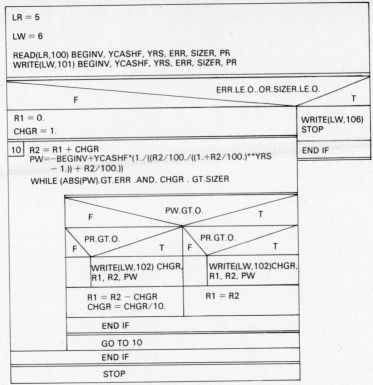

```
LR = 5

LW = 6

READ(LR,100) BEGINV, YCASHF, YRS, ERR, SIZER, PR
WRITE(LW,101) BEGINV, YCASHF, YRS, ERR, SIZER, PR
```

	ERR.LE.O..OR.SIZER.LE.O.
F	T

R1 = O. CHGR = 1.	WRITE(LW,106) STOP
10　R2 = R1 + CHGR PW=−BEGINV+YCASHF*(1./((R2/100./((1.+R2/100.)**YRS 　− 1.)) + R2/100.)) WHILE (ABS(PW).GT.ERR .AND. CHGR . GT.SIZER	END IF

	PW.GT.O.	
F		T
PR.GT.O.		PR.GT.O.	
F	T	F	T
WRITE(LW,102) CHGR, R1, R2, PW		WRITE(LW,102)CHGR, R1, R2, PW	
R1 = R2 − CHGR CHGR = CHGR/10.		R1 = R2	
END IF			
GO TO 10			
END IF			
STOP			

FIGURE 7-6 Modified Nassi-Shneiderman chart for program RATE

```
PROGRAM RATE

C        --- GIVEN: BEGINING INVESTMENT (BEGINV)
C        ---        RATE OF REPAYMENT (YCASHF,
C        ---          'YEARLY CASH FLOW')
C        ---        YEARS OF REPAYMENT (YRS)
C        --- FIND:  COMPOUND INTEREST RATE RECEIVED (R2);
C        ---        R1 IS PREVIOUS VALUE COMPUTED
C        ---        BY THE ITERATION PROCESS)
C        --- USE:   INTERATION PROCESS WITH CHANGE IN RATE
C        ---        BETWEEN R2 AND R1 CALLED CHGR
C        ---        ATTEMPTING TO GET PRESENT WORTH (PW) = 0
C        --- SUBJECT TO:
C        ---    (1) MINIMUM CHGR LIMITED BY SIZER
C        ---    (2) 'CLOSE TO ZERO' ESTABLISHED BY ERR
C        --- NOTE:  BOTH CONTROLS (SIZER,ERR) ARE READ
C        ---        AS INPUT VALUES (MUST BE GTR 0)
      LR=5
      LW=6
      READ(LR,100)BEGINV,YCASHF,YRS,ERR,SIZER,PR
      WRITE(LW,101)BEGINV,YCASHF,YRS,ERR,SIZER,PR

      IF(ERR.LE.O .OR. SIZER .LE. O.) THEN
         WRITE(LW,106)
  106    FORMAT(////' ERR AND SIZER MUST BE INPUT GREATER THAN O')
         STOP
      END IF
```

LISTING 7-3 Program RATE

170　　　　　　　　　　　　　　　　　　**Chapter 7 Synthesis and Examples**

```
C               --- SET INITIAL 'GUESS' OF INTEREST RATE (R1) TO 0
C               --- SET INITIAL INCREMENT ON INTEREST RATE TO 1
      R1=0.
      CHGR= 1.

C                  --- INCREMENT 'OLD' RATE (R1) BY CHGR
C                  ---      TO GET 'NEW' RATE (R2)
C                  --- THEN COMPUTE PRESENT WORTH(PW)
   10 R2= R1 + CHGR
      PW=-BEGINV+YCASHF*(1./((R2/100./((1.+R2/100.)**YRS-1.))+R2/100.))
C                  ---IF:(1)PRESENT WORTH(PW) CLOSE
C                  ---     ENOUGH TO 0 (ESTABLISHED BY ERR)
C                  --- OR (2)CHANGE IN STEP SIZE(CHGR)
C                  ---     EXCEEDS ALLOWABLE (SIZER)
C                  --- THEN: ANSWER OBTAINED, OUTPUT AND STOP
C                  --- OTHERWISE:ENTER BLOCK-IF
      IF(ABS(PW).GT.ERR .AND.CHGR .GT. SIZER) THEN

C                  --- IF PW REMAINS POSITIVE, CHANGE 'NEW'
C                  ---     RATE(R2) INTO 'OLD' RATE(R1) --AND--
C                  ---     GO BACK TO START OF LOOP
C                  --- OTHERWISE
C                  --- IF PW CHANGES SIGN, SET 'OLD' RATE(R1)
C                  ---     BACK TO LAST (+) VALUE --CHANGE.
C                  ---     STEP SIZE CHGR--AND LOOP AGAIN

         IF(PW .GT. 0.) THEN
            IF(PR.GT.0.)WRITE(LW,102)CHGR,R1,R2,PW
            R1=R2
         ELSE
            IF(PR.GT.0.)WRITE(LW,102)CHGR,R1,R2,PW
            R1=R2-CHGR
            CHGR= CHGR/10.
         END IF

         GO TO 10
      END IF

      WRITE(LW,103)CHGR,R1,PW,R2

  100 FORMAT( 6F8.0)
  101 FORMAT('1BEGINNING INVESTMENT = $',F10.2/
     1        '     YEARLY CASH FLOW = $',F10.2/
     2        '       PERIOD IN YEARS = ',F10.0/
     4        ' ERR IN PRESENT WORTH = $',F10.3,' MAXIMUM'/
     5        '     ERROR IN INTEREST = ',F10.6,' PERCENT MAXIMUM'/
     6        '         PRINT CONTROL = ',F10.1, ///)
  102 FORMAT(' CHG IN RATE=',F10.6,' RATE 1=',F6.3,/
     1        '          ',10X,  ' RATE 2=',F6.3,' PW 1= $',F10.2/)
  103 FORMAT('         CHANGE IN RATE = ',F10.6/
     1        ' RATE OF INTEREST # 1 = ',F10.6,'PERCENT'/
     2        '     PRESENT WORTH # 1 = $',F10.2//
     3        ' RATE OF INTEREST # 2 = ',F10.6,' PERCENT'/)

      STOP
      END
```

LISTING 7-3 *(continued)*

rate is to be computed. The magnitude of SIZER is also a function of user requirements.

An additional input value is print-control (PR), which determines whether intermediate values or only the final answer are to be output by the program. In normal use, the value of PR would be set to zero by simply leaving it blank and only important input values and final answers would print.

```
BEGINNING INVESTMENT = $     .........
     YEARLY CASH FLOW = $     2800.00
       PERIOD IN YEARS =         10.
ERR IN PRESENT WORTH = $      .001 MAXIMUM
    ERROR IN INTEREST =      .000100 PERCENT MAXIMUM
        PRINT CONTROL =         1.0

CHG IN RATE=  1.000000 RATE 1=  .000
                       RATE 2= 1.000 PW 1= $   11519.63

 ⌐ IN RATE=  1.000000 RATE 1= 1.000
                       RATE 2= 2.000 PW 1= $   10151.23

        ⌐E=  1.000000 RATE 1= 2.000
                       RATE 2= 3.000 PW 1= $    8884.56

CHG IN .        ↓    ⌐0000 RATE 1= 3.000
                       RATE 2= 4.000 PW 1= $    7710.50

CHG IN RATE=  .         TE 1:  ⌐00
                          2= ↓        PW 1= $    6620.86

CHG IN RATE=  1.000000      1=
                       RA   2=10.⌐               5608.24

CHG IN RATE=  1.000000 RATE 1=10.000
                       RATE 2=11.000 PW 1          ↓  03

CHG IN RATE=  1.000000 RATE 1=11.000
                       RATE 2=12.000 PW 1= $

CHG IN RATE=  1.000000 RATE 1=12.000
                       RATE 2=13.000 PW 1= $     193.48

CHG IN RATE=  1.000000 RATE 1=13.000
                       RATE 2=14.000 PW 1= $    -394.88

CHG IN RATE=  .100000 RATE 1=13.000
                      RATE 2=13.100 PW 1= $     132.95

CHG IN RATE=  .100000 RATE 1=13.100
                      RATE 2=13.200 PW 1= $      72.81

CHG IN RATE=  .100000 RATE 1=13.200
                      RATE 2=13.300 PW 1= $      13.04

CHG IN RATE=  .100000 RATE 1=13.300
                      RATE 2=13.400 PW 1= $     -46.34

CHG IN RATE=  .010000 RATE 1=13.300
                      RATE 2=13.310 PW 1= $       7.09

CHG IN RATE=  .010000 RATE 1=13.310
                      RATE 2=13.320 PW 1= $       1.14

CHG IN RATE=  .010000 RATE 1=13.320
                      RATE 2=13.330 PW 1= $      -4.81

CHG IN RATE=  .001000 RATE 1=13.320
                      RATE 2=13.321 PW 1= $        .54

CHG IN RATE=  .001000 RATE 1=13.321
                      RATE 2=13.322 PW 1= $       -.05

        CHANGE IN RATE =      .000100
RATE OF INTEREST # 1 =    13.321000PERCENT
    PRESENT WORTH # 1 = $        .48

RATE OF INTEREST # 2 =    13.321100 PERCENT
```

LISTING 7-4 Output from program RATE

7-3.4 Choosing Test Data by Book Examples

The example in this section was taken directly from an economics book, which has the advantage of saving time. Before using the example, however, the final result presented in the economics book was checked longhand by use of appropriate theory and without reference to the equations shown. Such precautions are necessary to detect typographical or other errors that do occur.

Using examples from books to test programs has two other serious pitfalls. First, book examples used to test programs may not thoroughly test the computer program because the examples are not sufficiently inclusive. Second, use of book examples in an attempt to bypass understanding a problem is almost certain to lead to serious programming errors and waste of time.

In summary, using examples from books to validate computer programs can often save a great deal of time, but only when the examples are well chosen, carefully checked, and provide generality sufficient to test the program completely.

7-4 PROGRAM CUES—SOLUTION FOR ROOTS BY ITERATION

The method of iteration for roots is a simple, direct technique for solving a number of complex problems involving roots of equations. (Iteration is also useful in a number of other contexts.) It is used quite often because of its mathematical simplicity and applicability to a large range of problems. The method of iteration has two drawbacks: it does not guarantee an answer, and only a single answer is produced even though there may be a number of correct answers to a problem. The method of iteration can be applied to finding roots to equations such as the following.

$$a\left(P + \frac{a}{v^2}\right)(v - b) - RT = 0 \quad \text{(for } v\text{)}$$

$$a\cos y + b\ln y - c \qquad = 0 \quad \text{(for } y\text{)}$$

$$ax^2 + be^{-x} - c \qquad = 0 \quad \text{(for } x\text{)}$$

$$ax - b\log_{10}x - c \qquad = 0 \quad \text{(for } x\text{)}$$

$$x^3 - 5x^2 - 16x + 80 \qquad = 0 \quad \text{(for } x\text{)}$$

The last equation in this list, the cubic equation, is chosen as the example for this section because of its mathematical simplicity.

7-4.1 The Iteration Process

The iteration process involves four general steps.

1. First, the equation is rearranged so that a single unknown appears on the left of the equal sign and the remainder of the equation appears to the right of the equal sign. For example, for the cubic equation

$$ax^3 + bx^2 + cx + d = 0$$

the general solution is:

$$x(ax^2 + bx + c) + d = 0$$

$$x = \frac{-d}{ax^2 + bx + c}$$

2. Once the formula has been arranged in the proper fashion, a value for x is "guessed." This guessed value of x is used to perform calculations on the right side of the equation and results in an answer that may or may not be the true value of x.
3. After the computation, a comparison is made to see how the computed value of x compares to the estimated (guessed) value of x. If the guessed value of x and the computed value of x are identical, the answer is correct. If the guessed value of x and the computed value of x are not the same, they may still be "close enough" for purposes of the user. If the guessed value of x does not produce an answer that is "close enough" to the resulting computed x, then the computed value of x is used on the right side of the equation to compute another "new" x.
4. The process of repeatedly using the computed "old" x to find a "new" x is an iteration process. This iteration process continues until the value used for x on the right side of the equation yields a result "close enough" to the guessed value of x for the purposes for which the answer is intended. On many occasions, and for various types of problems, the computed value of x will never be "close enough" to the value of x used to compute it. In such cases, the problem is said to diverge and no solution is possible. (See Section 7-4.2.)

Table 7–3 summarizes the iteration process for solution of the cubic equation using algebraic notation. Because the mathematical computations are carried out a number of times, the denominator is written in nested form to decrease the number of mathematical operations required.

To aid in the transition from the algebraic solution of Table 7–3, the steps are repeated in Table 7–4 using FORTRAN symbols. (Some insight into the convergence process is given in the following subsection.)

The definition sheet for program CUES is shown in Table 7–5, p. 176, and the coding is given in Listing 7–5. Before studying the coding, use the "start-in-the-middle" technique of the last section and develop an appropriate diagram or chart to formalize necessary programming steps. Now, compare your work to the coding of program CUES. Did you

---

Table 7-3 Algebraic Formulation for Cubic Equation by Iteration

$$ax^3 + bx^2 + cx + d = 0$$

$$ax^3 + bx^2 + cx = -d$$

$$x(ax^2 + bx + c) = -d$$

$$x = \frac{-d}{(ax^2 + bx + c)}$$

$$x = \frac{-d}{(x(ax + b) + c)}$$

Table 7-4 Iteration Procedure Using FORTRAN Symbols

XN = -D/(XO * (A * XO + B) + C)

X—New

X—Old

1. Try XO and compute XN.
2. XO $\doteq$ XN? YES → STOP
   NO ↓
3. Replace XO by XN and try again.

miss some important points? Is your algorithm better than the one used in this text? Remember, many correct ways are available for writing almost any program. Why do you think one might be better than another?

7-4.2 Convergence of the Iterative Process (Optional)

The expression *right of the equal sign* used for the iterative process is often expressed as $\phi(x)$. Thus, for this particular problem,

$$\phi(x) = \frac{-d}{ax^2 + bx + c} = \frac{-(-80)}{x^2 - 5x - 16}$$

and the derivative of $\phi(x)$ is expressed as

$$\phi'(x) = \frac{80(2x - 5)}{(x^2 - 5x - 16)^2} = \frac{160x - 400}{(x^2 - 5x - 16)^2}$$

If the absolute value of $\phi'(x)$ is less than one in the vicinity of a root, then convergence is guaranteed. If this criteria is not met, then the iteration process will diverge.

Page 178 shows the cubic equation used as an example in this subsection plotted to scale. Also shown is the curve representing the values of the first derivative of ϕ, $\phi'(x)$. From this, it can be seen that the method of iteration will yield only the answer $x = 4$. Iteration will not find the other two roots at $x = 5$ and at $x = -4$. The exercises suggest several values that could be used to investigate for rate of convergence or for divergence.

7-4.3 Controlling an Iteration Process

In general, the iteration process should be controlled by values read in as data. Two different controls are normally required: one to restrict the number of loops permitted and the other to terminate the run when the answer gets "close enough."

In this computer program, the variable CNTMAX is used to restrict the number of loops. It is compared in an IF statement to the counter CR, which is increased by one during each individual loop cycle of the program.

To see if the answer is "close enough," the absolute value of the "new" x minus the "old" x divided by the "new" x, all times 100, is compared with the input value stored in location ERR. This form uses percentage to compare the difference between the "old" and

Table 7-5 Definition Sheet for Program CUES

Program: CUES

Purpose: An iterative procedure is used to find (at most) one real root of the cubic equation $ax^3 + bx^2 + cx + d = 0$. (A good initial guess is desirable, but even then an answer is not assured.)

Descriptive Items:

	Variable Name	Symbol	Meaning
Input:	A	a	Coefficient of x^3
	B	b	Coefficient of x^2
	C	c	Coefficient of x
	D	d	Constant term
	XO	x	Trial guess, subsequently, latest machine generated guess; X-Old
	ERR		Percent ERRor permitted in answer
	CNTMAX		Maximum number of iterations permitted.
	PR		Print Control
Output:	XN	x	X-New; the location where each solution is stored; ultimately the final solution if one is obtained
	CR		Counts the number of iterations actually used.
Auxiliary:	LR		Logical Unit Number for READ
	LW		Logical Unit Number for WRITE

```
          PROGRAM CUES

C          PURPOSE: AN ITERATIVE PROCEDURE IS USED TO FIND(AT MOST)
C                   ONE REAL ROOT OF THE CUBIC EQUATION
C                   A * X**3 + B * X**2 + C * X + D = 0.
C                   (A GOOD INITIAL GUESS IS DESIRABLE, BUT EVEN
C                   THEN AN ANSWER IS NOT ASSURED.)

C          PARAMETERS:

C             VARIABLE NAME:      DEFINITION:

C             INPUT:    A          COEF. OF X ** 3
C                       B          COEF. OF X ** 2
C                       C          COEF. OF X
C                       D          CONSTANT TERM
C                       ERR        PERCENT ERROR PERMITTED IN ANS
C                       XO         TRIAL GUESS, SUBSEQUENTLY LATEST
C                                  MACHINE GENERATED GUESS; X-OLD
C                       CNTMAX     MAX NUMBER ITERATIONS PERMITTED
C                       PR         PRINT CONTROL

C             OUTPUT:   XN         X-NEW; LOCATION WHERE EACH SOLUTION
C                                  IS STORED--ULTIMATELY FINAL SOLUTION
C                                  IF ONE IS OBTAINED
C                       CR         COUNTS THE NUMBER OF ITERATIONS
C                                  ACTUALLY USED
```

LISTING 7-5 Program CUES with output and echoed input

```
C          AUXILARY:      LR          LOGICAL UNIT NUMBER FOR READ
C                         LW          LOGICAL UNIT NUMBER FOR WRITE

        LR=5
        LW=6

        CR=0.
        READ(LR,1000)A,B,C,D,ERR,XO,CNTMAX,PR

    20 XN= -D/(C +XO * (B + A * XO))
        CR=CR+1.
        IF(CR.LE.CNTMAX .AND. ABS((XN-XO)/XN)*100. .GT. ERR) THEN
            IF(PR.GT.0.)WRITE(LW,1003) CR,XO,XN
  1003     FORMAT(" COUNT=",F4.0," OLD X=",F10.4, " NEW-X=",F10.4)
            XO=XN
            GO TO 20
        END IF

        CR=CR-1.
        WRITE(LW,1001) A,B,C,D,ERR,CNTMAX,CR,XO,XN
  1001 FORMAT("1 COEFS OF A*X**3 + B*X**2 + C*X +D =0 ARE"/1X,
      14F12.4/" PERCENT ERROR PERMITTED IS", F8.4 /
      2" MAX LOOPS PERMITTED IS", F4.0/
      3" ACTUAL LOOPS USED WAS ", F4.0/
      4" PREVIOUS X WAS=",F10.4, " LAST X=",F10.4 )
  1000 FORMAT(10F8.0)

        STOP
        END
```

Output:

```
COUNT=  1. OLD X=      3.0000 NEW-X=      3.6364
COUNT=  2. OLD X=      3.6364 NEW-X=      3.8170
COUNT=  3. OLD X=      3.8170 NEW-X=      3.8995
COUNT=  4. OLD X=      3.8995 NEW-X=      3.9426
COUNT=  5. OLD X=      3.9426 NEW-X=      3.9665
COUNT=  6. OLD X=      3.9665 NEW-X=      3.9802
COUNT=  7. OLD X=      3.9802 NEW-X=      3.9882
COUNT=  8. OLD X=      3.9882 NEW-X=      3.9930

COEFS OF A*X**3 + B*X**2 + C*X +D =0 ARE
      1.0000      -5.0000     -16.0000      80.0000
PERCENT ERROR PERMITTED IS    .1000
MAX LOOPS PERMITTED IS 10.
ACTUAL LOOPS USED WAS    8.
PREVIOUS X WAS=    3.9930 LAST X=    3.9958
```

LISTING 7-5 *(continued)*

the "new" computed values of x. Percentage error is usually preferred rather than absolute error. For example, if an absolute error of 1 were established with XOLD of 1863974723 and XNEW computed as 1863974893, these answers are not "close enough." In fact, no adequate ("close enough") answer could be obtained because of the machine limitation of significant figures. By contrast, if XOLD of 0.000637 were used to compute XNEW of 0.013295, these answers would be "close enough" if criteria were established by an absolute error of 1. In both of these cases, the use of percent error appears to be highly preferable:

$$\left| \frac{1863974893 - 1863974723}{1863974893} \right| \times 100 = 9.12 \times 10^{-6}\%$$

$$\left| \frac{0.013295 - 0.000637}{0.013295} \right| \times 100 = 95.2\%$$

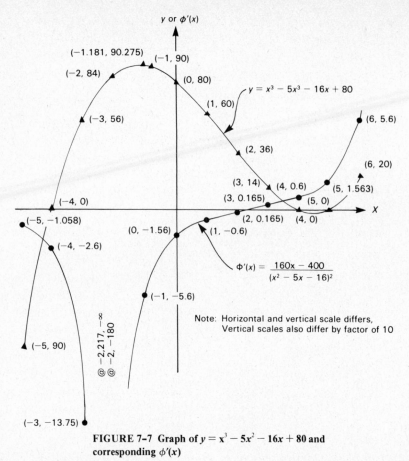

FIGURE 7-7 Graph of $y = x^3 - 5x^2 - 16x + 80$ **and corresponding** $\phi'(x)$

The percent error shows that the former is actually a very small difference, while the latter is a very large difference.

The question of what is "close enough" is difficult to answer in a general way. In specific cases, however, the user knows the sort of accuracy that is required. Since requiring more precision than necessary may increase run-time cost appreciably, it is desirable to have the "close enough" value used for comparison read in with data for each run.

7-4.4 Test Data

To test the cubic equation of program CUES, a "reverse" technique of the quadratic equation is also useful. The following are the necessary formulas.

$$-a_1 = x_1 + x_2 + x_3$$
$$+a_2 = x_1 x_2 + x_2 x_3 + x_3 x_1$$
$$-a_3 = x_1 x_2 x_3$$

In addition, it may be desirable to check if $|\phi'(x)| < 1$ in the neighborhood where an answer is anticipated. More often, however, it is easier (less costly in time and money) to simply try the iterative process rather than to check the derivative of $\phi(x)$.

Although an answer can be checked by back substituting into the original equation, this is not usually the best way to test a program for general validity. Do you see why?

7-5 PROGRAM CUBIC—ROOTS OF CUBIC EQUATION BY CARDAN'S METHOD (OPTIONAL)

This section introduces variables and constants of type complex, which provides a direct method for representing complex variables and constants.* Also, some indication of the unexpected complications that can occur in writing programs is illustrated. The advantage of program CUBIC is that all three roots are found for any cubic equation with real coefficients. The program is very simple and straightforward because of a convenient set of equations developed by Cardan.

7-5.1 Type Complex and the Cube Root

Use of type complex is similar in many respects to using either type real or type integer. There are three variations.

1. Complex variables must be declared either implicitly or explicitly (see Section 4-4) before the variables are used within a given program. Typically

   COMPLEX VAR
   IMPLICIT COMPLEX (C)

2. Complex constants are written in a special form. A complex constant occurs in a FORTRAN computer program written as two numerical values, separated by commas, and enclosed in parentheses. The first number represents the real part and the second number represents the imaginary part of a complex number. Thus (2, 3) stands for $2 + 3i$, and (6.23, -1.4) stands for $6.23 - 1.4i$.
3. Formats for complex variables and constants must always use two locations, because one position is necessary for the real part and one position is necessary for the imaginary part.

The three cube roots of the number 8 are shown in Table 7–6. These roots are shown to be correct by multiplication. In general, the three cube roots of a real number are expressed as follows (easily verified by comparing with results of Table 7–6).

$$\text{Principal root:} \quad R_1 = r$$

$$\text{Second root:} \quad R_2 = r\left(\frac{-1 + i\sqrt{3}}{2}\right)$$

$$\text{Third root:} \quad R_3 = r\left(\frac{-1 - i\sqrt{3}}{2}\right) \left.\right\} \text{complex conjugates}$$

Program TCCR of Listing 7–6 is a simple program that takes the cube roots of 8 and -8 by raising the numbers to the one-third power. In accordance with the ANSI Specification, the result of exponentiation is the principal value determined by

*A complex number has the general form $a + ib$ where a and b are real numbers and $i^2 = -1$.

$$X ** Y = EXP (Y * LOG (X))$$

Principal value is defined as: a result having a real part greater than or equal to zero—and if the real part is zero, the imaginary part must be greater than or equal to zero. Therefore, the cube root of $+8$ (see Table 7-6) has a principal value of $+2$. The three cube roots of -8 are -2, $+1+i\sqrt{3}$, $+1-i\sqrt{3}$, so that the principal value is output as $+1+i\sqrt{3}$ (rather than the -2 which you might have expected). Any complex result obtained when extracting the cube root can, however, be converted to the real root by multiplying the real part of the

---

Table 7-6 Cube Roots of 8

Principal	Complex conjugates	
2	$\dfrac{2(-1 - i\sqrt{3})}{2}$	$\dfrac{2(-1 + i\sqrt{3})}{2}$
	$= -1 - i\sqrt{3}$	$= -1 + i\sqrt{3}$
	$\doteq -1 - 1.732i$	$\doteq -1 + 1.732i$

Check:

$$2 \times 2 \times 2 = 8$$

$$
\begin{array}{r}
-1 - i\sqrt{3} \\
\times \underline{-1 - i\sqrt{3}} \\
1 + i\sqrt{3} \\
\underline{i\sqrt{3} + 3i^2} \\
1 + 2i\sqrt{3} - 3
\end{array}
$$

$$
\text{or}
\begin{array}{r}
-2 + 2i\sqrt{3} \\
\times \underline{-1 - i\sqrt{3}} \\
2 - 2i\sqrt{3} \\
\underline{2i\sqrt{3} - 2i^2(3)} \\
2 \qquad + 6 = 8
\end{array}
$$

```
      PROGRAM TCCR
      IMPLICIT COMPLEX(A-D)

C           --- STORE + AND - 8
      A=-8.
      B=8.

C           --- TAKE CUBE ROOTS
      C=A**(1./3.)
      D=B**(1./3.)

C           --- OUTPUT RESULTS
      PRINT *,A,B
      PRINT *,C,D
      STOP
      END
```

Output:

```
(-8.0000000   ,  .00000000  ) ( 8.0000000   ,  .00000000   )
( 1.0000000   , 1.7320508   ) ( 2.0000000   ,  .00000000   )
```

LISTING 7-6 Program TCCR with output

Chapter 7 Synthesis and Examples

complex result by -2 and setting the imaginary part of the complex result to zero. Using the latter procedure, the complex result $+1+i\sqrt{3}$ converts to the real result -2.

7-5.2 Two Subroutines for Cube Root

Listing 7–7 shows a small program that uses two different subroutines (Listings 7–8 and 7–9) to obtain real cube roots using complex exponentiation to the one-third power. This program shows that the same results can be obtained by two different methods that entail considerable difference in programming effort. Also note that the names of the arguments in the calls within the program do not necessarily match the names as they are defined in the subroutine statements. Variables in these argument lists must, however, agree in meaning and in type in a one-to-one relationship.

```
      PROGRAM TESTCR
      IMPLICIT COMPLEX (R,V)
C            --- CUBE ROOTS OF TYPE COMPLEX V FOUND:
C                  (1)  R BY SUBROUTINE CUBERT
C                  (2)  RR BY SUBROUTINE CBROOT

      LR=5

10 READ(LR,*,END=30) V
      CALL CUBERT(R,V)
      CALL CBROOT(RR,V)
      PRINT *,'INPUT VALVE=',V,'  CUBE ROOT=',R, RR
      GO TO 10

30 STOP
   END
```

LISTING 7-7 Program TESTCR

```
      SUBROUTINE CUBERT(R,V)
C     **** PRINCIPAL CUBE ROOT OF COMPLEX
C     **** -OR- REAL ROOT IF IMAGINARY PART OF RADICAL IS 0
      IMPLICIT  COMPLEX (R,V)

      P=1./3.

C     **** IF IMAG PART EXISTS, TAKE ROOT
      IF(AIMAG(V).NE.0.)THEN
         R= V**P
      ELSE
C     **** WORK WITH REAL ONLY
         T= REAL(V)
         IF(T.GT.0.) THEN
            T = T**P
         ELSE IF(T.LT.0.) THEN
            T =-((-T)**P)
         ELSE
            T= 0.
         END IF

         R=T
      END IF

      RETURN
      END
```

LISTING 7-8 Subroutine CUBERT

```
    SUBROUTINE CBROOT(R,V)
C   *** RETURNS PRINCIPAL ROOT OF COMPLEX NUMBER
C   *** --EXCEPT--  IF IMAGINARY PART OF COMPLEX
C                   NUMBER IS 0, RETURNS REAL ANSWER

    IMPLICIT COMPLEX (R,V)
    R= V**(1./3.)
    IF(AIMAG(V).EQ.0..AND.REAL(V).LT.0.)R=-2.*REAL(R)
    RETURN
    END
```

LISTING 7-9 Subroutine CBROOT

7-5.3 Cardan Solution of the Cubic Equation

The basic formulas for the Cardan solution to the cubic equation $x^3 + a_1x^2 + a_2x + a_3 = 0$ are summarized using a very convenient series of intermediate formulas to simplify the computational process.

$$Q = \frac{3a_2 - a_1{}^2}{9}$$

$$R = \frac{9a_1a_2 - 27a_3 - 2a_1{}^3}{54}$$

$$SQ = Q^3 + R^2$$

$$SR = \sqrt{SQ} = \sqrt{Q^3 + R^2}$$

$$S = (R + SR)^{1/3}$$

$$T = (R - SR)^{1/3}$$

$$x_1 = \frac{S + T - a_1}{3}$$

$$x_2 = -\frac{S + T}{2} - \frac{a_1}{3} - \frac{\sqrt{-3}\,(S - T)}{2}$$

$$x_3 = -\frac{S + T}{2} - \frac{a_1}{3} + \frac{\sqrt{-3}\,(S - T)}{2}$$

The preceding set of equations is coded into the program of Listing 7-10 and typical results are shown in Listing 7-11 for a representative set of cubic equations. (See pages 184 and 185.)

7-6 EXERCISES

1. Modify program SIMLR of Listing 7-1 so that it prints out a table similar to that shown in Table 7-1. Verify your program by running a reasonable set of data.

2. Delete the IF statement from program SIMLR of Listing 7-1 and add END = 40 to the appropriate control information list. Be sure to establish a proper statement labeled 40.

3. Prepare a definition sheet for program SIMLR of Listing 7-1.

4. Prepare a machine-oriented flow diagram and human-oriented flow diagram for program SIMLR of Listing 7–1.

5. Prepare a modified Nassi-Shneiderman chart for program SIMLR of Listing 7–1.

6. Make a definition sheet for program QUAD of Listing 7–2.

7. Rewrite program QUAD of Listing 7–2 using type Complex as shown in Section 7–5. Caution: The computer can take $\sqrt{(-1., 0)}$ but not $\sqrt{-1.}$.

8. Make program QUAD into a subroutine by doing each of the following.
   (a) Changing the first statement from a PROGRAM statement to a SUBROUTINE statement.
   (b) Deleting LR = 5 and the corresponding READ statements.
   (c) Deleting LW = 6 and the WRITE statements, or precede all WRITE statements by IF (PR.GT..0), with PR placed in the argument list of the subroutine.
   (d) Changing STOP to RETURN.
   In addition, write a test program that reads the three coefficients (a, b, and c), calls the subroutine with an argument list (A, B, C, X, Y, Z, PR), and outputs the results.

9. Prepare a more suitable ending for program RATE of Listing 7–3. (See the output of Listing 7–4 to see what improvements are needed.)

10. Modify program RATE of Listing 7–3 so that
    (a) it starts with zero percent interest;
    (b) it starts with a preset minimum interest; or
    (c) so that it solves several sets of problems.

11. Will program RATE of Listing 7–3 actually find the interest rate if the correct answer is 6.003%?

12. Find the values of x that make y zero (that is, the roots) from a formula such as $y = ax^3 + bx^2 + cx + d$ by a method similar to that used in Listing 7–3. Note there are four main differences between this exercise and program RATE of Listing 7–3:
    (a) The step size should change when the sign changes, not just from plus to minus but also from minus to plus.
    (b) Once a root is found, the process must continue to search for the next root.
    (c) It is possible to miss a root if the step size is too large; that is, the search may "step" over an answer if roots are very close together.
    (d) The program needs to have the beginning, ending points, and step size for the search read as input data.
    A search of this sort is typically called *Regula-Falsi*.

13. Run program CUES of Listing 7–5 with the following values of x.
    (a) 1.   (b) 2.7   (c) 3.8   (d) 4.57   (e) 4.53
    (f) 5.05   (g) −3.98   (h) −4.02   (i) −6.   (j) −2.21

14. Write a program using the Regula-Falsi method (see Exercise 12) to solve one of the equations shown in the first paragraph of Section 7–4.

15. Change program CUES of Listing 7–5 to
    (a) add flexibility so that different "guesses" can be used for the same formula;
    (b) add flexibility to accommodate more sets of a, b, c, and d coefficients; or
    (c) add flexibility by providing for more sets of coefficients of a, b, c, and d with more than one guess per set of coefficients.

16. Prepare a Nassi-Shneiderman chart for program CUBIC of Listing 7–10.

17. Prepare a definition sheet for program CUBIC of Listing 7–10.

18. Prepare a machine-oriented flow diagram for program CUBIC of Listing 7–10.

19. Study the examples from program CUBIC shown in Listing 7–10 to see if all program paths have been adequately tested. Suggest any other cases that should be tried to insure program generality.

20. In program CUBIC of Listing 7–10, does the solution still work if the coefficient *a* is zero? If not, would it be useful to add the subroutine QUAD? How would this be done?

21. Change program CUBIC of Listing 7–10 into a subroutine by changing the PROGRAM statement to a SUBROUTINE statement. Delete the READS, add print-control to the WRITE (or delete the WRITE), and change the STOP to a RETURN.

```
      PROGRAM CUBIC

C              --- SOLVE FOR 3 ROOTS OF X FROM
C                  X**3 + A1*X**2 + A2*X + A3 = 0

      IMPLICIT COMPLEX (X,S,T)

      LR=5
      LW=6

   10 READ(LR,1000) A1,A2,A3
      IF(A1.NE.9999.99) THEN

C              --- COMPUTE TYPE REAL Q, R, AND QR
      Q =(3.*A2 - A1**2)/9.
      R =(9.*A1*A2 -27.*A3 -2.*A1**3)/54.
      QR= Q**3 + R**2

C              --- CHANGE TYPE QR(REAL) TO SR(COMPLEX)
C                  TAKE SQUARE ROOT OF + OR - VALUE
      SQ= QR
      SQ= SQRT(SQ)

C              --- COMBINE R(REAL) AND SR(COMPLEX)
C                  TO GET COMPLEX S1 AND T1
      S1= R + SQ
      T1= R - SQ

C              --- TAKE CUBE ROOTS OF S1 AND T1
C                  USING SUBROUTINE CBROOT
      CALL CBROOT(S,S1)
      CALL CBROOT(T,T1)

C              --- COMPUTE THREE ROOTS OF EQUATION
C                  AND OUTPUT EQUATION, INTERMEDIATE
C                  RESULTS AND SOLUTIONS
      X1= S + T -A1/3.
      X2= -(S+T)/2. -A1/3. +(0.,1.)/2.*SQRT(3.)*(S-T)
      X3= -(S+T)/2. -A1/3. -(0.,1.)/2.*SQRT(3.)*(S-T)
      WRITE(LW,1001)A1,A2,A3,Q,R,QR,SQ,S,T,X1,X2,X3

C              --- LOOP BACK FOR ANOTHER SET OF
C                  COEFFICIENTS FOR ANOTHER SOLUTION
      GO TO 10
      END IF

 1000 FORMAT(3F8.0)
 1001 FORMAT(//' X**3 +(',F10.2,')*X**2 +(',F10.2,')*X +(',F10.2,') = 0'
     1/' Q=',F10.3,'  R=',F10.3,'   QR=',F10.3/
     2' SQ=',2F10.3,'  S=',2F10.3,'  T=',2F10.3/
     3' X1=',2F10.3,'  X2=',2F10.3,'  X3=',2F10.3/)

      STOP
      END
```

LISTING 7–10 Program CUBIC (calls subroutine CBROOT of Listing 7–9)

```
x**3 +(     -6.00)*x**2 +(     11.00)*x +(     -6.00) = 0
Q=    -.333  R=     .000  QR=    -.037
SQ=    .000     .192  S=    .500     .289  T=    .500    -.289
x1=   3.000     .000 x2=   1.000     .000 x3=   2.000     .000


x**3 +(      2.00)*x**2 +(     -5.00)*x +(     -6.00) = 0
Q=   -2.111  R=    1.037  QR=   -8.333
SQ=    .000    2.287  S=   1.333     .577  T=   1.333    -.577
x1=   2.000     .000 x2=  -3.000     .000 x3=  -1.000     .000


x**3 +(     -4.00)*x**2 +(      9.00)*x +(    -36.00) = 0
Q=    1.222  R=   14.370  QR=  208.333
SQ=  14.434     .000  S=   3.065     .000  T=   -.399     .000
x1=   4.000     .000 x2=     .000   3.000 x3=     .000  -3.000


x**3 +(     -7.00)*x**2 +(     17.00)*x +(    -15.00) = 0
Q=     .222  R=     .370  QR=     .148
SQ=    .385     .000  S=    .911     .000  T=   -.244     .000
x1=   3.000     .000 x2=   2.000   1.000 x3=   2.000  -1.000


x**3 +(     -8.00)*x**2 +(     21.00)*x +(    -18.00) = 0
Q=    -.111  R=    -.037  QR=     .000
SQ=    .000     .000  S=    .167     .289  T=    .167    -.289
x1=   3.000     .000 x2=   2.000     .000 x3=   3.000     .000


x**3 +(     -6.00)*x**2 +(     12.00)*x +(     -8.00) = 0
Q=     .000  R=     .000  QR=     .000
SQ=    .000     .000  S=    .000     .000  T=    .000     .000
x1=   2.000     .000 x2=   2.000     .000 x3=   2.000     .000


x**3 +(      6.00)*x**2 +(     12.00)*x +(      8.00) = 0
Q=     .000  R=     .000  QR=     .000
SQ=    .000     .000  S=    .000     .000  T=    .000     .000
x1=  -2.000     .000 x2=  -2.000     .000 x3=  -2.000     .000


x**3 +(      4.00)*x**2 +(     -3.00)*x +(    -18.00) = 0
Q=   -2.778  R=    4.630  QR=     .000
SQ=    .000     .000  S=   1.667     .000  T=   1.667     .000
x1=   2.000     .000 x2=  -3.000     .000 x3=  -3.000     .000


x**3 +(      .00)*x**2 +(     -1.00)*x +(       .00) = 0
Q=    -.333  R=     .000  QR=    -.037
SQ=    .000     .192  S=    .500     .289  T=    .500    -.289
x1=   1.000     .000 x2=  -1.000     .000 x3=     .000     .000


x**3 +(      .00)*x**2 +(      .00)*x +(    -27.00) = 0
Q=     .000  R=   13.500  QR=  182.250
SQ=  13.500     .000  S=   3.000     .000  T=    .000     .000
x1=   3.000     .000 x2=  -1.500   2.598 x3=  -1.500  -2.598


x**3 +(      3.00)*x**2 +(      .00)*x +(       .00) = 0
Q=   -1.000  R=   -1.000  QR=     .000
SQ=    .000     .000  S=  -1.000     .000  T=  -1.000     .000
x1=  -3.000     .000 x2=     .000     .000 x3=     .000     .000


x**3 +(      2.00)*x**2 +(     -3.00)*x +(       .00) = 0
Q=   -1.444  R=   -1.296  QR=   -1.333
SQ=    .000    1.155  S=    .833     .866  T=    .833    -.866
x1=   1.000     .000 x2=  -3.000     .000 x3=     .000     .000


x**3 +(      .00)*x**2 +(      2.00)*x +(     -3.00) = 0
Q=     .667  R=    1.500  QR=    2.546
SQ=   1.596     .000  S=   1.457     .000  T=   -.457     .000
x1=   1.000     .000 x2=   -.500   1.658 x3=   -.500  -1.658
```

LISTING 7-11 Output of three roots of cubic equation from program CUBIC

Chapter **8**

Program Looping
With DO-Loops

Since Chapter 2, you have been seeing and using loops. In this chapter, a more convenient form is introduced which combines built-in initialization, comparison (as if by a built-in IF statement), and incrementation.

8-1 INTRODUCTION TO THE DO-LOOP

To help you become more proficient in their use, DO-loops are developed in four simple steps within this section.

8-1.1 DO-Loop Represented by Human-Oriented Flow Diagrams

The human-oriented flow diagram for DO-loops may be expressed in several ways; common forms are illustrated in Figure 8-1. Double arrowheads delineate the beginning and ending of each DO-loop mini-module. A hexagonal box is used to indicate the controls for the DO-loop, and sometimes for the loop itself. The line along the left edge of the figure represents the "main line" of the program.

8-1.2 DO-Loop Represented by Machine-Oriented Flow Diagram

Figure 8-2 illustrates the logic of a DO-loop in two ways. The hexagonal box indicates the following. (Page 188)

1. Entrance into the top of the hexagonal box produces initialization.
2. The middle statement is a built-in IF statement. Flow is to the right (activating a loop cycle) when the comparison is false and to the left (leaving the mini-module) when the IF statement is true.
3. After calculations are performed within any loop cycle, re-entrance is at the bottom of the hexagonal box. Incrementation takes place there before another comparison can occur.

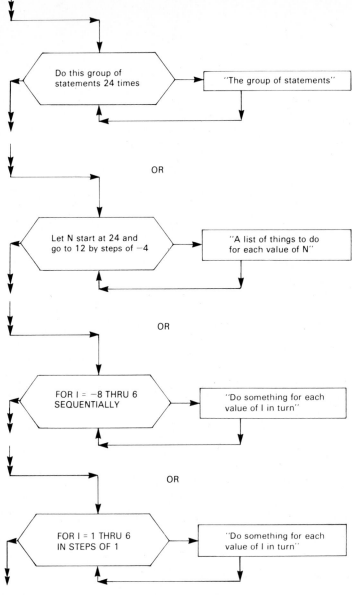

FIGURE 8-1 Some typical human-oriented flow
diagrams for DO-loops

4. After incrementation, the built-in IF statement is reactivated to determine whether the loop is to be executed again or the mini-module is to be exited.

In the second part of Figure 8–2, FORTRAN coding (showing the loop indices NB, NE, and NS) is linked directly to the machine-oriented flow diagram. Flow into the top of the hexagonal box initializes I to the value stored in NB. This value of I is compared with

NE to determine whether the first loop cycle is to be performed or the DO is to be exited without ever activating the loop cycle. If the first loop cycle is performed, flow returns to the bottom of the hexagonal box where I is incremented by the value stored in NS. Flow then returns to the built-in IF statement to decide if another loop cycle is to be performed, or the DO-loop exited.

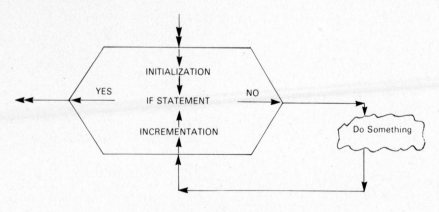

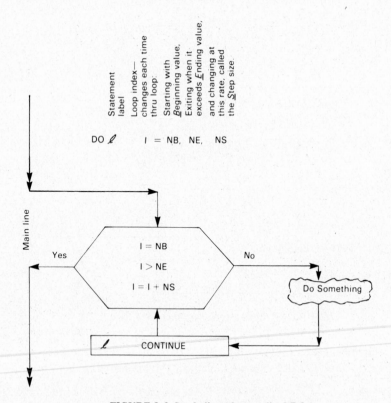

FIGURE 8–2 Symbolic and generalized DO-loop

8-1.3 DO-Loop Coding and Restrictions

More detailed descriptions of rules for the FORTRAN formulation of a DO statement for Subset FORTRAN 77 are shown in Table 8-1. Extensions permitted by Full Language FORTRAN 77 are presented in Section 16-1.3.

The word DO is always used to specify the start of a DO-loop.* DO is followed by a fixed-point constant that specifies the label of the last statement within the loop—preferably a CONTINUE statement. Legally, the terminal statement for a DO-loop can be almost any executable statement, except another DO, GO TO, IF statement of any kind (except a logical IF), RETURN, STOP, or END. To maintain consistency and to preclude difficulties that can be caused by use of these "legal" statements, it is strongly recommended that DO-loops terminate with a labeled CONTINUE statement.

The statement label in the DO is followed by a nonsubscripted, integer variable (called the DO-variable) which is used as the loop index (counter or incrementer). Although not required, the value of the loop index may be used within the loop. The loop

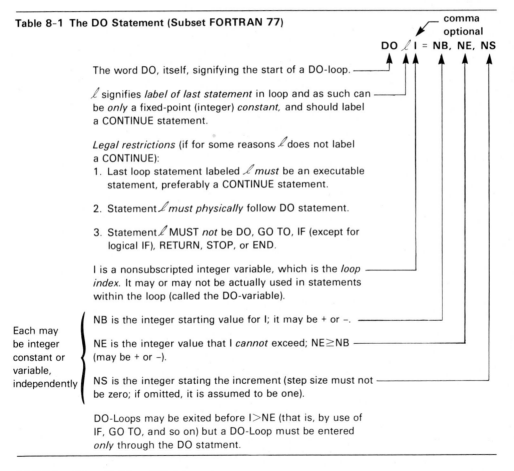

Table 8-1 The DO Statement (Subset FORTRAN 77)

comma optional

$$DO \; \ell \; I = NB, NE, NS$$

The word DO, itself, signifying the start of a DO-loop.

ℓ signifies *label of last statement* in loop and as such can be *only* a fixed-point (integer) *constant,* and should label a CONTINUE statement.

Legal restrictions (if for some reasons ℓ does not label a CONTINUE):
1. Last loop statement labeled ℓ *must* be an executable statement, preferably a CONTINUE statement.

2. Statement ℓ *must physically* follow DO statement.

3. Statement ℓ MUST *not* be DO, GO TO, IF (except for logical IF), RETURN, STOP, or END.

I is a nonsubscripted integer variable, which is the *loop index.* It may or may not be actually used in statements within the loop (called the DO-variable).

NB is the integer starting value for I; it may be + or –.

Each may be integer constant or variable, independently

NE is the integer value that I *cannot* exceed; NE≥NB (may be + or –).

NS is the integer stating the increment (step size must not be zero; if omitted, it is assumed to be one).

DO-Loops may be exited before I>NE (that is, by use of IF, GO TO, and so on) but a DO-Loop must be entered *only* through the DO statment.

*A DO-loop is specified by a DO statement

index retains its last defined value on exit from the loop; its value cannot be changed by any statements within the loop.

The loop index is followed by an equals sign which, in turn, is followed by three positive or negative integer variables or constants, separated by commas. The first of these integers indicates the starting value for the loop index; that is, it performs initialization. The second represents an integer value that places a limit on the loop index used by the built-in IF to make comparisons. The last integer constant, or variable, specifies the step size used for incrementation; if not specified, a *default* value of 1 is used.

Because the loop indices may be either positive or negative, a criterion is established by FORTRAN 77 to determine the number of loops to be performed. Looping criteria can be explained from equations involving the loop indices of a typical DO-loop form such as

$$DO \quad 10 \quad I = IB, IE, IS$$

The number of cycles is determined from the loop indices and is the maximum of either $(IE - IB + IS)/IS$ or zero. Thus if the quantity $(IE - IB + IS)/IS$ is negative, no loops are executed.

8-1.4 DO-Loop Represented by Modified Nassi-Shneiderman Chart

In languages where the DO-WHILE is incorporated as a statement, the DO-loop may be included as a special form. The modified Nassi-Shneiderman chart resembles a DO-WHILE, but it does not represent the flow as clearly as a machine-oriented flow diagram. Once the DO-loop is understood, however, the modified Nassi-Shneiderman (Figure 8-3) provides an important tool.

8-2 DO-LOOP EXAMPLES

A representative set of human-oriented flow diagrams, machine-oriented flow diagrams, modified Nassi-Shneiderman charts, and coding for several typical DO-loops are shown in this section.

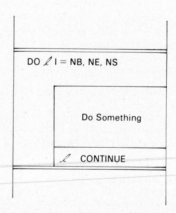

FIGURE 8-3 Generalized DO-loop, modified Nassi-Shneiderman chart

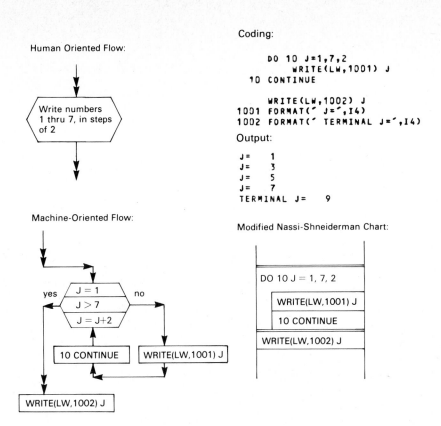

FIGURE 8-4 Loop index used within DO-loop

8-2.1 DO-Loop Using Counter Within The Loop

In Figure 8-4 the counter (loop index or incrementer) is used in a loop that writes numbers from 1 through 7 in steps of 2. Note that the terminal value of J is 9, not 7; the DO-loop executes until the counter *exceeds* the maximum value.

8-2.2 DO-Loop With Counter Not Used in Loop

In Figure 8-5, the number of cards to be read (N) is the first value input. The counter (I) is not used within the DO-loop. Note that the step size is automatically set at 1 because it was left undefined. Upon exiting the DO-loop, the value of I is one greater than N.

8-2.3 Counting, Summing, and Accumulative Multiplication

In Figure 8-6, a simple DO-loop is used to count, accumulate the sum of, and accumulate the product of a series of numbers between 16 and 54, taken in steps of 8. The variable names used for counting and for accumulating the sum are initialized at zero. The variable name used for accumulating products, however, is initialized to 1; otherwise, the resulting product would always be zero. The last value of K used within the loop is 48 because adding 8 to 48 gives 56, which becomes the terminal value of the loop index as it exceeds the limit of 54.

Human-Oriented Flow Diagram:

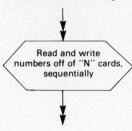

Coding:

```
      READ(LR,1003) N
      DO 20 I=1,N
          READ(LR,1003) JK
          WRITE(LW,1004) JK
  20  CONTINUE

      WRITE(LW,1005) N,I
1003  FORMAT(I4)
1004  FORMAT(' JK=',I4)
1005  FORMAT(' INITIAL N=',I4/
     1'  TERMINAL I=', I4)
```

Output:

```
JK=   17
JK=    6
JK=   -3
JK=   99
INITIAL N=   4
 TERMINAL I=   5
```

Machine-Oriented Flow Diagram:

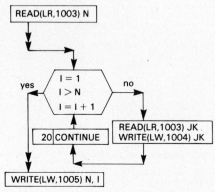

Modified Nassi-Shneiderman Chart:

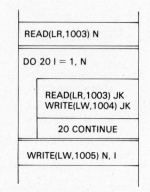

FIGURE 8–5 Sequential DO-loop, counter not used within loop

8–2.4 Obtaining Special Sequences

In certain applications, the sequence $2i - 1$ and $2i$ must be obtained from an i that is incremented by ones. Listings of page 194 show several such examples.

Listing 8–1 shows a technique that yields 1 and 2 for 1, 3 and 4 for 2, 5 and 6 for 3, and so on. Several exercises at the end of this chapter deal with problems of this general type.

The Fibonacci series begins with 0 and 1. Each subsequent term is obtained by adding the two previous terms. Thus, the Fibonacci series is 0, 1, 1, 2, 3, 5, 8, ... Listing 8–2 produces a Fibonacci series by use of a DO-loop. Can you do the same thing with one less variable?

Listing 8–3 produces part of Table 7–1 by using a DO-loop to replace a large segment of program SIMLR of Listing 7–1. Are necessary comment statements missing from this program segment? What are they?

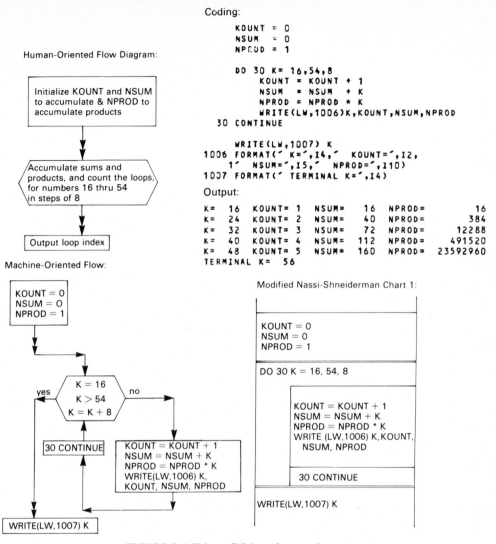

Coding:

```
         KOUNT = 0
         NSUM = 0
         NPROD = 1

         DO 30 K= 16,54,8
             KOUNT = KOUNT + 1
             NSUM  = NSUM  + K
             NPROD = NPROD * K
             WRITE(LW,1006)K,KOUNT,NSUM,NPROD
      30 CONTINUE

         WRITE(LW,1007) K
    1006 FORMAT(' K=',I4,'   KOUNT=',I2,
         1' NSUM=',I5,' NPROD=',I10)
    1007 FORMAT(' TERMINAL K=',I4)
```

Human-Oriented Flow Diagram:

Initialize KOUNT and NSUM to accumulate & NPROD to accumulate products

Accumulate sums and products, and count the loops, for numbers 16 thru 54 in steps of 8

Output loop index

Machine-Oriented Flow:

```
KOUNT = 0
NSUM = 0
NPROD = 1
```

```
K = 16
K > 54
K = K + 8
```
yes   no

```
30 CONTINUE
```

```
KOUNT = KOUNT + 1
NSUM = NSUM + K
NPROD = NPROD * K
WRITE(LW,1006) K,
KOUNT, NSUM, NPROD
```

```
WRITE(LW,1007) K
```

Output:

```
K=   16  KOUNT= 1  NSUM=    16  NPROD=          16
K=   24  KOUNT= 2  NSUM=    40  NPROD=         384
K=   32  KOUNT= 3  NSUM=    72  NPROD=       12288
K=   40  KOUNT= 4  NSUM=   112  NPROD=      491520
K=   48  KOUNT= 5  NSUM=   160  NPROD=    23592960
TERMINAL K=  56
```

Modified Nassi-Shneiderman Chart 1:

```
KOUNT = 0
NSUM = 0
NPROD = 1
```

```
DO 30 K = 16, 54, 8
```

```
KOUNT = KOUNT + 1
NSUM = NSUM + K
NPROD = NPROD * K
WRITE (LW,1006) K,KOUNT,
   NSUM, NPROD
```

```
30 CONTINUE
```

```
WRITE(LW,1007) K
```

FIGURE 8-6 Using a DO-loop for counting, summing, and accumulative multiplication

8-2.5 "Artificial" Type Real Loop Indices

In this subsection, a loop is developed that begins, ends, and is incremented by type real variables, any or all of which may be fractional and positive or negative. Listing 8-4 shows two possible methods that satisfy these criteria. (Full Language FORTRAN allows real indices and "artificial" indices are not required.) See page 195.

In one method, the terminal loop index N is calculated by computing "the difference between actual real ending and beginning sizes (END-BEG), dividing by "the step size

```
      WRITE(LW,9000)
9000 FORMAT(5X,'1I',4X,'2I-1',4X,'2I'/)

      DO 110 I=1,5
         K=2* I
         J=K- 1
         WRITE(LW,1016)I,J,K
  110 CONTINUE

      WRITE(LW,1017) I
1016 FORMAT(' I=',I3,' J=',I3,' K=',I3)
1017 FORMAT(' TERMINAL I=',I4)
```

Output:

```
         1I     2I-1     2I

I=   1  J=   1  K=   2
I=   2  J=   3  K=   4
I=   3  J=   5  K=   6
I=   4  J=   7  K=   8
I=   5  J=   9  K=  10
TERMINAL I=    6
```

LISTING 8-1 Special series

```
      I=0
      WRITE(LW,1018) 1,I
      J=1
      WRITE(LW,1018) 2,J

      DO 120 L=1,8
         K=I+J
      WRITE(LW,1018) L+2,K
         I=J
         J=K
  120 CONTINUE

1018 FORMAT(' FIBONACCI TERM NUMBER',I2,' =',I3)
```

Output:

```
FIBONACCI TERM NUMBER 1 =   0
FIBONACCI TERM NUMBER 2 =   1
FIBONACCI TERM NUMBER 3 =   1
FIBONACCI TERM NUMBER 4 =   2
FIBONACCI TERM NUMBER 5 =   3
FIBONACCI TERM NUMBER 6 =   5
FIBONACCI TERM NUMBER 7 =   8
FIBONACCI TERM NUMBER 8 = 13
FIBONACCI TERM NUMBER 9 = 21
FIBONACCI TERM NUMBER10 = 34
```

LISTING 8-2 Fibonacci series

```
      SUMX2= 0.
      SUMXY= 0.
      SUMY = 0.
      SUMX = 0.
      WRITE(LW,1019)

      DO 140 I=1,8
         READ(LR,1020) X,Y
         X2   = X**2
         XY   = X*Y
         SUMX2= SUMX2 + X2
         SUMXY= SUMXY + XY
         SUMY = SUMY  + Y
         SUMX = SUMX  + X
         WRITE(LW,1021)X,Y,X2,XY
  140 CONTINUE

      WRITE(LW,1022)SUMX,SUMY,SUMX2,SUMXY
1019 FORMAT(9X,'X',5X,'Y',4X,'X SQD',4X,'X*Y'/)
1020 FORMAT(10F8.0)
1021 FORMAT(F11.1,F6.1,2F8.2)
1022 FORMAT(/' SUMS=',F5.1,F6.1,2F8.2)
```

Output:

```
         X      Y    X SQD    X*Y

        .0    2.0     .00     .00
       2.0    8.0    4.00   16.00
       6.0   20.0   36.00  120.00
       1.2    5.6    1.44    6.72
      -3.1   -7.3    9.61   22.63
       4.0   14.0   16.00   56.00
       7.0   23.0   49.00  161.00
      -8.0  -22.0   64.00  176.00

SUMS=  9.1   43.3  180.05  558.35
```

LISTING 8-3 Table 7-1 using DO-Loop

```
          DO 100 I=1,6
C                              --- READ AND OUTPUT TYPE
C                                  REAL LOOP INDICES
          READ(LR,1012) BEG,END,STEP
          WRITE(LW,1013)I, BEG,END,STEP

C                              --- INITIALIZE, METHOD 1
          N=(END-BEG)/STEP +1.001

C                              --- INITIALIZE, METHOD 2
          B=BEG-STEP

          DO 90 J=1,N

C                              --- INCREMENT, METHOD 1
             A= J-1
             A= BEG+STEP*A

C                              --- INCREMENT, METHOD 2
             B= B+ STEP

C                              --- OUTPUT BOTH VALUES
C                                  FOR COMPARISON
             WRITE(LW,1014) J,A,B
   90        CONTINUE

             WRITE(LW,1015) J
  100 CONTINUE

 1012 FORMAT(3F8.0)
 1013 FORMAT(/' I=',I3,'   BEG=',F5.1,
     1' END=',F5.1,'  STEP=',F5.1/)
 1014 FORMAT(' J=',I4,'  A=',F6.1,'  B=',F6.1)
 1015 FORMAT(' TERMINAL J=',I4)
```

Output with echoed input

```
I=  1  BEG=  1.4  END=  2.7  STEP=   .5

J=   1  A=   1.4  B=   1.4
J=   2  A=   1.9  B=   1.9
J=   3  A=   2.4  B=   2.4
TERMINAL J=   4

I=  2  BEG=  2.7  END=  1.4  STEP=  -.5

J=   1  A=   2.7  B=   2.7
J=   2  A=   2.2  B=   2.2
J=   3  A=   1.7  B=   1.7
TERMINAL J=   4

I=  3  BEG= -1.4  END= -2.7  STEP=  -.5

J=   1  A=  -1.4  B=  -1.4
J=   2  A=  -1.9  B=  -1.9
J=   3  A=  -2.4  B=  -2.4
TERMINAL J=   4

I=  4  BEG= -2.7  END= -1.4  STEP=   .5

J=   1  A=  -2.7  B=  -2.7
J=   2  A=  -2.2  B=  -2.2
J=   3  A=  -1.7  B=  -1.7
TERMINAL J=   4
```

LISTING 8-4 "Artificial" real loop indices

```
I=   5  BEG=-27.0  END= 27.0  STEP= 25.0

J=   1  A= -27.0  B= -27.0
J=   2  A=  -2.0  B=  -2.0
J=   3  A=  23.0  B=  23.0
TERMINAL J=   4


I=   6  BEG= 27.0  END=-27.0  STEP=-25.0

J=   1  A=  27.0  B=  27.0
J=   2  A=   2.0  B=   2.0
J=   3  A= -23.0  B= -23.0
TERMINAL J=   4
```

LISTING 8-4 (*continued*)

(STEP)", and then adding one plus a small fraction to overcome possible losses due to roundoff. Within the loop itself, the artificial index A is determined by a two-step calculation. Six typical cases of "artificial" loop indexing are illustrated by the output shown in Listing 8–4.

Although the method described above works, a much simpler method is available. The alternate solution uses the variable B, where B is originally set as the difference between the initial value (BEG) and the step size (STEP). Within the loop, B is determined by adding STEP during each cycle.

The output of Listing 8–4 demonstrates that the signs of type real loop indices are immaterial. Furthermore, it is evident that N can only become negative when the indices have been chosen erroneously. The program could be modified to insure that N is positive before entering the loop. If a negative N were encountered, an error message could be output and the run terminated.

The results of both methods using "artificial" type real loop indices are identical, but the amount of computation involved is significantly different. Thus, Listing 8–4 points out that almost any working program can be made more efficient and effective. Except in special circumstances, however, such improvements are usually not cost effective.

8–2.6 Special Considerations With Regard To DO-Loops

The nested DO-loops of Listing 8–5 (flow diagrammed in Figure 8–7) are presented in three formats. All are "legally" correct. Statements grouped under MARK = 1 are in good form. Statements grouped under MARK = 2 are poor form because CONTINUE statements should terminate DO's and each DO should have its own labeled CONTINUE as a terminal statement.

Statements grouped under MARK = 3 are bad form because they lack even the rudiments of style and are therefore difficult to read and comprehend.

It is constructive to mentally calculate the values output as I, J, K, L, and N in Listing 8–5. If you encounter any trouble in verifying that the results are correct, trace the machine-oriented flow diagram of Figure 8–7, page 199.

The program segment of Listing 8–6 shows more clearly why the statements under MARK = 2 of Listing 8–5 are poor practice. The statement DO 200 K = 5, 1 of Listing 8–6 is never executed (is a null loop) because 5 is always greater than 1, without regard to the value of the loop index I. Because the second DO never executes, L is left undefined and the statement N = N + 1 is never activated.

```
       MARK=1
       N=0

       DO 220 I=1,10
           J=I

              DO 215 K=1,5                    Good form
                  L=K
                  N=N+1
215           CONTINUE

220 CONTINUE

       WRITE(LW,1029)I,J,K,L,N,MARK
1029 FORMAT(' I=',I3,' J=',I3,' K=',
     1I3,' L=',I3,' N=',I3,' MARK=',I2/)



       MARK=2
       N=0                                    Poor form

       DO 230 I=1,10
           J=I
           DO 230 K=1,5
               L=K
230            N=N+1

       WRITE(LW,1029)I,J,K,L,N,MARK



       MARK=3                                 Bad form
       N=0
       DO 240 I=1,10
       J=I
       DO 240 K=1,5
       L=K
240 N=N+1
       WRITE(LW,1029)I,J,K,L,N,MARK

       WRITE(LW,1000)
```

Output:

```
I= 11 J= 10 K=  6 L=  5 N= 50 MARK= 1

I= 11 J= 10 K=  6 L=  5 N= 50 MARK= 2

I= 11 J= 10 K=  6 L=  5 N= 50 MARK= 3
```

LISTING 8-5 Nested DO-loops showing variations

8-2.7 DO's in Combination With Block IF's

DO's within block IF statements must be located entirely within the block. That is, a DO statement located following an IF-THEN, ELSE IF, or ELSE must have the terminal statement (labeled CONTINUE) located before the ELSE IF, ELSE, or END IF which ends the block. Likewise, block IF's within the limits of a DO-loop must be completely contained between the DO and its terminal statement.

Figure 8–8 shows flow diagrams and charts for a program segment that counts, sums, and accumulates products by using a DO-loop within a DO-WHILE mini-module. Coding and output are shown in Listing 8–7. Data for Listing 8–7 is chosen to illustrate the effect of sign changes on the loop control parameters. Most of the looping is self-evident. The fourth set of data, however, results in no looping at all (See Section 8–1.3).

By contrast, Figure 8–9 and Listing 8–8 show a do nothing program segment that has a block IF located within a DO-loop. In addition, DO-loops are located within two of the blocks themselves. Output from the program segment traces the flow to help clarify the process, often called program tracing. (Pages 202 and 203.)

In addition to showing nested loops, this program illustrates a method of writing that locates the output source within the program. The value LOC indicates the block IF by its hundreds digit; it also shows the DO-loop number in the units digit. Both programs of this section illustrate program tracing.

8-3 PROGRAM LOOP

The schematic for Program LOOP is shown on page 204 and the definition sheet is shown in Table 8–2. Computer output from the program itself has been annotated by naming several of the constants. The $\underline{N}$umber of $\underline{S}$ub$\underline{G}$roups $\underline{W}$ithin any $\underline{G}$roup (NSGWG) and the $\underline{N}$umber of $\underline{S}$ETS within any subgroup NSETS are input values. Sets of values, FT ($\underline{F}$irst $\underline{T}$erm) and ST ($\underline{S}$econd $\underline{T}$erm), are read and summed into a location called SUM. Within a subgroup, these sets of numbers are added together and shown as a $\underline{S}$ub$\underline{G}$rou$\underline{P}$ $\underline{S}\underline{U}\underline{M}$ in location SGPSUM. Thus in Listing 8–9, $2 + 4 = 6$, $3 + 5 = 8$, $2 + 6 = 8$, and $1 + 7 = 8$ represent the four sets in the first sub-group. The total of these values, $6 + 8 + 8 + 8$, or 30, is stored in location SGPSUM. This process is repeated for each of the three subgroups of the first group, yielding values in SGPSUM of 30, 13, and 28, respectively. The sum of these 3 values ($30 + 13 + 28$, or 71) is stored as the $\underline{G}$rou$\underline{P}$ $\underline{S}\underline{U}\underline{M}$ in location GPSUM.

The calculations performed with FT and ST are trivial so that the process for nested looping will not be obscured. The simple calculation of adding FT and ST could, of course, be replaced by any set of complex calculations that would lead to the solution of real-world problems.

Observe that the number of sets within each subgroup varies, as does the number of subgroups within each group. The number of groups is determined by the use of a trailer card which, when not signaling program termination by a zero, establishes the number of subgroups.

As in every case of programming, it is vitally important to understand the problem. In this case, the calculations are quite simple, but the program is reasonably complex. It may be approached in either a top-down or a *bottom-up* manner.

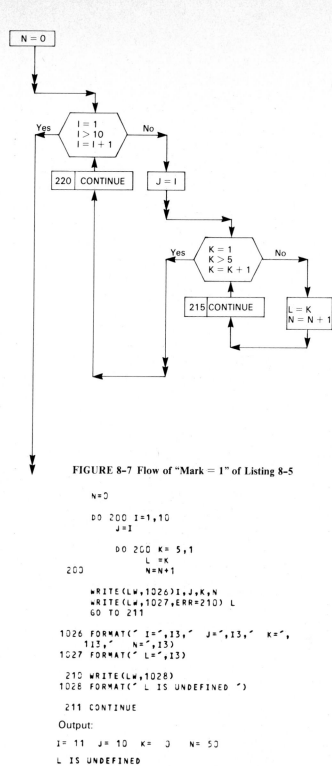

FIGURE 8-7 Flow of "Mark = 1" of Listing 8-5

```
       N=0

       DO 200 I=1,10
           J=I

           DO 200 K= 5,1
               L =K
200            N=N+1

       WRITE(LW,1026)I,J,K,N
       WRITE(LW,1027,ERR=210) L
       GO TO 211

1026 FORMAT(' I=',I3,'   J=',I3,'   K=',
       113,'    N=',I3)
1027 FORMAT(' L=',I3)

 210 WRITE(LW,1028)
1028 FORMAT(' L IS UNDEFINED ')

 211 CONTINUE
```

Output:

```
I= 11   J= 10   K=  0   N= 50

L IS UNDEFINED
```

LISTING 8-6 Null loop

Machine-Oriented Flow Diagram

Modified Nassi-Shneiderman Chart

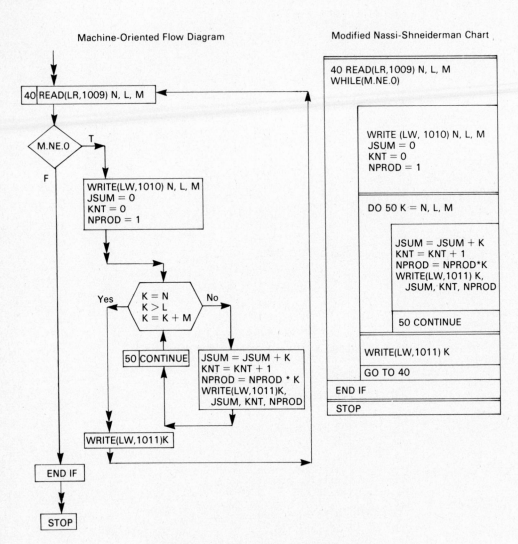

FIGURE 8-8 DO-Loop within DO-WHILE mini-
module

```
        WRITE(LW,1008)
C                        --- START LOOP
     40 READ(LR,1009) N,L,M
C                        --- START BLOCK-IF
        IF(M .NE. 0) THEN
           WRITE(LW,1010) N,L,M
           JSUM  = 0
           KNT   = 0
           NPROD = 1

C                        --- START NESTED-DO LOOP
           DO 50 K =N,L,M
C                        --- ACCUMULATE SUMS
              JSUM  = JSUM  + K
C                        --- COUNT OPERATIONS
              KNT   = KNT   + 1
C                        --- ACCUMULATIVE MULTIPLICATION
              NPROD = NPROD * K
              WRITE(LW,1011)K,JSUM,KNT,NPROD
     50       CONTINUE

           WRITE(LW,1011) K
           GO TO 40
        END IF

 1008 FORMAT(3X,´N´,3X,´L´,3X,´M´, 3X,´K´,2X,
     1 ´NSUM´,1X,´KNT´,2X,´NPROD´/)
 1009 FORMAT (3I4)
 1010 FORMAT(I5,2I4)
 1011 FORMAT(13X,I4,I5,I4,I8)
```

Output:

N	L	M	K	NSUM	KNT	NPROD	
3	8	3					
			3	3	1	3	
			6	9	2	18	
			9				
1	3	1					
			1	1	1	1	
			2	3	2	2	
			3	6	3	6	
			4				
4	-4	-2					
			4	4	1	4	
			2	6	2	8	
			0	6	3	0	
			-2	4	4	0	
			-4	0	5	0	
			-6				
-8	-9	1					
			-8	-8	1	-8	NO LOOPING OCCURS!
			-7				
-9	-8	1					
			-9	-9	1	-9	
			-8	-17	2	72	
			-7				

Input

LISTING 8-7 Summing, counting, and accumulating products

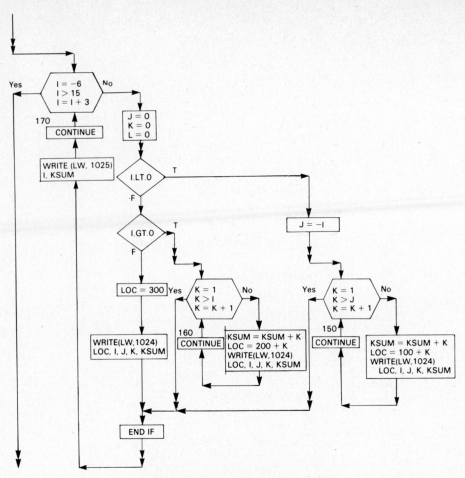

FIGURE 8–9 (a) Nested DO, block IF, DO
Machine-oriented flow diagram

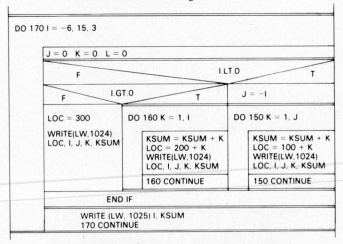

FIGURE 8-9 (b) Nested DO, block IF, DO Modified
Nassi-Shneiderman chart.

```
            WRITE(LW,1023)

        DO 170 I= -6,15,3
            J=0
            K=0
            L=0

            IF(I.LT.0) THEN
                J= -I

                DO 150 K=1,J
                    KSUM = KSUM + K
                    LOC = 100 + K
                    WRITE(LW,1024) LOC,I,J,K,KSUM
150             CONTINUE

            ELSE IF(I.GT.0) THEN

                DO 160 K= 1,I
                    KSUM = KSUM + K
                    LOC = 200 + K
                    WRITE(LW,1024) LOC,I,J,K,KSUM
160             CONTINUE

            ELSE
                LOC = 300
                WRITE(LW,1024) LOC,I,J,K,KSUM
            END IF

            WRITE(LW,1025)I,KSUM
170     CONTINUE
1023 FORMAT('1LOCATION I  J  K  KSUM'/)
1024 FORMAT(I7,I4,2I3,I5)
1025 FORMAT(/' OUT OF BLOCK IF WITH I=',I3,' KSUM=',I4/)
```

Output:

```
LOCATION I  J  K  KSUM

    101  -6  6  1    1
    102  -6  6  2    3
    103  -6  6  3    6
    104  -6  6  4   10
    105  -6  6  5   15
    106  -6  6  6   21

OUT OF BLOCK IF WITH I= -6 KSUM=  21

    101  -3  3  1   22
    102  -3  3  2   24
    103  -3  3  3   27

OUT OF BLOCK IF WITH I= -3 KSUM=  27

    300   0  0  0   27

OUT OF BLOCK IF WITH I=  0 KSUM=  27

    201   3  0  1   28
    202   3  0  2   30
    203   3  0  3   33

OUT OF BLOCK IF WITH I=  3 KSUM=  33

    201   6  0  1   34
    202   6  0  2   36
    203   6  0  3   39
    204   6  0  4   43
    205   6  0  5   48
    206   6  0  6   54
```

LISTING 8-8 Nested DO, Block IF, DO

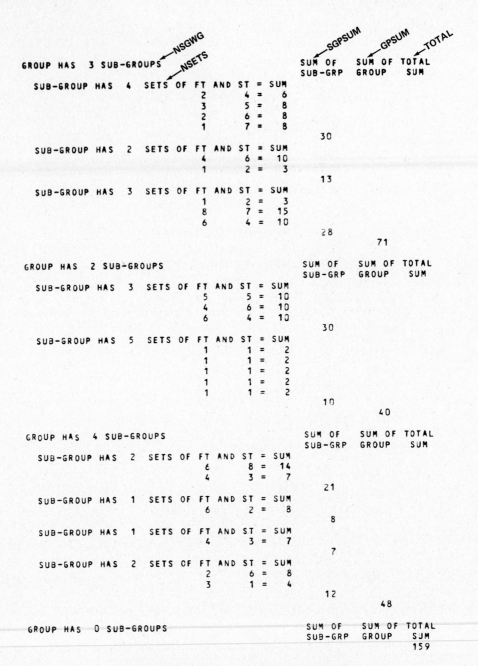

```
                                  ←NSGWG
GROUP HAS  3 SUB-GROUPS     ←                 SGPSUM      GPSUM      TOTAL
                                  ←NSETS                  ←          ←
                                                 SUM OF   SUM OF  TOTAL
                                                 SUB-GRP  GROUP    SUM
   SUB-GROUP HAS  4  SETS OF FT AND ST = SUM
                                2      4 = 6
                                3      5 = 8
                                2      6 = 8
                                1      7 = 8
                                                   30

   SUB-GROUP HAS  2  SETS OF FT AND ST = SUM
                                4      6 = 10
                                1      2 = 3
                                                   13

   SUB-GROUP HAS  3  SETS OF FT AND ST = SUM
                                1      2 = 3
                                8      7 = 15
                                6      4 = 10
                                                   28          71


GROUP HAS  2 SUB-GROUPS                           SUM OF   SUM OF  TOTAL
                                                 SUB-GRP  GROUP    SUM

   SUB-GROUP HAS  3  SETS OF FT AND ST = SUM
                                5      5 = 10
                                4      6 = 10
                                6      4 = 10
                                                   30

   SUB-GROUP HAS  5  SETS OF FT AND ST = SUM
                                1      1 = 2
                                1      1 = 2
                                1      1 = 2
                                1      1 = 2
                                1      1 = 2
                                                   10          40


GROUP HAS  4 SUB-GROUPS                           SUM OF   SUM OF  TOTAL
                                                 SUB-GRP  GROUP    SUM

   SUB-GROUP HAS  2  SETS OF FT AND ST = SUM
                                6      8 = 14
                                4      3 = 7
                                                   21

   SUB-GROUP HAS  1  SETS OF FT AND ST = SUM
                                6      2 = 8
                                                    8

   SUB-GROUP HAS  1  SETS OF FT AND ST = SUM
                                4      3 = 7
                                                    7

   SUB-GROUP HAS  2  SETS OF FT AND ST = SUM
                                2      6 = 8
                                3      1 = 4
                                                   12          48


GROUP HAS  0 SUB-GROUPS                           SUM OF   SUM OF  TOTAL
                                                 SUB-GRP  GROUP    SUM
                                                                  159
```

**LISTING 8-9 Output from program LOOP with
echoed input data**

Table 8-2 Program Loop Definition Sheet

Program: LOOP

Purpose: To obtain the total of the sums of a large number of sets of FT and ST, at the same time obtaining subtotals for certain groups and subgroups.

Descriptive Items:

FT	First Term of input per set.
ST	Second Term of input per set.
SUM	SUM of a set: SUM = FT + ST
SGPSUM	Sum of the SUMs in a subgroup: SubGrouP SUM
GPSUM	Sum of the SUMs in a group: GrouP SUM
TOTAL	Sum of the SUMs for entire input
NSGWG	The Number of SubGroups Within any Group.
NSETS	The Number of SETS of FT and ST within any subgroup.
K	A counter that shows how many subgroups have been considered in any group.

In the top-down approach, it would be necessary to read NSGWG, the number of subgroups present within the group, and either perform some operations within the group or stop the program. (Since summations are involved, it is likely that some values will also have to be initialized.) Stated in a little more detail, the following must be done:

Initialize.
Read and echo NSGWG.
If NSGWG

        is greater than zero for a particular group,
        then work with NSGWG subgroups.

ELSE

        output total sum (TOTAL) and

STOP.

The human-oriented flow diagram of Figure 8-10(a) shows these same requirements.
The work that is to be performed within the NSGWG subgroups must next be inserted. (It is likely that some initialization will have to be performed and also that a count of the subgroup might be desirable for use in terminating a particular loop.) Within each loop, it is necessary to work with NSETS sets of FT and ST.

"Work with NSGWG subgroups:"
Initialize.
Increment count of subgroups.
IF another subgroup exists

        THEN work with NSETS set of FT and ST.

ELSE

        Output sum of group (GPSUM).

A specific outline of these concepts is given in flow diagram form in Figure 8–10(b).

Work related to the NSGWG sets within the subgroup involves reading and echoing the variable NSETS and a loop that reads and sums FT and ST into SUM and accumulates the appropriate subgroup sums (SGPSUM), group sums (GPSUM), and the total for the whole set of data (TOTAL). The values FT and ST are output with their immediate sum, SUM. When all of the sets of FT and ST have been processed, the sum of the subgroup is output and reinitialized. In summary:

"Work with the NSETS sets of FT and ST:"
Read and echo NSETS, the number or sets within the subgroup
For each set, in turn, within any particular subgroup
Read and sum FT and ST into SUM.
Accumulate sum of subgroup into SGPSUM
sum of group into GPSUM and
sum of all values into TOTAL.
Output FT, ST, and their sum (SUM).
Output sum of subgroup (SGPSUM).
Re-initialize sum of subgroup (SGPSUM=0).

This process is illustrated in Figure 8–10(c).

The program can also be developed in a bottom-up manner by reversing the process and looking at the innermost set of calculations. One could decide that it was necessary to read NSETS and for each set, in turn, to: read and sum FT and ST into SUM; accumulate sums for the subgroup, groups and total sum; and output FT and ST and their sum, SUM. After doing this loop, the value of the sum of subgroup would need to be reinitialized. In such a case, the flow diagram of Figure 8–10(c) would be constructed first. Once this was completed, then the next step would be to work with NSGWG subgroups, involving initialization, counting the subgroups and (when subgroups exist) processing as outlined in the flow diagram of Figure 8–10(b). When all subgroups have been accounted for, the sum of the group should be output (GPSUM), as represented in the flow diagram of Figure 8–10(b). Finally, the total picture would be put together as in Figure 8–10(a).

For either case, Figure 8–11 shows the total human-oriented flow diagram.

You may have noticed that this program could have been done just as well by using a second DO-loop that loops on NSGWG. Such a modification is left as an exercise.

Translation of the human-oriented flow diagram to the machine-oriented flow diagram or modified Nassi-Shneiderman chart of Figure 8–12 (pages 210, 211) is relatively simple, and the coding (see Listing 8–10, page 209) follows naturally.

8–4 HALT METHODS

This section compares different methods of looping and also illustrates several logical ways for terminating a FORTRAN program. Machine-oriented flow diagrams and codings are shown.

8–4.1 Error Halt Or Control Information List Specifier END

The type of program illustrated in Figure 8–13 usually results in an error message when no more data is available at run-time. It is poor programming since there is no logical means

Program LOOP

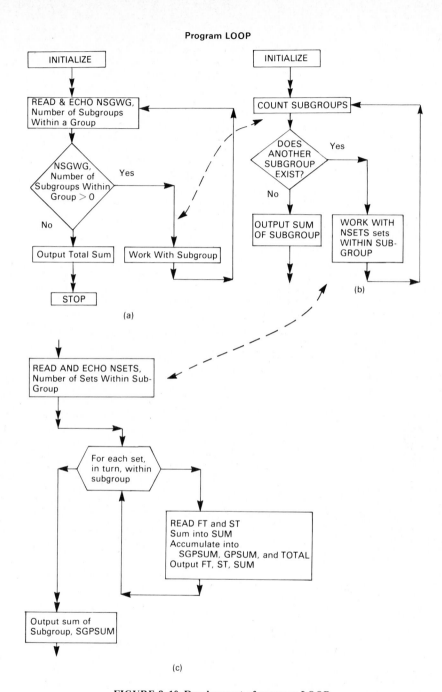

FIGURE 8-10 Development of program LOOP

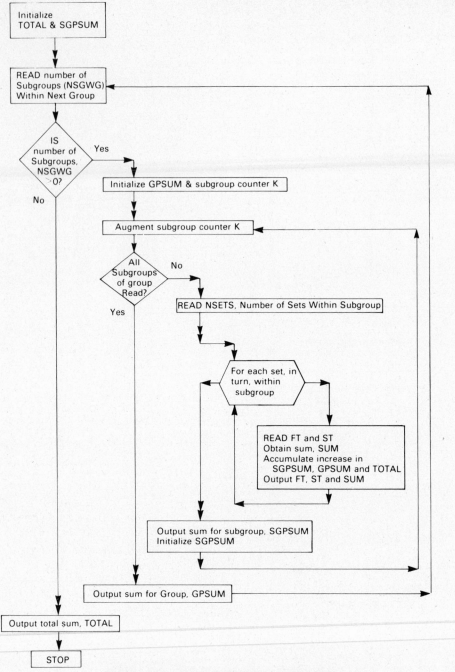

FIGURE 8-11 Human-oriented flow diagram for
program LOOP

Chapter 8 Program Looping With DO-Loops

```
       PROGRAM LOOP
C      ---      FT = FIRST TERM
C      ---      ST = SECOND TERM
C      ---     SUM = SUM OF FIRST (FT) AND SECOND (ST) TERMS
C      ---   NSGWG = NUMBER OF SUB-GROUPS WITHIN GROUPS
C      ---   NSETS = NUMBER OF SETS WITHIN A PARTICULAR SUB-GROUP
C      --- SGPSUM = SUB-GROUP SUM
C      ---   GPSUM = GROUP SUM
C      ---   TOTAL = TOTAL

       IMPLICIT INTEGER(F,G,S,T)
       LR=5
       LW=6

       TOTAL= 0
       SGPSUM  = 0

    10 READ(LR,1000) NSGWG
       WRITE(LW,1001) NSGWG
       IF(NSGWG.GT.0) THEN
           GPSUM=0
           K = 0

    20     K=K+1
           IF(K.LE.NSGWG) THEN
                  READ(LR,1000) NSETS
                  WRITE(LW,1002) NSETS

                  DO 40 I=1,NSETS
                       READ(LR,1000) FT,ST
                       SUM= FT+ ST
                       SGPSUM = SGPSUM+ SUM
                       GPSUM= GPSUM+ SUM
                       TOTAL = TOTAL + SUM
                       WRITE(LW,1003) FT,ST,SUM
    40            CONTINUE

                  WRITE(LW,1004) SGPSUM
                  SGPSUM =0
                  GO TO 20
           END IF

           WRITE(LW,1005) GPSUM
           GO TO 10
       END IF

       WRITE(LW,1006) TOTAL

  1000 FORMAT(2I4)
  1001 FORMAT(/' GROUP HAS',I3,' SUB-GROUPS',22X,
      1'SUM OF',3X,'SUM OF',1X,'TOTAL'/
      246X,'SUB-GRP',2X,'GROUP',3X,'SUM')
  1002 FORMAT(3X,'SUB-GROUP HAS',I3,'  SETS OF FT AND',
      1' ST = SUM')
  1003 FORMAT(28X,I3,4X,I3,' =',I4)
  1004 FORMAT(47X,I4)
  1005 FORMAT(56X,I4)
  1006 FORMAT(62X,I4)

       STOP
       END
```

LISTING 8-10 Program LOOP coding

Program LOOP

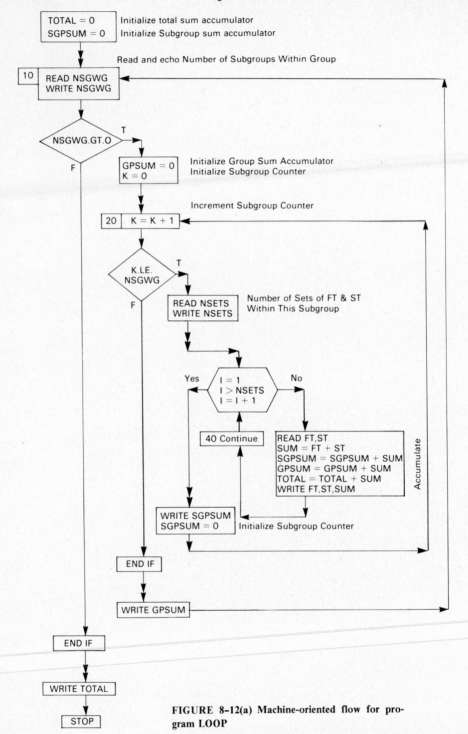

FIGURE 8–12(a) Machine-oriented flow for program LOOP

Program LOOP

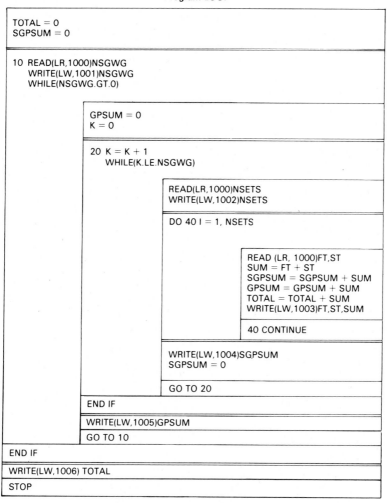

```
TOTAL = 0
SGPSUM = 0

10  READ(LR,1000)NSGWG
    WRITE(LW,1001)NSGWG
    WHILE(NSGWG.GT.0)

        GPSUM = 0
        K = 0

        20  K = K + 1
            WHILE(K.LE.NSGWG)

                READ(LR,1000)NSETS
                WRITE(LW,1002)NSETS

                DO 40 I = 1, NSETS

                    READ (LR, 1000)FT,ST
                    SUM = FT + ST
                    SGPSUM = SGPSUM + SUM
                    GPSUM = GPSUM + SUM
                    TOTAL = TOTAL + SUM
                    WRITE(LW,1003)FT,ST,SUM

                    40 CONTINUE

                WRITE(LW,1004)SGPSUM
                SGPSUM = 0

                GO TO 20

        END IF

        WRITE(LW,1005)GPSUM
        GO TO 10

END IF

WRITE(LW,1006) TOTAL

STOP
```

**FIGURE 8-12(b) Modified Nassi-Shneiderman
chart for program LOOP**

to arrive at the STOP statement in this program; it is in an endless loop.

The programming error depicted in Figure 8–13 can be eliminated by changing the input statement to

$$\text{READ (LR, 1000, END = 30) A, B}$$

and adding statement label 30 to the STOP statement.

8–4.2 Constant Count Halt

The constant count halt, shown on the left of Figure 8–14, represents a typical loop that is always executed a fixed number of times. Because any change in the required number of loops necessitates reprogramming, this method is usually undesirable. The exact number of cards to be read must be known and cards, therefore, must be counted before the program is run. The program in Figure 8–14 requires ten cards.

8–4.3 Variable Count Halt

The variable count halt, illustrated on the right of Figure 8–14, is similar to the constant count halt. A precise card count (N) is needed before the program can be run. For any run, N can be filled with any positive value, thus providing much more flexibility than in the constant count halt.

ERROR HALT . . .

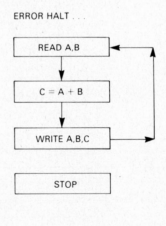

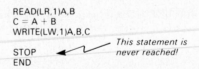

FIGURE 8–13 Error halt

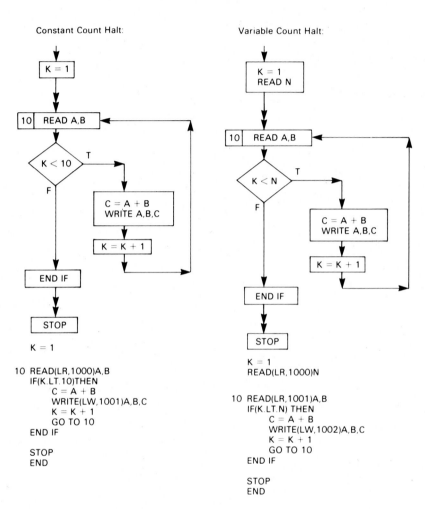

Constant Count Halt:

```
K = 1
10  READ A,B
    K < 10    T
    F
          C = A + B
          WRITE A,B,C
          K = K + 1
    END IF
    STOP
```

```
    K = 1
10  READ(LR,1000)A,B
    IF(K.LT.10)THEN
        C = A + B
        WRITE(LW,1001)A,B,C
        K = K + 1
        GO TO 10
    END IF

    STOP
    END
```

Variable Count Halt:

```
K = 1
READ N
10  READ A,B
    K < N    T
    F
          C = A + B
          WRITE A,B,C
          K = K + 1
    END IF
    STOP
```

```
    K = 1
    READ(LR,1000)N
10  READ(LR,1001)A,B
    IF(K.LT.N) THEN
        C = A + B
        WRITE(LW,1002)A,B,C
        K = K + 1
        GO TO 10
    END IF

    STOP
    END
```

FIGURE 8-14 Constant and variable count halts

8-4.4 Constant DO-Loop Halt

The constant DO halt is illustrated on the left of Figure 8-15. The results obtained by the constant DO-loop itself are exactly the same as for the constant count halt, except that a DO statement is used rather than a separate initializer, incrementer, and counter. The constant DO halt, therefore, suffers from the same difficulties as the constant count halt. The number of cards to be read is fixed from one run to the next, unless the program is rewritten. Ten cards are read by the program of Figure 8-15.

8-4.5 Variable DO-Loop Halt

The right side of Figure 8-15 illustrates a typical variable DO halt, which parallels the variable count halt previously discussed. As written, it reads N cards.

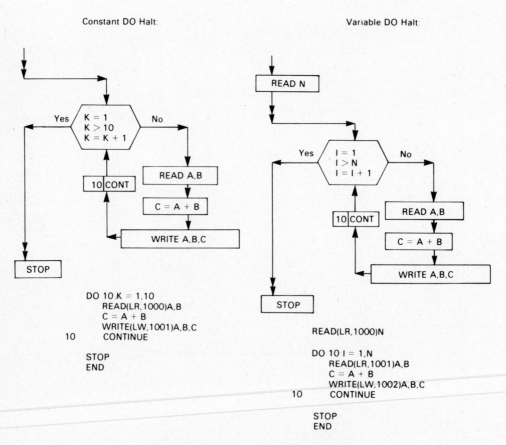

FIGURE 8-15 Constant and variable DO halt

8-4.6 Trailer Card Halt

Figure 8–16 shows a typical trailer card halt in the form of a DO-WHILE mini-module. This is usually a very satisfactory method for program control because data cards do not have to be counted and the program may be terminated by simply adding an appropriate card to the end of the data deck. Trailer cards are usually blank to represent zeros. In cases where zero is not a valid quantity, however, another scheme is required. Program SIMLR (Listing 7–1) uses a pair of numbers input simultaneously as the trailer card. Sometimes any negative (or positive) value suffices. On other occasions, a special (often large) value, such as 99999.E21 or −98765.E-43 is picked.

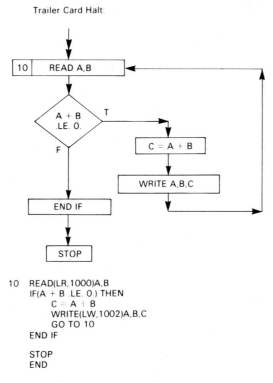

Trailer Card Halt:

```
10   READ(LR,1000)A,B
     IF(A + B .LE. 0.) THEN
         C = A + B
         WRITE(LW,1002)A,B,C
         GO TO 10
     END IF

     STOP
     END
```

FIGURE 8-16 Trailer card halt

8-5 EXERCISES

1. Write a DO-loop in which the loop counter is incremented by 1 on each cycle so that it outputs each of the following.
   (a) 4 and 7 for loop 1, 11 and 14 for loop 2, 18 and 21 for loop 3, and so on.
   (b) 1, 2, −1, −2 for loop 1; 3, 4, −3, −4 for loop 2; 5, 6, −5, −6 for loop 3; and so on.
   (c) The square, cube, square root, and cube root of each loop counter in each cycle. (*Warning:* Be careful of mixed modes.)
   (d) The square of the loop counter and the sum of the squares of the loop counters through and including the "present" loop itself.

2. Use only positive integers for loop indices and simulate

$$\text{DO 10 J} = 12, 3, -1$$

or

$$\text{DO 20 J} = -17, -34, -3$$

Check your results by using negative loop indices as shown in the preceding DO statements.

3. Write a small DO-loop that prepares a table for sine, cosine, and tangent for angles varying between BTHETA and ENDTH in steps of STEPT. Input angles in degrees. (*Caution:* Functions require angles in radian measure.) Make output meaningful and clear.

4. Use a DO-loop to convert angles expressed in degrees and decimal parts of a degree into degrees, minutes, and seconds. Make angular ranges input variables. A typical test range might be from 28.16° to 29.21°, in steps of 0.01°.

Chapter **9**

Single-Dimensional Arrays

Arrays can increase both the power and versatility of many computer programs because access to several related entities can be gained using only one symbolic name and appropriate subscripts. Arrays are often called *tables* or *matrices*.

9-1 THE CONCEPT OF SINGLE-DIMENSIONAL ARRAYS

As a simple example, consider programming involving the ages of six different people: (1) Ida, (2) Jack, (3) Kim, (4) Louis, (5) Mary, and (6) Nancy. Rather than using each person's name as a variable to store his or her age, a symbolic name (such as NAME) could be used for all six. To obtain the age of IDA, one would then use NAME(1) and to refer to Louis, one would use NAME(4). (Mathematically, $NAME_1$ = Ida, $NAME_4$ = Louis, and so on.)

Within computer programs, a location is often defined in a more general form as NAME(J); the choice of age to be used then depends upon the current value stored in J. If J were 3, then NAME(J) would represent (store) the age of KIM. If J were 6, then NAME(J) would represent NAME(6), or the age of Nancy.

Thus a single-dimensional array may be thought of as a column or row of locations, called by a single symbolic name, and referenced by subscripts enclosed in parentheses.

9-2 DIMENSION STATEMENT

A FORTRAN program deck enters into the computer during the compilation state. As you recall (see Figure 1–6 and Table 4–1), during this first stage the computer sequentially translates the FORTRAN statements into its own language and allocates storage locations. An array element name (subscripted variable) gives no indication of the total array size, or number of elements in the array. Yet, in order for a FORTRAN program to compile, it must have all storage locations allocated before proceeding to the second stage, execution.

To allocate space for arrays, the FORTRAN language includes a DIMENSION statement which takes the form

DIMENSION NAME(6), GRADE(6)

where the following are true.

1. Array names are formed using the same rules as for variables; that is, array names must start with a letter of the alphabet, contain only letters and numbers, and be limited to six characters.
2. The size of the array is shown by integer (fixed-point) constants within the parentheses that follow the array name in a DIMENSION statement.

DIMENSION statements in FORTRAN programs must physically precede any *executable* statement. When a computer program is in the compilation stage, the DIMENSION statement is used by the processor to establish sufficient locations for all array elements to be stored within each specific array.

Dimension can also be declared in type statements. For the preceding declaration, the following would suffice:

INTEGER NAME (6)
REAL GRADE (6)

Some programmers prefer to use type statements to the exclusion of DIMENSION statements.

9-3   ARRAY ELEMENTS; SUBSCRIPTED VARIABLES

Access to values currently stored in any array location is gained by using the name of the array followed by a subscript (in parentheses) of the element of the array that you wish to use. Thus RSLT(6) refers to the sixth location of the array RSLT. Likewise TOTAL(J) refers to the Jth location of array TOTAL, where the subscript J is evaluated by the current numerical value stored in location J.

Although values following the name of an array in the DIMENSION statement must always be integer constants, a subscript expression may be any integer expression (which, in Subset FORTRAN, does not contain array elements or functions). A DIMENSION statement has only one purpose—to allocate sufficient spaces to store all elements of an array. Every required space must be specified at compilation time and must, therefore, be defined by a numerical constant. If a variable name were used within a DIMENSION statement, the numerical value of that variable would be unknown until after the compilation stage, requiring additional allocation of storage during the execution stage. (Such a procedure, called *dynamic storage,* is possible in some languages, such as ALGOL. In FORTRAN, however, the DIMENSION statement must declare array sizes absolutely.)

By contrast, once the size of an array has been established, an integer expression can be evaluated to give the location of any array element and is, therefore, a logical extension of the FORTRAN language. It is important to insure that computed subscripts are within limits imposed by array dimensions. On some FORTRAN compilers, if a subscript is out of range, storage locations that should be left intact are changed and no error is indicated. A more detailed discussion of errors produced when subscripts are out of range may be found in Section 10–3.3.

9-4 I/O OF SINGLE-DIMENSIONAL ARRAYS

It is helpful to see single-dimensional arrays used in READ and WRITE statements. Three independent methods are available to input/output arrays: The DO-loop, the whole array method, and the implied-DO loop.

Figure 9–1 illustrates the use of a DO-loop to read one value from each of a *sequence* of data cards. Each time the READ statement is executed, the FORMAT statement is re-initiated. The WRITE statement in this case uses the same FORMAT statement as does the READ statement.

As shown in Figure 9–1, one value is read from each card and then that single value is immediately echoed on an independent line of high-speed printer output. The DO-loop reads and writes N lines, where N is less than or equal to the array size as defined in a previous DIMENSION statement. If N exceeds the array size, some computers may output an error message, but most will store the values in incorrect locations, causing problems at some place and time.

The whole array can also be read or written at one time by simply using the array name without subscripts. Thus,

READ(LR,10) A

reads all values of the array A, in order, in accordance with the FORMAT statement. If the FORMAT statement is 10F8.0 and array A has 26 locations, ten values are read from the first card, ten from the second, and six from the third. Conversely, if array A has 26 locations with format 5F10.0, then five values would be read from five cards in sequence and the 26th value would be read from the sixth card.

WRITE(LW,10) A

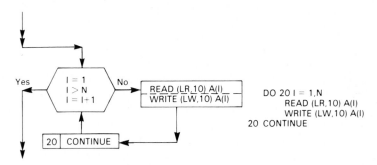

FIGURE 9-1 I/O of single-dimensional array, DO-loop method

follows a similar pattern, the FORMAT statement being exhausted and then re-initiated until all values of the array have been output. For an array of 26 locations with a format of 9F8.0, output would occur on three lines: nine values on the first line, nine values on the second line, and eight values on the third line.

The implied-DO loop is an additional useful technique for input and output of arrays, and appears as follows.

$$READ(LR,10) (A(I), I = 1, N)$$
$$WRITE (LW,10) (A(I), I = 1, N)$$

The first of these statements causes N values of A to be read from an appropriate input device in accordance with the format specified by the statement labeled 10. Output occurs in the same fashion.

The following input/output examples involve single-dimensional arrays used with the special set of data shown in Figure 9–2. All input data may be left-justified for reading by format 10F8.0, because each value includes a decimal point. The data of Figure 9–2 are sequential (1 through 50) so that the values that are read indicate their location in the array. Use of such artificially ordered data helps clarify both the I/O operations and use of single-dimensional arrays.

9–4.1 Reading the Whole Array At One Time

The DIMENSION statement of Listing 9–1 assigns nine locations to array A. The FORMAT statement specifies that, at most, four values can be read from a single card. The READ statement indicates that all nine values are to be read, because A is not

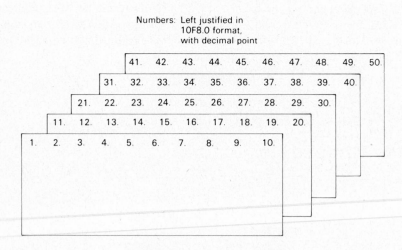

FIGURE 9–2 A special set of data

subscripted. Thus values are stored in the nine locations of array A as shown in Listing 9–1. The first four values, 1 through 4, are taken from the first data card (line of data) of Figure 9–2. The next four locations, 5 through 8, take their values of 11 through 14 from the second data card. Finally, the ninth element of array A (21) is taken from the first location of the third card. All other data on the first three cards are ignored; data beyond column 32 are not within the format specification defined by Statement 10.

9–4.2 DO-Loop Used To Read An Array

Listing 9–2 illustrates an array read by the use of a regular DO-loop. Array B has only four locations specified by the DIMENSION statement. FORMAT Statement 10

```
     DIMENSION A(9)
     LR = 5
10   FORMAT (4F8.0)
     READ(LR,10)A
```

Stored as:

A (1)	1.
A (2)	2.
A (3)	3.
A (4)	4.
A (5)	11.
A (6)	12.
A (7)	13.
A (8)	14.
A (9)	21.

LISTING 9–1 Reading an entire single-dimensional array by one symbol

```
     DIMENSION B(4)
     LR = 5

     DO 12 J = 1, 4
         READ (LR,1000) B (J)
     CONTINUE

10   FORMAT (F8.0)
```

Stored in B as:

```
B (1) =  1.
B (2) =11.
B (3) =21.
B (4) =31.
```

LISTING 9–2 Reading an array with a DO-loop

specifies that only one value can be read from each card. The DO-loop index, J, goes sequentially from 1 to 4. Initial execution of the DO-loop fills variable J with the value 1, so that B(J) represents B(1). The number 1 is then read from the first data card and stored in B(1). Subsequently, J becomes 2 and a value of 11 is read from the second data card and stored in B(2). The balance of the array is read in a similar manner. The last nine values on each of the first four cards are ignored because they are beyond the field width of the FORMAT statement.

9-4.3 The Implied-DO Loop

A form of the implied-DO loop is illustrated and explained in Table 9-1.

Listing 9-3 uses the implied-DO loop to both read and write. Array A has nine locations allocated by the DIMENSION statement. The FORMAT statement, on the other hand, allows input or output of only five values per card or line. The READ statement uses the implied-DO loop to read nine values sequentially, A(1), A(2), A(3), . . . , A(9). As shown in Listing 9-3, values are read and stored from the first two cards. Because the WRITE statement outputs only four of the input values, the single line of output displays the contents of A(1), A(2), A(3), and A(4) as 1., 2., 3., and 4..

Table 9-1 Implied-DO List (Subset FORTRAN 77)

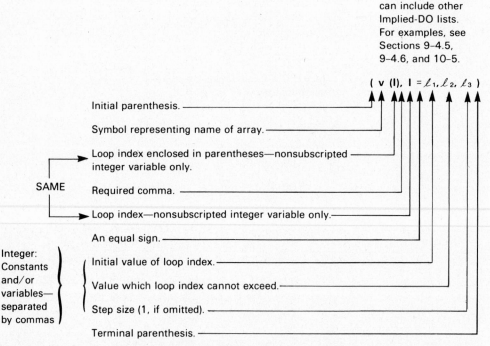

In general this can be any list and can include other Implied-DO lists. For examples, see Sections 9-4.5, 9-4.6, and 10-5.

$$(\ v \ (I), \ I = \ell_1, \ell_2, \ell_3 \ )$$

Initial parenthesis.

Symbol representing name of array.

Loop index enclosed in parentheses—nonsubscripted integer variable only.

SAME

Required comma.

Loop index—nonsubscripted integer variable only.

An equal sign.

Integer: Constants and/or variables— separated by commas

Initial value of loop index.

Value which loop index cannot exceed.

Step size (1, if omitted).

Terminal parenthesis.

Note: In Full Language I may be integer, real or double precision ℓ_i may be an integer, real or double precision expression ℓ_i have their types automatically converted to agree with type of I

```
      DIMENSION A(9)
      LW = 6
      LR = 5
   10 FORMAT (5F8.0)
      READ (LR,10) (A(I), I = 1,9)
      WRITE (LR,10) (A(I), I = 1,4)
```

Stored in A as:

A(1) = 1.	A(6) = 11.
A(2) = 2.	A(7) = 12.
A(3) = 3.	A(8) = 13.
A(4) = 4.	A(9) = 14.
A(5) = 5.	

Output:

```
   1.    2.    3.    4.
```

LISTING 9-3 Reading an array with an implied-DO

```
      DIMENSION A(11)
      LW = 6
      LR = 5
   10 FORMAT (2F8.0)
   11 FORMAT (3F8.0)
      READ (LR, 10)(A(I), I = 1,9)
      WRITE (LW, 11)(A(I), I = 3,9,2
      WRITE (LW, 11) A
```

Stored in A as:

A(1) = 1.	A(4) = 12.	A(7) = 31.
A(2) = 2.	A(5) = 21.	A(8) = 32.
A(3) = 11.	A(6) = 22.	A(9) = 41.

Output:

```
   11.    21.    31.
   41.
    1.     2.    11.
   12.    21.    22.
   31.    32.    41.
```

Boom!

LISTING 9-4 I/O with an anomaly

9-4.4 Mixed I/O Forms

Listing 9–4 shows array A with 11 locations, use of two FORMAT statements, use of two implied-DO loops, and output of a whole array. The nine values stored in locations A(1) through A(9) are taken from the first five cards: two values each from the first two locations on each of the first four cards and the last value from the first location on the fifth card. All other values on these five cards are ignored because they are beyond field widths specified by the FORMAT statement.

The first WRITE statement sets I to 3 and writes A(3), increments I by 2 to yield 5 and writes A(5), increases I to 7 and writes A(7), and finally increments I to 9 and writes A(9). Because FORMAT Statement 11 allows output of only three values per line, 11, 21, and 31 occur on the first line and 41 occurs on the second line.

The last WRITE statement says to output all of array A, displaying three values per line. Thus output shows 1, 2, and 11 on the third line, 12, 21, and 22 on the fourth line, and 31, 32, and 41 on the fifth line—and then the program has difficulties. Values of A(10) and A(11) are not defined. Attempting to output undefined entities usually results in some type of anomaly, the precise nature of which depends upon the processor.

9–4.5 Length of Implied-DO Established Within READ

Statements such as

        READ(LR, 1000) N, (K(I), I = 1, N)
        READ (LR, 1000) NB, NE, NS, (K(I), I = NB, NE, NS)

are legal in FORTRAN 77 because all items are transmitted prior to the processing of any succeeding list item.

In the first of the preceding READ statements, if N were input as 9, nine values would be read sequentially into K(1), K(2), . . . , K(9).

In the second READ statement, input data values of 4, 9, 2, 7, 11, and −8 would store 7 into K(4), 11 into K(6), and −8 into K(8).

9–4.6 Multiple Entity Implied-DO Lists

Statements such as

        READ(LR, 1000) (K(I), J(I), I = 1, 5)
        READ(LR, 1000) NB, NE, NS, (K(I), J(I), I = NB, NE, NS)
        READ(LR, 1000) N, (K(I), I = 1, N), (J(I), I = 1,N)
        WRITE(LW, 1001) (I, K(I), J(I), I = 1, N)

are also legal in FORTRAN 77. The first of these statements would read and store values sequentially into K(1), J(1), K(2), J(2), . . . , J(5). Assuming input values established NB as 1, NE as 5, and NS as 1, the second statement would also store values in K(1), J(1), K(2), J(2), . . . , J(5). With N equal to five, the third statement would store values sequentially in K(1), K(2), K(3), K(4), K(5), J(1), . . . , J(5).

Assume the first five values stored in array K are 5, 10, 15, 20, and 25 and the first five values stored in array J are 2, 4, 6, 8, and 10. Then, if N is 5, the WRITE statement will output the following (in the format specified by Statement 1001).

1	5	2
2	10	4
3	15	6
4	20	8
5	25	10

9–5 BUBBLE-SORT ALGORITHM
USING SINGLE-DIMENSIONAL ARRAYS

Computer programs are frequently required to sort random data into an ordered sequence. Proper choice of an efficient and effective algorithm is dependent upon both the size and characteristics of the data set. The bubble-sort algorithm is a common technique.

9-5.1 Understanding the Bubble-Sort Algorithm

The bubble-sort algorithm has two parts.

1. Each value of the sequence is compared with the next value in line; if necessary, the two are interchanged.
2. Whenever two values within the sequence are interchanged, and before making the next comparison in the sequence, the interchanged value is "bubbled-up." The bubble-up process is performed by comparing values sequentially in the reverse order and interchanging values that are out of order.

The following simple example should help clarify the algorithm. Assume we are given the numbers ⑦, ③, 3, 8, 9, 10, 10, 12, 3, 5. The following steps are used to sort this data in ascending order, in accordance with the bubble-sort algorithm.

1. Compare the first entry with the next in line. Because 7 and 3 are not in ascending order, rearrange them. Thus we have

$$③, ⑦, 3, 8, 9, 10, 10, 12, 3, 5$$

2. Compare the second entry with the next in line. Again, 7 and 3 are not in ascending order; rearrange them. The second entry, 7, must be interchanged with the third entry, 3.

$$3, 3, 7, 8, 9, 10, 10, 12, 3, 5$$

   (a) If no rearrangement occurs, proceed directly to the next entry.
   (b) If rearrangement does occur, bubble the rearranged value to the top if it is less than any preceding entry. (In this case, the 3—originally in the third location and now moved to the second location—is not less than the 3 in the first location, and no bubble-up occurs.) Proceed to the next entry in line.

3. Compare the third entry with the next in line. The order (7, 8) is correct.
4. Compare the fourth entry with the next in line. The order (8, 9) is correct.
5. Continue to compare entries one by one.
6. Compare the eighth entry, 12, with the next in line, 3. Rearrange the 12 and 3 because they are not in ascending order, giving

$$3, 3, 7, 8, 9, 10, 10, ③, 12, 5$$

   (a) Bubble the 3 upwards by interchanging 10 and 3, resulting in

$$3, 3, 7, 8, 9, 10, ③, 10, 12, 5$$

   (b) Continue bubbling the 3 upwards until it is no longer less than a previous entry:

$$3, 3, 7, 8, 9, ③, 10, 10, 12, 5$$
$$3, 3, 7, 8, ③, 9, 10, 10, 12, 5$$
$$3, 3, 7, ③, 8, 9, 10, 10, 12, 5$$
$$3, 3, ③, 7, 8, 9, 10, 10, 12, 5$$

7. Now compare the ninth entry with the next in line, continuing until all entries are in sequential order.

This example is shown in more detail by the output of program BBSRT1 in Listing 9–6, displayed in the form of program tracing. Interchange of previously untouched entries is indicated by crossed arrows. The bubble-up process is indicated by arched, two-headed arrows. Original line numbers are shown (left of a colon) for each entry on each line of output. (The WRITE statements that display Listing 9–6 are shown in the diagram and chart of Figure 9–3 and the coding of Listing 9–5, pages 231, 228, 230, respectively.)

9–5.2 Development of Program BBSRT1

The first part of the bubble-sort algorithm can be accomplished fairly readily by the following.

Read and echo sequence of numbers.

For each number of the sequence, in turn,

>> Compare each term with next term in sequence:

>> If first term is smaller than second, no action is required.

>> If first term is larger than second, interchange terms.

Before proceeding, it is important to check these pseudocode statements. Do you see that the second line is in error? As written, the last number in the sequence would be compared with a number "beyond the sequence." Also, the bubble-up process can be indicated in the pseudocode to show the second part of the algorithm.

Read and echo sequence of numbers.

For each number of the sequence (except the last), in turn,

>> Compare each term with next term in sequence:

>> If first term is smaller than second, no action is required.

>> If first term is larger than second, interchange terms and bubble-up as necessary.

Sometimes it is necessary to visualize an intermediate form of coding before proceeding with the details. In this case, the statements could be represented by

```
DO 40 I = 1, number of terms in sequence less 1
    IF   (i+1)st number in sequence < ith number in sequence, THEN
         interchange (i+1)st and ith terms.
    ELSE
         do nothing
40 CONTINUE
```

This leads to the question of how the $(i+1)$st and ith terms can be interchanged. If it is assumed that the sequence is stored in a single-dimensioned array called INFO, the process could be performed in the following manner.

$$\text{ITEMP} = \text{INFO (I)}$$
$$\text{INFO(I)} = \text{INFO (I+1)}$$
$$\text{INFO(I+1)} = \text{ITEMP}$$

That is, the number in the first location is temporarily stored in ITEMP. Once this is accomplished, the next value in the sequence is stored in the preceeding location. Finally, the value of the first number in the sequence (previously stored in ITEMP) can be placed in the second location, and the interchange is complete. The temporary storage location ITEMP has to be used so that the values will not be lost during the interchange process.

The bubble-up process is the reverse of the first part of the algorithm, that is, the interchange process is performed by comparing entries sequentially, but in reverse order. This suggests use of a DO-loop that has its upper limit based on the "current position" used in the sequence by the first part of the algorithm and its step size set at −1. These considerations give the following coding.

```
    DO 40 I=1, Number of terms in sequence less 1
        DO 30 J = I, 1, −1
                    IF(INFO(J+1).LT.INFO(J)) THEN
                                ITEMP = INFO(J)
                                INFO(J) = INFO(J+1)
                                INFO(J+1)= ITEMP
            ELSE
                        What is needed here?
            END IF
30                  CONTINUE
40 CONTINUE
```

Note that the IF statement will always be executed at least one time by DO-loop 40, because J is initialized with I. If no interchange is required, the bubble-up process will not occur. If an interchange is required, then the bubble-up process will start with J=I−1 and continue until no more interchanging is required.

After the ELSE statement, a branch is needed to exit the loop. A GO TO 40 is used, although the use of a GO TO in this manner is not considered desirable by many programmers. It is left as an exercise to rewrite this portion so that a GO TO will not be needed.

The program is essentially complete, but it is often desirable to carry line numbers along with corresponding information. This is presented in either the machine-oriented flow diagram or modified Nassi-Shneiderman chart of Figure 9–3, or the coding of Listing 9–5. Note that two parts are involved: first, the line numbers are initialized by a DO-loop (just after input and echoing of the data) and second, the line numbers are interchanged parallel to the interchange of information inside the block IF. This results in a program that includes everything except the program line numbers within a circle or square in Listing 9–5.

Section 9-5 Bubble-Sort Algorithm

227

Program BBSRT1

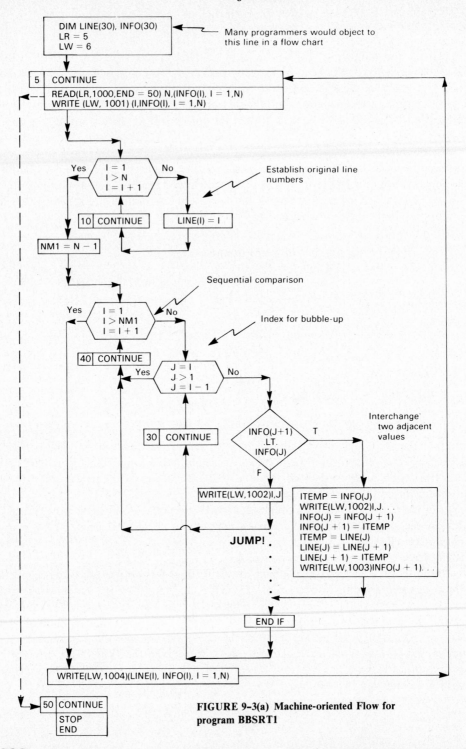

DIM LINE(30), INFO(30)
LR = 5
LW = 6

Many programmers would object to
this line in a flow chart

5 | CONTINUE
READ(LR,1000,END = 50) N,(INFO(I), I = 1,N)
WRITE (LW, 1001) (I,INFO(I), I = 1,N)

Yes ← I = 1
I > N
I = I + 1 → No

Establish original line
numbers

10 | CONTINUE   LINE(I) = I

NM1 = N − 1

Sequential comparison

Yes ← I = 1
I > NM1
I = I + 1 → No

Index for bubble-up

40 | CONTINUE

Yes ← J = I
J > 1
J = I − 1 → No

30 | CONTINUE

INFO(J+1)
.LT.
INFO(J) → T

Interchange
two adjacent
values

F

WRITE(LW,1002)I,J

ITEMP = INFO(J)
WRITE(LW,1002)I,J. . .
INFO(J) = INFO(J + 1)
INFO(J + 1) = ITEMP
ITEMP = LINE(J)
LINE(J) = LINE(J + 1)
LINE(J + 1) = ITEMP
WRITE(LW,1003)INFO(J + 1). . .

JUMP!
.
.
.
.
.

END IF

WRITE(LW,1004)(LINE(I), INFO(I), I = 1,N)

50 | CONTINUE
STOP
END

FIGURE 9-3(a) Machine-oriented Flow for
program BBSRT1

Chapter 9 Single-Dimensional Arrays

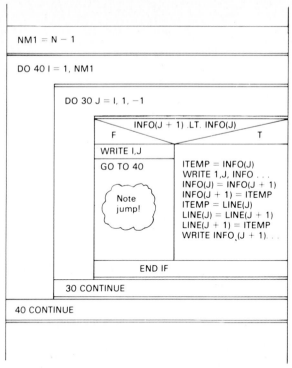

FIGURE 9–3(b) Partial modified Nassi-Shneiderman Chart for program BBSRT1

9–5.3 Coding and Output for Program BBSRT1

The coding of Listing 9–5 shows line numbers associated with the FORTRAN statements. Line numbers 13, 14, 77 and 78 are circled to emphasize their part in creating a major loop. Addition of lines 13 and 77, plus adding END = 50 to line 14 and a statement label 50 to line 78, allows the program to use multiple sets of data on each run. For improved style, lines 14 through 66 should be indented five more spaces and lines 68 through 75 should be placed between lines 78 and 79.

Lines 49, 55, 56, 58, and 71 through 73 have been added to provide a program trace to assist in debugging without hampering the sorting process. Line 49 produces output only when an entry must be moved. Each time line 49 executes, output is also obtained from lines 55 and 56. During each such process, the first line outputs the values of I and J, the values of the two entities that must be interchanged, and the line number stored in the temporary location ITEMP. The second output line shows the values interchanged and the entire array in its current position (with each entry preceded by its original line number and a colon.)

Note that the three statement "interchange" sequence is performed twice, once for the entry and once for its original line number. Typically, (1) LINE(J) is stored in ITEMP so that its value is not lost when (2) LINE(J + 1) is stored in LINE(J). (3) LINE (J + 1) is then reset by filling it with the value previously stored in ITEMP.

When I = J and no reordering is required, line 58 outputs the identical values of I and J.

```
1            PROGRAM BBSRT1
2     C            --- PERFORMS BUBBLE SORT ON SINGLE DIMENSIONED ARRAY
3     C            --- INFO(30): ARRAY TO BE SORTED
4     C            --- LINE(30): USED TO CARRY ORIGINAL LINE NUMBERS
5     C            ---          ASSOCIATED WITH ARRAY INFO
6     C            --- N : NUMBER OF ELEMENTS TO BE SORTED
7     C            ---  ITEMP : TEMPORARY LOCATION USED DURING INTERCHANGES
8
9            DIMENSION LINE(30),INFO(30)
10           LR=5
11           LW=6
12
13      5 CONTINUE
14         READ(LR,1000,END=50) N,(INFO(I),I=1,N)
15         WRITE(LW,1001) (I,INFO(I),I=1,N)
16
17    C            --- ESTABLISH ORIGINAL LINE NUMBERS IN ARRAY LINE
18    C            ---    CORRESPONDING TO ORIGINAL LOCATIONS IN ARRAY INFO
19           DO 10 I=1,N
20               LINE(I)=I
21      10 CONTINUE
22
23    C                     (IN FULL LANGUAGE FORTRAN 77: )
24    C                     (   DELETE: NM1 = N-1         )
25    C                     (            DO 40 I=1,NM1     )
26    C                     (   REPLACE BY:                )
27    C                     (            DO 40 I=1,N-1     )
28         NM1= N-1
29
30    C                --- I PROCEEDS SEQUENTIALLY THROUGH LIST OF ARRAY INFO
31           DO 40 I=1,NM1
32
33    C                    --- J PRODUCES 'BUBBLE-UP' EFFECT BY INCREMENTING
34    C                    --- 'BACKWARDS' FROM LOCATION I OF ARRAY INFO
35             DO 30 J= I,1,-1
36
37    C                        --- INTERCHANGE OCCURS IF:
38    C                            (1) SEQUENTIAL COMPARISON CALLS FOR IT
39    C                                (NOTE: IN SECOND DO, J STARTS WITH I)
40    C                            (2) BUBBLE-UP REQUIRED
41    C                        --- FIRST 3 STMTS INTERCHANGE ELEMENTS OF
42    C                            ARRAY INFO, USING ITEMP FOR TEMPORARY
43    C                            STORAGE OF FIRST ELEMENT
44    C                        --- SECOND 3 STMTS USED TO INTERCHANGE
45    C                            ELEMENTS OF LINE, ALSO USING ITEMP
46
47               IF(INFO(J+1).LT.INFO(J)) THEN
48                   ITEMP= INFO(J)
49                   WRITE(LW,1002)I,J,INFO(J+1),INFO(J),ITEMP
50                   INFO(J)  =INFO(J+1)
51                   INFO(J+1)=ITEMP
52                   ITEMP    =LINE(J)
53                   LINE(J)  =LINE(J+1)
54                   LINE(J+1)=ITEMP
55                   WRITE(LW,1003)INFO(J+1),INFO(J),
56        1               (LINE(K),INFO(K),K=1,N)
57               ELSE
58                   WRITE(LW,1002) I,J
59                   GO TO 40
60               END IF
61
62      30    CONTINUE
63
64      40 CONTINUE
65
66         WRITE(LW,1004)(LINE(I),INFO(I),I=1,N)
67
68    1000 FORMAT(20I4)
69    1001 FORMAT('1 I  J INFO(J+1) INFO(J) ITEMP  LINE NUMBER: VALUE'/
70        1       3(30X,10(I2,':',I2,1X)/))
71    1002 FORMAT(2I3,I6,2I8)
72    1003 FORMAT(6X,I6,I8,10X,10(I2,':',I2,1X)/
73        1       2(30X,10(I2,':',I2,1X)/))
74    1004 FORMAT(////' ORDERED ARRAY WITH ORIGINAL LINE NUMBERS '
75        1' BEFORE COLONS'/3(1X,10(I2,':',I2,1X)/))
76
77         GO TO 5
78      50 CONTINUE
79         STOP
80         END
```

LISTING 9-5 Coding for program BBSRT1
(bubble-sort)

```
 I   J  INFO(J+1)  INFO(J)  ITEMP   LINE NUMBER: VALUE
                                    1: 7   2: 3   3: 3   4: 8   5: 9   6:10   7:10   8:12   9: 3  10: 5
 1   1     3          7        7
           7          3        2: 3   1: 7   3: 3   4: 8   5: 9   6:10   7:10   8:12   9: 3  10: 5

 2   2     3          7        7
           7          3        2: 3   3: 3   1: 7   4: 8   5: 9   6:10   7:10   8:12   9: ③  10: 5

 2   1
 3   3
 4   4
 5   5
 6   6
 7   7
 8   8     3         12       12
          12          3        2: 3   3: 3   1: 7   4: 8   5: 9   6:10   7:10   9: ③   8:12  10: 5

 8   7     3         10       10
          10          3        2: 3   3: 3   1: 7   4: 8   5: 9   6:10   9: ③   7:10   8:12  10: 5

 8   6     3         10       10
          10          3        2: 3   3: 3   1: 7   4: 8   5: 9   9: ③   6:10   7:10   8:12  10: 5

 8   5     3          9        9
           9          3        2: 3   3: 3   1: 7   4: 8   9: ③   5: 9   6:10   7:10   8:12  10: 5

 8   4     3          8        8
           8          3        2: 3   3: 3   1: 7   9: ③   4: 8   5: 9   6:10   7:10   8:12  10: 5

 8   3     3          7        7
           7          3        2: 3   3: 3   9: ③   1: 7   4: 8   5: 9   6:10   7:10   8:12  10: 5

 8   2
 9   9     5         12       12
          12          5        2: 3   3: 3   9: 3   1: 7   4: 8   5: 9   6:10   7:10  10: 5   8:12

 9   8     5         10       10
          10          5        2: 3   3: 3   9: 3   1: 7   4: 8   5: 9   6:10  10: 5   7:10   8:12

 9   7     5         10       10
          10          5        2: 3   3: 3   9: 3   1: 7   4: 8   5: 9  10: 5   6:10   7:10   8:12

 9   6     5          9        9
           9          5        2: 3   3: 3   9: 3   1: 7   4: 8  10: 5   5: 9   6:10   7:10   8:12

 9   5     5          8        8
           8          5        2: 3   3: 3   9: 3   1: 7  10: 5   4: 8   5: 9   6:10   7:10   8:12

 9   4     5          7        7
           7          5        2: 3   3: 3   9: 3  10: 5   1: 7   4: 8   5: 9   6:10   7:10   8:12

 9   3
```

```
ORDERED ARRAY WITH ORIGINAL LINE NUMBERS  BEFORE COLONS
  2: 3   3: 3   9: 3  10: 5   1: 7   4: 8   5: 9   6:10   7:10   8:12
```

**LISTING 9–6 Typical output from bubble-sort
program BBSRT1**

Output shown in Listing 9–6 traces the BBSRT1 program for the data discussed in Section 9–6.1. Once the major loop is complete, the reordered array is output with original line numbers.

9–6 A SEARCH PROGRAM

Often it is desirable to search for a specific value within a data set. Many differing techniques have been developed to search a diverse range of data groups efficiently. The *binary search,* which is illustrated schematically in Table 9–2, is useful for smaller sets of data. For large sets of data requiring many operations, other methods must be used.

The first column of Table 9–2 shows 14 elements, all constants, stored in an array called INFO. The second column shows the locations of the constants in the array INFO, as well as the initial values stored in three variables called ITOP, MID, and IBOT.

The initial scan searches the whole field, so ITOP is set at zero and IBOT is set at one more than the number of elements to be searched. The midpoint is located in MID, as $(ITOP + IBOT)/2$; in the first case, this yields $MID = 7$ (shown in the second column). A comparison is then made between the information stored in element 7 of array INFO and the value being sought (in this case, 131). Since 121 (INFO(7)) is less than 131, the number sought must lie in the lower half of the list. Therefore ITOP is changed from 0 to MID, reducing the scanning area to be searched to the lower half of the sequence.

MID is computed again: $(7 + 15)/2 = 11$. INFO(MID) = INFO (11) is 133, which is now greater than the sought value of 131. Thus 131 must lie above this last computed

Table 9-2 Searching for J = 131 in Array INFO, Schematic

Constants stored in Array INFO	Constants in ITOP, MID, IBOT and Locations in Array INFO			
	0 ········ITOP			
10	1			
13	2			
17	3			
73	4			
84	5	┌INFO(MID)		
111	6		┌J	
121	7 ········ MID 121<131 so → ITOP ···················· ITOP			J = 131 found in INFO(MID)
130	8			
131	9		MID 131 = 131	INFO(9) = 131
132	10			
133	11 ······················· MID 133>131 so → IBOT			
134	12		└┐J	
160	13	└INFO(MID)		
190	N = 14			
	15 ······· IBOT ················ IBOT			

Number of elements in Array INFO

First search between elements 0 and 15 narrows search limits to between elements 7 and 15.

Second search between elements 7 and 15 narrows search limits to between elements 7 and 11.

Third search between elements 7 and 11 finds value sought.

midpoint. For this reason, IBOT is set at MID and the search is now continued between location 7 and 11 of the array INFO.

MID is recomputed and this time INFO (MID) = INFO (9) = 131 = J, so the value sought has been found.

This process leads to a solution unless the value sought is less than the lowest value in the list, the value sought is greater than the largest number in the list, or the value sought is not contained in the list.

9–6.1 Formulation of Binary Search

Figure 9–4 summarizes the binary search algorithm. The values to be searched are stored in ascending order in array INFO and the value sought is stored in location J. The program is written to accommodate multiple sets of data for storage in INFO and for different "sought values (J)" for each set. The outer DO-WHILE mini-module depends upon N; the value read into N establishes the number of entries for INFO or terminates the run (when N is zero). The inner DO-WHILE mini-module controls the search (for J if the value input is not equal to -123), or controls the exit from the search portion (if J is -123).

When J is less than the first data entry or greater than the last data entry, an appropriate message is output and the search is terminated. Otherwise, upper and lower limits are established for search boundaries within the data set in subsequent looping. When upper and lower limits become adjacent within array INFO, the value sought (J) does not exist. After output of a suitable message, the search is terminated (the WRITE following the innermost DO-WHILE). Within the innermost DO-WHILE, labeled 30, the initial values of IBOT and ITOP always encompass all entries in array INFO. As the loop cycles, IBOT or ITOP changes each time the value sought is not found. Each change in IBOT or ITOP halves the area to be searched. If values exist in array INFO between locations ITOP and IBOT (when IBOT $-$ ITOP is greater than or equal to 2), the midpoint location is computed and stored in MID.

J is then compared with the value stored in location INFO(MID). If J is less than INFO(MID), IBOT is set to MID and values in array INFO below location MID are subsequently ignored. If J exceeds INFO(MID), ITOP is set to MID so that no values in array INFO above INFO(MID) are searched. In either case, the area to be searched is cut in half and flow is back to Statement 30 to continue searching for J.

By contrast, when J equals INFO(MID), the value sought has been located and, after appropriate output, control transfers out of the inner loops to the DO-WHILE next to the outside. (Such jumps are not allowed by staunch proponents of structured programming; how could it be eliminated?)

9–6.2 Program SEARCH

Coding for the search is shown in Listing 9–7. Typical output for Program SEARCH is shown in Listing 9–8. Searches include numbers sought that are too small, too big, nonexistent, first in the list, last in the list, and within a sequence. Is this sufficient for a thorough test? Why or why not? Do you like the form for output? Does it give you the information you need and want? If not, what would you do differently?

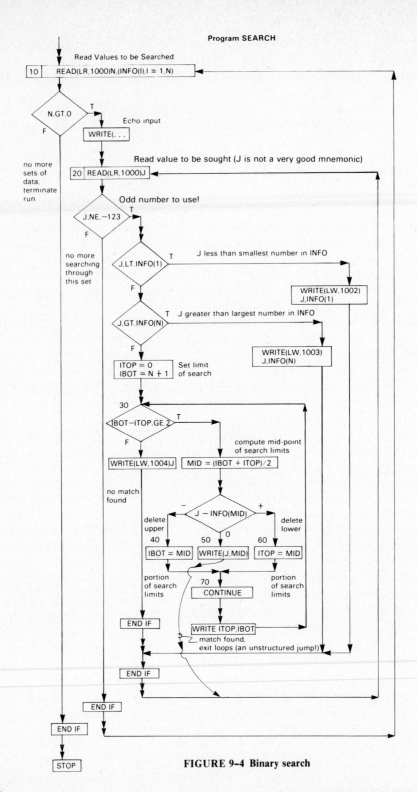

FIGURE 9-4 Binary search

```
      PROGRAM SEARCH

C---                  --- SEARCH FOR A SPECIFIC VALUE (J) ---
C---                  --- FROM VALUES READ INTO ARRAY (INFO) ---
      DIMENSION INFO(30)
      LR=5
      LW=6


C---                  --- READ N VALUES TO BE SEARCHED ---
   10 READ(LR,1000)N,(INFO(I),I=1,N)
      IF(N.GT.0) THEN
C---                  --- ECHO INPUT ---
          WRITE(LW,1001)(I,INFO(I),I=1,N)


C---                  --- READ VALUE TO BE SOUGHT ---
   20     READ(LR,1000) J
          IF(J.NE.-123) THEN

              IF(J.LT.INFO(1)) THEN
C---                  --- J LESS THAN SMALLEST NUMBER IN INFO ---
                  WRITE(LW,1002) J,INFO(1)
              ELSE IF(J.GT.INFO(N)) THEN
C---                  --- J GREATER THAN LARGEST NUMBER IN INFO ---
                  WRITE(LW,1003) J,INFO(N)
              ELSE
C---                  --- SET LIMITS OF SEARCH
                  ITOP = 0
                  IBOT = N+1

   30             IF(IBOT-ITOP.GE.2) THEN
C---                  --- COMPUTE MID-POINT OF SEARCH LIMITS ---
                      MID =(IBOT+ITOP)/2

                      IF(J.LT.INFO(MID)) THEN
C                 --- DELETE UPPER PORTION OF SEARCH LIMITS ---
                          IBOT = MID
                      ELSE IF(J.EQ.INFO(MID)) THEN
C                 --- MATCH FOUND, EXIT LOOPS ---
                          WRITE(LW,1005) J,MID
                          GO TO 80
                      ELSE
C                 --- DELETE LOWER PORTION OF SEARCH LIMITS ---
                          ITOP = MID
                      END IF

   70                 CONTINUE
                      WRITE(LW,1006) ITOP,IBOT
                      GO TO 30
                  ELSE
                      WRITE(LW,1004) J
                  END IF

              END IF

   80         GO TO 20
          END IF

          GO TO 10
      END IF

 1000 FORMAT(10I4)
 1001 FORMAT('1 LIST OF KEYS PRECEDED BY LINE NUMBER'//
     130(I4,':',I5/))
 1002 FORMAT(/' NO MATCH, SEARCHING FOR',I4,2X,
     1'WHICH IS LESS THAN',I4///)
 1003 FORMAT(/' NO MATCH, SEARCHING FOR',I4,2X,
     1'WHICH IS MORE THAN',I4///)
 1004 FORMAT(/' SEARCH TERMINATED, NUMBER',I4,2X,'NOT FOUND'////)
 1005 FORMAT(/ I4,' FOUND ON LINE',I4 ///)
 1006 FORMAT(5X,' IN SEARCH BETWEEN LINES',I4,' AND',I4)

      STOP
      END
```

LISTING 9-7 Coding for program SEARCH

```
LIST OF KEYS PRECEDED BY LINE NUMBER

  1:    10
  2:    13
  3:    17
  4:    73
  5:    84
  6:   111
  7:   121
  8:   130
  9:   131
 10:   132
 11:   133
 12:   134
 13:   160
 14:   190


NO MATCH, SEARCHING FOR   8  WHICH IS LESS THAN   10



NO MATCH, SEARCHING FOR 200   WHICH IS MORE THAN 190



     IN SEARCH BETWEEN LINES    7 AND   15
     IN SEARCH BETWEEN LINES    7 AND   11
     IN SEARCH BETWEEN LINES    7 AND    9
     IN SEARCH BETWEEN LINES    7 AND    8

SEARCH TERMINATED, NUMBER 129   NOT FOUND



     IN SEARCH BETWEEN LINES    7 AND   15
     IN SEARCH BETWEEN LINES    7 AND   11

131 FOUND ON LINE    9



     IN SEARCH BETWEEN LINES    7 AND   15
     IN SEARCH BETWEEN LINES   11 AND   15
     IN SEARCH BETWEEN LINES   11 AND   13
     IN SEARCH BETWEEN LINES   12 AND   13

SEARCH TERMINATED, NUMBER 135   NOT FOUND



     IN SEARCH BETWEEN LINES    0 AND    7
     IN SEARCH BETWEEN LINES    3 AND    7

84 FOUND ON LINE    5



     IN SEARCH BETWEEN LINES    0 AND    7
     IN SEARCH BETWEEN LINES    0 AND    3

10 FOUND ON LINE    1



     IN SEARCH BETWEEN LINES    7 AND   15
     IN SEARCH BETWEEN LINES   11 AND   15
     IN SEARCH BETWEEN LINES   13 AND   15

190 FOUND ON LINE   14
```

LISTING 9-8 Output for program SEARCH

9-7 SUBROUTINE—BEST STRAIGHT LINE THROUGH SET OF DATA PAIRS (OPTIONAL)

Program SIMLR of Listing 7–1 had severe limitations, and single-dimensional arrays can overcome one of them. Listing 9–9 shows coding for program TLR (Test Linear Regression) similar to that of Listing 7–1. The program merely reads sets of data pairs, calls a subroutine which does the work, and outputs the best linear equation for the given data. A major difference from program SIMLR is that X and Y now represent arrays, and access to individual x's and y's is gained by using array elements within the subroutine.

The statement that gives access to the subroutine is

CALL LR(X, Y, PR, N, A, B)

where the following hold.

LR is the name of the subroutine.
X   is an array storing a maximum of 30 x's.
Y   is an array storing a maximum of 30 y's.
PR is the print-control value controlling the amount of output produced by the subroutine.
N   is the number of data pairs.
A   is the value computed within the subroutine for a in the equation $y = a + bx$
B   is the value computed within the subroutine for b in the equation $y = a + bx$

Calculations are performed within the subroutine LR when it is "called" by the main program, TLR. Arrays in the argument list of subroutine LR should have the same dimensions as the corresponding arrays in TLR. Arguments in this program and subroutine happen to agree in name, but such agreement is not necessary. Arguments must, however, agree in meaning, type, and size; one-to-one order is mandatory.

Within the subroutine of Listing 9–10, computations are very similar to those performed by program SIMLR of Listing 7–1. The major exception is that access to x and y is gained from corresponding arrays in subscripted form as X(I) and Y(I). Also,

```
      PROGRAM TLR
      DIMENSION X(30),Y(30)
      LRU=5
      LWU=6

10    CONTINUE
      READ(LRU,1000) N,PR,(X(I),Y(I),I=1,N)

      IF(N.GT.0) THEN
          CALL LR(X,Y,PR,N,A,B)
          WRITE(LWU,1001)A,B
          GO TO 10
      ENDIF

1000  FORMAT(I1,7X,9F8.0:2(/10F8.0))
1001  FORMAT(////' A=',F10.3,2X,'AND B=',F10.3/
     1' IN EQUATION Y= A + B*X' //)

      STOP
      END
```

LISTING 9–9 Coding for program TLR

```
          SUBROUTINE LR(X,Y,PR,N,A,B)
    C         --- OBTAINS A AND B OF Y=A+BX
    C         --- FOR X-Y COORD PAIRS STORED IN
    C         --- ARRAYS X AND Y, SEQUENTIALLY
    C         --- OUTPUTS:
    C         ---   (1)TABLE OF X,Y,XY AND X-SQUARED
    C         ---        (WHEN PR GTR OR EQL 2.)
    C         ---   (2)EQUATION (IF PR GTR OR EQL 1.)
          DIMENSION X(30),Y(30)

          LWU=6

          SUMX  = 0.
          SUMY  = 0.
          SUMXY = 0.
          SUMX2 = 0.

          DO 10 I=1,N
              XY    = X(I)*Y(I)
              X2    = X(I)**2
              SUMX = SUMX + X(I)
              SUMY = SUMY + Y(I)
              SUMXY= SUMXY + XY
              SUMX2= SUMX2 + X2
              IF(PR.GE.2.)WRITE(LWU,1000) X(I),Y(I),XY,X2
     10   CONTINUE

          B=(SUMX*SUMY- N*SUMXY)/(SUMX**2-N*SUMX2)
          A=(SUMY- 3* SUMX)/N
          IF(PR.GE.1.) WRITE(LWU,1001)A,B

     1000 FORMAT(' X=',F8.2,2X,'Y=',F8.2,2X,'X*Y=',F10.2,2X,
          1'X**2=',F10.2)
     1001 FORMAT(///' BEST STRAIGHT LINE THRU POINTS IS'/
          11X,F10.3,' + ',F10.3,' * X = Y' )

          RETURN
          END
```

LISTING 9–10 Coding for subroutine LR

intermediate values of xy and x^2 are temporarily stored during each cycle in locations XY and X2 for ease of output.

If PR is less than 1, subroutine LR does not produce output. When PR is 2 or more, subroutine LR outputs the table of values of x, y, xy and x^2 (one line during each cycle) plus the linear equation $a + bx = y$ (with a and b expressed numerically). If PR is input as 1, only the linear equation is output by subroutine LR.

9–8 EXERCISES

1. Answer each of the following if the order of data cards in Figure 9–2 is reversed.
  (a). Determine the values stored in A of Listing 9–1.
  (b). Determine the values stored in B of Listing 9–2.
  (c). Determine the values stored in A of Listing 9–3 and sketch the corresponding output.
  (d). Determine the values stored in A of Listing 9–4 and show the appearance of the corresponding outputs.

In exercises 2–5, make the following assumptions: (1) The FORMAT statement matches input data appropriately; (2) The DIMENSION statement is large enough so that bounds are not overrun; and (3) All data are not necessarily needed for any statement. Data sets are:

(a)	8	3	2	−6	1	2	−1	4	6
(b)	4	2	6	8	3	1	2	−5	2
(c)	7	−3	−4	7	6	−2	1	8	−4
(d)	6	3	4	5	−5	−4	−3	2	0
(e)	5	0	1	2	3	2	1	0	7

What values would be stored in which elements of what array using data sets (a), (b), (c), (d), or (e) with the following statements?

2. READ(LR, 1000) N, (LV(L), L = 1, N)

3. READ(LR, 1000) NS, (LL(M), M = 1, 12, NS)

4. READ(LR, 1000) (K(I), I = 1, 3), (L(J), J = 1, 4)   (*Note:* I could be used in place of J.)

5. READ(LR, 1000) (K(I), L(I), I = 2, 9, 3)

6. Alter program BBSRT1 so that it writes the data in descending order.

7. At a certain installation, tables are needed for x and various corresponding functions, together with first and second derivatives. Although combinations of terms are variable, the terms themselves are restricted to the following: ax^3, bx^2, cx, d, $e \sin fx$, $g \cos hx$, and re^{tx}. The coefficients a, b, c, d, e, f, g, h, r, and t are read sequentially into a linear array F. Then

$$f(x) = ax^3 + bx^2 + cx + d + e \sin fx + g \cos hx + re^{tx}$$

is written as

> FX = F(1)*X**3+F(2)*X**2+F(3)*X+F(4)+F(5)*SIN(F(6)*X)
> +F(7)*COS(F(8)*X)+F(9)*EXP(F(10)*X)

Likewise, the first derivative is

> FPX = 3.*F(1)*X**2+2.*F(2)*X+F(3)+F(5)*F(6)*COS(F(6)*X)
> −F(7)*F(8)*SIN(F(8)*X)+F(9)*F(10)*EXP(F(10)*X)

Input data for $3x + 7 \sin 2x$ would be

> 0.   0.   3.   0.   7.   2.   0.   0.   0.   0.

Input data for $5x^3 + 17 - 8e^{4x}$ would be

> 5.   0.   0.   17.   0.   0.   0.   0.   −8.   4.

Figure 9–5, on page 240, shows the human-oriented flow diagram. Prepare a machine-oriented flow diagram ready for key-punching or entry at a remote terminal.

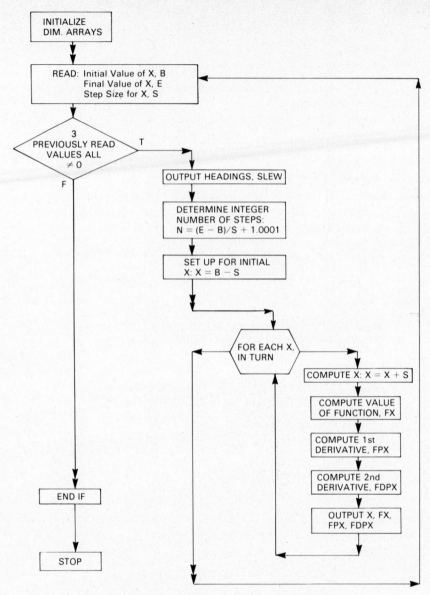

FIGURE 9–5 Human-oriented flow diagram for Exercise 7

Chapter 9 Single-Dimensional Arrays

The Data Statement, Arrays, and Nested DO-Loops

This chapter introduces the DATA statement and amplifies the concepts of arrays and nested DO-loops.

10-1 THE DATA STATEMENT

Much of the data required for use within computer programs can be efficiently and effectively generated. For example, it is more economical to compute the sine of an angle than to look it up in a stored table. On the other hand, certain data cannot be generated by any mathematical function. Wind pressure on buildings (Section 10–2) is typical of such data.

Nonprofessional programmers, experienced in their particular area of expertise, occasionally write inefficient programs because they input tables into DATA statements rather than generating values as needed. Remember, expressions too complicated for routine longhand computations are often very easy to program. The DATA statement should only be used to establish data that cannot be efficiently and effectively generated in the computer program itself.

Characteristics of the DATA statement are summarized in Table 10–1. The three most important considerations are: (1) a one-to-one relationship must be established between variable names, sequential elements of an array, or array element names in the list and constants supplied to fill them, (2) mixing of type is not allowed between variable names, array names, or array element names and the corresponding constants which are assigned, and (3) the total number of variables, elements of a named array, and array element names must equal the number of constants supplied.

DATA statements must follow DIMENSION statements, and they must precede any executable statement. (See Section 16–1.4 for extension permitted by Full Language FORTRAN 77.)

Listing 10–1 illustrates four (among many) possible ways to use a DATA statement to

Table 10-1 The DATA Statement (Subset FORTRAN 77)

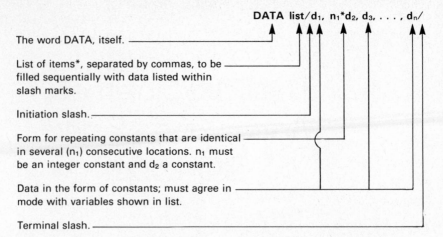

$$\text{DATA list}/d_1, \; n_1 {}^* d_2, \; d_3, \; \ldots , \; d_n /$$

The word DATA, itself.

List of items*, separated by commas, to be filled sequentially with data listed within slash marks.

Initiation slash.

Form for repeating constants that are identical in several (n_1) consecutive locations. n_1 must be an integer constant and d_2 a constant.

Data in the form of constants; must agree in mode with variables shown in list.

Terminal slash.

Storage locations represented by the list must exactly equal the number of data values within the slashes.

*Variable names, array names, or array element names in Subset FORTRAN 77; full language also allows substring names and implied-DO lists.

```
DIMENSION M(3), Q(2)
DATA M/16, −3, 12/, Q/4.3, −0.016/, PI/3.1415926/, N/17/
```

or

```
DIMENSION M(3), Q(2)
DATA PI/3.1415926/, Q/4.3, −0.016/, M/16, −3, 12/, N/17/
```

or

```
DIMENSION M(3), Q(2)
DATA M,Q,N,PI/16, −3, 12, 4.3, −0.016, 17, 3.1415926/
```

or

```
DIMENSION M(3), Q(2)
DATA Q,N,PI/4.3, −0.016, 17, 3.1415926/, M/16, −3, 12/
```

All result in

```
M(1) = 16      Q(1) = 4.3      PI = 3.1415926
M(2) = −3      Q(2) = −0.016   N = 17
M(3) = 12
```

LISTING 10-1 Examples of the DATA statement

prescribe constants for arrays M and Q, and for variables PI and N. Because the one-to-one relationship is essential, many programmers prefer the first or second of the forms shown. Every element of any array shown in the list without subscripts must be entirely filled. It is also possible to assign values to single elements of arrays, such as

$$\text{DATA M(1)}/6/,\ \text{P(3)}/17.26/$$

When constants repeat, the alternate form is useful. Thus, for an array L of dimension 26,

$$\text{DATA L}/1,2,20*3,4,3*5/$$

stores 1 in L(1), 2 in L(2), 3 in L(3) through L(22) inclusive, 4 in L(23), and 5 in L(24) through L(26) inclusive.

10-2 PROGRAM WIND

Buildings are designed for wind loads in accordance with specifications such as the *Uniform Building Code.* Such specifications provide precise loadings that safely represent constant, design wind forces for various elevations and for different geographical regions within the United States. Figure 10-1 shows design wind forces applied to a typical seven-story building. Program WIND is written to find the total load on a vertical strip 1 foot wide for each wall between each set of floors. Clearly, a generalized program would have to provide correct results for buildings with any number of floors, and any spacing between floors.

10-2.1 Illustration of Longhand Solution for Wind Force on Buildings

Output from program WIND (Listing 10-2) is shown for the building in Figure 10-1. The top floor (roof) has a height above ground of 105 feet. Wind pressure changes from 45 to 40 pounds per square foot at 100 feet above ground. Finally, the second floor from the top has a height of 90 feet. Wind force is computed as "height of wall" times "wind pressure":

$$(105 - 100)\ 45 = 225 \text{ pounds}$$
$$(100 - 90)\ 40 = \underline{400} \text{ pounds}$$
$$\text{Total wall force} = 625 \text{ pounds per one-foot strip}$$

For the next wall down, wind pressure remains constant so that total wind force is the height of floor at top of wall minus the height of floor at bottom of wall times wind pressure.

$$\begin{array}{r} 90 \text{ feet} \\ -75 \text{ feet} \\ \hline 15 \text{ feet} \\ \times\ 40 \text{ pounds per square feet} \\ \hline 600 \text{ pounds per one-foot strip} \end{array}$$

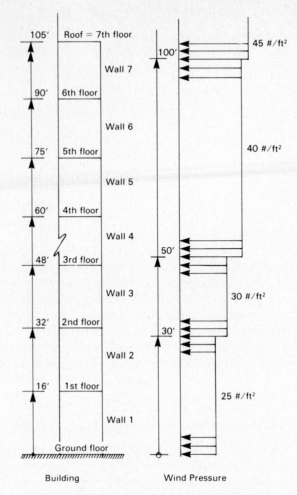

FIGURE 10-1 Wind Pressure on Building

10-2.2 Formulating the Computer Program

A review of the longhand solution used in conjunction with the sketch of Figure 10-1 suggests that a computer program must establish wind pressures and corresponding heights, establish the building geometry, and then determine the forces on each wall. This can be described in more detail in the following manner.

    Establish wind pressures and corresponding heights.
    Read number of floors in building
           IF number of floors is positive, building data exists.
                    From top floor to bottom floor, one floor at a time:
                            Determine height of top of wall;
                            Determine height of bottom of wall;
                            Determine wind pressure(s) for wall.
                            If wind pressure changes over wall height:

Compute force above change;
Compute force below change;
Add forces to obtain the force
on the wall.
ELSE if wind pressure constant:
Compute force on the wall.
Cycle back to next lower floor.
Cycle to next building.
If floor number is 0, STOP.

```
TOP FLR =  105.00 FT.
                        WIND= 45.   FORCE=  225.0 LBS.
MID FLR =  100.00 FT,
                        WIND= 40.   FORCE=  400.0 LBS.
BOT FLR =   90.00 FT.


TOP FLR =   90.00 FT.
                        WIND= 40.   FORCE=  600.0 LBS.
BOT FLR =   75.00 FT.


TOP FLR =   75.00 FT.
                        WIND= 40.   FORCE=  600.0 LBS.
BOT FLR =   60.00 FT.


TOP FLR =   60.00 FT.
                        WIND= 40.   FORCE=  400.0 LBS.
MID FLR =   50.00 FT,
                        WIND= 30.   FORCE=   60.0 LBS.
BOT FLR =   48.00 FT.


TOP FLR =   48.00 FT.
                        WIND= 30.   FORCE=  480.0 LBS.
BOT FLR =   32.00 FT.


TOP FLR =   32.00 FT.
                        WIND= 30.   FORCE=   60.0 LBS.
MID FLR =   30.00 FT,
                        WIND= 25.   FORCE=  350.0 LBS.
BOT FLR =   16.00 FT.


TOP FLR =   16.00 FT.
                        WIND= 25.   FORCE=  400.0 LBS.
BOT FLR =     .00 FT.


FLOOR  HEIGHT   FORCE
  7    105.00   625.0
  6     90.00   600.0
  5     75.00   600.0
  4     60.00   460.0
  3     48.00   480.0
  2     32.00   410.0
  1     16.00   400.0
```

LISTING 10-2 Output from program WIND

A possible definition sheet for program WIND is shown in Table 10-2. Relate the variables in the remaining formulation to the definition sheet; it may also be helpful to sketch a human-oriented flow diagram.

Using Figure 10-1, wind pressure and height can be related in two arrays.

Wind pressure	Stored	Range of height	Upper height	Stored in
25 lb/ft^2	W(1)	0 → 30 ft	30	HZ(1)
30	W(2)	30 → 50	50	HZ(2)
40	W(3)	50 → 100	100	HZ(3)
⋮	⋮	⋮	⋮	⋮

These relationships remain constant, but cannot be related algebraically. Therefore it is appropriate to establish wind pressures and corresponding (upper limits to) heights by a DATA statement. It is also helpful to highlight the relationships between pressure and height by use of spacing within the DATA statement itself.

A major loop is suggested for each building "signified" by reading the number of existing floors, N (a DO-WHILE). Within this major loop, floor heights would then have to be read and a secondary loop entered to work on one floor at a time, top to bottom (I=N,1,−1)(a DO-Loop).

Table 10-2 Definition Sheet for Program WIND

Program:	WIND
Purpose:	This program determines wind forces for a one foot strip on each wall of a building having up to 20 floors using UBC wind loads based on 30 psf at 30 feet above ground level.

Descriptive Items:

HZ(6)	Array containing upper limits on height above ground for each wind pressure; corresponds one-to-one with pressures in array W. HZ(I) is upper height of *i*th wind pressure.
W(6)	Array containing wind pressures for each segment of height above ground; corresponds one-to-one with height in array HZ. W(I) is wind pressure of *i*th height.
H(20)	Floor heights measured from ground, in feet, lowest floor first. H(I) is height of *i*th floor.
WF(20)	Wind forces computed for each wall by program WIND.
N	Number of stories in building, limited to 20.
K	A pointer that "points to" an element of array HZ (for elevation) and an element of array W (for wind pressure).
HT	Height of floor above wall under consideration, in feet.
HB	Height of floor below wall under consideration, in feet.
HI	Height of change in wind pressure IF such a change occurs between the upper and lower heights of wall under consideration.
LR	Logical unit number for input device.
LW	Logical unit number for output device.

Within the secondary loop, four specific values are needed:

HT, height of top of the wall (from floor height above wall)
HB, height of bottom of the wall (from floor height below wall)
HI, height where wind pressure changes over height of wall (if such occurs)
K, a subscript expression that points to the proper wind pressure and corresponding height above ground

The subscript expression K is determined by a terciary loop (a DO-WHILE), which compares the height at the top of the wall (HT) with upper heights corresponding to changes in wind pressure (array HZ). Such a comparison can lead to the difficulty of K becoming zero. An IF statement can use two comparisons: one to find K and the other to preclude the difficulty of a zero value.

The second loop must split into two paths to allow for the two types of calculations required: when wind pressure is constant over wall height, or when wind pressure changes over wall height.

Figure 10–2 gives the machine-oriented flow diagram and modified Nassi-Shneiderman chart for program WIND. Look at the form of output used by the program given in Listing 10–2. Do you think such a presentation is worth the effort involved? Does the format of output have any effect on user confidence in program reliability?

10-2.3 Summary of Program WIND

The DATA statement of Listing 10–3 establishes height above ground for corresponding wind pressures in arrays HZ and W, respectively. Is it clearly evident that these two arrays establish wind pressure of 25 pounds per square foot up to 30 feet, 30 pounds per square foot from 30 feet to 50 feet, 40 pounds per square foot from 50 feet to 100 feet, and so on?

Statement 10 begins the major DO-WHILE, which activates only when the number of floors is positive, signifying that data for a building exists; floor heights are read into array H, bottom floor first.

The major loop computing wall forces is a DO-loop, terminating with 30 CONTINUE. This DO-loop starts at the top of the building and works down (I = N, 1, −1). For each wall, in turn, K is set to point to the upper value of both height and wind pressure as stored in arrays HZ and W. Heights of floors above and below the wall are stored temporarily in HT and HB.

The DO-WHILE initiated at Statement 20 establishes which elements of array HZ and W are to be used, corresponding to upper and lower wall heights.

The IF-THEN-ELSE divides computations into two types: those in which wind pressure changes within the wall height, and those in which wind pressures are constant over the entire wall between floors. In the former, W1 and W2 are computed and summed into WF(I) as the wall force. In the latter, the wall force is stored directly into WF(I), where I signifies the wall number counted from the ground upwards.

10-3 ARRAYS (TABLES OR MATRICES)

In previous chapters, single-dimensional arrays—visualized as rows or columns containing numerical values—were used. Two-dimensional arrays can be visualized as tables or

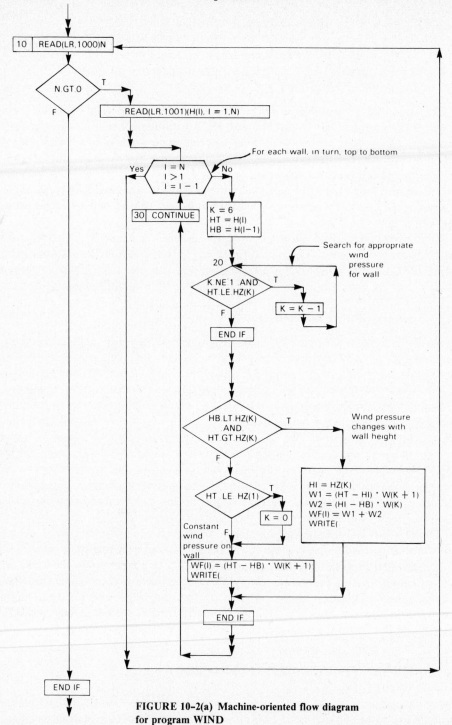

Program WIND

**FIGURE 10–2(a) Machine-oriented flow diagram
for program WIND**

Chapter 10 The Data Statement, Arrays, and Nested DO-Loops

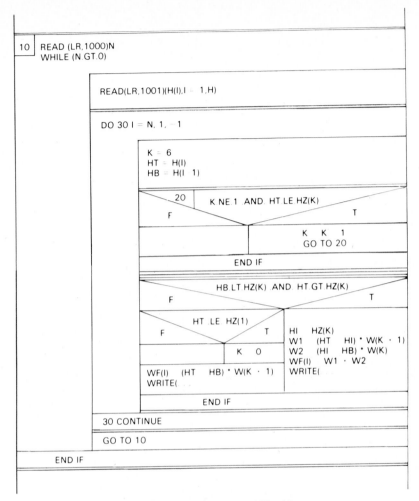

FIGURE 10–2(b) Modified Nassi-Shneiderman chart for program WIND

matrices, and three-dimensional arrays can be visualized as a related series of tables contained on several pages or as matrices. (Extensions to the capabilities of arrays by Full Language FORTRAN 77 are discussed in Section 16–1.2.)

10–3.1 Dimensions

Before the first executable statement within any FORTRAN program, the dimensions of all arrays must be established using only numerical integer constants. Typical form is illustrated by the following (a type statement could also be used).

DIMENSION NAME (6,3), TABLE (10,4,3), INFO(7)

This is in accordance with the rules specified in Table 10–3.

Section 10-3 Arrays (Tables or Matrices)   **249**

```
          PROGRAM WIND

C (THIS PROGRAM DETERMIES WIND FORCES ON BUILDING WALLS)
C (SEE DEFINITION SHEET FOR DETAILS AND DESCRIPTIONS    )

          DIMENSION HZ(6),W(6),H(20),WF(20)
          DATA HZ/30.,50.,100.,500.,1200.,100000./,
        1       W/25.,30., 40., 45.,  55.,    60./

          LR=5
          LW=6

       10 READ(LR,1000) N
          IF(N.GT.0) THEN
              READ(LR,1001) (H(I),I=1,N)

C                 --- DO FOR EACH WALL IN TURN
C                 --- (TOP TO BOTTOM)
              DO 30 I= N,1, -1
                  K =6
                  HT=H(I)
                  HB=H(I-1)

C                 --- SEARCH FOR APPROPRIATE WIND
C                 ---          PRESSURE FOR WALL

       20         IF(K.NE.1 .AND. HT.LE.HZ(K)) THEN
                    , K = K-1
                      GO TO 20
                  END IF

                  IF(HB.LT.HZ(K) .AND. HT.GT.HZ(K)) THEN

C                         --- WIND PRESSURE CHANGES
C                         --- WITHIN WALL HEIGHT
                      HI = HZ(K)
                      W1 = (HT-HI)* W(K+1)
                      W2 = (HI-HB)* W(K)
                      WF(I)=W1+W2
                      WRITE(LW,1002) HT,W(K+1),W1,HI,W(K),W2,HB
                  ELSE

C                         --- WIND PRESSURE REMAINS
C                         --- CONSTANT OVER WALL HEIGHT
                      IF(HT.LE.HZ(1))K=0
                      WF(I)=(HT-HB)* W(K+1)
                      WRITE(LW,1003) HT,W(K+1),WF(I),HB
                  END IF

       30     CONTINUE

              WRITE(LW,1004) (I,H(I),WF(I),I=N,1,-1)
              GO TO 10
          END IF

1000 FORMAT(I4)
1001 FORMAT(10F5.0)
1002 FORMAT(//' TOP FLR =',F8.2,' FT.'/24X,'WIND=',F4.0,3X,
        1'FORCE=',F7.1,' LBS.'/' MID FLR =',F8.2,' FT.'/24X,
        2'WIND=', F4.0,3X,'FORCE=',F7.1,' LBS.'/' BOT FLR =',
        3F8.2,' FT.'/)
1003 FORMAT(//' TOP FLR =',F8.2,' FT.'/24X,'WIND=',F4.0,3X,
        1'FORCE=',F7.1,' LBS.'/' BOT FLR =',F8.2,' FT.'/)
1004 FORMAT(//' FLOOR  HEIGHT  FORCE'/20(I5,F8.2,F7.1/))

     STOP
     END
```

LISTING 10-3 Coding for program WIND

Chapter 10 The Data Statement, Arrays, and Nested DO-Loops

Table 10-3 The DIMENSION Statement

Separation by commas

DIMENSION	$W_1(R)$,	$W_2(R, C)$,	$W_3(R, C, P)$
	1-dim. array named W_1 with R rows	2-dim. array named W_2 with R rows, C columns	3-dim. array named W_3 with R rows, C columns, P pages

W_1, W_2, and W_3 represent symbolic names that:

1. start with a letter;
2. contain only letters and numbers;
3. are limited to 6 characters;
4. establish type by first letter.

    I, J, K, L, M, or N   INTEGER (fixed-point)

not I, J, K, L, M, or N   REAL (floating-point)

R, C, T represent integer (fixed-point) constants or variables*
    that establish size of arrays

First constant	Rows
Second constant	Columns
Third constant	Pages

  with constants separated by commas

*Arithmetic expressions containing only integer constants, integer symbolic names of variables, and integer variables are allowed in the Full Language but not in the subset. See Section 16-1.2 for other extensions.

Array NAME is two-dimensional, array TABLE is three-dimensional, and array INFO is single-dimensional.

The first array, NAME, is an integer array because it starts with N. This array has six rows and three columns.

Array TABLE stores real values in ten rows and four columns, on three separate pages (conceptually).

Finally, array INFO has seven (integer) locations, arranged in a single column (or row).

All DIMENSION statements must precede the first executable statement in the program, but order or combination of the DIMENSION statements themselves, or the array names within DIMENSION statements, is not important. Thus either of these alternate forms is also permissible.

      DIMENSION INFO(7)
      DIMENSION NAME(6,3), TABLE(10,4,3)

DIMENSION NAME(6,3), INFO(7)
DIMENSION TABLE(10,4,3)

Dimension statements must be defined by integer constants because they are used to assign locations for arrays during the first stage, compilation.

The size of an array is equal to the number of elements in the array. Thus the size of INFO(7) is seven and the size of NAME (6,3) is $6 \times 3 = 18$. The size of the three-dimensional array TABLE is $10 \times 4 \times 3 = 120$.

10–3.2 Array Elements; Subscripted Variables

Figure 10–3 illustrates single-, two-, and three-dimensional arrays. In each case, the array is named A, although within any single program array and variable names must be distinct from one another. Subscripts must be integer (fixed-point) constants, variables, or arithmetic expressions.

Two different notations are used in Figure 10–3. One shows typical numerical values for elements of the array stored in particular locations, and the other depicts an array name, followed by the subscripts for the location of that particular element. Some of the numerical values stored in element locations are circled for use in the following discussion.

In the single-dimensional array, the number 54 is stored in location A(4).

Within the two-dimensional array, the circled 3 is stored in Row 4 and Column 3 and, the circled 9 is in Row 2 and Column 5; therefore, access can be gained by using A(4,3) and A(2,5), respectively.

In a three-dimensional array, the first subscript refers to the row, the second to the

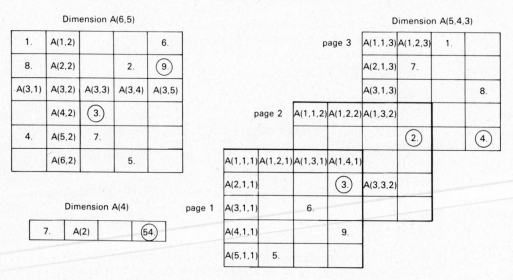

FIGURE 10–3 Locating elements within arrays

Chapter 10 The Data Statement, Arrays, and Nested DO-Loops

column, and the third to the page. Thus the circled 3 on Page 1 is in Row 2 and Column 4. For access, one would use A(2,4,1). Likewise, the circled 2 is in location A(2,4,2), while the circled 4 is stored in location A(5,4,3). Figure 10–3 contains one mistake. Knowing that the first subscript represents the row, the second the column, and the third the page, you should be able to find the mistake fairly easily.

10-3.3 Exceeding Array Limits

As with single-dimensional arrays, a common programming error when arrays have more than one dimension is to use subscripts that exceed the limits established by a DIMENSION statement.

Computer storage of two- and three-dimensional arrays can also be visualized as linear, with arrays stored sequentially by columns (rather than by rows). For example, the following 3×4 array

$$
\begin{array}{cccc}
1 & 2 & 3 & 4 \\
5 & 6 & 7 & 8 \\
9 & 10 & 11 & 12
\end{array}
$$

is stored sequentially as 1, 5, 9, 2, 6, 10, 3, 7, 11, 4, 8, 12.

A three-dimensional array is stored by columns, and then by pages. For example, a $4 \times 3 \times 2$ array with row, column, and page values of

$$
\begin{array}{ccc@{\qquad}ccc}
1 & 2 & 3 & 13 & 14 & 15 \\
4 & 5 & 6 & 16 & 17 & 18 \\
7 & 8 & 9 & 19 & 20 & 21 \\
10 & 11 & 12 & 22 & 23 & 24
\end{array}
$$

is stored sequentially as 1, 4, 7, 10, 2, 5, 8, 11, 3, 6, 9, 12, 13, 16, 19, 22, 14, 17, 20, 23, 15, 18, 21, 24.

Figure 10–4 shows an arrangement for a two-dimensional array with some other variables. (Numbers within boxes represent values *currently* stored.) Suppose a FORTRAN statement that exceeds the array size is encountered:

$$
E = A(3,1)
$$

Subscripts are not commonly checked automatically during the execution stage. So the computer considers A(3,1) to be the next location beyond A(2,3), meaning that E is actually stored with contents taken from B, shown with a current value of 13.

This error occurs most frequently when subscripts are computed, such as in

$$
E = A(2*I + I,J)
$$

If $I = 1$ and $J = 1$, E is not replaced by A(3,1) because A(3,1) does not exist, but instead is replaced by the current contents of B. Variable B is in the location A(3,1) would have

A(1,1)	A(1,2)	A(1,3)	A(2,1)	A(2,2)	A(2,3)	B	C	D	E
1.	3.	5.	7.	9.	11.	13.	15.	17.	19.

FIGURE 10-4 Schematic of variables in storage

occupied if array A had been given large enough dimensions. Of course, if A(3,1) were left of the equal sign, the value of B would be inadvertently changed.

10-3.4 Protection Against Exceeding Array Limits in DO-Loops

Array limits are exceeded most frequently when using DO-loops—the loop index goes out of bounds. This error can be precluded in Subset FORTRAN 77 by adding two IF statements in front of the typical DO-loop mini-module, as illustrated in the flow diagram of Figure 10–5. If the beginning value for the loop increment is negative or zero, flow continues along the main line and avoids the DO-loop entirely. The second IF statement compares the terminal value of the loop index (M) with the maximum dimension of the respective array dimension (MAXD). If the array limit is exceeded, an error message is output and the program terminates. (In some situations the two IF statements can be combined to terminate execution when either the initial or final value of the loop index is not within bounds.)

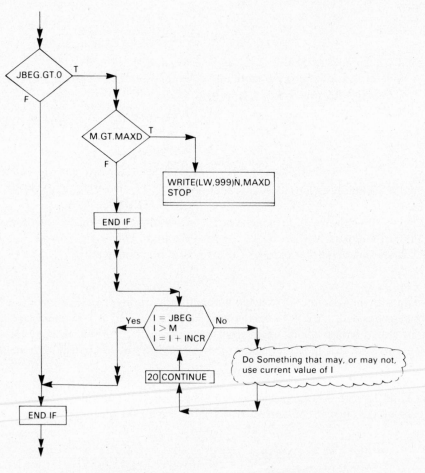

FIGURE 10–5 Protected DO-loop mini-module,
machine-oriented flow

Chapter 10 The Data Statement, Arrays, and Nested DO-Loops

Typical coding for the protected DO-loop mini-module is shown in Listing 10-4. Additional work, both in documentation and coding, is required to add the two IF statements. Furthermore, more computer time is required to execute the program. Yet some programmers feel that the mini-module has sufficient worth to more than compensate for such losses. (Automatic checking by the computer to insure that array elements do not exceed array limits can frequently be requested by the programmer.)

10-4 NESTED DO-LOOPS

Series of nested DO-loops are often used within FORTRAN programs. In such cases, the innermost loop is always completely exhausted before any successive step of the next higher loop is initiated. When the innermost loop is entered at any stage, it always starts from its beginning, and the complete series of loops is executed again.

10-4.1 A Simple Example

Figure 10-6 shows a simple, triple-nested DO-loop. The numbers on independent arrows are used to indicate the progress of the DO-loop in the semitabular form of Table 10-4. Numbers at the left of Table 10-4 correspond to the numbers on the arrows of Figure 10-6, which point to particular parts of the flow diagram. Statements associated with arrow numbers signify operations taking place as execution proceeds through each corresponding part of the flow diagram. The coding for Figure 10-6 is shown in Listing 10-5. A tabulated trace is shown in Table 10-5 and a typical set of output is displayed in Table 10-6.

A series of nested DO's can be terminated with a common CONTINUE statement. For consistency within the concept of mini-modules and structured programming, however, a separate, labeled, terminal CONTINUE statement is recommended for each independent DO-loop. (See Section 8-2.6.) Use of independent terminal CONTINUE statements is also helpful if additional statements need to be inserted into the program. For example, temporary WRITE statements are often used during particularly difficult debugging processes. A common CONTINUE statement makes such debugging additions tricky at best. (See Chapter 13.)

Complicated subscript expressions are often computed before being used to define

```
        IF (JBEG.GT.0) THEN

            IF (M.GT.MAXD) THEN
                WRITE(LW,999)M,MAXD
                STOP
            END IF

            DO 20 I = JBEG, M, INCR
                Do Something
20          CONTINUE

        END IF
```

LISTING 10-4 Protected DO-loop mini-module; coding

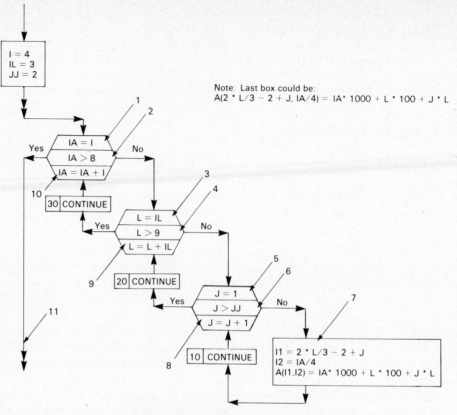

Note: Last box could be:
A(2 * L/3 − 2 + J, IA/4) = IA* 1000 + L * 100 + J * L

FIGURE 10-6 Triple-nested DO-loops—flow diagram with notation code

```
I = 4
IL = 3
JJ = 2

DO 30 IA = I, 8, I

    DO 20 L = IL, 9, IL

        DO 10 J = I, JJ
            I1 = 2 * L/3 −2 + J
            I2 = IA/4
            A (I1, I2) = IA* 1000 + L * 100 + J * L
10          CONTINUE

20      CONTINUE

30  CONTINUE


A(2 * L/3 − 2 + J, IA/4) = IA* 1000 + L * 100 + J * L
```

Alternate ←

LISTING 10-5 Triple-nested DO-loops; coding

Table 10-4 Semi-Tabular Trace of Triple Nested DO-Loop

1. IA is set equal to 4
2. Since IA not >8
3. L is set equal to 3
4. Since L not >9
5. J is set equal to 1
6. Since J not >2
7. A(2 * L/3 – 2 + J, IA/4) is set equal to IA * 1000 + L * 100 + J * L

   or A(1, 1) = 4303
8. J is incremented by 1; therefore J = 1 + 1 = 2
6. Since J not >2
7. A(2 * L/3 – 2 + J, IA/4) is set equal to IA * 1000 + L * 100 + J * L

   or A(2, 1) = 4306
8. J is incremented by 1; therefore J = 2 + 1 = 3
6. Since J >2
9. L is incremented by 3; therefore L = 3 + 3 = 6
4. Since L not >9
5. J is reset to 1
6. Since J not >2
7. A(3, 1) = 4606 (Equation evaluated with IA = 4, L = 6, and J = 1)
8. J is incremented by 1; therefore J = 1 + 1 = 2
6. Since J not >2
7. A(4, 1) = 4612 (Equation evaluated with IA * 4, L = 6, and J = 2)
8. J is incremented by 1; therefore J = 2 + 1 = 3
6. Since J>2
9. L is incremented by 3; therefore L = 6 + 3 = 9
4. Since L not >9
5. J is reset to 1
   Process then repeats until J = 3 and L = 12; then
4. Since L>9
10. IA is incremented by 4; therefore IA = 4 + 4 = 8
2. Since IA not >8
3. L is reset to 3
4. Since L not >9
5. J is reset to 1
   And process repeats until J = 3, L = 12, and IA = 12
2. Since IA>12, Loop is exhausted
11. Proceed to next instruction

Table 10-5 Trace of Triple Nested DO-Loop

A Tabulated Sequence of Calculations Would Appear:

IA	L	J	A(2 * L/3 − 2 × J, IA/4)	IA * 1000 × L * 100 × J * L	A(,) =
4	3	1	A(2 * 3/3 − 2 + 1, 4/4)	4 * 1000 + 3 * 100 + 1 * 3	A(1,1) = 4303
4	3	2	A(2 * 3/3 − 2 + 2, 4/4)	4 * 1000 + 3 * 100 + 2 * 3	A(2,1) = 4306
4	6	1	A(2 * 6/3 − 2 + 1, 4/4)	4 * 1000 + 6 * 100 + 1 * 6	A(3,1) = 4606
4	6	2	A(2 * 6/3 − 2 + 2, 4/4)	4 * 1000 + 6 * 100 + 2 * 6	A(4,1) = 4612
4	9	1	A(2 * 9/3 − 2 + 1, 4/4)	4 * 1000 + 9 * 100 + 1 * 9	A(5,1) = 4909
4	9	2	A(2 * 9/3 − 2 + 2, 4/4)	4 * 1000 + 9 * 100 + 2 * 9	A(6,1) = 4918
8	3	1	A(2 * 3/3 − 2 + 1, 8/4)	8 * 1000 + 3 * 100 + 1 * 3	A(1,2) = 8303
8	3	2	A(2 * 3/3 − 2 + 2, 8/4)	8 * 1000 + 3 * 100 + 2 * 3	A(2,2) = 8306

and so on. . . .

Table 10-6 Output From Triple Nested DO-Loop of Listing 10-5, page 256

Row/Column	1	2
1	4303	8303
2	4306	8306
3	4606	8606
4	4612	8612
5	4909	8909
6	4918	8918

array elements. If difficulties occur, additional statements can then be added to trace the subscript value if the loop terminates with a CONTINUE:

```
      I1 = 2*L/3 − 2 + J
      I2 = IA/4
      A(I1,I2) = IA*1000 + L * 100 + J * L
      WRITE (LW, 999) L, J, IA, I1, I2, A(I1, I2)
999   FORMAT (' L = ', I3, 2X, 'J = ', I3 . . .
10    CONTINUE
```

An alternate statement which uses subscript expressions rather than I1 and I2 is legal and is preferred by many programmers.

10–4.2 Some Typical Uses of Double-Nested DO-loops

A double-nested DO-loop can be utilized to sum all values in a two-dimensional table such as the one depicted by array IT in Table 10–7. The flow diagram of Figure 10–7 and the corresponding coding of Listing 10–6 indicate the process involved. The location for

Table 10-7 Two-Dimensional Table With Various
            Summations

Array IT(5, 6)   *Array NRSUM (5)*

1	3	9	6	9	8
0	4	7	9	3	6
2	3	9	2	0	1
2	6	5	3	7	3
9	5	8	9	2	2

36
29
17
26
35

(Sum of each row in array IT)

Array KSUM (6)

NSUM = 143

14	21	38	29	21	20

(Sum of all values in array IT)

(Sum of each column of array IT)

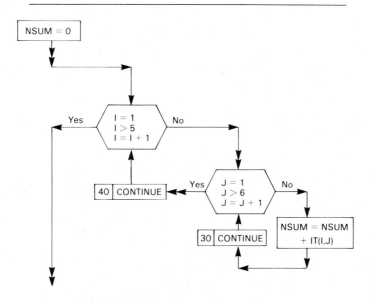

FIGURE 10-7 Flow diagram for summing two-dimensional table

accumulating the sum, called NSUM, is initialized (set to zero) before entering the double-nested DO-loop. One summation is performed for each element of the array, working on one row at a time (left to right) from the top down.

A similar process is shown in the flow diagram of Figure 10–8, where the objective is to obtain the sum of each row (in array NRSUM) and the sum of each column (in array KSUM). Coding for this program is shown in Listing 10–7.

Two solutions are shown. The first solution uses two independent DO-loops and sums rows completely before entering the second DO-loop to sum columns. The second

```
PROGRAM TBLSUM

DIMENSION IT(5,6),NRSUM(5),KSUM(6)
DATA IT/1,0,2,2,9,  3,4,3,6,5,  9,7,9,5,8,
1        6,9,2,3,9,  9,3,0,7,2,  8,6,1,3,2/,LW/6/

WRITE(LW,999)

NSUM = 0

DO 40 I=1,5

    DO 30 J=1,6
        NSUM = NSUM + IT(I,J)
        WRITE(LW,1000) I,J,IT(I,J),NSUM
30      CONTINUE

40 CONTINUE

999 FORMAT('1I J IT(I,J) NSUM'/)

1000 FORMAT(I2,I2,I5,I7)
```

Output:

```
I J IT(I,J) NSUM

1 1    1       1
1 2    3       4
1 3    9      13
1 4    6      19
1 5    9      28
1 6    8      36
2 1    0      36
2 2    4      40
2 3    7      47
2 4    9      56
2 5    3      59
2 6    6      65
3 1    2      67
3 2    3      70
3 3    9      79
3 4    2      81
3 5    0      81
3 6    1      82
4 1    2      84
4 2    6      90
4 3    5      95
4 4    3      98
4 5    7     105
4 6    3     108
5 1    9     117
5 2    5     122
5 3    8     130
5 4    9     139
5 5    2     141
5 6    2     143
```

LISTING 10-6 Summing two-dimensional table; coding and output

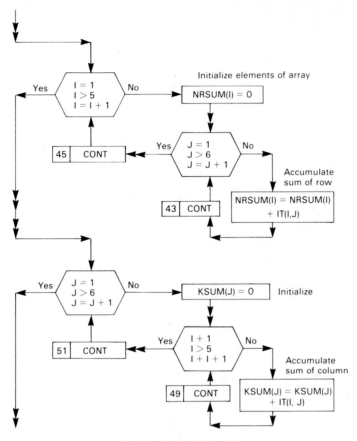

OR, IF [NRSUM] & [KSUM] ALREADY INITIALIZED:

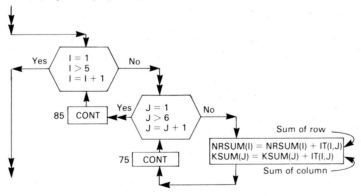

**FIGURE 10-8 Flow diagram for summing rows
and columns of two-dimensional array**

```
1001 FORMAT('1I J IT(I,J) NRSUM'/)
1002 FORMAT('1I J IT(I,J) KSUM    '/)
1003 FORMAT('1I J IT(I,J)    NRSUM        KSUM'/)

     WRITE(LW,1001)

     DO 45 I=1,5
        NRSUM(I)=0

        DO 43 J=1,6
             NRSUM(I) = NRSUM(I) + IT(I,J)
             WRITE(LW,1010) I,J,IT(I,J),I,NRSUM(I)
  43    CONTINUE

  45 CONTINUE

1010 FORMAT(2I2,I5,' NRSUM(',I1,') =',I3)
1011 FORMAT(2I2,I5,' KSUM(',I1,') =',I3)

     WRITE(LW,1002)

     DO 51 J=1,6
        KSUM(J)=0

        DO 49 I=1,5
             KSUM(J) = KSUM(J) + IT(I,J)
             WRITE(LW,1011) I,J,IT(I,J),J,KSUM(J)
  49    CONTINUE

  51 CONTINUE

     DO 70 I=1,5
        NRSUM(I)=0
  70 CONTINUE

     DO 71 J=1,6
        KSUM(J)=0
  71 CONTINUE

     WRITE(LW,1003)

     DO 85 I = 1,5

        DO 75 J = 1,6
             NRSUM(I) = NRSUM(I) + IT(I,J)
             KSUM(J)  =  KSUM(J) + IT(I,J)
             WRITE(LW,1012) I,J,IT(I,J),I,NRSUM(I),J,KSJM(J)
  75    CONTINUE

  85 CONTINUE

1012 FORMAT(2I2,I5,' NRSUM(',I1,')=',I3,' KSUM(',I1,')=',I3)
```

**LISTING 10–7 Coding, summing rows and
columns of two-dimensional array with outputs**

solution uses only one DO-loop to sum both rows and columns, assuming that arrays
NRSUM and KSUM have already been initialized.

10-5 I/O OF ARRAYS

A number of methods are available for the input and output of two-dimensional and
three-dimensional arrays. All are legally permissible, but only one yields human-oriented
results in essentially every conceivable situation.

Output:

```
I J IT(I,J) NRSUM
1 1   1 NRSUM(1) =  1
1 2   3 NRSUM(1) =  4
1 3   9 NRSUM(1) = 13
1 4   6 NRSUM(1) = 19
1 5   9 NRSUM(1) = 28
1 6   8 NRSUM(1) = 36
2 1   0 NRSUM(2) =  0
2 2   4 NRSUM(2) =  4
2 3   7 NRSUM(2) = 11
2 4   9 NRSUM(2) = 20
2 5   3 NRSUM(2) = 23
2 6   6 NRSUM(2) = 29
3 1   2 NRSUM(3) =  2
3 2   3 NRSUM(3) =  5
3 3   9 NRSUM(3) = 14
3 4   2 NRSUM(3) = 16
3 5   0 NRSUM(3) = 16
3 6   1 NRSUM(3) = 17
4 1   2 NRSUM(4) =  2
4 2   6 NRSUM(4) =  8
4 3   5 NRSUM(4) = 13
4 4   3 NRSUM(4) = 16
4 5   7 NRSUM(4) = 23
4 6   3 NRSUM(4) = 26
5 1   9 NRSUM(5) =  9
5 2   5 NRSUM(5) = 14
5 3   8 NRSUM(5) = 22
5 4   9 NRSUM(5) = 31
5 5   2 NRSUM(5) = 33
5 6   2 NRSUM(5) = 35
```

Output:

```
I J IT(I,J) KSUM
1 1   1 KSUM(1) =  1
2 1   0 KSUM(1) =  1
3 1   2 KSUM(1) =  3
4 1   2 KSUM(1) =  5
5 1   9 KSUM(1) = 14
1 2   3 KSUM(2) =  3
2 2   4 KSUM(2) =  7
3 2   3 KSUM(2) = 10
4 2   6 KSUM(2) = 16
5 2   5 KSUM(2) = 21
1 3   9 KSUM(3) =  9
2 3   7 KSUM(3) = 16
3 3   9 KSUM(3) = 25
4 3   5 KSUM(3) = 30
5 3   8 KSUM(3) = 38
1 4   6 KSUM(4) =  6
2 4   9 KSUM(4) = 15
3 4   2 KSUM(4) = 17
4 4   3 KSUM(4) = 20
5 4   9 KSUM(4) = 29
1 5   9 KSUM(5) =  9
2 5   3 KSUM(5) = 12
3 5   0 KSUM(5) = 12
4 5   7 KSUM(5) = 19
5 5   2 KSUM(5) = 21
1 6   8 KSUM(6) =  8
2 6   6 KSUM(6) = 14
3 6   1 KSUM(6) = 15
4 6   3 KSUM(6) = 18
5 6   2 KSUM(6) = 20
```

Output:

```
I J IT(I,J)   NRSUM        KSUM
1 1   1 NRSUM(1)=  1 KSUM(1)=  1
1 2   3 NRSUM(1)=  4 KSUM(2)=  3
1 3   9 NRSUM(1)= 13 KSUM(3)=  9
1 4   6 NRSUM(1)= 19 KSUM(4)=  6
1 5   9 NRSUM(1)= 28 KSUM(5)=  9
1 6   8 NRSUM(1)= 36 KSUM(6)=  8
2 1   0 NRSUM(2)=  0 KSUM(1)=  1
2 2   4 NRSUM(2)=  4 KSUM(2)=  7
2 3   7 NRSUM(2)= 11 KSUM(3)= 16
2 4   9 NRSUM(2)= 20 KSUM(4)= 15
2 5   3 NRSUM(2)= 23 KSUM(5)= 12
2 6   6 NRSUM(2)= 29 KSUM(6)= 14
3 1   2 NRSUM(3)=  2 KSUM(1)=  3
3 2   3 NRSUM(3)=  5 KSUM(2)= 10
3 3   9 NRSUM(3)= 14 KSUM(3)= 25
3 4   2 NRSUM(3)= 16 KSUM(4)= 17
3 5   0 NRSUM(3)= 16 KSUM(5)= 12
3 6   1 NRSUM(3)= 17 KSUM(6)= 15
4 1   2 NRSUM(4)=  2 KSUM(1)=  5
4 2   6 NRSUM(4)=  8 KSUM(2)= 16
4 3   5 NRSUM(4)= 13 KSUM(3)= 30
4 4   3 NRSUM(4)= 16 KSUM(4)= 20
4 5   7 NRSUM(4)= 23 KSUM(5)= 19
4 6   3 NRSUM(4)= 26 KSUM(6)= 18
5 1   9 NRSUM(5)=  9 KSUM(1)= 14
5 2   5 NRSUM(5)= 14 KSUM(2)= 21
5 3   8 NRSUM(5)= 22 KSUM(3)= 38
5 4   9 NRSUM(5)= 31 KSUM(4)= 29
5 5   2 NRSUM(5)= 33 KSUM(5)= 21
5 6   2 NRSUM(5)= 35 KSUM(6)= 20
```

LISTING 10-7 *(Continued)*

Listing 10-8, including study notes, is the coding of a FORTRAN program designed solely to indicate methods for the output of two-dimensional arrays. Headings for each form of WRITE statement specify the form actually used to output the array.

On lines 8 through 12 of the program, values are stored in an array of six rows and 23 columns. Values are entered so that the hundredths digit represents the stored row number. The tens and units digits show the column number where that particular constant is stored. Thus 423 is on the fourth row and in the 23rd column, while 106 is on the first row and in the sixth column. This technique is used to aid visualization of the two-dimensional output when written with various formatting schemes.

Output from line 27 is shown in Listing 10-9. This form of WRITE statement is quite simple to use and outputs the entire array, but it places the array in an order that is difficult to follow. The number 414 is circled to show where an element stored in Row 4, Column 14 occurs in the array output. To further illustrate the disadvantage of this method, try to quickly find the number 222 stored in the second row, 22nd column.

An alternate output of the entire array is shown (line 36 in Listing 10-10). In order to make the output more readable, the format has only six values per line, corresponding to the number of rows in the original matrix. Output in this case is transposed; that is, rows become columns and columns become rows. The elements are fairly easy to locate, but the transposed form may not be desirable. Also, if the number of rows in the matrix were to change, the format would have to change in a corresponding manner or the desirable ordering would be destroyed.

```
1            PROGRAM ARAYIO
2            DIMENSION A(6,23)
3
4     C      FILL ARRAY WITH NUMBERS SIGNIFYING THEIR SUBSCRIPTS
5     C           HUNDREDS DIGIT FOR ROW(LINE)
6     C           TENS & UNITS DIGIT FOR COLUMN
7
8            DO 2 I=1,6
9                DO 1 J=1,23
10                   A(I,J) = 100 * I + J
11        1        CONTINUE
12        2 CONTINUE
13
14    C      SET N AND M TO OUTPUT FULL ARRAY
15           N=6
16           M=23
17
18    C      ESTABLISH LOGICAL UNIT NUMBER FOR WRITE
19           LW=6
20
21    C---   WRITE AS FULL ARRAY USING 100 FORMAT(1X,10F6.0)
22
23
24           WRITE(LW,99)
25        99 FORMAT(1H1,"FULL ARRAY BY WRITE(LW,100)A; 100 FORMAT(1X,10F6.0 )"
26           1/1X,"NOTE ARRAY OUTPUT BY COLUMNS--HARD TO LOCATE ELEMENTS"//)
27           WRITE(LW,100)A
28       100 FORMAT(1X,10F6.0)
29
30    C---   WRITE AS FULL ARRAY WITH FORMAT EQUATING VALUES PER LINE TO TOTAL
31    C      NUMBER OF COLUMNS
32
33           WRITE(LW,101)
34       101 FORMAT(1H1,"FULL ARRAY BY WRITE(LW,102)A;   102 FORMAT(1X,6E11.3)"/
35           11X,"THIS IS TRANSPOSE OF ARRAY--ROWS & COLS INTERCHANGED"//)
36           WRITE(LW,102) A
37       102 FORMAT(1X,6E11.3)
38
39    C---   USE DOUBLE IMPLIED DO LOOPS--TWO WAYS
40
41           WRITE(LW,103)
42       103 FORMAT(1H1,"WRITE(LW,100)((A(I,J),I=1,N),J=1,M);(1X,10F6.0)"/
43           11X,"OBSERVE ORDER PRODUCED -- STILL HARD TO READ"//)
44           WRITE(LW,100)((A(I,J),I=1,N),J=1,M)
45
46           WRITE(LW,104)
47       104 FORMAT(1H1,"WRITE(LW,100)((A(I,J),J=1,M),I=1,N);(1X,10F6.0)"/
48           11X,"NOTICE DIFFERENCE IN ORDER -- STILL HARD TO READ"//)
49           WRITE(LW,100)((A(I,J),J=1,M),I=1,N)
50
51    C---   USE DO + IMPLIED DO FOR BETTER FORM
52
53           WRITE(LW,105)
54       105 FORMAT(1H1,3X,"DO 10 I=1,N"/1X,"    WRITE(LW,100)(A(I,J),J=1,M)",
55           1/1X,"10 CONTINUE",
56           22X,"100 FORMAT(1X,10F6.0)"/1X,"NOW MUCH EASIER TO READ"//)
57
58           DO 10 I=1,N
59               WRITE(LW,100)(A(I,J),J=1,M)
60        10 CONTINUE
61
62    C---   ADD NUMBERING OF LINES (ROWS)
63
```

LISTING 10-8 Coding for program ARAYIO

```
64              WRITE(LW,106)
65      106 FORMAT(1H1,3X,"DO 20 I=1,N"/1X,"    WRITE(LW,108)I,(A(I,J),J=1,M)",
66          1/1X,"20 CONTINUE",
67          22X,"108 FORMAT(I3,2X,10F6.0/10(5X,10F6.0))"/
68          31X,"THIS MAKES LOCATING ELEMENTS IN TABLES QUITE EASY"/
69          41X,"NOTE THAT FOR SIMPLICITY,FORMAT SHOULD ALLOW 10 VALUES/LINE"/
70          5/)
71
72              DO 20 I=1,N
73                  WRITE(LW,108)I,(A(I,J),J=1,M)
74      20 CONTINUE
75
76      108 FORMAT(I3,2X,10F6.0/10(5X,10F6.0))
77
78              CALL EXIT
79              END
```

LISTING 10-8 (*Continued*)

```
FULL ARRAY BY WRITE(LW,100)A; 100 FORMAT(1X,10F6.0 )
NOTE ARRAY OUTPUT BY COLUMNS--HARD TO LOCATE ELEMENTS

        101.  201.  301.  401.  501.  601.  102.  202.  302.  402.
        502.  602.  103.  203.  303.  403.  503.  603.  104.  204.
        304.  404.  504.  604.  105.  205.  305.  405.  505.  605.
        106.  206.  306.  406.  506.  606.  107.  207.  307.  407.
        507.  607.  108.  208.  308.  408.  508.  608.  109.  209.
        309.  409.  509.  609.  110.  210.  310.  410.  510.  610.
        111.  211.  311.  411.  511.  611.  112.  212.  312.  412.
        512.  612.  113.  213.  313.  413.  513.  613.  114.  214.
        314. (414.) 514.  614.  115.  215.  315.  415.  515.  615.
        116.  216.  316.  416.  516.  616.  117.  217.  317.  417.
        517.  617.  118.  218.  318.  418.  518.  618.  119.  219.
        319.  419.  519.  619.  120.  220.  320.  420.  520.  620.
        121.  221.  321.  421.  521.  621.  122.  222.  322.  422.
        522.  622.  123.  223.  323.  423.  523.  623.
```

414 is in
row 4
column 14

LISTING 10-9 Output of entire array, by array
name, without subscripts

Double implied-DO loops can also be used to output two-dimensional arrays. The output from line 44 is shown in Listing 10–11 and the output from line 49 in Listing 10–12. Observe the manner in which the nested implied-DO loops are activated. Also note that it is difficult to find a particular location unless the format is tied directly into the WRITE statement. For example, in both Listings 10–11 and 10–12, try to quickly find the number stored on the fifth row in the third column represented by 503.

We are oriented to numbers expressed in base 10. Therefore a format that shows ten values per line would be useful if it could be tied to the rows. Such an output is shown in Listing 10–13, from lines 58 and 59 of Listing 10–8, using a regular DO-loop plus an implied-DO loop.

The loop index of the regular DO-loop defines rows. The loop index of the implied-DO loop defines columns. Thus each time the loop cycles, the WRITE statement is executed for a single row of the array and the FORMAT statement starts from its beginning. Because there are 23 columns in the array and only ten values can be output per line, three lines are needed per row, with the final three values in the third line of output for each row.

FULL ARRAY BY WRITE(LW,102)A; 102 FORMAT(1X,6E11.3)
THIS IS TRANSPOSE OF ARRAY--ROWS & COLS INTERCHANGED

```
        .101+003    .201+003    .301+003    .401+003    .501+003    .601+003
        .102+003    .202+003    .302+003    .402+003    .502+003    .602+003
        .103+003    .203+003    .303+003    .403+003    .503+003    .603+003
        .104+003    .204+003    .304+003    .404+003    .504+003    .604+003
        .105+003    .205+003    .305+003    .405+003    .505+003    .605+003
        .106+003    .206+003    .306+003    .406+003    .506+003    .606+003
        .107+003    .207+003    .307+003    .407+003    .507+003    .607+003
        .108+003    .208+003    .308+003    .408+003    .508+003    .608+003
        .109+003    .209+003    .309+003    .409+003    .509+003    .609+003
        .110+003    .210+003    .310+003    .410+003    .510+003    .610+003
        .111+003    .211+003    .311+003    .411+003    .511+003    .611+003
        .112+003    .212+003    .312+003    .412+003    .512+003    .612+003
        .113+003    .213+003    .313+003    .413+003    .513+003    .613+003
        .114+003    .214+003    .314+003    .414+003    .514+003    .614+003
.215+03 is in  .115+003   (.215+003)   .315+003    .415+003    .515+003    .615+003
        .116+003    .216+003    .316+003    .416+003    .516+003    .616+003
row 2   .117+003    .217+003    .317+003    .417+003    .517+003    .617+003
        .118+003    .218+003    .318+003    .418+003    .518+003    .618+003
column 15  .119+003  .219+003   .319+003    .419+003    .519+003    .619+003
        .120+003    .220+003    .320+003    .420+003    .520+003    .620+003
        .121+003    .221+003    .321+003    .421+003    .521+003    .621+003
        .122+003    .222+003    .322+003    .422+003    .522+003    .622+003
        .123+003    .223+003    .323+003    .423+003    .523+003    .623+003
```

LISTING 10–10 Transposed array, using array name without subscripts

WRITE(LW,100)((A(I,J),I=1,N),J=1,M);(1X,10F6.0)
OBSERVE ORDER PRODUCED -- STILL HARD TO READ

```
        101.    201.    301.    401.    501.    601.    102.    202.    302.    402.
        502.    602.    103.    203.    303.    403.    503.    603.    104.    204.
        304.    404.    504.    604.    105.    205.    305.    405.    505.    605.
        106.    206.    306.    406.    506.    606.    107.    207.    307.    407.
        507.    607.    108.    208.    308.    408.    508.    608.    109.    209.
        309.    409.    509.    609.    110.    210.    310.    410.    510.    610.
        111.    211.    311.    411.    511.    611.    112.    212.    312.    412.
        512.    612.    113.    213.    313.    413.    513.    613.    114.    214.
        314.    414.    514.    614.    115.    215.    315.    415.    515.    615.
116 is in (116.)  216.    316.    416.    516.    616.    117.    217.    317.    417.
        517.    617.    118.    218.    318.    418.    518.    618.    119.    219.
row 1   319.    419.    519.    619.    120.    220.    320.    420.    520.    620.
column 16  121.  221.    321.    421.    521.    621.    122.    222.    322.    422.
        522.    622.    123.    223.    323.    423.    523.    623.
```

LISTING 10–11 Implied-DO loops

WRITE(LW,100)((A(I,J),J=1,M),I=1,N);(1X,10F6.0)
NOTICE DIFFERENCE IN ORDER -- STILL HARD TO READ

```
        101.    102.    103.    104.    105.    106.    107.    108.    109.    110.
        111.    112.    113.    114.    115.    116.    117.    118.    119.    120.
        121.    122.    123.    201.    202.    203.    204.    205.    206.    207.
        208.    209.    210.    211.    212.    213.    214.    215.    216.    217.
        218.    219.    220.    221.    222.    223.    301.    302.    303.    304.
        305.    306.    307.    308.    309.    310.    311.    312.    313.    314.
        315.    316.    317.    318.    319.    320.    321.    322.    323.    401.
        402.    403.    404.    405.    406.    407.    408.    409.    410.    411.
        412.    413.    414.    415.    416.    417.    418.    419.    420.    421.
        422.    423.    501.    502.    503.    504.    505.    506.    507.    508.
        509.    510.    511.    512.    513.    514.    515.    516.    517.    518.
        519.    520.    521.    522.    523.    601.    602.    603.    604.    605.
        606.    607.    608.    609.    610.    611.    612.    613.    614.    615.
        616.    617.    618.    619.    620.    621.    622.    623.
```

LISTING 10–12 Implied-DO loops, limits interchanged

Chapter 10 The Data Statement, Arrays, and Nested DO-Loops

```
      DO 10 I=1,N
      WRITE(LW,100)(A(I,J),J=1,M)
10 CONTINUE   100 FORMAT(1X,10F6.0)
NOW MUCH EASIER TO READ
```

101.	102.	103.	104.	105.	106.	107.	108.	109.	110.
111.	112.	113.	114.	115.	116.	117.	118.	119.	120.
121.	122.	123.							
201.	202.	203.	204.	205.	206.	207.	208.	209.	210.
211.	212.	213.	214.	215.	216.	217.	218.	219.	220.
221.	222.	223.							
301.	302.	303.	304.	305.	306.	307.	308.	309.	310.
311.	312.	313.	314.	315.	316.	317.	318.	319.	320.
321.	322.	323.							
401.	402.	403.	404.	405.	406.	407.	408.	409.	410.
411.	412.	413.	414.	415.	(416.)	417.	418.	419.	420.
421.	422.	423.							
501.	502.	503.	504.	505.	506.	507.	508.	509.	510.
511.	512.	513.	514.	515.	516.	517.	518.	519.	520.
521.	522.	523.							
601.	602.	603.	604.	605.	605.	607.	608.	609.	610.
611.	612.	613.	614.	615.	616.	617.	618.	619.	620.
621.	622.	623.							

— Easily located by visual inspection

(a) in row 4 → in group representing row 4
(b) in column 16 → in 2nd row, 6th location of the group which represents row 4

LISTING 10–13 Improved output of two-dimensional array

```
      DO 20 I=1,N
      WRITE(LW,108)I,(A(I,J),J=1,M)
20 CONTINUE   108 FORMAT(I3,2X,10F6.0/10(5X,10F6.0/))
THIS MAKES LOCATING ELEMENTS IN TABLES QUITE EASY
NOTE THAT FOR SIMPLICITY,FORMAT SHOULD ALLOW 10 VALUES/LINE
```

1	101.	102.	103.	104.	105.	106.	107.	108.	109.	110.
	111.	112.	113.	114.	115.	116.	117.	118.	119.	120.
	121.	122.	123.							
2	201.	202.	203.	204.	205.	206.	207.	208.	209.	210.
	211.	212.	213.	214.	215.	216.	217.	218.	219.	220.
	221.	222.	223.							
3	301.	302.	303.	304.	305.	306.	307.	308.	309.	310.
	311.	312.	313.	314.	315.	316.	317.	318.	319.	320.
	321.	322.	323.							
4	401.	402.	403.	404.	405.	406.	407.	408.	409.	410.
	411.	412.	413.	414.	415.	416.	417.	418.	419.	420.
	421.	422.	423.							
5	501.	502.	503.	504.	505.	506.	507.	508.	509.	510.
	511.	512.	513.	514.	515.	516.	517.	518.	519.	520.
	521.	522.	523.							
6	601.	602.	603.	604.	605.	606.	607.	608.	609.	610.
	611.	612.	613.	614.	615.	616.	617.	618.	619.	620.
	621.	622.	623.							

LISTING 10–14 Improved output with row number

Notice how easy it is to find a particular location using this format. For instance, the number 416, stored in Row 4, Column 16, is quickly found in the table.

An improved form is shown in Listing 10–14, from lines 72 and 73 of Listing 10–8. In this case, the row number itself is also output. This format makes it very easy to find a row number and then to locate the desired element in a particular column. Use of a ten-column format makes this method both efficient and effective.

Any of these methods for input and output of arrays may be acceptable, but the techniques shown in either Listing 10–13 or Listing 10–14 are usually preferred. This technique is also quite valuable when large arrays are input. Checking data using other schemes can be a tedious process prone to serious errors.

10-6 EXERCISES

1. Table 10–8 illustrates a two-dimensional, integer array ITBL, with seven rows and seven columns. What number is stored in each of the following locations?

(a) ITBL(2,3)   (b) ITBL(6,7)
(c) ITBL(1,1)   (d) ITBL(8,3)
(e) ITBL(5,4)   (f) ITBL(4,5)
(g) ITBL(3,7)   (h) ITBL(7,3)

2. Table 10–9 illustrates a three-dimensional integer array J with 5 rows, 5 columns, and 3 pages. What number is stored in each of the following locations?

(a) J(1,2,3)   (b) J(3,1,2)   (c) J(3,3,3)
(d) J(3,2,1)   (e) J(5,5,3)   (f) J(1,3,2)
(g) J(2,3,1)   (h) J(4,6,1)   (i) J(4,4,1)
(j) J(4,2,5)   (k) J(5,1,2)   (l) J(5,0,1)
(m) J(4,2,2)   (n) J(2,4,3)   (o) J(5,4,3)

3. Figure 10–9 illustrates a double nested DO-loop in which I1 and I2 are still undefined. Trace this flow diagram and show the resulting table in each case.

(a) I1 = 2 and I2 = 3   (b) I1 = 4 and I2 = 2   (c) I1 = 5 and I2 = 3

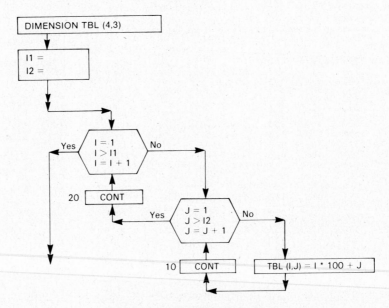

FIGURE 10-9 Double nested DO-loop

Table 10-8 Two-Dimensional Array

Array ITBL (7,7)

26	7	11	121	83	72	14
161	-9	-8	-11	12	-69	81
27	-27	32	-49	63	-52	43
102	-201	16	88	-77	4	0
111	91	-97	82	3	-2	5
55	-15	155	-115	105	35	-47
17	19	-21	-23	25	33	66

Table 10-9 Three-Dimensional Array

Array J(5,5,3)

Page 3

26	14	161	-9	72
-8	7	-11	12	-69
43	63	11	-52	81
-49	32	-27	121	27
4	-77	88	0	83

Page 2

-97	5	-47	35	16
17	82	55	-201	105
19	-21	102	-23	-115
9	111	-15	3	25
91	155	66	33	-2

Page 1

71	1	269	49	18
296	94	6	171	169
30	110	166	10	20
196	13	33	213	96
133	212	144	177	227

4. Given the following program segment.

$$\text{DIMENSION } I(8,5)$$

.
.

.

```
L =
IW =
LS =
ISW =
```
.

.

.

```
KNT = 0
DO 101 J = 1, L,LS
     DO 100 K = 1,IW, ISW
          KNT = KNT + 1
          I(J,K) = KNT
100      CONTINUE
101 CONTINUE
```

Assume that array I has been initialized to zero.

(a) Construct a machine-oriented flow diagram.

(b) Determine values stored in array I in each case.

(i)   L = 5,   IW = 4,   LS = 2,   ISW = 1
(ii) L = 8,   IW = 5,   LS = 3,   ISW = 2
(iii) L = 3,   IW = 2,   LS = 1,   ISW = 1
(iv) L = 6,   IW = 3,   LS = 4,   ISW = 1

(c) How could you skip over:

(i)   Rows 1 and 2?
(ii) Columns 1, 2, and 3?
(iii) Row 1 and Columns 1 and 2?

5. Given the program segment:

```
DO 101 I = 1,3
     DO 102 J = 1,4
          DO 103 K = 1,2
               IRRAY(I,J,K) = function
103           CONTINUE
102      CONTINUE
101 CONTINUE
```

Show array IRRAY(3,4,2) after the DO-loops for each definition of the function.

(a) 100*I + 10*J + K
(b) 100*J + 10*K + I
(c) I + J + K
(d) I*J+K

6. Show the appearance of output from the array ITBL(7,7) (illustrated in Table 10–8) for each of the following statements if 1001 FORMAT(4I5) is always used. (Hint: Remember that arrays have values stored sequentially by columns, not rows. See Section 10–3.3.)

(a)   DO 20 I = 2,4
          WRITE(LW,1001) (ITBL(I,J),J = 1,6)
      20 CONTINUE

(b)   DO 30 I = 1,7,2
          WRITE(LW,1001) (ITBL(I,J),J = 1,7,2)
      30 CONTINUE

(c)　DO 40 I = 4,7
　　　　　WRITE(LW,1001) (ITBL(I,J),J = 4,7)
　　40 CONTINUE
(d)　DO 50 I = 2,5,2
　　　　　WRITE(LW,100⊦) (ITBL(I,J),J = 1,7,3)
　　50 CONTINUE
(e)　WRITE(LW,1001)ITBL

7. Show the appearance of output from the three-dimensional array J(5,5,3)(illustrated in Table 10–9) for each of the following statements assuming 1000 FORMAT(5I4) is always used. (Hint: Refer to Section 10–3.3 for the sequence in which elements of a three-dimensional array are stored.)

(a)　WRITE(LW,1000) (J(I,I,I),I = 1,3)
(b)　DO 70 I = 1,5
　　　　　WRITE(LW,1000) (J(I,I,K),K = 1,3)
　　70 CONTINUE
(c)　WRITE(LW,1000) (J(4,IK,3),IK = 2,4)
(d)　WRITE(LW,1000) (J(3,2,I),I = 1,3)
(e)　DO 60 M = 3,5
　　　　　WRITE(LW,1000) (J(M,N,3),N = 1,5,2)
　　60 CONTINUE
(f)　DO 50 K = 1,3,2
　　　　　DO 40 I = 1,5,2
　　　　　　　WRITE(LW,1000) (J(I,L,K),L = 1,5,2)
　　40　　CONTINUE
　　50 CONTINUE
(g)　WRITE(LW,1000)J

Chapter 11

Examples Involving Two-Dimensional Arrays

The examples of this chapter are designed to help you become proficient in use of arrays. Section 11–1 discusses a program, DATAM, that performs various tasks on the data of a generalized table. The next section illustrates a simple conversion to change program WIND to program WINDZ, where WINDZ is more comprehensive than WIND because WINDZ takes geographical location into account. Program BBSRT1 (Section 9–5) is amplified in Section 11–3, providing two different versions of a bubble-sort for use with rows of tables. Finally, the last section develops the concept of matrix multiplication.

11-1 PROGRAM DATAM

Many practical programs require the manipulation of data within arrays. Program DATAM is to be written as a vehicle for studying such operations. The requirements for program DATAM are specified in the purpose shown in Table 11–1. It is assumed that Columns 1 and 2 of the first N rows of this array, called Z, are read into the program before any other operations start.

11-1.1 Formulation of Program DATAM

Consider the first requirement. For each of the first N rows of an array, Z, put the square of the values stored in Column 1 into Column 3. This suggests a simple DO-loop:

$$\text{DO 10 I=1,N}$$
$$Z(I,3) = Z(I,1)**2$$
$$\text{10 CONTINUE}$$

This could be followed by a second DO-loop that puts the square of the values stored in Column 2 into Column 4 for the first N rows of array Z.

Table 11-1 Definition Sheet for Program DATAM

Program: DATAM

Purpose:
1. Read values into the first two columns of the first N rows of array Z, a row at a time.

2. For each of 1st N rows of an array, Z
   (a) put the square of column 1 into column 3
   (b) put the square of column 2 into column 4
   (c) put the product of column 1 times column 2 into column 5

3. Count the number of negative values found in first N rows
   (a) of column 1 of array Z and store into KOUNT(1)
   (b) of column 2 of array Z and store into KOUNT(2)
   (c) of column 5 of array Z and store into KOUNT(3)

4. Sum the values of the first N rows (array Z)
   (a) of column 3 and store into SUM(1)
   (b) of column 4 and store into SUM(2)
   (c) of column 5 and store into SUM(3)

5. Accumulate products of values of the first N rows (array Z)
   (a) of column 1 and store into PROD(1)
   (b) of column 2 and store into PROD(2)

Descriptive Items:

Z(110,5)	Data array (N rows of Columns 1 and 2 are input). $Z(I,1) = X$ $Z(I,2) = Y$ $Z(I,3) = X^2$ $Z(I,4) = Y^2$ $Z(I,5) = XY$
N	Actual number of rows of array Z that are used.
KOUNT(3)	Counts negative values found in specific columns of array Z: KOUNT(1) for Column 1 KOUNT(2) for Column 2; KOUNT(3) for Column 5 of Z.
SUM(3)	Stores sums of values stored in Columns 3, 4, and 5 of array Z in locations SUM(1), SUM(2) and SUM(3), respectively.
PROD(2)	Stores accumulative product of numbers located in Columns 1 and 2 of array Z into locations PROD(1) and PROD(2), respectively.
NP	Print Control, output if: NP<1, no output at all; NP = 1, arrays KOUNT, SUM and PROD; NP≥2, array Z, all N-rows of all 5 columns.
LR	Unit number for card reader (=5).
LW	Unit number of high speed (line) printer (=6).

```
        DO 20 I=1,N
          Z(I,4) = Z(I,2)**2
     20 CONTINUE
```

A DO-loop could also be used for the product of Column 1 times Column 2, which is to be stored in Column 5. However, all three of these operations could be performed within the confines of a single DO-loop, at a considerable saving of computer time and cost.

The sum of Columns 3, 4, and 5 can be obtained either by a single or a double-nested DO-loop.

The first method would be to use the following.

$$DO\ 80\ I=1,N$$
$$SUM(1) = SUM(1) + Z(I,3)$$
$$SUM(2) = SUM(2) + Z(I,4)$$
$$SUM(3) = SUM(3) + Z(I,5)$$
$$80\ \ CONTINUE$$

It would also be possible to use:

$$DO\ 70\ I=1,N$$
$$DO\ 50\ J=1,3$$
$$SUM(J) = SUM(J) + Z(I,J+2)$$
$$50\ \ \ \ \ \ CONTINUE$$
$$70\ CONTINUE$$

Since SUM(J) appears on both sides of an equals sign, initialization is required. In fact, this shows that arrays KOUNT, SUM, and PROD must all be initialized.

The human-oriented flow diagram shown in Figure 11–1 helps check that all the necessary elements are included in the program; it also emphasizes that all the operations involving squaring and multiplying column entries, adding rows, counting values in rows, and accumulating the products of columns can be performed in one DO-loop. This human-oriented flow diagram is translated into a machine-oriented flow diagram in Figure 11–2. Final coding and output are shown in Listing 11–1.

11–1.2 Critique of Output

The typical set of output of Listing 11–1 shows the five values of both X and Y that were input. The values of X^2, Y^2, and XY shown in Columns 3, 4, and 5 were calculated line by line. The three asterisks may appear to signal an attempt to output a number using an edit descriptor with insufficient field width, but the asterisks actually act as flags to emphasize that the sums of Columns 3 through 5 are being shown. It is easy to verify the accumulative product for Column 1: $1 \times (-1) \times (-2) \times 2 \times 3 = 12$. Likewise, it is easy to visually inspect and count the negative values in Column 1. If the table were of maximum size however, such checking would be unrealistic. Although the output is complete, is it clear and unambiguous? Do you find the output "easily" readable? What would you do to improve the display of array Z and related solutions for program DATAM of Listing 11–1 on page 277?

11–1.3 Modifications to Program DATAM

Program DATAM works correctly and illustrates important methodologies. It can, however, be improved considerably. Consider what changes would be required if the array Z were single-dimensional, with only five locations. Typically

$$Z(I,3) = Z(I,1)**2$$

would become

$$Z(3) = Z(1)**2.$$

Study either of the flow diagrams or the coding, and consider why any difficulty would be encountered using this procedure. Basically, the only change is that the concept

Program DATAM

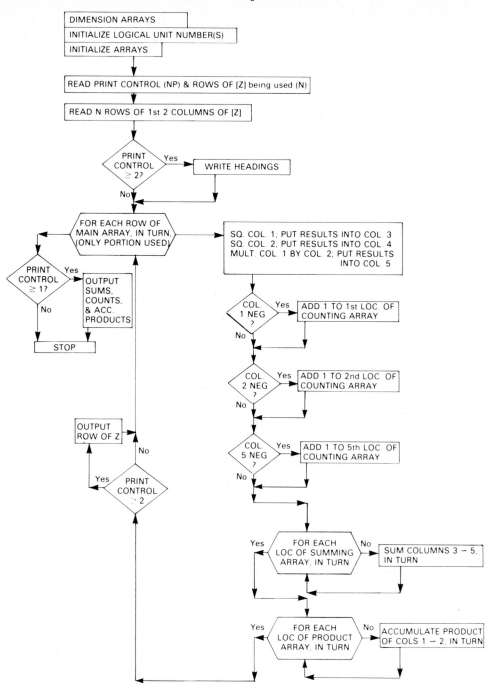

FIGURE 11-1 Human-oriented flow diagram for program DATAM

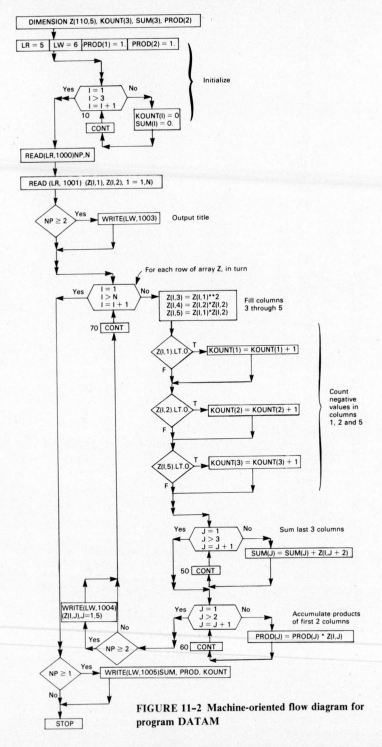

FIGURE 11-2 Machine-oriented flow diagram for program DATAM

```
        PROGRAM DATAM
        DIMENSION Z(110,5),KOUNT(3),SUM(3),PROD(2)
        LR=5
        LW=6

        PROD(1)=1.
        PROD(2)=1.

        DO 10 I=1,3
            KOUNT(I)=0
            SUM(I)=0.
  10    CONTINUE

        READ(LR,1000)NP,N
        READ(LR,1001)(Z(I,1),Z(I,2),I=1,N)
        IF(NP.GE.2) WRITE(LW,1003)

        DO 70 I=1,N
            Z(I,3)= Z(I,1)**2
            Z(I,4)= Z(I,2)* Z(I,2)
            Z(I,5)= Z(I,1)* Z(I,2)

            IF(Z(I,1).LT.0.) KOUNT(1) = KOUNT(1)+1
            IF(Z(I,2).LT.0.) KOUNT(2) = KOUNT(2)+1
            IF(Z(I,5).LT.0.)KOUNT(3)=KOUNT(3)+1

            DO 50 J=1,3
                SUM(J)=SUM(J)+Z(I,J+2)
  50        CONTINUE

            DO 60 J=1,2
                PROD(J)=PROD(J)*Z(I,J)
  60        CONTINUE

            IF(NP.GE.2)WRITE(LW,1004)(Z(I,J),J=1,5)
  70    CONTINUE

        IF(NP.GE.1)WRITE(LW,1005)SUM,PROD,KOUNT

1000 FORMAT(2I4)
1001 FORMAT(10F8.0)
1003 FORMAT(1H1,'   INPUT ARRAY CALLED Z'//
    15X,1HX,7X,1HY,7X,4HX**2,8X,4HY**2,9X,3HX*Y)
1004     FORMAT(2F8.2,3F12.4)
1005 FORMAT(8X,8H*** SUMS,3F12.4/2F8.2,' ----ACC',
    1'UMULATIVE PRODUCTS'/I6,I8,'   --COUNT '
    2'OF NEGATIVES',I10//)

        STOP
        END
```

Output:

```
INPUT ARRAY CALLED Z

    X        Y       X**2       Y**2        X*Y
  1.00     2.00     1.0000     4.0000     2.0000
 -1.00     2.00     1.0000     4.0000    -2.0000
 -2.00     1.00     4.0000     1.0000    -2.0000
  2.00    -1.00     4.0000     1.0000    -2.0000
  3.00     2.00     9.0000     4.0000     6.0000
         *** SUMS   19.0000    14.0000    2.0000
 12.00    -3.00 ----ACCUMULATIVE PRODUCTS
    2        1    --COUNT OF NEGATIVES                3
```

LISTING 11-1 Coding and output for program DATAM

of "rows" has been lost. But if the second READ statement of the program were deleted (the one which reads in array Z) and replaced by the statement

$$\text{READ (LR,1001) Z(1), Z(2)}$$

(placed just after DO 70), then the concept of "rows" would be taken care of automatically within the loop and a great deal of storage space could be saved.

It is important, particularly in large programs, to be aware of such ways to save space. Remember, however, such a technique is often inappropriate because the total array itself is sometimes needed for other valid reasons.

11-2 PROGRAM WINDZ

Program WIND of Listing 10–3 was written only for wind pressures specified at certain geographic locations. In practice, the proper wind zone, embodying appropriate wind pressures as a function of height above ground, is taken from a specially prepared map. Wind pressures are tabulated in the *Uniform Building Code* and shown in Table 11–2.

Only five modifications to program WIND are necessary to accommodate different geographic locations.

1. The program name is changed by adding Z (for Zone) to WIND: WINDZ.
2. Array W for wind pressure must be changed from a single-dimensional array to a two-dimensional array with six rows (corresponding to heights above ground) and seven columns (corresponding to wind zones): W(6,7).
3. The DATA statement must be modified to store 6×7 values.
4. The wind zone number, NZ, must be read at the same time as the number of stories in the building. Corresponding FORMAT statement 1000 must be modified to accept the additional input.
5. Every array element of W must have a second subscript expression added to accommodate the proper wind zone. Thus W(K+1) becomes W(K + 1, NZ) and W(K) becomes W(K,NZ).

Table 11-2 Uniform Building Code Wind Loads per Zone

Height Zones (in feet)	Wind-Pressure—Map Areas (pounds per square foot)						
	20	25	30	35	40	45	50
Less than 30	15	20	25	25	30	35	40
30 to 49	20	25	30	35	40	45	50
50 to 99	25	30	40	45	50	55	60
100 to 499	30	40	45	55	60	70	75
500 to 1199	35	45	55	60	70	80	90
1200 and over	40	50	60	70	80	90	100

*The figures given are recommended as minimum. These requirements do not provide for tornadoes.

This material is reproduced from the 1976 edition of the *Uniform Building Code,* copyrighted 1976, with permission of the publisher, the International Conference of Building Officials, Whittier, CA 90601.

Program WINDZ is shown in Listing 11–2 with these changes highlighted. The format and sequence used to store values in array W by a DATA statement needs careful consideration. First, values should be carefully spaced and aligned for ease of reading and checking. Second, entries in the list of the statement are by columns, not by rows. (For discussion, refer to Section 10–3.) Legally, entries in the DATA statement could be tightly packed onto a couple of lines if all "cosmetic" blank spaces were eliminated. When entries are large in number, such compactness may be required because all Subset FORTRAN 77 statements are limited to a maximum of nine continuation lines (Full Language to a maximum of 19).

```
      PROGRAM WINDZ

C     --- THIS PROGRAM USES WIND PRESSURES (W) AT ELEVATIONS CONTROLLED
C     --- BY ARRAY HZ TO DETERMINE WALL FORCES FOR A ONE FOOT STRIP IN
C     --- ARRAY WF FROM VALUES INPUT: NUMBER OF FLOORS IN N, WIND ZONE
C     --- IN NZ, AND FLOOR ELEVATIONS IN ARRAY H.

      DIMENSION HZ(6),W(6,7),H(20),WF(20)
      DATA HZ/30.,50.,100.,500.,1200.,100000./,
     1     W/15.,20.,  25., 30.,   35.,    40.,
     2       20.,25.,  30., 40.,   45.,    50.,
     3       25.,30.,  40., 45.,   55.,    60.,
     4       25.,35.,  45., 55.,   60.,    70.,
     5       30.,40.,  50., 60.,   70.,    80.,
     6       35.,45.,  55., 70.,   80.,    90.,
     7       40.,50.,  60., 75.,   90.,   100./

      LR=5
      LW=6

   10 READ(LR,1000) N,NZ
      WRITE(LW,1005) N,NZ
      IF(N.GT.0) THEN
         READ(LR,1001) (H(I),I=1,N)

C              --- DO FOR EACH WALL IN TURN (TOP TO BOTTOM)
         DO 30 I= N,1,-1
            K =6
            HT=H(I)
            HB=H(I-1)

C                 --- SEARCH FOR APPROPRIATE WIND PRESSURE FOR WALL
   20       IF(K.NE.1 .AND. HT.LE.HZ(K)) THEN
               K = K-1
               GO TO 20
            END IF

            IF(HB.LT.HZ(K) .AND. HT.GT.HZ(K)) THEN

C                    --- PRESSURE CHANGES WITHIN WALL HEIGHT
               HI = HZ(K)
               W1 = (HT-HI)* W(K+1,NZ)
               W2 = (HI-HB)* W(K,NZ)
               WF(I)=W1+W2
               WRITE(LW,1002) HT,W(K+1,NZ),W1,HI,W(K,NZ),W2,HB
            ELSE
C                    --- PRESSURE CONSTANT WITHIN WALL HEIGHT
               IF(HT.LE.HZ(1))K=0
               WF(I)=(HT-HB)* W(K+1,NZ)
               WRITE(LW,1003) HT,W(K+1,NZ),WF(I),HB
            END IF

   30       CONTINUE
            WRITE(LW,1004) (I,H(I),WF(I),I=N,1,-1)
            GO TO 10
      END IF

 1000 FORMAT(2I4)
 1001 FORMAT(10F5.0)
 1002 FORMAT(//' TOP FLR =',F8.2,' FT.'/24X,'WIND=',F4.0,3X,
     1'FORCE=',F7.1,' LBS.'/' MID FLR =',F8.2,' FT.'/24X,
     2'WIND=', F4.0,3X,'FORCE=',F7.1,' LBS.'/' BOT FLR =',
     3F8.2,' FT.'/)
 1003 FORMAT(//' TOP FLR =',F8.2,' FT.'/24X,'WIND=',F4.0,3X,
     1'FORCE=',F7.1,' LBS.'/' BOT FLR =',F8.2,' FT.'/)
 1004 FORMAT(//' FLOOR  HEIGHT  FORCE'/20(I5,F8.2,F7.1/))
 1005 FORMAT('1 NUMBER OF FLOORS =',I3/' WIND ZONE =',I3)

      STOP
      END
```

LISTING 11–2 Coding for program WINDZ

It is important to check the DATA statement by locating values using the following formula:

$$\text{Row Number} + (\text{Column Number} -1) \times$$
$$(\text{Rows dimensioned in DIMENSION statement})$$

Thus, when K = 3 and NZ = 4, W(K,NZ) represents W(3,4), or using the formula stated above:

$$3 + (4-1) \times (6) = 21$$

which corresponds to the 21st location, 45 pounds per square foot. Row 3, in Table 11–2, Column 4, shows 45 agreeing with the 45 stored in the 21st location of the DATA statement for array W as computed by the formula. Because 45 pounds per square foot occurs at several locations, a more positive proof can be obtained by using W(4,7), the only entry of 75 pounds per square foot. Then $4 + (7-1) \times 6 = 40$, which is the 40th location of the DATA statement for W, and has an entry of 75.

11-3   SORTING ROUTINES

Program BBSRT1 (Listing 9–5) was developed in Chapter 9 to sort entries within a single-dimensional array. The programs developed in this section will sort rows of tables in accordance with the values located within any column selected by the user.

11-3.1 Program BBSRT2

Listing 11–3 displays coding for program BBSRT2, a modification of program BBSRT1 that allows it to handle tables (arrays). The following program modifications are required.

1. The program name is changed from BBSRT1 to BBSRT2.
2. Array INFO is changed to two dimensions so that it can represent a table. As written, array INFO(30,7) allows a maximum table size of 30 rows and 7 columns. These limits can be exceeded only by changing the DIMENSION statement.
3. Initial I/O is modified in three ways.
   (a) A heading is output, always starting at the top of a new page for each independent table.
   (b) The actual number of rows to be used (NR), the actual number of columns to be used (NC), and the column to be used for ordering the table (LC) are input.
   (c) For each row, in turn, row entries are input and immediately echoed as output. For clarity, output also includes original line numbers.
4. DO-loop 10 and the computation for NM1 are altered to use NR (Number of Rows actually used) rather than N.
5. The major block IF requires two types of modifications. (Intermediate WRITE statements have also been deleted to shorten the program.)
   (a) The comparison between two adjacent entries is changed by adding a second

```
PROGRAM BBSRT2

C        --- SORTS ROWS OF AN ARRAY INFO USING BUBBLE SORT
C        --- SORTS ON COLUMN LC (LC IS READ AS INPUT DATA)
C        --- ACTUAL ROWS USED FOR DATA IN ARRAY INFO : NR
C        --- ACTUAL COLUMNS USED FOR DATA IN INFO : NC
C        --- ARRAY LINE STORES ORIGINAL LINE NUMBERS
C        --- DO 8 READS AND OUTPUT INFO LINE-BY-LINE
C        --- DO 10 ESTABLISHES ORIGINAL LINE NUMBERS
C        --- DO 40 USES I TO PROCEED SEQUENTIALLY THRU COL LC OF INFO
C        --- DO 30 USES J TO 'BUBBLE-UP' ROWS OF INFO (AND LINE)
C        --- DO 20 INTERCHANGES ROWS OF INFO
      DIMENSION LINE(30),INFO(30,7)
      LR=5
      LW=6

    5 CONTINUE
      WRITE(LW,1003)
      READ(LR,1000,END=50) NR,NC,LC

      DO 8 I=1,NR
          READ(LR,1000) (INFO(I,J),J=1,NC)
          WRITE(LW,1001) I,(INFO(I,J),J=1,NC)
    8 CONTINUE

      DO 10 I=1,NR
          LINE(I)=I
   10 CONTINUE

      NM1= NR-1

      DO 40 I=1,NM1

          DO 30 J= I,1,-1

              IF(INFO(J+1,LC).LT.INFO(J,LC)) THEN

                  DO 20 K=1,NC
                      ITEMP       =INFO(J,K)
                      INFO(J,K)   =INFO(J+1,K)
                      INFO(J+1,K)=ITEMP
   20             CONTINUE

                  ITEMP       =LINE(J)
                  LINE(J)     =LINE(J+1)
                  LINE(J+1)=ITEMP
              ELSE
                      GO TO 40
              END IF

   30     CONTINUE

   40 CONTINUE

      WRITE(LW,1004) LC
      DO 45 I=1,NR
          WRITE(LW,1001) LINE(I),(INFO(I,J),J=1,NC)
   45 CONTINUE

 1000 FORMAT(20I4)
 1001 FORMAT(I4,':',7I4)
 1003 FORMAT('1ORIGINAL ARRAY WITH LINE NUMBERS'/)
 1004 FORMAT(////' ORDERED ARRAY WITH ORIGINAL LINE NUMBERS
     1' BEFORE COLONS'/,' ORDERED ON COLUMN',I2//)

      GO TO 5
   50 CONTINUE
      STOP
      END
```

LISTING 11-3 Coding for program BBSRT2

subscript expression, LC. In this way, ordering is only predicated upon the values located in column LC of array INFO.

(b) When adjacent entries in column LC are out of order, a DO-loop is entered that "trades" entries of every column of the two rows involved, a column at a time. For example, when LC = 3, rows two and three would go through the following transformations:

```
 42    27    17     6    600    Values in Column 3 are out of order, 3 is less
 63    21     3     1    100    than 17.

 63    27    17     6    600
 42    21     3     1    100

 63    21    17     6    600
 42    27     3     1    100

 63    21     3     6    600
 42    27    17     1    100

 63    21     3     1    600
 42    27    17     6    100

 63    21     3     1    100    Rows 2 and 3 are now interchanged.
 42    27    17     6    600
```

6. Output of the solution is modified to state which column (LC) is used for the sorting process and to output the table in an easily read format.

Listing 11–4 shows output from program BBSRT2.

11–3.2 Program BBSRT3

BBSRT2 works correctly, but interchanging and bubbling rows consumes large amounts of computer time because every entry in a row must be moved whenever adjacent values in column LC are out of order. An alternate approach is therefore desirable. As a possibility, consider sorting a designated column in an auxiliary array, and never sorting the table at all! For this procedure to be successful, the table could be output by a proper ordering of the sequence of rows to be printed. In addition, a facility could be added to make it possible to output tables which are "apparently" sorted on the basis of several different independent columns. Listing 11–5 shows the coding for program BBSRT3.

The following steps can be used to change BBSRT1 into BBSRT3.

```
        ORIGINAL ARRAY WITH LINE NUMBERS

        1:   21   26    8    3 300
        2:   42   27   17    6 600
        3:   63   21    3    1 100
        4:   84   23    5    2 200
        5:  105   24   16    5 500
        6:  126   28    8    4 400
        7:  147   25   21    7 700


        ORDERED ARRAY WITH ORIGINAL LINE NUMBERS   BEFORE COLONS
        ORDERED ON COLUMN 3

        3:   63   21    3    1 100
        4:   84   23    5    2 200
        1:   21   26    8    3 300
        6:  126   28    8    4 400
        5:  105   24   16    5 500
        2:   42   27   17    6 600
        7:  147   25   21    7 700
```

LISTING 11-4 Output from program BBSRT2

1. Change the title from BBSRT1 to BBSRT3.
2. Add a new array for the table, IN(30,7).
3. Modify initial I/O by:
    (a) Adding a title;
    (b) Reading actual number of rows (NR), number of columns (NC), and column used to sort table (LC);
    (c) Entering a DO-loop that
        (i) reads a row of the table, sequentially
        (ii) echos the row of the table just read, and
        (iii) puts contents of column LC into auxiliary single-dimensional array INFO.
4. Change N to NR as appropriate.
5. Do *not* change the sorting process. Instead, use array LINE to store "*pointers*", in this case sorted row numbers that point to a properly ordered sequence within array INFO. For the first example shown, array INFO is originally filled sequentially with 8, 17, 3, 5, 16, 8, 21 (taken from Column 3 of array IN and shown in Column 4 of first table of Listing 11–6). Upon exit from the sorting process, array INFO contains 3, 5, 8, 8, 16, 17, 21 (which corresponds to an appropriately reordered Column 3 of array IN as shown in the second table of Listing 11–6) and, more importantly, array LINE (Column 1 of the second table on Listing 11–6) contains the "pointers" 3, 4, 1, 6, 5, 2, 7, which point to the rows of IN in a sequence that results in proper ordering. Meanwhile, entries in the third (LC) column of array IN are actually unaltered and *remain* stored as 8, 17, 3, 5, 16, 8, 21 (Column 3 of array IN, Column 4 in the first table of Listing 11–6).

    Table 11–3 illustrates a graphical summary of the process as we attempt to work out an appropriate algorithm. Pointers, line numbers of array IN, are stored sequentially in array LINE, and point, sequentially, to the line numbers (rows) of Column 3 of array IN that would result in a sorted set. For example, LINE (2) of Table 11–3 contains the number 4 which points to the fourth row of Column 3 of array IN. The fourth row of Column 3 contains the second value in the sequence 5. Next, LINE (3) contains 1, which points to the location of the next number (8) of a sorted sequence in Column 3 of array IN. Likewise, LINE (4) contains 6 and points to IN (6,3), storing an 8 (the fourth value in the sorted sequence). In summary, row numbers stored sequentially in array LINE *point* to the sorted set to be constructed from Column 3 of array IN.

    In Table 11–3, the two arrays are related by arrows that point to the proper sorting sequence, DO-loops that output column LC (Column 3 in this case) of array IN in the proper order (one for Subset and one for Full Language) and a trace of the output process, which shows clearly that no values have actually been rearranged within array IN.
6. Output is modified to show the table in accordance with the row numbers stored in array LINE. The process is quite similar to that of Table 11–3, except an entire row is output on each cycle through the loop.
7. Subsequent values of LC (defining the column to be used for sorting) can be input for each table.
    (a) If LC is less than or equal to zero, control passes to reading a new table.

```
PROGRAM BBSRT3
C        --- IN(30,7) TO BE OUTPUT WITH ROWS ORDERED ON COLUMN LC
C        --- LINE(30) STORES ORIGINAL LINE NUMBERS
C        --- INFO(30) USED TO STORE COLUMN LC OF ARRAY IN FOR SORTING
C        --- NR= ROWS OF IN, LINE INFO ACTUALLY USED
C        --- NC= COLUMNS OF IN ACUTALLY USED
      DIMENSION LINE(30),INFO(30),IN(30,7)
      LR=5
      LW=6

    5 CONTINUE
      WRITE(LW,1003)
      READ(LR,1000,END=50) NR,NC,LC

C        --- READ AND ECHO DATA
C        --- STORE COLUMN LC INTO LINE FOR SORTING
      DO 8 I=1,NR
      READ(LR,1000,END=50) (IN(I,J),J=1,NC)
      WRITE(LW,1001) I,(IN(I,J),J=1,NC)
      INFO(I)=IN(I,LC)
    8 CONTINUE

C        --- SORT INFO AND LINE SO THAT ARRAY LINE
C        --- HAS ORIGINAL LINE NUMBERS SORTED IN
C        --- ACCORDANCE WITH COLUMN LC OF IN (INFO)
    9 DO 10 I=1,NR
      LINE(I)=I
   10 CONTINUE

      NM1= NR-1

      DO 40 I=1,NM1

        DO 30 J= I,1,-1

          IF(INFO(J+1).LT.INFO(J)) THEN
            ITEMP= INFO(J)
            INFO(J)  =INFO(J+1)
            INFO(J+1)=ITEMP
            ITEMP    =LINE(J)
            LINE(J)  =LINE(J+1)
            LINE(J+1)=ITEMP
          ELSE
            GO  TO 40
          END IF

   30   CONTINUE

   40 CONTINUE

C        --- OUTPUT ARRAY IN (NEVER REORDERED) BY
C        --- GETTING ORDERED LINE NUMBERS (STORED
C        --- SEQUENTIALLY IN ARRAY LINE) FROM K=LINE(I)
C            (IN FULL LANGUAGE FORTRAN 77 MAY          )
C            (REPLACE: K=LINE(I)                       )
C            (          WRITE(LW,1001) K,(IN(K,J),J=1,NC)  )
C            (BY:                                      )
C            (WRITE(LW,1001) LINE(K),(IN(LINE(K),J),J=1,NC)  )
      WRITE(LW,1004) LC

      DO 45 I=1,NR
      K=LINE(I)
      WRITE(LW,1001) K,(IN(K,J),J=1,NC)
   45 CONTINUE

C        --- SECTION TO PERMIT REORDERED OUTPUT ON
C        --- ANOTHER COLUMN LC (IF LC=0, LOOP FOR NEW DATA)
      READ(LR,1000,END=50)LC
      IF(LC.LE.0) GO TO 5

      DO 46 I=1,NR
      INFO(I)=IN(I,LC)
   46 CONTINUE

      GO TO 9

 1000 FORMAT(20I4)
 1001 FORMAT(I4,":",7I4)
 1003 FORMAT(////" ORIGINAL ARRAY WITH LINE NUMBERS"/)
 1004 FORMAT(////" ORDERED ARRAY WITH ORIGINAL LINE NUMBERS
     1" BEFORE COLONS"/," ORDERED ON COLUMN",I2//)

   50 CONTINUE
      STOP
      END
```

LISTING 11-5 Coding for program BBSRT3

```
ORIGINAL ARRAY WITH LINE NUMBERS

1:   21   26    8    3 300
2:   42   27   17    6 600
3:   63   21    3    1 100
4:   84   23    5    2 200
5:  105   24   16    5 500
6:  126   28    8    4 400
7:  147   25   21    7 700


ORDERED ARRAY WITH ORIGINAL LINE NUMBERS  BEFORE COLONS
ORDERED ON COLUMN 3


3:   63   21    3    1 100
4:   84   23    5    2 200
1:   21   26    8    3 300
6:  126   28    8    4 400
5:  105   24   16    5 500
2:   42   27   17    6 600
7:  147   25   21    7 700


ORDERED ARRAY WITH ORIGINAL LINE NUMBERS  BEFORE COLONS
ORDERED ON COLUMN 1


1:   21   26    8    3 300
2:   42   27   17    6 600
3:   63   21    3    1 100
4:   84   23    5    2 200
5:  105   24   16    5 500
6:  126   28    8    4 400
7:  147   25   21    7 700


ORDERED ARRAY WITH ORIGINAL LINE NUMBERS  BEFORE COLONS
ORDERED ON COLUMN 5


3:   63   21    3    1 100
4:   84   23    5    2 200
1:   21   26    8    3 300
6:  126   28    8    4 400
5:  105   24   16    5 500
2:   42   27   17    6 600
7:  147   25   21    7 700


ORDERED ARRAY WITH ORIGINAL LINE NUMBERS  BEFORE COLONS
ORDERED ON COLUMN 2


3:   63   21    3    1 100
4:   84   23    5    2 200
5:  105   24   16    5 500
7:  147   25   21    7 700
1:   21   26    8    3 300
2:   42   27   17    6 600
6:  126   28    8    4 400
```

LISTING 11-6 Output from program BBSRT3

Table 11-3 Relationship Between Array LINE and Column LC(3) of Array IN

```
LINE(1) = 3 ─────────▶ IN(1,3) =  8
LINE(2) = 4 ───╲  ╱──▶ IN(2,3) = 17
LINE(3) = 1 ───╳─────▶ IN(3,3) =  3
LINE(4) = 6 ───╲─────▶ IN(4,3) =  5
LINE(5) = 5 ───────╳─▶ IN(5,3) = 16
LINE(6) = 2 ───╱─────▶ IN(6,3) =  8
LINE(7) = 7 ─────────▶ IN(7,3) = 21
```

Subset FORTRAN 77:

```
        DO 10  I = 1, 7              ┌─────────────────────────────┐
            K = LINE(I)             │ LINE(I) contains "pointer" K │
            WRITE(LW, 1000) IN(K, LC)│   to be used in IN(K, LC)    │
10      CONTINUE                     └─────────────────────────────┘
```

Assuming LC = 3, trace yields:

I	K	IN(K, LC)
1	3	3
2	4	5
3	1	8
4	6	8
5	5	16
6	2	17
7	7	21

Full Language FORTRAN 77:

```
        DO 10 I = 1, 7
            WRITE(LW, 1000) IN(LINE(I), LC)
10      CONTINUE
```

(b) If LC is greater than zero, the new column LC of array IN is transferred to array INFO for subsequent sorting.

(c) Transfer is to Statement 9 so that array LINE can be reinitialized.

Typical output for program BBSRT3 is shown in Listing 11–6. Remember, the table stored in array IN is *never* altered in any manner. Array IN is read row by row, sequentially, and is output a row at a time, with the sequence of rows to be output established by values stored within sequential elements of array LINE.

In general, program BBSRT3 is much more efficient than program BBSRT2. This increase in efficiency is primarily due to the use of a pointer, which substantially reduces the number of manipulations that must be performed. Any time that large quantities must be moved within a program, an auxiliary array that carries "pointers" yields the desired results with fewer calculations.

11-4 MATRIX MULTIPLICATION

Even for those unfamiliar with mathematics, matrix multiplication effectively illustrates the use of arrays and nested DO-loops. Matrix multiplication is also quite useful in many practical situations.

Matrix multiplication is frequently used in the solution of simultaneous equations, which occur in almost every academic field: in finding the best fitting polynomial curve to fit a set of data points, in solving D.C. and A.C. circuits, in certain types of optimization problems, in the design of space vehicles, and so on.

Since matrix multiplication also provides a good mechanism to bridge the gap between formal mathematics and computer programs, the following discussion has broader implications than the immediate problem.

Figure 11–3 illustrates two identical forms for any generalized matrix, *A*, that has *m* rows and *n* columns. A generalized matrix can often be visualized more easily if it is written in "expanded form," showing elements of the array, with their subscripts, all located within brackets. The first subscript of each element represents the row number and the second subscript is the column number. Vertical or horizontal dots are used to indicate that some elements are not shown and that the size of the array is variable. The actual number of elements depends upon the numerical values assigned to *m* and *n*. Within a computer program, such a matrix is represented by an array (a table), usually filled with numerical values.

Matrix multiplication is summarized in Figure 11–4. If matrix multiplication is to be defined for two matrices (arrays), the first must have exactly the same number of columns as the second has rows. Matrix multiplication is not commutative, so the order of the matrices in the matrix multiplication process is quite important.

11–4.1 Generalized Rules of Matrix Multiplication

Figure 11–5 gives the general rule for matrix multiplication. At first glance, the rule looks rather complicated. If taken one step at a time, however, the rule can be mastered by students with only a rudimentary background in algebra, and, in the process, students increase their ability to translate other formal mathematical expressions into FORTRAN.

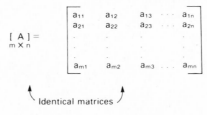

FIGURE 11–3 Generalized Matrix A

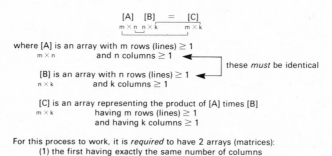

FIGURE 11–4 Matrix multiplication expressed symbolically

$$[A] \quad [B] \quad = \quad [C]$$
$$m \times n \quad n \times k \qquad m \times k$$

$$
\begin{bmatrix}
a_{11} & a_{12} & \cdots & a_{1n} \\
a_{21} & a_{22} & \cdots & a_{2n} \\
\cdot & \cdot & & \cdot \\
\cdot & \cdot & & \cdot \\
\cdot & \cdot & & \cdot \\
a_{m1} & a_{m2} & \cdots & a_{mn}
\end{bmatrix}
\begin{bmatrix}
b_{11} & b_{12} & \cdots & b_{1k} \\
b_{21} & b_{22} & \cdots & b_{2k} \\
\cdot & \cdot & & \cdot \\
\cdot & \cdot & & \cdot \\
\cdot & \cdot & & \cdot \\
b_{n1} & b_{n2} & \cdots & b_{nk}
\end{bmatrix} =
$$

where

COL 1   COL 2   COL K

$$
\underset{m \times k}{[C]} =
\begin{bmatrix}
c(1,1)=a_{11}b_{11}+a_{12}b_{21}+\cdots+a_{1n}b_{n1} & c(1,2)=\displaystyle\sum_{i=1}^{n} a_{1i}b_{i2} & \cdots & c(1,k)=\displaystyle\sum_{i=1}^{n} a_{1i}b_{ik} & \text{ROW 1} \\
c(2,1)=a_{21}b_{11}+a_{22}b_{21}+\cdots+a_{2n}b_{n1} & c(2,2)=\displaystyle\sum_{i=1}^{n} a_{2i}b_{i2} & \cdots & c(2,k)=\displaystyle\sum_{i=1}^{n} a_{2i}b_{ik} & \text{ROW 2} \\
\vdots & \vdots & & \vdots & \\
c(m,1)=\displaystyle\sum_{i=1}^{n} a_{mi}b_{i1} & c(m,2)=\displaystyle\sum_{i=1}^{n} a_{mi}b_{i2} & \cdots & c(m,k)=\displaystyle\sum_{i=1}^{n} a_{mi}b_{ik} & \text{ROW M}
\end{bmatrix}
$$

or considered by elements

$$C_{\ell i} = \sum_{i=1}^{n} a_{\ell i} b_{ij} \text{ FOR ANY ELEMENT IN [C]} \quad \begin{cases} \ell \text{ IS ROW OF [A] \& [C]} \\ \\ j \text{ IS COL OF [B] \& [C]} \end{cases}$$

FIGURE 11-5 Matrix multiplication in symbolic form

At the top of Figure 11–5,

$$[A] \quad [B] \quad = \quad [C]$$
$$m \times n \quad n \times k \qquad m \times k$$

represents multiplication of any matrices—in which the number of columns (n) of the first matrix is equal to the number of rows (n) of the second matrix. The answer, matrix C, will have the same number of rows as matrix A, m, and the same number of columns as matrix B, k. Note that these relationships are indicated by $m \times n$, $n \times k$, and $m \times k$ below each matrix, to show the number of rows and columns of arrays A, B, and C, respectively.

Array A is also shown in expanded form: a_{11} is the element in the first row and first column, a_{2n} is the element in the second row and nth (last) column, a_{m2} is the element in the mth (last) row and in the second column, and a_{mn} is the element in the mth (last) row and in the nth (last) column.

A similar expanded representation is given for B. The size of the array (matrix) is not specified until values of n and k are given. For instance, if B were 5×6 (5 rows by 6 columns), b_{nk} would become b_{56}.

Array $\underset{m \times k}{[C]}$ illustrates the computations required to obtain each element in C from appropriate elements of A and B. The value for any element of the answer matrix C, say $C_{\ell j}$, is computed by summing the products of corresponding elements of row ℓ of A times the corresponding elements of column j of B.

When ℓ is 1 and j is 1, element c_{11} is computed by adding the products of elements of Row 1 of A with the sequential elements of Column 1 of B. Thus the first subscript on an element a remains at 1, as the second subscript goes from 1 to n. Likewise, the second subscript of element b remains at 1, as the first subscript goes from 1 to n. The result is shown in location (1,1) of array C in Figure 11–5 as

$$a_{11}b_{11} + a_{12}b_{21} + \dots + a_{1n}b_{n1}$$

Note that the second subscript of element a always matches the first subscript of element b. For this reason, the sum of these products can be written using a summation sign, Σ. Thus:

$$c_{11} = \sum_{i=1}^{n} a_{1i}b_{i1}$$

The element $c(m,2)$ or C_{m2} is shown in summation form and can be expanded as

$$c(m,2) = \sum_{i=1}^{n} a_{mi}b_{i2} = a_{m1}b_{12} + a_{m2}b_{22} + a_{m3}b_{32} + a_{m4}b_{42} + \dots + a_{mn}b_{n2}$$

Observe that the row of A stays constant and defines the first subscript of the element of array C, the column of B stays constant and defines the second subscript of the element of array C, and successive multiplication goes one-to-one across the row of A and simultaneously down the column of B.

A typical computation for any element of product matrix C is shown at the bottom of Figure 11–5. The expression for C shows the computation of the element of array C located on the ℓ th row and the jth column, obtained by successive multiplication of the elements of the ℓ th row of matrix A by the elements of the jth column of B.

11–4.2 A Numerical Example of Matrix Multiplication

The simple example of Figure 11–6 should help clarify the process of matrix multiplication. Matrix A and matrix B both have nine elements.

To find the value of the element of the answer matrix in location (1,1), simply

A simple numerical example is:

$$[A][B] = \begin{bmatrix} 2 & -3 & 4 \\ 1 & 5 & -2 \\ -8 & 0 & -4 \end{bmatrix} \begin{bmatrix} 10 & 40 & -20 \\ 20 & -40 & 30 \\ -30 & -10 & 50 \end{bmatrix}$$

$$\begin{bmatrix} 2\cdot10 + (-3)\cdot20 + 4\cdot(-30) & 2\cdot40 + (-3)\cdot(-40) + 4\cdot(-10) & 2\cdot(-20) + (-3)\cdot30 + 4\cdot50 \\ 1\cdot10 + 5\cdot20 + (-2)\cdot(-30) & 1\cdot40 + 5\cdot(-40) + (-2)\cdot(-10) & 1\cdot(-20) + 5\cdot30 + (-2)\cdot50 \\ (-8)\cdot10 + 0\cdot20 + (-4)\cdot(-30) & (-8)\cdot40 + 0\cdot(-40) + (-4)\cdot(-10) & (-8)\cdot(-20) + 0\cdot30 + (-4)\cdot50 \end{bmatrix}$$

which reduces to

$$[C] = \begin{bmatrix} -160 & 160 & 70 \\ 170 & -140 & 30 \\ 40 & -280 & -40 \end{bmatrix}$$

FIGURE 11–6 Numerical example of matrix multiplication

multiply the elements of Row 1 of matrix A times elements of Column 1 of the second matrix, B: $2 \cdot 10 + (-3) \cdot 20 + 4 \cdot (-30) = -160$. This value is shown as C_{11} in the answer matrix at location (1,1).

To obtain -280 (in Row 3 and Column 2 of answer matrix C), sequentially multiply elements of the third row of the first matrix times elements of the second column of the second matrix: $(-8) \cdot 40 + 0 \cdot (-40) + (-4) \cdot (-10) = -280$.

You should check other elements of the answer matrix. For additional practice, see Exercise 5. Then return to Figure 11–5 and note that the symbols depict exactly the same process used in the example.

11–4.3 Programming Matrix Multiplication

A human-oriented flow diagram for the matrix multiplication process is shown in Figure 11–7; the process is expanded into a machine-oriented flow diagram in Figure 11–8 and coded in Listing 11–7.

The flow diagrams show the first DO-loop to be based upon the number of rows in matrix A (M). The second DO-loop is established by the number of columns in matrix B (K). The third DO-loop is dependent upon the number of columns (N) in the first matrix, which must be identical to the number of rows in the second matrix. If the number of columns in the first matrix does not equal the number of rows in the second matrix, matrix multiplication is undefined and the program will not work. Obviously, answer matrix C must have exactly the same number of rows as matrix A and exactly the same number of columns as matrix B.

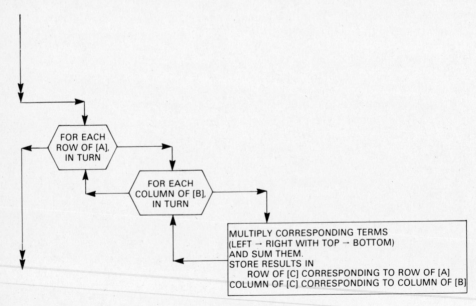

FIGURE 11–7 Human-oriented flow of matrix multiplication

Chapter 11 Examples Involving Two-Dimensional Arrays

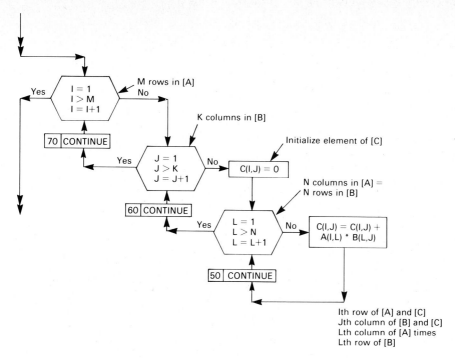

FIGURE 11-8 Machine-oriented flow of matrix
multiplication

```
PROGRAM MATMUL
DIMENSION A(10,10),B(10,10),C(10,10)
C ---                    --- M = ROWS OF MATRICES A AND C          ---
C ---                    --- N = COLUMNS OF MATRIX A -AND-         ---
C ---                            ROWS OF MATRIX B                  ---
C ---                    --- K = COLUNS OF MATRICES B AND C        ---
C ---                    --- SUMMARY:                              ---
C ---                            A(M X N)*B(N X K) = C(M X K)      ---

      DO 70 I=1,M

          DO 60 J=1,K
              C(I,J) = 0.

              DO 50 L=1,N
                  C(I,J) = A(I,L)*B(L,J)   +   C(I,J)
   50             CONTINUE
   60         CONTINUE
   70 CONTINUE
```

LISTING 11-7 Coding for matrix multiplication

11-5 EXERCISES

1. Modify the output from program DATAM, Listing 11–1, so that it more clearly indicates the process and results.

2. In reality, wind zones are not classified as 1, 2, 3, and so on. Rather, wind zones are specified by the tabulated wind pressure shown for 30 feet above ground. Modify program WINDZ, Listing 11–2, so that tabulated wind pressure at 30 feet above ground can be input rather than a wind zone number NZ.

3. Modify program BBSRT2 so that it will sort in each of the following ways.
   (a) In ascending order.
   (b) For different LC's for each table. (Be careful!)
   (c) In ascending or descending order.
   (d) In ascending or descending order for different LC's for each table.

4. Modify program BBSRT3 so that it will sort in each of the following ways.
   (a) In ascending order.
   (b) In ascending or descending order for any LC used with any table.

5. Perform the implied matrix multiplication (without use of a computer).

$$(a) \begin{bmatrix} 1 & 2 & 1 \\ 2 & -1 & 2 \\ 4 & 2 & 1 \end{bmatrix} \begin{bmatrix} 1.6 \\ 4.8 \\ -3.2 \end{bmatrix}$$

$$(b) \begin{bmatrix} 1 & 2 & 1 \\ 2 & -1 & 2 \\ 4 & -2 & -1 \end{bmatrix} \begin{bmatrix} 0.2 & 0 & 0.2 \\ 0.4 & -0.2 & 0 \\ 0 & 0.4 & -0.2 \end{bmatrix}$$

$$(c) \begin{bmatrix} 2 & -4 & 6 \end{bmatrix} \begin{bmatrix} -2 \\ 2 \\ 4 \end{bmatrix}$$

$$(d) \begin{bmatrix} -2 \\ 2 \\ 4 \end{bmatrix} \begin{bmatrix} 2 & -4 & 6 \end{bmatrix}$$

$$(e) \begin{bmatrix} 1 & 2 & 3 \\ 8 & 1 & 9 \end{bmatrix} \begin{bmatrix} -1 & -5 & -2 \\ -1 & 1 & 4 \\ 1 & 1 & 2 \end{bmatrix}$$

$$(f) \begin{bmatrix} 1 & 2 \\ -2 & -3 \end{bmatrix} \begin{bmatrix} 2 & 1 & 0 & 4 \\ -5 & 1 & 0 & 2 \end{bmatrix}$$

6. Write a program to do matrix multiplication. Although useful as an educational exercise, does such a program have real value? What limits program usefulness?

7. Write a subroutine to do matrix multiplication. Write a small I/O program to CALL your subroutine. What limits the usefulness of your subroutine? In later chapters, it is shown that dimensions within subroutines may be established by variable names carried through the argument list. Would such a change increase the usefulness of your program? If so, why? If not, why not?

Chapter **12**

Utilizing Characters

Full Language FORTRAN 77 usually provides additional flexibility by decreasing the number of restrictive rules contained in Subset Fortran. Utilizing characters, however, is a special case and the differences between Full Language and Subset FORTRAN 77 are much more pronounced (although each uses type character). The older FORTRAN Standard (ANSI X3.9–1966) treated characters differently, using a Hollerith data type. This old form of utilizing characters is included as Appendix C in the newer FORTRAN 77 Standard. Because characters are important, and because of the major differences between Subset FORTRAN 77, Full Language FORTRAN 77 and Appendix C (which relates to the earlier FORTRAN Standard), this chapter treats each as a separate topic.

Input and output of both character type and Hollerith data type are by A-Format. The A-Format edit descriptor is very similar to the integer edit descriptor, except that the letter *A* is used in place of the letter *I*. A summary of the alphanumeric edit descriptor is shown in Table 12–1. Characteristics associated with the integer constant that represents the specified field width differ between the various dialects of FORTRAN and are considered separately in each of the following subsections.

12–1 USING SUBSET FORTRAN 77

Subset FORTRAN 77 has four types of data: integer, real, logical, and character. The first two types have been used extensively throughout this text; type character is the primary subject of this chapter.

12–1.1 Fundamental Rules, Program CHRBAS

Type character can be represented by constants, variables, or arrays, which can be used in replacement statements, DATA statements, and relational operations.

**Table 12-1 Edit Descriptor for Type CHARACTER
(and for Hollerith Data Type)**

Alphanumeric Edit Descriptor

(Used for I/O of alphanumeric characters into
or out of locations specified by lists in READ/
WRITE statements.)

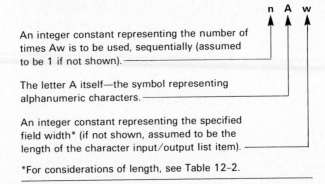

An integer constant representing the number of
times Aw is to be used, sequentially (assumed
to be 1 if not shown).

The letter A itself—the symbol representing
alphanumeric characters.

An integer constant representing the specified
field width* (if not shown, assumed to be the
length of the character input/output list item).

*For considerations of length, see Table 12-2.

(a) *Character Constant.* A character constant is formed by a series of characters enclosed in apostrophes. The characters located between the beginning and ending apostrophe are called a *string* and are numbered consecutively 1, 2, 3, . . ., to indicate their sequential positions from left-to-right. The string of characters may contain blanks, but it cannot be completely empty.

Because apostrophes are used to specify character constants, an apostrophe within the string of a character constant is represented by two apostrophes adjacent to each other. Double apostrophes, representing a single apostrophe character, are recognizable by the processor only because all character constants must contain nonempty strings.

The length of a character constant is the number of characters contained between the delimiting apostrophes, including blanks and counting double apostrophes as only one character. The delimiting apostrophes are not counted. Thus the character constant '123' has length 3. A character constant 'AB   CD' has length 6 because the two blank characters are counted. The character constant 'ABE''S' has length 5 because the double apostrophes count as only one character. Because a character constant cannot be empty, the length of a character constant is always greater than zero.

(b) *Form of a CHARACTER Type-Statement.* A variable name (or array) may be declared as type character by either an explicit CHARACTER statement or an IMPLICIT statement. The length of character string to be used may be specified by following the variable (or array) name by first an asterisk and then an unsigned, nonzero, integer constant that specifies length within the type-statement. If the asterisk and length immediately follow the word CHARACTER, then that length is the length of each entity within the statement that does not have its own length specified independently.

All characters in an array must have exactly the same length. If a length is not specified for any item, a length of 1 is assigned by default. For example, the length of character strings for the variable VAR, and of each element of arrays ARRAY and TABLE, may be established as five by either:

CHARACTER *5 VAR, ARRAY(6), TABLE(4,3)
CHARACTER VAR*5, ARRAY(6)*5, TABLE(4,3)*5

An IMPLICIT statement could also be used.

IMPLICIT CHARACTER *5 (A, T, V)

Such a statement establishes all entities, not otherwise explicitly defined, that start with the letters A, T, or V as type character with a length of five.

The next two examples show type statements that specify variable VAR to have a length of 5, all elements of array TABLE to have lengths of 4, and variable NAME and all elements of ARRAY to have lengths of 8.

CHARACTER *8 VAR*5, ARRAY(6), NAME, TABLE (4,3)*4
CHARACTER VAR*5, ARRAY(6)*8, NAME *8, TABLE (4,3)*4

Because the length of character strings is often a critical factor, many programmers would write the preceding type statements on three separate lines (each line representing only variables and arrays, which are actually elements of the array, with identical lengths):

CHARACTER *4 TABLE(4,3)
CHARACTER *5 VAR
CHARACTER *8 NAME, ARRAY(6)

(c) *Establishing Data in Type-Character Variables.* The data within character type arrays and variables is established by character assignment statements, DATA statements, or by input from READ statements. Mixing of types is not permitted in either replacement or DATA statements when type character variables are involved. Thus if variables VAR and array TABLE have been specified as type character, the following type character assignment statements are valid:

VAR = TABLE(I,J)
TABLE(2, I + 1) = '123'
TABLE(3, I + 2) = 'ABC'

On the other hand, the following three statements are not valid.

TABLE(2, I + 1) = 123.   (Not valid because 123 is type integer.)
TABLE(2, I + 1) = 123.   (Not valid because 123. is type real.)
TABLE(2, I + 1) = NONCHR   (Not valid if NONCHR has not been specified as
                                          type character.)

(d) *Treatment When Type-Character Lengths are Unequal to Each Other.* Table 12–2 illustrates the effect of unequal lengths in replacement statements, DATA statements, and input/output statements.

(e) *Relational Operations.* Type character variables and constants can be compared with each other in relational expressions. The results will be .TRUE. or .FALSE. depending upon the collating sequence. If the two character expressions to be compared are not of the same length, the shorter one will be extended to the right by blanks until it is the same length as the longer one.

The collating sequence depends primarily on the processor. If your machine uses the

American National Standard Code for Information Exchange, ANSI X3.4-1977 (typically referred to as ASCII), and often pronounced as'-key, then the ASCII typical, and partial, collating sequence is:

blank " # $ % & ( ) * + , − . /
0 1 2 3 4 5 6 7 8 9 : ; = ? @
A B C D E F G H I J K L M N O P Q R S T U V W X Y Z

Another widely used system is the Extended Binary-Coded-Decimal Interchange Code (typically called EBCDIC), and often pronounced ebb'-sea-dick, which has the following EBCDIC typical, and partial, collating sequence:

blank ? . (+ & $ *) ; − / , % " : # @ =
A B C D E F G H I J K L M N O P Q R S T U V W X Y Z
0 1 2 3 4 5 6 7 8 9

In both the ASCII and EBCDIC collating sequences, the numeral 8 is always higher than the numeral 3 and the letter H is always higher in a collating sequence than the letter

---

**Table. 12-2 Treatment of Unequal Lengths for
Type CHARACTER**

(*Note:* LEN(v) means the length of variable *v* (number of characters specified for variable *v* in an explicit or IMPLICIT type statement).)

Character assignment statement

   v = e

if LEN(v) > LEN(e)	v = e + trailing blanks
LEN(v) < LEN(e)	v = e with its rightmost characters deleted

Data statement

  DATA v/'constant'/

if LEN(v) > LEN ('constant')	v = "constant" + trailing blanks
LEN(v) < LEN ('constant')	NOT ALLOWED (in Full Language FORTRAN 77: v = "constant" with its rightmost characters deleted)

Input Character *Constant* Into Variable Using Format Aw

if LEN(v) > w of Aw	v = input data + trailing blanks
LEN(v) < w of Aw	v = rightmost characters from within field width w, and with leftmost characters ignored

Output Character *Constant* From Variable v

if LEN(v) > w of Aw	output = v with its rightmost characters deleted
LEN(v) < w of Aw	output = leading blanks + v

D. By contrast, in EBCDIC, numerals are always higher than letters, whereas numerals are always lower than letters in ASCII. To add to the confusion, nonalphanumeric characters are not ordered in the same way in the two collating sequences. For many programs, only letters or numerals are used and the type of collating sequence is essentially immaterial. To illustrate, assuming A contains only letters of the alphabet,

$$IF(A.LT. \; 'H') \; J = J + 1$$

is true when A contains any character A through G. On the other hand, if the character constant stored in A is any letter H through Z, then the expression A.LT.'H'is false and J is not incremented.

In the statement

$$IF(CHAR.GT. \; 'B3C7') \; K = K + 1$$

results depend upon which collating sequence is being used, that is, whether letters are higher or lower than numerals. Four intrinsic lexical functions are supplied to overcome this difficulty: LGE, LGT, LLE, and LLT (lexically greater than or equal to, greater than, less than or equal to, less than, respectively). These functions insure that the ASCII collating sequence is used. Subset FORTRAN 77 requires the operands to be of the same length. (Full Language FORTRAN extends blanks to the right of the shorter operand until it agrees in length with the longer operand.) Using an intrinsic function, the previous statement becomes

$$IF(LGT(CHAR, \; 'B3C7')) \; K = K + 1$$

To insure machine independence, these four intrinsic functions should be used rather than .GE., .GT., .LE., and .LT.. Equality and inequality (.EQ., .NE.) are independent of the processor because collating sequence plays no part in these two relational operations.

(f) *Example.* Program CHRBAS (CHaRacter BASics) is a simple example that illustrates most of the rules discussed in this section. SHORT, RIGHT, and LONG display similar results because they all have a length of 5. When '123' is stored into SHORT, character positions 4 and 5 are filled with blanks. When '09876543' is stored into LONG, the character constant is truncated to '09876'. When the field width exceeds 5, leading blanks are output. Careful study of Listing 12–1 in conjunction with Table 12–2 can help eliminate many programming difficulties.

12–1.2 Counting Letters, Program ALPHA1

The flow diagram of Figure 12–1, as well as coding and output of Listing 12–2, show a program called ALPHA1. This program reads a line of alphanumeric data, numbers the line, counts the number of *T*'s in the line, and outputs the line number, the line itself, and the number of times the letter *T* is found within that line. The program continues to execute and read data until it encounters a trailer card (line) containing only blanks.

Line numbers are counted in the variable LINE; the number of *T*'s on each line is accumulated in the variable NUMBT. LINE is initialized before the loop is entered, but NUMBT is initialized for each line in turn.

The first DO-loop checks each space of a given line, in turn, to see if it is other than blank. (This sequence terminates execution of the program when all 80 input characters are blank.) On the other hand, when any nonblank is encountered on any line, a second

```
      PROGRAM CHRBAS

 C            --- CHARACTER BASICS
 C            --- ***        ***
      CHARACTER *2 FI
      CHARACTER *5  GO , SHORT,RIGHT,LONG
      CHARACTER *8 ARRAY(3,2)

      DATA FI/'-'/, GO/'ABCDEFG'/,
     1ARRAY/'1,1-234-','2,1''56789','3,1''''''''8',
     2'ROW1COL2','ROW2COL2','ROW3COL3'/, LW/6/

      SHORT = '123'
      RIGHT = 'ABCDE'
      LONG  = '09876543'

      WRITE(LW,100) (SHORT,RIGHT,LONG,I=1,3)
  100 FORMAT(/////3X,'SHORT',5X,'RIGHT',5X,'LONG'/
     1' 12345678  12345678  12345678'/
     21X,3(A3,7X)/1X,3(A5,5X)/1X,3(A8,2X)//////)

      DO 101 I=1,3
          WRITE(LW,102) (ARRAY(I,J),J=1,2)
  101 CONTINUE
  102 FORMAT(1X,2(A8,2X)/)

      WRITE(LW,102) FI,GO

      STOP
      END
```

Output:

```
  SHORT      RIGHT      LONG
 12345678   12345678   12345678
 123        ABC        098
 123        ABCDE      09876
    12'          ABCDE       09876




 1,1-234- ROW1COL2

 2,1'5678 ROW2COL2

 3,1''''8 ROW3COL3

     -    ABCDE
```

LISTING 12-1 Coding of program CHRBAS with output

DO-loop is entered that compares each character on that line with the letter *T* (established in the DATA statement). Every time that the character stored in location J(L) is equal to *T* in location K(2), then NUMBT is increased by one. When all 80 spaces on a line have been searched for the letter *T*, then the line number, the line itself, and a count of the number of *T*'s found within that line is output.

It may seem wasteful of computer time for the first DO-loop to check all 80 locations before terminating the program. However, this DO-loop cycles a very limited number of times; the loop is exited when I gets to 6 for the first data card. I never exceeds 1 for data cards 2 through 6. Only on the final (trailer) card does the loop check all 80 positions. By starting the nested loop with I, duplicate looping is avoided.

Chapter 12 Utilizing Characters

Program ALPHA1

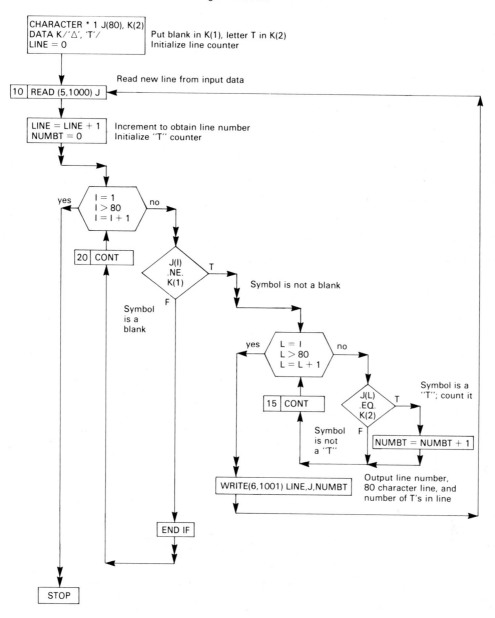

FIGURE 12-1 Program ALPHA1

```
      PROGRAM ALPHA1
      CHARACTER*1 J(80) , K(2)

C---              --- STORE CHARACTER "BLANK" AND "T" INTO K(1),K(2) ---
      DATA K/" ","T"/
      LINE = 0

   10 READ( 5,1000) J
      LINE = LINE + 1
      NUMBT = 0

      DO 20 I=1,80
C---              --- LOOK FOR FIRST CHARACTER "NON-BLANK" ON INPUT LINE J
          IF(J(I).NE.K(1)) THEN

              DO 15 L=1,80
C---                      ---COUNT T'S ON LINE---
                  IF(J(L).EQ.K(2)) NUMBT= NUMBT+1
   15         CONTINUE

              WRITE( 6,1001) LINE, J, NUMBT
              GO TO 10
          END IF

   20 CONTINUE

 1000 FORMAT(80A1)
 1001 FORMAT(1X,I3,3X,80A1," NUMBER T'S=",I4)

      STOP
      END
```

Output:

```
1      THIS IS THE DATA FOR PROGRAM ALPHA WHICH NUMBERS THE LINES, OUTPUTS THE      NUMBER T'S=   7
2  LINE, AND COUNTS THE NUMBER OF TIMES THAT THE LETTER T OCCURS IN EACH LINE OF    NUMBER T'S=   9
3  INPUT DATA.  THIS IS A RELATIVELY SIMPLE PROGRAM, BUT YOU MAY PREFER MORE        NUMBER T'S=   5
4  COMMENT STATEMENTS.  NOTE THAT THE FIRST LOOP IS USED VERY LITTLE BECAUSE WHEN A NUMBER T'S=  11
5  NON-BLANK IS ENCOUNTERED CONTROL PASSES TO THE LOOP TO COUNT T'S---AND THEN OUT  NUMBER T'S=   9
6  OF THE LOOP TO READ A NEW LINE.                                                  NUMBER T'S=   2
```

LISTING 12-2 Coding of program ALPHA1 with
output

12-1.3 Counting Words, Program CNRBG1

Program CNRBG1 (Count Number of Red, Blue, and Green) counts the number of cards
with the words *red, blue,* and *green* input as data. When errors are encountered, the card
number is shown with the material actually punched in the card. Table 12-3 shows the
input cards used to test the program. Three cards are in error. The words *red* and *blue*
occur with leading blanks, which is not permitted. In addition, *blue* is mispelled as BLVE
on one card. Output from program CNRBG1 (Listing 12-3) shows the erroneous cards
numbered 7, 14, and 15. The erroneous data is lined up for output under column numbers
corresponding to actual character positions on the input cards. The total number of cards
read was 17; 4 were red, 5 were blue, 5 were green and 3 were none of these.

Program CNRBG1 is rather simple. A separate DIMENSION statement and the
type statement are used, although this is not necessarily desirable. The three permissible
colors as well as a five-character blank string to be used for comparison with a terminal
card, are defined in the DATA statement. Cards are counted in KNT, and a count of each
of the three colors is stored in the respective locations of array KOUNT. The first WRITE
statement outputs the heading that shows column numbers.

The primary loop starts with Statement 20; a single data card is read. If that data card contains a blank, transfer is to the END IF, and subsequently to the final WRITE statement and STOP.

If the input value is not blank, the input card is counted and the second DO-loop is entered; the color written on that card is compared with the three colors stored by the DATA statement in array COLOR. If the data on the card is neither blank nor any of the three permissible colors; then the characters on the card are output beside the card number.

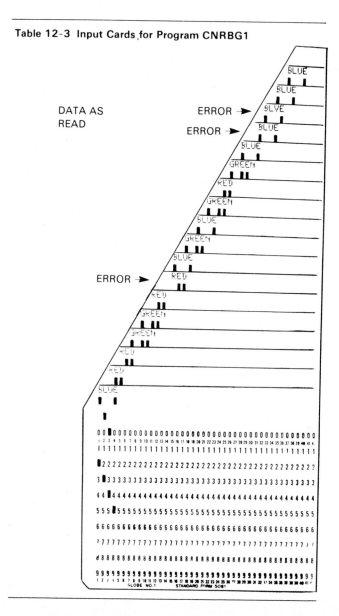

Table 12-3 Input Cards for Program CNRBG1

12-1.4 Sorting A List Containing Alphanumerics, Program CHSORT

The previous examples are trivial to provide simple examples for study. By contrast, program CHSORT (Listing 12–4) is both useful and important. The program is coded directly from program BBSRT1 of Listing 9–5.

Alterations include the following.

1. The program name is changed.
2. Array INFO is declared in a CHARACTER statement, as is the new temporary storage location for characters (called TEMP). Within the DO-loop and beyond the IF statement that compares INFO elements, ITEMP is changed to TEMP (for the first three statements) so that the replacement statements are of the same type.
3. ITEMP is maintained to assist in the three-line process that reorders line numbers.
4. WRITE statements are eliminated because they are unnecessary.
5. FORMAT statements are changed to output character variables by A-format.

Output (Listing 12–5) shows input on lines 1 through 10. The ordered array is then displayed with the original line number followed by the name of the person and his or her social security number.

The ASCII or EBCDIC collating sequences will both give the same results because numerals and letters are compared only with themselves at any level. Note that lines 2 and 6 contain people with identical names but different social security numbers. Because the social security number on line 2 is higher than the social security number on line 6, these two are reversed in the ordering process.

12-2 VARIATIONS OF OUTPUT, PROGRAM VAROUT

Although not precisely related to utilizing characters, this section is included at this point to summarize several troublesome points and to clearly delineate between Subset and Full Language FORTRAN 77.

12-2.1 Format Identifiers

Chapter 6 introduced statement labels and asterisks as *format identifiers.* Chapter 17 demonstrates several uses for specific needs. This subsection summarizes the rules. A format identifier, of course, identifies the type of format to be used and is always the second item in the control information list unless used in the form (Full Language only) FMT = f, where f is the format identifier.

Five types of format specifiers are available: (1) a statement label, (2) an integer variable that has received an appropriate statement label from an ASSIGN statement (Section 16–2.2), (3) a character constant (in Full Language, also a character expression except when *concatenation* occurs with operands whose length is specified by an asterisk), (4) a character array name (Full Language only), and (5) an asterisk that specifies list-directed formatting (Full language only). Several of these rules are demonstrated within this section.

In addition to implied-DO lists, the following table indicates allowable items for input/output lists.

```
          PROGRAM CNRBG1
C         COUNT NUMBER OF RED,BLUE AND GREEN USING ARRAYS
C         *       *         *   *          *

          DIMENSION COLOR(4),KOUNT(3)
          CHARACTER COLOR * 5, COLORI * 5
          DATA COLOR/'RED  ','BLUE ','GREEN','     '/

          LR=5
          LW=6
          KNT=0

C---            --- INITIALIZE ARRAY WHICH COUNTS COLORS FOUND ---
          DO 1 I=1,3
             KOUNT(I)=0
        1 CONTINUE

          WRITE(LW,1000)

       20 READ(LR,1001) COLORI
          IF(COLORI .NE. COLOR(4)) THEN
C---            --- COUNT TTHE TOTAL NUMBER OF CARDS READ ---
          KNT = KNT + 1

             DO 30 I=1,3
C---            --- IF COLOR MATCHES, ADD COUNT TO PROPER
C---            --- ELEMENT OF ARRAY KOUNT ---
                IF(COLORI .EQ. COLOR(I)) KOUNT(I)=KOUNT(I)+1
       30    CONTINUE

C---            ---IF NO MATCH FOUND, OUTPUT INCORRECT VALUE
C---            --- WHICH WAS INPUT ALONG WITH CARD NUMBER SO
C---            --- IT CAN BE EASILY LOCATED.
             IF(COLORI .NE. COLOR(1) .AND.
        1       COLORI .NE. COLOR(2) .AND.
        2       COLORI .NE. COLOR(3)) WRITE(LW,1002) COLORI,KNT
             GO TO 20
          END IF

     1000 FORMAT('1 ENTRIES ON FOLLOWING CARDS INCORRECT'/
        1        ' CARD COLUMNS: 12345')
     1001 FORMAT(A5)
     1002 FORMAT('                      ',A5,' ON CARD NUMBER',I3)
     1003 FORMAT(/' TOTAL NUMBER OF CARDS READ=',I3/
        U,' OF WHICH',I3,' ARE RED'/,I12,' ARE BLUE'/,I12,' ARE GREEN')

          WRITE(LW,1003) KNT,(KOUNT(I),I=1,3)
          STOP
          END
```

Output:

```
 ENTRIES ON FOLLOWING CARDS INCORRECT
CARD COLUMNS: 12345
                  RED ON CARD NUMBER  7
                 BLUE ON CARD NUMBER 14
                 BLVE  ON CARD NUMBER 15

TOTAL NUMBER OF CARDS READ= 17
OF WHICH  4 ARE RED
          5 ARE BLUE
          5 ARE GREEN
```

LISTING 12-3 Coding of program CRNBG1 with
output

```
PROGRAM CHSORT

C                                    ( USES:                )
C                                    (      LEXICAL         )
C                                    ( INTRINSIC FUNCTION   )
C                                    (      LLT(EXP)        )

      DIMENSION LINE(30)
      CHARACTER*30 INFO(30),TEMP
      LR=5
      LW=6

    5 CONTINUE
      READ(LR,1000,END=50) N,(INFO(I),I=1,N)
      WRITE(LW,1001) (I,INFO(I),I=1,N)

      DO 10 I=1,N
          LINE(I)=I
   10 CONTINUE

      NM1= N-1

      DO 40 I=1,NM1

          DO 30 J= I,1,-1

              IF(LLT(INFO(J+1),INFO(J))) THEN
                  TEMP= INFO(J)
                  INFO(J)  =INFO(J+1)
                  INFO(J+1)=TEMP
                  ITEMP    =LINE(J)
                  LINE(J)  =LINE(J+1)
                  LINE(J+1)=ITEMP
              ELSE
                  GO  TO 40
              END IF

   30     CONTINUE

   40 CONTINUE

      WRITE(LW,1004)(LINE(I),INFO(I),I=1,N)

 1000 FORMAT(I4/30(A/))
 1001 FORMAT(' LINE   NAME'/30(I4,3X,A/))
 1004 FORMAT(///' ORDERED ARRAY WITH ORIGINAL LINE NUMBERS '
     1//' LINE   NAME'/30(I4,3X,A/))

      GO TO 5
   50 CONTINUE
      STOP
      END
```

LISTING 12-4 Coding of program CHSORT

List Item:	Subset		Full Language	
	Input	Output	Input	Output
1. Variable Name*	yes	yes	yes	yes
2. Array Element Name*	yes	yes	yes	yes
3. Array Name*	yes	yes	yes	yes
4. Character Substring Name	no	no	yes	yes
5. Other Expressions	no	no	no	yes

*Variable Names, Array Element Names, and Array Names may
include type character.

```
LINE   NAME
  1    STRAUSS, TOM D. III  460-71-832
  2    PHILMONT, JOHN JR.   425-89-636
  3    GRAN, BOOBZIE        243-49-357
  4    GRAN, BOOAZIE        460-83-832
  5    ZINK, ROGER T.       744-93-962
  6    PHILMONT, JOHN JR.   163-40-159
  7    ZINK, R. G.          376-21-882
  8    AUTHER, CEIIL R.     359-62-448
  9    ARTHUR, CECIL V.     631-49-168
 10    ZINK, R. G. JR.      716-36-732

ORDERED ARRAY WITH ORIGINAL LINE NUMBERS

LINE   NAME
  9    ARTHUR, CECIL V.     631-49-168
  8    AUTHER, CEIIL R.     359-62-448
  4    GRAN, BOOAZIE        460-83-832
  3    GRAN, BOOBZIE        243-49-357
  6    PHILMONT, JOHN JR.   163-40-159
  2    PHILMONT, JOHN JR.   425-89-636
  1    STRAUSS, TOM D. III  460-71-832
  7    ZINK, R. G.          376-21-882
 10    ZINK, R. G. JR.      716-36-732
  5    ZINK, ROGER T.       744-93-962
```

LISTING 12-5 Input/output of program CHSORT

Other expressions can include function references and character expressions involving concatenation, except when an operand has an asterisk length specification (but the symbolic name of a constant can have its length specified by an asterisk).

The first WRITE statement of program VAROUT (Listing 12-6) is the most common form. Note that the apostrophe within the string ISN'T is represented by a double apostrophe because the character constant is delineated by apostrophes.

In the second WRITE statement, a character constant is used instead of the label of a FORMAT statement. Thus the actual apostrophe between ISN and T is nested two deep and must be represented by four apostrophes. That is, the apostrophe within the string is itself within a string. This form of the WRITE statement, using a character constant, is particularly advantageous for debugging processes. The third WRITE statement is also of the most common form, except it uses the H-edit descriptor (*Hollerith*), which was used extensively in older FORTRAN and is still legal in FORTRAN 77. The H-edit descriptor establishes a character string by preceding the string by H, where n is an integer constant that defines the number of characters in the string. Thus 6H ISN'T outputs a space followed by ISN'T. The H-edit descriptor leads to errors because n must exactly specify the count of characters (including blanks) to follow. The H-edit descriptor will probably disappear from future FORTRAN language standards.

The fourth write statement is similar to the third, except that the format is provided by a character constant in the WRITE statement. Although the 5H would suggest that only a single apostrophe should be needed, two apostrophes are actually required because the entire expression is itself a character constant set off by apostrophes.

12-2.2 Full Language FORTRAN 77

The next two statements of Listing 12-6 demonstrate that Full Language FORTRAN 77 allows output of expressions (a character constant and an integer constant are shown).

Formats are included within the WRITE statement although a separate FORMAT statement could be referred to by a statement label appearing within the WRITE statement. Of course, WRITE statements valid for Subset FORTRAN 77 are also valid in the Full Language.

12-2.3 Calculator Mode

The last four statements of Listing 12–6 are sometimes called *calculator mode*. The reason for this term is obvious. The PRINT statement requires only the FORMAT and variables to be output. The format is provided by a character constant that outputs

$$21.2 + 32.3 =$$

followed by the answer obtained from the expression $21.2 + 32.3$. On the next line, the WRITE statement is used for a similar process.

The last two output statements are list directed, that is they use an asterisk in place of the FORMAT statement. (Also see Listing 6–6.) In this case, strings are also output. Note that the fourth from the last output statement could have been written as:

PRINT '(////A,F5.1)', '21.2 + 32.3 = ', 21.2 + 32.3

When working from a remote terminal, calculator mode is quite useful for solving complicated problems that produce a single result. With the advent of hand held electronic calculators, however, the value of calculator mode on large computers has diminished drastically.

12-3 USING FULL LANGUAGE FORTRAN 77 WITH SUBSTRINGS

In the Full Language, the length of a character string may also be established by an integer constant expression enclosed in parentheses following the asterisk. The PARAMETER statement of Section 16–1.1(a) can have its length established, or can be used to form a character constant expression to establish the length of another entity.

PARAMETER (LJ = 4)
CHARACTER *(3*LJ) V, A (6,5)

In addition, character entities may have their lengths specified by an asterisk enclosed in parenthesis following the asterisk within functions and procedures, as used in Section 14–6.1.

Full Language FORTRAN 77 extends type character capabilities in several important ways. First, the Full Language allows use of substrings, which can add flexibility and decrease space requirements for a given program. In addition, substrings can be combined to form new substrings, increasing the power of utilizing characters by an order of magnitude. Finally, Full Language FORTRAN includes an intrinsic function to determine the length of any entity of type character.

12-3.1 Fundamental Rules, Programs CONCAT and LEN

This subsection deals with the rules applicable to extensions of character operations in the Full Language.

```
          PROGRAM VAROUT
      C-------VALID SUBSET FORTRAN 77:---
          DATA I,J,K,L,M/2,3,4,5,6/
   1      WRITE(6,100) I,J
      100 FORMAT(///1X,I1,1X,'ISN''T',1X,I1)
   2      WRITE(6,'(1X,I1,1X,''ISN''''T'',1X,I1)') J,K
   3      WRITE(6,200) K,L
      200 FORMAT(1X,I1,6H ISN'T,1X,I1)
   4      WRITE(6,'(1X,I1,1X,5HISN''T,1X,I1)') L,M
      C-------VALID FULL LANGUAGE FORTRAN 77 ONLY:---
   5      WRITE(6,'(///A)')  ' 6 ISN''T 7'
   6      WRITE(6,'(1X,I1,A,I1)') 2,  ' ISN''T ',4
      C-------CALCULATOR MODE---
   7      PRINT '(////'' 21.2 + 32.3='',F5.1)', 21.2 + 32.3
   8      WRITE(6,'('' 20 + 30='',I3)') 20 + 30
   9      PRINT *,'24.2 + 32.3=', 24.2 + 32.3
  10      WRITE(6,*) '20 + 300=', 20 + 300
          STOP
          END
```

Output:

```
2 ISN'T 3
3 ISN'T 4
4 ISN'T 5
5 ISN'T 6

6 ISN'T 7
2 ISN'T 4

21.2 + 32.3= 53.5
20 + 30= 50
24.2 + 32.3=  56.500000
20 + 300=         320
```

LISTING 12–6 Program VAROUT with output

(a) *Substrings.* A substring name is formed by following the name of a character variable (or element of a character array) by two optional integer expressions, enclosed in parentheses and separated by a colon. The first integer expression specifies the leftmost character position of the substring; the second specifies the rightmost position. If the first expression within the parentheses is missing, the default value is 1, signifying the leftmost character position. If the last expression is missing, the default value is the length of the variable or array element. Table 12–4 summarizes these relationships.

Examples summarizing the rules for substrings are shown in Table 12–5. The material represents only a portion of a computer program and the strings stored in each location are shown (on the right hand side of the table) for each assignment statement. The character string stored in variable L8 is sequentially altered by a series of substring changes taken from element 2,1 of the array AR.

When using substrings in assignment statements, the same positions cannot be shown on both sides of the equal sign. Thus, while

$$A(3:5) = A(7:9) \qquad \text{(Legal)}$$

is legal, it is not legal to write

Section 12-3 Using Full Language FORTRAN 77 With Substrings

307

$$A(5:9) = A(8:12) \quad \text{(Illegal)}$$

because characters 8 and 9 are referenced on both sides of the equal sign. The latter could be accomplished with the following two statements.

$$ALT = A(8:12)$$
$$A(5:9) = ALT$$

(b) *Concatenation* (To Link Together). The concatenation operator is $//$ with a significance for character types very similar to a plus sign for type integer or real. As a simple example, consider the following sequence of statements:

CHARACTER A*2, B*3, C*4, D*9
A = '12'
B = '345'
C = '6789'
D = A//C//B yields '126789345' in D

Concatenation is a powerful technique, as shown by program CONCAT of Listing 12–7. The program contains three arrays with 30 locations each, but the elements of each array

Table 12–4 Definition of A Substring

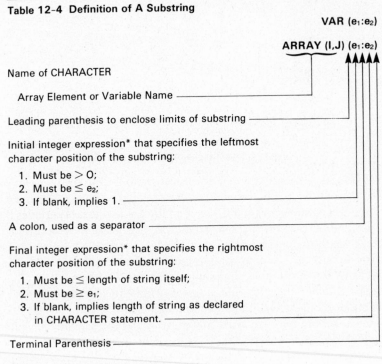

VAR $(e_1:e_2)$

ARRAY (I,J) $(e_1:e_2)$

Name of CHARACTER

Array Element or Variable Name

Leading parenthesis to enclose limits of substring

Initial integer expression* that specifies the leftmost character position of the substring:

1. Must be > 0;
2. Must be $\leq e_2$;
3. If blank, implies 1.

A colon, used as a separator

Final integer expression* that specifies the rightmost character position of the substring:

1. Must be $\leq$ length of string itself;
2. Must be $\geq e_1$;
3. If blank, implies length of string as declared in CHARACTER statement.

Terminal Parenthesis

Note:

1. Length of CHARACTER Substring $= e_2 - e_1 + 1$;
2. VAR $\equiv$ VAR(:);
3. ARRAY (I,J) (:) = ARRAY (I,J).

*May include integer array element and function references.

Table 12-5 Examples of CHARACTER Strings

Given:

```
CHARACTER *3 L3
CHARACTER *4 L4
CHARACTER *5 L5, AR(4,2)
CHARACTER *8 L8, NAM
```

NAM   = '12345678'

AR(2,1) = '12345'

Then:

L3	= NAM(4:6)	yields L3 = '456'
L4	= NAM(:4)	yields L4 = '1234'
L5	= NAM(4:)	yields L5 = '45678'
L8	= NAM(:)	
	or	yields L8 = '12345678'
L8	= NAM	

L8(2:3) = AR(2,1) (4:5) yields L8(2:3) = '45'
so that now L8 = '14545678'

L8(6:) = AR(2,1) (:3) yields L8(6:8) = '123'
so that now L8 = '14545123'

```
      PROGRAM CONCAT

C     CHARACTER NAME(30)*20, SSN(30)*11 , CODE(30)*6
      CHARACTER*20 NAME(30)
      CHARACTER*11 SSN(30)
      CHARACTER*6 CODE(30)

      LR=5
      LW=6

      DO 10 I=1,30
         READ(LR,'(2A)',ERR=30) NAME(I),SSN(I)
         CODE(I)(:)  = NAME(I)(1:3)//SSN(I)(9:11)
         WRITE(LW,'(2X,A,4X,A,4X,A)') NAME(I),SSN(I),CODE(I)
   10 CONTINUE

   30 STOP
      END
```

Output:

```
STRAUSS, TOM D. III     460-71-8324     STR324
PHILMONT, JOHN SR.      125-89-6364     PHI364
GRAN, BOOBZIE           243-49-3572     GRA572
GRAN, BOOAZIE           460-83-8325     GRA325
ZINK, ROGER T.          744-93-9625     ZIN625
PHILMONT, JOHN JR.      163-4 -1594     PHI594
ZINK, R. G.             376-21-8824     ZIN824
ARTHUR, CEIIL R.        359-62-4482     ART482
ARTHUR, CECIL V.        631-49-1683     ART683
ZINK, R. G. JR.         716-36-7324     ZIN324
```

LISTING 12-7 Coding of program CONCAT with output

have a different character length. The second line of Listing 12–7 is a comment line and could be used to replace the three CHARACTER type statements shown. A comment line is used so that both forms can be shown within a single program.

The DO-loop reads a name and a social security number, concatenates the first three letters of the last name and the last three numbers of the social security number into array CODE, and outputs the results showing the name, social security number, and the concatenated code consisting of the first three letters of the last name and the last three numbers of the social security number.

(c) *Determining Length of Strings.* Full Language FORTRAN 77 includes the intrinsic function LEN, illustrated in Listing 12–8. Although this function may appear to be insignificant, it is extremely useful when character strings are used as *arguments* of subroutines. The value of LEN is illustrated in program CHGNAM (Section 14–6), which also summarizes uses and characteristics of characters.

12–3.2 Counting Letters, Program ALPHA2

Program ALPHA2 of Listing 12–9 repeats the processes of Listing 12–2, using substrings. No arrays are necessary because J is defined as the string with a length of 80 characters, and K as a string of 2 characters. In the DATA statement, a blank is stored in the first location of K, and a T in the second location.

The entire line is read as a string into J. In program ALPHA2, comparisons are made between characters within strings. Use of substrings with a length of 1 character makes elements of arrays unnecessary. Use of substrings saves computer storage space and can (but may not) also increase the speed of execution.

12–3.3 Counting Words, Program CNRBG2

The program of Listing 12–10 reproduces the solution of program CNRBG1 (Listing 12–3), again using substrings in place of array elements. In addition, the original IF

```
      PROGRAM LEN
*
      CHARACTER L20*20, L5*5, L*1
*
      DATA L20, L5, L / 'ABCDEFGH', 'IJKLMNOP', 'QR' / , LW/6/
*
      LL20 = LEN(L20)
      LL5  = LEN(L5)
      LL   = LEN(L)
*
      WRITE(LW, '(3(I4,2X,A/))' ) LL20, L20, LL5, L5, LL, L
*
      STOP
      END
```

Output

```
20  ABCDEFGH
 5  IJKLM
 1  Q
```

LISTING 12–8 Coding of program LEN and partial
output

statements are combined into a more efficient IF-THEN-ELSE construct. The results are identical but computer storage is reduced and speed of operation is enhanced somewhat.

12–3.4 Program SEEK

Listing 12–11 is included to show a search for various combinations of characters from different elements of the same array. The first WRITE statement causes a slue to the top of a new page before output commences. The DO-loop that reads the array also echoes it to provide easy visibility. (See pages 314 and 315.)

Nested loops are designed to read a three-letter combination and to search every element of the array HOST for that three-letter combination. The first value input to FIND was the three-letter combination ABC, found in eleven locations of array HOST.

The innermost DO-loop increments K from 1 to 18 (rather than 1 to 20) so that the strings within array elements will not be overrun. Study of this program and I/O of Listing 12–12 will help insure that you understand how to use character strings.

12–4   USING HOLLERITH (Optional)

This optional section is included because of the diverse nature of Hollerith and its use in so many existing programs. Character data processing is definitely superior to the Hollerith data capability that existed in ANSI X3.9-1966, but the latter capability has also been included with Fortran 77 in Appendix C.

```
      PROGRAM ALPHA2
      CHARACTER J*80 , K*2

C---               --- STORE ´BLANK´ INTO FIRST LOCATION OF STRING K -AND-
C---               --- A CHARACTER ´T´ INTO SECOND LOCATION
      DATA K/´ T´/
      LINE = 0

   10 READ( 5,1000) J
      LINE = LINE + 1
      NUMBT = 0

      DO 20 I=1,80
C---               --- J(I:I) SEARCHES EACH LOCATION OF STRING J,
C---               --- SEQUENTIALLY, FOR A ´BLANK´ CHARACTER WHICH IS
C---               --- STORED IN K(1:1)--FIRST LOCATION OF STRING K.
C---               --- K(:1) COULD BE USED RATHER THAN K(1:1)
          IF(J(I:I).NE.K(1:1)) THEN

              DO 15 L=1,80
C---                   ---COUNT T´S ON LINE---
                  IF(J(L:L).EQ.K(2:2)) NUMBT= NUMBT+1
   15         CONTINUE

              WRITE( 6,1001) LINE, J, NUMBT
              GO TO 10
          END IF

   20 CONTINUE

 1000 FORMAT(A80)
 1001 FORMAT(1X,I3,3X,A80,´ NUMBER T´´S=´,I4)

      STOP
      END
```
LISTING 12–9 Coding of program ALPHA2

```
      PROGRAM CNRBG2
C     USE STRINGS TO COUNT NUMBER OF
C     READ, BLUE, AND GREEN READ ON INPUT

      DIMENSION KOUNT(3)
      CHARACTER COLOR * 17, COLORI * 5

C               --- STORE                INTO         OF
C               --- CHARACTER STRINGS:   LOCATIONS:   THE STRING COLOR
C               ---                      RED          1-3
C               ---                      BLUE         4-7
C               ---                      GREEN        8-12
C               ---          5 BLANKS    13-17
      DATA COLOR/'REDBLUEGREEN      '/

      LR=5
      LW=6
      KNT=0

C---              --- INITIALIZE ARRAY WHICH COUNTS COLORS FOUND ---
      DO 1 I=1,3
          KOUNT(I)= 0
    1 CONTINUE

      WRITE(LW,'(''1 ENTRIES ON FOLLOWING CARDS INCORRECT''/
     1'' CARD COLUMNS: 12345''//)')

   20 READ(LR,'(A )') COLORI
      IF(COLORI .NE. COLOR(13:17)) THEN
C---              --- WHEN PREVIOUS CARD READ IS NOT A BLANK,
C---              --- THEN COUNT NUMBER OF CARD READ
          KNT=KNT + 1

C ---             --- CHECK CARD JUST READ AND ADD COUNT TO:
C ---             --- KOUNT(1) IF ' RED' , KOUNT(2) IF ' BLUE' AND
C ---             --- KOUNT(3) IF 'GREEN'.  IF NONE OF THESE-- THEN --
C ---             --- OUTPUT CONTENTS OF CARD AND ITS NUMBER WITHIN
C ---             --- THE DECK SO THAT IT CAN BE READILY LOCATED.
      IF(COLORI .EQ. COLOR(1:3)) THEN
          KOUNT(1) = KOUNT(1) + 1
      ELSE IF(COLORI .EQ. COLOR(4:7)) THEN
          KOUNT(2) = KOUNT(2) + 1
      ELSE IF(COLORI .EQ. COLOR(8:12)) THEN
          KOUNT(3) = KOUNT(3) + 1
      ELSE
          WRITE(LW,'(15X,A,'' ON CARD NUMBER'',I3)') COLORI,KNT
      END IF

      GO TO 20
      END IF

      WRITE(LW,'(/'' TOTAL NUMBER OF CARDS READ='',I3/
     1'' OF WHICH'',I3,'' ARE RED''/I12,'' ARE BLUE''/I12,
     2'' ARE GREEN''///)') KNT,(KOUNT(I),I=1,3)
      STOP
      END
```

LISTING 12–10 Coding of program CNRBG2

12-4.1 Fundamental Rules

Although Hollerith is a data (for Appendix C definition only) type, no symbolic names can be declared as type Hollerith. Instead, Hollerith data are identified under the guise of names that are type integer or real. In general, Hollerith strings are stored in type integer or real variables by means of a DATA or READ statement. Usually, a Hollerith constant can be used only in a DATA statement with a form quite similar to that of the H-editing discussed for formats in Section 6–1.3. That is, a Hollerith constant takes the form $nHh_1h_2 \ldots h_3$, where blanks are significant.

Figure 12–2 illustrates input and output of a Hollerith using A-Format. (Observe that for this machine, the logical unit number for input is 2 and for output is 3.) Following the coding of this program segment, a typical data card shows blanks in the first two locations, the letters ST in locations 3 and 4, the letters ST repeated again in locations 5 and 6, blanks in Columns 7, 8, and 9 and the letters QUE in Columns 10, 11 and 12. When read using 3A4 Format, the characters are stored as shown in the middle table, with spaces represented by small triangles.

Output from the two WRITE statements is also shown, with column locations listed across the top of the page. The first WRITE statement shows $\triangle$QUEST$\triangle\triangle$, corresponding to the characters stored in locations A(3) and A(2). The second set of output shows $\triangle$QUE$\triangle\triangle$ST, corresponding to characters stored in locations A(3) and A(1). Blanks are counted and are important with A-Formats.

The simple program of Listing 12–13 on page 316 illustrates characteristics of the data statement in conjunction with the A-Format. This program has only four entities, two integer and two real, with one of each kind being an array. Once the dimensions of the two arrays have been established, their values are given by a DATA statement. A Hollerith AB is stored in the location M(1), a Hollerith 123 in M(2), and an integer constant 123 in M(3). Notice that although M is type integer, it actually stores two Hollerith strings and one integer. The edit descriptor recommended by Appendix C of ANSI X3.9–1978 is that used to define M(1). The integer in front of the H indicates precisely how many characters are required to follow and be defined for that location. (The apostrophe edit descriptor has often been allowed throughout the industry.)

The first location of Q stores a Hollerith IZ and the second location the real number 16.3. An integer 4 is stored in location N and a real 4. in location P. All of the data is

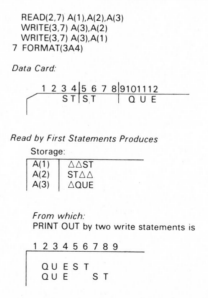

```
READ(2,7) A(1),A(2),A(3)
WRITE(3,7) A(3),A(2)
WRITE(3,7) A(3),A(1)
7 FORMAT(3A4)
```

Data Card:

1 2 3 4	5 6 7 8	9 10 11 12
ST	ST	QUE

Read by First Statements Produces
Storage:

A(1)	$\triangle\triangle$ST
A(2)	ST$\triangle\triangle$
A(3)	$\triangle$QUE

From which:
PRINT OUT by two write statements is

1 2 3 4 5 6 7 8 9
QUEST
QUE   ST

FIGURE 12–2 Input/output of Hollerith using A-Format

```
      PROGRAM SEEK

C --- THIS PROGRAM READS AND ECHOS A 2-DIMENSIONAL CHARACTER ARRAY(HOST)
C     WHICH STORES 20 SYMBOLS INTO CHARACTER STRINGS (HAVING LENGTH=20)
C     OF EACH OF THE 12 ELEMENTS, 3 EACH ON 4 LINES.
C --- A LOOP IS THEN ENTERED WHICH:
C         (1) READS CHARACTER VARIABLE FIND, HAVING LENGTH=3 --AND--
C         (2) SEARCHES THROUGH:
C             (A) EACH ELEMENT OF ARRAY HOST --AND--
C             (B) THRU EACH STRING OF EACH ELEMENT --FOR--
C             (C) CHARACTER STRING(S) MATCHING THE CHARACTER STRING
C                 WHICH WAS LAST READ INTO CHARACTER VARIABLE FIND
C         (3) OUTPUTS
C             (A) SUBSCRIPTS I AND J OF CHARACTER ARRAY HOST
C             (B) THE CHARACTER STRING LOCATED IN ELEMENT HOST(I,J)
C             (C) AND THE STRING SOUGHT AS DEFINED IN FIND

      CHARACTER*20 HOST(4,3),FIND*3

      LR=5
      LW=6
      WRITE(LW,'(''1'')')

      DO 10 I=1,4
         READ(LR,'(3A20)') (HOST(I,J),J=1,3)
         WRITE(LW,'(3(3X,A)///)') (HOST(I,J),J=1,3)
   10 CONTINUE

   20 READ(LR,'(A)',ERR=100) FIND

         DO 50 I=1,4

            DO 40 J=1,3

               DO 30 K=1,18
                  IF(FIND( : ) .EQ. HOST(I,J)(K:K+2)) THEN
                     WRITE(LW,'('' ROW'',I2,  '', COL'',I2,
     1               '' WITH '',A,'' HAS '',A,'' STARTING IN''
     2               '' LOCATION'',I3)')  I,J,HOST(I,J),FIND
     3               ,K
                  END IF
   30          CONTINUE
   40       CONTINUE
   50    CONTINUE

      GO TO 20

  100 STOP
      END
```

LISTING 12-11 Coding of program SEEK

output in a single WRITE statement using the FORMAT Statement 10. (Such combinations are poor practice.)

Output from Listing 12–13 is annotated in Figure 12–3. Observe that the field width for the A edit descriptor must agree exactly with the field width specified within the DATA statement. Thus the field width for M(1), which contains the Hollerith AB, is output with edit descriptor A2. Use of A1, A3, or any other field width with the edit descriptor would normally result in a run-time error when output was attempted. The Hollerith 123, the second location of array M, is output using edit descriptor A3, whereas

Input:

```
ABCDEDABCQRABCBBCABCAZQBABCOTZ:3MAN.L136 .,$  L ZQBJ Z:3 ABC
T EZQBV JXZQ3RNU136I.,$ M136 $.,COT IABCSEZQBI 136 COT JRON
COT AZQB ABCOTOS$$Z:3MANZ:3COT H.,$OIN MAN Z:3ABCOTL LZQB.,$
.,$ NNCOTSR136I COTAUMAN EZ:3YABCOTAX136R COT OL ZQDDZ:3 ABC
ABC
COT
MAN
BOY
ZQB
136
.,$
Z:3
J Z
```

Output:

```
ABCDEDABCQRABCBBCABC     AZQBABCOTZ:3MAN.L136     .,$  L ZQBJ Z:3 ABC


T EZQBV JXZQBRNU136I     .,$ M136 $.,COT IABC     SEZQBI 136 COT JRON


COT AZQB ABCOTOS$$Z:     3MANZ:3COT H.,$OIN M     AN Z:3ABCOTL LZQB.,$


.,$ NNCOTSR136I COTA     UMAN EZ:3YABCOTAX136     R COT OL ZQDDZ:3 ABC
```

```
ROW 1, COL 1 WITH ABCDEDABCQRABCBBCABC HAS ABC STARTING IN LOCATION  1
ROW 1, COL 1 WITH ABCDEDABCQRABCBBCABC HAS ABC STARTING IN LOCATION  7
ROW 1, COL 1 WITH ABCDEDABCQRABCBBCABC HAS ABC STARTING IN LOCATION 12
ROW 1, COL 1 WITH ABCDEDABCQRABCBBCABC HAS ABC STARTING IN LOCATION 18
ROW 1, COL 2 WITH AZQBABCOTZ:3MAN.L136 HAS ABC STARTING IN LOCATION  5
ROW 1, COL 3 WITH  .,$  L ZQBJ Z:3 ABC HAS ABC STARTING IN LOCATION 18
ROW 2, COL 2 WITH .,$ M136 $.,COT IABC HAS ABC STARTING IN LOCATION 18
ROW 3, COL 1 WITH COT AZQB ABCOTOS$$Z: HAS ABC STARTING IN LOCATION 10
ROW 3, COL 3 WITH AN Z:3ABCOTL LZQB.,$ HAS ABC STARTING IN LOCATION  7
ROW 4, COL 2 WITH UMAN EZ:3YABCOTAX136 HAS ABC STARTING IN LOCATION 11
ROW 4, COL 3 WITH R COT OL ZQDDZ:3 ABC HAS ABC STARTING IN LOCATION 18
ROW 1, COL 2 WITH AZQBABCOTZ:3MAN.L136 HAS COT STARTING IN LOCATION  7
ROW 2, COL 2 WITH .,$ M136 $.,COT IABC HAS COT STARTING IN LOCATION 13
ROW 2, COL 3 WITH SEZQBI 136 COT JRON  HAS COT STARTING IN LOCATION 12
ROW 3, COL 1 WITH COT AZQB ABCOTOS$$Z: HAS COT STARTING IN LOCATION  1
ROW 3, COL 1 WITH COT AZQB ABCOTOS$$Z: HAS COT STARTING IN LOCATION 12
ROW 3, COL 2 WITH 3MANZ:3COT H.,$OIN M HAS COT STARTING IN LOCATION  8
ROW 3, COL 3 WITH AN Z:3ABCOTL LZQB.,$ HAS COT STARTING IN LOCATION  9
ROW 4, COL 1 WITH .,$ NNCOTSR136I COTA HAS COT STARTING IN LOCATION  7
ROW 4, COL 1 WITH .,$ NNCOTSR136I COTA HAS COT STARTING IN LOCATION 17
ROW 4, COL 2 WITH UMAN EZ:3YABCOTAX136 HAS COT STARTING IN LOCATION 13
ROW 4, COL 3 WITH R COT OL ZQDDZ:3 ABC HAS COT STARTING IN LOCATION  3
ROW 1, COL 2 WITH AZQBABCOTZ:3MAN.L136 HAS MAN STARTING IN LOCATION 13
ROW 3, COL 2 WITH 3MANZ:3COT H.,$OIN M HAS MAN STARTING IN LOCATION  2
ROW 4, COL 2 WITH UMAN EZ:3YABCOTAX136 HAS MAN STARTING IN LOCATION  2
ROW 1, COL 2 WITH AZQBABCOTZ:3MAN.L136 HAS ZQB STARTING IN LOCATION  2
ROW 1, COL 3 WITH  .,$  L ZQBJ Z:3 ABC HAS ZQB STARTING IN LOCATION  9
ROW 2, COL 1 WITH T EZQBV JXZQBRNU136I HAS ZQB STARTING IN LOCATION  4
ROW 2, COL 1 WITH T EZQBV JXZQBRNU136I HAS ZQB STARTING IN LOCATION 11
ROW 2, COL 3 WITH SEZQBI 136 COT JRON  HAS ZQB STARTING IN LOCATION  3
```

LISTING 12-12 Input/output of program SEEK

the integer 123 (the third location of array M) could have been output in any I edit descriptor that had sufficient field width for the size of the number involved.

12-4.2 Simple Examples, Programs DSAF and UNIA

Program DSAF (Data Statement And Formatting) is shown in Listing 12–14, with the output, and annotated in Listing 12–15. Use the program with comments as extra assistance only if you need it. Note that both programs terminate logical operations by CALL EXIT rather than STOP. Use of this non-standard alternate form is encouraged in some computer environments.

The most frequent difficulties encountered when using DATA statements and the A-Format are mixing types or having nonmatching field widths. (It is often necessary to add blanks in order to keep field widths identical in length.) The length of Hollerith words is processor dependent, and on some machines the possible lengths differ for storage in entities of type integer or type real.

Machine independence can never be assured, but restricting word lengths to four characters is helpful if it is anticipated that the program will run on more than one machine over a period of time. This causes additional complications, as illustrated by program UNIA in Listing 12–16. Twelve spaces are desired for each name, with the maximum possible word length considered to be four. Therefore each name requires three locations of the array NAME. In the DATA statement, all four spaces must be used for each element of the array, even when all four spaces are blank. If blanks were not used, serious troubles would occur and any results would be erroneous. Within the DO-loop, beginning and ending array elements are computed for each name based on the order of the names as denoted by the loop index I. It is usually important to spot check this type of coding to be sure that it satisfies beginning and ending locations. For instance, when I is 3, the ending location defined by JEND equals 3 times I, or 9, and the beginning location (JBEG) is 7. Locations 7 through 9 in the DATA statement show LEAV, followed by ETTS, followed by ΔJ.Δ. This, therefore, yields the third name: LEAVETTS, J. .

```
C   |  PROGRAM DATA
    |  DIMENSION M (3), Q (2)
    |  DATA M/2HAB, '123', 123/,
  1 |  Q/'IZ',16.3/,N/4/,P/4./
    |  WRITE (6,10)M,Q,N,P
 10 |  FORMAT (1X,A2,1X,A3,1X,I3,1X,A2,
  1 |  1X,F5.1,1X,I3,1X,F4.2)
    |  STOP
    |  END
```

LISTING 12-13 Coding of program DATA

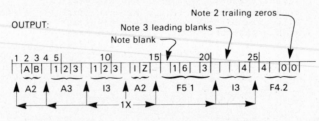

FIGURE 12-3 Output from program DATA

```
        PROGRAM DSAF
C       --- DATA STATEMENT AND FORMATS FOR HOLLERITH
C           *     *       *     *
        DIMENSION K(80),L(10)
        LW=6
        DATA L / 1H ,1H*,1H+,3HACE,1HT,4HKING,1,88,999,0/

        DO 20 I=1,80
            K(I)=L(1)
  20 CONTINUE

        K(10)=L(2)
        K(20)=L(3)
        K(30)=L(7)
        K(40)=L(5)

        WRITE(06,40) K
  40 FORMAT(1H1,1X,29A1,I1,50A1//)

        DO 50 I=1,80
            K(I)=L(1)
  50 CONTINUE

        K(10)=L(4)
        K(15)=L(5)
        K(30)=L(8)
        K(25)=L(6)
        K(40)=L(9)

        WRITE(06,60)(K(I),I=1,40)
  60 FORMAT(1X,9A1,A3,14A1,A4,4A1,I4,9A1,I4//)

  70 FORMAT(1X,A3,A1,A4,A1,I3//)
        WRITE(LW,70) L(4),L(3),L(6),L(2),L(9)
        WRITE(LW,70) K(10),L(3),K(25),L(2),K(40)

        DO 80 I=1,10
            IF(K(25).EQ.L(I)) WRITE(LW,90) I
  80 CONTINUE
  90 FORMAT(1X,'KING IS FOUND IN L(',I2,')')

        CALL EXIT
        END
```

Output:

```
          *           +           1           T


          ACE     T           KING        88          999


ACE+KING*999


ACE+KING*999


KING IS FOUND IN L( 6)
```

LISTING 12-14 Program DSAF with output

```
            PROGRAM DSAF
C---     ---PROVIDE STORAGE LOCATIONS FOR 2 INTEGER ARRAYS
         DIMENSION K(80),L(10)
         LW=6
C---     ---STORE DATA IN ARRAY L BY DATA STATEMENT
C---     --- A BLANK IN L(1)      WORD KING IN L(6)
C---     --- AN *  IN L(2)    INTEGER CONSTANTS: 1 IN L(7)
C---     --- A +   IN L(3)                      88 IN L(8)
C---     ---WORD ACE IN L(4)                    999 IN L(9)
C---     ---LETTER T IN L(5)                      0 IN L(10)
         DATA L / 1H ,1H*,1H+,3HACE,1HT,4HKING,1,88,999,0/
C---     ---NOTE THAT BLANK,SYMBOLS,LETTERS AND WORDS,IE,
C---     ---    ALPHANUMERIC ESTABLISHED BY HOLLERITH H
C---     ---INTEGER CONSTANTS ARE SIMPLY LISTED
C---     ---ARRAYS FOR DATA STATEMENTS MAY ALSO BE FLOATING POINT

C---     ---NOW,BLANK OUT 80 CHARACTER SPACES IN AN ARRAY LINE___

         DO 20 I=1,80
            K(I)=L(1)
     20 CONTINUE

C---     ---NOW AN * IN K(10):
         K(10)=L(2)
C---     ---NOW A + IN K(20):
         K(20)=L(3)
C---     ---NOW INTEGER CONSTANT 1(ONE) IN K(30)
         K(30)=L(7)
C---     ---NOW LETTER T IN K(40)
         K(40)=L(5)

C---     ---OUTPUT LINE OF 80 CHARACTERS FROM ARRAY K:
         WRITE(06,40) K

C---     ---IN FORMAT: 1 ST 29 SPACES ALPHANUMERIC --     29A1
C---     ---           30 TH SPACE IS FOR INTEGER CONSTANT -- I1
C---     ---        LAST 50 SPACES FOR ALPHANUMERIC AGAIN --  50A1
C---     ---                            TOTAL FIELD WIDTHS=80
     40 FORMAT(1H1,1X,29A1,I1,50A1//)

C---     ---BLANK OUT K-ARRAY AGAIN

         DO 50 I=1,80
            K(I)=L(1)
     50 CONTINUE

C---     ---NOW PUT WORD ACE IN K(10)
         K(10)=L(4)
C---     ---NOW PUT LETTER T IN K(15)
         K(15)=L(5)
C---     ---PUT WORD KING IN K(25)
         K(25)=L(6)
C---     ---PUT INTEGER CONSTANT 88 IN K(30)
         K(30)=L(8)
C---     ---PUT INTEGER CONSTANT 999 IN K(40)
         K(40)=L(9)
```

LISTING 12-15 Program DSAF with extensive comments

12-4.3 Counting Letters, Program ALPHA3

The program of Listing 12–17 is included for comparison with its counterparts in Listings 12–2 and 12–9. Note the similarities and differences between program ALPHA3 and the programs ALPHA1 and ALPHA2.

```
C---    ---WRITE A LINE USING 1 ST 40 LOCATIONS OF K:
        WRITE(06,60)(K(I),I=1,40)

C---    ---FORMAT: 1 ST 9 LOCATIONS= SINGLE CHARACTER BLANKS    9A1
C---    ---          K(10) HAS WORD ACE= 3 CHARACTERS             A3
C---    ---          K(11) THRU K(24)= SINGLE CHAR:BLANK OR T   14A1
C---    ---          K(25) HAS KING= 4 CHARACTERS                 A4
C---    ---          K(26)-K(29) SINGLE CHAR BLANKS             4A1
C---    ---          K(30) INTEGER CONSTANT,FIELD .GE. 2 FOR 88  I4
C---    ---          THEN 9 MORE SINGLE CHAR BLANKS             9A1
C---    ---          K(40) INT CONST,FIELD .GE. 3 FOR 999         I4
C---    ---                               TOTAL FIELD WIDTHS= 51
   60 FORMAT(1X,9A1,A3,14A1,A4,4A1,I4,9A1,I4//)

C---    ---WRITE ACE+KING*999   FIRST USE L, THEN RE-DO USING K IF ABLE
   70 FORMAT(1X,A3,A1,A4,A1,I3//)
        WRITE(LW,70) L(4),L(3),L(6),L(2),L(9)
        WRITE(LW,70) K(10),L(3),K(25),L(2),K(40)

C---    ---COMPARE KING IN K(25) TO L(1-10),OUTPUT LOCATION OF L WHERE
C---    ---                            KING IS FOUND

        DO 80 I=1,10
           IF(K(25).EQ.L(I)) WRITE(LW,90) I
   80 CONTINUE

   90 FORMAT(1X,'KING IS FOUND IN L(',I2,')')
C---    ---NOTE HOW VARIABLE ANSWER IS IMBEDDED IN HOLLERITH
C---    ---WARNING: THIS TECHNIQUE SIMPLY WILL NOT WORK WITH MIXED MODES.

        CALL EXIT
        END
```

LISTING 12-15 *(continued)*

```
        PROGRAM UNIA
C           USING-NAMES-IN-ARRAYS
        DIMENSION NAME(12)
        DATA NAME /4HJOHN,4HS, T,4HOM  ,4HKOP,,4H ROG,
       14HER  ,4HLEAV,4HETTS,4H, J.,4HMO ,4HTIM ,4H    /
C       WRITE OUT NAMES IN ORDER:

        DO 10 I=1,4
           JEND= 3*I
           JBEG= JEND-2
           WRITE(06,1000)(NAME(J),J=JBEG,JEND)
   10      CONTINUE

 1000 FORMAT(///1X,3A4//)
        STOP
        END
```

Output:

```
JOHNS, TOM




KOP, ROGER




LEAVETTS, J.




MO, TIM
```

LISTING 12-16 Coding of program UNIA with output

```
      PROGRAM ALPHA3
      DIMENSION J(80),K(2)
C---            --- TYPE INTEGER ARRAY K IS DEFINED WITH HOLLERITH
C---            --- 'BLANK' IN K(1) AND 'T' IN K(2)
      DATA K/' ','T'/
      LINE = 0

   10 READ( 5,1000) J
      LINE = LINE + 1
      NUMBT = 0

      DO 20 I=1,80
C---            --- EACH HOLLERITH WHICH WAS READ INTO TYPE INTEGER
C---            --- ARRAY J IS COMPARED WITH 'BLANK' HOLLERITH DEFINED
C---            --- IN TYPE INTEGER K(1).
      IF(J(I).NE.K(1)) THEN

          DO 15 L=1,80
C---                 ---COUNT T'S ON LINE---
             IF(J(L).EQ.K(2)) NUMBT= NUMBT+1
   15     CONTINUE

          WRITE( 6,1001) LINE, J, NUMBT
          GO TO 10
      END IF

   20 CONTINUE

 1000 FORMAT(80A1)
 1001 FORMAT(1X,I3,3X,80A1,' NUMBER T''S=',I4)

      STOP
      END
```

LISTING 12-17 Coding of program ALPHA3

12-5 EXERCISES

1. Given: CHARACTER * 3 C3
           CHARACTER * 4 C4
           CHARACTER *10 C10
           C3 = 'ABC'
           C4 = '1234'
           C10 = C3//C4//C3
           C10 (:3) = C4 (2:)
           C10 (6:7) = C3 (2:3)
           C10 (8:8) = C4 (3:3)
   Show variations in C10.

2. Given: CHARACTER TWO * 2, THREE * 3, EIGHT * 8
           TWO = '.,'
           THREE = 'XYZ'
           EIGHT = '12345678'
           EIGHT (3:5) = THREE (:1)//TWO (1:1)//THREE (3:)
           EIGHT (7:) = THREE (2:2)//TWO (2:2)
           EIGHT (1:2) = EIGHT (7:7)//THREE (:1)
           EIGHT (3:7) = EIGHT (4:8)
   Show variations in EIGHT.

Chapter **13**

Recapitulation and Synthesis

By now, it is important to be able to clearly distinguish between formal FORTRAN 77 and items that are matters of style and good practice. In addition, it is now appropriate to use another perspective in consideration of problem formulation, program verification, and input/output.

13-1 FORMAL FORTRAN 77

A processor is a combination of a data processing system and the mechanisms by which programs are transformed for use on that data processing system. The processor transforms an executable program composed of one, and only one, main program and any number (including none) of external procedures and subprograms. A main program, an external procedure, a block data subprogram, and a subroutine are each called a program unit and each consists of a series of FORTRAN statements (including comment lines), always terminating with an END statement. Only the main program can have a PROGRAM statement as its first statement, having the form PROGRAM *pgm* where *pgm* represents the symbolic name of the program.

13-1.1 Summary of Syntactic Items

Syntactic items are formed from the FORTRAN character set (Table 4-2). Syntactic items are the following.

Constants
> Integer, real, logical, character, complex, and double precision

Symbolic names (1 to 6 letters or digits, first must be a letter)
> Names of:
> array, block data subprogram, common block, constant (only if it appears as a symbolic name in PARAMETER statement), dummy

procedure, external function, intrinsic function, main program, statement function, subroutine, or variable.

Statement labels

Keywords

such as GO TO, READ, FORMAT
(whether these entities are keywords or symbolic names is determined by context.)

Operators

$+ \quad - \quad * \quad / \quad ** \quad //$

Special characters

Variables, array elements, or substrings are either defined or undefined. Typically, they become defined by DATA statements (initially defined), assignment statements, association, and so forth. When any reference is made to an entity, it must be defined.

13-1.2 Summary of Data Types

Executable programs in Subset FORTRAN 77 operate with four data types: integer, real, logical, and character. Full Language FORTRAN 77 includes two additional data types: complex and double precision. Unless otherwise declared in an explicit type statement or implicitly, integers start with one of the letters *I, J, K, L, M,* or *N* and type real starts with letters of the alphabet other than these six. Types integer and real can be changed from their default identities by using type statements; double precision, complex, logical, and character types must all be declared.

13-1.3 Order and Classification of Statements

Table 13-1 groups the keywords and assignment statements according to their general classifications, and in the order in which they must be used. Among the major groupings (PROGRAM and subprogram statements, IMPLICIT specification statements, other specification statements, statement function statements, DATA statements, and executable statements) the keywords and/or assignment statements can be used in any order. The primary sections of this book in which each keyword is discussed are given. Note that all statements start with keywords except assignment and statement function statements.

The nonexecutable statements may be labeled, but such labels cannot be used to control the sequence of execution. The nonexecutable statements classify program units, specify entry points within subprograms, contain information for editing, specify arrangements, specify characteristics, specify statement functions, and specify initial values. Executable statements provide the action and establish the flow of the program logic.

13-1.4 Assignment Statements: Order of Evaluation and Conversion of Type

Precedence of operators is as follows.

Innermost parentheses
exponentiation   (right to left)   (*Note:* This is the reverse of the usual order.)

Table 13-1 Order and Classification of Statements

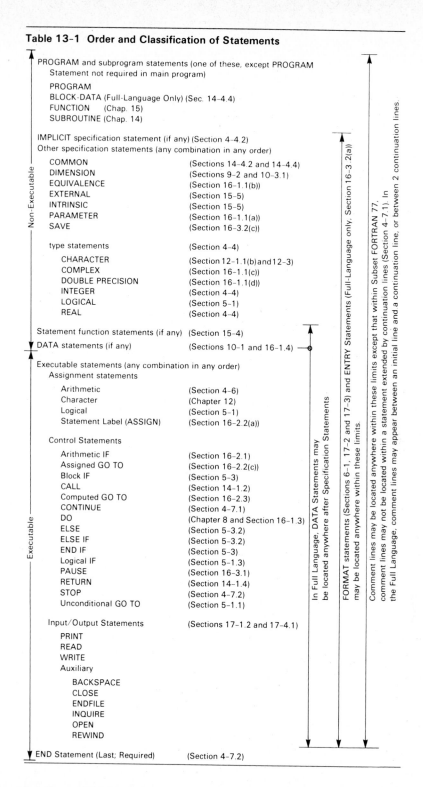

PROGRAM and subprogram statements (one of these, except PROGRAM
Statement not required in main program)

PROGRAM
BLOCK-DATA (Full-Language Only) (Sec. 14-4.4)
FUNCTION   (Chap. 15)
SUBROUTINE (Chap. 14)

IMPLICIT specification statement (if any) (Section 4-4.2)
Other specification statements (any combination in any order)

COMMON	(Sections 14-4.2 and 14-4.4)
DIMENSION	(Sections 9-2 and 10-3.1)
EQUIVALENCE	(Section 16-1.1(b))
EXTERNAL	(Section 15-5)
INTRINSIC	(Section 15-5)
PARAMETER	(Section 16-1.1(a))
SAVE	(Section 16-3.2(c))
type statements	(Section 4-4)
CHARACTER	(Section 12-1.1(b) and 12-3)
COMPLEX	(Section 16-1.1(c))
DOUBLE PRECISION	(Section 16-1.1(d))
INTEGER	(Section 4-4)
LOGICAL	(Section 5-1)
REAL	(Section 4-4)

Non-Executable

Statement function statements (if any) (Section 15-4)
DATA statements (if any)   (Sections 10-1 and 16-1.4)

Executable statements (any combination in any order)
Assignment statements

Arithmetic	(Section 4-6)
Character	(Chapter 12)
Logical	(Section 5-1)
Statement Label (ASSIGN)	(Section 16-2.2(a))

Control Statements

Arithmetic IF	(Section 16-2.1)
Assigned GO TO	(Section 16-2.2(c))
Block IF	(Section 5-3)
CALL	(Section 14-1.2)
Computed GO TO	(Section 16-2.3)
CONTINUE	(Section 4-7.1)
DO	(Chapter 8 and Section 16-1.3)
ELSE	(Section 5-3.2)
ELSE IF	(Section 5-3.2)
END IF	(Section 5-3)
Logical IF	(Section 5-1.3)
PAUSE	(Section 16-3.1)
RETURN	(Section 14-1.4)
STOP	(Section 4-7.2)
Unconditional GO TO	(Section 5-1.1)

Input/Output Statements   (Sections 17-1.2 and 17-4.1)

PRINT
READ
WRITE
Auxiliary

BACKSPACE
CLOSE
ENDFILE
INQUIRE
OPEN
REWIND

Executable

END Statement (Last; Required)   (Section 4-7.2)

In Full Language, DATA Statements may be located anywhere after Specification Statements

FORMAT statements (Sections 6-1, 17-2 and 17-3) and ENTRY Statements (Full-Language only, Section 16-3.2(a)) may be located anywhere within these limits.

Comment lines may be located anywhere within these limits except that within Subset FORTRAN 77, comment lines may not be located within a statement extended by continuation lines (Section 4-7.1). In the Full Language, comment lines may appear between an initial line and a continuation line, or between 2 continuation lines.

* and /	(left to right)
+ and −	(left to right) includes negation
//	(left to right)
.NOT.	(left to right)
.AND.	(left to right)
.OR.	(left to right)
.EQV. or .NEQV.	(left to right)

The actual order of evaluation by the processor may differ from the order indicated by this precedence. For instance, $A + B$ can be evaluated by the processor as $B + A$ and $A * C + A * D$ can be evaluated by the processor as $A * (C + D)$. In such alternate forms, the mathematical values must be equal, although the relative size of the numbers involved can produce different results from mathematically equivalent arithmetic expressions. In any critical cases in which the order of operation is mandatory for the accuracy desired, use parentheses to establish the order. Alternate forms are not allowed for mixed types where the results would be different. For instance, $A*M/N$ cannot be evaluated as $A*(M/N)$. Similar alterations are allowed in the evaluation of character, relational, and logical expressions.

When either two integer entities or two real entities are combined by $+, −, *$, or $/$, no change in type occurs. When an integer entity and a real entity are added, subtracted, multiplied or divided (in either order), the integer entity is converted to real before the operation is performed. Mixed types become double precision or complex if either type is present (double precision and complex cannot be used together in the same expression).

When any type entity is raised to an integer power, no conversion of type occurs. Also, no conversion occurs when a real entity is raised to a real power; however, an integer entity raised to a real power is first converted to real. Thus

$$R = I_1 ** R_2 \quad \text{is evaluated as} \quad R = REAL(I_1)**R_2$$

Mixed types raised, or raising, entities to double precision or complex are converted to double precision or complex before the operation is performed (double precision and complex cannot be mixed in exponentiation).

13-2 STYLE AND GOOD PRACTICE

Wide variations of style exist among competent programmers; a consistent style used habitually can greatly facilitate programming in all of its aspects. This section comments on the styles presented within this text. Because style is personal, you will have to use these concepts to formulate your own consistent procedures that make up your style.

13-2.1 Supportive Documentation

The amount and type of supportive documentation varies with personal preference and requirements of various computer installations. In the author's experience, the four-step procedure involving a definition sheet, human-oriented flow diagram, machine-oriented flow diagram, and coding processed directly from the machine-oriented flow diagram has been very effective. Typically, the final supportive documentation in this case includes a comprehensive definition sheet and a machine-oriented flow diagram, with the human-oriented comments written in script beside the process boxes.

Such procedure, however, is not standard and is only one style. At the far extreme, many programmers use no supportive documentation, relying solely on comment lines within the program to perform this function. (Variations on this theme are discussed in the next subsection.)

The American National Standards Institute, Inc.* publishes "Flow Chart Symbols and Their Usage in Information Processing," (ANSI X3.5–1970). These symbols are widely used. As previously discussed, however, they are not used in this text because students who take only one course in computer programming find the simplified symbols used within this text easy to remember and easy to adapt to the standard symbols.

The style of flow diagrams also varies widely. In this text, structured flow diagrams are used. Such structuring provides a main line (which flows vertically down the left side of the sheet) with loops separated from each other and nested loops indicated by indented vertical lines. The use of double arrow heads to offset mini-modules not only aids in formulation, but gives a direct signal that blank lines and indentation are needed in the coding.

The author's strong personal preference is to keep flow diagrams on a single sheet of paper and to connect all boxes with flow lines. (Some programmers show breaks in the flow diagrams by arrows pointing to circles containing a letter, with the same letter in a circle in another part of the program to show a branch.) Though not everyone agrees, the flow diagramming techniques in this text are useful in both the formulative process and as permanent documentation.

13–2.2 Coding

Variations in the layout and styling of FORTRAN coding are almost unlimited. In this text, a uniform style is used for coding of FORTRAN statements, but various styles are used for comment lines.

(a) *Documentation with Comment Lines.* A wide variety of strong opinions exist about how comment lines should be used within FORTRAN programs.

1. *None:* Some programmers feel that the coding should be done so well that no comments are necessary and that the structure and good style of a FORTRAN program can actually be destroyed by insertion of comment lines.
2. *Definition Sheet Approach:* Other programmers feel that the program is not complete unless it contains a definition sheet, in the form of comment lines, near the beginning of the program. Often such programmers define the problem and the variables used within the program at the beginning of the program, and then use no other comment lines.
3. *Captions:* Some programmers feel that it is important to use titles or captions for various modules as they are entered and exited.

*1430 Broadway, New York, N.Y. 10018

4. *Explanations:* Some programmers like to give a detailed explanation of the program, some emphasizing the coding itself and others the algorithm being used.
5. *Extensive Comments:* Finally, some programmers feel that a program is not completely coded unless it has comment lines that display the complete definition sheet and explain the program in detail.

Examples of all of these forms are shown in this text. Also, the comments are set off in several different ways. Many programmers prefer to use the asterisk rather than a capital C in Column 1 and to carry the asterisk theme throughout the comment lines. Using such a plan, it is possible to draw boxes around various elements of the program; some put boxes around the major groupings of Table 13-1. (See Listing 7-1.) Your final decision will probably be a function of both personal preference and installation practice.

(b) *Spacing and Indentation.* Throughout this text, spacing has been used in a uniform manner. Such spacing becomes habitual with a minimum amount of practice and relates directly to the flow diagrams. The programs in this text are indented to start in Columns 11, 16, 21, and so on. (Spacing for this indentation was originally based on coding forms containing heavy lines between Columns 10 and 11, Columns 15 and 16, and so on.) Because the first permissible column of a FORTRAN statement is 7, many programmers prefer to indent to Columns 12, 17, 22, and so on. In general, a five-space indentation seems to be commonly used, although indentations of either four or six spaces have been observed. The number of spaces used for an indentation is relatively unimportant, so long as it is standardized in your programs; it is important to faithfully use indentation to highlight mini-modules.

(c) *Special Considerations.* The use of LR and LW to specify the units used for reading and writing is a personal habit; any other set of integer variables could be used. It is a good idea to pick a set of symbols to use consistently (rather than using constants within READ and WRITE statements) so that your programs are readily transportable.

Programs can often provide much more flexibility if variables (rather than constants) are used within DO-loop and relational expressions. Thus it is definitely worth the effort necessary to consciously consider using variables in place of constants for such operations.

(d) *Computer Cards.* Although the type and color of computer cards makes no difference to the card reader, it is often helpful for people to use color coding. Although any system will do, one that works well is to use red for control cards, green for FORTRAN cards, yellow for *debugging* cards (see Section 13-5) and a natural color for data cards.

Columns 73 through 80 on FORTRAN cards are used for identification only. Such identification is useful if you accidently drop the deck, when you are making changes, and for identifying portions of the program in future modifications. A typical scheme is to put the first three digits of the program's name within Columns 73 to 75 and to number the cards by tens, right justified to Column 80. Numbering the cards by tens makes it possible to insert intermediate cards without destroying the numerical sequence.

13-3 PROBLEM FORMULATION

Following the development of subroutines in the next chapter, the concepts of top-down and bottom-up programming are discussed. These techniques are applicable to any programming, but particularly to large-scale projects.

For smaller programs that involve rather complex logic, two simplified procedures can also produce reliable results in a reasonable amount of time.

13-3.1 Input-Output; Link

Often, comprehension of the program can be gained by first considering the form and type of input and output. Input should be considered by asking questions such as: What is included? What form will it have? Can all of the input data be read at once, or is a special sequence required? Ask questions about output such as: What output should be included? What form should the output take? Can all of the output be printed at once, or is a special sequence required for printing the output? Should different levels of output be provided for, depending upon the user's desires for any particular run?

Insight can be gained by actually writing the form in which the data is to be input and by laying out the form for output of answers. Once this step is completed, the intermediate calculations emerge as a link between the input and output in an intuitively clear manner.

13-3.2 Starting in the Middle

Sometimes, when problem formulation is particularly complex, it is helpful to start in the middle. Using this technique, the simple core of the problem is pseudoprogrammed. From this intermediate solution, coding for intermediate ramifications of the problem can be developed. By repeating this process, the core of the solution grows until it finally encompasses the entire problem.

It cannot be overemphasized that the primary requirement for formulating any computer program is to thoroughly understand the problem itself. Any technique—input-output; link, starting in the middle, or human-oriented flow diagrams—that clarifies the program can be used. Nassi-Shneiderman charts or machine-oriented flow diagrams are used by many programmers for this purpose. Others develop programs using formal FORTRAN coding, fragments of FORTRAN coding, or a *pseudocode* that informally indicates the process involved. In the author's experience, coding with a well-thought-out plan, however formalized, is always most effective and efficient.

13-4 INPUT/OUTPUT

Many FORTRAN texts subordinate input/output to a secondary position, because it is, undoubtedly, the most difficult concept for a neophyte programmer. Nonetheless, a strong emphasis has been placed on the development of good input/output techniques from the beginning of this text. When a computer is used in calculator mode, there is no necessity for output that is carefully developed. On the other hand, the power and versatility of a computer is truly utilized in programs that far outstrip calculator mode, and in such programs the form used for the input and the display of output is very important.

13–4.1 Input Considerations

Most of the programs in this text use 10F8.0 as the input edit descriptor. Section 10–5 gives a comprehensive discussion of the output of arrays. A few additional comments can be made, however.

The use of input forms that require users to "fill in the boxes," particularly when left- or right-justification of entries is a requirement should be discouraged. Judicious use of edit descriptors, including the use of floating point numbers or BN and BZ edit descriptors (see Chapter 17) can relieve many restrictions often applied to human users. It is important not to impose rigid requirements on program users through lack of careful attention to detail.

13–4.2 Using a Layout to Format Output

Figure 13–1 illustrates a four-step development of a WRITE statement and its corresponding FORMAT statement.

In the first step, typical numerical values are written on a coding form. The titles will be headings over the columns of numerical values and are written on lines 2 and 3. In the process, it is clear that more spacing is required for the titles to "fit" the numerical data. Thus the layout must be redone in the second group of three lines. The second group appears to be a satisfactory solution until we observe that the numerical values shown under CALIBRATION could actually be much greater or smaller than those shown. This suggests the use of E-format, and the three lines are rewritten with the proper spacing.

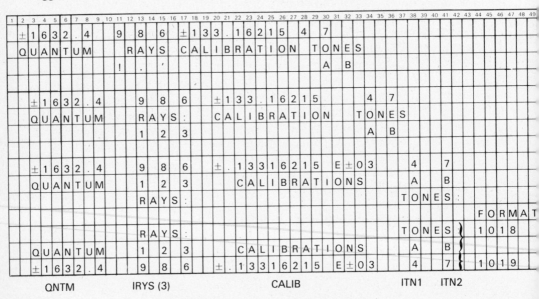

FIGURE 13–1 Using a layout to format output

The last set of three lines shows the titles in their proper positions, with typical numerical values shown along with names of the storage locations. The first two lines are formatted by Statement 1018 and the numerical values are output using Format 1019, written as follows.

```
1018 FORMAT (12X, 'RAYS:', 19X,'TONES:'/' QUANTUM  1 2 3',
      14X,'CALIBRATIONS',4X,'A',2X,'B'/)
1019 FORMAT (1X,F8.1,I4,2I2,E17.8,I4,I3)
     WRITE (LW,1019) QNTM,IRYS,CALIB,ITN1,ITN2
```

A coding form used to lay out the formats makes it relatively simple to write the correct formats by inspection, reducing errors and saving time and effort.

13-4.3 Print-Control

Print-control is not a formal part of FORTRAN 77. Nonetheless, print-control is used within many of the programs displayed in this text and is discussed at some length in Chapter 6. In large programs that require substantial debugging, print-control statements have sometimes been eliminated by putting a C in Column 1 to make them comment lines. Even in such cases, however, they are seldom completely removed from the program. Print-control is not a legal requirement, but its use has many advantages.

13-5 PROGRAM VERIFICATION

Unfortunately, it is not easy to verify that any given computer program works perfectly; often a great deal of time and effort must be spent in validating programs.

13-5.1 Choosing Test Data

Several methods of choosing test data have already been demonstrated. A preselected set of data was used to test program SIMLR. The reverse approach, using reverse equations, was used to verify programs QUAD and CUBIC. Book examples were used to verify program RATE. In Chapter 15, subprogram AREA2 is verified by choosing a set of areas, all located within a simple square, that satisfy all possible criteria.

No precise rules exist to determine which type of test is most appropriate for your program. Nonetheless, it is important to test all aspects of each program, particularly near the boundaries or limits of your formulations. For example, programs for trigonometric functions may malfunction at critical points near angles approaching zero or $\pi/2$.

13-5.2 Typical Errors

Recall that errors may be classified as logic, compilation, or run-time errors. Most compilation and run-time errors are detected by the processor and error messages are output. In some cases, however, errors in a program can confuse the processor so that it outputs error messages that are not indicative of the actual problems in the program.

A common difficulty is to exceed the limits of an array, most often within a DO-loop or implied-DO loop. This can lead to a "strange conglomeration" of error messages, which should lead you to suspect that you have overrun an array. Depending upon the processor, information that is being output into nonexisting portions of an array may go into other locations. The locations receiving this information may contain other data, or possibly even part of the program instructions themselves. Thus overrunning the dimensions of arrays can produce errors that output error messages far from the point of the actual problem.

Another source of difficulty is accidently mixing modes. A thorough understanding of the order of evaluation and conversion of type can prevent such errors. However, extreme care must be used. For instance, if I is less than J, then

$$(I/J)*R$$

is always 0.

$$1.*(I/J)*R$$

is also always 0, but

$$1.*I/J*R$$

multiplies R by the real fraction I/J.

An error that occurs occasionally, usually by spuriously adding a variable as an afterthought, is the attempt to call an array and a variable by the same name. In such a case, what the programmer considers to be a variable is, in fact, an array. For example, a programmer states: READ (LR, 1000) A, B, with anticipation that single values are to be read into A and B. If A (which the programmer is considering to be a variable) has already been declared in a DIMENSION statement, the READ statement will attempt to read values into every element of array A. This can precipitate a very confusing situation.

Sometimes names can be changed inadvertently, either by poor typing and proof-reading, or by poor spelling. The incorrectly spelled type statement

INTERGER COUNT

leaves COUNT a real number but makes RCOUNT an integer. Did you notice that this would occur? (This type of situation can happen with many processors that do not "read" every character in keywords.) Because blanks are ignored, the processor in such a case considers R COUNT as the integer variable RCOUNT.

The fact that blanks are ignored can also lead to strange errors when values that were intended to start in Column 73 actually start in 72. In such a case, the expression

INTEGER RATE

would leave RATE a real variable, but make RATEI an integer (assuring an I in Column 72).

Sometimes such errors can confuse the processor into believing that you are calling a function. For instance, if you have dimensioned

DIMENSION TABLE (16,3)

and use

VALUE = TABEL (I,J)

the computer will expect TABEL to be a function statement or a function subprogram, rather than an array. This is true because TABEL has not been dimensioned.

Although subroutines are not considered extensively until the next chapter, it is important to note that a very common error, even by more experienced programmers, occurs when actual arguments of subprograms do not match dummy arguments.

Other miscellaneous errors can also cause rather unpleasant difficulties. First, if a variable or an array element is not defined, it cannot be output. Also, the DO variable within a DO-loop cannot be changed within the loop (this is particularly troublesome to some programmers familiar with other languages).

Finally, FORTRAN cannot perform operations that are mathematically impossible. Values cannot be divided by 0. Zero cannot be raised to a nonpositive power. A negative number cannot be raised to a real power. Unfortunately, when anything can go wrong within a computer program, it usually does. So it is important to be particularly careful in using division and exponents to be sure you do not use valid operations that become mathematically impossible during execution.

13–5.3 Tracing Techniques

Sometimes, even after inspecting for some of the classical errors discussed earlier, programs still fail to work correctly. In any such cases, program logic, rather than the program syntax, should be reviewed. Basically, if the computer program does not do what you want, it is because you are not giving it proper instructions. Nonetheless, several techniques do exist for helping locate errors when all else fails.

A number of processors provide built-in trace mechanisms, sometimes used in conjunction with the PAUSE statement described in Chapter 16. The form and variety of these traces is quite varied. Characteristics and methods of implementation for traces must be obtained from the local installation. Trace programs may give an amount of output that exceeds your expectations.

Tracing can also be built into FORTRAN programs; in fact, Program BBSRT1 provides a program trace. In general, the form recommended in this text involves duplicating a series of statements that have only a single value changed for each line or card. A typical such statement might appear as

WRITE (LW,'('' LOC=006,'' I4,3F6.1,3I2)')I,A,B,C,J,K,L

Obviously, the number following LOC is changed on each card to give a counting sequence. When the program runs, the first position on every line will then show a location at which the variables (in this case I, A, B, C, J, K, L) are being output. Again, such a technique can sometimes produce amounts of data so large as to be almost useless.

Chapter 14

Subroutines

Subroutines provide one means for segmenting large and complex computer programs into smaller parts, or modules. Such segmenting is both necessary and desirable for two compatible, but divergent, reasons.

1. Subroutines can be developed for direct, unaltered use in many different programs.
2. Subroutines allow programs to be written and tested in units that can be sized to accommodate efficient and effective mental capacity, saving both clock and calendar time.

A subroutine falls into a category of subprograms called *procedures*. Three other procedures, collectively referred to as functions, are discussed in the next chapter: intrinsic functions, statement functions, and external functions. There is some overlap in this terminology because subroutines and external functions are often referred to collectively as external procedures. Thus an external function is called both a function and an external procedure.

14-1 CONSTRUCTION AND USE OF SUBROUTINES

A subroutine is a complete program, and differs from a main program in only three important ways:

1. The first statement must name the subroutine, as illustrated in Table 14–1.
2. The subroutine cannot be used alone. Subroutines must be "called" by another program using a statement of the form shown in Table 14–2.
3. The subroutine usually terminates its execution with the word RETURN rather than STOP.

Thus a subroutine differs from a main program because it has a special entrance and exit form, and because it cannot stand alone—it must be called by another program in order to execute.

14-1.1 Form of a Subroutine

The first statement of a subroutine starts with the word SUBROUTINE itself, followed by the name of the subroutine and a list of (dummy) arguments, separated by commas and enclosed in parentheses. The list of arguments represents the "door" between the calling program and the subroutine and (except for use of COMMON discussed in Section 14-4.2) is the only way that the information can pass between the two. When writing subroutines, it is assumed that all values in the argument list are defined and that they contain the necessary information for the program to execute. (See Table 14-1 for a detailed summary.)

Subroutine I/O is identical to that for main programs. Because label numbers are unique within a subroutine, however, all subroutine READ/WRITE statements must

Table 14-1 SUBROUTINE Statement, Always the First Statement of A Subroutine

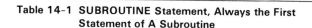

SUBROUTINE NAME(list)

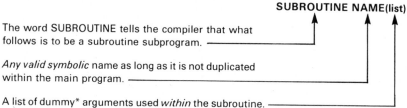

The word SUBROUTINE tells the compiler that what follows is to be a subroutine subprogram. ⎯⎯⎯⎯

Any valid symbolic name as long as it is not duplicated within the main program. ⎯⎯⎯⎯

A list of dummy* arguments used *within* the subroutine. ⎯⎯⎯⎯ List serves as the "door" between the calling program and the subroutine, and it is the most important way information can pass between the two. (Entities used within the subroutine that do not need to be obtained from, or used by, the calling program should not be in the list.) Lists in SUBROUTINE statements may include:

> variables
> arrays
> dummy procedure names
> in Full Language only, an asterisk

but *not*

> constants
> elements of arrays (subscripted variables)

Symbolic names within the list must be separated by commas and contained within the single set of parentheses.

*For additional information, see Section 14-1.3.

have their own FORMAT statements within the subroutine itself. Although no restrictions are placed upon reading and writing in subroutines, relatively few appear to contain READ statements, whereas many contain WRITE statements. In design of large programs, it is often desirable to have an input module (an independent subroutine which reads all input data) and an output module (an independent subroutine which produces well ordered output).

Although STOP is usually replaced by RETURN, it is legal and may be reasonable to use STOP within a subroutine. For example, if a run-time error occurs that obviates need for all further calculations in both the subroutine and main program, then it may be appropriate to output an error message and use STOP to terminate the run.

Because a subroutine is a complete program, the last line of coding should always be the word END.

14-1.2 Calling a Subroutine

In the calling program, a statement like that of Table 14–2 is used when a subroutine is needed. The statement contains the word CALL itself, followed by the name of the subroutine and the list of (actual) arguments, separated by commas and enclosed in

Table 14-2 Method for Calling A Subroutine

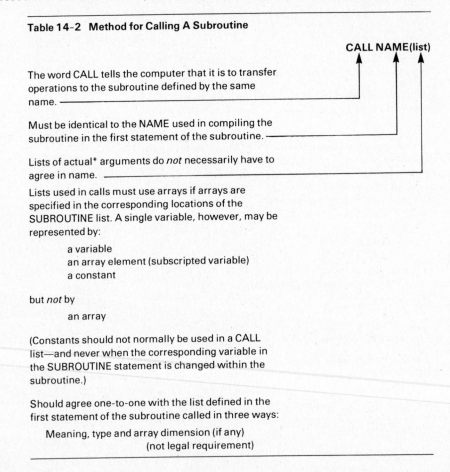

CALL NAME(list)

The word CALL tells the computer that it is to transfer operations to the subroutine defined by the same name.

Must be identical to the NAME used in compiling the subroutine in the first statement of the subroutine.

Lists of actual* arguments do *not* necessarily have to agree in name.

Lists used in calls must use arrays if arrays are specified in the corresponding locations of the SUBROUTINE list. A single variable, however, may be represented by:

> a variable
> an array element (subscripted variable)
> a constant

but *not* by

> an array

(Constants should not normally be used in a CALL list—and never when the corresponding variable in the SUBROUTINE statement is changed within the subroutine.)

Should agree one-to-one with the list defined in the first statement of the subroutine called in three ways:

> Meaning, type and array dimension (if any)
> > (not legal requirement)

parentheses. The argument list used in the CALL statement must agree on a one-to-one basis with the argument list in the subroutine in three important ways: arguments must have identical meanings, the type of the arguments must be identical, and the size of the arguments should be identical (not a specification requirement). They do not need to agree, however, in a very important way: the dummy argument of the subroutine does not need to use the same symbolic name as the actual argument in the calling program.

Use of different names for corresponding arguments is particularly advantageous when a team is working on a segmented program in a parallel fashion. The fact that corresponding argument names must agree only in meaning, type and size—but not name—is even more important because it allows subroutines to be used in many different programs.

14–1.3 Actual versus Dummy Arguments

Actual arguments are used in the CALL. Usually they are expressions (variable names and array elements are most common) or array names. Intrinsic function names and external procedure names (subroutines and function subprograms) and dummy procedure names are also permitted.

Subroutines use dummy arguments. Every time a dummy argument occurs within the subroutine, values are obtained from, or returned to, its associated actual arguments. The association between arguments is defined by one-to-one relationship in the argument lists of the subroutine and CALL, respectively. The following are permissible associations.

Actual Argument in CALL:	Dummy Argument in Subroutine:
Variable	
Array Element	Variable Name
Expression	
Array	Array Name
Intrinsic Function	
External Function	
Subroutine	Dummy Procedure Name
Dummy Procedure	

ANSI X3.9–1978 (section 15.9.3.3) states: "The number and size of dimensions in an actual argument array declaration may be different from the number and size of the dimensions in an associated dummy array declarator." Also, (Section 15.9.3.3, paragraph 3) "the size of the dummy argument array must not exceed the size of the actual argument array." Nonetheless, experience suggests that actual and associated dummy array declarators should always match in number and size. Until one becomes an experienced programmer, variations in number and size of array dimensions between corresponding arguments is almost certain to cause substantial difficulty.

Some care must be used in establishing argument names. For example, the dummy variable name in the subroutine cannot have its value changed when associated with an actual expression in the CALL from the main program. (See Section 14–4.)

14-1.4 RETURN

Logical termination of the execution for a subroutine is signaled by the word RETURN. When a RETURN statement is reached during execution of the subroutine, control returns to the statement immediately following the CALL statement in the calling program. When this occurs, any items in the subroutine argument list that have changed during the subroutine's execution will also have been changed in the main program. All other items in the subroutine will have absolutely no effect on the main program, even if item names are identical. Of course, a subroutine may have more than one RETURN in the same way that a program can have more than one STOP.

14-1.5 Nested CALLS

Subroutines can call other subroutines, which in turn can call still other subroutines, and so on. The only restriction is that no subroutine can call itself, that is, subroutines are not *recursive*. This restriction applies at any level. Subroutine A can call subroutine B, which in turn can call subroutines C and D. But, A, B, C, and D cannot call A, and B, C, and D cannot call B. Subroutine A can, however, call subroutines B, C, and D even though B calls C and D or C calls D or D calls C. Figure 14-1 shows four of these cases of nesting, two legal and two illegal.

14-1.6 Elimination of Error

The most common, and the most serious, error encountered when using subroutines is poorly matched argument lists. Before running a program using subroutines, take time to do the following once again.

1. Count the number of arguments in the CALL list to see that they exactly match the number of arguments in the SUBROUTINE statement list.
2. Check that the type of each argument agrees in a one-to-one order (that is, real in CALL matched by real in SUBROUTINE or integer in CALL matched by integer in SUBROUTINE, and so on).
3. Check every argument representing an array to be sure that the dimension size in the main program agrees exactly with the size dimensioned within the subroutine. (This is not a legal requirement.)
4. *Remember*—argument names do *not* have to be the same. If a variable name A is listed in the CALL statement, it may be matched with a B in the subroutine argument list. At execution, the value stored in A in the main program will be used everyplace that B is specified within the subroutine. If B changes its value within the subroutine, the value of A in the main program will, in essence, also be simultaneously changed to agree exactly.
5. Errors between lists of CALL and SUBROUTINE statements will, in general, NOT be flagged by the processor. Thus incorrect results can be obtained without producing an error message.
6. *Check arguments* in lists of CALL and SUBROUTINE to be sure they agree in *meaning, type* and *dimension*.
7. *Check argument lists!*

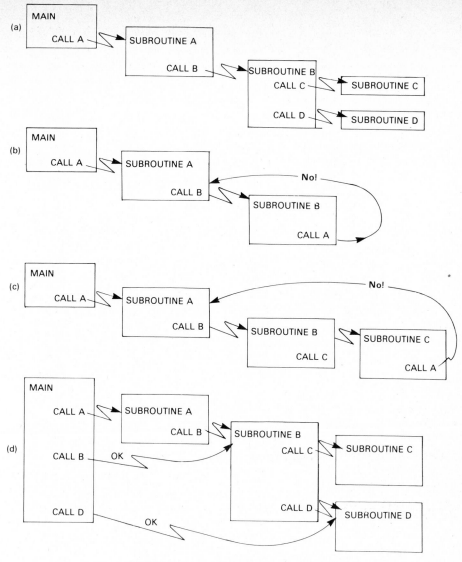

FIGURE 14-1 Schematics of legal and illegal subroutine calls

14-2 A SIMPLE EXAMPLE: SUBROUTINE DEMO

In a certain activity, three similar computations are required, each based upon the results obtained from a previous set of calculations. A typical set of such mathematical operations is shown in Table 14–3. Values for each set are always determined by summing the squares of three values, summing the same three values, and determining their accumulative product. The only variation between the three different sets of three

Table 14-3 Three Sets of Three Similar Equations

Statement 20:

$$R = B^2 + X^2 + G^2$$
$$S = B + X + G$$
$$T = B * X * G$$

Statement 21:

$$E = R^2 + S^2 + T^2$$
$$F = R + S + T$$
$$G = R * S * T$$

Statement 22:

$$U = B^2 + R^2 + E^2$$
$$Y = B + R + E$$
$$W = B * R * E$$

computations shown in Table 14–3 is in the names of the variables used. Such similarity suggests that a subroutine would prove useful. Subroutine DEMO is coded in Listing 14–1 to solve any one set of the three equations. A test program and output is also shown.

The first line of the subroutine contains the word SUBROUTINE, followed by the name of the subroutine, DEMO, and then a list of arguments separated by commas and enclosed in parentheses. Variables X, Y, and Z of the argument list provide "input" from the main program. Results are stored in variables A, B, and C for return to the main program. NP is a print control value obtained from the calling program.

The next three statements in subroutine DEMO perform the necessary calculations. A is determined by summing the squares of the values currently stored in the locations called X, Y, and Z. The sum of X, Y, and Z is stored in location B. The accumulative product (X times Y times Z) is computed and subsequently stored in C.

The last variable in the argument list, the print control NP, merely controls output within the subroutine. During execution, the subroutine terminates and control is returned to the calling program when the statement RETURN is reached. END signifies the physical end of the subprogram and terminates compilation.

The test program, TDEMO, is independent of the subroutine. It reads four values, B, X, G, and H. H is used as a print control value in floating point format within the program and is converted to integer, NP, for use in the subroutine. The print control value is also used to control termination of the program. Statements 20, 21, and 22 effect computations shown in Table 14–3 by using subroutine DEMO.

At Statement 20, the current value stored in the main program at location B is used in the subroutine wherever X is shown, that is, B is the first actual argument in the calling program list and provides the value for dummy argument X that is in the first location of the argument list of the subroutine. Likewise, the second actual argument in the call list of the main program is X, so the value stored in X of the main program is used in the subroutine at every place where the variable name Y occurs.

The result obtained by the subroutine for the sum of the squares of the three values

```
      PROGRAM TDEMO

10  READ(5,11) B,X,G,H
      NP=H
      IF (H.LT.-9.) STOP

20  CALL DEMO(B,X,G,R,S,T,NP)
      IF (H.GT.2.) WRITE (6,14) R,S,T,B,X,G

21  CALL DEMO (R,S,T,E,F,G,NP)
      IF (H.GT.1.) WRITE (6,13) E,F,G

22  CALL DEMO (B,R,E,U,V,W,NP)
      IF (H.GT.0.) WRITE (6,12) U,V,W

      GO TO 10

11  FORMAT(10F8.0)
12  FORMAT(/' U,V,W=',3E20.6////)
13  FORMAT(/' E,F,G=',3E20.6)
14  FORMAT(/' R,S,T=',3E20.6/' B,X,G=',3E20.6)

      END

      SUBROUTINE DEMO(X,Y,Z,A,B,C,NP)
      A = X**2+Y**2+Z**2
      B = X+Y+Z
      C = X*Y*Z
      IF(NP.GE.3) WRITE(6,10) X,Y,Z,A,B,C
10  FORMAT(//1X,'INSIDE DEMO INPUT VAR=',
     13E20.8/12X,'OUTPUT VAR=', 3E20.8//)
      RETURN
      END
```

Output:

```
INSIDE DEMO INPUT VAR=         .40000000+001          .60000000+001          .80000000+001
            OUTPUT VAR=        .11600000+003          .18000000+002          .19200000+003


R,S,T=          .116000+003          .180000+002          .192000+003
B,X,G=          .400000+001          .600000+001          .800000+001


INSIDE DEMO INPUT VAR=         .11600000+003          .18000000+002          .19200000+003
            OUTPUT VAR=        .50644000+005          .32600000+003          .40089600+006


E,F,G=          .506440+005          .326000+003          .400896+006


INSIDE DEMO INPUT VAR=         .40000000+001          .11600000+003          .50644000+005
            OUTPUT VAR=        .25648282+010          .50764000+005          .23498816+008


U,V,W=          .256483+010          .507640+005          .234988+008



E,F,G=          .506440+005          .326000+003          .400896+006
U,V,W=          .256483+010          .507680+005          .469976+008
```

LISTING 14-1 Coding of Program TDEMO and Subroutine DEMO With Output

Section 14-2 A Simple Example: Subroutine DEMO

339

called B, X, and G in the main program (called X, Y, and Z in the subroutine) are stored in subroutine location A. But A is the fourth (dummy) argument in the subroutine list, corresponding to location R (real argument) in the main program. Thus in the main program, R has the value $B^2 + X^2 + G^2$.

Calling subroutine DEMO with different variable names for the arguments makes it possible to work all three sets of three problems with a single, identical, subroutine. It is instructive to trace calculations performed by Statements 20, 21 and 22 of program TDEMO to verify that, with the help of subroutine DEMO, all of the calculation of Table 14-3 are performed correctly.

14-3 A MORE USEFUL EXAMPLE: SUBROUTINE QUAD

Coding of subroutine QUAD is shown in Listing 14-2. A comparison between this subroutine and program QUAD of Listing 7-2 shows that the conversion took place by doing the following.

1. Replacing

   C   PROGRAM QUAD

   by

                    SUBROUTINE QUAD (A, B, C,
                1 XR1, XI1, XR2, XI2, NP, LW)

   where

QUAD	is the name of the subroutine;
A, B, and C	are coefficients of the quadratic equation $ax^2 + bx + c = 0$;
XR1 and XI1	are real and imaginary parts of one solution;
XR2 and XI2	are real and imaginary parts of a second solution;
NP	is the print control which: if ≤ 0, allows no output from subroutine; if ≥ 1, output A, B, C and answers from subroutine.
LW	Unit number for output

2. Deleting the READ statement labeled 1 and corresponding FORMAT statement 1001.
3. Replacing STOP with RETURN.
4. Deleting LR and LW. (LW is carried through the argument list).
5. Preceding all WRITE statements by a logical IF statement to control output.

```
      SUBROUTINE QUAD(A,B,C,XR1,XI1,XR2,XI2,NP,LW)

C             --- A,B,C: COEFS IN A*X**2 + B*X + C = 0
C             --- XR1,XI1: REAL, IMAGINARY PARTS OF FIRST X
C             --- XR2,XI2: REAL, IMAGINARY PARTS OF SECOND X
C             --- NP: PRINT CONTROL, OUTPTS ONLY IF GTR 0
C             --- LW: LOGICAL UNIT NUMBER FOR OUTPUT

      IF(NP.GT.0) WRITE(LW,1000)

      IF(A.NE.0. .OR. B.NE. 0.)THEN

          IF(A.EQ.0.) THEN

              XR1= -C/B
              IF(NP.GT.0) WRITE(LW,1002)A,B,C,XR1

          ELSE IF(B.EQ.0.) THEN
              D = -C/A

              IF(D.LT.0.) THEN
                  XI1= SQRT(-D)
                  XI2= -XI1
                  IF(NP.GT.0) WRITE(LW,1003)A,B,C,XI1,XI2

              ELSE IF(D.EQ.0.) THEN
                  XR1= 0.
                  XR2= 0.
                  IF(NP.GT.0) WRITE(LW,1002)A,B,C,XR1,XR2

              ELSE
                  XR1= SQRT(D)
                  XR2= -XR1
                  IF(NP.GT.0) WRITE(LW,1002) A,B,C,XR1,XR2

              END IF

          ELSE
                  D= B**2 -4.*A*C
                  A2= 2.*A
                  XR1= -B/A2
                  XR2= XR1

              IF(D.LT.0.) THEN
                  XI1= SQRT(-D)/A2
                  XI2= -XI1
                  IF(NP.GT.0) WRITE(LW,1004)A,B,C,XR1,XI1,XR2,XI2

              ELSE IF(D.EQ.0) THEN
                  IF(NP.GT.0) WRITE(LW,1002)A,B,C,XR1,XR2

              ELSE
                  E= SQRT(D)/A2
                  XR1= XR1+E
                  XR2= XR2-E
                  IF(NP.GT.0) WRITE(LW,1002)A,B,C,XR1,XR2

              END IF

          END IF

      END IF

 1000 FORMAT(' SOLUTION OF QUADRATIC EQUATION'/
     1  15X,'A',10X,'B',10X,'C',15X,'X1',20X,'X2'/
     2  36X,'REAL',8X,'IMG',7X,'REAL',8X,'IMG'/)
 1002 FORMAT(1X,4E11.4,11X,E11.4)
 1003 FORMAT(1X,3E11.4,2(11X,E11.4))
 1004 FORMAT(1X,7E11.4)

      RETURN
      END
```

LISTING 14-2 Coding of subroutine QUAD

Listing 14–3 shows a possible test program, TQUAD. The print control value is read in type real to enable use of a *drum card* and left-justified real (floating point) numbers. Print control is subsequently changed to integer for use in the subroutine CALL. The argument list contains all variables, listed in a one-to-one order, corresponding in meaning and type (size is automatically satisfied because no arrays exist.)

Subroutine QUAD does not always compute values for all four of the possible answers: AA, AB, BA, and BB. In such cases, the values of these variables should be zero. For this reason, AA, AB, BA, and BB are set to zero after each CALL so that answers from a previous CALL will not "appear" to be answers for the current CALL.

An alternate test program is shown in Listing 14–4. In test program QUADT, the coefficients (*a, b,* and *c*) are stored in array COEF which has three locations. The answer is returned in array ANS, which has four locations: the first two locations for storage of the real and imaginary parts of the first X, and the second two locations for the real and imaginary parts of the second X. The call list, therefore, uses elements of arrays COEF and ANS, with their current contents used in the subroutine QUAD when it is executing.

```
       PROGRAM TQUAD

C              PROGRAM TESTS SUBROUTINE QUAD USING VARIABLE ARGUMENTS BY:
C              (1) READING COEF A, B, AND C OF A*X**2 + B*X + C = 0
C              (2) CALLING SUBROUTINE QUAD
C              (3) OUTPUTING FOUR VALUES:
C                  (A) FIRST X, REAL PART          AA
C                  (B) FIRST X, IMAGINARY PART     AB
C                  (C)SECOND X, REAL PART          BA
C                  (D)SECOND X, IMAGINARY PART     BB
C                  (NOTE:  NON-EXISTING VALUES APPEAR AS ZEROS)
C              (4) INITIALIZES AA, AB, BA, AND BB SO THEY WILL NOT
C                  APPEAR IN 'NEXT' SOLUTION.  THIS IS NECESSARY
C                  BECAUSE ALL FOUR VALUES ARE NOT ALWAYS COMPUTED
C              (5) LOOPS FOR NEW PROBLEM UNTIL A AND B BOTH ZERO

       LR=5
       LW=6

    9  READ(LR,10)A,B,C,ANP
       IF(A.EQ.0.0.AND.B.EQ.0.0) STOP

       WRITE(LW,11)A,B,C
       NP=ANP
   10  FORMAT(1GF8.0)
   11  FORMAT(//////1X,'A=',E20.8,4X,'B=',E20.8,4X,'C=',E20.8/)

C      COMPUTE ROOTS OF QUADRATIC
       CALL QUAD(A,B,C,AA,AB,BB,BA,NP,LW)

       WRITE(LW,13)AA,AB,BB,BA
   13  FORMAT(1X,'REAL=',E20.8,4X,'IMAG=',E20.8,/,
      1        ' REAL=',E20.8,4X,'IMAG=',E20.8)

       AA=0.
       AB=0.
       BB=0.
       BA=0.

       GO TO 9

       END
```

LISTING 14–3 Coding of test program TQUAD

```
              PROGRAM QUADT

C                PROGRAM TESTS SUBROUTINE QUAD USING
C                    (1) ELEMENTS OF ARRAYS FOR ARGUMENTS
C                    (2) CONSTANT FOR ARGUMENT
C                    (3) VARIABLE FOR ARGUMENT
C                BY:
C                    (1) READING COEF ARRAY FORMING EQUATION:
C                        COEF(1)*X**2 + COEF(2)*X + COEF(3) = 0
C                    (2) CALLING SUBROUTINE QUAD
C                    (3) RETURNING AND OUTPUTING X'S IN ARRAY ANS:
C                        (A) FIRST X, REAL PART        ANS(1)
C                        (B) FIRST X, IMAGINARY PART   ANS(2)
C                        (C)SECOND X, REAL PART        ANS(3)
C                        (D)SECOND X, IMAGINARY PART   ANS(4)
C                        (NOTE: NON-EXISTING VALUES APPEAR AS ZEROS)
C                    (4) INITIALIZES ARRAY ANS IN CASE SOME ARE NOT
C                        ZERO AND ARE NOT COMPUTED FOR NEXT SOLUTION
C                    (5) LOOPS FOR NEW PROBLEM WHEN COEF(1) = 0
C                                AND SIMULATANEOUSLY COEF(2) = 0

           DIMENSION COEF(3),ANS(4)

           LR=5
           LW=6

        9  READ(LR,10)COEF
           IF(COEF(1).EQ.0.0.AND.COEF(2).EQ.0) STOP

           WRITE(LW,11)COEF
        10 FORMAT(1CF8.0)
        11 FORMAT(//////1X,'3 COEFS OF QUAD=',3E20.8/)

C          COMPUTE ROOTS OF QUADRATIC
           CALL QUAD(COEF(1),COEF(2),COEF(3),ANS(1),ANS(2),
          1ANS(3),ANS(4),4,LW)

           WRITE(LW,13)ANS
        13 FORMAT(/1X,'REAL AND IMAG ANS, 1 PER LINE',
          1       /2E20.8/2E20.8)

           DO 14 I=1,4
               ANS(I)=0.
        14 CONTINUE

           GO TO 9

           END
```

LISTING 14-4 Coding of an alternate test program QUADT

The print control argument uses a constant rather than a variable. Although this is legal, it is not good practice. Using a constant is illegal if the value of this constant is changed within the subroutine in any way. (In some compilers, when this is done, the value of the constant itself is changed in the main program. This is a very serious error that is extremely difficult to locate. For example, assume that a variable in an argument list of a subroutine were replaced by a constant such as the number 1 in its call. If within the subroutine, the variable represented by this constant changed its value to 3, every time the numerical integer constant 1 was used in the main program, it would (in fact) have a value of 3 rather than 1. This error occurs without an error message and is obviously very frustrating.

14-4 MORE ABOUT ARGUMENTS

Variables and arrays within subroutines are local (only defined within the subroutine) unless they appear in the argument list or a COMMON statement. Arrays that are used in the argument list, therefore, must be dimensioned both in the calling and the called program.

Two techniques are available: (1) the use of adjustable dimensioning, and (2) the use of COMMON. (Of course, arrays within subroutines can also be dimensioned by integer constants.)

14-4.1 Adjustable Dimensioning

All arrays in any main programs written in FORTRAN must be dimensioned by integer constants. This is necessary because, as you recall, FORTRAN is a two-stage operation. At the time of compilation, storage locations are allocated while the FORTRAN is translated into the machine's own language. The only way that adequate storage can be allocated is if the arrays are dimensioned by numerical constants within the main program (using DIMENSION, type, or COMMON statements). In the subroutine, however, the size of an array can be tied to the size of an array in the main program by the use of adjustable dimensioning. This is possible because as the subroutine is being compiled, rather than allocating storage for an array that is adjustably dimensioned, a pointer is designated to "tell the subroutine" to use a particular array that has been dimensioned by numerical constants within the main program.

Thus arrays in the main program must always be fixed in size by numerical integer constants by DIMENSION, type, or COMMON statements, located before the first executable statement. Arrays of subroutines may, however, have adjustable sizes if both the name and the dimensions are carried through the argument list. In such a case, a typical subroutine DIMENSION statement could be:

```
      DIMENSION ARY (ILARY,IWARY), IKC(ILIKC,IWIKC),
    1 KB(6,IWKB), COEF(39)
```

Array limits so defined should agree exactly with dimensions defined by constants in the main program, and must be integers carried in the list of arguments.

Although not required, some programmers form variables defining array limits in a standard way. The following is a typical plan.

For row dimensions:
    IL + first three characters in array name
      signifies length of array

For column dimensions:
    IW + first three characters in array name
      signifies width of array

And for the third dimension (page):
    IP + first three characters in array name
      signifies page of array

Use of adjustable dimensions requires longer argument lists because all variables defining dimensions must be included.

In the preceeding example, arrays ARY and IKC must be dimensioned by integer constants in the main program. Also, ILARY, IWARY, ILIKC, and IWIKC should be set in the main program to correspond exactly to the integer constants used in the DIMENSION statement. Again, the names used for actual and dummy arguments do not have to be identical.

Furthermore, the actual argument corresponding to dummy argument KB must also be defined in the main program, even though one of its dimensions is a constant. This is necessary because only arrays defined by numerical integer constants in the main program and carried through the argument list can have any adjustable dimensions in subroutines. Conversely, the array COEF, if not listed in the argument list, is defined only within the subroutine. If the array COEF is to be listed in the argument list, it should match with a real array in the main program that also has 39 locations (not a specification requirement).

To maintain the one-to-one relationship in the size of arrays when using adjustable dimensions, it is good practice to define the array sizes by showing their adjustable dimensions in a comment line and numerically define variables representing adjustable dimensions immediately after such comment lines.

An example of this technique is shown in Listing 14–5. In this case, the lengths of arrays SUM and ACCUM are tied with the second and third dimensions, respectively, of the array named TABLE. For this reason, the dimensions for SUM and ACCUM are not shown as ILSUM nor ILACC, although such names would be satisfactory (and necessary if dimensions of the second two arrays were not tied absolutely to the dimensions of the first array). The only reason for not using the additional names ILSUM and ILACC is to reduce the length of the argument lists.

Notice that a comment line specifies very clearly what do do in case dimensions change. For instance, if the second dimension of the array TABLE and the dimension of

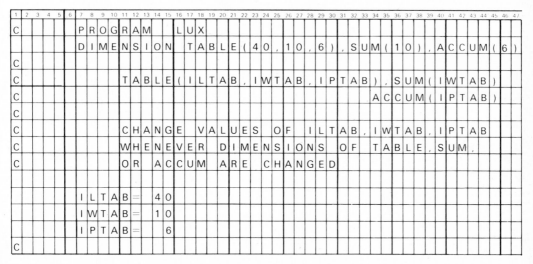

LISTING 14–5 Controlling adjustable dimensions in the main program

SUM were to change to 12, then the 10 in both places on line 2 would be changed to a 12. Also, IWTAB would be set to 12. By this process, the subroutine array dimensions are guaranteed to match the dimensions of the calling program. Also, see the use of PARAMETER in Section 16–1.1(a).

14-4.2 BLANK COMMON

Items that are to be associated in different program units, use the same locations, and do not have to be listed as arguments, must be declared in a COMMON statement of the form

COMMON list

where *list* is a listing of only those items to be in common, separated by commas. To eliminate errors, it is usual practice to punch a basic common card and to duplicate it for use in each subroutine. This, however, has the disadvantage of requiring that item names used in common must have the same meaning in all calling and called programs.

Actually, it is the order of items in the list that is important, not the names of items. Thus

COMMON A,B(6,3,2),I,K,G(14)

and

COMMON R,G(6,3,2),LL,LV,A(14)

would be compatible so long as either

A, I, K, R, LL, and LV are variables

or

A and R are both dimensioned identically

or

I and LL are both dimensioned identically

or

K and LV are both dimensioned identically

In general, an array can be dimensioned in either a COMMON, a DIMENSION, or a type statement, but only once. Also, COMMON statements must appear in all subprograms that use even one of the items carried through common.

Items defined by COMMON statements are not used in argument lists of subroutines or function subprograms. This is the only exception to the rule that argument lists act as the "door" between calling and called programs.

14-4.3 Comparisons Between COMMON and Adjustable Dimensioning

Many programmers have a decided preference for COMMON because it shortens argument lists. To foster structured programming, others always prefer to carry arguments through lists, and so prefer adjustable dimensioning. The following examples indicate how each might be used.

Program MAIN1 of Listing 14–6 illustrates the use of COMMON. Note in particular that a one-to-one correspondence must exist between the entities used in each COMMON statement. Note how the arrays are also dimensioned in either COMMON or DIMENSION statements but not in both. (Many programmers prefer to dimension arrays in type statements.)

By contrast, program MAIN2 of Listing 14–7 illustrates the use of adjustable dimensioning. In this case, the size of the arrays in the main program and all subroutines can be changed by changing only the first few statements within the main program itself. This is very advantageous because the subroutines have great modularity; all arrays and their corresponding dimensions must, however, be carried through the argument list.

It is valuable to check the arguments and array dimensions of Listing 14–7 since mismatched arguments are a common and serious error. With names that are not identical, this can be tricky. A typical procedure is as follows:

1. Count arguments of SUB1 in the subroutine and in the CALL to be sure they agree.
2. In the subroutine, note that R represents an array with length ILR (first and fourth arguments). In the CALL, the first and fourth arguments are A and ILA. This checks, because A is a single-dimensional array with 17 locations and ILA = 17.
3. Continue checking all arguments until everything is completely verified.

```
C      PROGRAM MAIN1 USING COMMON
C---   USING COMMON
       COMMON A, B, C(6,7), J(2,4) , K
       DIMENSION K(25), A(17)
       ------
       CALL SUB1
       ------
       CALL SUB2
       ------
       ------
       END

       SUBROUTINE SUB1
       COMMON A(17), B, C, J(2,4), K
       DIMENSION K(25), C(6,7)
       ------
       RETURN
       END

       SUBROUTINE SUB2
       COMMON R, B, A, KK, K
       DIMENSION R(17), A(6,7), KK(2,4), K(25)
       ------
       RETURN
       END
```

LISTING 14–6 Program and two subroutines demonstrating COMMON

```
C       PROGRAM MAIN2
C---    USING ADJUSTABLE DIMENSIONS
        DIMENSION C(6,7), A(17), J(2,4), K(25)
        ILC = 6
        IWC = 7
        ILA = 17
        ILJ = 2
        IWJ = 4
        ILK = 25
        ------
        CALL SUB1 (A, B, J, ILA, ILJ, IWJ)
        ------
        CALL SUB2 (A, C, J, K, ILA, ILC, IWC, ILJ, IWJ, ILK)
        ------
        END

        SUBROUTINE SUB1(R, S, K, ILR, ILK, IWK)
        DIMENSION R(ILR), K(ILK, IWK)
        ------
        RETURN
        END

        SUBROUTINE SUB2(R, T, K, KAK, ILR, ILT, IWT,
     1  ILK, IWK, ILKAK)
        DIMENSION R(ILR), T(ILT, IWT), K(ILK, IWK),
     1  KAK(ILKAK)
        ------
        RETURN
        END
```

LISTING 14-7 Program and two subroutines demonstrating adjustable dimensions

Listing 14-8 is a program segment that indicates how adjustable dimensioning facilitates use of the same subroutine with different size arrays in the same calling program. It is relatively difficult to use common to perform this same mission as efficiently, although the block data program (Section 14-4.4) helps.

The advantages and disadvantages of common and adjustable dimensioning are illustrated in Table 14-4. Although it is legal to mix adjustable dimensioning and COMMON statements within the same program, the table assumes that each is used independently.

Adjustable dimensions can be applied to writing FORTRAN computer programs using structured programming with modules. Subprograms with adjustable dimensions can be used in any number of calling programs without recompilation of the subroutines themselves. Use of subprograms that are dependent upon common, however, usually require changes in COMMON statements and, therefore, recompilation before using with other calling programs.

14-4.4 Two Forms of Common and the Block Data Subprogram

FORTRAN has two forms of common: named common and blank common. Named common is established in a COMMON statement if the list is preceded by the name enclosed in slashes. Thus

```
C     PROGRAM MAIN3
C     ADJUSTABLE DIMENSIONS
C     MULTIPLE USE OF SUBROUTINES
      DIMENSION SMALL(3,3), SM(3,3), AVG(6,6),
     1 AVEG(6,6), BIG(100, 100), GRT(100,100)
      LD = 3
      MD = 6
      LS = 100
      ------
      ------
      CALL INV(SMALL, SM, LD)
      ------
      ------
      CALL INV(SM, SMALL, LD)
      ------
      CALL INV(AVG, AVEG, MD)
      ------
      CALL INV(BIG, GRT, LS)
      ------
      ------
      END

      SUBROUTINE INV(ARRAY, AINV, NDIM)
      DIMENSION ARRAY(NDIM, NDIM), AINV(NDIM,
     1 NDIM)
      ------
      ------
      RETURN
      ------
      ------
      END
```

LISTING 14-8 Multiple use of subroutines using adjustable dimensions

---

Table 14-4 Comparison Between COMMON and Adjustable Dimensions

	COMMON	*Adjustable Dimensions*
1. Argument LISTS	Shorter	Longer
2. Transfer between calling and called Program	*Not* limited to argument list (may increase debugging difficulties)	Limited to argument list (an advantage in long run for structured programming).
3. Name independence	Can be maintained with added burden of being sure that one-to-one relationship is maintained—not usual because of practice of duplicating COMMON statement for use in main and all subprograms.	Maintained.
4. System development	Because COMMON statements must agree in a one-to-one relationship, subroutines must usually be recompiled if used with other calling programs so that COMMON statements will match. Use of named COMMON can help overcome this difficulty somewhat.	Ideal because of *name* independence and establishment of array dimensions by statements in main program *only*.

$$\text{COMMON A } (6,9), C (7,3) / \text{BLK1}/I (12), J (17)/ \text{BLK9}/R (34)$$
$$1 \quad / \quad /T (43) / \text{LST}/\text{LIST} (20,12), \text{VAL}, \text{TOM}$$

places arrays A, C, and T, sequentially in blank common (note that the blank space between the two slashes before T(43) signifies blank common). Arrays I and J are in named common BLK1, array R in BLK9 common, and array LIST, VAL, TOM in LST common.

Differences between blank common and named common include.

	Blank Common	Named Common
may be undefined after RETURN or END	never	sometimes
must be of same size in all program units	no	yes
can be initialized by DATA statement in block data subprogram	no	yes

Block data subprograms allow use of DATA statements to establish initial values in entities of named common (but not blank common). The first statement of a block data subprogram is the BLOCK DATA statement, which has the form

BLOCK DATA name

where name is an optional global name (no name is required).

Block data subprograms are nonexecutable and their purpose is to establish initial values.

The only statements that can occur in the main body of a block data subprogram are COMMON, DATA, DIMENSION, END, EQUIVALENCE, PARAMETER, SAVE and type statements. Note that the DATA statement can be used only with named common.

14-5 SUBROUTINE PLOT, A REVIEW

The large amount of data generated by computer programs are often hard to interpret without plotting the data in graphical form. Subroutine PLOT is designed to plot data using different symbols for the various columns of an array.

Development of a rudimentary plot routine is quite valuable because it provides an unusually complete review of computer programming. Before beginning the formulation process, several basic decisions are required. How will the graph be oriented? What grid or grids will be used? What will be the scale of the graph? What scale factor, if any, is required? What process will be utilized for the storage mechanism?

14-5.1 Basic Considerations

On the usual graph, the x-axis (abscissa) is located parallel to the bottom of the page and y-axis (ordinate) is located parallel to the left side of the page. For some plot routines, this orientation is both desirable and possible. However, for a rudimentary plot, which provides considerable generality, it is desirable to rotate the axis 90°. Thus the x-axis should be parallel to the left side of the page and the y-axis parallel to the top of the page. Standard orientation for the computer output is, therefore, obtained by a counterclockwise rotation of 90°.

The range associated with the y-axis has precise, finite limits, whereas the x-axis may continue from page to page and is essentially unlimited.

Orientation of the axes is related to the question of the storage mechanism to be used. With the axes rotated 90°, a line of output can be stored in a single-dimensional character array (or character variable in Full Language) and output for each x, in turn.

For simplicity, the y scale ranges from zero to 100, requiring 101 locations. Although of limited use, this y-scale is valid for plotting positive percentages. Furthermore, the scale can be generalized by use of offset and scale factors discussed following the development of subroutine PLOT.

Grids should be provided to make graphs more readable. Assume that both the vertical and horizontal grid are spaced ten units apart. Minus signs make presentable horizontal grid lines and plus signs can provide the vertical grid lines. (The colon is often used as an alternate character for vertical grid lines.) The spacing of grid lines can be adjusted easily once the concepts of a plot routine are thoroughly understood. For this first program, x is to start with zero and be incremented by 1 for each line of output.

An example of the desired output is shown in Figure 14–2. Four figures are plotted: two straight lines, one concave curve, and one convex curve. Note that although the straight lines appear to be straight, the curves are actually composed of straight line segments. Such segments occur within the curved portions because of the fixed lateral position of high-speed printer type. By using a pen or pencil, a smooth curve can easily be drawn through the given points, resulting in a more accurate representation with very little additional work. (An improved form of graphical output can be obtained by using other peripheral devices. The technique is roughly comparable to that used for subroutine PLOT, but a number of subroutines are provided to assist in specifying details from generalized concepts. Mastery of such plotting subroutines takes some time, but should be relatively easy once you have completed this text.)

14–5.2 FORMULATION

(The formulation of this and the following section are based on the limitations of Subset FORTRAN 77. If Full Language FORTRAN 77 is used, each reference to a character array can be replaced by a character variable. For completeness, two listings are shown in Listing 14–9, one for the Subset and the other for Full Language FORTRAN 77.)

Consider the process needed to obtain the results of Figure 14–2. (See Table 14–5.) In every case, just one line at a time, corresponding to a particular x value, is to be output. Therefore it is reasonable to store the necessary information in a character array called LINE. To initialize LINE, the process starts by blanking out the entire array. The line (array LINE) can then be filled with minus signs to represent a horizontal grid, but only if it is a tenth row. To establish the vertical grid, the line is filled with a plus sign for each column in the tenth location of every row. Finally, it is necessary to store appropriate characters into array LINE to represent locations corresponding to the four curves. Once filled, array LINE can be output and the process repeated. (Note that every time a

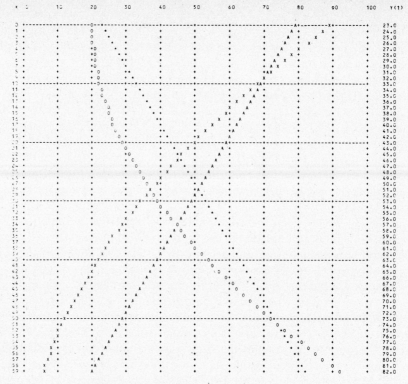

FIGURE 14-2 Output by specialized test program using PLOT subroutine

character is loaded into array LINE, any character previously stored in that location is replaced, that is, essentially erased.) A summary of this process is presented in Table 14–5.

More specifically, character array LINE needs 101 locations. This array must first be blanked out, then filled as appropriate with minus and plus signs to form a grid. Appropriate characters can then be stored to correspond to the y locations associated with the particular x under consideration. Once all characters have been placed into array LINE, it can be output on the high-speed printer to form one row of the graph. The total process is then repeated for the next value of x, and so on, until all rows have been sequentially output for every value of x.

Table 14-5 Process Used to Output A Single Line of Graph

Line by line:

1. Blank out entire line.

2. If Row 0, 10, 20, . . . , fill entire line with minus signs.

3. If Column 0, 10, 20, . . . , enter a plus sign.

4. Finally, enter appropriate characters to show where curve intersects the axis represented by the line.

14–5.3 Toward a Computer Solution

Once a formulation procedure (an algorithm) has been chosen, a definition sheet for subroutine PLOT is started as shown in Table 14–6. The subroutine name is followed by the argument list, in parentheses. The purpose, in accordance with the previous discussion, should indicate precisely what the subroutine can, and cannot, accomplish. It is sometimes helpful if descriptive items are classified as either input, output, or internal. The values to be plotted are accessed by the subroutine by an input array XY that stores values of Y associated with integer values of X (XY has ILXY rows and IWXY columns). The number of Y's associated with any given X cannot be infinite, so IWXY sets an upper limit of four.

ILXY and IWXY define the size of array XY as dimensioned in the main program. In many cases, the entire array will not be needed, so arguments NE and NY are added to indicate how much of array XY is actually being used *this time* within subroutine PLOT. In general, when adjustable dimensions are used, one variable establishes the dimensions in the main program and a second variable establishes the actual amount of space within the array to be used.

Internal to the subroutine, two character arrays are used that need not be defined in the main program and which, therefore, should not be shown in the argument list. Array LINE is needed with 101 locations to store and output results that are plotted line-by-line. Another character array, NAME, is needed to store the characters used within subroutine PLOT.* Referring to Figure 14–2, a blank, +, −, A, O, * and X are needed, suggesting an array with seven locations.

Table 14–6 Definition Sheet of Subroutine Plot

Subroutine Plot (XY, NE, NY, ILXY, IWXY)

Purpose:		To plot a graph of Y versus X, where X is incremented from 0 by steps of 1 and Y is a percentage between 0 and 100.
Descriptive Items:		
Input:	XY	(ILXY, IWXY) Array having NE rows, the columns corresponding to different sets of Y, in a one-to-one relation to X, as described by their location.
	NE	Number of entries of Y in any one column.
	NY	Number of independent columns of Y (limited to 4).
	ILXY	Length of XY array as defined in calling program.
	IWXY	Width of XY array as defined in calling program (limited to 4).
Internal:	LINE	(101) Storage array used to store appropriate symbols to print a line.
	NAME	(7) Symbols to be plotted, * for first column of XY, A for second column of XY, 0 for third column of XY, and X for fourth column of XY. Fifth location is –, sixth is + and seventh is a blank.

---

*See discussion at end of this section.

A human-oriented flow diagram can be constructed (see Figure 14–3) by following the schematic of Table 14–5 very closely.

A major DO-loop is suggested by the requirement of proceeding one line at a time. The MOD function provides a means to output the horizontal grid of minus signs for only every tenth line. Once the grid has been established, two steps are required for each Y corresponding to any particular X: (1) a computation must determine where a character should be stored within array LINE, and (2) the appropriate character must be stored within the computed location.

Table 14–7 illustrates how subscript locations for use in array LINE are computed to correspond to appropriate Y-grid locations. Two operations are involved: an offset because the first location of array LINE is 1, while the first location corresponding to the Y-grid is zero; and roundoff because of the fixed position of printer characters and array locations. Thus 1.0 must be added to any Y-coordinate being plotted to account for the necessary offset. Locations within the array are integer. To plot as closely as possible to the correct location, therefore, 0.5 must be added to the Y-coordinate to provide proper roundoff.

Subroutine PLOT (XY, NE, NY, ILXY, IWXY) Human-oriented flow

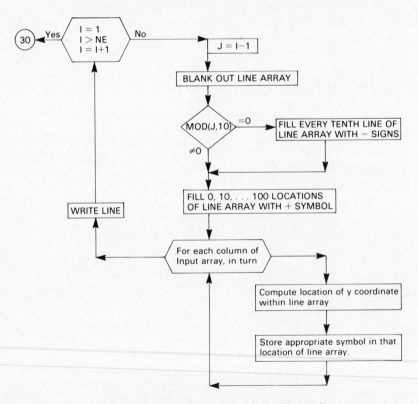

FIGURE 14–3 Human-oriented flow diagram for subroutine PLOT

Table 14-7 Calculation for Position to Store Plot Symbol

Array LINE	1	2	3	4	5	6	7	8	9	10	11	12	13	14	··· ▶ ··· ▶

Corresponding X-GRID location	0	1	2	3	4	5	6	7	8	9	10	11	12	13	··· ▶ ··· ▶

Number to be plotted:		Offset between array LINE and Corresponding X-GRID location:		To account for necessary round off:		Location in array LINE:
11.6	+	1.0	+	0.5	=	$13.1 \rightarrow 13$
11.2	+	1.0	+	0.5	=	$12.7 \rightarrow 12$

It is always wise to check procedures such as these. For example, when 1.5 is added to the Y value 11.6, the result is 13.1, or 13 when converted to integer. Thus the thirteenth location in the array corresponds to the twelfth position on the Y-axis grid and is the closest point for plotting 11.6. Likewise, $11.2 + 1.5 = 12.7$, truncates to 12, so the symbol is stored in the twelfth location of array LINE to plot 11.2.

A machine-oriented flow diagram (see Figure 14-4) shows the details of these computations. The appropriate character is stored in array LINE for plotting and is obtained from array NAME, which has its characters established in a DATA statement.

Subroutine PLOT is coded in Listing 14-9(a). Comments are given to help clarify the process. The subroutine uses two CHARACTER arrays local to the subroutine and an array XY of adjustable dimension. (The last two arguments in the list, ILXY and IWXY, establish dimensions of array XY.) Listing 14-9 is on pages 358 and 359.

Subroutine PLOT uses character array NAME for three reasons. First, use of arrays helps to reinforce understanding of the DATA statement. Second, the use of such an array provides flexibility in use of characters when it is carried through the argument list, as suggested in Section 14-5.5. Third, such an array makes DO-loop 40 practical. If these three considerations are rejected, then in DO-loop 10,

$$\text{LINE (K)} = \text{NAME (7)}$$

would be replaced by

$$\text{LINE (K)} = \text{'}\Delta\text{'} \quad (\Delta \text{ represents a single blank space})$$

Likewise, in DO-loop 20,

$$\text{LINE (K)} = \text{NAME(5)}$$

would be replaced by

$$\text{LINE (K)} = \text{'}-\text{'}$$

DO-loop 40, however, still requires use of array NAME and the DATA statement unless it is replaced by a series of logical or block IF's containing statements such as the following.

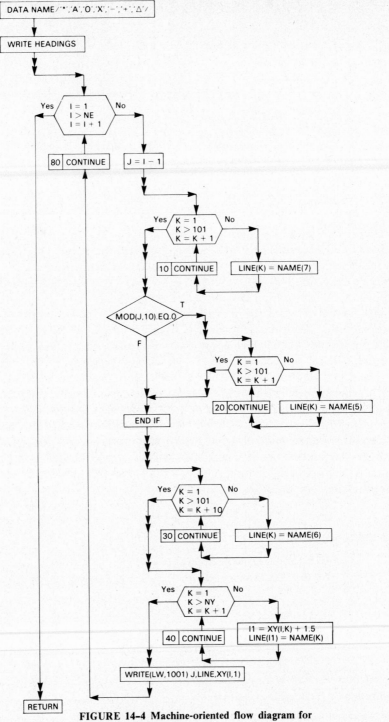

FIGURE 14-4 Machine-oriented flow diagram for subroutine PLOT

$$LINE (I1) = `*`$$
$$LINE (I1) = `A`$$

Listing 14–9(b) illustrates a revision of the PLOT subroutine to take advantage of Full Language FORTRAN 77. Character arrays NAME and LINE are changed to character variables. Then character replacement statements of the subset such as

$$LINE (K) = NAME (6)$$

are changed to represent substrings in the Full Language by

$$LINE (K:K) = NAME (6:6)$$

Finally, on output, 101A1 is replaced by A101.

14–5.4 Testing Subroutine PLOT

A specialized test program can be coded (see Listing 14–10) to output the graph of Figure 14–2. To eliminate the need for input data, values to be plotted are determined by a DO-loop. Constants are used for some arguments in the CALL statement, although this can be a dangerous practice. (See page 360.)

A more generalized test program may sometimes be useful (see Listing 14–11), but preparing input data is required before the test program can be used. In general, one or the other of these methods should be used to test each complex subroutine before it is used within a parent program. (See the discussion in Section 14–7.)

14–5.5 Generalizing Subroutine PLOT

Subroutine PLOT can be generalized rather easily. First, horizontal grid lines can be spaced at different intervals by changing MOD(J,10) so 10 is represented by a variable that is carried through the argument list. Likewise, vertical grid lines can be spaced at different intervals by changing the DO-loop so that the increment size 10 is replaced by a variable name, also carried through the argument list.

It is also desirable to have scales with the range for y other than zero to 100. Also, x's are seldom incremented by exactly one for each line of the plot. If such changes are made, however, an additional subroutine should be used to establish appropriate scales, preferably using increments of one, two, four, or five times some power of 10 to permit easy interpolation. (See Exercise 7 of Section 3–8.) Computations for location of the Y-coordinate within the LINE array are then adjusted by changing the offset and/or changing the scale factor.

For instance, to accommodate a Y-scale ranging from 0 to 10,000, it would be necessary to use a scale factor. The location for a character to plot within array LINE, I1, would be computed as

$$I1 = XY(I,K)*.01+1.5 \quad \text{or} \quad I1 = XY(I,K)/100.+1.5$$

The scale factor (*.01 or /100.) is the ratio of 100 to 10,000.

If the scale were changed to range between −50 and +50, a change in offset is required. Because the beginning value is now −50, +50 would have to be added to the offset so that the value −50 would be in the first location of the array LINE. Then I1 would be computed as

```
            SUBROUTINE PLOT(XY,ILXY,IWXY,NE,NY,LW)

            DIMENSION XY(ILXY,IWXY)
            CHARACTER*1 NAME(7) , LINE(101)

C---              ---PUT SYMBOL INTO ARRAY NAME---
            DATA NAME/'*','A','O','X','-','+',' '/

C---                ---OUTPUT HEADING---
            WRITE(LW,1000) (I,I=0,100,10)

C---              ---FOR ONE LINE AT A TIME---
C---                ---IN SEQUENCE---
            DO 80 I=1,NE
            J= I-1

C---                   ---BLANK OUT ENTIRE LINE---
            DO 10 K= 1,101
                  LINE(K) = NAME(7)
      10    CONTINUE

C---                   ---CHECK TO SEE IF A GRID LINE---
C---                   ---GRIDS OCCUR EVERY TENTH LINE---

C--                    ---IF(J-J/10*10.EQ.0) THEN IS VALID---
C--                    ---PARENTHESES ADDED FOR CLARITY---
            IF((J-(J/10)*10).EQ. 0) THEN
C---                   ---GRID LINE, FILL WITH MINUS(-) SIGNS---
                  DO 20 K=1,101
                        LINE(K) = NAME(5)
      20          CONTINUE
            END IF

C---              ---PUT + SIGN IN EVERY 10 TH COL FOR GRID---
            DO 30 K=1,101,10
                  LINE(K) = NAME(6)
      30    CONTINUE

C---                   ---GRID COMPLETE(FOR THIS LINE) NOW---
C---                   ---GET LOCATION(S) OF POINT(S) TO PLOT---
C---                    ---ADD 1.0 TO VALUE TO OFFSET BY 1---
C---                    ---ADD 0.5 TO ROUND OFF PROPERLY---
C---                    ---CONVERSION TO INTEGER RESULTS IN---
C---                    ---PROPER LOCATION FOR PLOTTING POINT---

            DO 40 K=1,NY
                  I1 = XY(I,K)+1.5
                  LINE(I1) = NAME(K)
      40    CONTINUE

C---                    ---LINE 'LOADED' AND READY---
C---                    ---THEREFORE, OUTPUT LINE---

            WRITE(LW,1001) J, LINE, XY(I,1)
        80 CONTINUE

     1000 FORMAT('1GRAPH OF Y VS. X'//4X,'X ',10(I2,8X),I3,4X,
          1'Y(1)'//)
     1001 FORMAT(I5,1X,101A1,F8.1)

            RETURN
            END
```

LISTING 14-9 (a) Coding of Subroutine Plot

Chapter 14 Subroutines

```
        SUBROUTINE PLOT(XY,ILXY,IWXY,NE,NY,LW)

        DIMENSION XY(ILXY,IWXY)
        CHARACTER NAME*7 , LINE*101

C---            ---PUT SYMBOL INTO ARRAY NAME---
  .    DATA NAME/'*AOX-+ '/

C---            ---OUTPUT HEADING---
       WRITE(LW,1000) (I,I=0,100,10)

C---          ---FOR ONE LINE AT A TIME---
C---          ---IN SEQUENCE---
       DO 80 I=1,NE
           J= I-1

C---              ---BLANK OUT ENTIRE LINE---
        DO 10 K= 1,101
            LINE(K:K) = NAME(7:7)
   10   CONTINUE

C---              ---CHECK TO SEE IF A GRID LINE---
C---              ---GRIDS OCCUR EVERY TENTH LINE---

C--               ---IF(J-J/10*10.EQ.0) THEN IS VALID---
C--               ---PARENTHESES ADDED FOR CLARITY---
        IF((J-(J/10)*10).EQ. 0) THEN
C---                  ---GRID LINE, FILL WITH MINUS(-) SIGNS---
            DO 20 K=1,101
                LINE(K:K) = NAME(5:5)
   20           CONTINUE
        END IF

C---              ---PUT + SIGN IN EVERY 10 TH COL FOR GRID---
        DO 30 K=1,101,10
            LINE(K:K) = NAME(6:6)
   30   CONTINUE

C---              ---GRID COMPLETE(FOR THIS LINE) NOW---
C---              ---GET LOCATION(S) OF POINT(S) TO PLOT---
C---                  ---ADD 1.0 TO VALUE TO OFFSET BY 1---
C---                  ---ADD 0.5 TO ROUND OFF PROPERLY---
C---                  ---CONVERSION TO INTEGER RESULTS IN---
C---                  ---PROPER LOCATION FOR PLOTTING POINT---

        DO 40 K=1,NY
            I1 = XY(I,K)+1.5
            LINE(I1:I1) = NAME(K:K)
   40   CONTINUE

C---              ---LINE 'LOADED' AND READY---
C---              ---THEREFORE, OUTPUT LINE---

       WRITE(LW,1001) J, LINE, XY(I,1)
   80 CONTINUE

 1000 FORMAT('1GRAPH OF Y VS. X'//4X,'X ',10(I2,8X),I3,4X,
     1'Y(1)'//)
 1001 FORMAT(I5,1X,A101,F8.1)

       RETURN
       END
```

LISTING 14–9 (b)

```
      PROGRAM PLOTT
C---           ---PROGRAM GENERATES DATA---
C---           ---TO TEST SUBROUTINE PLOT---
      DIMENSION R(80,4)
C---           ---LOAD ARRAY WITH---
C---               ---2 STRAIGHT LINES---
C---               ---2 CURVES, CONCAVE,---
C---               ---        CONVEX---
      DO 10 I=1,60
         R(I,1) = I+22
         R(I,2) = 80-I
         R(I,3) = I*I/50. + 20.
         R(I,4) = (80-I)**2/70.
   10 CONTINUE

      CALL PLOT(R,80,4,60,4,6)

      STOP
      END
```

LISTING 14-10 Coding of test program PLOTT

```
      PROGRAM TPLOT
C---           ---GENERAL TEST FOR SUBROUTINE PLOT---
      DIMENSION A(100,4)
      ILA=100
      IWA=4
C---        ---TO CHANGE SIZE---
C---           ---CHANGE DIMENSIONS OF ARRAY A---
C---           ---AND VALUES OF ILA AND IWA WHERE---
C---           ---DIMENSION A(ILA,IWA)---
      LR=5
      LW=6

   20 READ(LR,1000) NE,NY
C---        ---NE= NUMBER OF ROWS OF ARRAY A ACTUALLY USED---
C---        ---NY= NUMBER OF COLS OF ARRAY A ACTUALLY USED---
C---        ---NE MUST BE .LE. ILA---
C---        ---NY MUST BE .LE. IWA---

      IF(NE.GT.0) THEN

C---           ---READ ARRAY A OF VALUES TO BE PLOTTED---
      DO 30 I=1,NE
         READ(LR,1001)(A(I,J),J=1,NY)
   30 CONTINUE

C---           ---CALL SUBROUTINE AND PLOT ARRAY A---
      CALL PLOT(A,ILA,IWA,NE,NY,LW)

C---           ---CYCLE BACK FOR ANOTHER ARRAY TO PLOT---
      GO TO 20
      END IF

 1000 FORMAT(2I4)
 1001 FORMAT(10F8.0)

      STOP
      END
```

LISTING 14-11 Coding of alternate test program
TPLOT

$$I1 = XY(I,K)+51.5$$

If the scale were to vary from −500 to +500, both an offset and a scale factor are necessary. The difference between −500 and +500 is 1000, and leads to the scale factor of 1000:100, or 10. Dividing −500 by this scale factor of 10 shows that an offset of +50 is again needed. Thus

$$I1 = XY(I,K)/10. + 51.5 \quad \text{or} \quad I1 = XY(I,K)* 0.1 + 51.5.$$

For each change of offset or scale factor, it is important to check the upper and lower limits to insure that values fall within end points of array LINE. The lowest value to be plotted must result in an I1 value of 1. The highest value to be plotted must yield 101 as the value of I1. If either is untrue, an error has been made. As examples:

$$\text{If } XY(I,K) = -500 \quad I1 = -500./10. + 51.5 = 1 \quad (\text{not } 1.5)$$
$$\text{If } XY(I,K) = +500 \quad I1 = +500./10. + 51.5 = 101 \quad (\text{not } 101.5).$$

To alter the values of x, the DO-loop could use type real loop indices (Full Language) or convert integers to real numbers within the loop.

Alternately, a column could be added to array XY for designation as the X-coordinate. Such a change would require a change in the DO-loop. (Any column could be designated as the X column by a variable carried through the argument list.)

For complete generality and modularity, this program should have an internal check to insure that the value of NE never exceeds the value of ILXY. Likewise, it is important to insure that the value of NY does not exceed the width of the array XY, as defined by IWXY. If either situation occurs, the program may continue to operate, but results would probably be erroneous and the error difficult to locate.

This program has modularity because it uses adjustable dimensioning. Modularity can be greatly increased by adding the following to the argument list: variables that adjust the horizontal and vertical scales, a scale factor, an offset value, and an array of characters to add flexibility of output and to provide an additional number of curves.

This section has reviewed much of the material covered in the text to this point, and modifications to the plot routine provide a wealth of examination material. It is suggested, therefore, that you study this section until you thoroughly understand it, even if you will not use the plot routine in the near future.

14-6 TEXT EDITING

Suppose you are the manager of a computer center for a firm that has just merged with three other firms. Each firm has a file with information about their customers formatted in a different way. The one thing that the formats have in common is that the last name is first and that any suffix (such as Jr. or Sr.) follows the middle name or initials. You wish to make address labels and to write each person's name in the correct form: first name first, followed by the last name, followed by a comma and the suffix, if one exists. Furthermore, it is important that the rearranged names be spaced in a standard format.

One firm followed the last name by a comma and then the first name. Another firm started the first name consistently in the same column, but did not use a comma between the last and first name. The third firm used random formatting for input. We conclude from all of this that names take the following form.

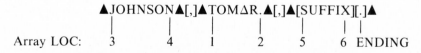

The solid black triangles represent any number of blank spaces, including none. The open triangle represents exactly one blank space.

The brackets enclose either a comma, a period, or the word SUFFIX. This symbolism indicates that the comma, period or suffix may or may not exist.

Below this typical name are six numbers that represent locations within an array called LOC. Thus location 3 of array LOC stores the position of the first letter of the last name. Likewise, the fifth position of array LOC stores the position of the first letter of the suffix, if any exists. The variable ENDING is used to store a period if a suffix that exists requires a period but does not contain one.

A study of the six locations suggests that the column locations to be stored in the array LOC are obtained in the following manner.

LOC 3 is defined as the first nonblank.

LOC 4 is defined as the first nonblank located left of the first comma (or left of a blank if no comma exists) following the last name, when written first.

LOC 1 is the first nonblank located right of the comma (or blank if no comma exists) following the last name, when written first.

LOC 5 equals the first character of the suffix.

LOC 6 equals the last character of the suffix, including a period if the period exists.

LOC 2 represents the first nonblank/noncomma left of the suffix if it exists, otherwise the first nonblank left of the character farthest right in the total string.

Output of this name would be in the following form.

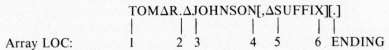

(*Note:* The first letter of the first name starts in the first column, only one space exists between the middle name or initials and the last name, any existing suffix is preceded by a comma and a single blank space, and all suffixes are followed by a period if a period is required.)

Once we have decided how to distinguish the string locations for the beginning and ending of various parts of the name, it is clear that some method must be determined for finding particular substrings of characters within a character string. This suggests that a subroutine, FNDCHR, be developed to locate substrings within strings. Such a subroutine should be thoroughly tested (by a program called TFC, for Test Find Characters) before proceeding. Once the subroutine FNDCHR is perfected, it can then be used in a subroutine (NAMLOC) to determine the string locations and store them in the array LOC as described above. This subroutine also must be tested by a program CHGNAM (CHanGe NAMe). Note: FNDCHR, FiND CHaRacter; NAMLOC, NAMe LOCation.

14-6.1 Subroutine FNDCHR

Since it is often desirable to be able to find substrings within strings, often with specific limits, the subroutine should be written in a more generalized manner than needed to satisfy the minimum requirements of the present program. A reasonable name for the string to be searched is SAMPLE, and the substring being sought could be named SOUGHT. When the substring SOUGHT is found in the string SAMPLE, the location of its first character and last character needs to be stored.

(Full Language FORTRAN 77 has the intrinsic function INDEX which can be used for this purpose. If LOC is the location of the first character of SOUGHT in SAMPLE, the intrinsic function would be used.

$$LOC = INDEX (SAMPLE, SOUGHT)$$

If SOUGHT occurs more than once, only the first occurance is flagged; zero is returned if SOUGHT is not in SAMPLE or if

LEN (SAMPLE) < LEN(SOUGHT). INDEX is not as general as FNDCHR.)

Possible names of such locations are

LOCBEG (LOCation,BEGinning) and LOCEND (LOCation, END of string).

The area to be searched should be controlled by lower and upper limits, with names like LIMLOW and LIMUP. Two additional arguments appropriate to the subroutine are NP, to control output, and LW, to provide the logical unit number for output. Most of the preceeding information should be presented by comment lines within the subroutine.

Using these arguments gives the first line of the subroutine as follows.

```
    SUBROUTINE FNDCHR
   1 (SAMPLE,SOUGHT,LOCBEG,LOCEND,LIMLOW,LIMUP,NP,LW)
```

The first two arguments are type character and the last six are type integer. When type character variables are carried through the argument list, their lengths must be carried with them, by a CHARACTER statement using their names followed by an asterisk and an asterisk in parentheses[*(*)]. Showing character length in this way is much the same as using adjustable dimensions for arrays of type real and integer, that is, the length of the character is established in the main program (or possibly in the calling subprogram). Typically

```
    CHARACTER ROSE*(*), RATZ(6,3)*(*)
    CHARACTER ARAY (ILARA, IWARA)*(*)
              or
    CHARACTER *(*) ROSE, RATZ(6,3) ARAY(ILARA, IWARA)
```

The lengths of character variable SAMPLE and SOUGHT are determined by using the intrinsic function LEN, because these lengths will be needed in the computations that follow.

To develop a formulation procedure, it is useful to work with some typical values. As an example, let:

```
SAMPLE = 'ABCDEFGHIJKLMNOPQRST'  so that   LENSAM = 20
SOUGHT = 'IJK'                    so that   LENSOU = 3
LIMLOW = 5 signifying to start search at 'E' within SAMPLE
   LIMUP = 14 signifying to stop search at 'N' within SAMPLE
```

```
       SUBROUTINE FNDCHR(SAMPLE,SOUGHT,LOCBEG,LOCEND,MLIMLO,MLIMUP,
      1                  NP,LW)
       CHARACTER SAMPLE *(*),SOUGHT *(*)

C---      LOCBEG SHOWS POSITION WHERE 'SOUGHT' STARTS IN 'SAMPLE',---
C---      AND LOCEND POSITION WHERE 'SOUGHT' ENDS IN 'SAMPLE'---
C---      LIMLOW AND LIMUP ARE LOWER AND UPPER LIMITS WHICH CAN---
C---      BE SEARCHED WITHIN 'SAMPLE', IF 0 LIMLOW DEFAULTS TO 1---
C---      IF 0, LIMUP DEFAULTS TO LAST POSITION OF 'SAMPLE'---
C---      NP IS PRINT CONTROL AND LW IS LOGICAL OUTPUT NUMBER---

       LENSAM = LEN(SAMPLE)
       LENSOU = LEN(SOUGHT)

       IF(MLIMLO.EQ.0) THEN
           LIMLOW = 1
       ELSE
           LIMLOW = MLIMLO
       END IF

       IF(MLIMUP.EQ.0) THEN
           LIMUP = LENSAM
       ELSE
           LIMUP = MLIMUP
       END IF


C---      SET UPPER LIMIT ON LOOP INDEX SO 'SAMPLE' LENGTH---
C---            NOT EXCEEDED DURING SEARCH---

       LOOPI = LIMUP - LENSOU + 1

C---      BEGIN SEARCH FOR 'SOUGHT' WITHIN ' SAMPLE'---

       DO 10 I = LIMLOW,LOOPI

           IF(SAMPLE(I:I+LENSOU-1).EQ.SOUGHT(:)) THEN
               LOCBEG = I
               LOCEND = I + LENSOU - 1
               IF(NP.GE.2) WRITE(LW,'(/1X,A,'' FOUND IN LOCATIONS''
      1        ,I3,'' THRU'',I3,'' WITHIN '', A,/
      2        '' WHICH IS FOUND BETWEEN POSITIONS '',I2,'' AND '',
      3        I2,'' OF SAMPLE '', A/)') SOUGHT,LOCBEG,LOCEND,
      4        SAMPLE(LIMLOW:LIMUP),LIMLOW,LIMUP,SAMPLE
               RETURN

C---              NOTE 'RETURN' WITHIN LOOP---
           END IF

   10 CONTINUE

C---      IF PROGRAM REACHES THIS POINT, 'SOUGHT' NOT IN 'SAMPLE'---

       LOCBEG = 0
       LOCEND = 0
       IF(NP.GT.0) WRITE(LW,'(//'' ***CHARACTERS '', A ,
      1'' SOUGHT IN SAMPLE '',A ,'' NOT FOUND '')')
      2SOUGHT,SAMPLE

       RETURN
       END
```

LISTING 14-12 Coding for program FNDCHR

```
      PROGRAM TFC
C---      TEST SUBROUTINE 'FNDCHR'---

      CHARACTER  C20*20, C5*5, C4*4 , C2*2 , C*1

      LR=5
      LW=6

      DO 10 I= 1,4
        READ(LR,'(5A)',ERR=50)C20,C5,C4,C2,C
        WRITE(LW,'(//'' C20= '',A,'' C5= '', A, ''  C4= '',A,
     1          '' C2= '',A,'' C= '',A/)')C20,C5,C4,C2,C

        CALL FNDCHR(C20,C5,LB,LE, 0, 0,2,LW)
        CALL FNDCHR(C20,C4,LB,LE,10, 0,2,LW)
        CALL FNDCHR(C20,C2,LB,LE, 4,17,2,LW)
        CALL FNDCHR(C20,C ,LB,LE, 0, 0,2,LW)
 10   CONTINUE

 50   CALL FNDCHR('ABCDEFG','CD',LB,LE,2,6,2,LW)
      CALL FNDCHR('12341234','23',LB,LE,0,0,2,LW)
      CALL FNDCHR('12341234','23',LB,LE,0,2,LW)
      CALL FNDCHR('12341234','23',LB,LE,LE,0,2,LW)

      STOP
      END
```

Input:

```
12345678901234567890345671234019
ABCDEFGHIJKLMNOPQRSTIJKLMFGRSTUF
ABCDEFGHIJKLMNOPQPSTPQRSTPQRSSTT
•,()+-*135AQVMPZRLMV*135A()+-5A.
```

Output:

```
C20= 12345678901234567890   C5= 34567   C4= 1234 C2= 01   C= 9


34567 FOUND IN LOCATIONS  3 THRU  7 WITHIN 12345678901234567890
WHICH IS FOUND BETWEEN POSITIONS  1 AND 20 OF SAMPLE 12345678901234567890


1234 FOUND IN LOCATIONS 11 THRU 14 WITHIN 01234567890
WHICH IS FOUND BETWEEN POSITIONS 10 AND 20 OF SAMPLE 12345678901234567890


C1 FOUND IN LOCATIONS 10 THRU 11 WITHIN 45678901234567
WHICH IS FOUND BETWEEN POSITIONS  4 AND 17 OF SAMPLE 12345678901234567890


9 FOUND IN LOCATIONS  9 THRU  9 WITHIN 12345678901234567890
WHICH IS FOUND BETWEEN POSITIONS  1 AND 20 OF SAMPLE 12345678901234567890



C20= ABCDEFGHIJKLMNOPQRST   C5= IJKLM   C4= PQRS C2= TU   C= F


IJKLM FOUND IN LOCATIONS  9 THRU 13 WITHIN ABCDEFGHIJKLMNOPQRST
WHICH IS FOUND BETWEEN POSITIONS  1 AND 20 OF SAMPLE ABCDEFGHIJKLMNOPQRST


PQRS FOUND IN LOCATIONS 16 THRU 19 WITHIN JKLMNOPQRST
WHICH IS FOUND BETWEEN POSITIONS 10 AND 20 OF SAMPLE ABCDEFGHIJKLMNOPQRST



***CHARACTERS TU SOUGHT IN SAMPLE ABCDEFGHIJKLMNOPQRST NOT FOUND

F FOUND IN LOCATIONS  6 THRU  6 WITHIN ABCDEFGHIJKLMNOPQRST
WHICH IS FOUND BETWEEN POSITIONS  1 AND 20 OF SAMPLE ABCDEFGHIJKLMNOPQRST
```

**LISTING 14-13 Coding of Program TFC, With
Input and Selected Output**

The idea is to compare the string 'IJK' contained in SOUGHT with the reduced string 'EFGHIJKLMN' in SAMPLE. This suggests use of a DO-loop with an IF statement used for comparison. The lower limit on this DO-loop would be LIMLOW. The upper limit, however, would not be LIMUP because SOUGHT has a length of three. The last valid comparison, would be between 'IJK' of SOUGHT and 'LMN' of SAMPLE. Therefore, the upper limit of the DO-loop is computed as LIMUP minus LENSOU plus 1 (to avoid the *one-off error*). For this particular case, we have the following.

$$LOOPI = LIMUP - LENSOU + 1$$

or

$$LOOPI = 14 - 3 + 1 = 12$$

Twelve represents the twelfth location of SAMPLE, which is the letter L; the last comparison in the loop would then be 'IJK' with 'LMN', which is the correct.

These statements are coded in Listing 14–12, where the sought string within SAMPLE has its initial point defined in LOCBEG and its ending point defined in LOCEND.

In case the string sought within the sample is not found, LOCBEG and LOCEND are both set equal to zero and a provision is made to output that fact within the subroutine. Listing 14–13 shows a typical program that could be used to test this subroutine, along with input data and a partial set of output. The subroutine has two block IF statements that were not discussed; these are to illustrate the kind of difficulties that can happen during the development process.

This subroutine was originally run with two statements to adjust LIMLOW and LIMUP:

IF(LIMLOW.EQ.0) LIMLOW = 1
IF(LIMUP.EQ.0) LIMUP = LENSAM

When the first call is made by program TFC using these statements, LIMLOW is changed to 1. The important point is that the constant zero was used in the call as an actual argument rather than a variable name. Thus, in the subroutine, when LIMLOW was changed to 1, the constant zero in the main program was also changed to 1. At the next step in the subroutine, the expression LIMUP.EQ.0 then actually represented the statement LIMUP.EQ.1 because zero had been changed to 1 within the main program for use as an actual argument for LIMUP. Thus you should be cautious about using actual arguments that are either constants or expressions, since such constants or expressions cannot be changed within the subroutine without dire consequences.

Program TFC is a dummy program constructed solely to test subroutine FNDCHR, but it is a time-saving device that is well worth the effort because it helps validate the subroutine. Once program TFC has thoroughly tested the subroutine, it is then reasonable to proceed to the next step in the overall programming project.

14–6.2 Subroutine NAMLOC

In accordance with the earlier discussion, subroutine NAMLOC (Listing 14–14) needs five arguments. The first argument, NAME, is for the string that contains a name, stored with the last name first. The second argument is the array LOC, needing six locations to store the end points of the last name, the first name and any middle name(s) or initials, and the suffix, if any. The third argument, ENDING, stores a period for any suffix that was input without one, even though one was required. The fourth and fifth arguments control both the amount of output and the output device to be used.

The subroutine must perform the steps outlined in the introduction to this section.

Find the first nonblank character by searching each character, in turn, of the variable NAME. When a nonblank is found, this location represents the value to be stored in the third location of array LOC.

Next, it is necessary to find either the first comma or blank that exists after the last name. A reasonable place to start the search is in LOC(3), thereby ignoring any leading blanks. Two searches are required, one for a blank and the other for a comma. LOCEND can be used to store the location of the first blank after the last name, and LOCE can be used for the first comma after the last name. If the comma is located ahead of the blank, however, LOCE is moved into location LOCEND. Thus LOCEND stores the position that contains the first blank or comma located after the last name.

Once LOCEND is found, the first nonblank left of it will be the last character of the last name, which suggests using a DO-loop starting left of the blank or comma just found. When the location of the last character of the last name is found, it can be stored in element LOC(4). Starting from one position beyond the previously found blank or comma, another DO-loop can search for the first nonblank, which signifies the first letter of the first name for storage into LOC(1).

The search for the suffix can also be used to determine whether or not a final required period is missing. To do this, the variable ENDING can be filled with a blank and LOC(6) with a zero. Subroutine FNDCHR can then be called to look for the string 'JR.' If found, LOC(6) is no longer zero and no more searching is required. Otherwise, each of the subsequent suffixes must be sought. By judiciously ordering the calls, the variable ENDING can be filled with a period to go with JR or SR (without the required period) if they are found. If the search is completed and no suffixes are found, so that LOC(6) is still zero, ENDING needs to be reset to a blank.

Everything has now been located except the end of the first name and initials or middle names. If no suffix exists, then LOC(6) is still zero and the "far right search limit" is equal to the total length of NAME. Otherwise, the far right search limit is equal to the location of the leftmost character of the suffix, less one. Either of these values can be stored in a variable, say M, and used in a loop to search leftward for the first nonblank that is not a comma, representing the endpoint to be stored in LOC(2). To help in debugging, if the print control is greater than or equal to one, the string can be output above a row of column numbers that can be used to compare the six locations stored in array LOC.

The subroutine should be tested before using it in the major program configuration. This can be done by a program such as CHGNAM, using an input character array(ARRAY) with ten rows and two columns, each with space for 20 characters. The first column of array ARRAY contains the names to be reorganized. The second column of the array has some comments about what is encountered in the reorganization of that name.

The program (see Listing 14–15) can be written as essentially one large DO-loop that first reads a line of the array. It could then call the subroutine NAMLOC to obtain the

```
      SUBROUTINE NAMLOC(NAME,LOC,ENDING,NP,LW)
C---      USED TO LOCATE LIMITS OF PARTS OF NAMES,GIVEN---
C---      LAST NAME FIRST SO NAME CAN BE WRITTEN FIRST---
C---      NAME FIRST. NAMES MAY BE SEPARATED BY COMMAS---

C---      AND/OR BLANKS.  SUFFIX NAMES MAY INCLUDE A---
C---      ERIOD OR NOT,'ENDING' CARRIES BLANK OR PERIOD---
C---      TO PROVIDE PROPEX ENDING.---

      CHARACTER NAME *(*) , ENDING *(*)
      DIMENSION LOC(6)
      LENNAM = LEN(NAME)

C         FIND FIRST NON-BLANK------
      DO 5 I= 1,LENNAM

         IF(NAME(I:I).NE.' ')THEN
            LOC(3)=I
            GO TO 6
         END IF

    5 CONTINUE

    6 CONTINUE

C---      FIND FIRST COMMA OR BLANK AFTER THE LAST NAME---

      CALL FNDCHR(NAME,' ',LCB,LOCEND,LOC(3),0,NP,LW)
      CALL FNDCHR(NAME,',',LOCB,LOCE,LOC(3),0,NP,LW)
      IF(LOCE.GT.3 .AND. LOCE.LT.LOCEND) LOCEND=LOCE
C---      LOCATE END POINT OF LAST NAME, STORE IN LOC(4)---
C---      SEARCH FOR FIRST NON-BLANK LEFT OF LOCEND---

      L = LOCEND - 1
      DO 10 I= L,1,-1

         IF(NAME(I:I).NE.' ') THEN
            LOC(4) = I
            GO TO 20
         END IF

   10 CONTINUE

C---      LOCATE BEGINNING POINT OF FIRST NAME INTO LOC(1)---

   20 L = LOCEND + 1
      DO 30 I= L , LENNAM, 1

         IF(NAME(I:I).NE.' ') THEN
            LOC(1) = I
            GO TO 40
         END IF

   30 CONTINUE
   40 CONTINUE
```

LISTING 14-14 Coding of program NAMLOC

locations of the beginning and ending characters of the different parts of the name. Using these locations, the first name (and middle name(s) or initials) can be concatenated with a blank and the last name. These results can be stored in a temporary location NTEMP, needed because of the restriction on replacement statements that use overlapping parts of the same substring. The sixth location of array LOC can then be checked and if not zero, the first name, middle name and initials, and last name (previously stored in NTEMP)

```
C---        FIND SUFFIX, IF ANY,  BEGINNING AND ENDING LOC(5)(6)---
C---        SET 'ENDING' TO BLANK IF SUFFIX HAS PERIOD---
C---                        OR IF SUFFIX NON-EXISTENT---
C---        IF SUFFIX HAS PERIOD MISSING, SET PERIOD INTO 'ENDING'---

        ENDING = ' '
        LOC(6) = 0

        CALL FNDCHR(NAME,'JR,',LOC(5),LOC(6),L,0,NP,LW)
        IF(LOC(6).EQ.0)CALL FNDCHR(NAME,'SR.',LOC(5),LOC(6),L,0,NP,LW)
        IF(LOC(6).EQ.0)CALL FNDCHR(NAME,'III',LOC(5),LOC(6),L,0,NP,LW)
        IF(LOC(6).EQ.0)CALL FNDCHR(NAME,'II' ,LOC(5),LOC(6),L,0,NP,LW)
        IF(LOC(6).EQ.0) ENDING = '.'
        IF(LOC(6).EQ.0)CALL FNDCHR(NAME,'JR' ,LOC(5),LOC(6),L,0,NP,LW)
        IF(LOC(6).EQ.0)CALL FNDCHR(NAME,'SR' ,LOC(5),LOC(6),L,0,NP,LW)
        IF(LOC(6).EQ.0) ENDING = ' '


C---        WORK BACK FROM BEGINNING OF SUFFIX TO FIND END OF---
C---        FIRST NAME + INITIAS AND/OR MIDDLE NAMES IN LOC(2)---

        IF(LOC(6).EQ.0) THEN
            M = LENNAM
        ELSE
            M = LOC(5) - 1
        END IF .

        DO 60 I = M,L,-1

            IF(NAME(I:I).NE.' '  .AND
    1         NAME(I:I).NE.',') THEN
                LOC(2) = I
                GO TO 70
            END IF

     60 CONTINUE
     70 CONTINUE

        IF(NP.GE.1) WRITE(LW,'(/1X,A/1X,4(''1234567890'')/'' LOC(1 THRU'',
    1'' 6)= '',6I4/)') NAME,(LOC(I),I=1,6)

        RETURN
        END
```

LISTING 14-14 *(continued)*

are concatenated with a comma, a blank, the suffix, and the blank or period stored in ENDING.

To provide a ready check, it is useful to output the first two columns of the array followed by the name in its rearranged position. (Do not forget that NAME and NTEMP must be blanked out so that they will be available for the next reordering of a name within the loop.)

Typical output is shown in Listing 14-16. The first column shows the name as input, the second column lists some characteristics about the name, and the third column shows the rearranged name. Intermediate output is shown when the print control level is sufficiently high.

Once these tests have been completed, the subroutine CHGNAM is ready for use in the larger complex of programs. Notice that it has a great deal of modularity and flexibility. It can seek and find any size character string within any size character string. If

```
      PROGRAM CHGNAM
C---      CHANGE NAME ORDER FROM LAST, FIRST TO---
C---                              FIRST LAST

C---      NTEMP: TEMPORARY STORAGE FOR BUILDING NAME
C---      NAME:  FIRST NAME FIRST
C---      ARRAY(10,2): COLUMN 1 HAS LAST NAME FIRST
C---                   COLUMN 2 DESCRIBES CHANGES NEEDED
C---      LOC(6): LOCATES POSITIONS OF NAME IN COLUMN 1 OF ARRAY
C---           WITH LOC(1)= BEGINNING LOCATION OF FIRST NAME
C---                LOC(2)= ENDING LOCATION OF FIRST NAME
C---                LOC(3)= BEGINNING LOCATION OF LAST NAME
C---                LOC(4)= ENDING LOCATION OF LAST NAME
C---                LOC(5)= BEGINNING LOCATION OF JR, SR, ETC(IF ANY)
C---                LOC(6)= ENDING LOCATION OF SUFFIX JR, SR, ETC(IF ANY)
C---      ENDING: STORES A . IF NEEDED WITH SUFFIX AND NOT ALREADY SHOWN
      DIMENSION LOC(6)
      CHARACTER*20 ARRAY(10,2) , NAME, NTEMP
      CHARACTER ENDING*1
      LR = 5
      LW = 6

      DO 10 I= 1, 10
C---              --- READ NAME(LAST NAME FIRST) AND CHANGES NEEDED
      READ(LR,'(2A)') (ARRAY(I,J),J=1,2)
C---              --- FIND 6 VALUES FOR LOC PLUS VALUE FOR ENDING
      CALL NAMLOC(ARRAY(I,1),LOC,ENDING,I-8,LW)
C---              --- CONCATENATE FIRST AND LAST NAME
      NTEMP=ARRAY(I,1)(LOC(1):LOC(2))//' '//
     1      ARRAY(I,1)(LOC(3):LOC(4))
C---              --- COMPUTE LENGTH OF STRING STORED IN NTEMP
      LNT = LOC(2) - LOC(1) + LOC(4) - LOC(3) + 3
C---              --- STORE NTEMP INTO NAME FOR OUTPUT IF NO SUFFIX
      NAME=NTEMP
C---              --- CONCATENATE SUFFIX AND ENDING(IF ANY) TO NAME
      IF(LOC(6).NE.0) NAME= NTEMP(1:LNT)//', '//
     1                ARRAY(I,1)(LOC(5):LOC(6))//ENDING
      WRITE(LW,'(3(3X,A20))') ARRAY(I,1),ARRAY(I,2),NAME

C---              --- BLANK-OUT NAME AND NTEMP FOR NEXT NAME PROCESS
      DO 9 J=1,20
        NTEMP(J:J) = ' '
        NAME(J:J) = ' '
9     CONTINUE

10 CONTINUE

      STOP
      END
```

LISTING 14-15 List of program CHGNAM

the character string sought for is longer than the character string in which the search is to be conducted, the length counter is established to show automatically that the string cannot be found.

In addition, the search can be performed within any specified limits. This makes it possible to write a small subroutine to find all occurrences of a particular substring within a single given string. Inclusion of the print control is often useful, particularly when problems are encountered in debugging a larger complex of programs that use this subroutine. Note that the subroutine CHGNAM can be used to search in any column of any array and therefore provides great power and flexibility. Because variables SAMPLE and SOUGHT can be represented by any subscripted array elements, flexibility of this program is essentially unlimited.

```
HENRY, JOHN D. III       1 COMMA, INITIAL W/.     JOHN D. HENRY, III
HOLLY BOB J. K., JR      NEED . ON JR, NO,        BOB J. K. HOLLY, JR.
HSU.TU WU SR             NO COMMA, NO .           WU HSU.TU, SR.
HITE   ,   TOM   SR.     EXTRA BLANKS             TOM HITE, SR.
LURTZ    ,J.K.,  III     2, EXTRA BLANKS          J.K. LURTZ, III
FRY,JORGE T. ,JR.        EXTRA SPC BEFORE JR.     JORGE T. FRY, JR.
JON, JOHN G.,II          3 NEARLY SAME:           JOHN G. JON, II
JON, JOHN V., II            BETTEN SPACE          JOHN V. JON, II


***CHARACTERS JR, _ SOUGHT IN SAMPLE JON, JOHN T,     II  NOT FOUND


***CHARACTERS SR. _ SOUGHT IN SAMPLE JON, JOHN T,     II  NOT FOUND


***CHARACTERS III _ SOUGHT IN SAMPLE JON, JOHN T,     II  NOT FOUND
JON, JOHN T,     II
12345673901234567890123456789012345567890
LOC(1 THRU 6)=    6  11   1   3  18  19

  JON, JOHN T,     II      TOO MUCH SPACE        JOHN T JON, II

   _ FOUND IN LOCATIONS 11 THRU 11 WITHIN TROUBLE, J. Q.
WHICH IS FOUND BETWEEN POSITIONS  3 AND 20 OF SAMPLE   TROUBLE, J. Q.


,  _ FOUND IN LOCATIONS 10 THRU 10 WITHIN TROUBLE, J. Q.
WHICH IS FOUND BETWEEN POSITIONS  3 AND 20 OF SAMPLE   TROUBLE, J. Q.


***CHARACTERS JR, _ SOUGHT IN SAMPLE   TROUBLE, J. Q.     NOT FOUND


***CHARACTERS SR. _ SOUGHT IN SAMPLE   TROUBLE, J. Q.     NOT FOUND


***CHARACTERS III _ SOUGHT IN SAMPLE   TROUBLE, J. Q.     NOT FOUND


***CHARACTERS II  _ SOUGHT IN SAMPLE   TROUBLE, J. Q.     NOT FOUND


***CHARACTERS JR  _ SOUGHT IN SAMPLE   TROUBLE, J. Q.     NOT FOUND


***CHARACTERS SR  _ SOUGHT IN SAMPLE   TROUBLE, J. Q.     NOT FOUND
  TROUBLE, J. Q.
12345678901234567890123456789012345567890
LOC(1 THRU 6)=   12  16   3   9   0   0

  TROUBLE, J. Q.       LEADING BLANK ERROR    J. Q. TROUBLE
```

LISTING 14-16 Typical output from program CHGNAM

14-7 SEGMENTING FOR EASE AND FLEXIBILITY

Earlier it was stated that efficient and effective use of subroutines saves both work and time. It seems appropriate to discuss such comments in the light of the developments presented in this chapter. In addition, advantages of subroutines will be amplified and discussed in terms of a systems approach.

14-7.1 Saving Time

In the context of computer programming, saving time means saving money. Two types of time exist: clock time and calendar time. Clock time refers to the actual number of hours required to complete a particular project. Calendar time refers to the overall period of time needed to complete a project in terms of real, continuous time. For example, the clock time required to complete a particular program might be 20 hours. Because of the creative nature of the endeavor, however, the job might well take 3 weeks of calendar time. That is, 20 consecutive hours would not suffice because a person is often not capable of doing creative work on such a consistent basis. It is possible that the job could not even be completed at the rate of 4 hours a day for 5 days. Calendar time can be shortened or lengthened by the number and quality of people used on the project, whereas clock time is relatively fixed.

(a) *Segmenting to Save Clock Time*. The curve in Figure 14–5 represents a possible relationship between the time required to write a program and its length. This curve was constructed by assuming that the length of time necessary to complete a correctly working program increases as the square of program length, which is probably a conservative estimate. That is, the amount of time needed to write a program probably increases faster than the square of program length.

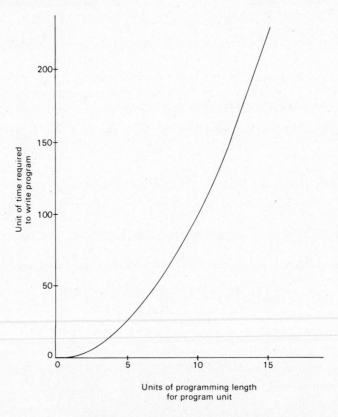

FIGURE 14–5 Time versus program length

As an illustration, consider a specific single program that is 15 units long. Using Figure 14–5, development of such a program would require 225 units of time. This program of 15 units could be segmented into three separate parts, each part approximately 5 units long. As seen in this chapter, it would seem reasonable to test each part by a dummy program which could increase the length of time needed for each segment by 20%. Each 5-unit segment would then require the time of a 6-unit segment. From Figure 14–5, each 6-unit segment would require 36 units of time. To complete all three segments would take 3×36 units, or 108 total units of time.

If Figure 14–5 is correct, the program can be written in less than half the time by segmenting it into three parts, even when 20% is added to the development length of each segment to permit independent testing.

Although the values used are hypothetical, the results are quite realistic. For this reason, many installations set the optimum length for any program or subprogram at no more than 50 FORTRAN statements. Other commonly applied rules of thumb state that "a program must be completely listed on only one page of high speed printer output", or that a program must be concerned with only one primary subject. Although these rules are not inviolable, the conclusion is that a program should be broken into segments when it becomes longer than about 50 FORTRAN statements. By so doing, many hours of valuable human time can be saved.

(b) *Segmenting for Calendar Time.* When a number of programmers work together as a team, segmenting programs is essentially mandatory. By segmenting, individual programmers can work in parallel and overall calendar time for obtaining a successful program can be contained within reasonable bounds. Such efforts, of course, require very careful planning and probably need top-down programming by the team leader(s). In engineering and scientific applications, careful analysis is also required to determine which segments need to be tested in a bottom-up fashion before being added to the entire program complex. Top-down and bottom-up programming are discussed later in this section.

(c) *Segmenting for Visualization.* Even if time were no object and money was bountiful, it would still be necessary to segment programs, because no single human being has the mental capacity to visualize a very large complex program in its entirety. In fact, limitation of modules to about 50 FORTRAN statements is also predicated upon the amount of program that most people can "see" at any given time. Even if you can see a larger program, others who use your work need to be considered.

Segmenting should take place during early developmental stages, often in human-oriented (gross) flow diagrams. During this initial stage, it is important to pinpoint areas that contain potential hazards or programming anomalies and to note locations that require further study. Time spent at this stage is almost always time well spent. Segmenting, conscientiously used, can truly optimize your programming capabilities and save time.

14–7.2 Systems Approach

The word *systems* has a multitude of definitions. As used here, a systems approach embodies two concepts.

1. Any programming unit must be viewed in a holistic manner, relating individual projects, problems, and programs to an overall plan, preferably with an eye to the future.
2. Every program should be written to be an integral part of the overall plan, as envisioned for both present and future use.

The time, and consequently money, associated with programming can be classified into four mutually interelated activities.

1. Development time
2. Debugging time
3. Maintenance-updating-revision time
4. Computer (machine) time

In general, either inadequate or excessive time usage in any of these four classifications has a significant impact on time usage in the others. In a sense, these time related interconnections have been the catalyst for wide-ranging discussions of top-down and bottom-up programming, as discussed in this section.

(a) *Not a New Program Every Time.* In the earliest days of computer programming, it was necessary to write a routine for finding the sine of a number within the program. Such activities are now completely routine, because of built-in intrinsic function subprograms. In the same way, many installations have greatly increased their efficiency and effectiveness by giving careful thought to the development of subroutines that can be used within many diverse programs. Figure 14-6 represents a typical solution space for a large component of engineering problems. One axis represents required mathematical formulations, one axis represents required analytical techniques, and one axis represents design requirements. Although difficult to adequately set up and carry through, such thinking does lead to very valuable results. The idea suggests that programs can be developed in a linear fashion along each of the three axes, typically in the form of subroutines. Combination of these subroutines results in solutions to a wide range of problems represented by the space between the three axes. Thus, using this organized

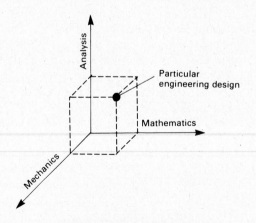

FIGURE 14-6 Solution space

technique, each new problem is solved by using existing modules and developing additional modules in a generalized way so that they can be used in still more problems. This approach contrasts drastically with the hit-and-miss methods of writing a special-purpose program for each particular problem as it is encountered. In the generalized formulation, each new module increases the capacity of the system to solve many more problems. Thus, development within such a systems context can actually provide exponential growth simply by planned linear development.

(b) *Top-Down Programming.* The ideas discussed in the previous paragraphs embody the concept of top-down programming. That is, the entire program complex is considered before any individual parts are contemplated. Top-down programming has proven to be extremely beneficial even in moderately sized program complexes involving about fifty subroutines.

This technique was recently used for a program to automatically design high-rise masonry shearwall buildings. Broad, major steps were first considered and organized into a reasonable sequence. Each of these broad areas was then considered in a little more detail and subsequently divided into smaller increments. At this stage, the type of data structure to be used throughout the program was considered. Each of these stages was documented in the form of gross human-oriented flow diagrams.

Once the overall pattern was mentally tested, each of the subareas was divided into groups of proposed subroutines. At this point, all of the subroutines were given names. Definition sheets that listed the arguments to be used within the subroutines, as well as the purpose of the subroutine itself, were established. The main program was written at this time to call the major subroutines. Dummy subroutines were utilized in the test program.

Dummy subroutines used the names of real subroutines, with complete argument lists, but the dummy subroutines performed only a limited and artificial purpose. Some of these subroutines simply contained an output message such as, "You are now in subroutine NAME." Other dummy subroutines returned preconceived values that were established in the subroutine as constants (rather than by computations). This process insured that the overall program would fit together and that the data structure was adequate for the problem.

A number of the subroutines were written and tested directly within the program because the program automatically generated the large quantities of data that were necessary for such testing. Some of the subroutines, however, were logically quite complex and needed a great deal of thorough testing before they could be used with confidence in the overall program. (This is the concept of bottom-up programming, which will be discussed in the next section.)

In this top-down approach, a number of errors that would have been extremely difficult to correct during the programming process were uncovered. In general, every subroutine was represented by a human-oriented flow diagram and was cross-checked by an individual other than the one who wrote it. Only when complete agreement was obtained on human-oriented flow diagrams were the machine-oriented flow diagrams processed. These went through a similar checking process before the coding was punched (directly from the flow diagrams). Thus the total program was conceived and developed by a top-down process using a holistic view of the entire problem throughout. For reasons that are discussed in the next section, however, certain areas of the program received thorough bottom-up testing before being included in the overall program complex.

(c) *Bottom-Up Programming.* To start with details and merge them into a whole is a bottom-up approach. The pitfalls of generalized bottom-up programming are legion. Programs written with such a myopic view usually do not contain the necessary modularity and flexibility required for efficient, effective programming in a systems context. Starting the program in a bottom-up mode is not recommended except in cases where development of theory is closely intertwined with program development. In such cases, there may be no other way to proceed except by such trial and error.

In scientific and engineering computer programming complexes, on the other hand, it is often necessary to do bottom-up programming for a limited number of particular segments that are discovered to be troublesome during the top-down programming development. This seems to be true for two primary reasons.

First, it is extremely time consuming and costly to thoroughly proof a program containing multiple paths when everything is done solely in the top-down programming mode. For example, it is almost impossible to adequately test four subroutines, each with ten separate logical paths. Conversely, it is relatively easy to test each of the subroutines to insure that it is correct. Such subroutines can then be used with confidence in the program and can be maintained with much less expenditure of money and time.

A second reason for bottom-up programming is for development of technically complex subroutines. Some crucial subroutines in a major programming effort may take nearly as much time to program as the rest of the project together. In such cases, it is valid to use a dummy test program to develop and verify these highly complex and technical subroutines.

(d) *Summary.* Although there is considerable disagreement, many top programmers champion the holistic view of top-down program development. The primary difficulty with such an approach is an apparently very slow start. Experience indicates, however, that this slow start almost always results in a more quick and satisfactory solution.

Bottom-up programming, however, is also a very viable component of program development, particularly in programs that are logically complex or technically difficult.

In all cases, none of these techniques would be viable approaches without the tremendous advantage supplied by the use of subroutines. In fact, it has been stated that programs written without subroutines are merely toys.

14-8 EXERCISES

1. Listing 14–17 shows eight sets of (a) a main program and (b) a subroutine (2 routines for sets d and h). Assume that the argument lists defined within the subroutine definitions are correct. Make necessary adjustments in calling program(s) to insure that argument lists match.

2. Listing 14–18 illustrates five sets of (a) a main program and (b) appropriate subroutine(s) using adjustable dimensioning. Assume that the main programs are correct—except for establishing correct array dimensions by variables that may need corrections—and adjust the subroutines to insure that argument lists match. (*Note*: This may require adjustment of DIMENSION statements within subroutines.)

3. If you were to prepare a scaling subroutine for a set of data (refer to Section 3–8.1, Problem 7, and Section 14–5).
   (a) What basis would you use for establishing a scale?
   (b) What arguments would you pass to a plot subprogram?

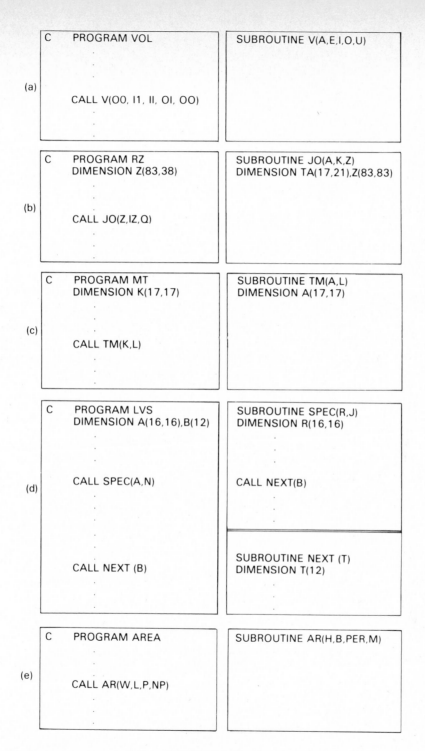

(a)
```
C       PROGRAM VOL                        SUBROUTINE V(A,E,I,O,U)
        .
        .
        CALL V(OO, I1, II, OI, OO)
        .
        .
```

(b)
```
C       PROGRAM RZ                         SUBROUTINE JO(A,K,Z)
        DIMENSION Z(83,38)                 DIMENSION TA(17,21),Z(83,83)
        .
        .
        CALL JO(Z,IZ,Q)
        .
```

(c)
```
C       PROGRAM MT                         SUBROUTINE TM(A,L)
        DIMENSION K(17,17)                 DIMENSION A(17,17)
        .
        .
        .
        CALL TM(K,L)
        .
        .
```

(d)
```
C       PROGRAM LVS                        SUBROUTINE SPEC(R,J)
        DIMENSION A(16,16),B(12)           DIMENSION R(16,16)
        .                                  .
        .                                  .
        CALL SPEC(A,N)                     CALL NEXT(B)
        .                                  .
        .                                  .
        .
        .                                  SUBROUTINE NEXT (T)
        CALL NEXT (B)                      DIMENSION T(12)
        .                                  .
        .
```

(e)
```
C       PROGRAM AREA                       SUBROUTINE AR(H,B,PER,M)
        .
        .
        CALL AR(W,L,P,NP)
        .
        .
```

LISTING 14–17

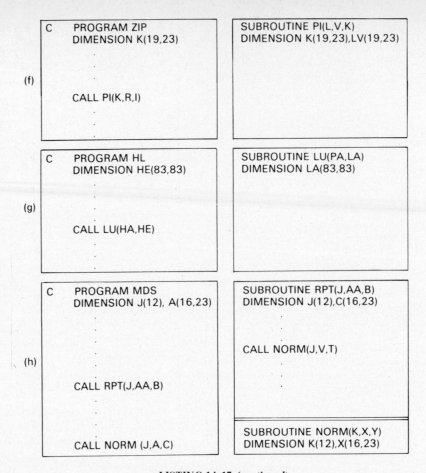

```
C    PROGRAM ZIP                    SUBROUTINE PI(L,V,K)
     DIMENSION K(19,23)             DIMENSION K(19,23),LV(19,23)

(f)
     CALL PI(K,R,I)
```

```
C    PROGRAM HL                     SUBROUTINE LU(PA,LA)
     DIMENSION HE(83,83)            DIMENSION LA(83,83)

(g)
     CALL LU(HA,HE)
```

```
C    PROGRAM MDS                    SUBROUTINE RPT(J,AA,B)
     DIMENSION J(12), A(16,23)      DIMENSION J(12),C(16,23)


                                    CALL NORM(J,V,T)
(h)

     CALL RPT(J,AA,B)

                                    SUBROUTINE NORM(K,X,Y)
     CALL NORM (J,A,C)              DIMENSION K(12),X(16,23)
```

LISTING 14–17 *(continued)*

4. Section 14–6 discusses a program that rearranges names according to common practice. The author, on the other hand, goes against convention and does not use a comma between Hill and Jr. Could you adjust the program to take care of such an anomaly? Can you think of other exceptions to common practice as it applies to names? How would you adjust the program for them?

5. In installations where text editing is widely used, modules are developed for general use. The following module is used to fill any desired portion of a string with a desired character.

```
SUBROUTINE FILL (C, STRING)
CHARACTER *1 C
CHARACTER *(*) STRING

DO 100 I = 1, LEN (STRING)
    STRING (I:I) = C
100 CONTINUE

RETURN
END
```

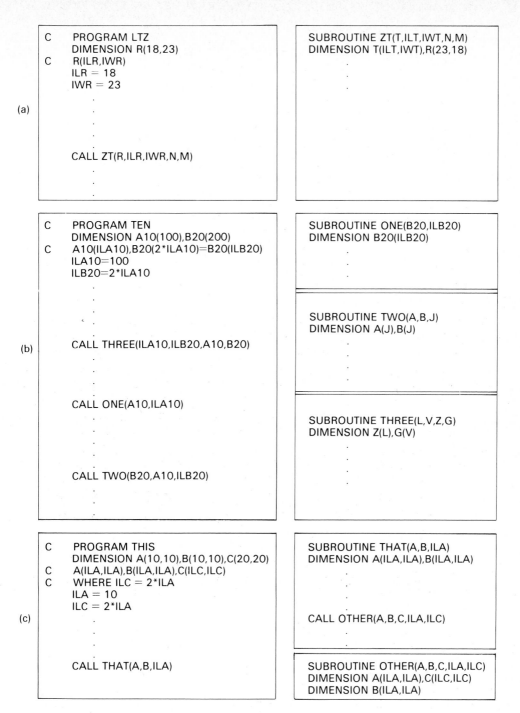

(a)

```
C     PROGRAM LTZ
      DIMENSION R(18,23)
C     R(ILR,IWR)
      ILR = 18
      IWR = 23
        .
        .
        .
      CALL ZT(R,ILR,IWR,N,M)
        .
        .
```

```
      SUBROUTINE ZT(T,ILT,IWT,N,M)
      DIMENSION T(ILT,IWT),R(23,18)
        .
        .
        .
```

(b)

```
C     PROGRAM TEN
      DIMENSION A10(100),B20(200)
C     A10(ILA10),B20(2*ILA10)=B20(ILB20)
      ILA10=100
      ILB20=2*ILA10
        .
        .
        .
      CALL THREE(ILA10,ILB20,A10,B20)
        .
        .
      CALL ONE(A10,ILA10)
        .
        .
        .
      CALL TWO(B20,A10,ILB20)
        .
        .
```

```
      SUBROUTINE ONE(B20,ILB20)
      DIMENSION B20(ILB20)
        .
        .
        .
```

```
      SUBROUTINE TWO(A,B,J)
      DIMENSION A(J),B(J)
        .
        .
```

```
      SUBROUTINE THREE(L,V,Z,G)
      DIMENSION Z(L),G(V)
        .
        .
        .
```

(c)

```
C     PROGRAM THIS
      DIMENSION A(10,10),B(10,10),C(20,20)
C     A(ILA,ILA),B(ILA,ILA),C(ILC,ILC)
C     WHERE ILC = 2*ILA
      ILA = 10
      ILC = 2*ILA
        .
        .
        .
      CALL THAT(A,B,ILA)
```

```
      SUBROUTINE THAT(A,B,ILA)
      DIMENSION A(ILA,ILA),B(ILA,ILA)
        .
        .
        .
      CALL OTHER(A,B,C,ILA,ILC)
        .
```

```
      SUBROUTINE OTHER(A,B,C,ILA,ILC)
      DIMENSION A(ILA,ILA),C(ILC,ILC)
      DIMENSION B(ILA,ILA)
```

LISTING 14-18

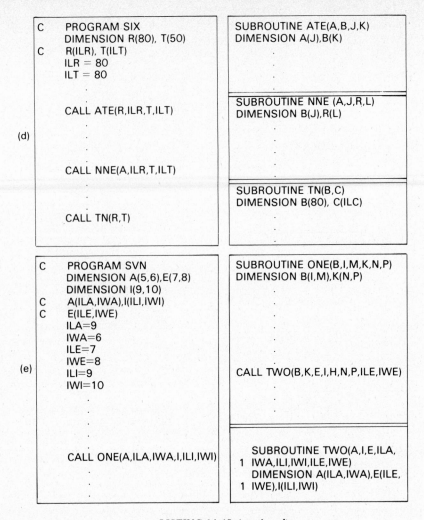

(d)

```
C      PROGRAM SIX
       DIMENSION R(80), T(50)
C      R(ILR), T(ILT)
       ILR = 80
       ILT = 80
       .
       .
       CALL ATE(R,ILR,T,ILT)
       .
       .
       .
       CALL NNE(A,ILR,T,ILT)
       .
       .
       .
       CALL TN(R,T)
```

```
       SUBROUTINE ATE(A,B,J,K)
       DIMENSION A(J),B(K)
          .
          .
          .
          .
```

```
       SUBROUTINE NNE (A,J,R,L)
       DIMENSION B(J),R(L)
          .
          .
          .
          .
```

```
       SUBROUTINE TN(B,C)
       DIMENSION B(80), C(ILC)
          .
```

(e)

```
C      PROGRAM SVN
       DIMENSION A(5,6),E(7,8)
       DIMENSION I(9,10)
C      A(ILA,IWA),I(ILI,IWI)
C      E(ILE,IWE)
       ILA=9
       IWA=6
       ILE=7
       IWE=8
       ILI=9
       IWI=10
       .
       .
       .
       .
       .
       CALL ONE(A,ILA,IWA,I,ILI,IWI)
       .
       .
```

```
       SUBROUTINE ONE(B,I,M,K,N,P)
       DIMENSION B(I,M),K(N,P)
          .
          .
          .
          .
          .
          .
       CALL TWO(B,K,E,I,H,N,P,ILE,IWE)
          .
          .
```

```
       SUBROUTINE TWO(A,I,E,ILA,
      1 IWA,ILI,IWI,ILE,IWE)
       DIMENSION A(ILA,IWA),E(ILE,
      1 IWE),I(ILI,IWI)
```

LISTING 14–18 *(continued)*

Show the contents of DOLLAR with a declared length of 10 after each of the following calls.

(a)   CALL FILL ('A', DOLLAR)

(b)   CALL FILL ('B', DOLLAR (2:2))

(c)   K = 7
      CALL FILL ('C', DOLLAR (K:))

(d)   M = 4
      CALL FILL ('$', DOLLAR (M:K–1))

Chapter **15**

Functions

FORTRAN 77 provides three types of functions: intrinsic functions, statement functions, and external functions (function subprograms). Although intrinsic functions were introduced in Chapter 4, additional considerations are discussed in this chapter. Intrinsic functions differ from the other two types because they are defined by the processor and are therefore available for any FORTRAN program. By contrast, function statements and external functions must be written by the user. Both intrinsic and external functions can be used with any program unit of an executable program, but function statements can be used only in the program unit in which they are defined.

15–1 REFERENCING A FUNCTION

All functions are referenced in an identical manner: the function name, followed by its actual arguments separated by commas and enclosed in parentheses. For instance, a function called HAPPY could be used in any of the following typical ways:

$$B = HAPPY(A,B,I,J)$$
$$C = R*HAPPY(R,R,KT,NB)/ST$$
$$Q = HAPPY(C,D,N,N)*HAPPY(D,C,M,M)$$

Intrinsic function names are global to FORTRAN, external functions (function subprograms) are global to an executable program, and statement functions are local entities within a program unit. Thus the name of an external function cannot be used as the symbolic name of any other entity within an executable program and use of the name of a function statement is restricted to the program unit defining it.

Actual arguments used to reference a function should agree in meaning, type, and size with dummy arguments, but need not agree in symbolic name.

Table 15–1 Summary of Intrinsic Functions

Classification of arguments

1. Actual arguments may be any expressions which agree in order, number and type with the dummy arguments shown in this table (except a character expression involving concatenation of an operand whose length specification is an asterisk in parentheses unless the operand is the symbolic name of a constant).

2. No mixed modes are allowed for arguments of an intrinsic function.

3. Dummy arguments are symbolized in this table as:

i integer	rd real or double precision
r real	ird integer, real, or double precision
d double precision	rdc real, double precision, or complex
c complex	$irdc$ integer, real, double precision, or complex
ch character	

Operation	Form of Intrinsic Function			Definitions, Notes, and Comments
	Subset	Full Language		
		Generic†	Specific*	
Type conversion				
to integer	INT(r)	INT($irdc$)		IFIX(r) and IDINT(d) not recommended
to real	REAL(i)	REAL($irdc$)		FLOAT(i) and SNGL(d) not recommended
to double precision		DBLE($irdc$)		converts real part of complex only
to complex		CMPLX($irdc$)		real part is REAL(ird), imaginary part is zero CMPLX(c) is c
		CMPLX(ird_1, ird_2)		real part is REAL(ird_1), imaginary part is REAL(ird_2) both arguments must be of the same type.
to integer	ICHAR(ch)	ICHAR(ch)		value of integer result is based on the position of the character in the processor collating sequence starting with position zero.
to character		CHAR(i)		function supplies character in ith position of collating sequence of processor; $0 \leq i \leq n-1$, where n = characters in collating sequence.

Adjusting values				
to nearest integer	NINT(r)	NINT(rd)	IDNINT(d)	if $rd \geq 0$ yields INT ($rd + 0.5$) if $rd < 0$ yields INT ($rd - 0.5$)
to nearest whole number	ANINT(r)	ANINT(rd)	DNINT(d)	if $rd \geq 0$ yields REAL (INT($r + 0.5$)) or DBLE(INT($d + 0.5$)) if $rd < 0$ yields REAL (INT($r - 0.5$)) or DBLE(INT($d-0.5$))
to truncated	AINT(r)	AINT(rd)	DINT(d)	yields REAL (INT(r)) or DBLE(INT(d))
Special Mathematics				
absolute value	IABS(i) ABS(r)	ABS($irdc$)	IABS(i) or DABS(d)	yields absolute value of ird yields real
			CABS(c)	$\sqrt{(\text{real part})^2 + (\text{imaginary part})^2}$ for c
remaindering	MOD(i,i_2) AMOD(r_1, r_2)	MOD(ird_1, ird_2)	AMOD(r_1, r_2) DMOD(d_1, d_2)	yields $ird_1 - \text{INT}(ird_1/ird_2) * ird_2$; undefined if $ird_2 = 0$
transfer of sign	ISIGN(i, i_2) SIGN(r_1, r_2)	SIGN(ird_1, ird_2)	ISIGN(i, i_2) DSIGN(d_1, d_2)	if $ird_2 \geq 0$ yields $|ird_1|$ if $ird_2 < 0$ yields $-|ird_1|$ if $ird_1 = 0$, no sign is transferred
positive difference	IDIM(i_1,i_2) DIM(r_1,r_2)	DIM(ird_1, ird_2)	IDIM(i_1, i_2) DDIM(d_1, d_2)	if $ird_1 > ird_2$ yields $ird_1 - ird_2$ if $ird_1 \leq ird_2$ yields zero
double precision product			DPROD(r_1, r_2)	yields double precision product of two reals
imaginary part			AIMAG(c)	yields real result as imaginary part of c
complex conjugate			CONJG(c)	yields a–bi from $c = a + bi$ or a + bi from a–bi
Selecting values				
largest value	MAX0($i, i_2, \ldots$)	MAX($ird_1, ird_2, \ldots$)	MAX0($i, i_2, \ldots$)	yields largest value from ird_1, $ird_2, \ldots$
	AMAX1($r, r_2, \ldots$)	AMAX1($r_1, r_2, \ldots$)	AMAX1($r_1, r_2, \ldots$)	use REAL(MAX($i, i_2, \ldots$)) for AMAX0($i, i_2, \ldots$)
			DMAX1($d_1, d_2, \ldots$)	use INT(MAX($r_1, r_2, \ldots$)) for MAXI ($r_1, r_2, \ldots$)
smallest value	MINO($i_1,i_2, \ldots$)	MIN($ird_1, ird_2, \ldots$)	MINO($i_1, i_2, \ldots$)	yields smallest value from ird_1, $ird_2, \ldots$

Section 15-2 Intrinsic Functions

Table 15-1 (continued)

Operation	Form of Intrinsic Function			Definitions, Notes, and Comments
	Subset	Generic†	Full Language Specific*	
	AMIN1($r_1, r_2, \ldots$)		AMIN1($r_1, r_2, \ldots$) DMIN1($d_1, d_2, \ldots$)	use REAL(MIN($i_1, i_2, \ldots$)) for AMINO($i_1, i_2, \ldots$) use INT(MIN($r_1, r_2, \ldots$)) for MIN1($r_1, r_2, \ldots$)
Mathematical functions				
square root	SQRT(r)	SQRT(rdc)	DSQRT(d) CSQRT(c)	yields $\sqrt{rd}$; rd must be ≥ 0. yield principal value of $\sqrt{c}$ with real part ≥ 0; if real part $= 0$ then imaginary part ≥ 0.
exponential	EXP(r)	EXP(rdc)	DEXP(d) or CEXP(c)	yields e^{rdc}
natural logarithm	ALOG(r)	LOG(rdc)	ALOG(r) or DLOG(d) CLOG(c)	yields $\log_e(rd)$; rd must be > 0. yields $\log_e(c)$; c must not be (0., 0.); imaginary part lies between $-\pi$ and π, being π only when real part of argument < 0 and imaginary part of argument $= 0$.
common logarithm	ALOG10(r)	LOG10(rd)	ALOG10(r) DLOG10(d)	yields $\log_{10}(rd)$; rd must be > 0.
sine	SIN(r)	SIN(rdc)	DSIN(d) or CSIN(c)	yields sine for any argument (radian, not degrees)
cosine	COS(r)	COS(rdc)	DCOS(d) or CCOS(c)	yields cosine for any radian argument
tangent	TAN(r)	TAN(rd)	DTAN(d)	yields tangent for any radian argument
arc sine	ASIN(r)	ASIN(rd)	DASIN(d)	yields arc sine with values from $-\pi/2$ through $\pi/2$ for $|rd| \leq 1$.
arc cosine	ACOS(r)	ACOS(rd)	DACOS(d)	yields arc cosine with values from 0 through π for $|rd| \leq 1$.
arc tangent	ATAN(r)	ATAN(rd)	DATAN(d)	yields arc tangent with values from $-\pi/2$ through $\pi/2$

				yields:
	ATAN2(r_1, r_2)	ATAN2(rd_1, rd_2)	DATAN2(d_1, d_2)	$0 < \text{ATAN2}(rd_1, rd_2) \leq \pi$ if $rd_1 > 0$. ATAN2$(0., rd_2) = 0$. if $rd_1 = 0$. and $rd_2 > 0$. ATAN2$(0., rd_2) = \pi$ if $rd_1 = 0$. and $rd_2 < 0$. $-\pi \leq \text{ATAN2}(rd_1, rd_2) < 0$. if $rd_1 < 0$. $\lvert \text{ATAN2}(rd_1, 0.) \rvert = \pi/2$ if $rd_2 = 0$. ATAN2$(0., 0.)$ is undefined.
hyperbolic sine	SINH(r)	SINH(rd)	DSINH(d)	yields hyperbolic sine of rd
hyperbolic cosine	COSH(r)	COSH(rd)	DCOSH(d)	yields hyperbolic cosine of rd
hyperbolic tangent	TANH(r)	TANH(rd)	DTANH(d)	yields hyperbolic tangent of rd
Character functions				
length			LEN(ch)	yields integer stating number of characters in ch
index of substring			INDEX(ch_1, ch_2)	yields integer stating starting position of substring ch_2 in string ch_1; first occasion only. If ch_2 not within ch_1 or if LEN(ch_1) < LEN(ch_2), yields 0
Lexical				
greater than or equal			LGE(ch_1, ch_2)	$ch_1 \geq ch_2$ yields .TRUE.
greater than			LGT(ch_1, ch_2)	$ch_1 > ch_2$ yields .TRUE.
less than or equal			LLE(ch_1, ch_2)	$ch_1 \leq ch_2$ yields .TRUE.
less than			LLT(ch_1, ch_2)	$ch_1 < ch_2$ yields .TRUE. otherwise, .FALSE.; all for collating sequence of American National Standard Code for Information Interchange, ANSI X3,4–1977 (ASCII).

*Only a specific intrinsic function name may be used as an actual argument when the argument is an intrinsic function. In all other cases, the generic name is preferred.

†For generic intrinsic functions, the type of the result (except for type conversion, adjusting values to nearest integer and the absolute value of a complex argument) is the same as the type of the argument.

15-2 INTRINSIC FUNCTIONS

A summary of the intrinsic functions is presented in Table 15-1.

Subset FORTRAN 77 supplies intrinsic functions with specific names that give type. Full Language FORTRAN also supplies intrinsic functions by generic names. For instance, the specific remaindering function for two integer arguments is MOD(NUMB1, NUMB2), but for two real arguments, MOD is preceded by an A—AMOD(FIRST, SECOND). In the Full Language, MOD is a generic function that receives its type from the type of its arguments. Thus MOD(NUMB1,NUMB2) produces an integer result, while MOD(FIRST, SECOND) produces a real result.

Arguments of intrinsic functions must agree in type. Except for the generic functions NINT, ABS (when used with a complex argument), INT, and REAL, results of generic functions have the same type as the arguments. A type statement is not sufficient to remove generic properties from a generic intrinsic function.

Local processors may supply additional, nonstandard intrinsic functions. To emphasize that such functions are not standard, they should be declared in an INTRINSIC statement. In addition, on such processors, all external functions should be declared in an EXTERNAL statement. Use of such statements provides appropriate and helpful error messages if the program is run with another processor.

To utilize EXTERNAL and INTRINSIC statements, follow the keyword by the name of the procedure being classified:

        EXTERNAL AREA, VOL
        INTRINSIC COSINH, COTH

The meanings of symbolic names for intrinsic functions can also be changed by EXTERNAL statements. For example, in a recently developed FORTRAN program, clock time was extremely crucial. Therefore a new sine function EXTERNAL SIN, was written to increase computer speed. Then, each time the computer encountered an expression such as SIN(X), it used the sine function developed by the user rather than the intrinsic sine function normally provided by the processor.

15-3 FUNCTION SUBPROGRAMS (EXTERNAL FUNCTION)

A function subprogram is much like a subroutine, but it returns only a single answer, and is used in the same manner as an intrinsic (built-in) function such as sine or cosine. If a set of computations that would otherwise require a subroutine returns only one answer, then an external function is usually preferable. It differs from a subroutine in only two ways:

1. The first line of an external function has the form FUNCTION NAME(list).
2. The value computed by the function subprogram must be set into NAME within the subprogram itself. For this reason, NAME must be of the correct type. In order to obtain its value, the function's name must occur left of an equal sign at least once within the subprogram; it may occur left on an equal sign any number of times. NAME must be the storage location for a simple variable, not an array.

    The type of a function subprogram must be specified either by default (first letter is I through N for integer or other than I through N for real), implicitly, by an EXPLICIT statement, or by a type statement preceding the FUNCTION statement:

> INTEGER FUNCTION THEONE(IN, LIN, OUT, LOUT)
> REAL FUNCTION POLYA(XY, ILXY, N, M)
> CHARACTER * 10 FUNCTION FILTER (NAME, PHONE, ADDR)

Type may be specified either internal to or external to the function subprogram. The type for a function, however, must be specified only once.

15-3.1 Formulating Function Subprogram AREA2

Function subprogram AREA2 computes the area of any irregular,multi-sided polygon. It is very useful in such situations as highway cut and fill, geological and mining surveys, mapping, or approximate integration. The basic equation for finding the area is

$$A = \frac{1}{2} \sum_{1}^{n} y_i(x_{i-1} - x_{i+1})$$

where:

n is the number of sides of polygon, and
x and y represent the x – and y – coordinates of polygon corners, numbered in counterclockwise order.

A simple example for a polygon with five sides is shown in Figure 15–1. Each corner is represented by a point P, with coordinates x and y. The positive values of x and y are to the right along the horizontal axis and upward along the vertical axis, respectively. The coordinates of each vertex are denoted both by symbols and by the corresponding numerical values. Thus P_1 has symbolic coordinates (x_1, y_1) corresponding to numerical coordinates (2,4).

The area is computed beneath the sketch of the polygon. The first line represents the summation in expanded form, using symbolic notation. The respective values of i are substituted in this equation on the second line; for example, y_2 ($i = 2$) gives $y_i(x_{i-1} - x_{i+1}) = y_2(x_{2-1} - x_{2+1})$, or $y_2(x_1 - x_3)$. One reason for examining a simple example is to look for irregularities. Two values of x are underscored in the second line to indicate such special situations. When $i = 1$, the subscript $i - 1$ yields zero. But no coordinate has a subscript of zero. Instead, this zero actually indicates the "last" position, which in this case is 5. The last x has a subscript of $5 + 1$, which yields 6. But for this example, the maximum n is 5. Six, therefore, signifies that the entire perimeter has been traversed and that the proper subscript is the first one, or x_1. In the third line of the equation, numerical values are substituted for the coordinates directly from the sketch. The equation is then simplified to obtain the final area for the polygon, 41.5.

15-3.2 Programming Function Subprogram AREA2

The layout of calculations shown in Figure 15–1 suggests a solution for the problem. The first and last terms must be taken into account:

> AREA2 = AREA2 + XY(1,2)*(XY(N,1)−XY(2,1))
> + XY(N,2)*(XY(N−1,1)−(XY(1,1))

This represents y ("upper" x − "lower" x). That is, y is stored in Column 2 of array XY and x is stored in Column 1 of array XY.

Once this computation has been performed, a DO-loop can be used for all intermediate values, going from 2 to one less than the number of vertices of the polygon. Symbolically, we have

$$\text{Area} = \text{Area} + y_i\,(x_{i-1} - x_{i+1})$$

as i goes from 2 to one less than the maximum number of vertices, or

$$\text{AREA2} = \text{AREA2} + \text{XY}(1,2)*(\text{XY}(I-1,1)-\text{XY}(I+1,1))$$

Figure 15-2 shows a machine-oriented flow diagram for the function subprogram AREA2. Arguments and internal variables are defined in the definition sheet of Table 15-2.

Function subprogram AREA2 is coded in Listing 15-1. Although the comments are fairly detailed, many programmers would include information from the definition sheet in comment statements located just after the FUNCTION statement line. Although not advocated, the RETURN statement has been omitted and is automatically evoked by the END statement.

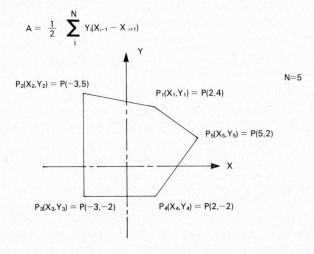

$$A = \frac{1}{2} \sum_i^N Y_i(X_{i-1} - X_{i+1})$$

$P_2(X_2,Y_2) = P(-3,5)$ $P_1(X_1,Y_1) = P(2,4)$ $N=5$

$P_5(X_5,Y_5) = P(5,2)$

$P_3(X_3,Y_3) = P(-3,-2)$ $P_4(X_4,Y_4) = P(2,-2)$

$$
\begin{aligned}
A ={}& \frac{1}{2}\ [Y_1(X_{1-1}-X_{1+1}) + Y_2(X_{2-1}-X_{2+1}) + Y_3(X_{3-1}-X_{3+1}) + Y_4(X_{4-1}-X_{4+1}) + Y_5(X_{5-1}-X_{5+1})] \\
={}& \frac{1}{2}\ [Y_1(\underline{X_5}-X_2) + Y_2(X_1-X_3) + Y_3(X_2-X_4) + Y_4(X_3-X_5) + Y_5(X_4-\underline{X_1})] \\
={}& \frac{1}{2}\ [4(5-(-3)) + 5(2-(-3)) + (-2)(-3-2) + (-2)(-3-5) + 2(2-2)] \\
={}& \frac{1}{2}\cdot\ [4(8) + 5(5) - 2(-5) - 2(-8) + 2(0)] \\
={}& 41\text{-}1/2
\end{aligned}
$$

FIGURE 15-1 Layout of computations for areas of polygons

Function Subprogram **AREA2 (XY, ILXY, IWXY, N, NP, LW)**

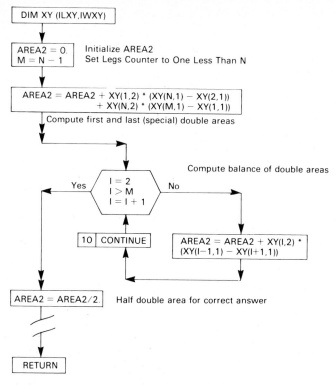

FIGURE 15–2 Machine-oriented flow diagram for
function subprogram AREA2

15–3.3 Testing Function Subprogram AREA2

Function subprogram AREA2 can be thoroughly tested by using a number of figures carefully drawn within the bounds of a 20 by 20 square (see Figure 15–3). These polygons have been selected to contain areas located in only one quadrant, in two quadrants, in three quandrants, and in all four quadrants (page 392).

To test the function subprogram, program TAREA2 was written to read in co-ordinates of these polygons and to add the areas obtained from each polygon. This test program is coded in Listing 15–2. Before each set of coordinates is read for any given polygon, the number of vertices is input along with the print control. If print control is zero (or blank), the program prints out only the final sum of an area. Output from this program using function subprogram AREA2 is shown in Listing 15–8. Because of a high print control value, coordinates of the first polygon, (located in the upper right corner of the square in Figure 15–3) are output along with the computed area, 12. For completeness, areas are output in both floating point and scientific notation (page 393).

Coordinates are also shown for the second area, and input/output is shown for a

Table 15-2 Definition Sheet for Subroutine AREA2

Function Subprogram AREA2 (XY, LXY, IWXY, N, NP)

Purpose:	Compute the area of a closed polygon of n sides from coordinates of the vertices, using:

$$A = \frac{1}{2} \sum_{i=1}^{n} y_i (x_{i-1} - x_{i+1}).$$

Descriptive Items:

XY (ILXY, IWXY)	Array storing coordinates in counterclockwise order. Column 1: $y_1, y_2, \ldots$ Column 2: $x_1, x_2, \ldots$
ILXY	Length of array XY
IWXY	Width of array XY = 2
N	Actual number of rows used in [XY], that is, the number of vertices = number of sides of polygon.
NP	Print Control ≤ 0 No output ≥ 1 Output area only ≥ 2 Output coordinates also
LW	Logical unit number for HSP output.
AREA2	Location to accumulate double area from summation, and eventually the actual area.
M	Auxiliary loop variable, $n - 1$, which allows looping for all except first and last elements by using I = 2, M.

counterclockwise order. The print control level was decreased for the remaining polygons so that only their areas were output.

The method used to test function subprogram AREA2 may be ideal, since every conceivable variation is tried, without trying every numerical value associated with each variation. In addition, the solutions are essentially machine tested, without need for other than mental calculations. The sum of the 13 areas is output as 400, which can be verified mentally for the 20 by 20 square into which all of the polygons fit. Of course, there could be two or more random errors that could lead to the correct results through compensating errors, although this is extremely unlikely. To insure that this is not the case, specific areas can also be spot checked mentally. For instance, Area 3 in the upper lefthand corner of the square 3×5, or 15, which verified by the output of Figure 15-3. Likewise, the triangle of Area 7 has a height of 3 and a base of 7, which corresponds to the area 10.5 shown on the output.

15-4 STATEMENT FUNCTION

A statement function must be located after any specification statements and before the first executable statement of the program unit. A statement function can be used only within the program unit in which it occurs. Its type may be specified with the FUNCTION statement.

If the entire computation required for a function subprogram can be done in a single FORTRAN statement, a statement function may be desirable. A statement function is used exactly as a function subprogram, but it is established by writing it in a form such as

$$PYT(A,B) = A**2 + B**2$$

where A and B are statement function dummy arguments.

The following represent typical uses of the preceding statement function.

$$Q = PYT(R,V) \qquad \text{meaning } Q = R^2 + V^2$$
$$S = R*PYT(A,C)/PYT(Q,A) \qquad \text{meaning } S = \frac{R(A^2 + C^2)}{(Q^2 + A^2)}$$

The general form of the function statement is

$$NAME(arg\ 1, arg\ 2, \ldots, arg\ N) = e$$

where NAME is the name of the statement function; arg 1, arg 2, . . ., arg N are dummy arguments used within expression e; and e is an expression. If one statement function is

```
      FUNCTION AREA2(XY,ILXY,IWXY,N,NP,LW)
      DIMENSION XY(ILXY,IWXY)
C---               ---INITIALIZE AREA2---
      AREA2 = 0.

C---               ---SET LOOP COUNTER TO---
C---               ---ONE LESS THAN N ---
      M=N-1

C---               ---COMPUTE FIRST AND LAST---
C---               ---(SPECIAL)DOUBLE AREAS---
      AREA2 = AREA2 + XY(1,2) * (XY(N,1)-XY(2,1))
     1                + XY(N,2) * (XY(M,1)-XY(1,1))

C---               ---COMPUTE BALANCE OF DBL AREAS---

      DO 10 I = 2,M
          AREA2 = AREA2 + XY(I,2) * (XY(I-1,1)-XY(I+1,1))
   10 CONTINUE

C---               ---HALF DBL AREA FOR CORRECT ANS---
      AREA2 = AREA2/2.
C---               ---OUTPUT IN ACCORDANCE WITH NP---
      IF(NP.GE.2) THEN
C---               ---OUTPUT X AND Y COORDINATES---
      WRITE(LW,1000)

      DO 20 I= 1,N
          WRITE(LW,1001) I,XY(I,1),XY(I,2)
   20     CONTINUE

      END IF

C---               ---OUTPUT AREA ONLY---
      IF(NP.GE.1) WRITE(LW,1002) AREA2,AREA2

 1000 FORMAT(///' COORDINATES: X        Y'//)
 1001 FORMAT( I10,2F7.2)
 1002 FORMAT(/' AREA =', F10.4 , E20.8)
      END
```

LISTING 15-1 Coding for function subprogram **AREA2**

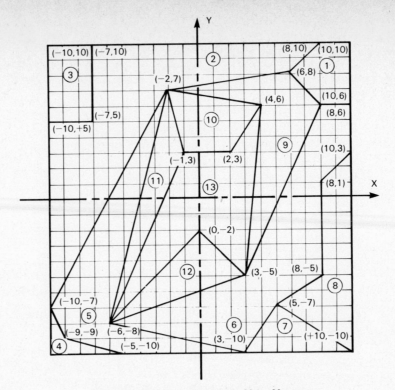

FIGURE 15-3 Test areas within 20 by 20 square

```
      PROGRAM TAREA2
C               --- ACCUMULATE SUM OF ARERAS OF POLYGONS ---
      DIMENSION POLY(20,2)
C---            ---POLY(ILPOLY,2):INSURE MATCH---
      DATA ILPOLY,LR,LW/20,5,6/
C---            ---INITIALIZE AND PROCEED---
      TSUM = 0.
      KNT = 0

C---            ---READ N AS NUMB COORD, NP PRINT CTRL---
   10 READ(LR,1000) N,NP
      IF(N.GT.0) THEN

C---            ---READ COORDINATES= X1,Y1,X2,Y2,X3,Y3...---
      READ(LR,1001)(POLY(I,1),POLY(I,2), I=1,N)
      KNT = KNT + 1

C---            ---SUM AREAS---
      TSUM = TSUM + AREA2(POLY,ILPOLY,2,N,NP,LW)

C---            ---CYCLE FOR NEW AREA---
      GO TO 10
      END IF

C---            ---OUTPUT SUM OF AREAS---
      WRITE(LW,1002)      KNT,TSUM,TSUM

 1000 FORMAT(2I4)
 1001 FORMAT(10F8.0)
 1002 FORMAT(//////" SUM OF",I3," AREAS =",F17.4,E20.8)

      STOP
      END
```

LISTING 15-2 Coding for test program TAREA2

```
COORDINATES: X       Y

          1   10.00    6.00
          2   10.00   10.00
          3    8.00   10.00
          4    6.00    8.00
          5    8.00    6.00
AREA  =    12.0000        .12000000+002


COORDINATES: X       Y

          1  -10.00   -7.00
          2   -2.00    7.00
          3    6.00    8.00
          4    8.00   10.00
          5   -7.00   10.00
          6   -7.00    5.00
          7  -10.00    5.00
AREA  =    87.0000        .87000000+002

AREA  =    15.0000        .15000000+002

AREA  =     4.0000        .40000000+001

AREA  =    47.0000        .47000000+002

AREA  =    68.0000        .68000000+002

AREA  =    10.5000        .10500000+002

AREA  =    28.5000        .28500000+002

AREA  =    33.0000        .33000000+002

AREA  =    16.0000        .16000000+002

AREA  =    15.5000        .15500000+002

AREA  =    18.0000        .18000000+002

AREA  =    45.5000        .45500000+002



SUM OF 13 AREAS =
          400.0000        .40000000+003
```

LISTING 15-3 Output for area of polygons

used in the expression of another statement function, then it must appear in a preceding line of that program unit.

A typical example are these two simple interest formulas.

$$F/P(i,n) = (1 + i)^n \quad \text{(single payment compound amount factor)}$$
$$P/F(i,n) = 1/(1 + i)^n \quad \text{(single payment present worth factor)}$$

These formulas can be represented by statement functions as

$$FOP(I,N) = (1. + I/100.)**N$$

and

$$POF(I,N) = 1./FOP(I,N)$$

where POF means P over F (P/F) and I is divided by 100. to convert it from a percent to a decimal fraction.

15-5 PROGRAM FOURIE AND DUMMY PROCEDURE CALLS

This section illustrates the use of procedures as dummy arguments. When they are used, the corresponding actual arguments must be an intrinsic function, an external function, a subroutine, or another dummy procedure. (The symbolic name for a function statement is not allowed as an actual argument.)

This example is chosen because it leads to results that are easily visualized by those with little mathematical background and has practical applications for students with proficiency in higher mathematics. Two cases are discussed before introducing a top-down formulation in Section 15-5.1.

When an external procedure (function subprogram) or a dummy procedure is used as an actual argument, the specific name must appear in an EXTERNAL statement within the calling program unit. Conversely, if an intrinsic function is used as an actual argument, the specific name must appear in an INTRINSIC statement within the calling program unit. (Intrinsic functions for type conversion, lexical relationships, and choosing the smallest or largest value cannot be used as actual arguments.)

Periodic functions (speaking loosely, those with plots that repeat their shapes at specific, fixed intervals) can be approximated by Fourier expansions. For instance, a straight line originating at the origin ($x = 0, y = 0$) which has a positive slope to the point where $x = L$ and $y = 1$ is approximately represented by

$$y = f(x) = \frac{1}{2} - \frac{1}{\pi} \sum_{n=1}^{\infty} \frac{1}{n} \sin \frac{n\pi x}{L}$$

Note that this equation states that y is a function of x, $f(x)$. (To provide generality, the term $f(x)$ is usually used rather than y.) Thus, using this formula, $y = f(x)$ can be found for any given x in expanded form; we have the following.

$$y = f(x) = \frac{1}{2} - \frac{1}{\pi}\left(\frac{1}{1}\sin\frac{1\pi x}{L}\right) - \frac{1}{\pi}\left(\frac{1}{2}\sin\frac{2\pi x}{L}\right) - \frac{1}{\pi}\left(\frac{1}{3}\sin\frac{3\pi x}{L}\right) - \cdots$$

$$\underbrace{\phantom{\frac{1}{2} - \frac{1}{\pi}\left(\frac{1}{1}\sin\frac{1\pi x}{L}\right)}}_{\text{1 term } (n = 1)}$$

$$\underbrace{\phantom{\frac{1}{2} - \frac{1}{\pi}\left(\frac{1}{1}\sin\frac{1\pi x}{L}\right) - \frac{1}{\pi}}}_{\text{2 terms } (n = 2)}$$

$$\underbrace{\phantom{\frac{1}{2} - \frac{1}{\pi}\left(\frac{1}{1}\sin\frac{1\pi x}{L}\right) - \frac{1}{\pi}\left(\frac{1}{2}\right)}}_{\text{3 terms } (n = 3)}$$

Likewise, a Fourier expansion of a rectangular wave, C units long, in expanded form is

$$y = f(x) = \frac{c}{L} + \frac{2}{\pi}\frac{(-1)^1}{1}\sin\frac{1\pi c}{L}\cos\frac{1\pi x}{L} + \frac{2}{\pi}\frac{(-1)^2}{2}\sin\frac{2\pi c}{L}\cos\frac{2\pi x}{L} + \cdots$$

$$\underbrace{\phantom{\frac{c}{L} + \frac{2}{\pi}\frac{(-1)^1}{1}\sin}}_{\text{1 term } (i = 1)}$$

$$\underbrace{\phantom{\frac{c}{L} + \frac{2}{\pi}\frac{(-1)^1}{1}\sin\frac{1\pi c}{L}\cos\frac{1\pi x}{L}}}_{\text{2 terms } (i = 2)}$$

As the number of terms increases, the approximation gets better. Nonetheless, Fourier expansions often exhibit "surprising" characteristics. To get an intuitive feel for how the approximation can be used in various circumstances to provide the most meaningful results, it is advantageous to compare plots of $f(x)$ for different numbers of terms in the series, and for different spacings of x values used to compute $f(x)$.

Therefore we want to write program(s) that provide the desired flexibility, including the ability to easily accommodate many different Fourier expansions. The following discussion uses a top-down approach toward a solution.

15–5.1 Top-Down Formulation

A comparison of the two typical expansions suggests the following.

1. Controls need to establish:
   (a) the constant c, if it exists (C);
   (b) the number of x's to be evaluated (N);
   (c) the maximum number of terms of the series to be used (MAXTRM);
   (d) the actual computation to be performed for a term in the series, which suggests use of EXTERNAL function subprograms for each different series (in the test case, only TRIANG and RECT2C).
2. It might be useful to store $f(x)$ for any given x in an array (TEMP) where

   TEMP $(1) = f_1(x)$ computed using only 1 term of the series
   TEMP $(2) = f_2(x)$ computed using only 2 terms
   TEMP $(3) = f_3(x)$ computed using only 3 terms

   and so on. In such a case, it could be helpful to be able to control the size of array TEMP from the main program, so define its length in LTEMP.

3. Thus the main program (FOURIE) might
   (a) establish TEMP

DIMENSION TEMP (7)

C   TEMP(LTEMP)

LTEMP = 7

.
.
.

   (b) establish EXTERNAL function subprograms

EXTERNAL RECT2C, TRIANG

.
.
.

   (c) establish controls and call a subroutine to perform operations

Call FEPF (C, TEMP, LTEMP, RECT2C, MAXTRM, N, LW)

.
.
.

It is desirable for subroutine FEPF to plot curves for any Fourier expansion. This can be accomplished by using a dummy procedure name for the dummy argument in the SUBROUTINE statement. Then the call could establish the proper function by using an EXTERNAL function for its actual argument. (In Step c above, RECT2C is the external function used as an actual argument for the dummy argument, procedure name DUMMY, in the SUBROUTINE FEPF statement shown next.) The first line of the subroutine would be

SUBROUTINE FEPF (C, TEMP, LTEMP, DUMMY, MAXTRM, N, LW)

Within a loop based on the number (N) of different x's, subroutine FEPF (Fourier Expansion of Period Functions) should perform three simple operations: compute x; fill TEMP with $f_1(x)$, $f_2(x)$, and so on, probably using a subroutine (TERM) to do this operation; and plot $f_1(x)$, $f_2(x)$, . . ., for a given x where $f_1(x)$ is for one term of the series, $f_2(x)$ is for two terms of the series, and so on.

Consider filling TEMP by use of a subroutine TERM. Information needed by the subroutine would include X, C, TEMP and its length LTEMP, and the maximum number of terms to be used, MAXTRM. In addition, an appropriate function subprogram is needed to do the proper computations. The call from FEPF could be

CALL TERM (X, C, TEMP, LTEMP, DUMMY, MAXTRM)

Note that DUMMY is a dummy procedure name and therefore must be delared within subroutine FEPF as

EXTERNAL DUMMY

The actual procedure used when the call is made will be established by "replacing" the external dummy procedure by either the external RECT2C or TRIANG, whichever is used as the actual argument in the main program FOURIE, which calls FEPF,—which, in turn, calls TERM.

Subroutine TERM fills array TEMP. Looking at the expanded forms of the Fourier series previously shown, (except for the initial constant) it appears that a DO-loop is appropriate. Inside the DO-loop, an actual term could be computed if X and C plus the term number (I), were known. So for the first term (excluding the constant)

$$TEMP\ (1) = DUMMY\ (X, C, I)$$

would transfer control to TRIANG or RECT2C, depending upon the actual argument used in program FOURIE. For instance, if

FOURIE uses TRIANG (external) as an actual argument in
    calling FEPF,

FEPF receives TRIANG for its dummy argument DUMMY (external).

FEPF then uses DUMMY as an actual argument (replaced by
    TRIANG) is calling TERM, and

TERM therefore receives DUMMY (TRIANG) for its dummy argument
    DUMMY (external).

TERM then uses TRIANG in place of DUMMY.

Note that a valid association can exist at the last (lowest) level only if a valid association exists at all intermediate levels.

15–5.2 Coding the Programs

Program FOURIE is the simple test program shown in Listing 15–4. Subroutine FEPF is coded in Listing 15–5. The plot routine is within DO-loop 10. The output array, LINE, is filled with blanks in DO-loop 8. Characters are entered in DO-loop 9. Note the scale and offset factors used. (No absolute grid is necessary because only a "picture" is desired.) Characters are obtained by relating the number of terms used for a particular $f(x)$ with the same number expressed in type character within the DATA statement. The FORMAT statement spaces output of lines containing characters to help provide a good mental image.

Subroutine TERM (Listing 15–6) is quite simple, using a dummy function subprogram for actual arguments for the computation of each term. As planned, this dummy argument can specify any desired Fourier expansion by using the correct actual argument in the main program, carried through the intermediate subroutines as a dummy procedure.

The two function subprograms are shown in Listing 15–7. Note that the problem is defined with a virtual sketch within comment statements of the function subprograms. Output for the call, using RECT2C, is shown in Listing 15–8.

```
          PROGRAM FOURIE
C ---       --- FOURIER SERIES SOLUTIONS AND PLOTS
C ---       --- FOR DIFFERENT NUMBER OF TERMS IN SERIES
C ---       --- --- A SIMPLE TESTING PROGRAM ---
C ---       --- --- FOR DEFINITION OF TERMS SEE:
C ---       --- --- SUBROUTINES TERM AND FEPF AND
C ---       --- --- FUNCTION SUBPROGRAMS RECT2C AND TRIANG

          EXTERNAL RECT2C, TRIANG
          DIMENSION TEMP(7)
C                   TEMP(LTEMP)
          LTEMP = 7
          LW = 6

C---       --- TEST RECT2C WITH 7 TERMS
C---       ---            AND 11 X´S (10 COMPUTED)
          C = .2
          MAXTRM = 7
          N = 10
C---       --- OUTPUT HEADINGS
          WRITE(LW,1000)
 1000 FORMAT(´1   FOURIER SERIES APPROX. FOR RECTANGLE´////11X,´0´,78X,
     1´1´/)
C---       --- CALL FEPF TO PLOT APPROXIMATION BY USE
C---       --- OF SUBROUTINE TERM AND DUMMY PROCEDURE
C---       --- ´DUMMY´ REPLACED BY FUNCTION SUBPROGRAM RECT2C
          CALL FEPF(C,TEMP,LTEMP,RECT2C,MAXTRM,N,LW)

C---       --- TEST TRIANG WITH 5 TERMS
C---       ---            AND 21 X´S (20 COMPUTED)
          WRITE(LW,1001)
 1001 FORMAT(´1   FOURIER SERIES APPROX. FOR TRIANGLE´////11X,´0´,78X
     1,´1´/)
          CALL FEPF(0,TEMP,LTEMP,TRIANG,5,20,LW)

          STOP
          END
```

LISTING 15-4 Coding for program FOURIE

15-6 EXERCISES

1. The volume of a circular (wine) barrel having sides with a parabolic curvature is

$$V = \pi h(8R^2 + 4Rr + 3r^2)$$

where

h = height of barrel
R = radius of barrel at midheight
r = radius of barrel at top or bottom

Write a program to compute this volume using (a) a function statement, (b) a function subprogram (external function), and (c) a subroutine. Also, write the necessary external procedures.

2. Convert external function AREA2 to a subroutine. Does such a conversion supply additional advantages? Disadvantages?

3. Would it be reasonable to make program QUAD (Listing 7–2), program RATE (Listing 7–3), program CUES (Listing 7–5), or program CUBIC (Listing 7–10) into (a) a subroutine or (b) a function subprogram (external procedure)? Why or why not?

```
            SUBROUTINE FEPF(C,TEMP,LTEMP,DUMMY,MAXTRM,N,LW)
C                   FOURIER EXPANSIONS, PERIODIC FUNCTIONS
C                   *        *         *        *

C             PLOT F(X)'S FOR EACH X OF A PARTICULAR FOURIER SERIES.
C             ESTABLISH THE PARTICULAR FOURIER SERIES BY USING 'AN
C             EXTERNAL PROCEDURE NAME' AS THE ACTUAL ARGUMENT(IN A
C             CALL TO THIS SUBROUTINE) FOR THE DUMMY ARGUMENT 'DUMMY'.
C             USE 'DUMMY' AS THE ACTUAL ARGUMENT TO CALL SUBROUTINE
C             TERM WHICH COMPUTES F(X) FOR A GIVEN X AND A SPECIFIC
C             NUMBER OF TERMS('DUMMY' IS NOW 'A DUMMY PROCEDURE NAME').

C             N = NUMBER OF DIFFERENT X'S FOR WHICH F(X) DESIRED
C             C, TEMP, LTEMP, DUMMY AND MAXTRM AS DEFINED
C             IN SUBROUTINE TERM
C           LINE = ARRAY FOR OUTPUT OF PLOT OF F(X)

      DIMENSION TEMP(LTEMP)

      CHARACTER*1 LINE(101),NTERMS(9)
      EXTERNAL DUMMY

      DATA NTERMS /'1','2','3','4','5','6','7','*',' '/
C---        --- FOR N X'S:
C---        ---     (1) COMPUTE X
C---        ---     (2) USE SUBROUTINE TERM TO COMPUTE F(X)
C---        ---             FOR 1,2,...MAXTRM TERMS OF SERIES
C---        ---     (3) STORE RESULTS INTO TEMP

      DO 10 I = 1,N
        X = 1.*I/N
        CALL TERM(X,C,TEMP,LTEMP,DUMMY,MAXTRM)

C---        --- INITIALIZE ARRAY LINE
        DO 8 II = 1,101
            LINE(II) = NTERMS(9)
    8   CONTINUE

C---        --- LOAD ARRAY LINE WITH SYMBOLS TO OUTPUT
C---        --- ARRAY TERM IN A GRAPHICAL FORM:
C---        ---     (1) USE LOGICAL SYMBOLS REPRESENTING
C---        ---             THE NUMBER OF TERMS USED IN SERIES
C---        ---             (WHICH EQUALS LOCATION IN ARRAY TEMP)
C---        ---     (2) IF POINT TO PLOT IS LESS THAN 1,
C---        ---             OUTPUT A * SIGN IN LOCATION 1 OF LINE
C---        ---     (3) IF POINT TO PLOT IS GREATER THAN 101
C---        ---             OUTPUT A * SIGN IN LOCATION 101 OF LINE

        DO 9 J = 1,MAXTRM
            LOC = 80. * TEMP(J) +11.5

            IF(LOC .LT. 1) THEN
                LINE(1) = NTERMS(8)
            ELSE IF(LOC .GT. 101) THEN
                LINE(101) = NTERMS(8)
            ELSE
                LINE(LOC) = NTERMS(J)
            END IF
    9   CONTINUE

C---        --- OUTPUT ARRAY LINE USING 101A1 FORMAT
C---        --- SO THAT POINTS WILL PLOT BY NUMBER OF
C---        --- TERMS USED.  ALSO, WHEN VALUES ARE
C---        --- OUT OF RANGE, VALUE TO BE PLOTTED IS
C---        --- AN *.
        WRITE(LW,1000) LINE
 1000   FORMAT(4(11X,':',78X,':'/),1X,101A1)
   10 CONTINUE

      RETURN
      END
```

LISTING 15-5 Coding for subroutine FEPF

```
            SUBROUTINE TERM(X,C,TEMP,LTEMP,DUMMY,MAXTRM)

C              FOR A GIVEN X, CALCULATE F1(X) FOR 1 TERM, F2(X) FOR
C              2 TERMS,...FMAXTRM(X) FOR MAXTRM TERMS OF A FOURIER
C              SERIES EXPANSION.  THE ACTUAL ARGUMENT USED FOR THE
C              DUMMY ARGUMENT 'DUMMY' IN THE CALL OF THIS SUBROUTINE
C              IS 'A DUMMY PROCEDURE NAME'.  THE FUNCTION DECALRED
C              'EXTERNAL DUMMY' REFERENCES 'A DUMMY PROCEDURE NAME'
C              FROM SUBROUTINE FEPF WHICH IN TURN REFERENCES 'AN
C              EXTERNAL PROCEDURE NAME' WHICH IS ESTABLISHED BY THE
C              REAL ARGUMENT RECT2C OR TRZANG IN PROGRAM FOURIE.

C              X = VARIABLE USED IN FUNCTION
C              C = CONSTANT USED IN FUNCTION
C          DUMMY = FUNCTION SUBPROGRAM WHICH USES X(ALWAYS)
C                  AND C(SOMETIMES, OTHERWISE ZERO) TO OBTAIN
C                  VALUE FOR FUNCTION AT THE GIVEN X; THIS
C                  IS A SYMBOLIC NAME DEFINING A DUMMY PROCEDURE
C                  SO THAT SEVERAL DIFFERENT FUNCTION SUBPROGRAMS
C                  CAN BE USED.
C           TEMP = ARRAY HAVING LENGTH LTEMP WHICH STORES F(X):
C                  FOR 1 TERM  OF SERIES IN TEMP(1),
C                  FOR 2 TERMS OF SERIES IN TEMP(2),
C                  FOR 3 TERMS OF SERIES IN TEMP(3),ETC.
C          LTEMP = LENGTH OF ARRAY  TEMP
C         MAXTRM = MAXIMUM TERMS TO BE USED IN SERIES

      DIMENSION TEMP(LTEMP)
      EXTERNAL DUMMY

C---            --- OBTAIN F(X) FOR 1 TERM OF SERIES IN TEMP(1)
      TEMP(1) = DUMMY(X,C,1)

C---            --- ACCUMULATE ADDITIONAL F(X) TERMS
      DO 10 I = 2,MAXTRM
          TEMP(I) = TEMP(I-1) + DUMMY(X,C,I)
   10 CONTINUE

      RETURN
      END
```

LISTING 15-6 Coding for subroutine TERM

```
      FUNCTION RECT2C(X,C,I)

C              :            2C          FOURIER SERIES APPROXIMATION
C          +1 +         --------
C      F(X)   :         :    :          I= TERM NUMBER IN SERIES
C              :         :    :
C          +----------+----------+---------X
C          0          L=1/2      2L=1

      PI = 3.1415926

C---            --- N(PI)C/L = I(PI)C/(1/2)
      ALPHA = I * PI * C * 2.
      RECT2C = 2/PI *(-1)**I/I * SIN(ALPHA) * COS(I*PI*X*2)

C---            --- ADD CONSTANT TERM C/L = C/(1/2)
C---            --- ONLY FOR FIRST TERM, I = 1
      IF(I.EQ.1) RECT2C = RECT2C + 2*C

      RETURN
      END
```

**LISTING 15-7 Coding for function subprograms
TRIANG and RECT2C**

```
FUNCTION TRIANG(X,C,I)
C              :                        *     FOURIER SERIES APPROX.
C          +1 +                   *     *
C      F(X)   :              *           *     I = TERM NUMBER OF SERIES
C              :         *                *     C = NOT USED
C              :    *                     *
C              +------------------------*----- X
C              0                        2L=1

      PI = 3.1415926
      TRIANG = -1/PI * SIN(2*I*PI*X)/I

C---              --- ADD CONSTANT ONLY FOR FIRST
C---              --- TERM WHEN I = 1
      IF(I.EQ.1) TRIANG = TRIANG + .5

      RETURN
      END
```

LISTING 15-7 *(continued)*

FOURIER SERIES APPROX. FOR RECTANGLE

LISTING 15-8 Output from program FOURIE

4. Construct a table with four columns. Fill the rows of Column 1 sequentially with the following captions: (a) Number of results; (b) Number of statements that can be used; (c) Where located; (d) Where accessible; (e) Restrictions on any symbolic names; and (f) How used. Title Columns 2, 3, and 4 Subroutines, Function Subprograms (External Function) and Function Statements, respectively. Fill in balance of the table with proper descriptions to match the captions in the rows of Column 1 with the titles of Columns 2 through 4.

Chapter **16**

Additional Features

This chapter summarizes the remaining features of FORTRAN 77, except for those features dealing with input/output contained in Chapter 17. Section 1 includes extensions beyond subset FORTRAN 77 which are provided by the Full Language. Several of these extensions are quite valuable in day-to-day programming situations, but were not discussed previously because they add complexity that can be excessive for the novice programmer. The second section discusses three statements that have been heavily used in FORTRAN programs for many years. However, these three statements—the arithmetic IF, the assigned GO TO, and the computed GO TO—are now being phased out of the FORTRAN language and will probably not be in the next ANSI specification. The final section describes another four statements that should be used only after careful consideration.

16–1 FULL LANGUAGE EXTENSIONS

Full Language FORTRAN 77 has more flexibility than Subset FORTRAN, particularly with respect to arrays and the DO-Loop. This section considers several of these extensions.

16–1.1 Miscellaneous

The diverse items of this subsection have been combined because each is relatively simple in concept and application.

(a) *PARAMETER Statement.* The PARAMETER statement is formed by using the word PARAMETER followed by one or more statements of the form with each statement separated by commas and the group of one or more statements enclosed in parentheses (see Table 16–1). Once defined in a PARAMETER statement, such a symbolic name can be used in any subsequent statement (except a format specification or as part of a complex constant) exactly as a constant. The PARAMETER statement, therefore, provides a very powerful tool for adjusting programs correctly with a minimum of change. (Also see Section 12–3.)

As an example consider the following program segments:

```
    IMPLICIT CHARACTER (A)
    PARAMETER (ILNAM = 400, IWNAM = 6, IWVAL = IWNAM *3
1  ,A8 = 'EIGHT', A11 = 'ELEVEN')
    CHARACTER*80 NAMES (ILNAM,IWNAM)
    CHARACTER*(3*IWNAM)ARRAY(ILNAM,IWVAL)
    DIMENSION VALUES (ILNAM,IWVAL)
    DATA SUB, SUPSET/IWVAL,ILARAY/
        .
        .
        .

    DO 100 I = 1, ILNAM
        DO 99 J = 1, IWNAM
        .
        .
        .
    CALL COMPUT(NAMES, ILNAM,IWNAM,VALUES,ILNAM,IWVAL)
        .
        .
        .
```

and

```
    SUBROUTINE COMPUT(CH,LCH,IWCH,VAL,LVAL,IWVAL)
    CHARACTER*(*) CH(LCH,IWCH)
    DIMENSION VAL(LVAL,IWVAL)
```

The CHARACTER, DIMENSION, and DATA statements, as well as loop indices and the value of actual arguments, can be changed by altering only the single PARAMETER statement! Thus, the PARAMETER statement is a powerful tool of FORTRAN 77.

(b) *EQUIVALENCE Statement.* To save storage space and to facilitate programming, the EQUIVALENCE statement is used so that more than one entity can share the same location. Table 16–2 shows the general form of the EQUIVALENCE statement. Because elements of arrays are stored sequentially, to make single elements of two different arrays equivalent automatically equivalences all of their sequentially overlapping elements.

Figure 16–1 is a symbolic representation of seven single-dimensional arrays and the array elements used in EQUIVALENCE statements to make them share the same storage

Table 16-1 General Form of PARAMETER Statement (Full Language)

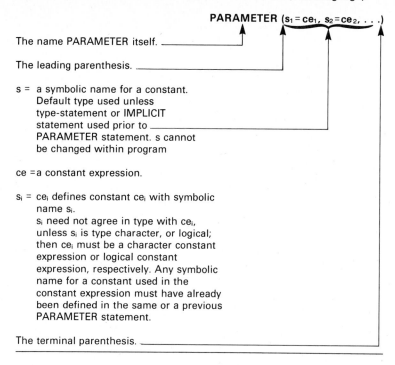

$$\text{PARAMETER } (s_1 = ce_1, \ s_2 = ce_2, \ \ldots)$$

The name PARAMETER itself.

The leading parenthesis.

s = a symbolic name for a constant.
Default type used unless
type-statement or IMPLICIT
statement used prior to
PARAMETER statement. s cannot
be changed within program

ce = a constant expression.

$s_i = ce_i$ defines constant ce_i with symbolic
name s_i.
s_i need not agree in type with ce_i,
unless s_i is type character, or logical;
then ce_i must be a character constant
expression or logical constant
expression, respectively. Any symbolic
name for a constant used in the
constant expression must have already
been defined in the same or a previous
PARAMETER statement.

The terminal parenthesis.

Table 16-2 General Form of EQUIVALENCE Statement

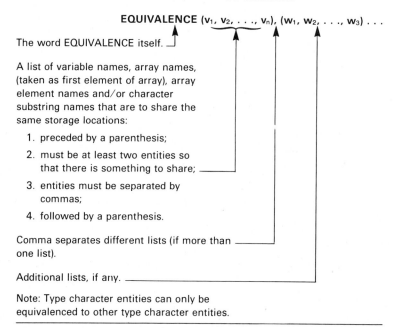

$$\text{EQUIVALENCE } (v_1, \ v_2, \ \ldots, \ v_n), \ (w_1, \ w_2, \ \ldots, \ w_3) \ \ldots$$

The word EQUIVALENCE itself.

A list of variable names, array names,
(taken as first element of array), array
element names and/or character
substring names that are to share the
same storage locations:

1. preceded by a parenthesis;

2. must be at least two entities so
   that there is something to share;

3. entities must be separated by
   commas;

4. followed by a parenthesis.

Comma separates different lists (if more than
one list).

Additional lists, if any.

Note: Type character entities can only be
equivalenced to other type character entities.

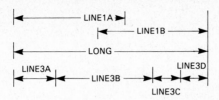

FIGURE 16-1 Symbolic representation of the EQUIVALENCE statement

location. Listing 16-1 is a small demonstration program that illustrates how the EQUIVALENCE statement works to relate these seven arrays.

In the EQUIVALENCE statement of program EQUIV, the first list (LONG, LINE3A, LINE1A), which equivalences the first location of each array, could be replaced by other lists such as (LONG(1), LINE3A (1), LINE1A (1)), which also equivalences first locations or, (LINE1A (3), LINE3A (3), LONG (3)), which equivalences third locations, and so on.

Because the two arrays LINE1A and LINE3B share common storage locations (LINE1A (6), LINE3B (3)), array LINE3B is mandated to share storage locations with array LONG even though it is equivalenced only to the array LINE1A.

To help illustrate the relationships, program EQUIV stores numbers sequentially into array LONG, which automatically means the same values are stored in the other arrays related by the EQUIVALENCE statement. The output parallels the input of Figure 16-1. Although arrays LINE1A and LINE1B are not related directly through a list of an EQUIVALENCE statement, nonetheless the last two locations of array LINE1A are shared with the first two locations of array LINE1B because both are equivalenced to array LONG.

EQUIVALENCE statements must be used judiciously so that two independent entities are not required to be in the same location, or elements of arrays are made nonconsecutive. For instance, in

DIMENSION ONE(4), TWO(5)
EQUIVALENCE (ONE(1), VAR), (ONE(3), VAR), (ONE(2), TWO(4)),
(ONE(3), TWO(3))

is illegal because ONE(1) and ONE(3) cannot be in the same location, and ONE(2), TWO(4) mandates that ONE(3) share its location with TWO(5) because of the consecutive ordering of arrays. Obviously, the same restrictions apply to common and equivalence.

Typical uses of the EQUIVALENCE statement are indicated by the following. When arrays of different types are needed to do "scratch" work in various portions of the program, the EQUIVALENCE statement can help save space. For example

$$\text{DIMENSION ITEMS(6,20),VALUES(4,3,7)}$$
$$\text{EQUIVALENCE(ITEMS,VALUES)}$$

saves 84 spaces ($6 \times 20 = 120$, $4 \times 3 \times 7 = 84$). Remember that type CHARACTER cannot be equivalenced to any other type.

The EQUIVALENCE statement is also used to force ordering, while allowing convenient name usage later in the program. For example

$$\text{COMMON/BIGFIL/SCRTCH(100)}$$
$$\text{EQUIVALENCE(COST,SCRTCH(7))}$$

allows COST to be used in computations and to be output in the required order by using array SCRTCH.

```
        PROGRAM EQUIV
C       --- ILLUSTRATING EQUIVALENCE

        DIMENSION LINE1A(8),LINE1B(8),LONG(14),LINE3A(3),
       1          LINE3B(7),LINE3C(2),LINE3D(2)

        EQUIVALENCE (LONG,LINE3A,LINE1A),(LINE1A(6),LINE3B(3)),
       1(LINE1B(5),LONG(11),LINE3C(1)),(LINE3D(1),LONG(13))

        DATA LONG/1,2,3,4,5,6,7,8,9,10,11,12,13,14/,LW/6/
        WRITE(LW,'(''1LINE1A='',8I3)') LINE1A
        WRITE(LW,'('' LINE1B='',8I3)') LINE1B
        WRITE(LW,'(''   LONG='',14I3)') LONG
        WRITE(LW,'('' LINE3A='',3I3)') LINE3A
        WRITE(LW,'('' LINE3B='',7I3)') LINE3B
        WRITE(LW,'('' LINE3C='',2I3)') LINE3C
        WRITE(LW,'('' LINE3D='',2I3)') LINE3D
        WRITE(LW,'(///'' LOCATIONS WITH RESPECT TO ARRAY LONG''/
       18X,'' 1  2  3  4  5  6  7  8  9 10 11 12 13 14''/ 8X,
       28I3/26X,8I3/2(8X,14I3/))') LINE1A,LINE1B,LONG,LINE3A,LINE3B,
       3LINE3C,LINE3D

        STOP
        END
```

Output:

```
LINE1A=  1  2  3  4  5  6  7  8
LINE1B=  7  8  9 10 11 12 13 14
  LONG=  1  2  3  4  5  6  7  8  9 10 11 12 13 14
LINE3A=  1  2  3
LINE3B=  4  5  6  7  8  9 10
LINE3C= 11 12
LINE3D= 13 14



LOCATIONS WITH RESPECT TO ARRAY LONG
         1  2  3  4  5  6  7  8  9 10 11 12 13 14
         1  2  3  4  5  6  7  8
                           7  8  9 10 11 12 13 14
         1  2  3  4  5  6  7  8  9 10 11 12 13 14
         1  2  3  4  5  6  7  8  9 10 11 12 13 14
```

LISTING 16-1 Coding for program EQUIV with output

```
      PROGRAM CQUAD
C     --- SOLUTION OF QUADRATIC EQUATION USING
C     ---     (1) TYPE COMPLEX
C     ---     (2) EQUIVALENCE STATEMENT FOR DEMONSTRATION PURPOSES

C     --- DECLARE VARIABLE D AS COMPLEX BY IMPLICIT STATEMENT
      IMPLICIT COMPLEX(D)
C     --- DECLARE VARIABLE E AS COMPLEX BY EXPLICIT STATEMENT
      COMPLEX E
      DIMENSION G(4)

C     --- STORE REAL PART OF D IN G(1) AND P
C     ---   IMAGINARY PART OF D IN G(2) AND Q
C     --- STORE REAL PART OF E IN G(3) AND R
C     ---   IMAGINARY PART OF E IN G(4) AND T
      EQUIVALENCE (D,G(1),P),(G(2),Q),(E,G(3),R),(G(4),T)

      LR=5
      LW=6

    1 READ(LR,1000) A,B,C

      IF(A.EQ.0. .AND. B.NE.0.) THEN
          S=-C/B
          WRITE(6,1002) A,B,C,S
          GO TO 1
      ELSE IF(A .EQ. 0. .AND. B .EQ. 0.) THEN
          STOP
      ELSE
          DS=(B**2-4.*A*C)
          DS= SQRT(DS)
          D=(-B+DS)/(2.*A)
          E=(-B-DS)/(2.*A)
          WRITE(LW,1001)A,B,C,D,E,G,P,Q,R,T
          GO TO 1
      END IF

 1001 FORMAT(////6X,'SOLUTION OF'//
     11X,'(',E14.8,')* X**2 +(',E14.8,')* X +(',E14.8,') = 0'//
     21X,'PROGRAM',12X,'FIRST X',24X,'SECOND X'/
     31X,'SYMBOLS',6X,'REAL',9X,'IMAGINARY',10X,'REAL',9X,'IMAGINARY'/
     41X,'D AND E',2X,2E14.8,4X,2E14.8/
     51X,'ARRAY G',2X,2E14.8,4X,2E14.8/
     61X,'P,Q,R,T',2X,2E14.8,4X,2E14.8///)
 1000 FORMAT(3F10.0)
 1002 FORMAT(/' LINEAR EQUATION WITH A,B,C =',3E20.8/'THEREFORE  X=',
     *E20.8/)
      END
```

LISTING 16-2 Coding for program CQUAD with output

The EQUIVALENCE statement is also useful in working with files or records that are of mixed type when obtained by an unformatted READ.

(c) *Complex Variables.* Program CUBIC of Section 7–5 obtains the three roots of cubic equations by Cardan's method. This section was optional, but included the definitions of complex constants and variables and their form of output. An additional example is shown in Listing 16–2 for program CQUAD. This program is more complicated than necessary because it also gives a second illustration of the use EQUIVALENCE. (See Section 17–2.3 for additional input/output considerations.)

(d) *Double Precision Variables.* Data that are of type double precision always require two consecutive storage units and therefore provide precision greater than that for type real. (See Section 17–2.3 for I/O considerations.)

Output:

```
      SOLUTION OF

  (-.83000000+002)* X**2 +( .00000000     )* X +( .14000000+002) = 0

  PROGRAM          FIRST X                       SECOND X
  SYMBOLS       REAL          IMAGINARY        REAL          IMAGINARY
  D AND E    -.41070025+000  .00000000      .41070025+000  .00000000
  ARRAY G    -.41070025+000  .00000000      .41070025+000  .00000000
  P,Q,R,T    -.41070025+000  .00000000      .41070025+000  .00000000




      SOLUTION OF

  ( .12000000+002)* X**2 +( .00000000     )* X +( .00000000     ) = 0

  PROGRAM          FIRST X                       SECOND X
  SYMBOLS       REAL          IMAGINARY        REAL          IMAGINARY
  D AND E     .00000000      .00000000      .00000000      .00000000
  ARRAY G     .00000000      .00000000      .00000000      .00000000
  P,Q,R,T     .00000000      .00000000      .00000000      .00000000




      SOLUTION OF

  ( .11200000+003)* X**2 +( .00000000     )* X +( .26000000+002) = 0

  PROGRAM          FIRST X                       SECOND X
  SYMBOLS       REAL          IMAGINARY        REAL          IMAGINARY
  D AND E     .00000000      .48181205+000  .00000000     -.48181205+000
  ARRAY G     .00000000      .48181205+000  .00000000     -.48181205+000
  P,Q,R,T     .00000000      .48181205+000  .00000000     -.48181205+000
                                 .
                                 .
                                 .
```

LISTING 16–2 *(continued)*

Double precision constants are formed like real constants in scientific notation, except the letter D is used instead of the letter E. Examples of double precision constants are:

$$26D14 \quad 123.4D\text{-}6 \quad 0.126D\text{+}03$$

Type double precision must be declared, either implicitly or explicitly, before being used within a given program. Thus any entity starting with D and the variables COMP and CONJ could be declared double precision by the following two statements. (See Section 4–4.)

IMPLICIT DOUBLE PRECISION (D)
DOUBLE PRECISION COMP, CONJ

In problems such as those involving determination of roots for polynomial equations and in the solution of eigenvalue problems double precision is almost always required.

Roots of polynomial equations are often located by a technique that raises coefficients of the equations to very large powers. In the eigenvalue problem, type real is inadequate because two numbers must be subtracted from each other, and usually they have the same leading digits. For example,

$$0.00369842178321$$
$$-0.00369842177983$$
$$0.00000000000338$$

This is zero if the numbers subtracted contain only eight significant figures.

Because variables and constants of type double precision require two storage locations each, such programs require more storage space. Often, to facilitate programming and to minimize storage requirements during the development stages, programs are written and debugged using real variables. When the program is essentially correct, an IMPLICIT statement is used to change all of the variables from type real to type double precision. This is an effective process because the *generic* intrinsic functions automatically take into account the type of the variables used as their arguments. Thus changing a program from type real to type double precision is a simple process.

(e) *Integer Constant Expression.* An integer constant expression contains only arithmetic operators, integer constants, and symbolic names of integer constants as established in a PARAMETER statement.

16–1.2 Arrays

Subset FORTRAN 77 allows a maximum of three dimensions and requires that the lower bound of the dimensions be one. The upper bound of the dimensions must be equal to or greater than 1. By contrast, Full Language FORTRAN 77 allows up to seven dimensions, a lower dimension bound that is positive, negative, or zero, and an upper dimension bound that must be equal to or greater than the lower dimension bound (it may, therefore, also be positive, negative, or zero). To declare array dimensions that have lower dimension bounds other than one requires two integer constants separated by a colon. The integer arithmetic expression left of the colon represents the lower dimension bound, and the integer arithmetic expression right of the colon represents the upper dimension bound. Thus A(6) can be written optionally as A(1:6) and B(4,3) as B(1:4, 1:3).

A four-dimensional array with

first dimension: lower bound = 0, upper bound = 7

second dimension: lower bound = −3, upper bound = 0

third dimension: lower bound = −11, upper bound = −4

fourth dimension: lower bound = −1, upper bound = 2

would be written in a dimension statement as:

$$\text{DIMENSION FOUND}(0{:}7, -3{:}0, -11{:}-4, -1{:}2)$$

Formally, array declarators establish the size of arrays in DIMENSION statements, type statements, or COMMON statements, but COMMON statements cannot be used as

Table 16-3 Relationships Between Subscripts and Elements of Arrays

Single-Dimensional Array:

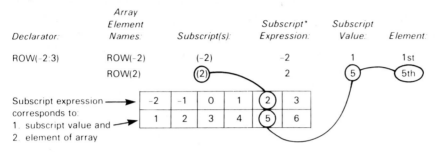

Declarator:	Array Element Names:	Subscript(s):	Subscript* Expression:	Subscript Value:	Element:
ROW(-2:3)	ROW(-2)	(-2)	-2	1	1st
	ROW(2)	(2)	2	5	5th

Subscript expression corresponds to:
1. subscript value and
2. element of array

-2	-1	0	1	2	3
1	2	3	4	5	6

Two-Dimensional Array:

Declarator:	Array Element Names:	Subscript(s):	Subscript* Expression:	Subscript Value:	Element:
BOX(4,3) or BOX(1:4,1:3)	BOX(3,1)	(3,1)	3 and 1	3	3rd
	BOX(2,3)	(2,3)	2 and 3	10	10th

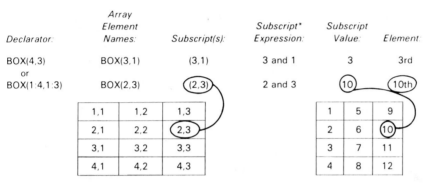

1,1	1,2	1,3
2,1	2,2	2,3
3,1	3,2	3,3
4,1	4,2	4,3

Subscript Expressions

1	5	9
2	6	10
3	7	11
4	8	12

Corresponds to: 1. subscript values and 2. elements of array

Three-Dimensional Array:

Declarator:	Array Element Names:	Subscript(s):	Subscript* Expression:	Subscript Value:	Element:
TBL (-2:3,-3:1)	TBL(-1,-3)	(-1,-3)	-1 and -3	2	2nd
	TBL(0,0)	(0,0)	0 and 0	21	21st
	TBL(2,-1)	(2,-1)	2 and -1	17	17th

-2,-3	-2,-2	-2,-1	-2,0	-2,1
-1,-3	-1,-2	-1,-1	-1,0	-1,1
0,-3	0,-2	0,-1	0,0	0,1
1,-3	1,-2	1,-1	1,0	1,1
2,-3	2,-2	2,-1	2,0	2,1
3,-3	3,-2	3,-1	3,0	3,1

Subscript Expressions

1	7	13	19	25
2	8	14	20	26
3	9	15	21	27
4	10	16	22	28
5	11	17	23	29
6	12	18	24	30

Corresponds to: 1. subscript values and 2. elements of array

*Integer expression containing only constants, symbolic names of constants, or variables in Subset; In Full Language may contain array elements and function references also.

dummy array declarators. A constant array declarator establishes dimensions with integer constant expressions such as (J, K, L, and N must have been previously defined by a PARAMETER statement)

$$\text{COMMON A(6), B}(-4\!:\!2, 7), \text{C}(3*J+2), \text{D}(K+L\!: 3*N+2)$$

An adjustable array declarator is used only as a dummy array declarator in a procedure such as discussed in Section 14–4.1. An assumed-size array declarator is also used as a dummy array declarator but has an asterisk as the upper dimension bound of the last dimension.

Each array element name contains a subscript expression enclosed in parentheses. (Note: The subscript expression with its enclosing parentheses is called simply the *subscript*.) Used in conjunction with a declaration, the subscript expression (within the subscript) results in a subscript value that identifies the element of the array being addressed. These relationships are summarized and illustrated for a few examples in Table 16–3. Full language FORTRAN 77 allows the integer expressions used for subscript expressions to include array element references and function references so long as the function does not alter the value of any other subscript expression within that same subscript.

16–1.3 DO-Loops

Full Language FORTRAN 77 relaxes the restrictions on DO-loops. The DO variable (loop index or counter) can be a real or double precision variable, as well as the integer variable required by subset FORTRAN. In addition, the loop controls which must be only integer constants or variables in subset FORTRAN may be expressions of type integer, real, or double precision in the Full Language.

This allows DO-loops of the following forms:

$$\text{DO 10 A} = 3.16, \text{A}+\text{C}**3, \text{STEP}$$
$$\text{DO 20 LOOPI} = \text{FUNI(K,Z)}, \text{I}+\text{J}/\text{I}*\text{I}$$
$$\text{DO 30 INDEX} = -(\text{J}/3), \text{K}**(\text{L}-\text{M}), \text{REAL1}$$

Such DO-Loops can often cause significant programming difficulties, particularly with respect to exceeding limits of any arrays which might be involved. In such cases, it is probably preferable to store results of the computations in a single variable, and use that variable within the loop (after checking to be sure that the subscript does not go out of range).

On the other hand, programming errors can often be lessened in cases such as those found in Listing 9–5 (program BBSRT1)

$$\text{NM1} = \text{N}-1$$
$$\text{DO 40 I} = 1,\text{NM1}$$

can be expressed by the more effective form of

$$\text{DO 40 I} = 1,\text{N}-1$$

As usual, the primary concern is to use FORTRAN capabilities in a manner that is easy to understand and which minimizes errors.

Extensions to the DO-loop also apply to the implied-DO Loops used in input/output Lists.

16-1.4 The DATA Statement

Table 10-1 summarized characteristics of the DATA statement for Subset FORTRAN 77. Full Language FORTRAN 77 extends the admissible list of variable names, or array names, or array element names to include substring names and implied-DO lists. In addition, the constant list may include symbolic names of constants as well. The requirement that type must agree between a constant and its corresponding element of the list is also relaxed. In this case, type must agree between corresponding elements of the list only when the type is either character or logical. For other types, arithmetic conversion is automatic. (For use of common, refer to Section 14-4.4)

The implied-DO used within a DATA statement is more restrictive than the general form. In the expression $I = NB, NE, NS$, capital I represents the implied-DO variable and must be an integer variable. The variables NB, NE, and NS must be integer constant expressions, except that they may also contain implied-DO variables of other implied-DO lists that have this implied-DO list within their ranges.

Study of program IIDLDS of Listing 16-3 should help clarify the use of implied-DO lists in DATA Statements (page 414).

Real array A is completely filled by two DATA statements. (*Note:* the three DATA statements in the program could be combined into one or divided into different groupings.) Several forms are used, but each item in the list of array elements is given an identical value. For example, the third item $(A(1,J),J=3,7)$ sets $A(1,3)$ through $A(1,7)$ to 4. Likewise, the fifth item

$$((A(I,J),I=2,4),J=6,7)$$

sets $3 \times 2 = 6$ elements to 5.

The third DATA statement stores asterisks according to array location, with the outer loop executed first.

J	I			
1	1	C(1,1) = '*'		
2	1,2	C(1,2) = '*'	C(2,2) = '*'	
3	1,2,3	C(1,3) = '*'	C(2,3) = '*'	C(3,3) = '*'

16-2 STATEMENTS THAT ARE NOW BEING PHASED OUT

Although the three statements discussed in this section are legal in FORTRAN 77, their use is decreasing. (In all likelihood, they will not be contained in the next ANSI standard.) They are included in this book because of their continued use in a great number of production programs, which you may be required to update.

16-2.1 The Arithmetic (Three-Way) IF Statement

Early versions of FORTRAN did not contain the logical IF. Many programmers, therefore, have become comfortable with the arithmetic IF (often called the three-way

```
      PROGRAM IIDLDS
C     --- ILLUSTRATING IMPLIED DO-LISTS IN DATA STATEMENTS
C          *          *      *  *       *     *

      INTEGER A
      DIMENSION A(6,7)
      CHARACTER *1 C(6,5)

      DATA A(1,1),A(1,2), (A(1,J), J=3,7),
     1 ((A(I,J),I=2,4),J=1,5), ((A(I,J),I=2,4),J=6,7),
     2     A(5,1),A(5,2),A(5,3) / 3,3,5*4,15*2,6*5,6,7,8/
      DATA A(6,1),A(6,2),A(6,3),((A(I,J),I=5,6),J=4,7)
     1  / 9,10,11,8*12/
C                               ---TWO PRECEDING STATEMENTS COULD
C                               ---BE COMBINED(OR SPLIT IN ANY WAY)
C                               ---WITH NEXT ONE ---
      DATA ((C(I,J),I=1,J),J=1,5) / 15* '*'/, LW/6/

C     --- OUTPUT ARRAY A COMPLETELY DEFINED BY DATA STMTS
      WRITE(LW,'(''1 '',7I3/5(2X,7I3/)//////)')((A(I,J),J=1,7)
     1  ,I=1,6)

C     --- ARRAY C IS NOT COMPLETELY DEFINED BY DATA STATEMENT
C     ---SO IF ELEMENT NOT EQUAL '*', STORE '-' INSTEAD.

      DO 20 I = 1,6

         DO 19 J = 1,5

            IF(C(I,J).NE.'*') C(I,J) = '-'

   19    CONTINUE

   20 CONTINUE

C     --- OUTPUT ARRAY C
      DO 30 I = 1,6
         WRITE(LW,'(/5(1X,A1))') (C(I,J),J=1,5)
   30 CONTINUE

      STOP
      END
```

Output:

```
3   3   4   4   4   4   4
2   2   2   2   2   5   5
2   2   2   2   2   5   5
2   2   2   2   2   5   5
6   7   8  12  12  12  12
9  10  11  12  12  12  12


*  *  *  *  *

-  *  *  *  *

-  -  *  *  *

-  -  -  *  *

-  -  -  -  *

-  -  -  -  -
```

LISTING 16-3 Coding for program IIDLDS with output

IF). In FORTRAN 77, the arithmetic IF is standard, but more and more programmers use the logical IF.

The basic form of the IF statement is summarized in Table 16–4. Note that all of these statement labels must be integer constants, not variables and not real numbers.

Figure 16–2 represents a simple two-way branch. The first statement label, 66, indicates the location for transfer of flow when J is negative; the second, 12, when J is zero; and the third, 12, when J is positive. Although not a legal requirement, the arithmetic IF should usually be used as a mini-module, terminated by a labeled CONTINUE statement. In older production programs, such branches are often difficult to follow because the mini-module concept was not adhered to and programs are not in structured form.

Figure 16–3 illustrates a slightly more complex three-way IF. During the execution stage, the current value of V and the current value stored in location T are used to evaluate the expression. If the result of this evaluation is negative, flow is to Statement 111. If the evaluation yields exactly zero, Statement 9 is subsequently executed and, if positive, flow is to Statement 8.

This arithmetic IF can cause difficulties. When $V + T^2$ is "supposed" to be zero, roundoff error (resulting from a computation) can yield a small number instead. If such error occurs, transfer is to Statement 111 if the expression is evaluated as a small negative

Table 16-4 Arithmetic (Three-Way) IF Statement

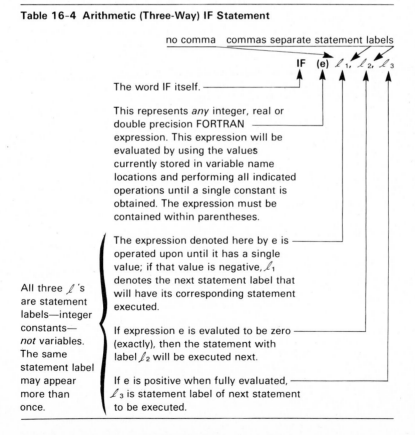

no comma   commas separate statement labels

IF (e) ℓ_1, ℓ_2, ℓ_3

The word IF itself.

This represents *any* integer, real or double precision FORTRAN expression. This expression will be evaluated by using the values currently stored in variable name locations and performing all indicated operations until a single constant is obtained. The expression must be contained within parentheses.

The expression denoted here by e is operated upon until it has a single value; if that value is negative, ℓ_1 denotes the next statement label that will have its corresponding statement executed.

All three ℓ's are statement labels—integer constants— *not* variables. The same statement label may appear more than once.

If expression e is evaluted to be zero (exactly), then the statement with label ℓ_2 will be executed next.

If e is positive when fully evaluated, ℓ_3 is statement label of next statement to be executed.

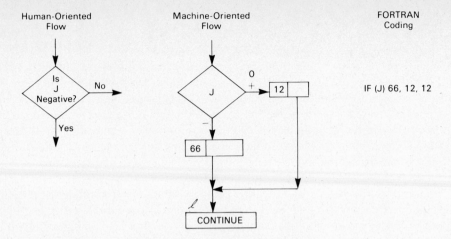

FIGURE 16-2 Simple two-way branch

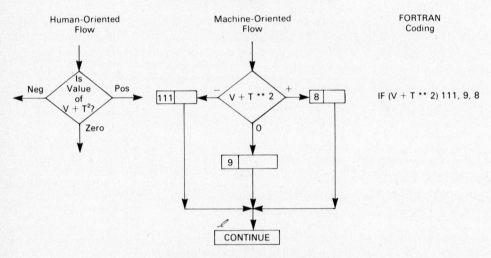

FIGURE 16-3 Simple three-way branch

number but to Statement 8 if the resulting small value is positive. For this reason, during the compilation stage many machines output a precautionary message such as "branch on real expressions may not be meaningful because of roundoff error."

Figure 16-4 shows a comparison between the block IF of the binary search program and an equivalent arithmetic IF. Situations such as this seem to be natural for the use of the arithmetic IF because branches are required based upon negative, zero, or positive results. Nonetheless, the block IF does this job very well.

16-2.2 The ASSIGN Statement and the Assigned GO TO Statement

The assigned GO TO is particularly troublesome to proponents of structured programming because the statement masks flow and has the ability to make multiple, drastic, discontinuous jumps.

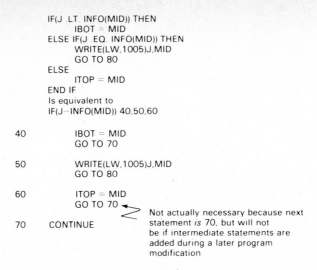

```
        IF(J .LT. INFO(MID)) THEN
                IBOT = MID
        ELSE IF(J .EQ. INFO(MID)) THEN
                WRITE(LW,1005)J,MID
                GO TO 80
        ELSE
                ITOP = MID
        END IF
        Is equivalent to
        IF(J—INFO(MID)) 40,50,60

40              IBOT = MID
                GO TO 70

50              WRITE(LW,1005)J,MID
                GO TO 80

60              ITOP = MID
                GO TO 70        Not actually necessary because next
                                statement is 70, but will not
70      CONTINUE                be if intermediate statements are
                                added during a later program
                                modification
```

**FIGURE 16–4 Comparison between a block IF
and an equivalent arithmetic IF**

(a) *Formulation of the ASSIGN Statement.* Table 16–5 summarizes the ASSIGN statement. Note, in particular, that the integer variable to which a label is assigned can be used for no other purpose. The statement label must be the label of an executable or FORMAT statement. The ASSIGN statement is also called the Statement Label Assignment Statement.

(b) *Use of the ASSIGN Statement to Control Formats.* The ASSIGN statement is used (see Listing 16–4) in conjunction with an arithmetic IF to control the format of a WRITE statement. When I is negative, L is assigned a value of 1000 and the statement

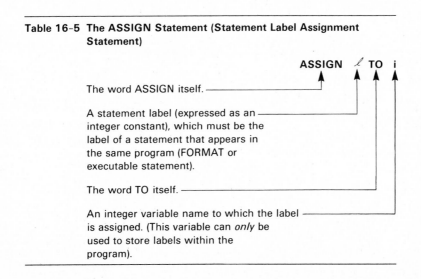

**Table 16-5 The ASSIGN Statement (Statement Label Assignment
Statement)**

ASSIGN ℓ TO i

The word ASSIGN itself.

A statement label (expressed as an integer constant), which must be the label of a statement that appears in the same program (FORMAT or executable statement).

The word TO itself.

An integer variable name to which the label is assigned. (This variable can *only* be used to store labels within the program).

WRITE(LW,L) uses FORMAT 1000. The other two formats are used when L is assigned values of 1001 or 1002. Compare the output of Listing 16–4 with corresponding FORMAT statements to clarify these concepts.

(c) *Formulation of the Assigned GO TO Statement.* The assigned GO TO is summarized in Table 16–6. Note, in particular, that the variable *i* must be assigned by an ASSIGN statement prior to reaching the assigned GO TO, and must have a matching statement label contained within the list displayed within parentheses.

16–2.3 The Computed GO TO Statement

The computed GO TO provides an "arithmetic" way to do a series of block IF's. It can provide structured programming when used judiciously, but the computed GO TO appears to have no advantages over a series of block IF's.

When used, the computed GO TO should be in mini-module form, always terminating with a labeled CONTINUE statement. Flow diagrams in the form of horizontal and vertical "ladders" are shown in Figure 16–5, page 420.

Rules for formulating the computed GO TO are summarized in Table 16–7. Using these rules, Figure 16–5 would be coded as shown in Listing 16–5. If K is less than 1 or

```
        PROGRAM ASSIGN
        LW=6

        DO 100 I=-2,2,2

            IF(I) 10,20,30

    10          ASSIGN 1000 TO L
                GO TO 40

    20          ASSIGN 1001 TO L
                GO TO 40

    30          ASSIGN 1002 TO L
                GO TO 40

    40      CONTINUE

C                   L HAS BEEN ASSIGNED
C                   L IS STATEMENT LABEL
C                   L THEREFORE ESTABLISHES
C                       WHICH FORMAT IS TO BE USED
        WRITE(LW,L)
   100 CONTINUE

  1000 FORMAT(////' I HAS A VALUE OF -2')
  1001 FORMAT(' NOW, I= 0')
  1002 FORMAT(' IN THIRD LOOP, I= 2')

        STOP
        END
```

Output:

```
I HAS A VALUE OF -2
NOW, I= 0
IN THIRD LOOP, I= 2
```

LISTING 16–4 Program using ASSIGN to control output (displayed)

Table 16-6 The Assigned GO TO Statement

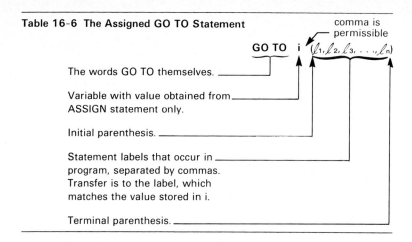

greater than the maximum number of entries in the list, it is treated as a CONTINUE statement. In the subset, K must be an integer variable; in Full Language, K may be an integer expression.

The assigned GO TO and the computed GO TO differ in two important ways: The "transfer variable" in an assigned GO TO statement must obtain its value from a previous ASSIGN statement, but the "transfer variable" in the computed GO TO is simply an

Table 16-7 Computed GO TO Statement

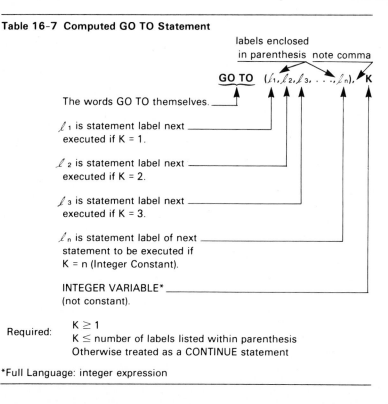

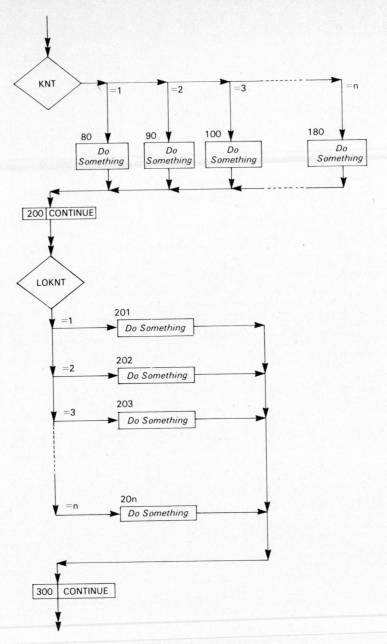

FIGURE 16-5 Computed GO TO, Flow Diagram

integer variable. The "transfer variable" in an assigned GO TO must be one of the statement labels contained in the list, while the "transfer variable" in the computed GO TO simply states (by direct count) which statement label in the list is to be used to make the jump in flow.

```
                   GO TO (80, 90, 100, . . ., 180), KNT

        80          Do Something
                    GO TO 200

        90          Do Something
                    GO TO 200

       100          Do Something
                    GO TO 200

                            .

                            .

       180          Do Something
                    GO TO 200

       200   CONTINUE

                   GO TO (201,202,203, . . . 20n),LOKNT

       201          Do Something
                    GO TO 300

       202          Do Something
                    GO TO 300

                            .

                            .

       20n          Do Something
                    GO TO 300

       300   CONTINUE
```

LISTING 16-5 Coding of computed GO TO

16-3   ADDITIONAL STATEMENTS

The statements contained in this section are legal FORTRAN 77, but their use is recommended only after careful consideration.

16-3.1 The PAUSE Statement

Either of the following is a form of the PAUSE statement.

PAUSE
PAUSE n

Here n is a string of not more than 5 digits or a character constant. This statement causes the computer program to stop execution, with restart of the program beyond control of the program itself. In the early days of computing, the PAUSE statement was frequently used, particularly in conjunction with built-in program trace mechanisms. For today's computers, however, the PAUSE statement is normally undesirable because better ways exist for human interaction.

The string of no more than 5 digits or the character constant represented by n has no precise meaning in the specification and its use is strictly processor dependent.

16–3.2 Additional Statements Related To Procedures

The ENTRY statement and the alternate RETURN statement are used in conjunction with procedures. The SAVE statement is used to preserve the value of local variables from one subprogram call to another.

(a) *The ENTRY Statement.* The ENTRY statement converts a subroutine or function subprogram mini-module into a pseudo mini-module because it provides more than one entrance. The ENTRY statement has the form

$$\text{ENTRY NAME } (V_1, V_2, \dots, V_3)$$

where NAME is a symbolic name for entry into a subroutine or function subprogram and is either: a subroutine name if ENTRY is within a subroutine; or an external function name if ENTRY is within a function subprogram, and V_1, V_2, . . . represent a list of arguments in which the list does not have to agree with the list of arguments of the subroutine or function subprogram where the ENTRY statement is located.

In the calling program, the entry name and its corresponding argument list is used in exactly the same as a subroutine is called or a function subprogram is accessed. When such an action occurs, the subroutine or function subprogram is entered at the statement immediately following the ENTRY statement located within it. In effect, the ENTRY statement makes it possible for a function subprogram or a subroutine to be several function subprograms or several subroutines all within one program unit.

(b) *The Alternate RETURN Statement.* The RETURN statement normally transfers control to the calling program just after the point where the function subprogram or subroutine is referenced. The alternate RETURN makes it possible for resumption of flow in the calling program to start at alternate locations. The form of a RETURN statement is

$$\text{RETURN } n$$

where if n is less than 1, a normal return occurs; if n is at least 1 but not more than the number of asterisks in its dummy argument list, control returns to the nth statement label (preceded by *) in the actual argument list of the calling program that corresponds to the nth * in the dummy argument list; if n is more than the number of asterisks in its dummy argument list, a normal return occurs.

For example, if the reference statement in the calling program is

$$\text{CALL KITE(R,ILR,IWR,N,M,*260,*320,*440)}$$

corresponding to

$$\text{SUBROUTINE KITE(T,ILT,IWT,N,M,*,*,*)}$$

then

$$\text{RETURN 2}$$

in the subroutine will return control to Statement 320 (the second * position) of the calling program,

RETURN 3

in the subroutine will return control to Statement 440 (the third * position) of the calling program, and either

$$\text{RETURN } -1 \text{ or}$$
$$\text{RETURN } 4$$

produces a normal return

(c) *The SAVE Statement.* The SAVE statement makes it possible to retain the definition status of entities after the RETURN statement of function subprograms or procedures, even when these entities are not carried through the argument list and are not in a COMMON statement. The form of the SAVE statement is

$$\text{SAVE } v_1, v_2, \ldots$$

where $v_1, v_2, \ldots,$ are:

1. named common blocks preceded and followed by a slash;
2. variable names; or } Full Language only
3. array names.

When used as

$$\text{SAVE}$$

the entire list of allowable items is assumed. If a named common block is SAVEd in one subprogram, it must be SAVEd in every subprogram where it appears.

The SAVE statement makes it possible to keep local variables of a procedure unchanged between calls. (Without the SAVE statement, such an assumption is unwarranted.) This feature is useful in procedures that: use the number of times they have been called as a variable in computations; initiate a search between limits that can be diminished between successive calls of the procedure, if saved; involve portions of identical involved computations that need not be redone, if saved; and so on.

16-4 EXERCISES

1. Given:

$$\text{DIMENSION L(10), M(7), N(21)}$$
$$\text{EQUIVALENCE (L(7), M(7)), (M(4), N(3))}$$

What elements of M and N are stored with L(6)?
What elements of M and L are stored with N(2)?
What elements of L and N are stored with M(4)?

2. In your field of study or expertise, name six commonly used tables, three of which could be easily generated within a computer program and three which would require use of a DATA statement. Study the three tables that require input by a DATA statement. What characteristics do they possess that makes their generation impossible? Have you changed your mind?

3. Trace the flow of Figure 16–6, which sums positive numbers, counts zeros, and accumulates products of negative numbers for data sets *a, b, c,* or *d.*

4. Use a Logical or block IF to perform the task shown in Figure 16–6.

Program EXER2

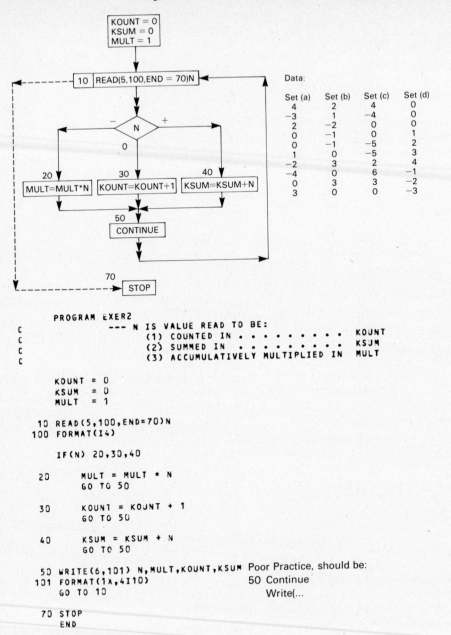

Data:

	Set (a)	Set (b)	Set (c)	Set (d)
	4	2	4	0
	−3	1	−4	0
	2	−2	0	0
	0	−1	0	1
	0	−1	−5	2
	1	0	−5	3
	−2	3	2	4
	−4	0	6	−1
	0	3	3	−2
	3	0	0	−3

```
      PROGRAM EXER2
C            --- N IS VALUE READ TO BE:
C                (1) COUNTED IN . . . . . . . . . . KOUNT
C                (2) SUMMED IN . . . . . . . . . . KSUM
C                (3) ACCUMULATIVELY MULTIPLIED IN   MULT

      KOUNT = 0
      KSUM  = 0
      MULT  = 1

   10 READ(5,100,END=70)N
  100 FORMAT(I4)

      IF(N) 20,30,40

   20    MULT = MULT * N
         GO TO 50

   30    KOUNT = KOUNT + 1
         GO TO 50

   40    KSUM = KSUM + N
         GO TO 50

   50 WRITE(6,101) N,MULT,KOUNT,KSUM     Poor Practice, should be:
  101 FORMAT(1X,4I10)                    50 Continue
         GO TO 10                        Write(...

   70 STOP
      END
```

FIGURE 16-6 Arithmetic IF in program to count, sum, and multiply accumulatively

Chapter 17

Additional
Input/Output

All of Section 17–1 and the first two subsections of Section 17–2 can be used with no knowledge beyond Chapter 6. Section 17–3 requires some knowledge of type CHARAC-TER before it can be used. Finally, Section 17–4 considers concepts of file management made available by Full Language FORTRAN 77.

17–1 SIMPLE FILE MANAGEMENT USING SUBSET FORTRAN 77

Although using only the concepts of Subset FORTRAN 77, this section is applicable to most programs involving the utilization of files on and off of disks, tapes, and so on. The numerical calculations performed in the example programs of this section are extremely simple, allowing emphasis to be placed upon file management rather than complex FORTRAN coding for solutions.

17–1.1 Terminology

In order to understand file management, it is essential to understand the terms *character, item, record,* and *file.*

A *character* is a single symbol such as

A   or   3   or   *

An *item* is a string of characters that represents the name of something or a numerical value, such as:

TOM JONES   or   WATCHES   or   263.12   or $17.42

A *record* is a group of sequentially interrelated items that can be considered collectively to be a single unit, such as

TOM JONES 369-26-8493 4.63 163 1896.42

or

WATCHES, SWISS A6B4397 0.001 SECOND ACCURACY $476.00

A *file* is a group of sequentially interrelated records that can be considered collectively to be a single unit, such as

TOM JONES	369-26-8493	4.63	163	1896.42
BILL KING	291-34-8612	5.21	163	2231.64
JIM LEWIS	876-79-8432	7.12	211	4168.32

or

WATCH, SWISS	A6B4397	0.001	SECOND ACCURACY	$476.00
WATCH, ZEISS	Z17K83L	MOST ACCURATE		$974.00
WATCH, ZODIAC	RBY1783C	NOVELTY		$117.50

In computer parlance, a file is associated with some form of mechanical device such as a card reader, remote terminal, high speed printer, disk, drum, magnetic tape, and so forth. The connection between a file and its associated "hardware" is through the unit specifier. Typically, the unit specifier for a card reader or remote terminal for input is specified in this text by 5 (that is, $LR = 5$).

Because files are always associated with a mechanical device, students sometimes confuse a file with the device that stores, inputs, or outputs the file. But in FORTRAN, a file is always "a sequence of records."

By contrast, a record in FORTRAN is simply a sequence of values or a sequence of characters. In practice, a record may be stored on a single card and a file may be stored on a sequence of cards. But records and files do not necessarily correspond to physical entities.

(a) *Record.* FORTRAN records are of three kinds.

1. *Formatted records* are a sequence of characters capable of representation by the processor. Formatted records must be capable of being read and written by (and only by) formatted input/output statements.
2. *Unformatted records* are a sequence of values in a processor-dependent form (sometimes called *binary*). The values contained in unformatted records may be characters or noncharacter representations. Large quantities of data are efficiently transferred between physical storage units in unformatted form.
3. FORTRAN has a special type of record called the *endfile*. This record is used only as the last record of a (sequential) file to indicate that no more additional data exist in the file. (See below.)

(b) *File Properties.* FORTRAN files have properties that are often processor-dependent. Such properties include allowable methods of access, forms, kinds, lengths, and possibilities for names.

1. *Allowable access methods.* These methods depend upon both the processor and the file itself. A file used with *sequential access* might be represented symbolically as:

   [Record 1 | Record 2 | Record 3 | . . . | Record n | Endfile Record]

   Such files are read and written (strictly) in a sequential manner. Thus Record 3 cannot be accessed without first reading Record 1 and Record 2. (In general, the endfile record is required.)

   A file used with *direct access* might be represented symbolically as

   [1, Record 1 | 2, Record 2 | 3, Record 3 | . . . | n, Record n]

   Any record of such a file is read directly by using the record number that defines it. Thus only Record 3 can be read by using the record number itself during input/output operations. Because of this feature, direct access is often called *random access*. Note that each record of files connected for direct access have the same length. Because all records of a file connected for direct access are uniquely identified by a record number (positive integer), and because records can be written in any sequence, records are ordered by the order of their record numbers.

   Some mechanical devices allow files to be connected either for sequential or direct access, while some restrict the access method. For instance, some processors will not permit magnetic tapes to be connected for direct access because of the excessive time required to search back and forth through them. Disks, however, were developed for random entry points and are therefore readily applicable to direct access.

2. *Allowable forms.* All files must be either formatted or unformatted.

3. *Allowable kinds* (not processor dependent). *External files* are located on physical devices not associated with program variables or arrays, such as cards, remote terminals, high speed printers, disks, drums, magnetic tapes, and so forth.

   Internal Files are type CHARACTER variables, array elements, arrays, or substrings contained within the program itself. They are used extensively when rescanning input characters after they have been stored in an internal file when changing types, and so on. Section 17–3.4 illustrates use of internal files to replace the (deleted from FORTRAN 77) ENCODE and DECODE statements of FORTRAN IV.

4. *Allowable lengths.* These are processor dependent. Lengths of records within files are dependent upon the form of the file. Formatted record length is measured in characters. Unformatted record length is measured in processor-dependent units.

5. *File names.* These are permissible only in Full Language FORTRAN, and their form is processor-dependent.

(c) *Mechanical Devices* are constantly changing. The oldest device is a computer card with attendant card reader and card puncher. Remote terminals come in many styles, providing hard copy (results on paper) or a visual display. Paper tape is sometimes used with remote terminals, but less often directly with computers. Paper tape stores symbols by using coded punched holes.

Magnetic tapes come in several varieties, and are not always directly transferable from one machine to another. Input/output of magnetic tape is performed by tape handlers (typically shown on television to represent the computers themselves) which wind and rewind the magnetic tape between the parent tape spool and an auxiliary tape spool.

Drums were introduced to increase storage capacity without the time delay caused by winding and rewinding magnetic tapes. Disks were introduced to provide direct (random) access.

Disks are of many forms; some are portable. "Floppy" *disks* are used to replace the storage capability of magnetic tapes and to supply direct (random) access capability.

Auxiliary external storage devices are likely to continue to change and improve, but the techniques of file management will remain applicable to each. The primary change will be increased speed and flexibility combined with reduced capital, maintenance and operating costs.

17-1.2 Input/Output Statements and Control Information Lists

Subset FORTRAN 77 contains six input/output statements.

> *Data Transfer* (must refer only to files that exist)
> > READ
> > WRITE
> *Auxiliary* (may refer to files which do or do not exist)
> > OPEN
> *File Positioning* (must refer to sequential access files only)
> > BACKSPACE
> > ENDFILE
> > REWIND

From previous use, you are familiar with the data transfer statements READ and WRITE. These, along with the new INPUT/OUTPUT statements ENDFILE, REWIND, BACKSPACE, and OPEN are summarized with their permissible control information list items in Table 17-1.

The unit specifier, u, is required as the first item of every control information list. ENDFILE, REWIND, and BACKSPACE use only the unit specifier, so it is not placed within parentheses.

All other specifiers are optional, except that REC (which specifies the record number to be accessed) must be used with any file we OPEN to make direct access. Direct access files are unformatted, by default.

Files that do not use OPEN are sequential access files, but may be either formatted or unformatted, depending upon the control information list of the WRITE statement that builds them. If the FMT item (or second item in the list) is used in a WRITE that creates a file, the file is formatted; otherwise it is unformatted.

The unit specification should always be set at the beginning of the main program.

$$LR = 5$$
$$LW = 6$$

$$ITAPE = 10$$
$$IDISC = 20$$

are typical entries. Then, (note that file positioning statements can only be used with sequential access)

ENDFILE ITAPE means put an end-of-file on tape ITAPE.

REWIND ITAPE means rewind the tape, that is, position the tape at its initial point—the beginning of the first record.

BACKSPACE ITAPE means back the tape up to the initial point of the preceding record.

To open a file, all three items of the control information list are required. Thus,

OPEN(IDISC, ACCESS = 'DIRECT', RECL = 20)

means open the file on disk for direct access, allocating 20 processor-dependent units for the length of each record. Note, by default, that this file is unformatted.

A typical WRITE and READ to the disk opened by the preceding statement might be

WRITE(IDISC, REC = 4) VAR1, VAR2

which means write contents of VAR1 and VAR2 into Record 4 of the disk file in unformatted form.

READ(IDISC, REC=2) THIS, THAT

means read the contents of record number 2 of the disk file (in unformatted form) and store in variables THIS and THAT. Note that END = 5 cannot be used because direct access files do not allow end-of-file records.

These INPUT/OUTPUT statements and their corresponding control information lists are discussed in Sections 17–1.4 and 17–1.5. In Sections 17–1.6 and 17–1.7, user requirements dictate formulation of two programs that use these statements and control information list items to manage data passed between external devices such as a remote terminal, cards, magnetic tape, disk, and high-speed printer.

17–1.3 Special, Processor-Dependent Information Required

The ease with which processor-dependent information can be obtained depends in a large measure upon the attitude of the personnel in your computer center, your communication with those personnel, and the method by which material is organized. Most personnel will be helpful when you communicate with them through well-thought-out, pertinent questions. Before you will be able to run disks or tapes, it will be necessary to learn something about their processor-dependent characteristics. Three particular items are important.

1. If you are using a magnetic tape processed on another computer, you must be sure that it will work within the operating system of your present computer.
2. If you are using direct access files, you must know how to compute and define a length for the records of that file.

Table 17-1. SUMMARY SUBSET FORTRAN 77 INPUT/OUTPUT STATEMENTS AND CONTROL INFORMATION LISTS

Items: Control Information List	Data Transfer		Input/Output Statements — Auxiliary — File Positioning, Sequential Access Only			OPEN by Unit	Form, Definition and Comments
	READ	WRITE	ENDFILE	REWIND	BACKSPACE		
UNIT Note: u must be first item in control information list.	Required	Required	All have a single form with UNIT following name and not enclosed in parentheses. Let UNIT = u, then: ENDFILE u (Next record becomes endfile record.)	REWIND u (Position to Initial Point in File.)	BACKSPACE u (File positioned before preceding record; if no preceding record, position unchanged. If preceding record is an endfile record, file is positioned immediately before endfile record.)	Required	u ≡ *EXTERNAL* UNIT IDENTIFIER expressed as : (1) integer constant or variable ≥ 0 or : (2) * which signifies (a) processor dependent, (b) preconnected external unit, (c) formatted for (d) sequential access. u ≡ *INTERNAL* UNIT IDENTIFIER expressed as : (1) character variable or : (2) array element of character type.
FMT Note: f must be second item in control information list if it exists.	Optional	Optional					f ≡ FORMAT SPECIFIER expressed as : (1) statement label or : (2) integer variable previously assigned with a statement label, or : (3) character constant. Comment : If FMT exists, file is formatted; otherwise, file is unformatted.
REC	Optional	Optional					REC = rn ≡ RECORD SPECIFIER, that is, specifies record, by number, to be I/O expressed as : (1) integer constant or : (2) integer variable Comment : (1) direct (random) access if REC exists, otherwise sequential access (2) used only if ACCESS = 'DIRECT' within control information list of OPEN statement.

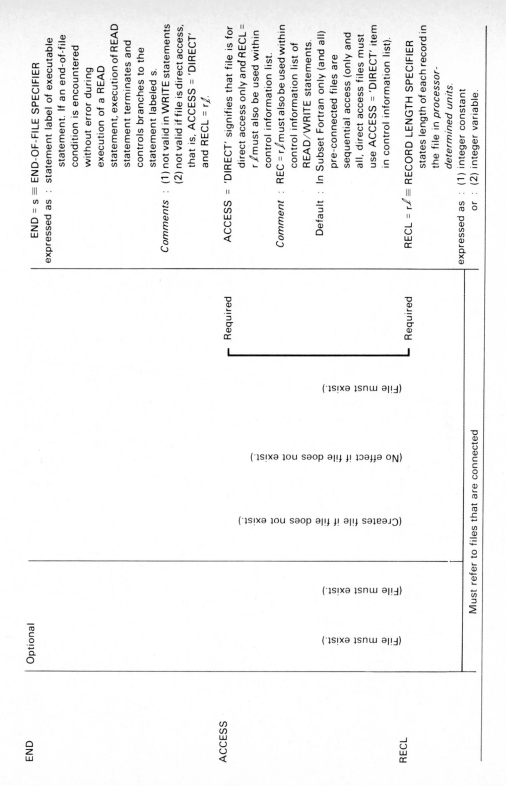

END = s ≡ END-OF-FILE SPECIFIER

expressed as : statement label of executable statement. If an end-of-file condition is encountered without error during execution of a READ statement, execution of READ statement terminates and controls branches to the statement labeled s.

Comments : (1) not valid in WRITE statements
(2) not valid if file is direct access, that is, ACCESS = 'DIRECT' and RECL = $r\ell$.

ACCESS = 'DIRECT' signifies that file is for direct access only and RECL = $r\ell$ must also be used within control information list.

Comment : REC = $r\ell$ must also be used within control information list of READ/WRITE statements.

Default : In Subset Fortran only (and all) pre-connected files are sequential access (only and all, direct access files must use ACCESS = 'DIRECT' item in control information list).

RECL = $r\ell$ ≡ RECORD LENGTH SPECIFIER states length of each record in the file in *processor-determined units.*

expressed as : (1) integer constant
or : (2) integer variable.

Required

Required

(File must exist.)

(No effect if file does not exist.)

(Creates file if file does not exist.)

(File must exist.)

Optional

(File must exist.)

(File must exist.)

Must refer to files that are connected

END

ACCESS

RECL

3. You must know the range (and any other restrictions) on numbers that can be used for unit processors and how these numbers are related to the external units to which they apply.

If you are in an unfamiliar computer center, then page 437 can be used to guide your questioning. Figure 17–1 graphically displays the external devices that you are going to use and indicates when information is going to or from the devices. In addition, the unit specifier is named and a tentative number is assigned. Also, the file on that unit is identified as formatted or unformatted, sequential or direct. A pertinent question is "Would you show me how to access these external units for this computer program written in Subset FORTRAN 77?" The answer might be directions to a specific reference or help in making appropriate control cards to use for the operation. (As soon as possible, of course, it is desirable to read the specifications for yourself.)

Once you have this information, then you will also need to find out how to give a reasonable length for any records of direct access files.

Terminology applied to file management can prove quite troublesome because of the wide variations in operations between different computer centers, and between different processors within the same computer center. Two particularly troublesome concepts are unit connection and file existence. Within FORTRAN, an attempt has been made to standardize these definitions, but because many characteristics of file management are external to the FORTRAN language itself, a wide variety of nuances continue to exist.

Fundamentally, *connection* means that a physical unit is connected to the computer so that information can be input/output to the file (tape, disk, cards, and so on) currently stored on that unit. During such connections, the file is designated by the unit on which it is stored.

Existence is a property of the file itself. A file exists when it can be, potentially, processed by an executable program. A file without information does not exist except when created by an OPEN statement.

Information on a magnetic tape represents an existing file, but until the magnetic tape can be accessed for input/output, the file (unit) is not connected. A disk may be preconnected so that it can be read from and written upon, but if it contains no information the disk (unit) is connected but the file does not exist.

Within the context of FORTRAN 77, files may be connected in three ways: preconnection (typically by job control action or default), OPEN by unit, and (Full Language only) OPEN by name. Files may be created (come to exist) either by writing upon preconnected files or by use of OPEN statements.

17–1.4 Program SOMNUM, Output Some Numbers to External File

Listing 17–1 of program SOMNUM demonstrates how values can be calculated and output on a magnetic tape, disk, or other external device. The unit specification number is stored in integer UNITSP and set with a numerical value of 20. The tape is rewound before its initial use so that it will be positioned correctly. If the tape is already positioned correctly, then no action will occur.

The DO-loop computes a series of integer values and outputs them on the external device specified by UNITSP. Each time a value is calculated, it is output and the device is automatically positioned ready for the next value. Once all the computations have been

```
      PROGRAM SOMNUM
C     --- OUTPUT SOME NUMBERS(GENERATED BY FORMULA) INTO AN EXTERNAL
C     --- FILE WHICH MAY BE A MAGNETIC TAPE, DISC, ETC.  ACTUAL UNIT
C     --- USED IS PROCESSOR-DEPENDENT UPON UNIT SPECIFIER:
      INTEGER UNITSP
      UNITSP = 20

C     --- SET TAPE TO ITS ORIGIN
      REWIND UNITSP

C     --- COMPUTE AND WRITE VALUES
      DO 10 I=1,100
          NUM =(I-I/3*3)*100 + (I-I/7*7)*10 + I-I/13*13
          WRITE(UNITSP) NUM
   10 CONTINUE

C     --- PUT END-OF-FILE ONTO FILE SO END OF DATA CAN BE DETECTED
      ENDFILE UNITSP

C     --- REWIND FILE SO IT WILL BE PROPERLY POSITIONED FOR NEXT RUN
      REWIND UNITSP

      STOP
      END
```

LISTING 17-1 Coding of program SOMNUM

performed and the values output within the DO-loop, and end-of-file has to be set on the unit so that the tape will have a logical end. Finally, the tape is rewound so that it is properly positioned for a subsequent use.

In every case, it is desirable to rewind external devices at the beginning and end of programs to insure proper positioning. Note that the WRITE statement contains no format, so the file is output in unformatted form. In Subset FORTRAN 77, when the program stops executing the file on the external device will be in the 'KEEP' mode and will, therefore, be available for reading by a subsequent program.

17-1.5 Program AVG, Obtain Average of Numbers
   Taken from an External File

This program (Listing 17–2) demonstrates the reverse of the process depicted by program SOMNUM. In this case, values are read from a file and output to a high-speed printer or a remote terminal for inspection by the user.

The unit specification is designated by UNITSP and is set to the integer value ten. Two values are initialized, one to count the number of entries read from the external device and the other to sum them. The unit is rewound to insure that it is at its initial point.

The DO-loop reads values from the external device, counts them, and sums them. It continues to do this until an end-of-file is reached (in which case control transfers to Statement 20). Note that the variable VALUE has been declared type INTEGER so that it can be read from the file created by program SOMNUM. In both cases, the files are used in unformatted form, but input/output cannot be of mixed types.

Once all of the values have been read, counted and summed, their average is computed in Statement 20 and output on the high-speed printer or remote terminal by a WRITE statement. Finally, the external device is rewound for subsequent use, still containing the data that was read from it (including the endfile record).

```
          PROGRAM AVG
C    --- READ NUMBERS FROM FILE, COUNT THEM, AND GET AVERAGE
C    --- EXTERNAL FILE MAY BE DISC, TAPE, ETC.  PRECISE UNIT IS
C    --- SPECIFIED BY UNIT SPECIFIER(PROCESSOR-DEPENDENT):
          INTEGER UNITSP,VALUE
          UNITSP = 10
          LW =6

          KOUNT = 0
          SUM   = 0.

          REWIND UNITSP

   10 READ(UNITSP,END=20) VALUE
          KOUNT = KOUNT + 1
          SUM   = SUM + VALUE
          GO TO 10

   20 AVG = SUM/KOUNT

          WRITE(LW,100) SUM, KOUNT, AVG
  100 FORMAT('1 SUM/KOUNT = AVG:',F12.3,'/',I3,' = ',F7.3////)

          REWIND UNITSP
          STOP
          END
```

Output:

```
          SUM/KOUNT = AVG:   13561.000/100 = 135.610
```

LISTING 17-2 Coding of program AVG

17-1.6 Program PAY1, Simplistic Payroll Program Using Tape, Disk, Card, and High-Speed Printer

The requirements for this program are spelled out in the following statements.

1. Use a master file stored on a magnetic tape that contains (in formatted form)
   (a) Employee's name (listed alphabetically, last name first);
   (b) Accumulated hours worked;
   (c) Rate of pay, in dollars per hour;
   (d) Accumulated pay.
2. Create a new master file on another tape that is updated from time cards of individual employees, (arranged in alphabetical order, last name first), but with cards missing for employees who were absent during pay period).
      Time cards contain:
   (a) Employee's name (last name first, deck in alphabetical order with some names missing);
   (b) Hours worked this pay period;
   (c) Rate of pay in dollars per hour, if changed (if not changed, enter 0).
3. In addition, use a subroutine (not discussed or shown) that prints checks and check stubs from time card and master file information.
4. Also, output information from check stubs on high-speed printer. Because check output requires special forms, accumulate information from check stubs for output at end of program.

Formulation of the problem requires some preliminary planning to establish interaction between cards read and information obtained from the master file on tape. In addition, some thought must be given to where and when to output the updated master file and how to manage the check-stub information to be printed toward the end of the program.

First consider a case where every employee works at least some time during every pay period. In such a circumstance, each time card for each individual employee would be matched by a corresponding (and sequentially located) record on the master tape. For such data, a data card for an individual employee could be read, followed by a corresponding record from the master file. Then, using both sets of information (for the same employee), the employee's check for this pay period could be calculated. The check information could then be used by the subroutine to output the check and corresponding check stub. The check-stub information would have to be saved for the future; otherwise it would destroy the sequence of check printing operations. Finally, the master record would have to be updated and output on the second tape.

This process can be summarized only after making some decision about the external devices that will be used. Three basic decisions are required: (1) the symbolic name for the unit specifier and the numerical integer associated with it, (2) whether the file is to be accessed in the sequential or direct manner, and (3) whether the file is to be formatted or unformatted. The following list shows one possibility:

Master file (input)	ITAPET = 11	Sequential	Formatted
Master file (output)	ITAPE2 = 12	Sequential	Formatted
Time card (input)	LR = 5	Sequential	Formatted
Subroutine (output)	Unknown		
Check stub information (output/input)	IDISK = 20	Sequential	Unformatted
(Output)	LW = 6	Sequential	Formatted

For this program, only sequential access files are used so that the OPEN statement is not required. Formatted files are used rather extensively, although process time could be considerably shortened if unformatted files were used. (In this case, it is assumed that the original master file provided by the corporation had been supplied in formatted form.) The master files are on two tapes, so ITAPE1 and ITAPE2 were chosen as unit symbolic names for the unit specifiers. Obviously, any other integer variable could serve, but mnemonic names are usually preferred. Integer numbers associated with the unit specifiers are limited by different processors and are processor-dependent. The time cards are input using LR=5 in the usual fashion, and the check-stub output to the high speed printer is with LW=6. Intermediate to the output of check-stub information, data are stored sequentially in unformatted form on a disk (with a symbolic unit specifier of IDISK and an integer value of 20). This disk is used to both store and retrieve information within the program and has no use after the program terminates. Using Subset FORTRAN 77, however, no means exist for deleting this file upon termination of the program. Such deletion, therefore, must be handled external to the FORTRAN program itself.

Summarizing (and relating to symbolic unit specifiers): If every individual worked some time during every pay period, then a record could be read from ITAPE1 that corresponds to the time card for the same individual. Calculations would be performed. A subroutine would output the check with its check stub, and the check-stub information would be stored temporarily on IDISK. The loop would continue until all of the information from the master tape and from the individual time cards had been read. Once all of the information was read and processed, the check-stub information would be transferred from IDISK to the HSP.

Realistically, some individuals will not work during a particular pay period, and the Master File record from ITAPE1 for that individual should simply be transferred to ITAPE2 without change. This suggests that an inner DO-loop be constructed that compares the name read from the master file (from ITAPE1) to the name read from an individual's time card.

This total process has been summarized in the flow diagram of Figure 17–1. The first box is utilized to remind us to always rewind tapes so that they will be at their initial point. The first loop reads an individual's time card, followed by a record for a person from the master file. The name received from the time card and from the master file are compared. If they are not the same, then the individual whose name appears on the master record did not work during that pay period, and that employee's record should simply be output unchanged to the master file of ITAPE2. Once this is done, a new record is read from the master file. When the names from the time card and the record of the master file do match, calculations are performed, a subroutine outputs the check with its check stub, and then the check-stub information is output to a disk for storage until the end of the program. (If you have studied the chapters on arrays, you will see that an array could be used in the place of the disk very easily. Nonetheless, with massive amounts of data it may be useful to use the disk in this manner.) Finally, within this loop, the changed master record is output to the new master tape ITAPE2 and flow returns to read the next individual's time card. This looping process continues until either no more cards exist or an end-of-file is read from the master file on ITAPE1. When an end-of-file is encountered in either case, control transfers to Statement 30, where an end-of-file is put on the disk and the disk is rewound for subsequent use. Then records are read sequentially from the disk and the output on the high-speed printer to provide the desired check-stub information. The final operation is to put end-of-file marks on the master tape and to rewind Tapes 1 and 2.

This flow diagram has been augmented to indicate the flow of information to and from devices, to catalog the unit specifications for the devices, and to show the method of access. The program, coded in Listing 17–3, contains extensive comments to help clarify several potentially troublesome issues.

Program PAY1 is quite realistic except for the actual calculations. Obviously, the system implied here is in a utopian state that does not require taxation or any other deductions. This simplistic approach is used, however, so that the details of file management are not lost in the myriad of details associated with realistic accounting for payroll operations. (This program does have a problem in logic; can you find it? See the exercises.)

17–1.7 Program PAY2, Simplistic Payroll Program Using Several External Files, Including a Remote Terminal

The preceding solution to the payroll problem has two major drawbacks. First, reading individual records from a tape with intermediate calculations is a slow process. Second, it

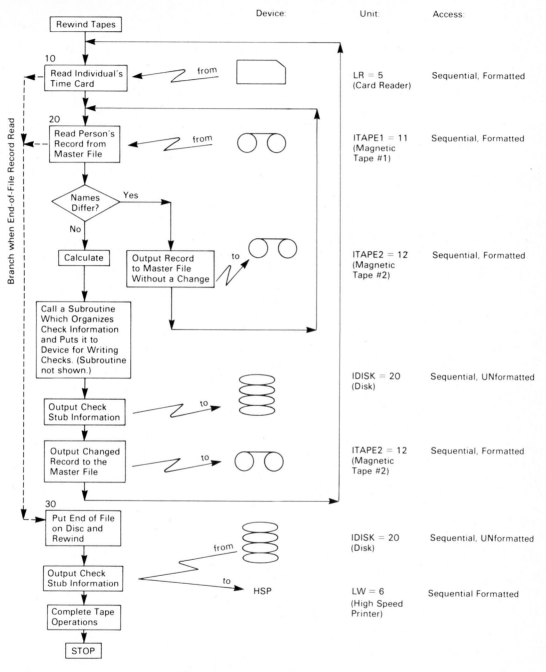

	Device:	Unit:	Access:

Rewind Tapes

10
Read Individual's Time Card ← from □ — LR = 5 (Card Reader) — Sequential, Formatted

20
Read Person's Record from Master File ← from ○○ — ITAPE1 = 11 (Magnetic Tape #1) — Sequential, Formatted

Names Differ? — Yes — No

Calculate

Output Record to Master File Without a Change — to ○○ — ITAPE2 = 12 (Magnetic Tape #2) — Sequential, Formatted

Call a Subroutine Which Organizes Check Information and Puts it to Device for Writing Checks. (Subroutine not shown.)

Output Check Stub Information — to ⊙ — IDISK = 20 (Disk) — Sequential, UNformatted

Output Changed Record to the Master File — to ○○ — ITAPE2 = 12 (Magnetic Tape #2) — Sequential, Formatted

30
Put End of File on Disc and Rewind — ⊙ — IDISK = 20 (Disk) — Sequential, UNformatted

Output Check Stub Information — from ... to → HSP — LW = 6 (High Speed Printer) — Sequential Formatted

Complete Tape Operations

STOP

Branch when End-of-File Record Read

FIGURE 17-1 Flow of payroll program emphasizing I/O devices

```
      PROGRAM PAY1

C     --- PAYROLL PROGRAM--SUBSET FORTRAN 77
C     --- USING:  FORMATTED, SEQUENTIAL(DEFAULT) FILES (TAPE)
C     ---         UNFORMATTED, SEQUENTIAL DISC FILE

      CHARACTER *20 NAME, PERSON

C     --- ESTABLISH EXTERNAL UNIT IDENTIFIERS: (VALUES PROCESSOR DEPEND)
C               --- READ FROM CARDS:
      LR = 5
C               --- WRITE ON HIGH SPEED PRINTER
      LW = 6
C               --- USE MAGNETIC TAPE 1
      ITAPE1 = 11
C               --- USE MAGNETIC TAPE 2
      ITAPE2 = 12
C               --- USE DISC FILE
      IDISK = 20

C     --- REWIND TAPES TO INSURE THAT THEY START AT BEGINNING
      REWIND ITAPE1
      REWIND ITAPE2

C     --- START LOOP ---
C     --- READ INDIVIDUAL'S TIME CARD
C     --- WITH PERSON'S NAME(PERSON), HOURS WORKED(TIME),
C     ---      RATE OF PAY $/HR. (PAY) IF CHANGED, IGNORE
C     ---      IF BLANK OR ZERO
C     --- FROM COMPUTER(TIME) CARD

   10 READ(LR,1000,END=30) PERSON,TIME,PAY

C     --- START INNER LOOP ---
C     --- READ MASTER FILE:
C     ---      PERSON'S NAME(NAME), ACCUMULATED HOURS WORKED (HOURS),
C     ---      RATE OF PAY $/HR.(RATE),ACCUMULATED PAY (TOTPAY)
C     --- FROM TAPE 1 USING UNIT IDENTIFIER ITAPE1

   20 READ(ITAPE1,1000,END=30) NAME,HOURS,RATE,TOTPAY

C     --- COMPARE NAME READ FROM MASTER FILE (NAME)
C     ---     WITH NAME READ FROM COMPUTER(TIME)CARD (PERSON)

      IF( NAME .NE. PERSON) THEN

C           --- ALTHOUGH NOT A GOOD PRACTICE, FOR PURPOSES
C           --- OF ILLUSTRATING USE OF FILES, TIME CARDS
C           --- MUST BE SUBMITTED IN SAME ORDER AS USED
C           --- FOR NAMES IN MASTER FILE (ALPHABETICAL).
C           --- THUS, WHEN NO MATCH IS FOUND, EMPLOYE DID
C           --- NOT WORK AND MASTER FILE IS UNCHANGED.

C           --- UPDATED MASTER FILE IS OUTPUT ON ANOTHER
C           --- TAPE, TAPE 2 USING UNIT IDENTIFIER ITAPE2.
C           --- NOTE: NO CHANGE IN RECORD OF MASTER FILE

      WRITE(ITAPE2,1000) NAME,HOURS, RATE,TOTPAY

C           --- NOW, LOOP BACK TO READ ANOTHER PERSON'S
C           --- RECORD FROM MASTER FILE, STILL SEARCHING
C           --- FOR A MATCH WITH LAST TIME CARD READ.

      GO TO 20
      END IF
```

LISTING 17-3 Coding of program PAY1

```
           IF(PAY .GT. 0.) RATE = PAY
           HOURS = HOURS + TIME
           CHECK = RATE * TIME
C              --- CHECK CONTAINS AMOUNT OF CHECK IN DOLLARS
C              --- WITH ABSOLUTELY NO DEDUCTIONS. THIS UTOPIAN
C              --- SYSTEM IS USED BECAUSE THIS PROGRAM IS TO
C              --- EMPHASIZE FILE MANAGEMENT, NOT ACCOUNTING
C              --- AND TAXATION.
           TOTPAY = TOTPAY + CHECK

C              --- OUTPUT CHECK STUB AND CHECK ONTO HIGH SPEED PRINTER
           CALL CHECKO(PERSON,TIME,RATE,CHECK,LW)
C              --- OUTPUT CHECK STUB INFORMATION INTO DISC FILE
           WRITE(IDISK) PERSON,TIME,RATE,CHECK

C              --- OUTPUT UPDATED RECORD ONTO TAPE 2 FOR CREATION
C              --- OF NEW MASTER FILE
C              --- NOTE:  THIS TIME RECORD IS CHANGED

           WRITE(ITAPE2,1000) NAME,HOURS,RATE,TOTPAY

C              --- NOW LOOP BACK FOR A NEW TIME CARD
           GO TO 10

C       --- WHEN EITHER LAST TIME CARD IS READ OR END-OF-FILE REACHED ON
C       --- TAPE ITAPE1 ('OLD' MASTER FILE), THEN CONTROL TRANSFERED HERE.
C       --- READ CHECK STUB INFORMATION FROM DISC(AFTER ADDING END-OF-FILE
C       --- AND REWINDING DISC) AND OUTPUT ON HIGH SPEED PRINTER.
C       --- NOTE DISC USES UNFORMATTED I/O

    30 ENDFILE IDISK
       REWIND IDISK
       WRITE(LW,'(''1'')')
    35 READ(IDISK,END=40) PERSON,TIME,RATE, CHECK
       WRITE(LW,1002) PERSON,TIME,RATE,CHECK
       GO TO 35

C       --- REWIND TAPES SO THAT THEY WILL BE READY FOR NEXT RUN
    40 REWIND ITAPE1
C       --- PUT END-OF-FILE ON TAPE 2 BECAUSE IT IS SEQUENTIAL ACCESS.
       ENDFILE ITAPE2
       REWIND ITAPE2

       STOP

  1000 FORMAT(A20,3F10.2)
  1002 FORMAT(1X,A20,F8.2,' HOURS X $',F6.2,' PER HOUR = $',F8.2)

       END
```

Master File from Tape #1

```
    ABLE, TOM            163.2       3.42        558.14
    JOHNS, BILL         180.         5.16        873.12
    KING, JOE           143.         8.23       1176.89
    LEWIS, R. B.        180.         7.15       1287.00
    MIKOS, T            180.         6.23       1121.40
    PAUL, MIX           168.         5.49        871.30
    TAVAN, RAOL         170.         6.32       1074.40
```

Time Card Information

```
    ABLE, TOM            40.
    JOHNS, BILL          32.
    KING, JOE            40.         8.90
    MIKOS, T             48.
    PAUL, MIX            40.         6.00
    TAVAN, RAOL          30.
```

LISTING 17-3 *(continued)*

Section 17-1 Simple File Management Using Subset FORTRAN 77

439

Check Stub Information

```
ABLE, TOM          40.00 HOURS X $ 3.42 PER HOUR = $ 136.80
JOHNS, BILL        32.00 HOURS X $ 5.16 PER HOUR = $ 165.12
KING, JOE          40.00 HOURS X $ 8.90 PER HOUR = $ 356.00
MIKOS, T           48.00 HOURS X $ 6.23 PER HOUR = $ 299.04
PAUL, MIX          40.00 HOURS X $ 6.00 PER HOUR = $ 240.00
TAVAN, RAOL        30.00 HOURS X $ 6.32 PER HOUR = $ 189.60
```

Updated Master File to Tape #2

```
ABLE, TOM          203.20      3.42      694.94
JOHNS, BILL        212.00      5.16     1038.24
KING, JOE          183.00      8.90     1532.89
LEWIS, R. B.       180.00      7.15     1287.00
MIKOS, T           228.00      6.23     1420.44
PAUL, MIX          208.00      6.00     1111.30
TAVAN, RAOL        200.00      6.32     1264.00
```

LISTING 17-3 *(continued)*

is undesirable to require that individual time cards be submitted to the program in alphabetical order. Program PAY2 is to be designed to offset these two drawbacks.

Information can be passed directly from the tape, a record at a time, to a disk file (an array could serve the same function) that has direct access. The file numbers can be obtained by using a counter, I, which is initialized before the tape is read and can then be incremented after each record is read from Tape 1. When the process is complete, the master file would reside completely on Disk 1 in a sequential order, and records could be located by use of an appropriate record number. (Of course the information on the master file of Tape 1 is unchanged.)

In the second stage of the program, individual time-card information can be entered from a remote terminal and should include the record number associated with the particular employee. This assumes that the employees have record numbers that are directly associated (the record numbers are actually generated in the program) with the numbers of the records on disk. Although not an entirely satisfactory process, this serves to illustrate the use of direct access files and can be incorporated into large scale records without undue difficulties.

Once an individual's time-card information is read and his or her particular record is obtained from the master file stored on Disk 1, calculations can be performed for his or her check and check-stub information and is output to Disk 2 for future use. Check-stub summary information can then be output directly to the high-speed printer and an updated record for the master file accumulated on Disk 1. (Note that by this process, information on the master file in disk storage is changed within the program. If something goes wrong while the program is running, the basic master file is still safe on Tape 1.) Once information has been read for an individual, calculations have been performed, and information stored as necessary, the loop should proceed until the information for the last person is read.

At that time, control transfers to a statement that puts an end-of-file on Disk 2. Then the master file, which has been updated on Disk 1, is transferred to a new tape (Tape 2), and the final tape actions are taken to make them suitable for use during the next run.

Several observations are in order. First, for files that are not excessively large, Disk 1 could easily be replaced by an array, saving both time and money. Disk 2, which is saved for future use, is an efficient way to accumulate information for use in a subsequent program. Updating the master file from Tape 1 to Tape 2 is a reasonable way to "play safe." At the next operation, Tape 2 becomes Tape 1, and Tape 1 becomes Tape 2, by simply interchanging the units that process them. By this method, the tapes are used in a round-robin fashion so that recovery can be made without loss of information in case of any sort of computer failure.

A flow diagram of the process used by program PAY2 is shown in Figure 17–2, and the coding is given in Listing 17–4 (pages 442–444).

The program PAY2 is redone using Full Language FORTRAN 77 in Section 17–4. The Full Language version appears to be much more complicated but simply takes advantage of additional input/output statements and control information lists that make it possible to trace and eliminate errors occurring during the file management operations.

17-2 ADDITIONAL EDIT DESCRIPTORS

The remaining edit descriptors are described in this section. To save space, several edit descriptors are combined within each illustrative program. The following table summarizes

Edit Descriptors

	Repeatable		Nonrepeatable	
Subset	Full Language	Subset	Full Language
A,Aw	A,Aw	$'h_1h_2...h_n'$	$'h_1h_2...h_n'$
	Dw.d	$nHh_1h_2...h_n$	$nHh_1h_2...h_n$
Ew.d,Ew.dEe	Ew.d,Ew.dEe	BN,BZ	BN,BZ
Fw.d	Fw.d	kP	kP
	Gw.d,Gw.dEe	nX	nX
Iw	Iw,Iw.d	/	/
Lw	Lw		Tc,TLc,TRc
			:
			S,SP,SS

17-2.1 Logical, P (Scale Factor), BZ and BN Editing

The edit descriptors described in this subsection are available in Subset Fortran 77. Their use is demonstrated in Listing 17–5, page 445.

(a) *The L-Edit Descriptor.* The type logical variables and constants are input and output by use of L editing. The edit descriptor is a capital L, followed by an integer constant that specifies the field width. The only data available for logical input and output are the logical constants true (.TRUE.) and false (.FALSE.).

On input, the field may consist of any combination of the characters that make up the logical constants .TRUE. and .FALSE., so long as they contain either the T or F. Variations of input are indicated by the data used by the first READ statement of program LPBZBN. On output, type logical constants are always output as either T or F, right justified within the field width.

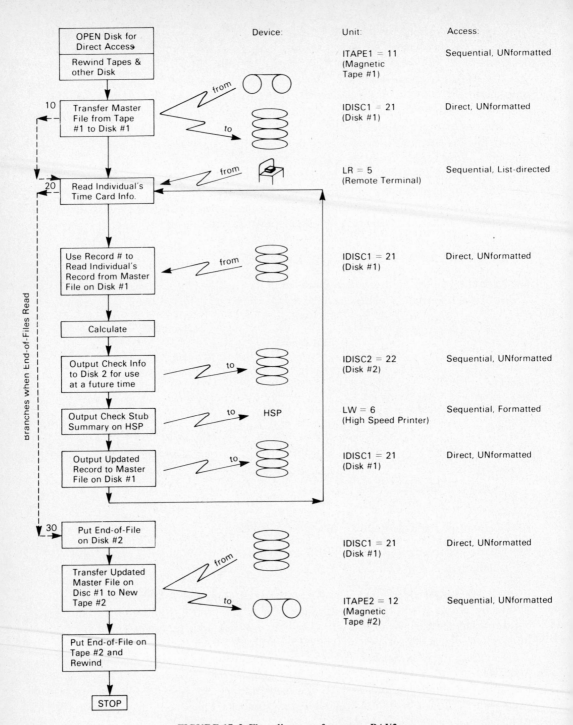

FIGURE 17–2 Flow diagram of program PAY2

```
      PROGRAM PAY2

C     --- ALTERNATE PAYROLL PROGRAM--SUBSET FORTRAN 77
C     --- DEMONSTRATES USE OF OPEN TO MAKE FILE DIRECT
C     --- (RANDOM) ACCESS.

      CHARACTER *20 NAME,PERSON


C     --- ESTABLISH EXTERNAL UNIT IDENTIFIERS: (PROCESSOR DEPENDENT)
      LR = 5
      LW = 6
      ITAPE1 = 11
      ITAPE2 = 12
      IDISC1 = 21
      IDISC2 = 22
C     --- ESTABLISH LENGTH OF RECORDS IN DIRECT ACCESS FILES
      LENGTH = 4

C     --- OPEN FILE TO HAVE DIRECT ACCESS ONLY
      OPEN (IDISC1, ACCESS='DIRECT', RECL=LENGTH)

C     --- REWIND FILES TO BE SURE THEY ARE AT INITIAL POINT
      REWIND ITAPE1
      REWIND ITAPE2
      REWIND IDISC2


C     --- READ MASTER FILE (SEQUENTIAL TAPE) ONTO DISK (DIRECT)
C     --- I IS INCREMENTED TO BE RECORD NUMBER
C     --- I BECOMES TOTAL NUMBER OF RECORDS

      I = 0

   10 READ(ITAPE1,END=20) NAME,HOURS,RATE,TOTPAY
      I = I+1
      WRITE(IDISC1,REC=I) NAME,HOURS,RATE,TOTPAY
      GO TO 10

C     --- MASTER FILE IS NOW ON DISC 1, EACH RECORD NUMBERED
C     --- ASSUME THAT EACH PERSON HAS AN ASSIGNED NUMBER WHICH
C     --- AGREES WITH THEIR RECORD NUMBER SO THAT THIS PROGRAM
C     --- WILL NOT BECOME TOO COMPLEX TO ILLUSTRATE IMPORTANT POINTS.

C     --- ENTER INFORMATION ON EACH EMPLOYE IN FREE FORMAT
C     --- FROM REMOTE TERMINAL (ON THIS PROCESSOR LR=5):
C     ---       J = RECORD NUMBER
C     ---       PERSON = PERSON'S NAME
C     ---       TIME = HOURS WORKED THIS PAY PERIOD
C     ---       PAY = RATE OF PAY $/HR (IF UNCHANGED, ENTER 0)

   20 READ(LR,*,END=30) J, PERSON,TIME, PAY

C     --- GET INDIVIDUAL'S RECORD FROM MASTER FILE ON DISC 1

      READ(IDISC1,REC=J) NAME,HOURS,RATE,TOTPAY

C     --- PERFORM NECESSARY CALCULATIONS:
C     ---     (1) ACCUMULATE HOURS WORKED, (2) SEE IF PAY RATE
C     ---     NEEDS TO BE CHANGED, CHANGE IF NECESSARY, (3) COMPUTE
C     ---     AMOUNT OF CURRENT CHECK, (4) ACCUMULATE TOTAL PAYMENTS
C     ---     MADE TO DATE
      HOURS = HOURS + TIME
      IF(PAY.GT.0.) RATE = PAY
      CHECK = RATE * TIME
      TOTPAY = TOTPAY + CHECK
```

LISTING 17-4 Coding of program PAY2

```
C       --- OUTPUT:
C       ---      (1) CHECK INFO ONTO FILE FOR FUTURE USE (DISC 2)
C       ---      (2) CHECK STUB SUMMARY (ON HIGH SPEED PRINTER)
C       ---      (3) UPDATED RECORD OF MASTER FILE (DISC 1)

            WRITE(IDISC2) NAME, RATE, TIME, CHECK
            WRITE(LW,1000) NAME, RATE, TIME, CHECK
            WRITE(IDISC1,REC=J) NAME, HOURS, RATE, TOTPAY

C       --- LOOP BACK FOR NEXT EMPLOYE INFORMATION FROM REMOTE TERMINAL
            GO TO 20

C       --- WHEN INPUT COMPLETE, CONTROL TRANSFERS HERE BY END IN READ
C       --- IN STATEMENT NUMBER 10

C       --- PUT END-OF-FILE RECORD ON SEQUENTIAL ACCESS DISC 2
     30 ENDFILE IDISC2

C       --- OUTPUT UPDATED MASTER FILE ON DISC 1 TO NEW TAPE 2. (USING
C       --- TWO TAPES IN ROUND-ROBIN FASHION HELPS ELIMINATE DIFFICULTIES
C       --- IF ANY GIVEN RUN IS ABORTED AND MUST BE DONE AGAIN.)

        DO 25 K = 1,I
            READ(IDISC1,REC=K) NAME,HOURS,RATE,TOTPAY
            WRITE(ITAPE2)      NAME,HOURS,RATE,TOTPAY
     25 CONTINUE

C       --- PUT END-OF-FILE RECORD ON SEQUENTIAL ACCESS TAPE 2
        ENDFILE ITAPE2
        REWIND ITAPE2


        STOP
   1000 FORMAT(1X,A20,' $',F6.2,'/HOUR FOR',F6.2,' HOURS = $',F8.2)

        END
```

LISTING 17-4 *(continued)*

(b) *BZ and BN Edit Descriptors.* The BZ and BN edit descriptors define whether trailing blanks are to be considered as zeros or are to be ignored. The BZ and BN edit descriptors are used only with input statements (they have no affect on output statements). BN and BZ affect only D, E, F, G, and I edit descriptors. BZ treats trailing blanks as zeros. BN treats trailing blanks as nonexistent so that the right point of the string of non-blank characters appears to be shifted to the rightmost position in the field width.

In the example, of Listing 17-5, the FORMAT statement 101 tells whether the output is controlled by BZ or BN. Furthermore, output describes the input by using B's to represent blanks within the field width. In the first case, with BZ active and F8.2, the value BB1BBBBB is equal to 1000.00, because the trailing blanks are treated as zeros and the FORMAT statement establishes the location of the decimal point. For the subsequent value, with BN in effect, the blanks following the 2 are ignored and the number read by F8.2 is considered to be 002, which is read .02 in accordance with the format. The third entry, still under the BN control, is not effected because a decimal point is included within the input data. Finally, with BZ in effect, the six trailing zeros after the 4 are treated as zeros, which with F8.0 yields the number 4 million.

The BN edit descriptor is particularly useful for reading real values in exponential form and integer values. Use of the BN edit descriptor makes it possible to left-justify both

```
      PROGRAM LPBZBN
C     --- LOGICAL, P(SCALE FACTOR), BZ AND BN EDITING EXAMPLES
C     --- *        *                    **      **

      IMPLICIT LOGICAL (L)
      INTEGER LR,LW
      LOGICAL TORF

      LR = 5
      LW = 6

C     --- DEMONSTRATE USE OF TYPE LOGICAL

      READ(LR,'(2L1,4L8)') L1,L2,L3,L4,L5,L6
      WRITE(LW,'(''1'',L1,L2,2L4,L6,L8)') L1,L2,L3,L4,L5,L6

      IF('A' .GT. '1') THEN
          TORF = .TRUE.
          WRITE(LW,'(//'' A IS GREATER THAN 1 IS'',L2)') TORF
      ELSE
          TORF = .FALSE.
          WRITE(LW,'(//'' A IS NOT GTR THAN 1, A GT 1 IS'',L2)')TORF
      END IF

C     --- DEMONSTRATE BZ AND BN: (NO EFFECT ON OUTPUT, USE W/INPUT ONLY)

      READ(LR,100) VAR1,VAR2,VAR3,VAR4
  100 FORMAT(BZ,F8.2,BN,F8.2,F8.0,BZ,F8.0)
      WRITE(LW,101)VAR1,VAR2,VAR3,VAR4
  101 FORMAT(////' BZ,F8.2 FOR BB1BBBBB=',F10.2/
     1           ' BN,F8.2 FOR BB2BBBBB=',F10.2/
     2           '    ,F8.0 FOR BB36.42B=',F10.2/
     3           ' BZ F8.0 FOR B4BBBBBB=',F10.2//)

C     --- DEMONSTRATE SCALE FACTOR (KP):

      READ(LR,102) V1,V2,V3,V4
  102 FORMAT(BN,2P4F8.0)
      WRITE(LW,103) V1,V2,V3,V4
  103 FORMAT(//' USING A SCALE FACTOR OF 2 WITH F8.0 YIELDS:'/
     1           ' 36.21   AS ',F10.4/
     2           ' 14.E1   AS ',E10.4/
     3           ' 47.9816 AS ',F10.4/
     4           ' 27.E-3  AS ',E10.4//)

      WRITE(LW,200)
  200 FORMAT(' FORMATS:'/5X,'F12.4',4X,'-4PF12.4',4X,'-2PF12.4',
     15X,'2PF12.4',5X,'F12.4',7X,'0PF12.4')
      WRITE(LW,104) V1,V1,V1,V1,V1,V1
  104 FORMAT(F12.4,-4PF12.4,-2PF12.4,2PF12.4,  F12.4,0PF12.4  )
      WRITE(LW,104) V2,V2,V2,V2,V2,V2
      WRITE(LW,201)
  201 FORMAT(' FORMATS:'/5X,'E12.4',4X,'-4PE12.4',4X,'-2PF12.4',
     15X,'2PE12.4',5X,'E12.4',7X,'0PE12.4')
      WRITE(LW,105) V2,V2,V2,V2,V2,V2
  105 FORMAT(E12.4,-4PE12.4,-2PE12.4,2PE12.4,  E12.4,0PE12.4//)

      STOP
      END
```

Input:

```
TF .TR     FALSE    .TRUE.  .FALSE.
   1      2          36.42  4
36.21    14.E1    47.9816 27.E-3
```

LISTING 17-5 Coding of program LPBZBN with
input and output

Output:

```
 T F    T    F      T           F


 A IS GREATER THAN 1 IS T


 BZ,F8.2 FOR BB1BBBBB=    1000.00
 BN,F8.2 FOR BB2BBBBB=        .02
   ,F8.0 FOR BB36.42B=      36.42
 BZ F8.0 FOR B4BBBBBB=4000000.00


 USING A SCALE FACTOR OF 2 WITH F8.0 YIELDS:
 36.21    AS      .3621
 14.E1    AS  .1400+003
 47.9816  AS      .4798
 27.E-3   AS  .2700-001


 FORMATS:
    F12.4        -4PF12.4      -2PF12.4      2PF12.4      F12.4      0PF12.4
      .3621          .0000        .0036     36.2100    36.2100        .3621
   140.0000          .0140       1.4000  14000.0000 14000.0000    140.0000
 FORMATS:
    E12.4        -4PE12.4      -2PF12.4      2PE12.4      E12.4      0PE12.4
 .1400+003************   .0014+005 14.0000+001 14.0000+001  .1400+003
```

LISTING 17-5 *(continued)*

integers and real numbers that are read in scientific notation, rather than tediously requiring right-justification.

The default value is usually BZ. (If a file is opened in Full Language FORTRAN 77, however, the method of treating blanks on input is controlled by control information list item BLANK, which has a default of NULL; this corresponds to BN rather than BZ. See Table 17–4.) When BZ or BN are encountered in a format specification, they remain in effect (within that FORMAT statement only) until altered by another BZ or BN.

(c) *Scale factor.* An optionally signed integer constant preceding a P specifies a scale factor. The scale factor relationships for F, E, D, and G type editing are summarized in Table 17–2.

Thus, on input, 36.21 yields

$$
\begin{array}{ll}
.3621 & \text{with scale factor of } 2 \\
.003621 & \text{with scale factor of } 4 \\
3621 & \text{with scale factor of } -2 \\
362100. & \text{with scale factor of } -4
\end{array}
$$

The preceding example corresponds to the first column and row of Table 17–2, where

$$
\left.\begin{array}{c}
\text{external} \\
\text{represented} \\
\text{number}
\end{array}\right\} = \left.\begin{array}{c}
\text{internal} \\
\text{represented} \\
\text{number}
\end{array}\right\} \times 10^{k}
$$

which for first case is

$$36.21 = 0.3621 \times 10^2$$

and for the last is

$$36.21 = 362100. \times 10.^{-4}$$

The next example corresponds to the last column of the first row of Table 17-2, where 54.32 is the "internal represented number" and the subsequent four versions are the "external represented numbers." Thus, for the first case,

$$5432. = 54.32 \times 10^2$$

and for the last,

$$0.005432 = 54.32 \times 10^{-4}$$

On output, 54.32 yields

$$
\begin{array}{ll}
5432. & \text{with scale factor of 2} \\
543200. & \text{with scale factor of 4} \\
.5432 & \text{with scale factor of } -2 \\
.005432 & \text{with scale factor of } -4
\end{array}
$$

On output, 17.21 E10 yields

$$
\left.
\begin{array}{ll}
1721.\text{E8} & \text{with scale factor of 2} \\
172100.\text{E6} & \text{with scale factor of 4} \\
.1721\ \text{E12} & \text{with scale factor of } -2 \\
.001721\ \text{E14} & \text{with scale factor of } -4
\end{array}
\right\}
\begin{array}{l}
\text{Number before E} \\
\text{multiplied by } 10^k, \\
\text{exponent reduced} \\
\text{by k.}
\end{array}
$$

Table 17-2 Scale Factor Relationships

Scale Factor Edit Descriptor: kP, k an optionally signed integer constant

Type Editing	Input — Without Exponent	Input — With Exponent	Ouput
F	external represented number } = internal represented number] $\times 10^k$	no effect	external represented number } = internal represented number] $\times 10^k$
E	external represented number } = internal represented number] $\times 10^k$	no effect	number before E multiplied by 10^k } and { exponent (after E) reduced by k
D	external represented number } = internal represented number] $\times 10^k$	no effect	number before E multiplied by 10^k } and { exponent (after E) reduced by k
G	external represented number } = internal represented number] $\times 10^k$	no effect	None, if within F editing range; Else use E output editing

Several other combinations are demonstrated in Listing 17–5. Note in particular that the scale factor remains in effect until it is changed. Thus the value 36.21, which is read as .3621, is output using six different scale factors on the same line. In the fifth location, the F12.4 retains the scale factor from the previous entry of 2P. Finally, on the last entry, the zero in front of the P returns the scale factor to zero, the normal position. Also note that on input, the scale factor has no effect with values that contain an exponent.

The form of constants input or output with exponents is changed, but their numerical values are not. Scale factors on input or output without exponents actually change values by some power of ten.

17–2.2 Positional (T, TL, TR) and Optional Plus Sign (S, SP, SS) Editing

These edit descriptors are available only in Full Language FORTRAN 77, and their use is demonstrated in program POPSE of Listing 17–6.
The following are the rules for position editing.

Tc = Position next character at c^{th} character position.

TLc = Position next character c characters backward (left) from the current position. (*Note:* If position specified is off left side of device, position next character to position 1.)

TRc = Position next character c characters forward (right) from current position.

T-editing is most useful for controlling the format of output, including printing several characters in the same location (some environments restrict such overprinting).

T-editing also makes it possible to do some other interesting things. For instance, the READ statement of program POPSE (Listing 17–6), uses FORMAT Statement 100 to read data into the character array CHARV from the first card (4A8). Once this is done, the TL32 edit descriptor transfers control back to the first position on the card, and four type real values are read into array REALV (from the beginning of that same card). Once the real array has been read, the edit descriptor TL28 returns control 28 locations to the left (still on that same card) so that the integers are read from fields 5 through 8, 9 through 12, 13 through 16 and 17 through 24. By this means, type character, real, and integer array elements were all read from the same data, on the same card.

Except for the T, TL, TR, X, slash, H, and apostrophe, file position is not changed by nonrepeatable edit descriptors. Position of T, TL, and TR is the subject of this section; X and slash edit descriptors have been discussed previously. After each apostrophe, H, or repeatable (A,D,E,F,G,I,L) edit descriptor has been processed, "the file is positioned after the last character read or written in the current record."

The second READ statement (after FORMAT statement 101) of program POPSE uses FORMAT statement 102 to input integers to array INTV. Edit descriptors T7,I1 cause the 7 from the seventh column of input to be stored in INTV(1). Once completed, the file is positioned to the 8th column. Then TL5,I1 causes the value for INTV(2) to be taken from location 8−5=3. Once completed, the file is positioned to column 4. Edit descriptor TR2,I1 then causes INTV(3) to be taken from location 4+2=6. (Note that INTV(3) of 6 is output by the last WRITE statement in the 23rd column by edit descriptors T20,I4 of FORMAT statement 103 because the left blank occurs in column

```
C     PROGRAM POPSE
C     ---   POSITIONAL(T,TL,TR)AND  OPTIONAL PLUS SIGN(S,SP,SS) EDITING
C     ---   *                  *         *    *              *

      CHARACTER *8 CHARV(4)
      DIMENSION REALV(4), INTV(4)

      LR=5
      LW=6

      READ(LR,100) CHARV,REALV,INTV
  100 FORMAT(4A8,TL32,F8.2,F8.4,F8.0,F8.6,TL28,3I4,I8)
      WRITE(LW,101) CHARV,REALV,INTV
  101 FORMAT('1 ALL OF THESE READ AND RE-READ FROM SINGLE CARD'/
     1        4(4X,A8)/4(4X,F20.6)/4(2X,I8)//)

      READ(LR,102) INTV
      WRITE(LW,102)INTV,INTV
  102 FORMAT(T7,I1,TL5,I1,TR2,I1,T9,I1,T20,4I1//)
      WRITE(LW,103) INTV
  103 FORMAT(SP,T7,I4,I6,SS,T20,I4, SP,T30,I2)

      STOP
      END
```

Input:

```
12345678901234567890123456789012                              POPSE D1
1234567890123                                                 POPSE D2
```

Output:

ALL OF THESE READ AND RE-READ FROM SINGLE CARD column-number diagram with values:
```
    12345678    9012345     78901234    56789012
         123456.780273            9012.345581         78901234.000000        56.789012
    5678        9012      3456   78901234

3  67 9            7369

     +7    +3      6      +9
 4 5     9 10  14 15   19 20  24 25  29 30 ←——Column numbers
```

LISTING 17-6 Coding of program POPSE with input and output

20, the second and third blanks in columns 21 and 22, and therefore the 6 in column 23. The one-off error is not uncommon when using T, TL, and TR edit descriptors.

Rereading of data can be useful when breaking apart compound code numbers such as X031RBT76389A471ZT43, which contain information about cost, physical description, available inventory, orders processed, and orders placed but not processed. (The same goal can also be accomplished by the use of internal files; see Section 17-3.4.) T-editing is also used to facilitate compounding entities of different length and type into one continuous string of output. For instance, if KEY1 = 157 and KEY2 = 3, the format I3,'.',I3 would yield 157. 3. If it is desired that the output should have the appearance 157.003, then the Iw.m edit description of Section 17-2.3 can be used in I3,'.',TL1,I4.3 to yield the proper result (assuming plus signs are not being printed). Some machines place a blank in the first space when w and m are equal. On other machines, the simple format I3,'.',I3.3 provides the same result.

The last WRITE statement outputs the integer array INTV using the edit descriptors which control the absence or inclusion of leading signs. The following is a summary of these edit descriptors.

On output only (no effect on input):

> S = output of optional + sign reverts to being processor-dependent
>
> SP = produce a + sign for all otherwise optional + signs.
>
> SS = do not produce a + sign for optional + signs.

The effect of these edit descriptors is apparent in the demonstration program POPSE (Listing 17–6). Note, however, that the S, SP, or SS edit descriptor remains in effect within a format until it is changed.

17–2.3 Numerical Editing Summarized, Including Full Language

In previous chapters, I, F and E edit descriptors have been used extensively. In this section, the effect of these edit descriptors on the form of output is discussed more precisely, and the D and G edit descriptors are introduced.

(a) *The Iw and Iw.m edit descriptors* are treated identically on input. On output, however, the Iw.m edit descriptor not only specifies a field of w but also specifies that "the unsigned integer constant must consist of at least m digits," where m must not be greater than w. If m is greater than the number of digits in the variables, leading zeros are added, and if m is zero, only blanks are output if the value of the integer is zero. The following are some examples.

Value or Integer	Edit Descriptor	Output Form
123	I5.4	ΔΔ0123
−123	I7.5	Δ−00123
0	I4.0	ΔΔΔΔ

(b) *The Fw.d edit descriptor* may be used to input values into real, complex, and double precision items using either a string of digits or an exponential form utilizing a signed integer constant, scientific notation using E, or scientific notation using D in place of E for double precision items. Typical examples for the same value are:

$$876.1 \quad 8.761+2 \quad 87.61E1 \quad 0.8761D3$$

On output, the internal value (modified by a scale factor if one is in effect) is rounded to d fractional digits. Complex always takes two edit descriptors.

(c) *Ew.d, Dw.d, and Ew.dEe edit descriptors* use the same form of input field as F-editing. On output, the general form is:

1. an optional + or − sign;
2. an optional zero;
3. a decimal point;
4. at most d significant digits of the value, after rounding;
5. an exponent that usually takes 4 spaces and has the typical form

$$E\pm87 \text{ or } \pm087, \quad \text{if } |\text{exponent}| \le 99$$
$$\pm876 \qquad\qquad\quad \text{if } 99 \le |\text{exponent}| \le 999$$

where for double precision, E is replaced by D.

Field width, w, should always be at least 1 (for a leading blank) plus 1 (for optional sign), plus 1 (for optional zero), plus 1 (for decimal print), plus 4 (for exponent with its sign) plus d, or d + 8.

On machines that allow exponents with absolute values greater than 999, the form Ew.dEe can be used for real values, but not for double precision. The integer e then indicates the number of digits to be displayed after the required plus or minus sign. A typical example is the following.

Value of Real Variable	Edit Descriptor	Output Form
-0.124×10^{3764}	E12.3E5	$-0.124 + 03764$

Field width must be at least $4 + d + e$.

(d) *The Gw.d or Gw.dEe edit descriptor* is allowed in the Full Language. Input editing is identical with F-editing, but representation of the output field depends upon the magnitude of the values.

If the value (more precisely, internal datum) is called N, then the following is true.

If	Then Gw.d is the same as	Example value	Output form if edit description is G10.4
$N < 0.1$	Ew.d	.024	.2400−001
$0.1 \leq N \leq 1.0$	F(w − 4) . d + 4 blanks	.7560	.7560⅃⅃⅃⅃
$1.0 \leq N \leq 10.$	F(w − 4) . (d − 1) + 4 blanks	−1.83	−1.830⅃⅃⅃⅃
$10. \leq N \leq 100.$	F(w − 4) . (d − 2) + 4 blanks	26.97	26.97⅃⅃⅃⅃
.			
.			
.			
$10**(d − 1) \leq N \leq 10**d$	F(w − 4) . 0 + 4 blanks	1216.23	1216.⅃⅃⅃⅃
$N > 10**d$	Ew.d	1837000.	1837+007

(Gw.dEe editing is the same as Gw.d, except that in the preceding example, the integer 4 subtracted from the field width and the integer 4 indicating the number of trailing blanks are replaced by e + 2.)

Program FLNE of Listing 17–7 is an example prepared to illustrate the rules of this section used most often.

17-3 ADDITIONAL FORMATTING TECHNIQUES AVAILABLE IN FULL LANGUAGE ONLY

While not essential, the techniques demonstrated in this section can prove quite useful during the input/output process.

17-3.1 Program COLON, Optional Format Termination

Program COLON of Listing 17–8 illustrates a common occurrence when information is output. In this case, it is desired to output the row number, the word ROW itself, a number signifying the element of array ROW, and the value associated with that location. This is accomplished by using a repeat FORMAT statement, which produces the word

```
      PROGRAM FLNE
C     --- FULL LANGUAGE(ONLY) NUMERICAL EDITING
C     --- *       *              *          *

      IMPLICIT COMPLEX(C), DOUBLE PRECISION(D)
      COMPLEX RPLUSI
      DOUBLE PRECISION BIGNUM

      LR= 5
      LW= 6

      RPLUSI = ( 34.63 , 11.21 )
      BIGNUM = 0.577215664901533
      WRITE(LW,99) RPLUSI, BIGNUM , BIGNUM , BIGNUM , BIGNUM
   99 FORMAT("1 COMPLEX RPLUSI = ", 2F8.2/
     1    "          BIGNUM = ", F25.16/
     2    "     10 X BIGNUM = ", 10P,F25.6/
     3    "     10 X BIGNUM = ",      E25.6/
     4    "          BIGNUM = ",   0P,E25.16///)
      READ(LR,"(F5.2,F7.3,F20.7)") CONJ, DBLZ
      WRITE(LW,"("" CONJ="", F8.3,F10.5/
     1          "" DBLZ="", D20.7 )") CONJ, DBLZ

C     --- G EDITING
      V1 = -.0000326
      V2 = .024
      V3 = .756
      V4 = -1.83
      V5 = 26.972
      V6 = 1836972.
      V7 = 8.4E21
      V8 = 7.3E-17
      WRITE(LW,100) V1,V2,V3,V4,V5,V6,V7,V8
      WRITE(LW,101) V1,V2,V3,V4,V5,V6,V7,V8
      WRITE(LW,102) V1,V2,V3,V4,V5,V6,V7,V8
      WRITE(LW,103) V1,V2,V3,V4,V5,V6,V7,V8
  100 FORMAT(////" G8.2:",8(2X,G8.2))
  101 FORMAT(    " G10.1:",8(2X,G10.1))
  102 FORMAT(    " G10.4:",8(2X,G10.4))
  103 FORMAT(    " G20.8:",/,(4(2X,G20.8)/))

      STOP
      END
```

Input:

```
12345678901234567890123456789012
```

Output:

```
COMPLEX RPLUSI =     34.63   11.21
        BIGNUM =            .5772156649015330
   10 X BIGNUM =       5772156649.015330
   10 X BIGNUM =    5772156649.015330-010
        BIGNUM =            .5772156649015330+000


CONJ= 123.450  6789.01202
DBLZ=        .3456789+013


  G8.2: -.33-004    .24-001    .76       -1.8        27.       .18+007   .84+022   .73-016
 G10.1:    -.3-004    .2-001    .8        -2.        .3+002    .2+007    .8+022       .7-016
 G10.4: -.3260-004  .2400-001  .7560     -1.830      26.97     .1837+007 .8400+022 .7300-016
 G20.8:
        -.32600000-004       .24000000-001       .75600000          -1.8300000

         26.972000            1836972.0           .84000000+022       .73000000-016
```

LISTING 17-7 Coding of program FLNE with
input and output

```
          PROGRAM COLON
C     --- DEMONSTRATE EFFECT OF COLON IN PLACE
C     --- OF COMMA IN FORMAT STATEMENT

      DIMENSION ROW(4)
      DATA ROW/1.,2.,3.,4./,LW/6/

      WRITE (LW,'(6('' ROW'',I1,'' = '',F4.1,2X))') (I,ROW(I),I=1,4)
      WRITE (LW,'(///
     1          6('' ROW'',I1,'' = '',F4.1:2X))') (I,ROW(I),I=1,4)
C                                              *
C                                              *
C                              FROM COMMA ,-: TO COLON

      STOP
      END
```

Output:

```
ROW1 =   1.0   ROW2 =   2.0   ROW3 =   3.0   ROW4 =   4.0   ROW

ROW1 =   1.0   ROW2 =   2.0   ROW3 =   3.0   ROW4 =   4.0
```

LISTING 17–8 Coding of program COLON with output

ROW after the last entry. The extraneous ROW occurs because of a (usually) desirable feature that provides for continuation of output until the end of the FORMAT statement after processing the last data.

To eliminate the extraneous ROW, the comma is replaced by a colon. Use of the colon signifies that the format is to terminate at that point if no more values are to be output. Any trailing comments are not printed after a colon unless additional numerical, logical, or character data exist to be output.

17–3.2 Program ADJFMT, Adjust Format Within the Program

Sometimes it is desirable to output a message at the right of a series of columns when the number of columns changes from run to run. For simplicity, a FORMAT statement using nF10.2, where n could be an integer variable specified at run time, would be desirable. Within the specifications for FORTRAN 77, however, this edit descriptor is not permitted and another technique must be employed.

The basic ingredients are a FORMAT statement that is established as a character constant, a value (called N) that tells how many columns are to be output, and the relationship established through a DATA statement that expresses the number of columns, N, in type character for use in the character constant representing the FORMAT statement.

Look at the program of Listing 17–9. The variable FMT is defined as type character, with a length of 30. In addition, character array NN (7 locations) is declared with one character per location. The DATA statement puts 1 through 7, in type character, into the seven locations of character array NN. The basic format is established as a character constant in variable FMT, with the number in front of the F descriptor left blank.

The number of columns, N, is input and the second location of the character constant FMT (which represents the format) is filled with the appropriate type character number corresponding to N, and is found in the Nth location of character array NN. The

```
      PROGRAM ADJFMT
C     --- OFTEN, IT IS DESIRABLE TO OUTPUT TEXTUAL MATERIAL AFTER
C     --- (TO THE RIGHT OF) COLUMNS OF FIGURES.  IF THE NUMBER OF
C     --- COLUMNS VARIES, THIS TECHNIQUE PROVIDES A SOLUTION.
C     --- FOR ILLUSTRATION, OUPUT OF AN ARRAY INPUT WITH N COLUMNS
C     --- IS SHOWN--THIS SIMPLISTIC PROGRAM IS USED TO ALLOW
C     --- CONCENTRATION ON THIS TECHNIQUE WITHOUT OTHER DISTRACTIONS.

      DIMENSION TBL(3,7)
      CHARACTER FMT*30

      CHARACTER *1 NN(7)
      DATA NN/'1','2','3','4','5','6','7'/,LR/5/,LW/6/

C     --- ESTABLISH BASIC OUTPUT FORMAT IN FMT
      FMT='( F10.2,'' KILOGRAMS PER ITEM'')'

C     --- READ NUMBER OF COLUMS TO BE READ, IF 0--PROGRAM STOPS

    5 READ(LR,'(I2)') N

C     --- ADJUST FORMAT STATEMENT: USE CHARACTER IN N-TH LOCATION OF NN
      FMT(2:2) = NN(N)

C     --- NOW, READ AND WRITE ARRAY TABLE, A LINE AT A TIME

      IF(N .GT. 0) THEN

          DO 10 I=1,3
              READ(LR,'(10F8.0)')(TBL(I,J), J=1,N)
              WRITE(LW,FMT=FMT)(TBL(I,J),J=1,N)
   10     CONTINUE

          GO TO 5

      END IF

      STOP
      END
```

Input:

```
 4
21.6    18.34   5.23    8.84
 2.1     2.2    2.3     2.4     2.5
 3.1     3.2    3.3     3.4     3.5
 2
41.1    41.2
42.1    42.2
43.1    43.2
 0
```

Output:

```
21.60       18.34       5.23        8.84 KILOGRAMS PER ITEM
 2.10        2.20       2.30        2.40 KILOGRAMS PER ITEM
 3.10        3.20       3.30        3.40 KILOGRAMS PER ITEM
41.10       41.20 KILOGRAMS PER ITEM
42.10       42.20 KILOGRAMS PER ITEM
43.10       43.20 KILOGRAMS PER ITEM
```

LISTING 17-9 Coding of program ADJFMT with
input and output

format FMT is now complete and has exactly enough columns for output of the columns of the array. As the table is read, it is output using the format FMT. As observed in the output of Listing 17–9, this makes it possible to include "kilograms per item" with every line, even though the number of columns changes between runs.

17-3.3 Program FMTINT, Format Obtained from Input Data

An extension of the requirements in the preceding section occurs when the data to be input (or output) must have a specific form that varies between users of the program. In such a case, the format can be read into the program by variables of type character, and used for either input or output as required. Listing 17–10 illustrates the method.

This technique is particularly useful when a master program is run for several different corporations, where each wants to input material in a different form and to have the results output according to their own particular requirements. In such a case, great flexibility can be obtained by this process, without necessitating large amounts of extra work.

```
      PROGRAM FMTINP
C     --- A LARGE PROGRAM MIGHT BE RUN FOR SEVERAL DIFFERENT FIRMS,
C     --- EACH REQUIRING DIFFERENT FORMATS FOR OUTPUT.  THIS SHOWS
C     --- A VERY SIMPLE INDICATION OF THE PROCESS BY USING FORMATS
C     --- READ INTO CHARACTER VARIABLES TO OUTPUT A SIMPLE TABLE.

      DIMENSION TBL(3,3)
      CHARACTER *80 FMT1,FMT2

      DATA TBL/1.1,2.1,3.1,2.1,2.2,2.3,3.1,3.2,3.3/,LR/5/,LW/6/

C     --- READ FORMATS FOR TITLE AND FOR TABLE OUTPUT
   10 READ(LR,'( A80 )',END=30) FMT1,FMT2

C     --- OUTPUT PROPERLY TITLED AND PROPERLY SPACED TABLE

      WRITE(LW,FMT1)
      DO 20 I = 1,3
         WRITE(LW,FMT2)(TBL(I,J),J=1,3)
   20 CONTINUE

      GO TO 10

   30 STOP
      END
```

Input:

```
('1THIS IS FIRST TITLE'/' TABLE AT 3F5.1'/)
(3F5.1)
(////' THIS IS SECOND TITLE'/' TABLE AT 3E10.2'/)
(3E10.2)
```

Output:

```
THIS IS FIRST TITLE
TABLE AT 3F5.1

1.1   2.1   3.1
2.1   2.2   3.2
3.1   2.3   3.3



THIS IS SECOND TITLE
TABLE AT 3E10.2

   .11+001    .21+001    .31+001
   .21+001    .22+001    .32+001
   .31+001    .23+001    .33+001
```

LISTING 17–10 Coding for program FMTINP
with input and output

However, this method is prone to error because it will not function as desired if the formats are not input correctly. If the number of users is not too great, and if the desired formats do not change from run to run, then a preferable procedure (much less error-prone) would be to store the required formats in character arrays within the program.

17-3.4 Program ENCODE, Using Internal Files for Encode and Decode Processes

Older versions of FORTRAN sometimes contained the statements ENCODE and DECODE. FORTRAN 77 allows these same operations by use of READ and WRITE statements, with less confusion about the way the data is being transmitted. The program ENCODE (Listing 17-11) is essentially self-explanatory, particularly when related to the program's output. (Reading and writing can only be by sequential access, formatted, input/output statements.)

The array TABLE could be output with an E-edit descriptor for essentially any accuracy desired. Sometimes, however, it is desirable to output the values located in a type real array (TABLE) in an integer format, with all values rounded to the nearest ten. In addition, when the numbers become too large or small or almost zero, it is often desirable to output words stating these facts rather than integer numbers. Without the use of internal files, there is no way FORTRAN 77 can do this operation without a great deal of data manipulation.

However, using the internal file INTFIL to store the character values from array ALTERS (or the integer values computed in variable INTEG) is permissible, because data conversion is provided by the use of internal files. Once completed, the internal file is

```
      PROGRAM ENCODE
C     --- ENCODE AND DECODE ARE NOT PART OF FORTRAN 77
C     --- BUT SAME EFFECT IS ACHIEVED BY USING INTERNAL FILES

C     --- USE CHARACTER VARIABLE INTFIL AS AN INTERNAL FILE

C     --- TO EMPHASIZE POINT, PROGRAM SIMPLY READS AND OUTPUTS A TABLE
C     --- TABLE READ IS OF TYPE REAL
C     --- ALTERATIONS:
C     ---   (1) IF GREATER THAN 100,000. OUTPUT 'TOO BIG'
C     ---   (2) IF LESS THAN -60,000. OUTPUT 'TOO LITTLE'
C     ---   (3) IF BETWEEN +20. AND -20. OUTPUT 'ALMOST 0'
C     ---   (4) OTHERWISE OUTPUT AS AN INTEGER TO NEAREST 10 UNITS

      DIMENSION TABLE(3,5)
      CHARACTER *10 ALTERS(3)
      CHARACTER *10 INTFIL(5)

C     --- ESTABLISH MESSAGES TO BE OUTPUT
      DATA ALTERS / '   TOO BIG','TOO LITTLE','  ALMOST 0'/
      DATA LW / 6 /

C     --- READ TABLE USING F-FORMAT BECAUSE TYPE OF ARRAY IS REAL
      DO 10 I=1,3
         READ( 5,1000)(TABLE(I,J),J=1,5)
   10 CONTINUE
```

LISTING 17-11 Coding for program ENCODE with input and output

output in A-format, and shows the values as they would appear in either integer or character format for this particular program.

Using internal files, tables with a combination of type real, type integer, type logical, type character, and so on, can be output without difficulty. This is possible because the various types are written into an internal file in their correct formats. In the process, data is converted into a suitable character format. Then, when the internal file is output using A-edit descriptors, the values "appear" to all be of the specific correct type.

17-4 FILE MANAGEMENT WITH FULL LANGUAGE FORTRAN 77

Full Language FORTRAN 77 contains three more INPUT/OUTPUT statements than Subset FORTRAN 77, and many additional items for the Control Information Lists. The nine INPUT/OUTPUT statements are classified as follows.

```
C        --- A LINE-AT-A-TIME, STORE ALTERED CHARACTERS INTO
C        --- INTERNAL FILE INTFIL

      DO 20 I=1,3

         DO 19 J=1,5

            IF(TABLE(I,J).GT.100000.) THEN
               WRITE(INTFIL(J),'(A10)') ALTERS(1)
            ELSE IF(TABLE(I,J).LT. -60000.) THEN
               WRITE(INTFIL(J),'(A10)') ALTERS(2)
            ELSE IF(TABLE(I,J).LT. 20. .AND.
     1            TABLE(I,J).GT.-20.) THEN
               WRITE(INTFIL(J),'(A10)') ALTERS(3)
            ELSE
               INTEG=(TABLE(I,J)+5.)/10.
               INTEG=INTEG*10
               WRITE(INTFIL(J),'(I10)') INTEG
            END IF

   19    CONTINUE

C        --- NOW OUTPUT ALTERED LINE, PRECEDED BY LINE NUMBER
      WRITE(LW,'(I3,5(2X,A10))') I,INTFIL

   20 CONTINUE

 1000 FORMAT(5F10.0)
      STOP
      END
```

Input:

```
163781.   19.999    -1637.    4         -3
-6.7      -67.      -676.     -6704.    -67000.
12.       124.      1206.     12008.    120000.
```

Output:

```
1    TOO BIG      ALMOST 0      -1630     TOO BIG    TOO LITTLE
2    ALMOST 0          -60      -670       -6690     TOO LITTLE
3    ALMOST 0          120      1210       12010        TOO BIG
```

LISTING 17-11 *(continued)*

Data Transfer (must refer only to files that exist and are connected)

      READ
      WRITE
      PRINT

Auxiliary (may refer to files that do not exist, except for BACKSPACE)

OPEN	(may refer to files that are not connected)
CLOSE	(the file must be connected)
INQUIRE	(may refer to files that are not connected)

File Positioning (the files must be connected and be sequential access)

ENDFILE	(creates a file that does not exist)
REWIND	(no effect if the file does not exist)
BACKSPACE	(the file must exist)

Section 17–4.1 discusses the FORTRAN rules for INPUT/OUTPUT statements and their corresponding control information lists, excluding INQUIRE. Section 17–4.2 uses Full Language FORTRAN 77 to rewrite program PAY2, previously discussed in Section 17–1.7. Finally, the last section considers the INPUT/OUTPUT statement INQUIRE.

17–4.1 INPUT/OUTPUT Statements and Corresponding Control Information Lists

Tables 17–3 and 17–4 summarize INPUT/OUTPUT statements and their corresponding control information lists. Only the highlights of these tables are discussed in the following subsections. (Pages 460–65.)

(a) *Data Transfer.* The three data transfer statements are quite similar to Subset FORTRAN 77, except that PRINT has been added to the INPUT/OUTPUT statements and four items are added to the control information list: UNIT, FMT, IOSTAT, and ERR. In addition, UNIT and FMT do not have to be the first and second items in the control information list if they are used as UNIT = u and FMT = f.

ERR is utilized in much the same manner as END, but is available for READ, WRITE and PRINT. In this case, however, transfer occurs if an error is detected during any READ or WRITE statement. IOSTAT is used to indicate the type of error condition which has been detected. If no error exists, ios, established by IOSTAT, is zero. If an error condition is detected, ios becomes a positive integer. If an end-of-file is detected, ios becomes a negative integer. The numerical value of ios is processor-dependent, and in any particular installation the value of these numbers indicates the type of error or end-of-file that has been detected.

(b) *The Auxiliary File Positioning INPUT/OUTPUT Statements.* (These are used with sequential access files only.) In addition to UNIT, the control information list items IOSTAT and ERR have been added to facilitate detection of any errors which might be encountered.

The summary in Table 17–3 will help you use these INPUT/OUTPUT statements effectively.

(c) *Auxiliary: CLOSE and OPEN.* Full Language FORTRAN 77 allows a number of additional items for the control information lists. In addition, OPEN can be used either by name or by unit. Note that STATUS has a different meaning for CLOSE than it does for OPEN (Table 17–4).

17–4.2 Program PAY3, Simplistic Payroll Program Using Features of Full Language FORTRAN 77

Program PAY3 (Listing 17–12) repeats program PAY2 of Section 17–1.7, using the expanded capabilities of Full Language FORTRAN 77. The program appears somewhat more complicated because of the extended use of OPEN and CLOSE statements and the longer control information lists. It has the advantage of providing additional flexibility and managing the program internally if any errors are detected. (Pages 466–68.)

17–4.3 The Auxiliary INPUT/OUTPUT Statement INQUIRE

The most complicated of the auxiliary INPUT/OUTPUT statements is INQUIRE, which has a large number of items available for the control information list. These items are summarized in Table 17–4. The INQUIRE statement is used to determine information about the characteristics of a file. (Pages 462–65.)

To illustrate the use of the INQUIRE statement, a partial listing of a subroutine called INQUIR is shown in Listing 17–13. A typical set of output that might come from such a subroutine is shown in Listing 17–14. It is left as an exercise to complete the subroutine. (Pages 468–70.)

17–5   EXERCISES

1. Program PAY1 (Listing 17–3) has an error in logic. Can you find it? This type of error is not uncommon when terminating merges and can go undetected for long periods of time.

2. Often a disk or tape is used to store information between runs. Typically, a program might contain a table (array) of names and grades. From time to time, new grades are added and new statistics computed. To eliminate handling old data over and over again, the entire table is stored between runs, ready for reading each time new information is to be added. Think of at least three circumstances where such storage of information between runs would be very beneficial.

3. When working from a remote terminal, some programmers use WRITE statements for output to devices other than the remote terminal and PRINT statements for output to the remote terminal. Can you see any advantages to this procedure? (Sometimes the same material is output on both a high-speed printer and the remote terminal. Sometimes different information is output on the two devices.)

4. Devise two schemes (one using adjustment of formats and one using input of formats) to read

```
DO 10 I = 1, N
READ(LR, ?) (IARAY(I,J),J=1,M), (RARAY(I,K),K=1,L)
```

where IARAY is an integer array, RARAY is a real array, M is number of columns of IARAY used (not the same on each run), and L is number of columns of RARAY used (not the same on each run).

5. Complete Subroutine INQUIR of Listing 17–13.

Table 17-3 Summary of Full Language Fortran 77 Input/Output Statements (excluding CLOSE, OPEN, and INQUIRE) and Control Information Lists

Items: Control Information List	Input/Output Statements						Form, Definition and Comments
	Data Transfer			Auxiliary File Positioning/ Sequential Access Only			
	READ	WRITE	PRINT	ENDFILE	REWIND	BACKSPACE	
UNIT *Note:* u must be first item in control information list if used alone; UNIT = u can have any position in list.	Required	Required	Required as u (without parentheses)	Required	Required	Required	UNIT = u ≡ EXTERNAL UNIT IDENTIFIER expressed as : (1) integer expression (2) * which signifies (a) processor dependent, (b) preconnected external unit, (c) formatted for (d) sequential access. or UNIT = u ≡ INTERNAL UNIT IDENTIFIER (may not be used with auxiliary I/O statements) expressed as : (1) character variable (2) character array (3) character array element (4) character substring
				(Next record becomes endfile record.)	(Position to Initial Point in File.)	(File positioned before preceding record; if no preceding record, position unchanged. If preceding record is an endfile record, file is positioned immediately before endfile record.)	
FMT *Note:* f must be second item in control information list if used alone; FMT=f can have any position in list.	Optional	Optional	Optional				FMT = f ≡ FORMAT SPECIFIER expressed as : (1) statement label (2) integer variable ASSIGNed with statement label (3) character array name (*Comment:* allows input of format so long as input list or any entity associated with it does not contain any portion of the format expression itself). (4) character expression (*Comment:* concatenation allowed except when LEN = *). (5) * which implies List-directed *Comments:* (a) cannot use FMT = * with internal file (b) cannot use REC = rn with FMT = * *Comment :* If FMT exists, file is formatted; otherwise, file is unformatted.

REC = rn ≡ RECORD SPECIFIER, i.e., specifies record, by number, to be I/O

expressed as : integer expression

Comment : (1) direct (random) access if REC exists, otherwise sequential access
(2) used only if ACCESS = 'DIRECT' within control information list or OPEN statement
(3) do not use END = s, end-of-file specifier.

IOSTAT = ios ≡ INPUT/OUTPUT STATUS, SPECIFIER

expressed as : (1) integer variable
(2) integer array element

YIELDS : (1) 0 if no error condition or end-of-file detected.
(2) +integer if error condition detected
(3) -integer if end-of-file detected
} values returned to ios are processor dependent

ERR = s ≡ ERROR SPECIFIER

expressed as : statement label of executable statement (within program unit)

RESULTS : (1) I/O statement terminates
(2) position of file becomes indeterminate
(3) if Control Information List contains IOSTAT=ios, ios becomes defined with +integer
(4) control BRANCHES TO STATEMENT s.

END = s ≡ END-OF-FILE SPECIFIER

expressed as : statement label of executable statement (within program unit)

RESULTS : (1) READ statement terminates
(2) if Control Information List contains IOSTAT=ios, ios becomes defined with -integer
(3) control BRANCHES TO STATEMENT s

Comment : Do not use with direct access files defined when REC = rn within Control Information List.

REC	Optional	Optional	Optional	
IOSTAT	Optional	Optional	Optional	Optional
ERR	Optional	Optional	Optional	Optional
END	Optional	Optional	Optional	
	Must refer only to files that exist.	Creates file if file does not exist.	No effect if file does not exist.	File must exist.

Must refer to files that are connected.

Table 17-4 Summary of Full Language FORTRAN 77 Auxiliary Input/Output Statements Other than File Positioning

Items: Control Information List	CLOSE	OPEN By Name	OPEN By Unit	INQUIRE By File	INQUIRE By Unit	Form	Type	Optional (Specifications)
FILE		Required		Required	Required	FILE=fin	character expression	
UNIT — Note: u must be 1st item in Control Information List if used alone. UNIT=u can have any position in list.	Required	Required	Required		Required	UNIT=u	(1) integer expression (2) * which signifies (a) processor-dependent. (b) preconnected external unit, (c) formatted for (d) sequential access.	
IOSTAT	Optional Return	Optional Return	Optional Return	Optional Return (Note: if error condition occurs, all inquiry specifiers become undefined except *ios*.)	Optional Return	IOSTAT = ios	(1) integer variable (2) integer array element	
ERR	Optional	Optional	Optional	Optional	Optional	ERR=s	statement label	
ACCESS		Optional	Optional	Optional Return	Optional Return	ACCESS=acc	(1) character variable (2) character array element	ACCESS='SEQUENTIAL' ACCESS='DIRECT'
RECL		Required if direct access	Required if direct access	Optional Return	Optional Return	RECL=rcl	integer expression > 0 (1) integer variable (2) integer array element	
STATUS	Optional					STATUS=sta	character expression	STATUS='DELETE' STATUS='KEEP'
STATUS		Optional	Optional			STATUS=sta	character expression	STATUS='OLD' STATUS='NEW' STATUS='SCRATCH' STATUS='UNKNOWN'
FORM		Optional	Optional	Optional Return	Optional Return	FORM=fm FORM=fm	character expression (1) character variable (2) character array element	FORM='FORMATTED' FORM='UNFORMATTED'

The following table summarizes the FORTRAN 77 file management specifiers (OPEN, CLOSE, and INQUIRE):

Specifier	OPEN	CLOSE	(status)	(status)	Specifier form	Variable / expression type
BLANK	Optional	Optional				BLANK='NULL' BLANK='ZERO'
				Optional Return	BLANK=blnk	character expression
			Optional Return	Optional Return	BLANK=blnk	(1) character variable (2) character array element
EXIST			Optional Return	Optional Return	EXIST=ex	(1) logical variable (2) logical array element
				Optional Return	EXIST=ex	(1) logical variable (2) logical array element
OPENED			Optional Return	Optional Return	OPENED=od	(1) logical variable (2) logical array element
				Optional Return	OPENED=od	(1) logical variable (2) logical array element
NUMBER			Optional Return	Optional Return	NUMBER=num	(1) integer variable (2) integer array element
NAMED			Optional Return	Optional Return	NAMED=nmd	(1) logical variable (2) logical array element
NAME			Optional Return	Optional Return	NAME=fn	(1) character variable (2) character array element
SEQUENTIAL			Optional Return	Optional Return	SEQUENTIAL=seq	(1) character variable (2) character array element
DIRECT			Optional Return	Optional Return	DIRECT=dir	(1) character variable (2) character array element
FORMATTED			Optional Return	Optional Return	FORMATTED=fmt	(1) character variable (2) character array element
UNFORMATTED			Optional Return	Optional Return	UNFORMATTED=unf	(1) character variable (2) character array element
NEXTREC			Optional Return	Optional Return	NEXTREC=nr	(1) integer variable (2) integer array element

OPEN statements are used to:
(1) connect existing file to unit
(2) create a preconnected file
(3) create a file and connect to a unit
(4) change certain specifiers of a connection between a file and a unit.

Implicit close at termination of execution is default condition of CLOSE; KEEP (except DELETE for 'SCRATCH' files.)

(each row continued on next page)

Table 17–4 (Continued)

Items: Control Information List	Optional Return	Comments	Default	Inquire by file *Assigned values only if file name fin is acceptable, otherwise become un-defined* [defined only if od = .TRUE.]	Inquire by unit *defined only if unit exists and file is connected*
FILE		Must be a form acceptable to processor for use as a file name.	Processor-determined	[fin]	
UNIT					
IOSTAT	0 + integer – integer	If no error condition or end-of-file detected If error condition detected } *Values returned to ios are* If end-of-file detected } *processor-dependent*			
ERR		Control branches to executable statement labeled s			
ACCESS	acc='SEQUENTIAL' acc='DIRECT' acc is undefined	Sequential access Direct (random) access No connection	SEQUENTIAL	acc	acc
RECL		Length of record: (1) number of characters if formatted. (2) processor dependent units if unformatted. (Undefined if od ≠ .TRUE.)		rcl	rcl
STATUS		File ceases to exist after execution of CLOSE File continues to exist after execution of CLOSE except 'KEEP' cannot be used with 'SCRATCH' files File must exist. FILE=fin must be used. File must not exist. File created and becomes 'OLD'. Cannot be used with named file. Exists only between OPEN and CLOSE. Processor-dependent.	'KEEP' except 'DELETE' for 'SCRATCH' files 'UNKNOWN'		
FORM	fm='FORMATTED' fm='UNFORMATTED' fm is undefined	Connected for formatted I/O only. Connected for unformatted I/O only. If file connected for formatted I/O only. If file connected for unformatted I/O only. If file is not connected.	'FORMATTED' for sequential access. 'UNFORMATTED' for direct access.	fm	fm

Specifier	Value	Description	Abbrev.
BLANK	blnk='NULL' blnk='ZERO' blnk is undefined	All blanks in numeric formatted input ignored (except field of all blanks has value of zero). All blanks other than leading blanks are treated as zeros. If NULL (see above) in effect. If ZERO (see above) in effect. If (1) no connection or (2) if not connected for formatted I/O. }Requires FORM='FORMATTED' 'NULL'	blnk blnk blnk
EXIST	ex=.TRUE. ex=.FALSE. ex=.TRUE. ex=.FALSE.	If file exists with specified name. If file does not exist. }Always become defined unless an error condition exists. If specified unit exists. If specified unit does not exist.	
OPENED	od=.TRUE. od=.FALSE. od=.TRUE. od=.FALSE.	If file connected to unit. If file not connected to unit. }Always becomes defined unless an error condition exists. If unit connected to file. If unit not connected to file.	[od]
NUMBER		Supplies external unit identifier number. If unit currently connected, otherwise num becomes undefined.	num num
NAMED	nmd=.TRUE. nmd=.FALSE.	If file has a name. If file does not have a name.	nmd nmd
NAME		Returns name if file has a name, otherwise fn becomes undefined. Note: if INQUIRE by file, name may not be name given in FILE=fin specifier because name may be altered in processor-dependent way. The name returned is, however, suitable for use as fin in FILE=fin.	fn fn fn
SEQUENTIAL	seq='YES' seq='NO' seq='UNKNOWN'	If file I/O can be SEQUENTIAL. If file I/O can not be SEQUENTIAL. If processor cannot determine if I/O can be SEQUENTIAL or not.	seq seq
DIRECT	dir='YES' dir='NO' dir='UNKNOWN'	If file I/O can be DIRECT. If file I/O can not be DIRECT. If processor cannot determine if I/O can be DIRECT or not.	dir dir
FORMATTED	fmt='YES' fmt='NO' fmt='UNKNOWN'	If FORMATTED I/O permitted. If FORMATTED I/O not permitted. If processor cannot determine if FORMATTED I/O permitted or not.	fmt fmt
UNFORMATTED	unf='YES' unf='NO' unf='UNKNOWN'	If UNFORMATTED I/O permitted. If UNFORMATTED I/O not permitted. If processor cannot determine if UNFORMATTED I/O permitted or not.	unf unf
NEXTREC	nr=n+1 nr=1 nr is undefined	If current record number is n of file connected for direct access. If file connected but no I/O since connection for direct access. If (1) file not connected for direct access or (2) position of file indeterminate due to previous error conditioning.	nr nr

```
      PROGRAM PAY3
C     --- ALTERNATE TO PROGRAM PAY2, USING FULL LANGUAGE FORTRAN 77

      CHARACTER *20 NAME, PERSON

C     --- ESTABLISH EXTERNAL UNIT IDENTIFIERS (PROCESSOR DEPENDENT)
      LR = 15
      LW = 6
      ITAPE1 =  11
      ITAPE2 =  12
      IDISC1 =  21
      IDISC2 =  22

C     --- ESTABLISH LENGTH OF RECORDS IN DIRECT ACCESS FILES
C     --- (PROCESSOR DEPENDENT)
      LENGTH = 4

C     --- OPEN TAPE 1 BY UNIT AND DISC 1 BY NAME

      OPEN(UNIT=ITAPE1, IOSTAT=IOS, ERR=10,ACCESS='SEQUENTIAL',
     1    STATUS='OLD', FORM='UNFORMATTED')
      GO TO 11
   10 WRITE(LW,'(''1 ERROR'',I4,'' WHEN OPENING TAPE 1'')') IOS
      STOP

   11 OPEN(FILE='MASTER', UNIT=IDISC1, IOSTAT= IOS, ERR=20,
     1    ACCESS='DIRECT', RECL='LENGTH', STATUS='NEW',
     2    FORM='UNFORMATTED')
      GO TO 21
   20 WRITE(LW,'(''1 ERROR'',I4,'' WHEN OPENING DISC 1'')') IOS
      STOP

C---   REWIND TAPE 1 TO INSURE PROPER POSITIONING

   21 REWIND(UNIT=ITAPE1, IOSTAT=IOS, ERR=40)
      GO TO 41
   40 WRITE(LW,'(''1 ERROR'',I4,'' ON REWIND OF TAPE 1'')') IOS

C     --- READ MASTER FILE (SEQUENTIAL) ONTO DISC (DIRECT)
C     --- I IS INCREMENTED TO BE RECORD NUMBER AND EVENTUALLY
C     --- BECOMES TOTAL NUMBER OF RECORDS

   41 I = 0

   42 READ(UNIT=ITAPE1, IOSTAT=IOS, ERR=50,END=80) NAME, HOURS, RATE,
     1TOTPAY
      GO TO 60
   50 WRITE(LW,'(''1 ERROR '',I4,'' ON READING TAPE 1'',
     1/'' IN LOOP NUMBER (I+1=)'',I4)') IOS, I+1
      STOP

   60     I = I+1
      WRITE(UNIT=IDISC1, REC=I, IOSTAT=IOS, ERR=61)
     1NAME,HOURS,RATE,TOTPAY
      GO TO 42
   61 WRITE(LW,'(''1 ERROR'',I4,'' WHILE WRITING ONTO DISC 1''/
     1'' IN LOOP NUMBER (I=))'',I4)') IOS, I
      STOP

C     --- REWIND AND CLOSE TAPE 1 FILE (NO ERROR MESSAGES--WHY NOT)
   80 REWIND(ITAPE1)
      CLOSE(UNIT=ITAPE1, STATUS='KEEP')

C     --- MASTER FILE IS NOW ON DISC 1, EACH RECORD NUMBERED
C     --- ASSUME THAT EACH PERSON HAS AN ASSIGNED NUMBER WHICH
C     --- AGREES WITH THEIR RECORD NUMBER SO THAT THIS PROGRAM
C     --- DOES NOT BECOME TOO COMPLEX TO ILLUSTRATE IMPORTANT POINTS.
```

LISTING 17-12 Coding for program PAY3

```
C     --- ENTER INFORMATION FROM REMOTE TERMINAL (LR=15 IS PROCESSOR
C     --- DEPENDENT) IN FREE FORMAT:
C     ---        J = RECORD NUMBER
C     ---        PERSON = INDIVIDUAL'S NAME
C     ---        TIME = HOURS WORKED THIS PAY PERIOD
C     ---        PAY = RATE OF PAY $/HR    (IF UNCHANGED, ENTER 0)

   81 READ(LR,*, IOSTAT=IOS, ERR=82, END= 100)J,PERSON,TIME,PAY
      GO TO 84
   82 WRITE(LR,'(''1 ERROR'',I4,'' ON READ FROM REMOTE TERMINAL'')')IOS
      STOP

C     ---   GET INDIVIDUAL'S RECORD FROM MASTER FILE ON DISC 1

   84 READ(IDISC1, REC= J, IOSTAT=IOS, ERR=85) NAME, HOURS, RATE, TOTPAY
      GO TO 90
   85 WRITE(LW,'(''1 ERROR'',I4,'' ON READ FROM RECORD'',I4,'' OF DISC 1
     1'')') IOS,J
      STOP

C     --- PERFORM NECESSARY CALCULATIONS:
C     ---        (1) ACCUMULATE HOURS WORKED, (2) CHANGE RATE OF PAY IF
C     ---        PAY .NE. ZERO, (3)FIGURE CURRENT CHECK DOLLARS,
C     ---        (4) ACCUMULATE TOTAL OF PAYMENTS FOR INDIVIDUAL TO DATE

   90     HOURS = HOURS + TIME
          IF(PAY .GT. 0.) RATE = PAY
          CHECK = RATE * TIME
          TOTPAY = TOTPAY + CHECK

C     --- OUTPUT:
C     ---        (1) CHECK INTO FILE OF DISC 2 FOR FUTURE USE
C     ---            OPEN FILE (MUST BE PRECONNECTED) WITH WRTIE
C     ---        (2) CHECK STUB SUMMARY ONTO HIGH SPEED PRINTER
C     ---        (3) UPDATE MASTER FILE ON DISC 1
C     --- USING SIMPLEST FORM.  (ASK YOURSELF IF THIS IS WISE.  IS USE
C     ---                       (OF IOSTAT AND ERR ALWAYS WORTH THE WORK

          WRITE(IDISC2) NAME, RATE, TIME, CHECK
          WRITE(LW,1000) NAME,RATE, TIME, CHECK
          WRITE(IDISC1,REC=J) NAME, HOURS, RATE, TOTPAY

C     --- LOOP BACK FOR INFO ON NEXT EMPLOYEE, USING REMOTE TERMINAL
      GO TO 81

C     --- WHEN INPUT COMPLETE, CONTROL TRANSFERS HERE BY END IN READ
C     --- PUT END-OF-FILE RECORD ON DISC2 WHICH IS SEQUENTIAL ACCESS
C     --- BY DEFAULT
  100 ENDFILE(UNIT=ITAPE2,IOSTAT = IOS, ERR= 101)
      GO TO 102
  101 WRITE(LW,'(''1 ERROR'',I4,'' ON ITAPE2 (TAPE 2) WHILE DOING ENDFIL
     1E'')') IOS

C     --- NOW OPEN TAPE 2 AND OUTPUT UPDATED MASTER FILE.
  102 OPEN(ITAPE2, STATUS='NEW')
      REWIND(ITAPE2)
C     --- WOULD YOU PREFER MORE ITEMS IN CONTROL INFORMATION LIST--WHY

      DO 120 K = 1,I
          READ(IDISC1, REC=K, IOSTAT=IOS, ERR= 110) NAME, HOURS, RATE,
     1    TOTPAY
          GO TO 111
  110     WRITE(LW,'(''1 ERROR'',I4,'' WHEN READING DISC 1 ON LOOP'',
     1    I4)') IOS, K
  111     WRITE(ITAPE2,IOSTAT=IOS, ERR= 115) NAME, HOURS, RATE, TOTPAY
          GO TO 116
  115     WRITE(LW,'(''1 ERROR'',I4,'' WHEN OUTPUTING TO TAPE 2 IN LOOP
     1    '')') IOS, K
  116     CONTINUE
  120 CONTINUE
```

LISTING 17-12 *(continued)*

```
C      --- PUT END-OF-TAPE FILE ON TAPE 2 AND REWIND AND CLOSE
       ENDFILE(ITAPE2)
       REWIND(ITAPE2)
       CLOSE(ITAPE2, STATUS='KEEP')

       CLOSE(IDISC1, STATUS='DELETE')
       ENDFILE(IDISC2)
       REWIND (IDISC2)
       CLOSE(IDISC2, STATUS = 'KEEP')

       STOP
1000   FORMAT(1X,A20,' $',F6.2,'/HOUR FOR',F6.2,' HOURS = $',F8.2)

       END
```

LISTING 17-12 *(continued)*

```
       SUBROUTINE INQUIR(FIN,U,LW)

C         --- THIS IS A GENERALIZED SUBROUTINE TO INQUIRE ABOUT FILES
C         --- WHICH MAY, OR MAY NOT, EXIST
C         --- FIN IS FILE NAME, IF DESIRE TO INQUIRE BY UNIT, USE BLANK
C         --- U IS UNIT NUMBER, IF NEGATIVE IMPLIES USE *
C         ---LW IS UNIT NUMBER FOR OUTPUT FROM SUBROUTINE

       CHARACTER FIN(*)
       INTEGER U

C         --- OTHER VARIABLE NAMES CORRESPOND TO LOWER CASE LETTERS
C         --- USED FOR ALL SPECIFIERS IN TABLE WHICH SUMMARIZES
C         --- THE AUXILARY INPUT/OUTPUT STATEMENT INQUIRE

       INTEGER IOS,NUM,RCL
       LOGICAL EX,NMD,OD
       CHARACTER *11 ACC,BLNK,DIR,FM,FMT,FN,NR,SEQ,STA,UNF

C         --- CHECK TO SEE IF FIN IS BLANK, SET NFN (NO FILE NAME) TO
C         --- 0 IF BLANK--OTHERWISE TO 1

       WRITE(LW,'(''1 INQUIRY ABOUT FILE'',2X,A,
      1        '' (IF BLANK, INQUIRY IS BY UNIT INSTEAD)''/
      2      9X,'' UNIT NUMBER'',I6,
      3        '' (IF NEGATIVE IMPLIES UNIT NUMBER = *)'')') FIN,U

       LFIN = LEN(FIN)

       DO 10 I= 1,LFIN

          IF(FIN(I:I).NE.' ') THEN
             NFN = 1
             GO TO 20
          END IF

10     CONTINUE
       NFN = 0

C         --- CHECK TO SEE IF UNIT HAS NUMBER (SET IT=1)
C         -                  OR ASTERICK (SET IT=0)

20     IT = 1
       IF(U .LT. 0) IT = 0
```

LISTING 17-13 Coding for subroutine INQUIR

```
C              --- USE INQUIRE AUXILARY INPUT/OUTPUT STATEMENT FOR ONE OF
C              --- FOUR CASES:(1) INQUIRE BY FILE , UNIT = *
C              ---             (2) INQUIRE BY FILE , UNIT = U
C              ---             (3) INQUIRE BY UNIT = *
C              ---             (4) INQUIRE BY UNIT = U
C              --- SPECIFY CASE NUMBER IN VARIABLE NCASE

  IF(NFN.EQ.1 .AND. IT .EQ. 0) THEN
        NCASE = 1
        INQUIRE(FILE=FIN, UNIT=*, IOSTAT=IOS, ERR=30, ACCESS=ACC,
1                         RECL=RCL, STATUS=STA, FORM=FM,
2                         BLANK=BLNK, EXIST=EX, OPENED=OD,
3                         NUMBER=NUM, NAMED=NMD, NAME=FN,
4                         SEQUENTIAL=SEQ, DIRECT=DIR,
5                         FORMATTED=FMT, UNFORMATTED=UNF,
6                         NEXTRC=NR)
  ELSE IF(NFN.EQ.1 .AND. IT .EQ. 1) THEN
        NCASE =2
        INQUIRE(FILE=FIN, UNIT=U, IOSTAT=IOS, ERR=30, ACCESS=ACC,
1                         RECL=RCL, STATUS=STA, FORM=FM,
2                         BLANK=BLNK, EXIST=EX, OPENED=OD,
3                         NUMBER=NUM, NAMED=NMD, NAME=FN,
4                         SEQUENTIAL=SEQ, DIRECT=DIR,
5                         FORMATTED=FMT, UNFORMATTED=UNF,
6                         NEXTRC=NR)
  ELSE IF(NFN.EQ.0 .AND. IT .EQ. 0) THEN
        NCASE =3
        INQUIRE(        UNIT=*, IOSTAT=IOS, ERR=30, ACCESS=ACC,
1                         RECL=RCL, STATUS=STA, FORM=FM,
2                         BLANK=BLNK, EXIST=EX, OPENED=OD,
3                         NUMBER=NUM, NAMED=NMD, NAME=FN,
4                         SEQUENTIAL=SEQ, DIRECT=DIR,
5                         FORMATTED=FMT, UNFORMATTED=UNF,
6                         NEXTRC=NR)
  ELSE
        NCASE =4
        INQUIRE(        UNIT=U, IOSTAT=IOS, ERR=30, ACCESS=ACC,
1                         RECL=RCL, STATUS=STA, FORM=FM,
2                         BLANK=BLNK, EXIST=EX, OPENED=OD,
3                         NUMBER=NUM, NAMED=NMD, NAME=FN,
4                         SEQUENTIAL=SEQ, DIRECT=DIR,
5                         FORMATTED=FMT, UNFORMATTED=UNF,
6                         NEXTRC=NR)

C            --- WHETHER AN ERROR HAS OCCURED, OR NOT, OUTPUT IOSTAT INFO

     IF(IOSTAT .GT. 0) THEN
        WRITE(LW,'('' ERROR CONDITION NUMBER'',I4,'' OCCURS'',
1            '' FOR CASE'',I2)') IOS,NCASE
        RETURN
     ELSE IF(IOSTAT .LT. 0) THEN
        WRITE(LW,'('' END-OF-FILE CONDITION DETECTED, IOS='',I4
1       ,'' OCCURS FOR CASE'',I2)') IOS,NCASE
     ELSE
        WRITE(LW,'('' NO ERROR CONDITIONS DETECTED'')')
     END IF

     WRITE(LW,'('' ACCESS IS '',A)', ERR = 40) ACC
     GO TO 50
 40  WRITE(LW,'('' ACCESS IS UNDEFINED'')')

 50  WRITE(LW,'('' RECORD LENGTH ='',I6)',ERR = 60) RCL
     GO TO 70
 60  WRITE(LW,'('' RECORD LENGTH IS UNDEFINED '')')
```

LISTING 17-13 *(continued)*

Section 17-4 File Management With Full Language FORTRAN 77

469

```
 INQUIRY ABOUT FILE  HIL4 (IF BLANK, INQUIRY IS BY UNIT INSTEAD)
UNIT NUMBER    301 (IF NEGATIVE IMPLIES UNIT NUMBER = *
NO ERROR CONDITIONS DETECTED
     ACCESS IS DIRECT
RECORD LENGTH =    40
STATUS IS KEEP
FORM IS FORMATTED
BLANK IS NULL
EXIST IS T
OPENED IS T
NUMBER IS 301
NAMED IS T
NAME IS CEEHIL4
SEQUENTIAL IS NO
DIRECT IS YES
FORMATTED IS YES
UNFORMATTED IS NO
NEXTRC IS     1
```

LISTING 17-14 Typical output from subroutine
INQUIR

Laboratory Projects

Objective of Laboratory Projects: Practice in Developing Programming Skills

The laboratory projects, the text material, and the lectures are often linked together as a homogeneous package, with each element designed to reinforce the learning taking place in the others. Thus it is essential to complete the laboratory projects at the indicated time and with the basic material specified as prerequisite.

(a) *Style of laboratory project definitions.*   Every item of information needed for any laboratory project is available, but it is woven into the computer problem formulations in ways you might not expect to find. This has been done to require you to define the problem for yourself, a procedure that is valuable in assisting you to ultimately overcome difficulties encountered in "problem definition."

(b) *How to approach a laboratory project.*   The early laboratory projects have sections designed to help you solve the problem in the most expeditious manner. You should read and study this material before proceeding with the laboratory project to make your effort most productive.

(c) *A helpful metaphor about laboratory projects.* Although the number and type of laboratory projects that you will be required to do may vary, the following metaphor illustrates what you might expect.

In Laboratory Project 1, you are like a passenger in an automobile who must do things such as open the door, get in, close the door, and instruct the driver where you wish to go. In Project 1, the program has already been written, so all you will do is use it. Your role will be to prepare input that controls your use of the program and supplies the necessary data, and then to use this input to run the existing program.

In Laboratory Project 2, you are a student driver, repeating what you have seen others do with some changes. You will obtain the concept for your laboratory project from program CUB, and then use program CUB in an imitative mode. In a sense, you are building a program, not "writing" one. And, although you imitate program CUB, you will have to make some significant changes because your program is a little more complicated.

Laboratory Project 3 can be compared to taking a driver's test, because it represents that stage in your own computer programming where you are proving your personal ability. You will write your own program, and it will seem hard to do at this stage.

Laboratory Project 4 is like taking a pleasure ride after you have passed your examination for a license. It is designed to give you more experience in programming with a minimum of effort and maybe even some fun.

Laboratory Project 5 is like going cross-country in a four-wheel drive vehicle. Although the road is difficult, you will be given a lot of assistance to make it easier for you.

By the time you get to Laboratory Project 6, you are for hire. You may be part of a team effort, but you will still be particularly responsible for your own special part.

Laboratory Project 7 is the one you have been looking for; you are now the boss. Everything, including defining the problem and formulating it, is up to you. It will be your responsibility to be sure that both input and output are human-oriented, and that all documentation can be easily followed by someone knowledgeable in the field for which you are programming.

If you choose to do Laboratory Project 8, it will be a busman's holiday. It is often given for extra credit, and gives you a chance to appraise your own ability in computer programming. This will be your chance to see, without penalty, how well you did in Laboratory Project 7.

(d) *Your N-Number.* A unique *N-number* will probably be assigned to you by your instructor so that each of these laboratory projects can provide uniquely individualized problems for you.

LABORATORY PROJECT 1*

This project is relatively easy and has three primary purposes.

1. To help you become familiar with the computer facilities, including keypunches or remote terminals.
2. To allow you to communicate with a computer.
3. To indicate the power and versatility of a computer.

The program has already been written so that it is unique for you. Your task will be to prepare and run two types of data sandwiched between appropriate control cards. Part of the input data is *alphanumeric* and will be output in a revised form by the computer. The other type of input data is numerical and provides the means to solve a problem. You will have to complete more than one run, but—it is hoped—not more than four, to solve your problem. If your answer is not satisfactory after four runs, seek help because additional learning is minimal and you will be wasting your time.

Your first laboratory project is to familiarize you with computer procedures; you are not expected to understand everything that takes place. Without this experience, however, class lectures will not have the import obtained when supplemented with your

---

*You are ready to proceed once you have read Sections 1-4 and 1-5.

personal, "hands-on" experience in using a computer. Even though you do, in fact, solve a problem, it is not the main reason for this laboratory project.

You cannot get the correct answer on your first run. You will have to make corrections to your data in order to proceed. Before you need a fifth run however, your answers should be correct and your material ready to submit for grading.

Toward a Solution—Reading and Understanding the Laboratory Project

Begin by reading the laboratory project through rather quickly to get an overview of what it contains. Once you have done this, reread it with aid of pencil and paper for understanding. These laboratory projects are designed to give you experience aimed at improving your ability to define problems.

This program is written; that is, it is a "canned" program. Some results are output in scientific notation, written as a decimal fraction times a power of 10.

You will encounter several possible sources of difficulty. Numbers are limited to a precise number of significant figures and therefore some roundoff will probably occur. In addition, output provided for you by the program does not show all the significant figures inherent in the results. Therefore you will not always be "seeing" the entire numbers for either input data or answers. Sometimes it is impossible to obtain the precise number desired for an answer. For example, zero might be impossible to obtain so that you will have to be content with a "sufficiently small number" instead.

Procedure:

1. A program exists for you to use; access is gained by proper "control cards."
2. You will prepare two types of data:
   (a) Personal data in the form requested;
   (b) Numerical data.
3. You will run the program "blind" the first time.
4. By changing data and rerunning you will eventually find the correct solution(s).
5. For the final run, use the discrete method for numerical data and show only the answer(s).

Deck Composition:

Your deck is composed of:

1. Leading control cards; no change between runs;
2. Personal data; no change between runs;
3. Numerical data; change before each run;
4. A blank card; no change between runs;
5. Trailing control cards; no change between runs.

Leading control cards establish who you are and which "canned" program you wish to use. Use the spaces at the top of page 475 to lay out the precise set needed for your computer installation.

Personal Data is to be prepared in accordance with the following.

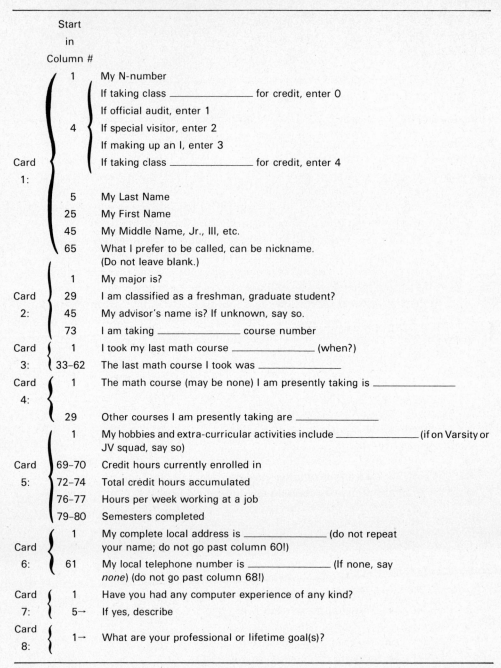

Start
in
Column #

Card 1:

Column	
1	My N-number
4	If taking class _____ for credit, enter 0 If official audit, enter 1 If special visitor, enter 2 If making up an I, enter 3 If taking class _____ for credit, enter 4
5	My Last Name
25	My First Name
45	My Middle Name, Jr., III, etc.
65	What I prefer to be called, can be nickname. (Do not leave blank.)

Card 2:

Column	
1	My major is?
29	I am classified as a freshman, graduate student?
45	My advisor's name is? If unknown, say so.
73	I am taking _____ course number

Card 3:

Column	
1	I took my last math course _____ (when?)
33–62	The last math course I took was _____

Card 4:

Column	
1	The math course (may be none) I am presently taking is _____
29	Other courses I am presently taking are _____

Card 5:

Column	
1	My hobbies and extra-curricular activities include _____ (if on Varsity or JV squad, say so)
69–70	Credit hours currently enrolled in
72–74	Total credit hours accumulated
76–77	Hours per week working at a job
79–80	Semesters completed

Card 6:

Column	
1	My complete local address is _____ (do not repeat your name; do not go past column 60!)
61	My local telephone number is _____ (If none, say *none*) (do not go past column 68!)

Card 7:

Column	
1	Have you had any computer experience of any kind?
5→	If yes, describe

Card 8:

Column	
1→	What are your professional or lifetime goal(s)?

Your grade may be reduced if you fail to answer any question. For instance, if you do not have a telephone, input NONE rather than leaving the entry blank. Otherwise, space your information in a normal way, that is, do not run words together.

This information does not change between runs and needs to be prepared only once.

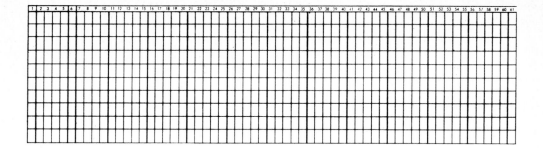

Misplaced or erroneous data, however, can cause you severe trouble because such information is used to make your problem individually unique.

Numerical data changes from run to run. The values that you guess depend upon the unique characteristics of the problem as individualized for you during your first run. Two methods are available to input numerical data: discrete and incremented. These two methods may also be used together, in any order, within any given run, so long as the specified maximum number of guesses is not exceeded.

Discrete Method—Input of Numerical Data

You may enter from 1 to 10 discrete values for your guesses on each card. You may use as many cards (lines) as you choose, so long as the number does not exceed any maximum which may be specified or the number of your guesses does not exceed the maximum permitted for any one run.

It is required that each number used for data contain a decimal point (2., 2.3, 4.67, for example). In addition, numbers must start, correspondingly, as:

Guess:	Must Start in Column:	Field is Columns:
1	1	1→8
2	9	9→16
3	17	17→24
4	25	25→32
5	33	33→40
6	41	41→48
7	49	49→56
8	57	57→64
9	65	65→72
10	73	73→80

Example:

3.16	7.94	8.31		
1.2				
3.				
4.				
1.6	2.19	7.83	16.23	18.91

Input of numerical data using the incremented method is particularly useful on your initial runs, saving you considerable time and effort.

Incremental Method—Input of Numerical Data

Starting in Column:	Put:
1	–1.
9	Lowest value of guess desired
17	Highest value of guess desired
25	Step size between guesses

For instance, the entry

–1.	10.	90.	10.

would produce x's successively equal to 10, 20, 30, 40, 50, 60, 70, 80 and 90. An entry such as

–1.	4	6.	.25

would produce x's successively equal to 4, 4.25, 4.5, 4.75, 5, 5.25, 5.5, 5.75 and 6.

Caution: Remember, the number of guesses for any one run is limited. Thus an entry such as

–1.	1.	99.	1.

would produce answers for guesses of 1., 2., 3., . . ., 40, but *no* answers for 41 through 99 if the number of guesses is limited to 40.

Discrete and incremented input can be mixed.

A valid entry scheme could be:

3.1	3.15	3.16	3.18	3.2	
–1.	14.	15.	.2		Mixed
2.					Input
5.					Scheme
–1.	80.	90.	5.		

which would produce guesses:

3.1, 3.15, 3.16, 3.18, 3.2, (all by line or Card 1)
14, 14.2, 14.4, 14.6, 14.8, 15., (all by line or Card 2)
2., 5., (by line or Cards 3 and 4)
80., 85. and 90. (by last line or card)

Three Real Roots

The objective is to find three numbers that are equal to or greater than 1 and less than or equal to 99, which make the equation $x^3 + ax^2 + bx + c$ almost equal to zero. For purposes of this project, it is best to approach this as a trial-and-error game and to neglect any mathematical implications. Your guesses may not contain more than two digits (only one if so specified by your instructor) after the decimal point.

You will run "blind" the first time because you will not know the numerical values assigned to the coefficients *a, b,* and *c.* They are output on each run although they do not change, and they need not be known to guess the three answers.

Because of roundoff error, you may get results which are not exactly zero. But, by changing data and rerunning, you should find the three correct results in about four separate runs.

You are limited to a maximum of 40 guesses on any one run. The number of numerical data cards is not restricted.

End of Deck

Follow the last line (card) of numerical data by a single blank line (card) every time you run.

The last line (card) in the deck is a terminal control card. Because control cards differ with machines and computer installations, you may wish to write the appropriate symbols for your last entry on this line.

$$\overline{123456789}$$

LABORATORY PROJECT 2*

Laboratory Project 2 is relatively simple if you follow the procedural steps quite carefully, aiming for only one target at a time. The laboratory project contains all information necessary for its solution and Chapter 2 contains all necessary FORTRAN techniques. You should, however, read the laboratory project very carefully until you understand all of its implications. Remember that laboratory projects are written to help you learn to define problems, not always in a logical and straightforward manner.

Once you have read Laboratory Project 2 thoroughly, it is important to begin construction of your own personal definition sheet. Start with the name of the program and a clear, precise definition of the problem. Occasionally, students use the purpose for which they are doing the program as the definition. That is incorrect. As written on the definition sheet, the purpose must state exactly what that particular program is supposed to do when it is executing. Do not proceed until you have written these two steps on a single sheet of paper.

When you have initiated your own personal definition sheet, you are ready for the second step, development of a human-oriented flow diagram with possible concurrent entries to the descriptive item list of the definition sheet.† At this stage, *do not* give any attention to the method of FORTRAN coding, input/output, or anything else except basic program logic. Simply concentrate on a flow diagram that solves the problem defined on your own definition sheet. Do not proceed until you are absolutely sure that your human-oriented flow diagram works adequately. If you encounter troubles, study program CUB (Section 2-2) very carefully.

---

*Study Section 2-2 before attempting this project. If Section 2-2 is not readily understood, then also study Section 2-3.

†These steps are the author's preference; your instructor may suggest a different way.

When you have a valid human-oriented flow diagram, proceed to development of the machine-oriented flow diagram. Leave input/output as a final consideration. Any time a computation is performed by the computer, the result must be stored in a computer location defined by a variable name or it will not be saved for subsequent use, including output. Every such variable name is to be immediately defined on the descriptive item list of your definition sheet. Only when the machine-oriented flow diagram is complete should you concentrate on the input/output.

The format to be used for reading input variables is specified to simplify grading and to aid in making each problem unique. Input is in real (floating point) form, so all variable names should start with letters other than I, J, K, L, M or N.

The purpose of this program is to evaluate formulas for different sets of input values. There is no relation between this program and Laboratory Project 1, where you used a prepared program. This time, you write the program itself. Although relatively simple, successful completion can help build your confidence and enhance your ability to learn more readily about computer programming. Use care in selecting trial data to test your program so that results are within the capacity of both the computer and formats which you use.

The Problem

Write a program that does the following.

1. Just after a comment line containing the program name, specifies the logical unit numbers for input and output, respectively, that is, defines LR and LW.
2. Outputs a heading, only once, at the beginning of each computer run with the following form:
   (a) a 1 in column 1 ['1',] (this causes the computer to *slue* to the top of a new page before starting to output the heading);
   (b) 2 blanks [2X,];
   (c) your "N" number ['nnn'];
   (d) 3 blanks [3X,];
   (e) the laboratory project number, that is, 2;
   (f) 4 blanks (Δ is a symbol used to represent a blank); $\Big\}$ [2$\Delta\Delta\Delta\Delta$',]
   (g) your last name, a comma, the name you like to be called for example, ['Hill, Louis'];
   (h) two slashes (this causes 2 carriage returns, resulting in two blank lines); typically

   ```
       WRITE (LW, 10)
   10  FORMAT ('1', 2X, '369', 3X, '2ΔΔΔΔ', 'HILL, LOUIS' //)
   ```

3. Reads 3 coefficients in the relative order shown in list below using FORMAT (10F8.0).
4. Stops working when all 3 coefficients are zero, else
5. Reads X and Y (10F8.0).
6. If X and Y are both zero, return to Step 3 to read three new coefficients, ELSE
7. Your particular equation will have three components chosen with the aid of your N-number using MOD calculations (see the end of this appendix of exercises.) To

determine which three components should be used to build your equation, compute MOD (N+K, 5) + 1 = _____, MOD (N+L, 4) + 6 = _____, and MOD(N+M+2,4)+10=_____.(Typically, a value of 4 signifies the use of dx or (COEFX)*X and a value of 10 signifies the use of qxy or (COFXY)*X*Y. You may call the coefficients by any name you choose, so long as the first letter is not an I, J, K, L, M, or N.) Use the computed values to select the components of your equation from the following.

Component Table

Alternate Forms of Components

Number Obtained by MOD Computation	Algebraic Form of Component of Equation	Single Letter Variable Name	Mnemonic Name (possibilities unlimited)
1	ax^4	A*X**4	COFX4*X**4
2	bx^3	B*X**3	COFX3*X**3
3	cx^2	C*X**2	CXSQD*X**2
4	dx	D*X	COEFX*X
5	e	E	CONST
6	fy^4	F*Y**4	YTO4*Y**4
7	gy^3	G*Y**3	YTO3*Y**3
8	hy^2	H*Y**2	YSQD*Y**2
9	py	P*Y	COEFY*Y
10	qxy	Q*X*Y	COFXY*X*Y
11	rx^2y	R*X**2*Y	COEF3*X**2*Y
12	sxy^2	S*X*Y**2	COF3*X*Y**2
13	tx^2y^2	T*X**2*Y**2	DBLC*X**2*Y**2 or DBLC*(X*Y)**2

---

8. Output an answer for each component on a line by itself showing:
   (a) the algebraic form of the equation;
   (b) the equation expressed numerically; and
   (c) the solution using both F (standard decimal form) and E (scientific notation) format specifications; then
   (d) follow these three lines with the sum of solutions for the three components, also using F and E format specifications. A typical output might look like the following.

E =   17.3 =   17.   "Follow by answers in

G * Y**3 =   41.7 * 16.1**3 =   174025.   scientific notation."

T * X**2 * Y**2 = 18.3 * 14.1**2 * 16.1**2 =   943064.

TOTAL = 1117107.

Make output readable. Put equal signs in vertical rows. Line up results and use spacing to enhance appearance of the output. Single space each set of data, that is, the three lines with information about the components and the fourth line with information about the total. Then, at least double space between sets of output. Test values used to grade your program all lie between −20.0 and +20.0. No test values will have more than one figure after the decimal point. Check to see that your output is truly human-oriented.

9. Read new values of X and Y and repeat Steps 6 through 9.

Some Comments

Choose test data that is sufficient to insure that the program works correctly. Only when you are confident that the program works for all possible data should you submit your program for grading, carefully following instructions.

Deck Set-up

Typical deck set-up is provided for your convenience, with cards left blank for entry of appropriate characters used at your computer center.

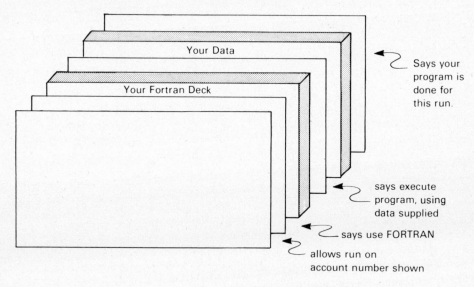

Generalized Deck Set-Up

LABORATORY PROJECT 3*

Laboratory Project 3 is not inordinately complex, but many students report that it causes them more difficulties than any other laboratory project because Laboratory Project 3 is the first requiring use of a formalized procedure in an effective and efficient manner. The

*You may start this project after completing Laboratory Project 2. Program CUES of Section 7–4 provides a model. You may find it helpful to study Chapters 3 through 6 as you work on Laboratory Project 3.

laboratory project is written so that you will have to work rather diligently to define the problem for yourself.

First, study the problem until you can write an accurate purpose on your definition sheet. Then proceed to the human-oriented flow diagram and a partial definition sheet. Be absolutely certain that the human-oriented flow diagram does what it should before proceeding. (Explain it to someone who is not a computer programmer.) Once the human-oriented flow diagram has been thoroughly checked, write the machine-oriented flow diagram, ignoring formatting. When the machine-oriented flow diagram satisfies your requirements completely, then, and only then, concentrate on the form for output. If you follow these steps*, Laboratory Project 3 should be a rewarding experience that does not cost you excessive time and effort. Shortcutting, however, may lead to frustration and failure.

This laboratory project is designed to reinforce your learning about the following concepts.

1. Looping.
2. Control of looping to obtain accuracy commensurate with the current data set, including
   (a) the need for counting loops;
   (b) the need for percentage rather than abolute comparisons; and
   (c) the need for initialization.
3. Reading a "print-control" that independently establishes the amount of output you will obtain on each run.
4. Using a control value, read as data, to work the problem of your choice.
5. Converting variables, when necessary, to avoid mixed modes.

The Problem

Write a program that does the following.

1. Just after the comment line bearing the program name, defines LR and LW to specify logical units to be used for input and output, respectively.
2. Prints a heading, only once, at beginning of each computer run that has the following form:
   (a) a 1 in column 1 ['1',] (this causes the computer to slue to the top of a new page before starting to output the heading);
   (b) 2 blanks [2X,];
   (c) your "N" number ['nnn'];
   (d) 3 blanks [3X,];
   (e) the laboratory project number, that is, 3;
   (f) 4 blanks (Δ is a symbol used to represent blank spaces); } ['3$\Delta\Delta\Delta\Delta$',]
   (g) your last name, a comma, the name you like to be called; for example, ['Hill, Louis'];

*Your instructor may want you to follow a different formulation procedure; if so, follow that procedure diligently.

(h) two slashes (this causes 2 carriage returns which result in 2 blank lines); typically

WRITE (LW,10)
10   FORMAT ('1', 2X, '369', 3X, '3ΔΔΔΔ', 'HILL, LOUIS' //)

3. Reads a data card containing five variables in format I2, 2F8.0, 2I4 (even if all are not needed in your program, all five variables must be read to facilitate grading). The meaning of the five values read from each data card depends upon the value contained in that card's first location, according to the following list (≠ means "not equal to").

type of problem (=17)	type of problem (≠ 17 and ≠ −6)
coefficient a	percent error permitted
coefficient b	value of x to be evaluated
power m	maximum number of loops permitted
power n	print control

To simplify the project, your instructor may designate 17 in the first location of the card to terminate the program instead of working the first type of problem.

4. (a) If the value read for "type of problem" is 17—and your instructor has not designated this to be a STOP—then solve one of the problems shown according to MOD(N,6)+ 1*. (The equations left of the equal sign produce results that are approximated by the expressions on the right for "reasonable" values of variables and powers.)

MOD(N,6) + 1:	Equation:
1	$(1 + a)^m \doteq 1 + ma$
2	$(1 - a)^m \doteq 1 - ma$
3	$(1 + a)^m (1 + b)^n \doteq 1 + ma + nb$
4	$(1 + a)^m (1 - b)^n \doteq 1 + ma - nb$
5	$(1 - a)^m (1 + b)^n \doteq 1 - ma + nb$
6	$(1 - a)^m (1 - b)^n \doteq 1 - ma - nb$
7	$\sqrt{ab} \doteq (a + b)/2$

m and n are to be positive integers

$\doteq$ means almost equal

Make only one evaluation of both equations. Form for the output is your choice, but it must be readily understandable and include independent solutions for both sides of the equation plus the percentage difference between the two results.

By using several sets of related data you may experiment to determine how large you can make coefficients a or b so that the exact solution (left of the equal sign) can be approximated by the expression right of the equal sign. Such an experiment is sometimes called a *parametric study or investigation*.

*For MOD definition, see end of this appendix of exercises.

A certain specific range of values can be found for each of the seven equations so that the approximations are relatively valid.

(b) If the value read for "type of problem" is neither 17 nor −6 and you have never had trigonometry, program a solution for one of these series according to MOD(N,4) + 1. (Each of these series representations are very useful in a number of practical applications, ranging from biology to social science and from engineering to business.)

Problem Choices for Students without Trigonometric Background when "Type of Problem" is not −17 nor 6.

MOD(N,4) + 1		Equation
1 with	$x < 1$ $x > 0$	$\dfrac{1}{1 + x} \doteq 1 - x + x^2 - x^3 + x^4 - x^5 + \ldots$
2 with	$x > -1$ $x < 0$	$\dfrac{1}{1 - x} \doteq 1 + x + x^2 + x^3 + \ldots$
3 with	$x < 1$ $x > 0$	$\dfrac{1}{(1 + x)^2} \doteq 1 - 2x + 3x^2 - 4x^3 + \ldots$
4 with	$x > -1$ $x < 0$	$\dfrac{1}{(1 - x)^2} \doteq 1 + 2x + 3x^2 + 4x^3 + \ldots$

Conversely, if you have had trigonometry, solve one of the trigonometric or logarithmic series according to MOD(N + 3,8) + 1. (Although these series do not precisely represent *algorithms* used by the computer to compute these functions, they are indicative of the process. They should suggest why built-in function statements are used instead of stored tables of sines, cosines, or other such functions. See table on the following page.)

(c) If the value read for "type of problem" is −6, then the program is to stop executing.

5. If the value read for "type of problem" is not −6, then a solution of some sort is required, after which flow is to return to Step 3.

6. Optionally, after READ statements, you may put in appropriate error messages when such things as the allowable number of loops or the values of X are in an unacceptable range.

Elaboration of Requirements

Choose trial values within the limits, if specified. Trial values for the trigonometric functions must be in radians. Although all real X are permitted for some series, anomalies may occur if X is quite large.

The objective of the second set of problems is to determine the number of terms required for an answer within the allowable percentage error specified by your data when the series solution is compared with the results of a built-in function. For example, if you were to solve $1/(1 + x)$, reasonable input data for a trial run could include an x of $\frac{1}{2}$ and a permitted error of, for example, 3%. The question then is, how many terms of $1 - x + x^2 - x^3$, with $\frac{1}{2}$ stored in location X, are necessary to get an answer which agrees within 3% of the answer obtained by using the same value of x in the expression $1./(1. + X)$?

Problem Choices for Student with
Trigonometric Background when
''Type of Problem'' is not −17 nor 6.

MOD(N+3,8) + 1	Equation	
1	$\sin x \doteq x - \dfrac{x^3}{3!} + \dfrac{x^5}{5!} - \dfrac{x^7}{7!} + \dots$	(all real x)
2	$\cos x \doteq 1 - \dfrac{x^2}{2!} + \dfrac{x^4}{4!} - \dfrac{x^6}{6!} + \dots$	(all real x)
3	$e^x \doteq 1 + x + \dfrac{x^2}{2!} + \dfrac{x^3}{3!} + \dfrac{x^4}{4!} + \dots$	(all real x)
4	$\log_e x \doteq \dfrac{x-1}{x} + \dfrac{1}{2}\dfrac{x-1}{x}^2 + \dfrac{1}{3}\dfrac{x-1}{x}^3 + \dots$	($x > 1/2$)
5	$\log_e x \doteq (x-1) - \dfrac{1}{2}(x-1)^2 + \dfrac{1}{3}(x-1)^3 - \dots$	($2 \geq x > 0$)
6	$\log_e x \doteq 2\dfrac{x-1}{x+1} + \dfrac{1}{3}\dfrac{x-1}{x+1}^3 + \dfrac{1}{5}\dfrac{x-1}{x+1}^5 + \dots$	($x > 0$)
7	$\sin^{-1} x \doteq x + \dfrac{x^3}{6} + \dfrac{1}{2}\cdot\dfrac{3}{4}\cdot\dfrac{x^5}{5} + \dfrac{1}{2}\cdot\dfrac{3}{4}\cdot\dfrac{5}{6}\cdot\dfrac{x^7}{7} + \dots$	($x^2 < 1$)
8	$\tan^{-1} x \doteq x - \dfrac{x^3}{3} + \dfrac{x^5}{5} - \dfrac{x^7}{7} + \dots$	($x^2 < 1$)

If you were to do the first problem for sin (x), you might fill x with $\pi/3$ radians and permit an error of 0.01%. The question would then be, how many terms of $x - x^3/3! + x^5/5! - x^7/7! + \dots$ are needed to get a value that is within 0.01% of the value obtained by using the same value of x in the built-in function SIN (X)?

You may output results in any organized manner of your choice, with only one exception. If, and only if, the print-control value read as input is equal to or greater than 1, then for that particular problem you must also write out within each loop: (1) the loop number; (2) the value of the term within that loop; and (3) the total value of the function as accumulated through that loop. All output, however, must be complete enough to be easily read and understood by anyone without referring to the program itself, program documentation, or this text.

Although you may not "like" the control parameters −6 and 17, they are used to help increase your consciousness of the need for a proper selection of such values in future programs which you both define and write.

Input to Laboratory Project 3

Depending upon your instructions, you may be solving one or two different types of problems in Laboratory Project 3. If you are solving two types, the scheme for data input may cause some difficulties. Each data card is to contain five values in a format that requires the first number to be integer, the next two to be real, and the last two to be integer. The meaning of values associated on a data card differs depending upon the type of problem to be solved, and careful selection of variable names is important.

Two approaches both reasonably efficient, are possible. The first method reads variables into five named locations. Each value is then transferred to another location that has a mnemonic name associated with the particular type of problem being solved. This has two disadvantages: additional storage locations are required and additional cards (lines) must be used in the FORTRAN program itself.

The second approach uses variables having mnemonic names that can stand for either meaning, depending upon the type of problem being solved. For example, the third variable to be read stores either coefficient B or the value of X to be evaluated. If the first value read from the card is a 17, the third value stands for B; if the first value read on that card is neither 17 nor −6, the third value on the card stands for X. Under such circumstances, a reasonable variable name is BX, standing for B when the first value read on that card is 17 and for X when the first value read on that card is neither 17 nor −6.

Mathematical Formulation

Signs alternate when $(-1)^n$ is used; it gives −1, 1, −1, 1, . . . for $n = 1, 2, 3, 4, ...$ Alternately, $J = J*(-1)$ can be used each time through the loop. The algorithm to use depends upon which function you are expanding. In general, use of $-1**N$ results in −1, but $(-1)**N$ alternates signs. Do you understand, in the light of hierarchy of computations, why this is true?

A number followed by an exclamation point means: multiply all counting numbers up to and including that number by each other. For instance, 3! means $1 \times 2 \times 3 = 6$, and 5! means $1 \times 2 \times 3 \times 4 \times 5 = 120$. 3! is read 3-factorial and 5! is read 5-factorial.

Some terms, or portions of terms, are dependent only upon their term numbers. For instance, in computing cos x, x is always raised to the power $2n - 2$. If $n = 1$, we have $2n - 2 = 0$, which gives a first term of x^0, or 1. If the term number (represented by n) is 2, $2n - 2 = 2$, and $x^{2n-2} = x^2$. When n is 3, $2n - 2 = 4$ and the third term equals x^{2n-2}, or x^4.

Conversely, some terms are found most simply by multiplying the preceding term by a specified value. For instance, in computing cos x, it is possible to find the power of x by simply multiplying the preceding term by x^2. Using either method, of course, you must include techniques for determining the appropriate factorials and signs.

For additional help in the mathematical formulation of the series represented in Laboratory Project 3, you may wish to refer to the exercises of Section 3–8.

Output

Presenting output in a human-oriented form may be the most difficult part of Laboratory Project 3. It requires careful thought to decide how the output should appear. It often helps to have typical output from your program read by someone not involved in computer programming. If such a person can understand what your program did, what the program used as input data, and what the answers are, your output is probably satisfactory.

LABORATORY PROJECT 4*

Concept

This program is designed to give you facility in the use of DO-loops and single-dimensional arrays. While the program has little intrinsic value, it demonstrates techniques that are valuable everyday tools used by programmers using all higher-level languages.

The Problem

Write a program that does the following.

1. Reads an integer print-control value in I4 format.
2. Stops working when the print-control value is negative or 0.
3. Uses four single-dimensional arrays:
   (a) the first array to be read by your program has a length computed by the formula $MOD(N+M,8)+3$, where M = _____;
   (b) the second array has a length computed by the formula $MOD(N+L+3,7)+2$, where L = _____;
   (c) the third array has a length defined by the equation $MOD(N+K+7,10)+1$, where K = _____;
   (d) the fourth array has a length of 6 and is used for storing answers which are to be output.
4. Reads these arrays as follows: The shortest of these three arrays is read by a single READ statement, indicating each element of the array independently. The longest of these arrays is read by another READ statement, using an implied-DO loop. The third of these arrays, the one of middle length, uses a READ statement that inputs the whole array using only the name of the array, without subscripting of any kind. If two or more arrays are of equal length, use the READ type of your choice with each array, as long as you use all three different types within the program.
5. Sums all of the values read for the array defined as the $MOD(N+M,3) + 1^{st}$, storing the results in the first location of the answer array. (M is defined in part (a) of Step 3.)
6. Accumulates the products of all values stored in the array read in as the $MOD(N+M+1,3) + 1^{st}$, storing the results in the second location of the answer array. (M is defined in part (a) of Step 3.)
7. For the $MOD(N+M+2,3)+1^{st}$ array read, counts the values evenly divisible by 3. Stores results in the third location of the answer array. (Again, M is defined in part (a) of Step 3.)
8. Divides the accumulated products of Step 6 by the sum of the values obtained in Step 5. Stores results in the fourth location of the answer array.

*You should have studied the text through Chapter 9.

9. Obtains the integer value of the quotient previously obtained in Step 8. Store in the fifth location of the answer array.
10. Adds the value of the count stored in the third location of the answer array to the value of the quotient stored in the fifth location of the answer array. Stores the results in the final location of the answer array, location 6.
11. Outputs your N-number (N), the values of M, L, and K assigned by your instructor (zero, if not otherwise assigned), the six values of the answer array and your N-number, repeated. Use the format I4, 3I3, F6.2, F10.0, F4.1, E20.8, F10.2, F10.2, I4.
12. Goes back and reads in a new value of print-control.
13. If the print-control value is 2 or greater, outputs the arrays immediately after they are read in, properly titled.

In addition, you should do the following.

14. Be sure to start your problem with a heading, sluing to a new sheet. For each set of results, however, do not slue to the next page.
15. Test your program with your own data. When you are certain everything is correct, obtain special test data to run for grading.

LABORATORY PROJECT 5*

Overview

Students of literature often want to find out who wrote a particular manuscript. To do so, they look for the repetition of certain expressions that are the "signature" of a particular author. A great deal of work has been done to determine if Shakespeare was actually another well-known author writing under a pseudonym. Biblical scholars also find this type of comparison useful in trying to determine whether or not Titus was written by Paul or by someone else.

In the field of coding and decoding, it is often useful to count the repetition of certain characters. Furthermore, at least one modern dictionary has used the computer to help insure accuracy of the current spelling and definition of all words displayed. Although it may be easier for us to work in English, national language is really immaterial for such work.

Materials Provided

Input data, completely textual in nature, is furnished either on cards or stored on disk. It is composed of the alphabet characters A through Z, blanks, periods, and commas. No other characters are used. In general, one space follows a comma and two spaces follow each period, although this is not guaranteed.

*Necessary background includes Section 12–1 (and Section 12–3 if you are using Full Language FORTRAN 77).

General Objective

Determine the following for each line of text provided (on disk or cards).

1. How many times does a specified vowel occur?
2. How many times does a specified consonant occur?
3. How many times does a specified two-letter pair occur?

Prepare the computer output in tabular form showing each line as it is read and echoed out, and—immediately to the right of each text line—also show the count, in columnar form, of the number of times the specified vowel is found on that line, the number of times the specified consonant occurs on that line, and the number of times the specified two-letter pair is found on that line. The specified vowel, consonant and two-letter pair are determined by using your MOD number.

The end of the data is signified by a line of data that starts with three blanks. When this occurs, output the total sum of the occurrence of your vowels, consonants and two-letter pairs.

Test data provided is a combination of words in a nonsensical pattern put together in correct grammatical form. The words in the data were chosen so that a great number of different combinations are available within a small data bank.

Be sure that you provide clear headings for output, and that it fits neatly on a single page. This single output page should also include necessary information about yourself, including your name and N-number.

Your Particular Problem

1. The vowel for which you are searching is determined by $MOD(N+K,5)+1$, where N is your N-number, $K = $ _____, and $1 = A, 2 = E, 3 = I, 4 = 0$, and $5 = U$.*

2. Your consonant is chosen by the function $MOD(N+L,21) + 1$, $L = $ _____. The relationship between the numbers that you obtain by this function and consonants of the alphabet are as follows.

$$
\begin{array}{lllll}
1 = B & 2 = C & 3 = D & 4 = F & 5 = G \\
6 = H & 7 = J & 8 = K & 9 = L & 10 = M \\
11 = N & 12 = P & 13 = Q & 14 = R & 15 = S \\
16 = T & 17 = V & 18 = W & 19 = X & 20 = Y \\
21 = Z
\end{array}
$$

3. The two-letter pair for which you will search is determined by the $MOD(N+M,33) + 1$, where $M = $ _____ and:

$$
\begin{array}{lllll}
1 = AL & 2 = AM & 3 = AN & 4 = AS & 5 = AT \\
6 = BE & 7 = DO & 8 = ED & 9 = EL & 10 = GO \\
11 = HA & 12 = HE & 13 = HO & 14 = ID & 15 = IF \\
16 = IN & 17 = IS & 18 = IT & 19 = JO & 20 = LA \\
21 = MA & 22 = ME & 23 = NO & 24 = OF & 25 = OH \\
26 = OK & 27 = ON & 28 = OR & 29 = PA & 30 = SO \\
31 = TO & 32 = US & 33 = WE
\end{array}
$$

*If they are not supplied, assume K, L, and M are zero.

4. For possible extra credit, (a) find your two-letter pair standing alone as a word, (b) find your two-letter pair starting a word, and/or (c) find your pair imbedded in a word (including the end of a word, but not the beginning of the word).

Thus in Step 3, if your two-letter pair was defined by the MOD function as IS, you are to determine how many times the combination IS occurs per line. In Step 4, you are to find how often the word IS occurs as a word in the line, how many times the word IS is the first part of a word (such as island), and/or how many times IS is imbedded in a word (such as Elvis).

Take into account the possibility of blanks, commas, and periods, as well as alphabetical characters, in your searching.

LABORATORY PROJECT 6*

Laboratory projects in this section involve use of subroutines and/or function subprograms. Many of them are suitable for teams of two or more students, while some can be handled easily by one person working alone.

Comments

Laboratory Project 6A involves the weighted scoring of tic-tac-toe games. The particular type of score weighting is controlled by your N-number in a MOD function. This laboratory project requires a single student to write a single subroutine. A main program, two auxiliary subroutines and data are furnished. The required subroutine must use each auxiliary subroutine one or more times, and is called by the main program.

Laboratory Project 6B is a team project involving elementary statistics. Although little mathematical background is required and the programs are simple to write, they are quite useful. It is anticipated that each team member will write one of the required subroutines, with two students collaborating to write the main program. The following modules are included:

6–B1 Subroutine to order rows numerically

6–B2 Subroutine for mean and median

6–B3 Subroutine for mode

6–B4 Subroutine for standard deviation

6–B5 Subroutine for geometric mean

6–B6 Main Program

Laboratory Project 6C involves the solution of simultaneous equations. This is a one-person project that involves writing a main program and a matrix multiplication subroutine. The inverse subroutine is usually supplied.

*Material from Chapters 14 and 15 is required for some of these projects.

Tic-Tac-Toe, Weighted Wins

The general concept of Laboratory Project 6A is to help you learn how to write subroutines that are called by a main program and which, in turn, call additional subroutines. In this particular problem, the main program and two subroutines, as well as data, have been provided on disk (or on cards). Your job is to write a *single* subroutine that is called by the main program, and that calls the two provided subroutines (probably more than once) in the order and manner necessary to solve your particular problem.

The data shows the results of a series of games of tic-tac-toe. The rules of the game, however, have been changed and are different for each person. Thus, in writing your subroutine, you will each have a different task to perform. The possible ways of winning by both *X* and *O* are specified by MOD functions.

Possible Wins, Set 1

In your laboratory project, only four of these possible combinations are actually called winners. The four that are used, based upon your N-number, are:

$$MOD\ (N,12)+1 \qquad MOD\ (N+6,12)+1$$
$$MOD\ (N+3,12)+1 \quad MOD\ (N+7,12)+1$$

Possible Vertical and Horizontal Wins

Possible Wins, Set 2

In addition to the four possible ways of winning discussed above, a win may occur in one additional way. This involves diagonals and is determined by the function $MOD(N,5) + 1$, with the number obtained related to these sketches. (If your MOD function calculation yields the number 5, there are two possible ways in which *X* can win on the diagonal. In all other cases, only one diagonal path is considered a winner.)

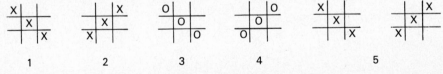

Possible Diagonal Wins

A definition sheet for the main program and two subroutines follow. (Your instructor may provide you with copies of flow diagrams or coding if they are desired.) The main program calls your subroutine by the statement

CALL SCORE (B, N, KSOL, ID)

where B, N, KSOL, and ID have the meanings specified in the Definition Sheet for Program TTTOE.

TTTOE—Definition Sheet

Program TTTOE

Purpose:

Reads in several tic-tac-toe boards and finds whether O's, X's or the cat wins on each board, then outputs result with total of each at end of printout. Also indicates "not a win" when a provided subroutine shows a win invalid for your N-number.

Descriptive Items:

Symbolic Name	Description
B (3×3)	Array storing X's and O's representing tic-tac-toe board.
OUT (3×15)	Array storing 5 sets of tic-tac-toe boards for output.
SOL (15)	Array storing 5 sets of solutions to board for output.
CHR (4)	Array of character words for output of solution.
RCD (6)	Array of character words indicating type of win.
KK (5)	Array for storing 5 game numbers.
NO	Number of O wins.
NX	Number of X wins.
NCAT	Number of CAT wins.
NSOL	Number of no SOLution wins.
NP	Print Control, (NP < −4) prevents more cards from being read.
K	Number of game.
N	Indicates type of win; N=1, X wins; N=0, cat wins; N=−1, O wins; N=−2, not a win, that is, subroutine indicates a win which is not valid for your N-number.
KSOL	Contains number of row or column. KSOL=0 when diagonal win, cat win, or not a win occurs.
ID	Contains number indicating type of win. ID=1, ROW ID=2, COL ID=3, Diagonal left to right (top to bottom) ID=4, Diagonal right to left (top to bottom) ID=5, CAT ID=6, NOT A WIN, that is, subroutine indicates a win not valid for your N-number.
BLK (5)	Store characters for solution messages.

Subroutine FIND—Definition Sheet

SUBROUTINE FIND (A,R,N,M,K)

Purpose:

Search for 3 *X*'s or 3 *O*'s in the rows or columns of a 3 × 3 array representing a tic-tac-toe board.

Descriptive Items:

Symbolic Name Description

A (3×3)   Array storing X's and O's on board.

R   Contains character X or O.

N   N=0 means search columns, N=1 means
                 search rows.

M   Indicates win (M=1), no win (M=0).

K   Indicates number of row or column with a win,
                 that is, with 3 X's or O's.

Subroutine FINDD—Definition Sheet

SUBROUTINE FINDD(T,R,KU,KD)

Purpose:

Search for X's and O's in a diagonal of a (3×3) array named T representing a tic-tac-toe board.

Descriptive Items:

Symbolic Name	*Description*
T (3×3)	Array containing X's and O's of tic-tac-toe board.
R	Contains character X or O.
KU	When returns 3, indicates right to left diagonal (top to bottom).
KD	When returns 3, indicates left to right diagonal (top to bottom).

Some Statistics

This relatively simple project requires very careful reading to insure that all of the ramifications are clearly understood. Data may be provided to test the program as shown in the table on the next page; if you do Subroutine 2 or 3, Subroutine 1 may be furnished to simplify your task.

Given:

1. A (floating point) array dimensioned   15 × 4 × 5.

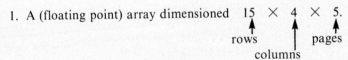

Test Data for Statistical Program

	Employee Number	Hourly Rate	Job Number	Years Employed	Page number = Site location number
	93	12.10	9	2	
	18	11.60	10	11	
	216	12.30	10	6	
	71	12.70	7	4	
	46	12.90	11	7	
	13	11.60	11	8	
	112	12.00	8	5	
	117	13.10	8	6	
	23	13.25	11	8	
	283	11.80	12	9	
	416	13.50	13	6	
	417	14.00	8	10	
	417	14.12	14	12	
	511	14.18	12	14	
	512	14.92	12	13	

(Left margin: Site 1 (page 1), Site 2 (page 2), Site 3 (page 3) with arrows.)

2. An integer showing how many pages are actually used.
3. An integer (fixed point) array (5) showing the actual number of rows used on each page, sequentially.
4. An integer indicating which column to operate upon.
5. An integer indicating which page to operate upon.
6. A print control variable, NP, which controls printing:

> if NP = 0, no output;
> if NP = 1, answer, with proper titles, only;
> if NP = 2, also intermediate values of major consequence;
> if NP = 3, also intermediate values of lesser consequence;
> if NP = 4, also intermediate values of lesser and lesser consequence.

General Requirements:

1. Each subroutine argument list is to use *all* variables shown above (in sequence). But, each subroutine is to use names known only to you.
2. In addition, each subroutine argument list is to include suitable variables for answers, added to argument lists sequentially:

> Subroutine 1: None
> Subroutine 2: Real variable for mean
>   Real variable for median
> Subroutine 3: Integer stating number of modes
>   Real array (3) for mode(s)
> Subroutine 4: Standard deviation
> Subroutine 5: Geometric mean

Special Requirements:

Subroutine 1 (6–B1): For the page controlled by "integer indicating which page to operate upon," rearrange the page so that values in the column controlled by "integer indicating which column to operate upon" are in numerical order, smallest value at the top. Keep information on each row together throughout the rearranging process. (For Column 1 *only,* if more than two numbers are identical, immediately print out both rows, indicating which row is to be deleted, and delete it. Remember to change number of rows in appropriate place.)

Subroutine 2 (6–B2): For column and page controlled by arguments: (a) determine the mean ((sum of values)/(number of values)), and (b) determine the median (the middle measure in a series in which all measures have been arranged according to size). A subroutine to order tables may be provided upon request.

Subroutine 3 (6–B3): For column and page controlled by arguments: (a) determine the mode (the value occurring most frequently), or (b) if more than one value occurs the same *maximum* number of times, determine the number of values so involved and store or list the values (max of 3).

Subroutine 4 (6–B4): For the column and page controlled by the arguments, compute the standard deviation as

$$\sqrt{\frac{\Sigma(X_i)^2 - \dfrac{(\Sigma X_i)^2}{N}}{N-1}}$$

Subroutine 5 (6–B5): For the column and page controlled by the arguments, compute the geometric mean as

$$\sqrt[n]{(X_1)(X_2)(X_3)\cdots(X_n)}$$

Subroutine 6 (6–B6): Make a master program that can use these 5 subroutines in a *simple* to use yet *very* flexible manner. Test by use of dummy subroutines (*Top-down* testing).

Simultaneous Equations

Your program should have built-in diversity as controlled by the first (header) card for each set of data. The header card will control the amount of input and the operations to be performed.

The main program uses two subroutines. The first subroutine may be provided, called by the following statement:

$$\text{CALL JNV (I, A, B , ILA, ILB)}$$

where I is *any* integer variable equal to or less than ILA and ILB defining the size of *square* matrices A and B. Matrices A and B may have any valid real variable name but *must* be dimensioned A(ILA, ILA), B(ILB, ILB) within the subroutine, with ILA and ILB defined in the main program so that array dimensions are compatible (identical between main program and subroutine). The subroutine inverts [A] and puts the results in [B]. If there is no inverse, an error message will be output. The second subroutine is to perform matrix multiplication of two (not necessarily square) matrices.

A header card is to read I, J, K, and L in 4I4 format. (Variables in your program do *not* have to be actually so named as long as they are integer.) All matrices are to be read one row at a time in 10F8.0 format.

If I = 0: STOP

If I = 1: Obtain the inverse of a square matrix.

    1. J defines the size of square matrices
       A and B (max size 5 × 5 is satisfactory, that is, ILA = ILB = 5).
    2. Read matrix [A].
    3. Output matrix $[A]^{-1} = [B]$.

If I = 2: Multiply two, not necessarily square, matrices.

    1. J, K, and L define dimensions of matrices to be input (maximum of 5 is satisfactory).
    2. Read matrix [A] having J rows and K columns.
    3. Read matrix [B] having K rows and L columns.
    4. Multiply [A] × [B] = [C].
    5. Output matrix [C] having J rows and L columns.

If I = 3: Solve a set of simultaneous equations.

    1. J and K define dimensions of matrices to be input.
    2. Read coefficient matrix [A] having J rows and columns.
    3. Read constant matrix [C] having J rows and K columns.
    4. Solve [A] [X] = [C] for matrix [X].
    5. Output matrix [X] having J rows and K columns.

The main program is to dimension three arrays corresponding to matrices [A], [B], [X], and/or [C]. However, you do *not* need to use these actual symbolic names.

LABORATORY PROJECT 7

Write an instructor approved laboratory project of your choice, using at least one more subroutine than the number of team members. To get ideas, think about your work, your hobbies, or your favorite courses. Be sure to generalize your project so that it has reasonably broad application, with size controlled only by arrays and corresponding array dimension lengths. Be careful not to restrict your program unnecessarily by using constants where variables would be preferable.

LABORATORY PROJECT 8

Efficient programming, with power and versatility, can often be learned most readily by using a previously developed program. Thus, Laboratory Project 8 involves creative use of Project 7. In the process, discover what you can learn about the *programmed problem* and also about the *value of the program itself.* Divide your report into three parts.

Part I should show the results obtained by using your program to learn about the programmed problem. Conclusions and observations drawn from these results should then be written. Document your statements by referring to results obtained. Include any necessary figures.

Part II should discuss what you have learned about programming because of performing Laboratory Project 8.

Part III should be a critique of Laboratory Projects 7 and 8, including such items as the following.

1. What would you do differently if you were to do them over again?
2. What would you do if you had more time to amplify and perfect them?
3. What are the strong and weak points of Laboratory Project 7? (*Note:* Comments such as, "I would throw Laboratory Project 7 into the wastebasket" will *not* detract from your grade. An honest appraisal is the only valid reason for Laboratory Project 8.)

Additional Programming is *not* required. However, if you do some additional programming to make your program more suitable for Laboratory Project 8, include documentation as Part IV.

THE MOD FUNCTION

The MOD function is more appropriately called the *modulo* or *remainder function*. It is a standard function available on FORTRAN compilers, but it is used in this text to enable everyone to have similar but different laboratory projects. Therefore the MOD function is not usually determined by the computer, but is calculated by each of you in the process of doing your laboratory project. The MOD function is used in the form MOD(N,L). To determine the particular numerical value represented by a MOD function, divide the first expression, N, by the second expression, L. The remainder of such division is the desired result.

$$
\text{MOD(N,L)} \quad \rightarrow R \quad \text{where } L \overline{)N} \overset{\text{A remainder R}}{}
$$

$$
\text{MOD(42,5)} \quad \rightarrow 2 \quad \text{where } 5 \overline{)42} \overset{8 \ R=2}{}
$$

$$
\text{MOD(37,N)} \quad \rightarrow 1 \quad \text{where if N} = 4,
$$
$$
4 \overline{)37} \overset{9 \ R=1}{}
$$

$$
\text{MOD(2N,N+3)} \quad \rightarrow 2 \quad \text{if N=1}
$$
$$
\rightarrow 0 \quad \text{if N=3}
$$
$$
\rightarrow 4 \quad \text{if N=7}
$$

$$
\text{MOD(N+8,4)+5} \rightarrow 8 \quad \text{where if N=3, } 4 \overline{)11} \overset{2}{}
$$
$$
R=3 \text{ and}
$$
$$
3+5=8
$$

In the table, MOD(42,5) is equal to 2, because when 42 is divided by 5, the answer of 8 (which is immaterial) produces a remainder of 2.

The combinations of expressions may become involved, but usually N stands for your N-number as assigned by your instructor. Study the examples and you should have no trouble—just remember that the solution is the remainder, not the quotient.

Answers
to Exercises

Chapter 1

1. IF YOU CAN TRANSLATE THIS, YOU ARE SUCCEEDING.
YOU HAVE THE RIGHT IDEA. **2.** 66473014 11304763 **3.** READING BACKWARDS IS EASY
FOR THE COMPUTER **6.** The number 1000 might be "close to zero" in many situations, such as when comparing to the number of grains of sand on a beach or comparing the distance to the nearest star in kilometers. When dealing with submicroscopic particles, the small fraction might not be "close to zero." This is also true in certain eigenvalue problems and other situations encountered in various fields.

Chapter 3

5. See Section 7–2. **7.** See Section 14–5.

8.

IKT	K	I	L	M	(3*I)	(2*I)	(K/3)	(L+4)	(IKT−3)
0 [1]	7 [2]	3 [3]			9 [4]				
1 [9]	16 [5]	0 [13]	1 [8]	0 [12]	0 [14]	6 [6]	5 [7]	+5 [11]	−2 [10]
2 [19]	16 [15]	8 [23]	−5 [18]	25 [22]	24 [24]	0 [16]	5 [17]	−1 [21]	−1 [20]
3 [29]	40 [25]	5 [33]	3 [28]	6 [32]	15 [34]	16 [26]	13 [27]	+7 [31]	0 [30]
4 [39]	55 [35]		−8 [38]			10 [36]	18 [37]		+1 [40]
			These numbers show sequence						
			of operations						

Expanded Form

IKT	K	I	L	M	(3*I)	(2*I)	(K/3)	(L+4)	(IKT−3)
0 [1]	7 [2]	3 [3]							
	16 [5]				9 [4]				
1 [9]			1 [8]			6 [6]	5 [7]		−2 [10]
		0 [13]		0 [12]				+5 [11]	
	16 [15]				0 [14]				
2 [19]			−5 [18]			0 [16]	5 [17]		−1 [20]
		8 [23]		25 [22]				−1 [21]	
	40 [25]				24 [24]				
3 [29]			3 [28]			16 [26]	13 [27]		0 [30]
		5 [33]		6 [32]				+7 [31]	
	55 [35]				15 [34]				
4 [39]			−8 [38]			10 [36]	18 [37]		+1 [40]

9.

J	K	L	M	N	(K−M)	(K²)	(M²)	(K−M)L
−4	0	3	1	0				
−3	0			−1	−1	0	1	
−2	−2			2	−3	4	1	
−1	−1			2	−2	1	1	
0	0			1	−1	0	1	
1	1			0				
2	2			4	+1			3
3	0			3	−1	0	1	
4								

10.

K	L	M	N
1	0	0	5
5			10
50	1		20
		25	25
		55	30
	2		20
100			2
			0

11.

I	A	J	B	C
0				
1	1.	1	1.	
2	2.	2		
3	3.	3	9.	−1.
4	4.	0	16.	
5	5.	1	25.	
6	6.	2		
7				

12.

I	AI=I+1	(AI²)	TERM	SUM	IF X=2	
					TERM	SUM
0				0.		0.
1	2.	4.	$4.X^0$	4.	4.	4.
2	3.	9.	$9.X^1$	$4.+9.X$	18.	22.
3	4.	16.	$16.X^2$	$4.+9.X+16.X^2$	64.	86.
4	5.	25.	$25.X^3$	$4.+9.X+16.X^2+25.X^3$	200.	286.
5	6.	36.	$36.X^4$	$4.+9.X+16.X^2+25.X^3+36.X^4$	576.	862.
6						

If X = .5 Terms are: 4., 4.5, 4., 3.125, 2.25 yielding
Sums: 4, 8.5, 12.5, 15.625, 17.875
If X = 1 Terms are: 4., 9., 16., 25., 36. yielding
Sums: 4., 13., 29., 54., 90.

13.

I	J	AJ	TERM	SUM	IF X= 0.5:	
					TERM	SUM
0				0.		.0
1	1	1.	$X^1/1$	X	.5	.5
2	3	3.	$X^3/3.$	$X+X^3/3.$	.041667	.541667
3	5	5.	$X^5/5.$	$X+X^3/3.+X^5/5.$	.006250	.547917
4	7	7.	$X^7/7.$	$X+X^3/3.+X^5/5.+X^7/7.$	.001116	.549033
5	9	9.	$X^9/9.$	$X+X^3/3.+X^5/5.+X^7/7.+X^9/9.$	.000217	.549250
6						

14.

I	A	FACT EXPANDED	AS STORED	SUM EXPANDED	AS STORED
0		1.	1.	0.	0.
1	1.	1.×1.	1.	1.	1.
2	2.	1.×2.	2.	1.+2.	3.
3	3.	1.×2.×3.	6.	1.+2.+6.	9.
4	4.	1.×2.×3.×4.	24.	1.+2.+6.+24.	33.
5	5.	1.×2.×3.×4.×5.	120.	1.+2.+6.+24.+120.	153.
6					

15.

I	A	FACT	(2I−1) B	(B+2.) (2I+1) C	TERM	SUM
0		1.				0.
1	1.	1.×1.=1.	1.	3.	1.×1.×3.=3.	3.
2	2.	1.×1.×2.=2.	3.	5.	2.×3.×5.=30.	3.+30.= 33.
3	3.	1.×1.×2.×3.=6.	5.	7.	6.×5.×7.=210.	3.+30.+210.= 243.
4	4.	1.×1.×2.×3.×4.=24.	7.	9.	24.×7.×9.=1512.	1755.
5	5.	1.×1.×2.×3.×4.×5.=120.	9.	11.	120.×9.×11.=11880.	13635
6						

Chapter 4

1.

	Valid Constant		Valid Variable		Why Invalid
	Integer	Real	Integer	Real	
$12.61		NO			$ invalid in constant
121.34E−17		YES			means 121.34×10^{-17}
JO+1			NO		+ sign invalid in variable name
FORM2				YES	
26E−4	NO				means 26×10^{-4}
(JOHN)			NO		( ) no good in variable (later used to indicate subscripts)
126.314.		NO			Two decimal points
JOHNSON			NO		More than 6 characters
12	YES				
1.+KL					?? Not variable, doesn't start with letter. ?? .+ ??
6.E431		NO			431 too large
.31E.26		NO			decimal point following E not allowed
JACK			YES		
SUM $				NO	$ sign illegal in variable name
BK				YES	
KB			YES		
2.61E4		YES			
IAAI			YES		
.24E+8		YES			
DIAMETER				NO	> 6 characters
2DKS					Variable name must start with letter
1286954					Depends on machine, may be too big
A123			YES		
F386			YES		
RUN				YES	But *not* good practice

	Valid		Comments
	Real	Integer	
CURR*RES	X		Means: multiply contents stored in location named CURR by contents stored in location named RES.
15.**4	X		Means: 15. × 15. × 15. × 15. Alternately, if decimal point were used after the 4, thus: 15.**4., would mean antilog (4. × log(15.)). Note: This is not same as 15.E4 which is a constant equal to 15.×10⁴.
JK3+321		X	Variables and constants may be added, same mode.
PRIN+INT			Mixed mode is not allowed in some courses. PRIN is floating point (real) and INT is fixed point (integer). Could say: PRIN+ANT (floating point—real), or NPIN+INT (fixed point—integer), etc.
Y–Y**2	X		Means: square contents stored in location called y and subtract from contents stored in location called y. During process, contents stored in y are *not* changed.
L/3.2			May want to change to type real, possibilities are such as: A/3.2 AL/3.2 CL/3.2 etc.
6A-5B			This is either 1. implied multiplication which is *not* allowed, i.e., 6A is *not* equal to 6 × A; also would be mixed mode —OR— 2. 5A and 5B are neither variables nor constants and therefore *not* syntactic items. Correct as either 1. 6.*A – 5.*B —OR— 2. A6 – B5
K+1,237			Would be all right except comma invalidates integer constant. Use K+1237
4–K+L/7		X	Means: Divide contents stored in location L by 7 and store results in accumulator. Then, subtract K from 4 and finally add the results of L/7 stored in accumulator to 4–K
15**4		X	Valid but dangerous! Can get too big too fast! Means 15 × 15 × 15 × 15
15**4.		NO	Integer changed to real before exponentiation
I**J		X	Valid but *very* dangerous! Can exceed range of integer values very fast.
B**(A/3.16)	X		Means: raise value stored in location B to power computed as the quotient of the contents of location A divided by 3.16.
π*D			π not valid character. In general, use 3.1415926 for π. Note 22/7 is not a good approximation. Also, precise value of π is needed when computing functions near 0 or 90 degrees.
(A)(B)/C			Implied multiplication is not allowed. Use (A)*(B)/C or, more simply A*B/C.
15.**4.	X		Means: antilog (4. × log 15.)
I*J/B			Mixed mode. Use something like I*J/KB or AI*AJ/B
J*–K			Operators can *not* be adjacent. Use J*(–K) or –J*K
4+SUMT			Mixed mode. Use 4.+SUMT
R+3.2E4/16.31	X		Means: $R + \dfrac{3.2 \times 10^4}{16.31}$

3.

Statement	Valid	Statement Rewritten Correctly
COST = $18.62		Bad constant, $ sign not allowed; use COST = 18.62
JNV = A*-B		Adjacent operators invalid. Note: *NOT* mixed mode. Use JNV = A*(–B). Computer will multiply contents stored in location named A by negative of contents stored in location named B. This result will then be changed from real to integer before storing in JNV. (Decimal values are "cut off.")
MAN = I+J+K+4	X	
AREA = π*R**2		Can not use π. Use AREA = 3.1415926*R**2 or PI = 3.1415926 AREA = PI*R**2 Computer will square value stored in location named R, multiply result by π and store result in location named AREA.
AREA = π*R*R		Same as above. Note R**2 is identical to R*R but *not* necessarily identical to R**2.; do you see why?
V = (R+U/T)**(T+V/G)	X	Means: $(R + U/T)^{(T+V/G)}$ which is perfectly valid as long as $(R + U/T)$ is greater than zero.
MAN = A+B+C+4		Mixed mode. Use A+B+C+4.
ROOT = JVK**.5		Integer changed to real before exponentiation.
PI= A+G+K+V+7.21		Mixed mode. Change K to floating point (real).
A(RECT) = B*H		Completely invalid at this point in course. Cannot use parentheses in word. However, parentheses will be used later to indicate subscripts, but subscripts are generally integer.
AREA = BH	X	All right. But simply puts contents stored in location named BH into location called AREA. If you want AREA = B × H, then use AREA = B*H.
HYPOTENUSE = (A**2+B*B)**.5		Variables limited to 6 characters. Use HYPOT = (A**2+B*B)**.5 which means HYPOT = $\sqrt{A^2 + B^2}$
AREA = L*W		Mixed mode. Either can change L to real (floating point) or W to integer (fixed point).
K=2.16E14/(A*B)		Possible trouble in size of result. Note that this is always a source of possible trouble when result is to be stored into an integer. Means $$K = \frac{2.16 \times 10^{14}}{A \times B}$$ Also, if A or B is zero, would be impossible division
R*B = C		No good! *ONLY* variable name is allowed left of equal sign. Probably mean C = R*B.
R*B = L		No good! Same as above. Probably mean L = R*B. (Note: *not* mixed mode.)
A = A+A**2	X	Means: 1. Take present value stored in location called A and square it, storing results in an accumulator. 2. Add *unchanged* value stored in location called A to results of A^2 stored in accumulator. Store total result in an accumulator. 3. Store final results from accumulator into location called A—WHICH NOW CHANGES VALUE STORED IN A.
R = N*(-4)	X	*Not* mixed mode. Mode can only be mixed in an expression.
N = N–3	X	Value stored in location called N is reduced by 3.
C=A/B/(A/B/C)	X	Means: 1. Divide (value stored in) A by B, store temporarily. 2. Divide result of A/B by C, store temporarily. 3. Now divide A by B, store temporarily. 4. Now divide stored value of A/B by stored value of (A/B/C) and store final results temporarily. 5. Now store final result into C, thereby *changing* value of C.
A = C+SQRT(-B)	X	In the case when B is negative, the result is an imaginary number. To take a root it must be real, therefore, take square root of –B because minus times minus is plus. An alternate form is A = C+SQRT(ABS(B)).

4. Note: Assumes maximum size of integer is 32000

Given:	Then:
R = 21/4 + 6/4	21/4 = 5 (not 5.25) 6/4 = 1 (not 1.5) 6 therefore R = 6.
J = 2/3	2/3 = 0, not .667. Therefore, J = 0
I = 2000*2000	2000 × 2000 > 32000; therefore results are not valid from standpoint of simple arithmetic. Value obtained will be meaningless without more understanding of machine and compiler.
A = 2000*2000	Same as above; even though A can be 4 × 10⁶, the result *cannot* be computed by integer arithmetic to be so stored.

N = 10.E2+699.	10.E2 = 1000. Note: In similar circumstances on some
	      699. machines, round off might cause 1000.
	    1699. to be 999.99999 which sums to
	Therefore N = 1699 1698.9999, making N = 1698

L = 3.*(2.E4/7.)	$\dfrac{2.E4}{7.} = \dfrac{20000.}{7.} = 2857.14\ldots$ —and— 3. × 2857.14 . . . $\doteq$ 8571.42 . . . Therefore L = 8571
R = 3.*(2.E4/7.)	Same as above except R $\doteq$ 8571.42 . . .
S = .21./4.+6./4.	21./4. = 5.25 6./4. = 1.5 6.75 Therefore S = 6.75
N = 21./4.+6./4.	Same as above, except N = 6
T = (1/8)*40	1/8 = 0 then 0 × 40 = 0; therefore T = 0.

Chapter 5

```
TOOK  PATH  1  WITH  I=  4,J=  4,K=  2--AND  TRUE  PATHS=   1,  FALSE  PATHS=   0
TOOK  PATH  1  WITH  I=  5,J=  3,K=  1--AND  TRUE  PATHS=   2,  FALSE  PATHS=   0
TOOK  PATH  1  WITH  I=  3,J=  0,K=  0--AND  TRUE  PATHS=   3,  FALSE  PATHS=   0
TOOK  PATH  1  WITH  I=  3,J=  3,K=  3--AND  TRUE  PATHS=   4,  FALSE  PATHS=   0
TOOK  PATH  1  WITH  I=  2,J=  2,K=  2--AND  TRUE  PATHS=   5,  FALSE  PATHS=   0
TOOK  PATH  1  WITH  I=  4,J=  4,K=  4--AND  TRUE  PATHS=   6,  FALSE  PATHS=   0
TOOK  PATH  1  WITH  I=  2,J=  2,K=  4--AND  TRUE  PATHS=   7,  FALSE  PATHS=   0
TOOK  PATH  1  WITH  I=  1,J=  2,K=  1--AND  TRUE  PATHS=   8,  FALSE  PATHS=   0
TOOK  PATH  1  WITH  I=  2,J=  2,K=  1--AND  TRUE  PATHS=   9,  FALSE  PATHS=   0
TOOK  PATH  1  WITH  I=  4,J=  1,K=  1--AND  TRUE  PATHS=  10,  FALSE  PATHS=   0
```

(e)
```
TOOK  PATH  1  WITH  I=  4,J=  4,K=  2--AND  TRUE  PATHS=   1,  FALSE  PATHS=   0
TOOK  PATH  1  WITH  I=  5,J=  3,K=  1--AND  TRUE  PATHS=   2,  FALSE  PATHS=   0
TOOK  PATH  1  WITH  I=  3,J=  0,K=  0--AND  TRUE  PATHS=   3,  FALSE  PATHS=   0
TOOK  PATH  2  WITH  I=  3,J=  3,K=  3--AND  TRUE  PATHS=   3,  FALSE  PATHS=   1
TOOK  PATH  2  WITH  I=  2,J=  2,K=  2--AND  TRUE  PATHS=   3,  FALSE  PATHS=   2
TOOK  PATH  2  WITH  I=  4,J=  4,K=  4--AND  TRUE  PATHS=   3,  FALSE  PATHS=   3
TOOK  PATH  1  WITH  I=  2,J=  2,K=  4--AND  TRUE  PATHS=   4,  FALSE  PATHS=   3
TOOK  PATH  2  WITH  I=  1,J=  2,K=  1--AND  TRUE  PATHS=   4,  FALSE  PATHS=   4
TOOK  PATH  1  WITH  I=  2,J=  2,K=  1--AND  TRUE  PATHS=   5,  FALSE  PATHS=   4
TOOK  PATH  1  WITH  I=  4,J=  1,K=  1--AND  TRUE  PATHS=   6,  FALSE  PATHS=   4
```

(f)
```
TOOK PATH 1 WITH I= 4,J= 4,K= 2--AND TRUE PATHS=   1, FALSE PATHS=  0
TOOK PATH 1 WITH I= 5,J= 3,K= 1--AND TRUE PATHS=   2, FALSE PATHS=  0
TOOK PATH 2 WITH I= 3,J= 0,K= 0--AND TRUE PATHS=   2, FALSE PATHS=  1
TOOK PATH 1 WITH I= 3,J= 3,K= 3--AND TRUE PATHS=   3, FALSE PATHS=  1
TOOK PATH 1 WITH I= 2,J= 2,K= 2--AND TRUE PATHS=   4, FALSE PATHS=  1
TOOK PATH 1 WITH I= 4,J= 4,K= 4--AND TRUE PATHS=   5, FALSE PATHS=  1
TOOK PATH 2 WITH I= 2,J= 2,K= 4--AND TRUE PATHS=   5, FALSE PATHS=  2
TOOK PATH 1 WITH I= 1,J= 2,K= 1--AND TRUE PATHS=   6, FALSE PATHS=  2
TOOK PATH 1 WITH I= 2,J= 2,K= 1--AND TRUE PATHS=   7, FALSE PATHS=  2
TOOK PATH 2 WITH I= 4,J= 1,K= 1--AND TRUE PATHS=   7, FALSE PATHS=  3
```

Chapter 6

2. (a) G = 9.16, H = −3.21, I = Mixed mode error. (b) T = 12.3, U = 17.60012, V = 34500041. (c) T = 1234.56, U = 2345.6, V = 1234.56, W = 2345.6, X = 1234.56. (d) T = 18.3, U = 4000., V = .1234, W = 2.7, X = 12.34.

3. (a)

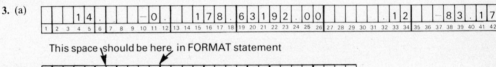

This space should be here, in FORMAT statement

(b)

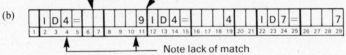

Note lack of match

(c)

Note: Field width needs to be increased in FORMAT statement

Lost leading 2—a substantial problem for any user of program.

(d)

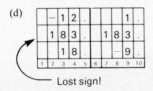

Lost sign!

4. (a)

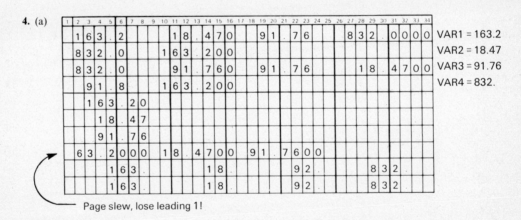

VAR1 = 163.2
VAR2 = 18.47
VAR3 = 91.76
VAR4 = 832.

Page slew, lose leading 1!

(b)

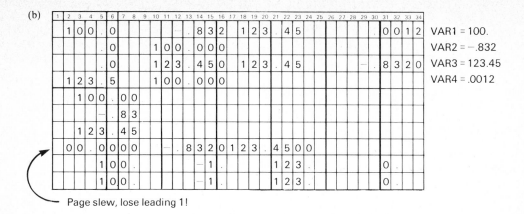

VAR1 = 100.
VAR2 = −.832
VAR3 = 123.45
VAR4 = .0012

Page slew, lose leading 1!

(c)

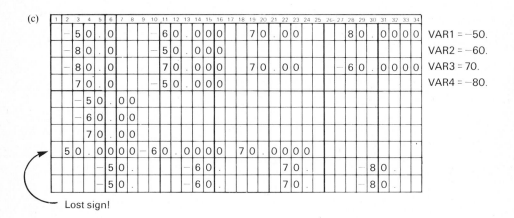

VAR1 = −50.
VAR2 = −60.
VAR3 = 70.
VAR4 = −80.

Lost sign!

(d)

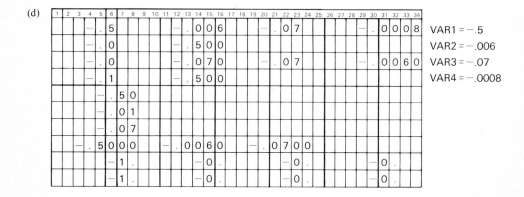

VAR1 = −.5
VAR2 = −.006
VAR3 = −.07
VAR4 = −.0008

Chapter 9

1. The appearance of input and output is according to the following table:

A(1)	41.	A(1)	41.	A(1)	41.	A(1)	41.
A(2)	42.	A(2)	31.	A(2)	42.	A(2)	42.
A(3)	43.	A(3)	21.	A(3)	43.	A(3)	31.
A(4)	44.	A(4)	11.	A(4)	44.	A(4)	32.
A(5)	31.			A(5)	45.	A(5)	21.
A(6)	32.			A(6)	31.	A(6)	22.
A(7)	33.			A(7)	32.	A(7)	11.
A(8)	34.			A(8)	33.	A(8)	12.
A(9)	21.			A(9)	34.	A(9)	1.
						A(10)	undefined
						A(11)	undefined

OUTPUT: (for c)
41. 42. 43. 44.

OUTPUT: (for d)
31. 21. 11.
1.
41. 42. 31.
32. 21. 22.
11. 12. 1.
BOOM!

(a)   (b)   (c)   (d)

Chapter 10

1. (a) −8 (b) −47 (c) 26 (d) illegal; 8 is beyond the array dimension. (e) 82 (f) −77 (g) 43 (h) −21   **2.** (a) 14 (b) 19 (c) 11 (d) 110 (e) 83 (f) −47 (g) 6 (h) illegal; 6 is greater than maximum dimension of 5. (i) 213 (j) illegal; 5 is beyond maximum dimension of 3. (k) 91 (l) illegal; 0 is below minimum dimension of 1. (m) 111 (n) 12 (o) 0   **3.** The trace for case (a) is shown here. For case (b) the results would be a table of 4 rows and 2 columns with the leading digit in each row being the number of that row and the trailing digit of each number being the number of that column. Part (c) will produce an anomaly because 11 of 5 is greater than the maximum dimension of the array which is 4.

I1	I2	I	J	TBL(I,J)
2	3	1	1	TBL(1,1) = 101.
			2	TBL(1,2) = 102.
			3	TBL(1,3) = 103.
			4	
		2	1	TBL(2,1) = 201.
			2	TBL(2,2) = 202.
			3	TBL(2,3) = 203.
			4	
		3		

4. (a)

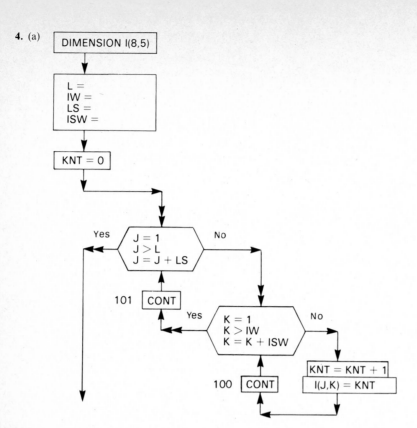

(b–i) Array I

1	2	3	4	0
0	0	0	0	0
5	6	7	8	0
0	0	0	0	0
9	10	11	12	0
0	0	0	0	0
0	0	0	0	0
0	0	0	0	0

(b–ii) Array I

1	0	2	0	3
0	0	0	0	0
0	0	0	0	0
4	0	5	0	6
0	0	0	0	0
0	0	0	0	0
7	0	8	0	9
0	0	0	0	0

(b–iii) Array I

1	2	0	0	0
3	4	0	0	0
5	6	0	0	0
0	0	0	0	0
0	0	0	0	0
0	0	0	0	0
0	0	0	0	0
0	0	0	0	0

(b–iv) Array I

1	2	3	0	0
0	0	0	0	0
0	0	0	0	0
0	0	0	0	0
4	5	6	0	0
0	0	0	0	0
0	0	0	0	0
0	0	0	0	0

(c–i) In the statement DO 101, make it J=3,L,LS—or define a new variable to use in place of the 1.
(c–ii) In DO 100, make it K=4,IW,ISW—or redefine 1 by a new variable.
(c–iii) In DO 101, change the 1 to a 2, and in DO 100, change the 1 to a 3—or use variables previously defined as 2 and 3 in place of the 1's shown in the current DO statements.

5. (a) IRRAY (3,4,2)

111	121	131	141		112	122	132	142
211	221	231	241		212	222	232	242
311	321	331	341		312	322	332	342

(b) IRRAY (3,4,2)

111	211	311	411		121	221	321	421
112	212	312	412		122	222	322	422
113	213	313	413		123	223	323	423

(c) IRRAY (3,4,2)

3	4	5	6		4	5	6	7
4	5	6	7		5	6	7	8
5	6	7	8		6	7	8	9

(d) IRRAY (3,4,2)

2	3	4	5		3	4	5	6
3	5	7	9		4	6	8	10
4	7	10	13		5	8	11	14

6. (a)

161	−9	−8	−11
12	−69		
27	−27	32	−49
63	−52		
102	−201	16	88
−77	4		

(b)

26	11	83	14
27	32	63	43
111	−97	3	5
17	−21	25	66

(c)

88	−77	4	0
82	3	−2	5
−115	105	35	−47
−23	25	33	66

(d)

161	−11	81
102	88	0

(e)

26	161	27	102
111	55	17	7
−9	−27	−201	91
−15	19	11	−8
32	16	−97	155
−21	121	−11	−49
88	82	−115	−23
83	12	63	−77
3	105	25	72
−69	−52	4	−2
35	33	14	81
43	0	5	−47
66			

7. (a) Since I goes from 1 to 3 by steps of 1, this outputs the values stored in J(1,1,1), then J(2,2,2) and finally J(3,3,3).

$$71 \quad 82 \quad 11$$

(b) K, the page number, is the innermost DO-loop. I is picking the values off the diagonals of each page, therefore the 15 values represent location 1,1 on page 1, page 2, page 3 and then location 2,2 on page 1, page 2, page 3, and so on.

71	−97	26
94	82	7
166	102	11
213	3	121
227	−2	83

(c) The row and page numbers are held constant while the column number changes from 2 to 4.

$$32 \quad -27 \quad 121$$

(d) The page number is changing and therefore the values stored in row 3, column 2 of pages 1, 2 and 3 are printed, in order.

$$110 \quad -21 \quad 63$$

(e) This prints out rows 3 through 5, columns 1, 3 and 5 of page 3 only.

```
 43    11 81
-49   -27 27
  4    88 83
```

(f) This writes out a row at a time, skipping every other value—that is, locations 1, 3 and 5 with the rows going by 1, 3 and 5 as for page 1. This is then repeated for page 3, skipping page 2.

```
 71 269   18
 30 166   20
133 144  227
 26 161   72
 43  11   81
  4  88   83
```

(g) Output in this manner shows how the array is stored in the computer sequentially.

71	296	30	196	133
1	94	110	13	212
269	6	166	33	144
49	171	10	213	177
18	169	20	96	227
−97	17	19	9	91
5	82	−21	111	155
−47	55	102	−15	66
35	−201	−23	3	33
16	105	−115	25	−2
26	−8	43	−49	4
14	7	63	32	−77
161	−11	11	−27	88
−9˙	12	−52	121	0
72	−69	81	27	83

Chapter 11

5. The solutions to each of the matrix multiplication problems are shown here. (a) This is a typical equation which had three unknowns evaluated as 1.6, 4.8 and −3.2. The results of the matrix multiplication should yield the original constants as a check on the solution for the unknowns.

$$\begin{bmatrix} 1 & 2 & 1 \\ 2 & -1 & 2 \\ 4 & 2 & 1 \end{bmatrix} \begin{bmatrix} 1.6 \\ 4.8 \\ -3.2 \end{bmatrix} = \begin{bmatrix} 1(1.6) + 2(4.8) + 1(-3.2) \\ 2(1.6) - 1(4.8) + 2(-3.2) \\ 4(1.6) + 2(4.8) + 1(-3.2) \end{bmatrix} = \begin{bmatrix} 1.6 + 9.6 - 3.2 \\ 3.2 - 4.8 - 6.4 \\ 6.4 + 9.6 - 3.2 \end{bmatrix} = \begin{bmatrix} 8.0 \\ -8.0 \\ 12.8 \end{bmatrix}$$

(b) This matrix multiplication leads to the *identity matrix.* An identity matrix is square, that is, it has the same number of columns as it has rows; it has 1's on the diagonal from the top left to the lower right and 0's every place else. These two matrices are the inverses of each other since their product yields the identity matrix.

$$\begin{bmatrix} 1 & 2 & 1 \\ 2 & -1 & 2 \\ 4 & -2 & -1 \end{bmatrix} \begin{bmatrix} 0.2 & 0 & 0.2 \\ 0.4 & -0.2 & 0 \\ 0 & 0.4 & -0.2 \end{bmatrix} =$$

$$\begin{bmatrix} 0.2 & +0.8 & +0 & 0 & -0.4 & +0.4 & 0.2 & +0 & -0.2 \\ 0.4 & -0.4 & +0 & 0 & +0.2 & +0.8 & 0.4 & -0 & -0.4 \\ 0.8 & -0.8 & -0 & 0 & +0.4 & -0.4 & 0.8 & -0 & +0.2 \end{bmatrix} =$$

$$\begin{bmatrix} 1 & 0 & 0 \\ 0 & 1 & 0 \\ 0 & 0 & 1 \end{bmatrix}$$

(c) A 1×3 times a 3×1 yields a 1×1.

$$\begin{bmatrix} 2 & -4 & 6 \end{bmatrix} \begin{Bmatrix} -2 \\ 2 \\ 4 \end{Bmatrix} = \begin{bmatrix} 12 \end{bmatrix}$$

$$(1 \times 3) \qquad (3 \times 1) \qquad (1 \times 1)$$

(d) A 3×1 times a 1×3 yields a 3×3. This shows that matrix multiplication is not commutative.

$$\begin{Bmatrix} -2 \\ 2 \\ 4 \end{Bmatrix} \begin{bmatrix} 2 & -4 & 6 \end{bmatrix} = \begin{bmatrix} -4 & 8 & -12 \\ 4 & -8 & 12 \\ 8 & -16 & 24 \end{bmatrix}$$

$$(3 \times 1) \qquad (1 \times 3) \qquad (3 \times 3)$$

(e)

$$\begin{bmatrix} 1 & 2 & 3 \\ 8 & 1 & 9 \end{bmatrix} \begin{bmatrix} -1 & -5 & -2 \\ -1 & 1 & 4 \\ 1 & 1 & -2 \end{bmatrix} = \begin{bmatrix} 0 & 0 & 0 \\ 0 & -30 & -30 \end{bmatrix}$$

$$(2 \times 3) \qquad (3 \times 3) \qquad (2 \times 3)$$

(f)

$$\begin{bmatrix} 1 & 2 \\ -2 & -3 \end{bmatrix} \begin{bmatrix} 2 & 1 & 0 & 4 \\ -5 & 1 & 0 & 2 \end{bmatrix} = \begin{bmatrix} -8 & 3 & 0 & 8 \\ 11 & -5 & 0 & -14 \end{bmatrix}$$

$$(2 \times 2) \qquad (2 \times 4) \qquad (2 \times 4)$$

Chapter 12

1. C10 = 'ABC1234ABC' = '2341234ABC' = '23412BCABC' = '23412BC3BC'   **2.** EIGHT = '12345678' = '12X.Z678' = '12X.Z6Y,' = 'YXX.Z6Y,'   Error! characters 4 thru 7 occur on both sides of equal sign.

Chapter 14

1. (a) The second variable in the subroutine argument list is real; therefore II in the call must be changed to a real variable. (b) TA is an array used only within the subroutine. The third argument represents the array Z which has 83 rows and 83 columns. In the main program the actual argument list does not agree because Z should be in the third location rather than the first in order to match. (c) The subroutine uses a real array. The call uses an integer array. This is mixed mode and is invalid. (d) When subroutine NEXT is called in the main program, array B has dimension 12, which corresponds to the subroutine definition for T (likewise of dimension 12). When a call is made to subroutine SPEC, however, although the array A is a $16 \cdot 16$—corresponding to R of the subroutine, which is $16 \cdot 16$—the array B is not carried through the argument list and is not dimensioned within the subroutine. Therefore when NEXT is called within subroutine SPEC, B is undefined or at best is a single variable name. This can be fixed by adding array B to the argument list of subroutine SPEC and adding a DIMENSION statement in subroutine SPEC for this array B having twelve locations. (e) The second arguments do not agree in mode. (f) CALL PI should have K in the third position of the argument list in order for the array sizes to match. (g) The subroutine has array LA(83,83) which is integer. Therefore, the main program must use an integer array rather than the real array HE, even though the sizes of the arrays appear to agree. (h) The subroutine NORM must have an integer 12-position array in the first location and an integer two-dimensional array $16 \cdot 23$ in the second location of its argument list. When called from the main program these conditions are satisfied. When called from the subroutine RPT, however, the second argument V has not been define and therefore creates an anomaly.

Chapter 16

3. (a)

4	1	0	4
-3	-3	0	4
2	-3	0	6
0	-3	1	6
0	-3	2	6
1	-3	2	7
-2	6	2	7
-4	-24	2	7
0	-24	3	7
3	-24	3	10

(b)

2	1	0	2
1	1	0	2
-2	-2	0	3
-1	2	0	3
-1	-2	0	3
0	-2	1	2
3	-2	1	6
0	-2	2	6
3	-2	2	9
0	-2	3	9

(c)

4	1	0	4
-4	-4	0	4
0	-4	1	4
0	-4	2	4
-5	20	2	4
-5	-100	2	4
2	-100	2	6
6	-100	2	12
3	-100	2	15
0	-100	3	15

(d)

0	1	1	0
0	1	2	0
0	1	3	0
1	1	3	1
2	1	3	3
3	1	3	6
4	1	3	10
-1	-1	3	10
-2	2	3	10
-3	-6	3	10

Chapter 17

1. If the last card read with personal data is not the last name in the list, control will pass to statement 30 *without* updating the Master File for output, and the record(s) on the end of the file will be lost. A suitable change would be to use END = 20 in statement 10.

Glossary

ALGOL   A language similar to FORTRAN, designed to solve scientific problems. The name comes from either ALGOrithmic Language or ALGebraic Oriented Language.

algorithm   A precise process that uses a well-defined set of rules to arrive at the solution to a given problem.

alphanumeric   In FORTRAN, a letter or a digit.

argument   In FORTRAN, the items in the list of a procedure that provide a means to communicate between the called and the calling program. For example in CALL SORT (LIST, VALUES), which calls SUBROUTINE SORT (FILE, AMOUNT), LIST and VALUES are actual arguments; corresponding dummy arguments are FILE and AMOUNT.

BASIC   A simple programming language; Beginners All-purpose Symbolic Instruction Code.

batch   Colloquially, the process of entering programs into a computer system by decks of cards.

binary   A system with the characteristic property of only two possible alternatives: 0 or 1; on or off; yes or no; or plus or minus. The binary number system uses 2 as its base. The counting sequence is 0, 1, 10, 11, 100, 101, 110, 111, corresponding to the decimals 0, 1, 2, 3, 4, 5, 6, 7, 8. Thus, 100_2 (100, base 2) represents decimal $2^2 = 4$ and 10000_2 represents $2^4 = 16$.

bit   The basic unit of computer memory, with a logical value of either 0 or 1 (on or off); a binary digit.

bottom-up   See Section 14–7.2.

branch   1. The point where a computer program deviates from the normal sequence of execution. or, 2. The subsequent instructions executed after such a branch is passed.

bug   Any type of error that keeps a program from operating correctly.

byte   A sequence of binary digits used collectively to represent information.

calls   The request by a computer program to have control transferred to another program in the operating system.

coding   In this text, to code is to write a program in the FORTRAN language, called *symbolic code*. The language into which FORTRAN is translated is called *object code*.

coding form   A form prepared to simplify the coding of FORTRAN programs.

compiler   In this text, the computer program that translates symbolic code (for example FORTRAN) into object code.

complex   A number with the general form $a + ib$, where a and b are real numbers and $i^2 = -1$.

concatenation   The process of linking or joining character strings or substrings.

constant   Three types of FORTRAN constants (arithmetic, logical, and character) that do not change values during execution of any given program.

control information list   In FORTRAN, a list that controls the manner and method of input/output.

CRT   Cathode ray tube, used to give a visual display at remote terminals.

debugging   Searching for, correcting, and eliminating errors in computer programs.

decision tables   A tabular, graphic form to represent the relationship between various items in a computer program, used as an aid in problem definition.

default   The value automatically assigned to an item if no specific assignment is made.

descriptive items   The list of all symbolic item names used in the computer program, together with corresponding mathematical symbols and complete descriptions (including formation of the mnemonic name).

disk, floppy   A somewhat slower, more portable, disk that receives its name from the flexible type of material used to construct it.

DO-WHILE   See Section 5–4.

documentation   In this text, definition sheets, flow diagrams or Nassi-Shneiderman charts, and comments included within the FORTRAN programs that are used to provide maximum program utility and as an aid to maintain, modify, and upgrade existing programs.

drum   A large cylinder that rotates very rapidly and stores data on its magnetic surfaces.

drum card   A computer card punched with appropriate coding for attachment to the small drum cylinder located within keypunch machines, used to provide supplementary controls, including setting tabs.

echo   An automatic repeat of a certain set of information. Typical examples: The echo received at a remote terminal from a computer when data are input in full duplex mode with echo on, and when input data are immediately displayed by a program to show that they were input correctly.

edit descriptor   Provides the explicit editing information needed for each item of information on input/output, including control of the carriage, optional signs, and the treatment of blanks.

entity   In FORTRAN, usually refers to variables, array elements, or substrings; but not to arrays.

executable   According to ANSI X3.9–1978 "specify actions and forms of an execution sequence in an executable program." See Table 13–1.

factorial n factorial is the product of $n(n-1)$ $(n-2)$ . . . 1. When n is 5, then 5 factorial is $5! = 5 \cdot 4 \cdot 3 \cdot 2 \cdot 1 = 120$; $1! = 1$ and $0! = 1$.

field width   The size in characters of a field.

flow   Used to indicate the sequence of events in a computer program or flow diagram.

flow diagram   A sketch that uses a specified symbology to give a visual presentation for an algorithm or computer program.

format identifiers   In FORTRAN, a statement label, an integer variable name with its value assigned in an ASSIGN statement, a character array name, a character expression, or an asterisk that identifies the type of format to be used.

FORMAT statement   See Section 6–1.2.

full-duplex Two-way, independent, and simultaneous transmission in both directions; As used with respect to a remote terminal, generally implies that the echo is on and that the material being displayed on the terminal is coming from the computer and not directly from the keyboard. (This makes it possible to type "ahead" of the remote terminal display.)

generic Usually refers to a general class or group as opposed to a special or specific class or group.

half-duplex Two-way transmission, but only one way at a time. On a remote terminal, a character is usually displayed on the terminal in direct response to entries at the keyboard.

hardware Physical equipment rather than computer programs: includes electronic, electrical, mechanical, and magnetic devices and physical support systems.

hexadecimal A number system using base 16. Counting numbers are $0, 1, 2, 3, 4, 5, 6, 7, 8, 9, A, B, C, D, E, F$, 10. Thus, 10_{16} corresponds to decimal 16 and 100_{16} is equivalent to $16^2 = 256$.

Hollerith An alphanumeric code invented by Dr. Herman Hollerith in 1889, shown in Figure 1–1.

I/O Input/output.

input Data information that has been or is to be transferred from some external storage medium (cards, remote terminal, disk, and so on) to the internal storage mechanism of the computer (Internal data).

internal datum The characters (numeral, alphabetic, or special) stored in locations referenced by a variable, array element, or substring name.

intrinsic function Functions supplied directly by the processor for use in any FORTRAN program.

item In FORTRAN, refers to a variable name, an array element, a character substring name or an array name (note that items could be considered as entities plus array names).

keypunch Mechanical device for putting the appropriate punched holes in a card while simultaneously printing the characters across the top of the card.

keyword In FORTRAN, except for assignment and statement function statements, a keyword or keywords begin every statement and are a specified sequence of letters such as DATA, GO TO, FORMAT, and so on.

label See statement label.

left-justified Positioning of a datum so that the first character is in the leftmost position of a field.

library function In FORTRAN, intrinsic functions.

list In ANSI X3.9–1978, a list is "a nonempty sequence of syntactic entities separated by commas."

lister A mechanical device that reads punched cards and outputs their contents, a line for each card, on a roll of continuous paper.

local An entity that has meaning only within a single program unit.

local extension ANSI X3.9–1978 FORTRAN 77 establishes a standard-conforming processor that accepts all standard-conforming programs and processes according to the rules of the standard. Some computers or installations add nonconforming rules that are called local extensions to standard FORTRAN 77 and will not work on many other standard-conforming processors.

logical expression The form of a logical computation that produces either of the logical results .TRUE. or .FALSE..

logical unit number In FORTRAN, a unit specifier and identifier (Typically UNIT = u) used to refer to a file, either external or internal. Sometimes used loosely to apply to the physical unit which contains the file.

mini-module See Section 5–2.

mnemonic   Usually an acronym or abbreviation intended to assist in memory of a concept.

MOD   See page 496

mode   Usually refers to a particular operational method, that is, using all type real or all type integer.

modular   See Sections 5–2 and 14–7.

module   In this text in the context of structured programming, a set of statements acting together to complete a specific task having only one entry and only one exit point.

Nassi-Shneiderman Chart   See Section 3–3.2.

negation   Changing the value of a constant or variable by preceding it with a minus sign.

nested   One module completely inside of another module.

nonexecutable   According to ANSI X3.9–1978, "specify characteristics, arrangement, and initial values of data; contain editing information; specify statement functions; classify program units; and specify entry points within subprograms." See Table 13–1.

object code   Produced from the FORTRAN source program by the processor, usually incomplete machine language representation of the program that lacks absolute addresses of storage locations, and so on. This representation of the program is processed by the loader (collector or linkage editor) to produce an executable program.

octal   A number system using base 8. Counting numbers are 0, 1, 2, 3, 4, 5, 6, 7, 10. Thus 10_8 represents decimal 8 and 100_8 represents $8^2 = 64$.

one-off error   An error that results in entities being one position out of phase, or numbers being computed one number off. A very common error in computer programming, especially by beginners.

operands   The quantities related by the mathematical operators when performing a mathematical operation. Thus in A * B, A and B are both operands and the asterisk is a mathematical operator.

operators   Mathematical and logical operations. In FORTRAN, they include $+, -, *$ (for multiplication), $/$ (for division), $**$ (for exponentiation) and $//$ (for concatenation). Also included are relational and logical operators.

PL/I   A computer language named from Programming Language I. It includes many features of FORTRAN, COBOL, and ALGOL.

pointers   In FORTRAN, an entity that points to the location where something is stored, found, or retrieved.

primary   In FORTRAN one of the arithmetic operands primary, factor, term, and arithmetic expression. For a complete explanation, refer to ANSI X3.9–1978.

procedure   In FORTRAN, subroutines, external functions, statement functions, and intrinsic functions.

process box   A rectangular box on a flow diagram that indicates an operation, or series of operations, to be performed.

processor   In FORTRAN, "a data processing system and the mechanism by which programs are transformed for use on that data processing system." In general, a program that translates FORTRAN into the machine's language.

program unit   Either a main program or a subprogram that consists of a sequence of statements, including optional comment lines.

pseudo-module   A series of statements that appear to be a module, but which have more than one entry and/or more than one exit point.

pseudocode   As used in this text, a series of English expressions that represent a desired set of computer operations.

record A sequence of characters or a sequence of values. See also Section 17–1.1.

recursive Loosely, the ability of a subprogram to call itself.

Regula-Falsi The oldest method for computing roots of numerical equations, the method of false position; based on interpolation between two points on a curve having opposite signs, considering the portion of the curve between the two points to be a straight line.

right-justified Positioning of a datum so that the last character is in the rightmost location of the field.

roundoff error A specific error occurring when the less significant digits are deleted from a quantity after it has been rounded off. Rounding to one decimal place differs from truncation because 3.76 would round to 3.8, but would be truncated to 3.7.

sequence An ordered set in a one-to-one correspondence with the numbers 1, 2, 3, ...

sigma, Σ The sum of a series.

slue or slew Colloquially, to advance the paper on the high-speed printer to the top of the next page.

software Computer programs, as contrasted with hardware or physical components of the computer.

statement label In FORTRAN, a sequence of one to five digits which identify a particular FORTRAN statement.

string A connected sequence of characters which, in FORTRAN, are set off by apostrophes. May be a constant, or stored in a variable name or an array element.

structured See Sections 5–2 and 14–7.

structured programming See Sections 5–2 and 14–7.

subprograms In FORTRAN, subprograms are procedures that cannot stand alone; they are not main programs and must be called by a main program or another subprogram.

subroutine See Section 14–1.

symbolic names Used to name variables, arrays, symbolic constants and substrings in FORTRAN programs.

syntactic In this text, an adjective for the noun syntax.

syntactic items In FORTRAN, constants; symbolic names of variables, arrays, and substrings; statement labels; key words; operators; and special characters.

syntax The rules and structure of FORTRAN concerning arrangement of syntactic items, specifying their mutual relations, and establishing the operations to be performed.

systems approach See Sections 5–2 and 14–7.

time-sharing A method of computer operation that, because of the high speed, makes it appear that services to several users are being performed simultaneously.

top-down See Section 14–7.2.

trace A longhand or machine-provided display of the values obtained while progressing through a flow diagram or computer program (or segment), also indicates branches taken.

trailer card A card used at the end of a set of data to indicate that it is the last item.

truncation Dropping digits after a specified number of significant figures; 3.17 truncated to 1 decimal place is 3.1. This contrasts to rounding, where 3.17 would round to 3.2.

turn-around time The elapsed time required from submitting a program until the results of the program are returned in usable form.

type See Section 4–2.4.

variable   In FORTRAN, an entity that has both a name and a type.

variable name   See Section 4–2.3.

verifier   A mechanical device that looks very much like a keypunch machine and is used to check data by retyping.

Index

526